CONTEMPORARY PERSONAL FINANCE

Louis E. Boone
University of South Alabama

David L. Kurtz
Seattle University

 **Random House Business Division**
New York

To Paul S. Donnelly,
whose energy, insight, and innovativeness have
made a profound impact on our careers.

First Edition
987654321
Copyright © 1985 by Random House, Inc.

All rights reserved under International and Pan-American Copyright Conventions.
No part of this book may be reproduced in any form or by any means,
electronic or mechanical, including photocopying, without permission
in writing from the publisher. All inquiries should be addressed to
Random House, Inc., 201 East 50th Street, New York, N.Y. 10022.
Published in the United States by Random House, Inc.,
and simultaneously in Canada by Random House of Canada Limited, Toronto.

Library of Congress Cataloging in Publication Data

Boone, Louis E.
    Contemporary personal finance.

    Includes index.
    1. Finance, Personal.   I. Kurtz, David L.
II. Title.
HG179.B583   1985   332.024   84-26236
ISBN 0-394-34282-8

Text Design: Suzanne Bennett

Cover Design: Lorraine Hohman

Cover Photo: Tom Norton

Manufactured in the United States of America

CONTEMPORARY PERSONAL FINANCE

Tony P O'Brien
243-8997

Preface

Our motivation for writing *Contemporary Personal Finance* is based on two beliefs. First, we recognize how important the study of personal finance is for college and university students. Few other courses can have such a profound effect on students for the remainder of their lives. One need only talk briefly with the typical business student to realize how little he or she knows about such fundamental personal finance topics as insurance, personal budgeting, checking and savings accounts, and investing. Too many of these students are well-versed on corporate finance but cannot prepare their own personal financial statements. They are at a major disadvantage compared to the student who has taken a quarter or semester of personal finance.

Second, we are concerned with the general quality of personal finance texts. Many are inadequately researched, poorly written, stodgy in appearance, and lacking in teaching materials and pedagogical aids. Some texts are similar to the numerous "how to" books that offer hundreds of suggestions but provide little or no conceptual foundations on which to base these suggestions. Other texts provide incomplete coverage, altogether ignoring or giving only superficial treatment to such important topics as mutual funds, the impact of career choice on personal finance, consumer decision making, and many types of nonstock investments. Still others, with their amateurish cartoons and drawings, look more like high school books than college texts.

We have written *Contemporary Personal Finance* to provide instructors with the kind of quality text that personal finance courses merit, one that provides a thorough, conceptually sound treatment of the subject. Concepts are reinforced by hundreds of real-life examples, up-to-date illustrations, and problem-solving approaches. The writing style, text organization, and emphasis on practical applications are designed to relieve students of the tedious, boring reading that has often characterized the study of personal finance.

A Readable Text with Personal Finance Concepts Emphasized by Real-World Examples

At first glance it is obvious that students will enjoy reading and studying *Contemporary Personal Finance*. Each chapter begins with a quiz, "Testing Your Personal Finance I.Q.," that provides a humorous pretest to materials covered in the chapter (answers to the quiz are near the end of each chapter). Following the quiz is a stop-action case involving an actual personal finance student who has a problem related to the chapter's topic. Later in the chapter the reader sees how the student applied the chapter materials to solve his or her problem. This technique is effective in showing students the immediate application of subjects discussed in class.

In addition, a number of interesting and reinforcing aids are included in each chapter. Photos and illustrations are used throughout the text to emphasize application of its various concepts. In addition, special focus boxes are included in each chapter. Examples include "What to Do When the IRS Calls," "Electronic Banking,"

"Protecting Yourself Against Credit Card Fraud," "How to Buy a Personal Computer," "Securities: Knowing When to Sell," "How to Find a Reliable Mechanic," "Investors' Most Common Mistakes," "How to Sell Collectibles and Come Out Ahead," "The Unisex Insurance Controversy," "How Much Life Insurance Should You Buy?" and "Building a Case for Term Insurance."

Stressing Pedagogical Soundness

Contemporary Personal Finance is designed to be an effective teaching and learning tool. It stresses pedagogical soundness by identifying specific learning objectives for each chapter. Key terms are defined and featured clearly in the margin of the page where they are discussed. The most recent statistics available are used throughout each chapter, and tables, figures, and other text data are clearly referenced. Summaries and end-of-chapter review questions reinforce student retention of the concepts developed in the chapter. Case problems and exercises are included at the end of each chapter for special student assignments and to stimulate class discussions.

Organization of Contemporary Personal Finance Provides Accepted, Orthodox Coverage

Surveys of personal finance instructors revealed a preference for ordering topics under the "life-cycle" approach. *Contemporary Personal Finance,* therefore, discusses topics in the following logical sequence: career choice; developing a financial plan; preparing personal financial statements and a budget; setting up checking and savings accounts; understanding the role of credit; making major purchases; purchasing protection in the form of different types of insurance; alternative investment considerations; investigating Social Security; making retirement plans; estate planning; and preparing a will. Professors who use the text in their courses will not face the problems involved in radically altering the sequence of topics covered.

Separate Chapter Coverage of Important Personal Finance Subjects

While many textbooks skim or altogether neglect several personal finance topics, we feel that the areas of investment clubs, mutual funds, career choice, consumer decision making, the transportation decision, Social Security, and nonstock investment alternatives are too important to ignore. Therefore, each of these subjects is given detailed treatment in its own chapter.

A Complete Instructional Support Package Is Available

Contemporary Personal Finance is available with a complete teaching/learning package, designed for both instructor and student. The package includes:

Instructor's Resource Manual. We have prepared the most complete manual available with any personal finance text. The manual includes a lecturer's guide, a section on organizing the course, and detailed materials for each chapter. The following sections are provided for every chapter:

- Overview
- Teaching Goals
- Testing Your Personal Finance I.Q.
- The Stop-Action Case

- Lecture Outline and Notes
- Introductory Examples
- Key Terms
- Answers to Review Questions
- Answers to Cases and Exercises
- Guest Speaker Suggestions
- Sources of Information
- Films for the Chapter

Test Bank. The 1,000-item Test Bank includes true/false, multiple choice, and essay questions. The Test Bank was prepared by Professor James W. Baird of Community College of the Finger Lakes.

Student Course Mastery Guide. This comprehensive aid for students was prepared by Professor Les R. Dlabay of Lake Forest College. It includes an array of text learning activities to reinforce material in the text, as well as enrichment activities to broaden the student's perspective and help bring the concepts to life.

Film Guide. A comprehensive film guide, containing descriptions of each film and mailing address of each film source, is included in the *Instructor's Resource Manual*.

Transparencies. A total of 100 transparency masters have been prepared to augment class lectures. Descriptions of each transparency are included at appropriate points in the lecture materials for each chapter. The transparency masters are included in the *Instructor's Resource Manual*.

The authors gratefully acknowledge the contributions of many people—colleagues, students, business professionals, government employees, members of trade associations, and the professionals at Random House—for their invaluable critiques, questions, and advice in making *Contemporary Personal Finance* a reality. We would also like to express our appreciation to Cindy Childree, Dot Martin, Jeanne Monk, Jane Sawyer, Kitty Sawyer, and Linda Troup for their invaluable assistance in typing the manuscript. The efficiency of our research associates, Judy Block, Shelly Orr, and Rose Burch Stabler, in updating statistical data greatly assisted in producing the most current book possible.

For their reviews of all or part of the manuscript or assistance in developing text materials, we would especially like to thank the following dedicated business professionals: Michael J. Ahern III, University of Toledo; James W. Baird, Community College of the Finger Lakes; Mark Bass, Texas Tech University; Robert Bohn, Golden Gate University; Harvey Bronstein, Oakland Community College; William Burr, University of Oregon; Les R. Dlabay, Lake Forest College; Michael Dohan, Queens College of the City University of New York; Bonnie Fletcher, Rainier Mortgage Company; George L. Granger, East Tennessee State University; David M. Hay, Dean Witter Reynolds Inc.; Roger P. Hill, University of North Carolina at Wilmington; Jerry L. Jorgensen, University of Utah; Peggy Keck, Western Kentucky University; Melvin J. Mallett, CPA, Mallet and Associates; Ethel C. Malloy, Suffolk County Community College; Craig C. Milnor, Clark College; Russell Ogden, Eastern Michigan University; Dennis Pappas, Columbus Technical Institute; Tena Perry, The Justin Agency; J. David Veitch, Rotan Mosle, Inc.; Taylor Waite, Jr., CPA, Mallet and Associates; Clyde D. Westwood, Utah Technical College; Ira Wilsker, Lamar University; and Gregory J. Worosz, Schoolcraft College.

Louis E. Boone, *Mobile, Alabama*
David L. Kurtz, *Seattle, Washington*

January 1985

Contents in Brief

Part One Overview of Contemporary Personal Finance — 1
Chapter One Introduction to Personal Finance — 2
Chapter Two Career Aspects of Personal Finance — 18

Part Two Financial Planning — 43
Chapter Three Personal Financial Statements and Records — 44
Chapter Four Financial Planning and Budgeting — 64
Chapter Five Taxes — 84

Part Three Managing Your Money — 123
Chapter Six Money Management — 124
Chapter Seven Borrowing: Obtaining Consumer Credit — 170

Part Four Effective Buying — 205
Chapter Eight The Informed Consumer — 206
Chapter Nine The Housing Decision — 242
Chapter Ten The Transportation Decision — 270

Part Five Purchasing Protection — 303
Chapter Eleven The Insurance Decision — 304
Chapter Twelve Life Insurance — 328
Chapter Thirteen Health Care Protection — 368
Chapter Fourteen Automobile, Homeowners, and Liability Insurance — 390

Part Six Investments — 413
Chapter Fifteen Stocks and Bonds — 414
Chapter Sixteen Buying and Selling Securities — 452
Chapter Seventeen Investment Clubs and Mutual Funds — 494
Chapter Eighteen Other Investment Alternatives — 522

Part Seven Financial Planning for Tomorrow — 555
Chapter Nineteen Social Security — 556
Chapter Twenty Retirement, Wills, and Estate Planning — 574

Notes — 605

Index — 610

Detailed Contents

Part One Overview of Contemporary Personal Finance 1

Chapter One
Introduction to Personal Finance 2

Testing Your Personal Finance I.Q. 2
Sharing a Personal Financial Decision with Professor Peggy Keck of Western Kentucky University 3
The Meaning and Importance of Personal Finance 4
The Role of Personal Goals in Financial Decision Making 5
  Shirley Chilton: Goal Setter par Excellence 5
  Personal Lifestyles: From Thelma to Scott 6
The Impact of Money 7
A Modern Personal Finance Model 11
An Outline of Personal Financial Decisions 13
Summary 16 / Review Questions 16 / Cases and Exercises 16 / How Jim Davis Reached His Personal Financial Decision 17

Chapter Two
Career Aspects of Personal Finance 18

Testing Your Personal Finance I.Q. 18
Sharing a Personal Financial Decision with Professor Michael Dohan of Queens College of the City University of New York 19
Career Choice Should Be Related to Personal Goals 20
Variables That Affect Income Potential 22
Choosing a Career 25
The Job Search 33

Summary 39 / Review Questions 39 / Cases and Exercises 40 / How Connie Ferrara Reached Her Personal Financial Decision 40

Part Two
Financial Planning 43

Chapter Three
Personal Financial Statements and Records 44

Testing Your Personal Finance I.Q. 44
Sharing a Personal Financial Decision with Professor Gregory J. Worosz of Schoolcraft College 45
The Importance of Developing Personal Financial Statements 47
The Income Statement 48
    Developing a Family Income Statement for the Chicago World's Fair 51
The Balance Sheet 53
    A Hard-Times Scorecard 55
Record Keeping 56
    Buying a Personal Computer 59

Summary 61 / Review Questions 61 / Cases and Exercises 62 / How Sherri Thompson Reached Her Personal Financial Decision 62

Chapter Four
Financial Planning and Budgeting 64

Testing Your Personal Finance I.Q. 64
Sharing a Personal Financial Decision with Professor Ethel C. Malloy of Suffolk County Community College 65
Some Basic Concepts 66
Financial Planning 67
Preliminary Budget Concerns 69
Budgeting 71
    The Martsens' Dilemma 76
    Life at the Top—Not as Easy as It Seems? 77
Credit Abuse: Common Characteristics of Individuals Who Ignore Financial Planning 78

Summary 81 / Review Questions 82 / Cases and Exercises 82 / How Tom Lee Reached His Personal Financial Decision 83

DETAILED CONTENTS

Chapter Five
Taxes 84
Testing Your Personal Finance I.Q. 84
Sharing a Personal Financial Decision with Professor Clyde D. Westwood of Utah Technical College at Provo 85
What Are Taxes? 86
Types of Taxes 89
    Taxing Crime 95
The Collection of Taxes 96
    Following Your Return Through the IRS 98
    What to Do When the IRS Calls 101
Preparing Your Federal Tax Return 104
    How Much Is Too Much? 111
Recent Changes in the Federal Tax System 111
Securing Competent Tax Advice 114
Tax Information Sources 117
Some Tax-Savings Tips 118
Summary 119 / Review Questions 120 / Cases and Exercises 120 / How Burt and Sally James Reached Their Personal Financial Decision 121

Part Three
Managing Your Money 123

Chapter Six
Money Management 124
Testing Your Personal Finance I.Q. 124
Sharing a Personal Financial Decision with Professor Robert Bohn of Golden Gate University 125
Why Maintain Money Balances? 126
Why Saving Is So Important 127
    Barter: An Alternative to Money 128
Types of Savings Instruments 130
    Keep Your Eye on the Real Rate 134
Financial Institutions of the 1980s: How They've Changed 137
    The Asset Management Account 144
Banking Services 146
    NOW Accounts: Compare How You'd Fare 148
The Electronic Revolution in Banking 151
    Chemical Bank's PRONTO System of Electronic Banking 153

DETAILED CONTENTS

How Safe Is Your Money?	154
Choosing the Right Place for Your Money	157
How to Use Checking, NOW, and Super-NOW Accounts	159
Special Types of Checks	163
How to Resolve Banking Problems	165

Summary 167 / Review Questions 168 / Cases and Exercises 168 / How Marcie Stillwell Reached Her Personal Financial Decision 169

Chapter Seven
Borrowing: Obtaining Consumer Credit 170

Testing Your Personal Finance I.Q.	170
Sharing a Personal Financial Decision with Professor Clyde D. Westwood of Utah Technical College at Provo	171
What Is Credit?	173
Securing Credit	174
How to Read a Credit Report	177
Sources of Credit	178
Types of Consumer Credit	181
Types of Consumer Credit Agreements	184
The Cost of Borrowing	185
Deciding How Much to Borrow	190
Right—and Wrong—Reasons for Borrowing	191
Credit Counseling: A Way Back	196
Legislation Governing Consumer Credit and Borrowing	197
Protecting Yourself Against Credit-Card Fraud	198

Summary 201 / Review Questions 203 / Cases and Exercises 203 / How Clark Boyd Reached His Personal Financial Decision 204

Part Four
Effective Buying 205

Chapter Eight
The Informed Consumer 206

Testing Your Personal Finance I.Q.	206
Sharing a Personal Financial Decision with Professor Ira Wilsker of Lamar University	207
The Consumer of the 1980s	208

The Changing Family Life Cycle	214
The Consumer Decision-Making Process	216
Consumer Fraud and Abuse	219
How Long Should Appliances Last?	223
Regulation: A Route to Consumer Protection	226
Getting Help: Additional Sources of Consumer Assistance	234
Suing the Product Raters	236
How to Complain and Get Action	237

Summary 239 / Review Questions 240 / Cases and Exercises 241 / How Floyd Campbell Reached His Personal Financial Decision 241

Chapter Nine
The Housing Decision 242

Testing Your Personal Finance I.Q.	242
Sharing a Personal Financial Decision with Professor William Burr of the University of Oregon	243
Personal Housing Requirements	244
Profile of the New Home Buyer	247
Sometimes It Is Tough to Buy a $1.8 Million Apartment	254
Buying a House	254
Have I Got a Deal for You!	256
Financing a Home	257
Building a Home	264
Selling a House	265
Purchasing a Second Home	266
Time Shares	267

Summary 267 / Review Questions 268 / Cases and Exercises 268 / How Alan Markus Reached His Personal Financial Decision 269

Chapter Ten
The Transportation Decision 270

Testing Your Personal Finance I.Q.	270
Sharing a Personal Financial Decision with Professor Michael J. Ahern III of the University of Toledo	271
The Transportation Alternatives	274
Purchasing an Automobile	279
The Growing Popularity of "Lemon Laws"	284
The "Blue Book"	286
How to Purchase an Automobile	287

xiv DETAILED CONTENTS

Financing the Automobile Purchase	291
What Car Ownership Really Costs	292
Auto Warranties	297
How to Find a Reliable Mechanic	298

Summary 299 / Review Questions 300 / Cases and Exercises 300 / How Bill Mikelson Reached His Personal Financial Decision 301

Part Five
Purchasing Protection   303

Chapter Eleven
The Insurance Decision   304

Testing Your Personal Finance I.Q.	304
Sharing a Personal Financial Decision with Professor Russell Ogden of Eastern Michigan University	305
What Is Insurance?	306
The Concept of Risk	308
Characteristics of Insurable Risk	311
The Boone and Kurtz List of Accidents and Disasters	315
Sex and Insurance	315
Types of Insurance	317
Basic Insurance Elements	319
Removing the Gobbledygook from Insurance Policies	321
The Insurance Purchase Process	323
Choosing and Talking to an Insurance Agent	324

Summary 326 / Review Questions 326 / Cases and Exercises 327 / How Greg Berger Reached His Personal Financial Decision 327

Chapter Twelve
Life Insurance   328

Testing Your Personal Finance I.Q.	328
Sharing a Personal Financial Decision with Professor Robert Bohn of Golden Gate University	329
The Life Insurance Decision	331
Determining the Need for Life Insurance	332
How Much Life Insurance Is Enough?	332
Basic Variables in Life Insurance Policies	336

DETAILED CONTENTS   XV

Types of Life Insurance Policies   336
   Life Insurance for Homemakers?   339
   Building a Case for Term Insurance   345
The Life Insurance Contract   353
Shopping for Rates   360
   Mail-Order Life Insurance: Is It a Bargain?   361
Summary 364 / Review Questions 364 / Cases and Exercises 365 / How Luis Sanchez Reached His Personal Financial Decision 365

Chapter Thirteen
Health Care Protection   368
Testing Your Personal Finance I.Q.   368
Sharing a Personal Financial Decision with Professor Gregory J. Worosz of Schoolcraft College   369
The Health Care Industry   370
Types of Health Insurance Coverage   371
   Hospice—Another Health Insurance Benefit?   375
Dental Insurance   376
Health Care Protection Plans   377
The Debate Over National Health Care   383
Developing a Personal Health Care Protection Plan   384
   The Man with the Artificial Heart   385
Summary 388 / Review Questions 388 / Cases and Exercises 388 / How Amy Shore Reached Her Personal Financial Decision 389

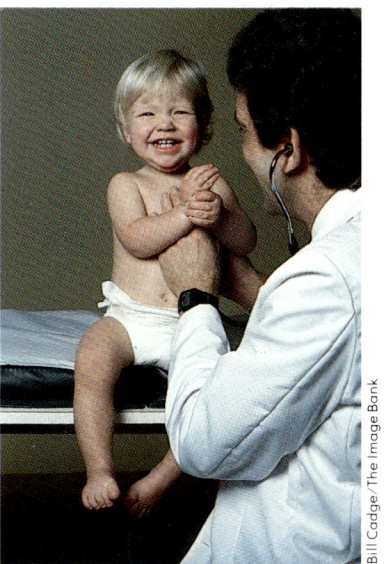

Chapter Fourteen
Automobile, Homeowners, and Liability Insurance   390
Testing Your Personal Finance I.Q.   390
Sharing a Personal Financial Decision with Professor Harvey Bronstein of Oakland Community College   391
The Concept of Liability   392
Personal Liability Insurance   393
   The Hyatt Regency Case   394
Homeowners Insurance   395
Automobile Insurance   400
   Auto Theft: A $3.27-Billion Financial Drain   403
   The Attack on DWIs   405

DETAILED CONTENTS

Reading the Insurance Policy	407
Making the Purchase Decision	409

Summary 409 / Review Questions 410 / Cases and Exercises 410 / How Sheldon Brown Reached His Personal Financial Decision 411

Part Six   Investments   413

Chapter Fifteen
Stocks and Bonds   414

Testing Your Personal Finance I.Q.	414
Sharing a Personal Financial Decision with Professor James W. Baird of Community College of the Finger Lakes	415
The Role of Stocks and Bonds in Modern Business	417
What Is an Investment?	418
Why People Invest	419
The Risk of Investing	421
"Corporate Triumph, Then Death in a Ferrari"	423
What Risks Can You Afford?	424
How the AT&T Breakup Affected Stockholders	425
Investing in Common Stocks	426
Investing in Preferred Stocks	437
Investing in Bonds	440
The Allure of Junk Bonds	448

Summary 449 / Review Questions 449 / Cases and Exercises 450 / How Linda Griffin Reached Her Personal Financial Decision 451

Chapter Sixteen
Buying and Selling Securities   452

Testing Your Personal Finance I.Q.	452
Sharing a Personal Financial Decision with Professor Russell Ogden of Eastern Michigan University	453
Securities Markets	455
America's Investors: Myths and Realities	457
The Securities Exchanges	458
Regulating the Securities Markets	462
The Crash of '29	464
Making Securities Transactions	465
Knowing When to Sell	469

DETAILED CONTENTS   **xvii**

What You Can Expect from Your Broker   471
Selecting a Stockbroker   474
Opening and Using a Brokerage Account   475
Sources of Investment Information   476
    Investors' Most Common Mistakes   478
Developing a Successful Investment Strategy   487
Summary 491 / Review Questions 491 / Cases and Exercises 492 / How Jennifer Powell Reached Her Personal Financial Decision 492

Chapter Seventeen
Investment Clubs and
Mutual Funds   494

Testing Your Personal Finance I.Q.   494
Sharing a Personal Financial Decision with Professor Mark Bass, CPA, of Texas Tech University   495
Investment Clubs   497
    Stock Analysis Checklist   498
Special Purchase Arrangements   499
What Are Investment Companies?   501
Load Versus No-Load Mutual Funds   506
Different Types of Mutual Funds   507
Mutual Fund Families   510
Special Features to Look for in Mutual Funds   511
Evaluating the Various Mutual Funds   513
    Good Advice for a Price   516
How to Read Mutual Fund Listings   517
Buying and Selling Mutual Funds   518
Summary 519 / Review Questions 520 / Cases and Exercises 520 / How Sam Johnson Reached His Personal Financial Decision 521

Chapter Eighteen
Other Investment Alternatives   522

Testing Your Personal Finance I.Q.   522
Sharing a Personal Financial Decision with Professor James W. Baird of Community College of the Finger Lakes   523
An Overview of Investment Alternatives   524
Real Estate   525
    Investing in the U.S. Postal Service?   526
Commodities   536
Options   539
Precious and Strategic Metals   543

xviii DETAILED CONTENTS

Diamonds and Gems	547
Art, Antiques, and Other Collectibles	550
How to Sell Your Collectibles and Come Out Ahead	551

Summary 552 / Review Questions 553 / Cases and Exercises 553 / How Ed and Marie Murphy Reached Their Personal Financial Decision 554

Part Seven
Financial Planning for Tomorrow 555

Chapter Nineteen
Social Security 556

Testing Your Personal Finance I.Q.	556
Sharing a Personal Financial Decision with Professor George L. Granger of East Tennessee State University	557
The Importance of the Social Security System	558
The Complexity of the Social Security System	559
The Evolution of the Social Security Act	559
Social Security Today	563
The Social Security Controversy	567
What Next for Social Security?	568
"But I Am Alive and Well"	570

Summary 571 / Review Questions 572 / Cases and Exercises 572 / How Estelle Cooper Reached Her Personal Financial Decision 573

Chapter Twenty
Retirement, Wills, and Estate Planning 574

Testing Your Personal Finance I.Q.	574
Sharing a Personal Financial Decision with Professor George L. Granger of East Tennessee State University	575
Retirement Planning	576
How Long Will You Live?	577
Sources of Retirement Income	581
Annuities	591
A Landmark Decision: *Norris* vs. *Arizona Governing Committee*	593

Estate Planning   594
    Silent Cal's Will—Brief as Usual   597

Summary 603 / Review Questions 603 / Cases and Exercises 604 / How Cindy Donovan Reached Her Personal Financial Decision 604

Notes   605

Index   610

About the Authors

Louis E. Boone (B.S., M.S., Ph.D.) holds the Ernest G. Cleverdon Chair of Business and Management at the University of South Alabama. He formerly chaired the Division of Management and Marketing at the University of Tulsa and has taught in Australia, Greece, and the United Kingdom.

Professor Boone has authored or coauthored a number of widely used textbooks. His research interests include the area of consumer decision making, and he has published articles in such journals as *Journal of Consumer Credit Management*, *Business Horizons*, *Journal of Business Strategy*, *Business*, and the *Journal of Business of the University of Chicago*.

David L. Kurtz (B.A., M.B.A., Ph.D.) is University Professor of Business Administration at Seattle University. He formerly held the Thomas F. Gleed Chair in Business and Finance at Seattle University and has previously taught at Eastern Michigan University, Caulfield Institute of Technology (Melbourne, Australia), the University of Arkansas, and Davis and Elkins College.

Professor Kurtz is the author or coauthor of numerous books, and more than forty articles, monographs, cases, book reviews, and computer simulations. He has been involved in consulting and training activities in business and has been the president of a small corporation.

PART ONE

OVERVIEW OF CONTEMPORARY PERSONAL FINANCE

LEARNING OBJECTIVES

1. To explain the concept of personal finance and its importance to contemporary society. / *2.* To outline the role of personal goals and priorities in financial decision making. / *3.* To describe the concept of money and its functions. / *4.* To develop a model of personal financial decisions. / *5.* To identify the basic steps in a financial plan.

TESTING YOUR PERSONAL FINANCE I.Q.

	FACT	FICTION
1. Money includes credit-union share drafts.	☐	☐
2. Unemployment benefits are not considered part of personal income.	☐	☐
3. Disposable income is often called take-home pay.	☐	☐
4. The cost of food has risen faster than the cost of fuel oil and coal.	☐	☐
5. The three-step approach to financial planning for anyone is to (a) obtain more money, (b) use money more effectively, and (c) monitor expenditures.	☐	☐

The materials in this chapter assist in separating fact from fiction. Your answers can be checked on page 17.

CHAPTER ONE

INTRODUCTION TO PERSONAL FINANCE

SHARING A PERSONAL FINANCIAL DECISION WITH PROFESSOR PEGGY KECK OF WESTERN KENTUCKY UNIVERSITY

At the start of a new semester of her personal finance course, Professor Peggy Keck threw out an intriguing question to her class: "Suppose that two companies offer you a job that you really want—the position of assistant manager. One job is in Nashville, Tennessee, for a salary of $21,000. The other is in Nome, Alaska, but the salary is $28,000. The work itself seems comparable. Which job would you take?"

Jim Davis didn't hesitate. Quickly he raised his hand. "I'd take the job in Alaska because it pays more," he asserted.

Professor Keck replied that Jim's answer was an obvious one, but wondered aloud whether he had fully thought it out. As individuals living in a complex society, we need to evaluate whether we are making the right financial decisions to achieve our personal goals. To do this, we have to weigh many factors.

At this point Jim raised his hand again. "My personal goal is to make as much money as possible," he declared. "I don't mind moving—even as far away as Alaska. It's the salary that counts."

If you were Professor Keck, what other considerations would you suggest Jim review before making his decision?

To find out how Professor Keck helped Jim with his personal financial decision, turn to page 17.

"If you can count your money, you don't have a billion dollars."
J. Paul Getty[1]

The young couple faced a variety of financial considerations. She had to give up her $4-an-hour job as a kindergarten assistant. And the job for which he had prepared himself would probably not become vacant for several years. Their new home would cost thousands of dollars to furnish. Even the new bride's homemaking abilities were in doubt—one cleaning lady had already quit working at her apartment because she and her roommates created such a mess.

Although these concerns may sound typical of those confronting any young couple, it is doubtful that Prince Charles and Lady Diana will ever have to worry about financial problems. As Prince of Wales, Charles receives no salary, but he does receive the income generated by the Duchy of Cornwall. The duchy's extensive holdings include 171 farms, London's Oval Cricket ground, and Dartmoor, which is leased to the government as a maximum-security prison. Net revenues are about $1.2 million annually, but the Prince donates half to the government (he is not required to pay taxes on the duchy's profits). Charles pays his staff from the half he keeps. The Prince also has earnings from investments (which are taxed).

Although the Princess of Wales (formerly Lady Diana Spencer) earned only $4 per hour as a kindergarten assistant when she was courted by Charles, she comes from a wealthy family. Her father even gives tours of his 300-year-old castle for $2 a person. Diana's apartment was a $150,000 gift from her parents.

The royal couple's new home required about $300,000 in furnishings. It is a nine-bedroom, six-bath estate situated on 347 acres. As for Diana's housekeeping, it is no longer a problem. The house is staffed with a cook, housekeeper, maid, and a special lady's maid![2]

THE MEANING AND IMPORTANCE OF PERSONAL FINANCE

Prince Charles may be relatively unconcerned about personal financial decisions, but that is not the case for most people. The economic environment of the past decade has made all Americans more conscious of the importance of personal finance. Up-to-date knowledge of personal finance has become a necessity of life.

Personal finance is the study of the economic factors and personal decisions that affect a person's financial well-being. Personal finance affects and is affected by many things we do. On one level, personal finance involves money know-how. It is essential to know how to earn money as well as how to save, spend, invest, and control it in order to achieve set goals. On another level, personal finance is intertwined with personal *lifestyle*. Our choice of careers, friends, hobbies, communities, cars, and clothes is determined by personal finances, and yet our personal finances can also determine our lifestyles.

If, for example, you are a college student living independently on a shoestring budget, you will probably have to make many financial sacrifices to achieve your educational goals. Where you live is determined by the school you attend and how much you can afford to pay for rent; your vacation is set by your academic schedule and your checkbook balance; your clothing depends on the climate and your limited budget. All these lifestyle decisions are partially determined by your personal finances.

personal finance: *the study of the economic factors and personal decisions that ultimately determine an individual's financial well-being.*

lifestyle: *the way we live our daily lives.*

THE ROLE OF PERSONAL GOALS IN FINANCIAL DECISION MAKING

It is impossible to explore personal finances without understanding the person's goals and priorities. We all need to make an honest assessment of our needs and wants in life, as well as what we are willing and able to do to achieve them.

Shirley Chilton—Goal Setter Par Excellence

Shirley Chilton started her career as a switchboard operator, and became chairman of Daniel Reeves and Company, which, until it was purchased by another company in 1984, was a member of the New York Stock Exchange. Chilton offers an excellent example of how goals can be used as a basis for personal decisions. She comments:

I've made goals for myself ever since childhood. When I was nine, my goal was to become the best student I possibly could and I ended up valedictorian of my class. Ever since then I've set short-term and long-term goals and I've tried my best to achieve each of them within a certain period of time. This is every bit as important after you've won a certain position as before. Right now I am planning what I'll do after I retire.

Shirley Chilton's goals have influenced her entire career. Her retirement goal is to write children's books on our economic system (she already has four co-authored books to her credit). No doubt this goal will underlie many of the personal decisions she will make in the future.

Source: Paula Nelson, *The Joy of Money: The Guide to Women's Financial Freedom* (New York: Bantam Books, 1980), p. 4.

SETTING PERSONAL GOALS

Suppose your long-range goal is to save enough money to open a television repair shop. Many intermediate objectives must first be achieved, such as obtaining the necessary technical training by attending a community college, a vocational school, or an industry-sponsored training program. You may also need to work for an established shop for on-the-job training and experience. The next consideration should be the determination of the amount of money needed to open the shop and how much of that money will come from savings and how much will be borrowed. Finally, you will need to determine the best location for your television repair shop. Some of the steps must be taken sequentially; you must complete one before starting the next. However, others can be accomplished simultaneously.

Personal Lifestyles: From Thelma to Scott

The term *lifestyle* simply refers to the way we live our daily lives. Lifestyle decisions are often based on the individual's personal goals and priorities. One study identified ten basic lifestyles (five for each sex):

Thelma, the old-fashioned traditionalist, *is a devoted wife, doting mother, and conscientious housekeeper. Thelma has few interests outside her own family. She does not condone sexual permissiveness or political liberalism, nor can she sympathize with women's libbers.*

Candice, the chic suburbanite, *is an urbane woman, well-educated, probably married to a professional man. She is a prime mover in her community and is active in club affairs.*

Mildred, the militant mother, *married early, had children and now wishes the women's liberation movement had happened in time to help her. She likes soap operas and lottery tickets because they help her escape into a fantasy world.*

Cathy, the contented mother, *married early, had a big family and likes it that way. She thinks women's liberation opposes biblical teachings, is trusting and relaxed, and buys only the cereals her children demand.*

Eleanor, the elegant socialite, *says women's liberation is unnecessary if a woman has a man to take care of her. She spends little time preparing meals but spends a lot of time and money on cosmetics and high-fashion clothes, and thinks face creams are better if they cost more.*

Herman, the retired homebody, *has opinions that conflict with nearly everything in the modern world. He can neither change the world nor cope with it. His favorite meal is a hearty breakfast. He uses low-cholesterol products, and he is very concerned about high prices. He distrusts foreign-made products.*

Dale, the devoted family man, *married early, fathered a family, and is happy. A blue-collar worker with a high school education, he is more interested in knowing what a product can do for him than what star endorses it and worries about excessive sex and violence on TV.*

Ben, the self-made businessman, *believes you get what you pay for, values his time, eats bacon and eggs despite his doctor's disapproval because "there's no substitute," and thinks government should keep its nose out of private industry.*

Fred, the frustrated factory worker, *married young and is now unhappy and cynical. He likes to think that he is a bit of a swinger; he fantasizes and goes to the movies to escape from his everyday world.*

Scott, the successful professional, *is much smoother; his speech is more confident and his manner sure. He carries three major credit cards and uses them primarily to pay for business travel.*

Source: Peter W. Bernstein, "Psychographics Is Still an Issue on Madison Avenue," *Fortune,* Jan. 16, 1978, pp. 78–84, reprinted by permission from FORTUNE Magazine; and "Film Findings Show Use of Lifestyle Research," *Marketing News,* June 17, 1977, p. 9, © American Marketing Association.

INTRODUCTION TO PERSONAL FINANCE

Personal goals change throughout an individual's lifetime, and for this reason they should be written down and reviewed periodically. To be effective, goals should reflect changes in circumstances, such as education, family situations, career advancement, the community, economic conditions, world events, and even your emotional and physical well-being.

THE IMPACT OF MONEY

Money is another important factor in most personal lifestyle decisions. First, you must acquire money through work, savings, investments, borrowing, or inheritance; then you allocate these funds among competing wants and needs. You must ask yourself whether a new tennis racket is more important than repairing the kitchen faucet, a $125 dinner for two at a French restaurant a higher priority than saving.

Whatever the answers—and these are private choices that only you can make—the focus on money remains. That is why it is important to understand what money is and how it is used to measure the nation's as well as personal wealth.

WHAT IS MONEY?

Money is an accepted and conventional medium of exchange. It includes currency, *demand deposits* (checking accounts at commercial banks), and other

money: an accepted and conventional medium of exchange.

demand deposits: checking accounts at commercial banks

Changing Lifestyles Are an Important Factor in Many Personal Financial Decisions.

Source: Drawing by Joseph Farris; © 1982 The New Yorker Magazine, Inc.

checking deposits, such as NOW, automatic-transfer, and credit-union share-draft accounts (see Chapter 6).

Whatever form money takes, it serves three vital functions. First, money is a convenient way of paying for goods and services. Money eliminates bartering transactions involving such items as livestock and grain—a form of exchange that was common in primitive societies. Money allows you to secure the necessities and comforts of life without worrying about supplying a specific item or service in return.

In its capacity as a means of payment, money is considered a liquid asset—that is, money is a direct means of payment whose nominal value does not change. If you buy a pair of shoes for $50, you can always be sure that 50 singles, 10 fives, a $50 check, or a $50 credit card charge will pay the bill. You cannot be sure of this constancy of nominal value if you are trying to exchange a diamond ring, a beach house, or a used car for money. Even though each of these items is a valuable asset, its worth may fluctuate up or down for a variety of reasons.

Second, money acts as a purchasing-power reserve fund. Because money can be stored until needed (unlike grain or livestock, which may lose their value if not bartered at a specific time), it eliminates the need for exact coordination between income and expenditures. If money could not be stored, every time you needed a loaf of bread, you would have to generate the income to pay for it. The money in your wallet or bank allows purchases to be made at any convenient time. However, it should be noted that a rising price level can significantly reduce the purchasing power of money.

Finally, money facilitates accounting for business activity. Because nearly every financial transaction in the United States is made in dollars, a total accounting of the goods and services bought and sold is possible. This accounting is vital to measuring the progress of the economy and deciding government economic policy. It also provides individuals with a yardstick for measuring their own economic progress.[3]

MONEY IN THE ECONOMY

Various economic concepts are expressed in monetary terms. Some of the more important concepts for personal finance are gross national product, personal income, disposable income, and discretionary income. These concepts entail the relative availability of money to purchase goods and services. The current status of these items is shown in dollars, which facilitates comparisons to earlier years.

gross national product:
the total value of all final goods and services produced in the economy during a specific period of time and expressed in current market prices.

Gross national product (GNP) is the total value of all final goods and services produced in the economy during a specific period of time and expressed in current market prices. Thus, the United States was a $3.3 trillion economy in 1983. Gross national product is the most accepted overall measure of the nation's economic performance, since it shows the overall output of the nation's economy.

Gross national product is an important determinant of *personal income,* the amount actually received by individuals. Personal income includes so-called *transfer payments* such as unemployment benefits. *Disposable income* is the amount left after income taxes are paid. Many people refer to this as *take-home pay,* although many paychecks are also subject to other payroll deductions like insurance premiums. *Discretionary income* is what remains after all necessary expenses have been paid. Necessary expenses are usually defined as those covering food, clothing, and shelter. Discretionary money is what we use to purchase entertainment, personal care items, and a new stereo.

All of these concepts have one thing in common. All are stated in terms of money—dollars in the United States, pesos in Mexico, and francs in France. Money is clearly the universally accepted method of keeping score in our economy.

THE CONSUMER PRICE INDEX SHOWS THE RELATIVE ABILITY OF MONEY TO PURCHASE GOODS AND SERVICES

Since 1919 the rise and fall of consumer prices have been measured by the *Consumer Price Index* (CPI). This index allows consumers to see how the value of a dollar changes over time. Specifically, the CPI measures the change in price over time of a fixed "market basket" of goods and services purchased by urban consumers to meet their day-to-day needs.

Over the years, the consumer purchasing power measured by the CPI has been ravaged by *inflation,* a term used to describe an increased price level. Between 1970 and 1982, for example, the CPI measure of food prices rose by nearly 102 percent; the cost of home ownership rose by 127 percent; and the cost of fuel oil and coal, by a whopping 208 percent (see Table 1-1). In 1983, however, the rate of inflation was only 3.8 percent, the lowest increase since 1972. Energy costs actually declined by 0.5 percent. While medical costs went up 6.4 percent, this was the best mark in a decade. Similarly, food costs recorded their smallest gain since 1976, a modest 2.7 percent.[4] Standard & Poor's, a financial reporting firm, pegged the 1984 inflation rate at 5.3 percent.[5]

Fluctuations in the CPI have a critical effect on personal finance. Social Security cost-of-living increases are tied to the CPI, as are federal retirement and food stamp benefits and the wages of union workers with cost-of-living clauses in their contracts. Because of the impact of the CPI on the economy, Department of Labor economists have attempted in recent years to correct measurement distortions, especially a major distortion in the measurement of housing costs.

Before 1983, the CPI measured four separate elements of home ownership: home prices, mortgage rates, financing costs, and property taxes. The

---

personal income: *the part of gross national product actually received by individuals.*

transfer payments: *payments such as unemployment benefits.*

disposable income: *the amount of personal income left after income taxes are paid.*

take-home pay: *a term used to describe a person's disposable income.*

discretionary income: *disposable income after all necessary expenses have been paid.*

Consumer Price Index: *the government's measure of consumer price changes.*

inflation: *a term used to describe rising price levels in the economy.*

Table 1-1
THE CONSUMER PRICE INDEX 1970–1982 (Selected Years)

[1967 = 100. Annual averages of monthly figures, except as indicated. Prior to 1965, excludes Alaska and Hawaii. 1965–1977 indexes reflect buying patterns of urban wage earners and clerical workers in the 1960's, including single workers living alone as well as families of two or more persons; indexes for prior years apply only to families of two or more persons; beginning 1978, reflects buying patterns of all urban consumers in the 1970's.]

ALL ITEMS	1970	1976	1978	1979	1980	1981	1982[1]
All items	**5.9**	**5.8**	**7.7**	**11.3**	**13.5**	**10.4**	**6.7**
Food	5.5	3.1	10.0	10.9	8.6	7.9	4.8
Housing:							
Rent, residential	4.2	5.4	6.8	7.3	8.9	8.7	7.7
Home ownership	10.8	5.6	10.9	15.5	19.7	12.3	9.4
Home purchase	8.0	5.1	9.6	13.4	14.0	5.3	6.2
Mortgage interest	10.1	−.8	5.9	12.7	18.6	16.2	7.2
Fuel oil and coal[2]	4.3	6.6	5.3	35.1	37.9	21.6	−6.0
Gas and electricity	4.4	11.4	9.0	10.8	17.1	14.6	14.4
Apparel and upkeep	4.1	3.7	3.5	4.4	7.1	4.8	2.7
Private transportation	4.3	9.9	4.8	14.8	17.4	11.4	2.0
Automobiles, new	3.1	6.3	7.6	7.9	8.0	6.1	3.5
Gasoline	.9	4.2	4.3	35.3	39.0	11.3	−11.1
Auto insurance rates	13.7	28.8	2.9	5.6	8.2	4.7	5.8
Public transportation	14.0	9.8	3.0	6.7	25.6	24.0	14.9
Intercity bus fare	7.0	5.9	7.5	8.2	14.3	14.4	9.8
Medical care	6.4	9.5	8.4	9.3	10.9	10.8	12.0
Entertainment	5.1	5.0	5.3	6.7	8.9	7.8	6.4
Personal care	3.6	6.5	6.5	7.6	8.8	8.9	6.9
All services	8.1	8.3	8.5	11.0	15.4	13.1	10.7
All commodities	4.7	4.3	7.1	11.4	12.2	8.4	3.8

[1] Change from May 1981–May 1982.
[2] Includes bottled gas.
Minus sign (−) denotes decrease.

Source: U.S. Bureau of Labor Statistics, cited in *Monthly Labor Review*; Bureau of the Census, *Statistical Abstract of the United States: 1982–1983*, (Washington, D.C.: U.S. Government Printing Office, 1983), p. 461.

assumption was made that every family bought and financed a new home each month, which, of course, was not the case. As a result, sharply rising mortgage rates overshadowed relatively moderate rises in the cost of goods and other staples, and the CPI climbed faster than it should have. To correct this distortion, the Department of Labor focused attention on the cost of renting, rather than owning, a home, which was regarded as a more accurate measure of actual month-to-month housing costs. Figure 1-1 shows that this change has had an important impact on the overall CPI. With the exception of 1982, the new method generally shows a more moderate level of inflation than the old.

Beyond the housing change, greater emphasis is now being placed on the cost of food, clothing, gasoline, and entertainment. By 1987, when all changes to the CPI are finalized, the index will more accurately reflect the cost of goods and services people actually buy in their day-to-day lives.

A MODERN PERSONAL FINANCE MODEL

While money is the essential topic in any discussion of personal finance, a variety of factors can affect our decisions about securing, investing, and allocating money. To be complete, a model of personal finance must focus on both environmental and personal decision factors.

Environmental factors are the general economic conditions that currently exist and must be considered in personal financial decisions. Personal decision factors include various aspects of individual and household financial behavior. Although individuals cannot change the environmental factors, they can make personal decisions about careers, investments, expenditures, tax planning, and personal values, goals, and priorities.

Figure 1-1
COMPARING THE METHODS OF CALCULATING THE CONSUMER PRICE INDEX

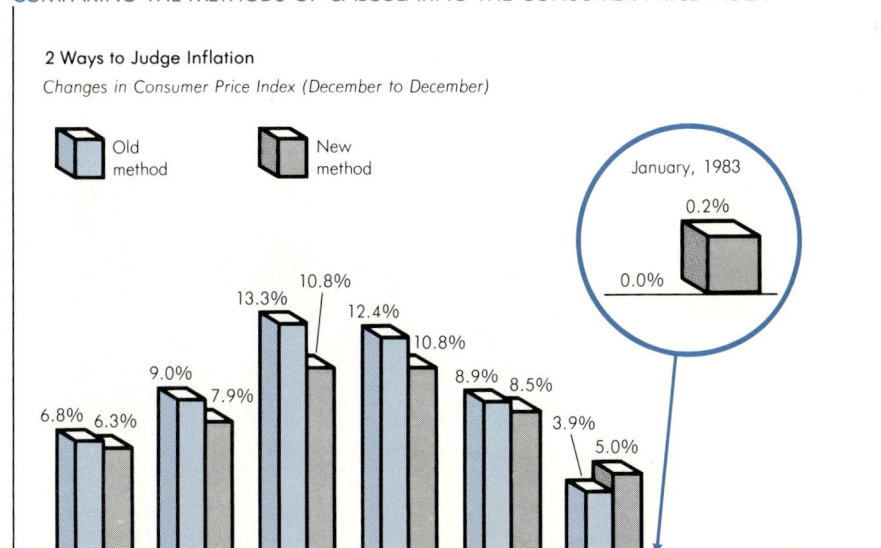

Source: Reprinted from *U.S. News & World Report* issue of March 7, 1983. Copyright, 1983, U.S. News & World Report, Inc.

12 OVERVIEW OF CONTEMPORARY PERSONAL FINANCE

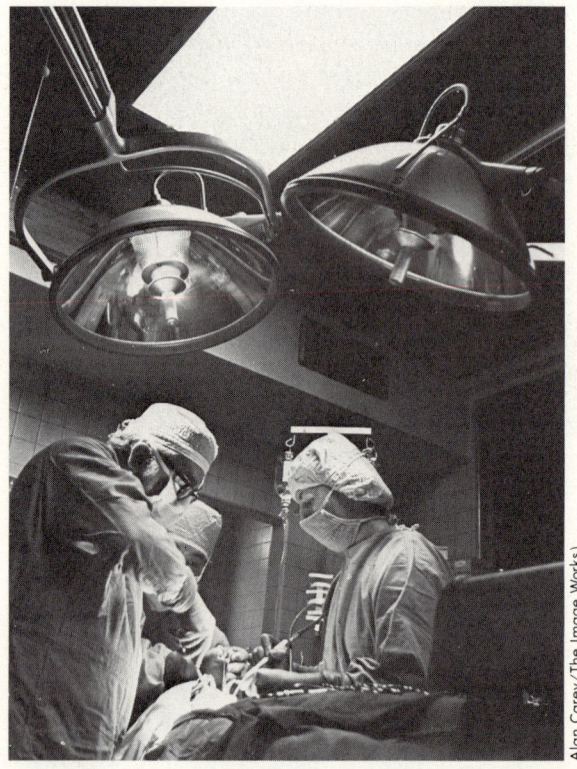

The Consumer Price Index (CPI) measures the change in price over time of specific goods and services—for example, food, housing, automobiles, and health care. When the CPI rises, it indicates that the economy is undergoing inflation.

Figure 1-2
THE MODERN PERSONAL FINANCE MODEL

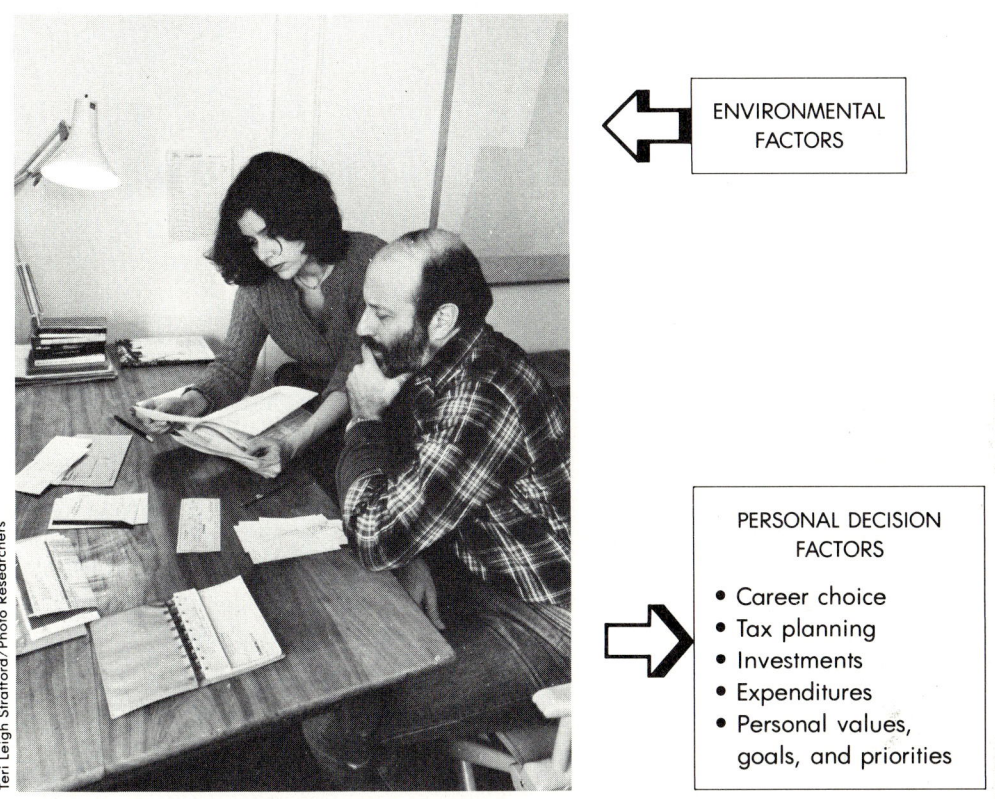

According to the modern personal finance model, our personal finance decisions, which reflect our individual goals and lifestyles, are strongly affected by environmental factors —general economic conditions that the individual cannot control.

Figure 1-2 shows the basic variables that affect personal financial decisions. Each influences the other. It would be foolish, for example, to make a major purchase without considering the availability and cost of credit. Similarly, savings and investment decisions should reflect one's personal goals and lifestyle. Personal financial decisions are the focus of this text. Let's look at a general outline of the decision areas you need to consider.

AN OUTLINE OF PERSONAL FINANCIAL DECISIONS

A person's economic future is charted via career, investment, spending, and tax-planning decisions. These decisions reflect the personal values and goals by which our economic lives are guided.

CAREER CHOICE

No factor exerts as strong an influence on an individual's personal finances as does the career choice. It is through work that we acquire the income needed to build a lifestyle; to buy goods and services, including insurance protection; to save and invest; and to plan for retirement. Chapter 2 focuses on the role a career plays in the personal finance picture. It also explains how education, occupation, and industry affect potential earnings, as well as the importance of and the best way to choose a career and find a job.

INVESTMENTS

Investments allow money acquired through work, inheritance, or other sources to be preserved and increased. Investments are tied to the things people want and expect out of life. A person who wants to become a millionaire will handle money differently from the person who wants only to "send the kids to college" and retire comfortably.

How many investment risks are taken depends on individual goals. A variety of options exist, including banks and money market funds, which enable cash to be invested with little risk. Stocks and bonds offer a higher potential yield but are a more precarious investment option. Mutual funds, commodities, futures, and collectibles, such as art and antiques, are other investment possibilities, but they require specialized knowledge in those areas.

EXPENDITURES

Managing one's money and spending it wisely are key factors in any personal financial plan. Without a clear, well-thought-out budget that reflects one's personal values and goals, any financial plan is sure to fail. Within personal budget limits, an individual exercises his or her rights as a consumer to select or reject the wide range of products and services that are available. As you purchase real estate, make major buying decisions, secure insurance protection, you can make the most of your money, or squander your valuable financial resources.

TAX PLANNING

Everyone is faced with paying a variety of taxes to the federal, state, and local governments, so personal financial plans must reflect these taxes and work to minimize the tax burden. The kinds of taxes we pay, including federal and state personal income taxes, sales taxes, property taxes, and so on, will be examined in Chapter 5, along with legal methods for minimizing one's tax load.

PERSONAL VALUES, GOALS, AND PRIORITIES

Underlying all these personal financial decisions are your values, goals, and personal financial priorities. Values define lifestyle by determining how you will live, the kind of work you will do, and how you will handle your money. Personal values also define long-range plans, ultimate goals, and financial priorities. A well-thought-out list of your values, goals, and priorities will give a financial plan direction and shape.

The challenge is to know what your values are so that they can be used in constructing an effective financial plan. The long-term economic benefits of a good financial plan are enormous, and the starting point for developing such a plan is to know your personal values, goals, and priorities.

DEVELOPING A FINANCIAL PLAN

Financial plans are discussed in detail in Chapter 4. Here we'll present the rudiments of such an effort. All financial plans involve three basic steps: (1) getting more money, (2) using your money more effectively, and (3) monitoring expenditures.

Step 1: Getting More Money. Work smarter; seek retraining for a better, higher-paying job; take career risks that may pay off in the long run; make sound, high-yielding investments—these are examples of the first step. The amount of money you earn is a vital part of any financial plan, and it is up to you to make the most of your opportunities.

Step 2: Using Your Money More Effectively. You must try to spend every dollar wisely and make every major buying decision part of your overall financial plan. That means no impulsive spending or giving in to the hard sell. It means discipline in sticking to a budget and a determination to succeed.

Step 3: Monitoring Expenditures. Budgeting is the key to controlling expenditures. A budget focuses on where the money is going and whether one's goals are being met. It also suggests appropriate times for reevaluating priorities. If your budget does not reflect what you want from life now and in the future, it should be changed. Information also enables expenditures to be kept under control. The more you know about real estate, consumer loans, different kinds of insurance, taxes, and major purchases, the more likely you are to spend the least money to purchase the greatest value.

Contemporary Personal Finance explores each of these basic steps in detail. Although the specific topics range from career-planning techniques to buying a new home, all are related to obtaining money, using money more effectively, or monitoring expenditures. Chapter 2 begins by focusing on the first of these basic actions: choosing a career.

SUMMARY

Personal finance is the study of the economic factors and personal decisions that affect a person's financial well-being. The study of personal finance is important since it provides a means to an improved lifestyle. In fact, all personal financial decisions should be based on a thorough assessment of the person's objectives and priorities.

Money is an important factor in lifestyle decisions. Money can be defined as an accepted and conventional medium of exchange. It consists of currency, NOW accounts, share-draft accounts, automatic-transfer accounts, and checking accounts. In terms of functions, money serves as a convenient way of paying for goods and services; it acts as a purchasing-power reserve fund; and it facilitates accounting for business activities. Money is also used to measure economic activity. Gross national product, personal income, disposable income, and discretionary income are all reported in monetary terms. The Consumer Price Index is used to show the relative ability of money to purchase goods and services.

The personal finance model developed in Chapter 1 outlines the various personal decision factors involved in financial decision making: career choice, investments, expenditures, tax planning, and personal values, goals, and priorities. These decisions must be made within the parameters of the current general economic environment.

Effective financial planning is a necessity in modern economic life. Such plans hinge on three basic steps: obtaining more money, using money more effectively, and monitoring expenditures. Each of these steps is discussed in detail in *Contemporary Personal Finance*.

REVIEW QUESTIONS

1. Briefly define the following terms:

   personal finance
   lifestyle
   money
   demand deposits
   gross national product
   personal income
   transfer payments
   disposable income
   take-home pay
   discretionary income
   Consumer Price Index
   inflation

2. Explain how the study of personal finance is important to a college student.
3. How are lifestyles influenced by money?
4. What is money?
5. What are the functions of money?
6. Outline the various economic concepts that are expressed in monetary terms.
7. Explain how the Consumer Price Index is used to show the relative ability of money to purchase goods and services.
8. Describe how the Consumer Price Index has been altered in recent years.
9. Briefly describe the modern personal finance model presented in Chapter 1.
10. Outline the three basic steps in any financial plan.

CASES AND EXERCISES

1. List your personal goals in order of priority. What must you do in order to reach these goals? Discuss.

2. A Gallup poll published in *Success* magazine asked over 2,500 people: "In your opinion, how much income per year does a person need to be considered a success in America today?" The median response was $37,000 annually. The response varied according to income levels. Those who made more had higher definitions of success. Respondents who earned $20,000 annually defined success as $34,000 a year, but people who earned $40,000 said success was $52,000 in annual earnings. When the responses were classified by age, there was little difference among the different age groups.[6] What is your definition of success? Why?

3. Respondents in the Gallup poll mentioned above were also asked to pick three factors that were most important in judging personal success. A list of twelve possible factors was provided.[7] The responses were:

Good health	58%
Enjoyable job	49%
Happy family	45%
Good education	39%
Peace of mind	34%
Good friends	25%
Intelligence	15%
Unlimited money	11%
Talent	7%
Luck	6%
Luxury car	2%
Expensive home	1%

4. Which of the personal lifestyles mentioned in the chapter—Thelma, Candice, Mildred, Cathy, Eleanor, Herman, Dale, Ben, Fred, or Scott—comes the closest to how you view yourself?

5. Some experts argue that the "market basket" of goods and services used to construct the Consumer Price Index is not appropriate for everyone. If so, what goods and services would you include if you were to develop a personal consumer price index? Trace the recent price history of these typical purchases. How does your consumer price index compare with the one developed by the government?

ANSWERS TO PERSONAL FINANCE I.Q. TEST

1. Fact. 2. Fiction. 3. Fact. 4. Fiction. 5. Fact.

HOW JIM DAVIS REACHED HIS PERSONAL FINANCIAL DECISION

Professor Keck was glad Jim had responded as he did. It helped her make a point she always tries to make to her personal finance classes at the outset: *understanding personal finance is understanding the relative value of money.* For Jim to reach his hypothetical decision, he must go beyond the dollar amount of the salary. Here are just a few of the questions he must ask:

1. What are the costs of living in Nashville compared with Nome? A salary might sound high, but if housing, food, and other basic costs in a city are also high, then the extra money will quickly disappear.

2. What is the career potential of the job? After a year or two, will Jim be able to advance to a higher-level position? Or is there nowhere to go?

3. Are there state and local taxes—and, if so, how much are they? A high tax rate will take a bite out of Jim's take-home pay. And sales taxes can add considerably to the cost of daily living expenses.

4. Does the company offer a health insurance plan and other benefits? Are there, for instance, any income-saving options? A good benefit package can increase the value of a salary.

5. Which city would Jim like living in the best? Even if his goal is making more money, he should consider his day-to-day environment as this can affect his attitude toward work. What kind of leisure activities are available? Is it easy to meet new people?

6. In addition, because Jim's family lives in Kentucky, he should figure out how much it will cost if he travels to see them a couple of times a year.

Professor Keck's point is that money is related to the goods and services it will purchase, so Jim must evaluate what the real money earned will be, not just income.

As the end of the class drew near, Jim raised his hand to say, "I guess I'll decide which job to take later. First, I think I'd better take this course."

LEARNING OBJECTIVES

1. To show that career choice is the most important financial decision anyone has to make, and that it should be related to personal goals. / 2. To outline the variables that affect a person's income potential. / 3. To explain the steps involved in choosing a career. / 4. To list the factors used to measure the potential of a particular career. / 5. To discuss the various aspects of the job search.

TESTING YOUR PERSONAL FINANCE I.Q.

	FACT	FICTION
1. A brain picker, legend maker, egg smeller, and slubber doffer are all jobs found in the American economy.	☐	☐
2. College students appear to be more materialistic than they were a decade ago.	☐	☐
3. Babe Ruth was poorly paid compared with today's athletes.	☐	☐
4. The service sector will show the highest rate of job growth in the 1980s.	☐	☐
5. College graduates do not earn appreciably more than high school graduates over their entire lifetime.	☐	☐
6. There are no practical limits to an individual's earning potential in the United States.	☐	☐

The materials in this chapter assist in separating fact from fiction. Your answers can be checked on page 40.

CHAPTER TWO

CAREER ASPECTS OF PERSONAL FINANCE

SHARING A PERSONAL FINANCIAL DECISION WITH PROFESSOR MICHAEL DOHAN OF QUEENS COLLEGE OF THE CITY UNIVERSITY OF NEW YORK

Professor Michael Dohan, who is also a financial planner with Family Financial Consultants, opens his personal finance course with a lecture on the value of time versus money. He discusses how to integrate these concepts into a financial plan which, starting now, helps students meet their long-term career goals and financial needs.

For many students, he explains, the key question in their financial plan involves a decision between working long hours in outside jobs and borrowing money to finance their education. In his experience, students who work more than ten hours per week are likely to see their grade-point average suffer. Yet many students have a bias against borrowing money, so Professor Dohan likes to discuss the implications of the borrowing versus study time versus work load decision with the following questions:

1. Is avoiding having to pay back a loan after graduation worth the time spent earning $3.50 or so per hour now? Compare your low wages now with your much higher income once you have a full-time job after you've earned your degree.
2. Are you working as an accounting clerk and planning to be an accountant, or are you working as a grocery clerk and planning to be an accountant? In other words, are you learning from your job? Will it help you in your career?
3. Is your course load too heavy given the time you have to study? If you must work, can you take fewer credits to allow yourself to learn more from each course even though it may take longer to get your degree? You need to evaluate the quality of the education you're getting. Remember, your performance in college plays a large role in later career or graduate school opportunities.

"Your earning power is affected by the level and quality of your education. Smart financial planning begins now, and takes this into account," Professor Dohan concludes.

A few days after hearing the lecture, Connie Ferrara sought out Professor Dohan's advice. His comments have made her re-evaluate her own situation, and she feels very confused. "This past summer my father retired and moved. Now I have to work 40 hours a week to support myself and pay tuition," she declares. "But I know it's affecting my learning because I hardly ever have the time or energy to study."

If you were Professor Dohan, what advice would you give to Connie?

To find out how Professor Dohan helped Connie with her personal financial decision, turn to page 40.

"How would you like a job where, if you made a mistake, a big red light goes on and 18,000 people boo?"
Jacques Plante, former hockey goalie[1]

The year was 1930 and the Great Depression was a fact of life. Factory workers earned about $1,600 a year, if they still had a job. College professors took in $3,100; lawyers, $5,500; and physicians, $5,200. But one wage earner stood out by receiving an amazing $80,000 that year. Babe Ruth's 1930 salary would be equal to $2.8 or $2.9 million today, after allowing for 50-plus years of inflation and the progressive income tax. As Ruth explained his career: "A man ought to get all he can earn. A man who knows he's making money for other people ought to get some of the profit he brings in. It's business, I tell you. There ain't no sentiment to it." Ruth understood the importance that one's career has for personal finance. He himself had come a long way from a Baltimore orphanage. Ruth began his career as a pitcher with the Boston Red Sox. But owner Harry Frazee traded him to the Yankees for a reported price of $400,000 so he could invest in Broadway plays. Six years later Frazee was rewarded when *No, No Nanette* became a smash hit. But one wonders how Frazee would have fared if the Babe had remained in Boston.[2]

Although few careers are as dramatic as that of Babe Ruth, it is clear that everyone's career is a crucial element of his or her personal finances. It is the primary source of most people's income, and it influences the very lifestyle they choose.

CAREER CHOICE SHOULD BE RELATED TO PERSONAL GOALS

The personal goals discussed in Chapter 1 provide the basis of the career selections we make. Consider the remarks of three University of Michigan students, and see how they might relate to their future careers.

- "Being materialistic is not necessarily an evil thing. It's just attaining something you'd like to have in life," commented Marc, an economics and psychology major.

- "My long-term goal is to get a job where I can be an entrepreneur, where I can plan programs and policies," explained Gail, a business major.

- "I want to be able to say to myself that I have cleaned up an environment that was hurting a lot of people," asserted Jim, a chemical engineering student.

These remarks illustrate differing emphases on money and financial security, job satisfaction, and social contribution. One's career choice is influenced by the weight one assigns to these personal financial goals.

MONEY AND FINANCIAL SECURITY

Wages and salaries provide the major source of income for two out of three Americans.[3] So earnings largely determine a person's standard of living. As inflationary pressures have increased, the desire for money has become a more important factor in job choice. According to Alexander Astin, a professor at the University of California, Los Angeles, who annually polls 200,000 college freshmen, "we've seen a steady rise in what I can only call materialism —an interest in money, power, and status." Astin's surveys show a dramatic increase in the number of college freshmen who feel that being "very well-off" financially is "very important" to them.[4]

JOB SATISFACTION

For many people, however, job satisfaction is even more important than income. These people seek a job that provides an intellectual challenge as well as a pleasant work environment with friendly co-workers. Donna Murray, a bookbinder, describes this goal in Studs Terkel's well-known book *Working*: "It's an alluring kind of thing, lovely, because you know . . . a book is a life, like one man is a life. Yes, yes this work is good for me. . . . If you bind good books you make something good, really and truly good."[5] Job satisfaction is also a critical ingredient in job success. One recent survey of executives found that all but a few truly enjoyed their jobs.[6]

SOCIAL CONTRIBUTION

The desire to contribute to society is an important career goal for many people. Chemical engineering student Jim Rubin's earlier comments reflect this goal. The need to contribute to society through work was also expressed by fireman Tom Patrick in Terkel's *Working*: "Last month there was a second alarm. I was off duty. I ran over there. I'm a bystander. I see these firemen on the roof, with the smoke pouring out around them, and the flames, and they go in. It fascinated me. [I realized] that's what I do! . . . The firemen, you actually see them come out with babies in their hands. You see them give mouth-to-mouth when a guy's dying. [When I'm old] I can look back and say, 'I helped put out a fire. I helped save somebody. It shows something I did on earth.'"[7]

OVERVIEW OF CONTEMPORARY PERSONAL FINANCE

A careful analysis of your personal goals in life represents a major step in clarifying your career choice. Whatever choice you make, pursue your career to its utmost. A person's career should be a primary source of personal satisfaction.

VARIABLES THAT AFFECT INCOME POTENTIAL

Part of the so-called American dream is the belief that there are no limits to an individual's earning potential. But this is only partly true. Several variables have a direct impact on how much a person can earn in a given occupation. These include education and occupational earning patterns (discussed below), as well as other factors like industry and geographical considerations (discussed later in this chapter).

EDUCATION

One of the most important factors affecting the level of annual income you can expect to earn is your educational background. College graduates over 25 average 44 percent higher yearly earnings than people with high school diplomas. And people with graduate degrees average 19 percent higher than those with bachelor's degrees.[8]

A college education is obviously the key to greater income potential, but it is becoming increasingly more costly to achieve. College costs have even outpaced inflation in recent years. According to one estimate, the annual cost of some prestigious colleges may exceed $30,000 by 1991.[9] Table 2-1 shows the annual costs at some selected schools from around the United States.

Financing Your Education. As college costs escalate, most students must find ways to finance their education. The need is critical, for college costs have become a huge expense for families to meet.

Students and their families can apply to a variety of sources for financial aid to meet college expenses. Since eligibility for many of these programs depends on family income, families are often required to reveal assets and sources of income and submit copies of their federal income tax return. The federal government itself offers several student assistance programs.[10] The more important ones are:

Pell Grants: *federal financial awards designed to assist needy students.*

Guaranteed Student Loan Program: *a program of federally insured loans for college students.*

1. *Pell Grants.* These federal awards are designed to help financially needy students, no matter what their grades are. In the year 1984–1985, if a student's family meets the family income requirements, the student is eligible to receive up to $1,900 for an academic year.

2. *Guaranteed Student Loan Program (GSLP).* This federal loan program is open to students whose families have incomes under $30,000 or meet the requirements of a needs test. Eligible students may receive up to $2,500 per

Table 2-1
UNDERGRADUATE TUITION COSTS FOR THE 1984–85 ACADEMIC YEAR

School	In-State	Out-of-State
Glendale Community College, CA	$ 100.00	$ 180.00
Western State College, CO	1,393.00	4,060.00
Georgetown University, DC	8,500.00	8,500.00
Hillsborough Community College, FL	480.00	1,056.00
University of Central Florida, FL	620.00	1,586.00
Ball State University, IN	1,464.00	3,360.00
Vincennes University, IN	1,108.00	3,128.00
Emporia State, KS	958.00	1,978.00
Western Kentucky University, KY	900.00	2,560.00
University of New Orleans, LA	984.00	2,294.00
Michigan State University, MI	1,476.00	3,258.00
Community College of the Finger Lakes, NY	1,224.00	2,248.00
Suffolk County Community College, Eastern Campus, NY	1,056.00	2,312.00
Appalachian State University, NC	771.50	3,082.50
University of North Carolina—Wilmington, NC	700.00	2,384.00
Columbus Technical Institute, OH	1,152.00	2,592.00
University of Cincinnati, OH	1,803.00	4,329.00
University of Toledo, OH	1,364.00	3,396.00
Portland State University, OR	1,413.00	4,038.00
Roane State University, TN	468.00	1,836.00
Lamar University, TX	490.00	1,570.00
Utah Technical College, UT	747.00	1,950.00
Old Dominion University, VA	1,502.00	2,800.00
Clark College, WA	580.50	2,284.50
University of Wisconsin—Oshkosh, WI	1,077.00	3,474.00

year (to a maximum of $12,500) while they are undergraduates, and an additional $5,000 per year for graduate work (up to a loan ceiling of $25,000 for both programs). Under the GSLP students are given federally insured loans from lending institutions at no interest while they are in school. Repayment with interest begins 6 months after graduation, and the loans must be repaid within 10 years.

3. *Auxiliary Loans to Assist Students* (formerly called the *Parent Loan for Undergraduate Students,* or *PLUS Loan*). This government program enables parents to borrow up to $3,000 a year per student from private lenders. Loan repayment must begin within 60 days of taking out the loan, but it can be spread over a period of up to 10 years.

Auxiliary Loans to Assist Students: a federal loan program to assist parents with college expenses.

Supplemental Education Opportunity Grants: a federal program designed to assist college students with exceptional financial needs.

College Work Study: a federal program that subsidizes some college student employment.

National Direct Student Loans: a federal loan program for students with special financial needs.

4. *Supplemental Education Opportunity Grants (SEOG).* These federal grants are available to students with exceptional financial needs. Students may receive up to $2,000 a year, which does not have to be repaid.

5. *College Work Study.* Under this federally subsidized program, needy students are paid for up to 20 hours of work per week on campus.

6. *National Direct Student Loans.* Designed to help students with special financial needs, these federal loans provide up to $6,000 for undergraduates and $12,000 for graduate students. Funds are available to students through their colleges. Repayment must begin 6 months after graduation, and needy students have up to 10 years to repay.

In order to be eligible for these federal programs, students must fill out various forms, which are available through the college financial aid office or high school counselors. This should be done as soon as possible because many of these programs are on a first-come, first-serve basis.

State governments also provide scholarships to some students. Awards are generally based on family income, but some states like California offer modest merit awards. Colleges and universities endowed by alumni contributions are another source of loans and scholarships. In addition, some corporations provide low-interest loans to employees who have children in college. At General Electric, for example, employees can borrow $1,500 a year per student, up to a maximum outstanding amount of $5,000 per student and a total ceiling of $10,000. Certain foundations, labor unions, and fraternal, religious, and ethnic organizations also offer scholarship assistance to qualified applicants.

Cooperative education program: an academic program that combines classroom instruction with paid on-the-job experience.

Another form of assistance, available at many institutions, is the *cooperative education program,* in which students attend class for part of the year and then earn tuition money by working part of the year in fields related to their studies. A different option is offered by the Reserve Officers Training Corp (ROTC), which provides students with substantial scholarship awards in exchange for a military service obligation.

You can learn more about these scholarship and loan programs by:

- Writing the college financial aid office for information.
- Reading *Don't Miss Out* (published by Octameron Associates, Box 3437, Alexandria, VA 22302).
- Writing the College Scholarship Service (Box 2700, Princeton, NJ 08540, or Box 1950, Berkeley, CA 94701).
- Reading *Financing College Education* by Kenneth A. Kohl and Irene C. Kohl (published by Harper & Row, NY).
- Consulting such companies as Scholarship Search (1775 Broadway, Suite 628D, New York, NY 10019); College Selection and Scholarship Services (PO Box 123M, Princeton, NJ 08540); or Academic Directions, Inc.

(575 Madison Ave., New York, NY 10022) for a computer analysis of the scholarships for which you might be eligible. These firms operate on a fee basis.

- Reading the *Selected List of Postsecondary Education Opportunities for Minorities and Women*, put out by the U.S. Department of Education. This guide provides financial aid information for Hispanics, blacks, native Americans, and women. It can be purchased from the Superintendent of Documents (U.S. Government Printing Office, Washington, DC 20402).

The Importance of Continuing Education. Even after you are established in a career, your need for education continues. Continuing education programs are available at many community colleges and other institutions of higher education. These programs are designed for working adults and are often scheduled at night and on weekends. In addition, specialized continuing education material is often available by mail.

OCCUPATIONAL EARNING PATTERNS

A person's occupation plays a large part in determining the individual's lifetime income level. Some occupations, like some industries, have traditionally paid more than others. These differences are an inherent aspect of the American workplace and must be recognized during the career-planning process.

CHOOSING A CAREER

The U.S. Department of Labor's *Dictionary of Occupational Titles* lists more than 20,000 different jobs, many of which are obscure, to say the least. Table 2-2 lists some of the more bizarre jobs.

The task of selecting a job should begin with a personal inventory. Then one must look at where the jobs will be in the future, measure the career potential of an occupation, and consider the benefits of preparation for an occupational cluster. Two alternatives to evaluate are self-employment and working at home. To do all of this effectively, one must become familiar with the various sources of career information.

Dictionary of Occupational Titles: a U.S. Department of Labor book that lists more than 20,000 different jobs.

A PERSONAL INVENTORY

Taking a personal inventory is an important step in career exploration. It helps you visualize clearly who you are and where you want to go.

1. **To start, define your career goals.** What kind of job would you like to have, and where do you see yourself in five years? Is any special training needed to reach your goal? Put these thoughts on paper.

Table 2-2
TWENTY-FIVE VERY ODD JOBS

1. BELLY BUILDER
   Assembles and fits interior parts, or the belly, of pianos.
2. BONE CRUSHER
   Tends the machine that crushes animal bones that are used in the manufacture of glue.
3. BOSOM PRESSER
   Clothing presser who specializes in pressing bosoms of blouses and shirts.
4. BRAIN PICKER
   Places animal head on a table or on hooks in a slaughterhouse, splits the skull, and picks out the brains.
5. BREAST BUFFER
   Buffs and smooths the shoe breast, which is the forepart of the heel.
6. CHICK SEXER
   Inserts a light to examine the sex organs of chicks, then separates the males from the females. A university degree in chick sexing is offered in Japan.
7. DOPE SPRAYER
   Sprays a solution, known as dope, on tanned hides in leather manufacturing.
8. DUKEY RIDER
   Couples and uncouples cars being moved in a railroad yard. Rides cars and turns hand brakes to control speed.
9. EGG SMELLER
   Smells eggs after they are broken open to check for spoilage.
10. FINGER WAVER
    Hairdresser who sets waves in with fingers.
11. FOOT STRAIGHTENER
    Straightens and screws into place the feet on watch and clock dials during assembly.
12. HEEL GOUGER
    Tends the machine that cuts a cavity to form the seat for a heel in shoe manufacturing.
13. HOG HEAD SINGER
    Singes hair from heads of hog carcasses in slaughterhouse with a torch.
14. HOOKER INSPECTOR
    Inspects cloth in a textile mill for defects by using a hooking machine which folds the cloth.
15. KISS MIXER
    Mixes the ingredients used in processing candy kisses.
16. LEGEND MAKER
    Arranges and mounts letters, logos, and numbers on paper backing to make signs and displays.
17. MOTHER REPAIRER
    Repairs metal phonograph record "mother" by removing dirt and nickel particles from sound-track grooves. Records are mass-produced by being pressed from the metal mother record.
18. MUCKER
    Shovels muck and other debris from work areas and ditches around construction sites and in mines.
19. NECKER
    Feeds cardboard and fabric into a machine that wraps them around each other to form the neck of a jewelry box. The neck is the filler between the case and the fabric lining.
20. PANTYHOSE-CROTCH-CLOSING-MACHINE OPERATOR
    Operates machine that sews pantyhose crotches closed.
21. SLUBBER DOFFER
    Doffs bobbins of yarn from spindles of slubber frames in a textile mill.
22. SQUEEGEE TENDER
    Tends a band-building machine that rolls squeegee, or bands or rubber, and gum strips together in tire manufacturing.
23. TOP SCREW
    Supervises cowboys—called screws.
24. VAMP CREASER
    Tends the machine that creases shoe vamps, the part of the shoe over the instep.
25. WOOD-CLUB-NECK WHIPPER
    Uses a machine to wind nylon cord around the neck of a wood golf club during its manufacture.

Source: "25 Very Odd Jobs" from *The Book of Lists #2* by Irving Wallace, David Wallechinsky, Amy Wallace, and Sylvia Wallace. Copyright © 1980 by Irving Wallace, David Wallechinsky, Amy Wallace, and Sylvia Wallace. By permission of William Morrow & Company.

2. Next explore your career interests. Ask yourself what you want from your work.

3. Then list your skills and special talents. It is important to determine your aptitude for specific careers. (A variety of tests exist for this purpose.)

4. Now list your educational background—the schools, colleges, and special training programs you have attended and any studies you plan to complete before starting a career. Try to apply your background to the job market.

5. Also write down the jobs you have held and the responsibilities of each job. Analyze what you liked and disliked about each.

6. Finally, explore your hobbies and personal interests.

A personal inventory should offer some clues about the types of careers that might be appropriate.

Help from Vocational Counseling. You may also want to consult a *vocational counselor,* someone who interviews, tests, and counsels clients on careers. The interview and testing process may take several days to complete. The tests measure such career-oriented abilities as verbal, computational, mechanical, social, sales, and supervisory skills. They also measure personality dimensions that affect job performance. Using the test results, the counselor assembles a profile that suggests ways you can apply your unique personality, skills, and interests to the job market. The counselor can also give advice on which jobs hold the greatest career opportunity.

Career counseling is available from private consultants, colleges, and various employment firms. Whether or not a career counselor is used, the objective of a personal inventory should be to set out what you really want from a job and to isolate those occupations that best meet your personal priorities.

vocational counselor: a consultant who interviews, tests, and counsels clients on careers.

WHERE THE JOBS WILL BE IN THE FUTURE

According to futurist Alvin Toffler, "both the office and the factory are destined to be revolutionized in the years ahead. The twin revolutions in the white-collar section and in manufacturing add up to nothing less than a wholly new mode of production for society—a giant step for the human race."[11] The changes that Toffler anticipates will create new job frontiers. But they will also eliminate or slow the demand for other jobs that have been the mainstay of the American economy.

According to the Bureau of Labor Statistics, the U.S. labor force will grow more slowly from 1985 to 1990 than it did from 1980 to 1985.[12] This decline is attributed to the fact that between 1980 and 1985 a decrease in younger workers was more than offset by an increase in women entering the labor force. Overall, employment opportunity will vary considerably among the different

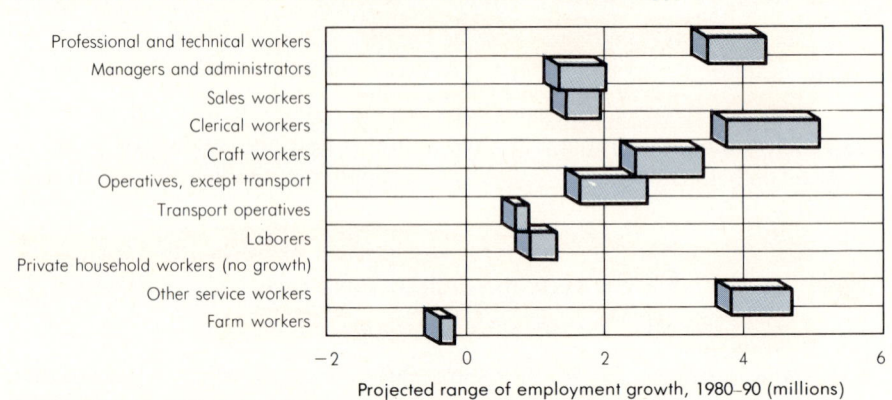

Figure 2-1
EMPLOYMENT CHANGES BY OCCUPATIONAL GROUPS IN THE 1980s

[Bar chart showing projected range of employment growth, 1980-90 (millions), with categories: Professional and technical workers, Managers and administrators, Sales workers, Clerical workers, Craft workers, Operatives except transport, Transport operatives, Laborers, Private household workers (no growth), Other service workers, Farm workers. X-axis ranges from -2 to 6.]

Source: U.S. Bureau of Labor Statistics, *Occupational Outlook Handbook: 1982–1983 Edition*, Bulletin 2200 (Washington, D.C.: U.S. Government Printing Office, 1982), p. 18.

occupational groups: white-collar, blue-collar, service, and farm. Changes in specific occupational groups are shown in Figure 2-1, although it should be remembered that specific career prospects can vary significantly within the various categories.

White-collar Occupations. White-collar occupations, which include professional, managerial, sales, and clerical jobs, make up about half of the work force. During the 1980s, up to 13.2 million new jobs will be added in the various white-collar occupations.

Blue-collar Occupations. Blue-collar occupations include craft, operative, and labor jobs. The Bureau of Labor Statistics predicts that blue-collar jobs will grow during the 1980s, although at a slower rate than the average white-collar job. This growth will create up to 8 million new blue-collar jobs.

Service Occupations. The service sector, which includes such jobs as cosmetologist and bartender, will show a high rate of growth during the 1980s. Up to 4.6 million new service jobs will become available during this decade.

Farm Occupations. Increased farm productivity has meant that fewer and fewer farmers are needed. It is anticipated that there will be between 300,000 and 500,000 fewer farmers at the end of the 1980s than there were at the beginning.

MEASURING CAREER POTENTIAL

It is also important to assess the career potential of various occupations. Choosing a career that is likely to grow in the future requires a focus on four critical factors: the occupation's growth prospects, the industry's growth prospects, job location, and the employer's growth prospects.[13]

The Occupation's Growth Prospects. Job opportunities are created by economic growth (an increased demand for a product or service) and by the need to replace workers who die, retire, or leave their jobs for other reasons. The careers with the greatest potential are those with more openings due to economic growth than to worker attrition. The best and worst growth prospects are shown in Table 2-3.

The Industry's Growth Prospects. Career prospects also depend on the health of the chosen industry. An industry on the wane offers little growth opportunity, while an expanding industry provides the greatest chance for

Table 2-3
THE BEST AND WORST JOBS FOR THE 1990s

The Good Jobs	% Job Growth, 1990s
Paralegal	109–139
Computer systems analyst	68–80
Occupational therapist	63–71
Physical therapist	51–59
Computer programmer	49–60
Speech pathologist/audiologist	47–50
Health services administrator	43–53
Aerospace engineer	43–52
Registered nurse	40–47
Licensed practical nurse	42
Dietician	38–46
Electrical/electronic engineer	35–47

No-Go Jobs	% Job Growth, 1990s
Secondary school teacher	−14
College and university teacher	−9
Historian	−9
School administrator	−1
Credit manager	0
Airline reservation and ticket agent	0–7
Soil conservationist	3
Librarian	3–5
Astronomer	5
Sociologist	6–8
Meteorologist	8

Source: Debra Kaplan Rubin, "Fifth Annual Salary Survey," *Working Woman,* January 1984, p. 63. Based on data from the U.S. Bureau of Labor Statistics. Reprinted with permission from *Working Woman.* Copyright © 1984 by Hal Publications, Inc.

OVERVIEW OF CONTEMPORARY PERSONAL FINANCE

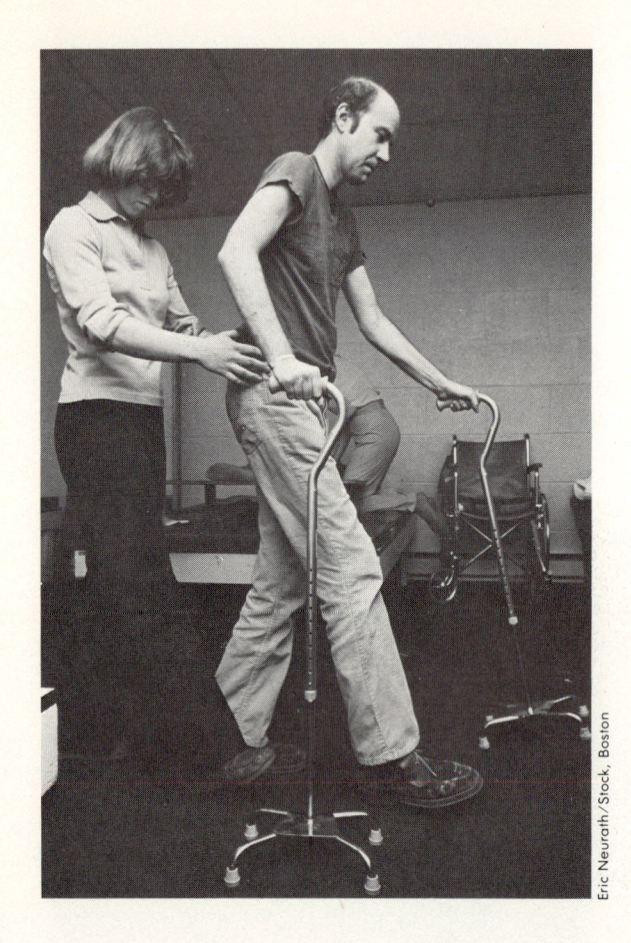

Physical therapists, paralegals, and computer analysts have excellent job prospects in today's labor market.

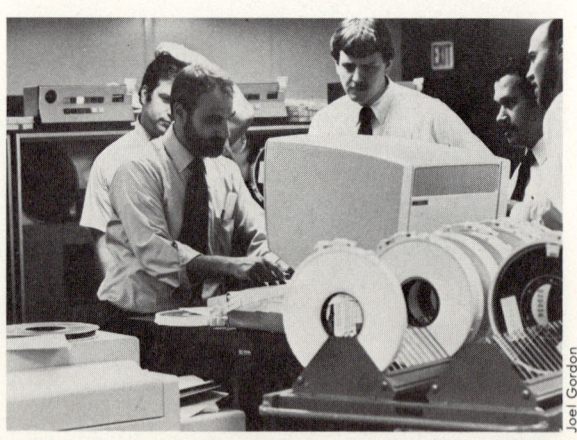

success. Over two-thirds of all current jobs are in service industries, and these jobs are expected to expand at a faster rate than goods-producing jobs.

Job Location. Career potential is influenced by the economic conditions of the area in which the industry is located. A depressed area will offer fewer economic opportunities than an area with a thriving economy. These economic differences may vary from region to region and even within states. Population growth patterns are good indicators of an area's economic health.

The Employer's Growth Prospects. The opportunity for success in any job partially depends on how well the company is managed, its past record of growth, and its future expectation of success. A company with a history of growth and plans for future expansion will offer the best career opportunities.

OCCUPATIONAL CLUSTER

One way to minimize your vulnerability to economic downturns that affect the work place is to prepare for a group of related jobs—an *occupational cluster*.[14] Dean L. Hummel of Virginia Polytechnic Institute and State University cites one example of how developing skills in several fields helped displaced employees: "When Boeing closed down in Seattle, a great many aerospace workers suddenly had no jobs. Those who had developed some talent in bricklaying, carpentry, plumbing, or electrical work were able to maintain themselves and a degree of self-worth. Those who did not were out of jobs."[15]

To prepare for an occupational cluster, a person must acquire both specific skills for a particular occupation and general knowledge that will enable the individual to transfer these skills from one field to another.

occupational cluster: a group of related jobs.

THE SELF-EMPLOYMENT OPTION

While many students believe that college will provide them with the necessary skills to compete in the job market, others see college as providing a broad-based education that will be helpful in running their own businesses. One of the more basic financial decisions a graduate has to make is whether to opt for self-employment.

Owning your own business directly links your efforts to company and personal profit; the harder you work, the more risks you take, the greater the potential reward. But owning a business is fraught with problems, and only a careful analysis of the pluses and minuses will enable you to decide whether it is the best route for you.

The greatest problem facing the self-employed is business failure. Half of

Increasing numbers of Americans are working at home, and the development of the desk-top personal computer, which can perform a wide range of office-related tasks, may encourage many others to do so, too.

all businesses that open their doors during the 1980s will not survive two years. The vast majority of failures are due to the owner's inexperience or incompetence.[16] Preventing business failure requires a great deal of preparation, knowledge, and hard work.

It should be noted, however, that collegiate business administration programs are often criticized for preparing students to be employees, usually for large corporations. The study of organizational behavior and administrative practices is often cited as an example of this tendency. Critics argue that little attention is given to smaller firms and to *entrepreneurship* (the risk taking associated with operating your own business). But this situation is changing. The study of small firms is being introduced into many business courses, and various colleges have started programs designed to prepare people to go into their own businesses. Today approximately 150 research centers and universities offer courses in entrepreneurship, compared with 6 in 1967.[17] Although no college course can guarantee someone's success in operating a business,

entrepreneurship: *the risk taking associated with operating your own business.*

today's entrepreneurship programs are an exciting new option on many campuses.

WORKING AT HOME: A NEW EMPLOYMENT TREND

Millions of self-employed people work at home on a full- or part-time basis, as do a number of salaried workers. Working at home frees workers from the drudgery and expense of commuting and gives them more time for work and personal commitments—taking care of young children, for example. Toffler argues that working at home is already a major employment alternative:

> An unmeasured but appreciable amount of work is already being done at home by such people as salesmen and saleswomen who work by phone or visit, and only occasionally touch base at the home office; by architects and designers; by a burgeoning pool of specialized consultants in many industries; by large numbers of human-service workers like therapists or psychologists; by music teachers and language instructors; by art dealers, investment counselors, insurance agents, lawyers, and academic researchers; and by many other categories of white-collar, technical, and professional people.
>
> These are, moreover, among the most rapidly expanding work classifications, and when we suddenly make available technologies that can place a low-cost "work station" in any home, providing it with a "smart" typewriter, perhaps, along with a facsimile machine or computer console and teleconferencing equipment, the possibilities for home work are radically extended.[18]

SOURCES OF CAREER INFORMATION

The best sources of career information are your library and the career guidance and placement center on your campus. The professionals who work in these areas are invaluable to any career information search. The library will probably contain the *Dictionary of Occupational Titles,* the *Occupational Outlook Handbook,* and other general career references. The career guidance and placement unit on campus should be able to provide more detailed information on the specific industries and firms in your area. Both of these sources will be able to suggest other information that might be available.

THE JOB SEARCH

Many people procrastinate when it comes to their own job search. But most authorities on the subject warn that job applicants need to start their job search as soon as possible. Employers favor applicants who are well organized, prepared, and informed about the job market, economic conditions, and the particular industry and firm. Some colleges even offer one-credit courses in job searching to prepare their students for this most important quest. Many offer workshops for students seeking jobs.

WHERE TO LOOK

Job contacts can be found in a variety of places. A logical starting point is with relatives, friends, and acquaintances. Simply tell people that you are seeking a position in a particular area and ask for their assistance. Many times associates can refer you to potential employers. But even when they are unable to help, most people will make a mental note of your request and refer future job contacts to you.

The campus career planning and placement office is another good starting point. Here you will need to set up a placement file—which usually includes a standard information sheet, transcripts, and references—in order to participate in campus interviews.

In addition, there are 2,150 public employment offices—called *job service centers*—which may have job listings of possible interest. For a fee, private placement agencies also try to match applicants with available positions.

Other sources include placement listings by professional associations and job advertisements in newspapers and trade publications. Another possibility is direct solicitation of local employers. For these contacts, you will usually need to present an effective résumé highlighting your strong points as well as a cover letter indicating your interest in a position and requesting a personal interview.

To be effective in your job search, you should contact all possible sources. The following is a handy checklist:

- Friends
- Acquaintances
- Relatives
- Campus career planning and placement office
- Job service centers
- Private placement agencies
- Professional association listings
- Newspaper advertisements
- Advertisements in trade publications
- Direct solicitations of employers

job service centers: *the 2,150 public employment offices in the United States.*

HOW TO WRITE AN EFFECTIVE RÉSUMÉ[19]

A *résumé* is a personal data sheet listing your employment qualifications. It's a selling document aimed at convincing prospective employers that you are right for their job. Your résumé must contain the following information:

- *Identification:* This section always appears first; it includes name, address, and telephone number.

résumé: *a personal data sheet listing a person's employment qualifications.*

- *Job objective:* This section defines the kind of job sought; it also pinpoints career goals.
- *Background:* These sections describe education, work experience, and may include pertinent facts about personal background.

In constructing your résumé, describe your job objective and past experience in terms of the skills the prospective employer is likely to want. Be as precise as possible in your language. If you are applying for different kinds of positions, you may have to use several forms of the same résumé—each focusing on the part of your background most relevant to the job.

As you list past experiences, remember that you may have gained valuable skills both in and out of structured job situations. Almost everything one does involves identifiable skills that can be transferred from one setting to another. If, for example, your objective is to become an office manager, mention all the organizational and management experience you have had, including organizing a successful block association or managing a local food co-op. This consideration is especially important if your formal work experience is limited or if you are changing your career.

Use a straightforward, factual presentation. Explain your accomplishments as exactly as possible, in quantitative terms. For example: "Sold $1 million in life insurance during 1984; trimmed yearly operating budget by $225,000 and staff by five people."

"I see in your résumé that from 1961 to 1982 you were at work. Can you be a little more specific?"

Some Résumés Are Limited Indeed!

Source: Reprinted with permission from *The Saturday Evening Post Society,* a division of BFL & MS, Inc. © 1984.

Try to limit your résumé to one typed page. Choose an easily readable type style and have your résumé professionally printed, if possible, on good-quality paper. Highlight headings with boldface print or capital letters and leave wide margins and spaces between paragraphs and sections. Employers, who may receive hundreds of résumés in response to job advertisements, respond to the appearance of a résumé. They know that a legible, well-organized résumé is a mark of professionalism.

Résumés may be written in two basic formats: the chronological format and the functional format.

The Chronological Résumé. As its name implies, the *chronological résumé* lists work and educational experience in chronological order, starting from the present and working backward (see Figure 2-2). It is the most commonly used résumé form and clearly presents the kinds of jobs you have held and how long you have held them.

Chronological résumés have the advantage of underlining long-term, steady employment, which increases your attractiveness to most employers. But they fail to highlight your most important job skills, since the same emphasis is placed on every job skill.

The Functional Résumé. The *functional résumé* solves this problem by emphasizing job-related skills, professional growth and development, and career goals (see Figure 2-3). It minimizes the importance of those jobs that are not directly related to career goals and hides a spotty employment record.

The functional résumé accomplishes this by eliminating specific chronological information, job titles and descriptions, and the names of companies where experience was gained. Be prepared, however, to provide this information to prospective employers during the job interview.

HANDLING THE INTERVIEW

The employment interview is your first face-to-face meeting with a prospective employer. It is the time when those all-important first impressions are made: you learn what it might be like to work in the company, and the interviewer decides whether your skills and personality are right for the job. The key to a successful interview is preparation. Study the firm's annual report to find out as much as you can about its products, locations, business philosophy, organizational structure, size, competition, financial status, and problems. Use this information to organize in your own mind how you might contribute to the company.

Approach the interview from a position of strength and self-confidence. Stress your qualifications. Discuss all aspects of your job history, educational background, community activities, and anything that might apply to the job. Avoid talking about your weaknesses, but if the interviewer brings them up,

---

chronological résumé: a résumé that lists work and educational experiences in chronological order, beginning with the most recent.

functional résumé: a résumé that emphasizes job-related skills, professional growth and development, and career goals.

Figure 2-2
THE CHRONOLOGICAL RÉSUMÉ

>
> Patricia Tait
> 150 Allerton Road
> Newton Highlands, Massachusetts 02159
> (617) 527-5334
> *Administrative Assistant*
>
> *Work Experience:*
>
> **1970–Present**   Administrative Assistant to President
> Western Technology, Inc.
> Lincoln, Massachusetts
> - Responsible for day-to-day operations of ten-person office.
> - Prepare annual stockholders' report.
> - Handle calendar, appointments and travel for president.
> - Authorize expenditures of $250,000 operating budget.
> - Review audits, projections and financial statements.
>
> **1968–1969**   Assistant to Chief Financial Officer
> Western Massachusetts Labs
> Andover, Massachusetts
> - Managed office.
> - Processed payroll, kept attendance records, ordered office supplies.
> - Set up appointments and meetings.
>
> **1967–1968**   Secretary/Assistant to President
> Techtronics Development Corp.
> Lincoln, Massachusetts
> - Directed president's office.
> - Served as liaison with stockholders.
> - Organized president's calendar and travel.
>
> *Education:*   B.S., Rice Institute, 1967.
> Electrical engineering major.

Source: Sarah Watt, "How to Write the Résumé That's Best for You," *Working Woman* (September, 1979), p. 43. Reprinted with permission from *Working Woman*. Copyright © 1979 by Hal Publications, Inc.

try to minimize their effect. If, for example, you are questioned about a lack of experience, you might point to community activities in which you have demonstrated similar skills. Always show an eagerness to learn.

Listen carefully to the interviewer and respond to the questions as directly as you can. Feel free to ask the interviewer questions about the company and

Figure 2-3
THE FUNCTIONAL RÉSUMÉ

> Kay Miniver
> 453 Van Buren Avenue
> Oakland, California 94610
> (415) 395-3165 (office)
> (415) 893-6609
>
> Qualifications and Experience:
>
> Project Development
> Conducted research into reading and learning problems of minority students in urban junior and senior high schools. Secured funding for major study in the field. Coordinated and administered the project. Was accountable for the $465,000 funding of the project. Project is being used as model for similar projects across the country. Developed reading-testing program for disadvantaged junior and senior high school students.
>
> Writing
> Published reports on evolution of projects. Specialist in grant projects.
>
> Research
> Gathered and processed wide variety of educational information. Working knowledge of statistical data processing.
>
> Administration and Management
> Organized research teams of up to 25 members.
>
> Public Relations
> Wide experience with speaking before community groups.
>
> Education:
> *Austin College*, B.A., American History, 1961
> *Columbia Teachers College*, M.A., Learning Disorders, 1962

Source: Sarah Watt, "How to Write the Résumé That's Best for You," *Working Woman*, September 1979, p. 43. Reprinted with permission from *Working Woman*. Copyright © 1979 by Hal Publications, Inc.

the job. Good questions show your interest and knowledge and often give the interviewer a sense of how you think. Your ability to express yourself, your enthusiasm, and your posture and dress also influence the interviewer's overall impression.

In addition to the interview, some companies require job applicants to take a series of intelligence or aptitude tests to determine their suitability. If you have targeted your career goals carefully and received the proper training, you should have little trouble with these tests.

Whatever happens—whether you get the job or not—think of each job interview as a learning experience. What you learn will help you present yourself more effectively in future business meetings.

DECIDING ON A JOB

If after one or more interviews a prospective employer feels you are qualified for a job, he or she will call you back for a hiring interview. It is during this interview that you must decide whether the job matches your career goals and whether the salary, benefits, and work environment are acceptable.

No job is perfect, but remember that a job can grow with you. Choose the best job you can and work hard to make it a successful experience. Success on the job has always been the basis of a secure financial future.

SUMMARY

For most people, choosing a career is the most important financial decision they have to make. The choice should be based on the individual's personal goals. Personal and financial goals include money and financial security, job satisfaction, and social contribution.

Several variables affect the amount of money a person can earn from a career. Education is one of the most important, and here several preliminary financial decisions are involved, including how to finance your education. Earnings potential also depends on the occupation and industry selected.

Career selection should begin with a personal inventory of one's strengths, weaknesses, and goals. A vocational counselor may be helpful in making such an assessment. In making a career decision, you should also consider the current and future status of various jobs. A career's potential is dependent on the growth prospects of the occupation, the industry, and the employer, as well as the geographical location of the job. Students are advised to prepare for employment in an occupational cluster of related jobs rather than a single occupation. The self-employment option is another route to consider.

In your job search you can find potential employers through the college placement office, direct job solicitations, the local job service center, and private employment agencies. An effective résumé that spells out your employment qualifications is a necessity. Job applicants are also advised to be well prepared for the personal interviews involved in the job search. A good career decision is the basis of sound personal finances.

REVIEW QUESTIONS

1. Briefly define the following terms:

   Pell Grants
   Guaranteed Student Loan Program (GSLP)
   Auxiliary Loans to Assist Students
   Supplemental Education Opportunity Grants
   college work study
   National Direct Student Loans
   cooperative education program
   Dictionary of Occupational Titles
   vocational counselor
   occupational cluster
   job service centers
   entrepreneurship
   résumé
   chronological résumé
   functional résumé

2. Discuss the various financial and personal goals that can have an impact on career decisions.

3. What are the variables that affect a person's income potential?

4. Describe the different methods of financing a college education.

5. Outline the steps involved in choosing a specific career.

6. How might a vocational counselor assist someone making a career decision?

7. Briefly describe the employment trends that are

expected to influence the job market in the late 1980s.

8. What factors should be considered in measuring a career's potential?

9. Why is it better to prepare for employment in an occupational cluster than in a specific job?

10. Explain how you will conduct your own job search.

CASES AND EXERCISES

1. A study by Catalyst, a New York center for professional women, has issued a report on two-career families that identifies some of the difficulties involved. Related productivity, morale, and recruiting problems are now widely recognized by industry. One-third of the firms surveyed reported that two-career families adversely affected their work environment.

   Many two-career couples believe that their situation has a negative effect on their career potential. Some 37 percent of the firms studied said that there were some executive positions that could not be reached by a man attempting to assume an equal parental role. Yet 80 percent of the companies recognized that males increasingly feel such an obligation.[20]

   Relate these conclusions to the topics presented in Chapter 2.

2. One firm reported that it lost an excellent executive because it could not locate an acceptable dental practice for her husband.[21] What are a company's responsibilities in such a situation?

3. Some firms are now offering job help to the so-called trailing spouse of an employee transferred overseas.[22] How would this effort differ from established domestic programs to place trailing spouses?

4. Prepare a three- to five-page report on a career field in which you are interested. What are the future job prospects in this field? What is the compensation level? What are the advancement opportunities? What job skills and education are required?

5. Develop a résumé that could be used in a job search. Ask other class members to critique your work.

ANSWERS TO PERSONAL FINANCE I.Q. TEST

1. Fact. 2. Fact. 3. Fiction. 4. Fact. 5. Fiction. 6. Fiction.

HOW CONNIE FERRARA REACHED HER PERSONAL FINANCIAL DECISION

Professor Dohan first asked Connie a few questions. He found out that she had an excellent grade-point average in high school and good SAT scores. She is putting herself through college with a job as a sales clerk at minimum wage and supports herself while living on her own. Right now Connie is planning on becoming a business major, and may also get an M.B.A.

Professor Dohan pointed out to Connie that as a first step she should make a financial and educational plan for the next five to seven years. What are her personal goals? What kind of job does she envision after she graduates? How much might she earn then? She should start by considering her work and course loads, and what borrowing would mean. Looking ahead at the long-term view, it might make sense to consider a student loan, which usually requires repayment after graduation.

Connie, however, indicated that the very thought of a loan frightens her. She doesn't want to incur any debts—it's hard enough to make ends meet now.

"That's why it's important to get the long-range picture in sight," replied Professor Dohan. "You'll be earning a higher income after you graduate so the real burden of a loan repayment will be less. A student education loan, especially if it's government subsidized, is really one of the best values around."

Professor Dohan added that even with a loan, Connie must evaluate the right balance between work and school. She should work enough hours to cover her expenses, but only take enough classes for which she has the time to do topnotch work. In addition, Connie needs to start thinking seriously about which area of business she wants to pursue. A good idea is to try to find a job in which she can gain some practical experience. That way, however long it takes her to finish school, she'll still be ahead.

Connie's conversation with Professor Dohan helped her see the many possibilities open to her. For the first time she realized that in taking Personal Finance 220, she is not just learning concepts for the future—she can apply those concepts now. Connie did make some changes. She took out a student loan for $2,000, and got a new job as a secretary in a small brokerage house, working fewer hours and getting less pay.

PART TWO

FINANCIAL PLANNING

LEARNING OBJECTIVES

1. To understand the importance of personal financial statements and how they are used. / *2.* To develop an income statement. / *3.* To calculate a person's net worth through the use of a personal balance sheet. / *4.* To discuss the importance and use of good records. / *5.* To determine where to keep personal financial records and for how long.

TESTING YOUR PERSONAL FINANCE I.Q.

		FACT	FICTION
1.	You can dispose of all tax records that are four years old or older.	☐	☐
2.	Americans spend a higher percentage of their family income on housing today than they did in 1893.	☐	☐
3.	The United States has one of the highest personal savings rates in the world.	☐	☐
4.	A person's will should be kept in a safe-deposit box for security reasons.	☐	☐
5.	Personal financial statements should be revised annually.	☐	☐
6.	Americans spend a higher percentage of their budgets on food today than they did in 1893.	☐	☐

The materials in this chapter assist in separating fact from fiction. Your answers can be checked on page 62.

CHAPTER THREE

PERSONAL FINANCIAL STATEMENTS AND RECORDS

**SHARING A PERSONAL FINANCIAL DECISION WITH
GREGORY J. WOROSZ OF SCHOOLCRAFT COLLEGE**

Sherri Thompson came to see Gregory Worosz, her personal finance instructor who is seasoned with 15 years experience, during his office hours. She was puzzled and frustrated. At her part-time job as a cashier, she earns good money every week, but she always feels broke. "I don't know where the money goes," Sherri confessed. "I live at home and eat most of my meals there, so it's not toward rent or food. My only real expense is my car—for gas and the monthly installment payments." Sherri paused. "Oh yes," she added with a sweeping gesture. "And there are the odd things—shampoo, a new T-shirt, going to the movies once in a while. But that can't amount to much."

Sherri explained to Mr. Worosz that she worked too hard to see it come to nothing. Yet she didn't know how to change things. She wondered if she could tap Mr. Worosz's knowledge and experience.

If you were Mr. Worosz, what steps would you recommend Sherri take?

To find out how Mr. Worosz helped Sherri with her personal financial decision, turn to page 62.

"Money is the barometer of society's virtue."
Ayn Rand[1]

After Gerald Ford assumed the presidency from Richard Nixon, former New York governor Nelson Rockefeller was nominated for the vice-presidency. Rockefeller filed a net-worth statement as part of the congressional approval process. This statement appears below. It shows a net worth of $62.6 million, over half of it in art. Adjusting for inflation, Rockefeller would have been worth about $134 million in today's prices.[2]

Table 3-1
NELSON ROCKEFELLER'S STATEMENT OF NET WORTH

Assets

Cash	$ 394,898
Cash advances	247,891
Notes receivable	1,518,270
Accounts receivable	713,326
New York State Retirement Fund (contributed cost)	21,803
Securities	12,794,376
Partnership interests	157,124
Art (estimated market value)	33,561,325
Real estate	11,252,261
Furnishings	1,191,328
Automobiles, other vehicles, boats and airplanes	1,767,900
Jewelry	521,136
Coins	12,600
Total	$64,154,238

Liabilities

Notes payable	$ 1,567,500
Miscellaneous accounts payable	5,513
Total	$ 1,573,013
Net worth	$62,581,225

Source: "Put a Finger on Your Financial Pulse," Changing Times, January 1979, p. 36.

While few Americans can ever hope to accumulate a net worth comparable to that of Nelson Rockefeller, the development of appropriate financial statements is critical for anyone interested in personal financial planning. Chapter 3 deals with the financial statements and records that are vital to this process.

THE IMPORTANCE OF DEVELOPING PERSONAL FINANCIAL STATEMENTS

Financial statements are assessments of the current status of one's personal finances. The two primary statements are the *income statement*, which traces the flow of income and expenditures, and the *balance sheet* (or statement of net worth), which lists the current value of assets and liabilities, as well as the person's net worth.

Financial statements serve several purposes. Basically, they are planning tools that enable better-informed decisions to be made. Specifically, financial statements will:[3]

- Provide an up-to-date evaluation of your financial well-being.
- Provide information for loan applications.
- Offer a starting point for estate planning.
- Serve as the basis for building future investment portfolios, which depend on your current financial status.
- Help detect potential financial problems.
- Provide necessary information for divorce and prenuptial agreements.

financial statements: assessments of the current status of one's personal finances.

income statement: a financial statement that traces the flow of personal income and expenditures.

balance sheet: a financial statement that lists assets, liabilities, and personal net worth.

HOW OFTEN SHOULD IT BE DONE?

Many people are very poor financial record keepers. According to a U.S. Department of Commerce estimate, fewer than 40 percent of all Americans regularly balance their checkbooks.[4] As a result, there is substantial procrastination when it comes to developing personal financial statements. How often should financial statements be revised? Touche Ross, an accounting firm, recommends that you do this annually at least.[5] Other financial experts suggest that revising financial statements be an ongoing effort. But regardless of the exact timing, the revision of these statements provides a regular checkup of one's financial health.

One of the hardest tasks is to gather all the data necessary for developing a complete set of financial statements.[6] Once this information is available, however, you can turn to preparing the income and net-worth statements on which your future personal financial planning should be based.

THE INCOME STATEMENT

A personal income statement traces a person or family's annual income, expenditures, and savings. Table 3-2 provides an example of such a statement. It shows that income less expenditures equals what is left for savings and investment. This figure then becomes an important factor in building one's net worth.

Consider a hypothetical young, married couple, Roger and Phyllis Morgan. Their income and expenses are shown in Table 3-2 as an example of a personal income statement. The starting point in constructing such a statement is the income section.

INCOME

Roger and Phyllis Morgan made $50,250 in salary during the year. He earned $29,750 in insurance sales, and she made $20,500 as a reporter for a local newspaper. In addition, they collected $600 in interest and from the auction sale of some books inherited from an estate of a distant relative, making their total income $50,850. After deducting their income taxes and Social Security taxes, the Morgans retained $42,195 to cover their expenditures.

EXPENDITURES

The Morgans were able to develop the "expenditures" part of their income statement largely on the basis of their checkbook, which they balanced as soon as their bank statement arrived each month. By carefully monitoring these expenditures, you can keep your financial plans on target.

Look at the various categories of expenditures noted in the Morgans' income statement.

Housing. As you can see in Table 3-2, the Morgans' largest expense for the year was housing. Their mortgage payments (including property taxes) amounted to $8,776, and their utilities costs (gas, electricity, and telephone) were $1,800. The repair of their porch steps and the removal of a dead tree on their property came to $400. Household insurance was $500, and the purchase and installation of a wood-burning stove came to $500. It is important to point out that some housing expenses (interest and property taxes) are tax-deductible; that is, they lower the amount of income tax the homeowner has to pay. Rent, by contrast, is not a tax-deductible expense. (Taxes are covered in detail in Chapter 5.)

Food. Food costs, tracked through checks written to supermarkets and specialty stores, were $3,975 for the year. What the Morgans cannot account for is the amount of cash paid for food. A quick stop made after work to pick up a

Table 3-2
INCOME STATEMENT FOR ROGER AND PHYLLIS MORGAN

Income

Wages earned		
Roger Morgan	$29,750	
Phyllis Morgan	20,500	
Other income		
Sale of books and interest	600	
Gross income		$50,850

Taxes

Less federal and state taxes	− 5,091	
Less Social Security taxes	− 3,564	− 8,655
Net income		$42,195

Expenditures

Housing		
Mortgage	8,776	
Utilities	1,800	
Maintenance	400	
Insurance	500	
Other	500	
		$11,976
Food		3,975
Clothing		2,850
Automobile and transportation		
Gasoline	1,352	
Repairs	550	
Insurance	680	
		2,582
Recreation, entertainment, and leisure-time pursuits		2,000
Medical expenses		
Professional services	250	
Medications	75	
		325
Cash allowances		5,000
Life insurance		420
Loan installment payments		1,250
Other		1,750
Total expenditures		− 32,128

Available for Savings and Investment $10,067

quart of milk and a loaf of bread, the occasional pizza brought home—these were paid for in cash and therefore do not appear in any records. The Morgans are also unable to account for the nonfood items included in the supermarket bills. Paper products, toiletries, and pet food are routinely purchased with their weekly groceries and do not appear as separate items in their accounting.

Clothing. The checkbook and monthly Visa and MasterCard statements usually provide a fairly complete record of expenditures for clothing. Here again, however, some impulse purchases (a shirt or tie, a blouse or scarf) may be paid for in cash. Overall, the Morgans estimated that they spent $2,850 on clothing during the past year.

Transportation. The Morgans own a four-year-old car, which Roger uses to drive to work. Phyllis walks to work in good weather and takes the bus when it rains or is very cold. Although the cost of repairs on the car was modest during the last year, the Morgans are concerned about what the coming year might bring. Such costs are difficult to predict. The Morgans are trying to decide whether it might be better to replace their car before it needs major repairs or to delay this purchase for another year. For many young couples, this is one of the most important personal financial decisions.

Recreation, Entertainment, and Leisure-Time Pursuits. The largest item in this category is most likely to be the annual vacation or an expensive hobby. Other expenditures included in the Morgans' statement are payments for participatory sports, such as tennis, bowling, and racquetball; tickets for plays, movies, and athletic events; and Phyllis's aerobic dance lessons.

Medical Expenses. The Morgans' checkbook and various receipts provided a record of medical expenses. If medical insurance payments are deducted from your paycheck or are paid separately, then these should be included in this category. The Morgans' medical insurance is fully paid by Roger's employer.

Cash Allowances. Usually called "spending money," this sum covers incidental day-to-day expenses. The Morgans discovered that they were each spending nearly $50 per week in this category and that they could not readily account for how the money was spent. Recording daily cash expenditures in a notebook can produce some interesting information for the ambitious budget balancer.

Life Insurance. These premiums are paid on a monthly, quarterly, or annual basis.

Developing a Family Income Statement for the Chicago World's Fair

Katherine Bement Davis developed the "New York State Workingman's Model Home" exhibit for the Chicago World's Fair in 1893. The exhibit included a model home and even the family budget. Davis estimated that the family could live well on a budget of $500 per year! Here is what the income statement of the hypothetical 1893 family looked like.

The 1893 budget allocated 40 percent of the family income to food; the comparable figure in the 1980s is 23 percent for middle-income families. Housing (rent) took up 24 percent of the family budget at the time of the Chicago World's Fair; today's figure is 21.8 percent for middle-income families. So even income statements have a historical perspective.

Income		$500
Expenditures		
Food	$200	
Rent	120	
Fuel	30	
Clothing	100	
Miscellaneous	50	$500
		-0-

Source: Based on an article by Joseph W. Barnes in *American Heritage* magazine. This article is discussed in "1893 Family's Income Lasts Just a Week Today," *Sentinel Star*, November 25, 1981, p. 8A; and U.S. Bureau of the Census, *Statistical Abstract of the United States: 1982–1983* (Washington, D.C.: U.S. Government Printing Office, 1982), p. 467.

At the time of the Columbian Exposition, which was held in Chicago in 1893, a typical American family could live on $500 a year!

Installment Loan Payments. Any loans not included under housing and transportation should be listed in this category.

Other. These expenses include contributions and other expenses that do not fit the categories listed above. The Morgans listed charitable donations, veterinarian bills, money sent to Phyllis's widowed mother, and the cost of firewood for their new stove.

AVAILABLE FOR SAVINGS AND INVESTMENT

At the end of the year, the Morgans had $10,067 to invest or save. This amount is arrived at by subtracting expenditures from income after taxes. In the Morgans' case, the figure is a positive one. In other words, they have money left over. If the figure had been negative—that is, if they had had expenditures greater than their income—they would have had to take money from savings accounts or other investments in order to meet their obligations.

An income statement outlines how much money you have received and spent during some past period of time, so it is useful in preparing a budget for

---

Americans Are Not Big Savers

Americans save a modest amount of their after-tax personal income ("disposable income") compared with people from many other nations. The U.S. rate of personal savings was 6.3 percent in 1950; 5.4 percent in 1955; 4.9 percent in 1960; 6.4 percent in 1965; 8.1 percent in 1970; 7.7 percent in 1974; and 5.6 percent at the beginning of the 1980s. The 1983 savings rate was 4.8 percent of disposable income, and the estimated 1984 rate is 4.9 percent. In comparison, the savings rates for Japan, France, the United Kingdom, and West Germany were all above 8 percent throughout the previous decade. In other words, the final figure in the income statement format presented in this chapter—the amount available for savings—is often zero.

There are many reasons for this situation. Some claim that easy credit has made Americans spenders rather than savers. It is also noted that interest rates in other countries, like Canada, are often higher than those in the U.S. Others blame the multitude of available products and aggressive marketing practices. Still others observe that Americans have little tax incentive to save. Most other free-world powers offer significant tax concessions for money earned on savings. Japan, for example, exempts the first $5,000 of interest earned by a family.

There have been many proposals to provide incentives for savings. One idea is to offer an exclusion of, say, $1,000. Others think long-term savings ought to be taxed at capital gains rates. Another proposal is to discount taxable interest by the current rate of inflation. Others have proposed tax credits for savings, and so on. The most significant change in recent years is the deregulation of savings institutions, which has allowed them to pay more competitive interest rates, thus generating more taxable interest.

How does your personal savings rate compare with the national average cited above?

Sources: U.S. Department of Commerce, Bureau of Economic Analysis, data presented in *Information Please Almanac, 1982* (New York: Simon and Schuster, 1981), p. 38; Citicorp, *United States Economic Forecast: 1983–1988* (December 7, 1983), p. 50; Linda Snyder Hayes, "How Americans Turned into Spendthrifts," *Fortune*, April 7, 1980, pp. 60, 62; Greg Heberlein, "Economic Recovery," *Seattle Times*, October 1, 1981, p. E1.

some future period. This budgeting process is discussed in Chapter 4. But as useful as a personal income statement is, it does not adequately assess one's present financial position. A balance sheet, or statement of net worth, is also required.

THE BALANCE SHEET

A balance sheet outlines what a person owns (*assets*) and what he or she owes (*liabilities*). The difference between these two items is *net worth* (also called equity)—the amount a person would have left after all assets were liquidated and all debts were paid off. In the case of Nelson Rockefeller, this figure was $62.6 million. For others, the figure may be negative; that is, their liabilities exceed their assets.

Let's see how a balance sheet would be constructed for our hypothetical couple, Roger and Phyllis Morgan. Table 3-3 shows what this statement of net worth would look like.

assets: the current value of what a person owns.

liabilities: the amounts that a person owes to other parties.

net worth: the amount a person would have left after all assets are liquidated and all debts are paid off.

Table 3-3
BALANCE SHEET (STATEMENT OF NET WORTH) FOR ROGER AND PHYLLIS MORGAN

Liquid Assets

Cash and cash equivalent	$ 2,475	
Savings account balance	9,248	
Cash surrender value of life insurance	200	$11,923

Fixed Assets

Market value of personal residence	87,000	
Market value of car	3,500	
Market value of furnishings and personal belongings	4,350	
Other (jewelry)	1,900	96,750

Total Assets $108,673

Liabilities

Current debts	322	
Loan installments	3,259	
Mortgage	57,000	

Total Liabilities   − 60,581

Net Worth $ 48,092

ASSETS

The Morgans began by counting their cash on hand and adding the balance available in their checking account. The balance in their savings account is another asset to be listed. If the Morgans had held certificates of deposit, money-market funds, U.S. savings bonds, stocks, or bonds, these items would also be listed under the first category on their balance sheet.

The cash value of their life insurance policy was determined by looking at the table included with the policy. The surrender value of annuities, the cash value of any pension plan, and the cash value of a profit-sharing plan would also be included in the balance sheet. The Morgans had none of these.

All of these assets are called *liquid assets* (or *quick assets*) because they are either cash or can be converted to cash quickly. Assets that take longer to convert to cash are labeled *fixed assets*.

The Morgans' largest fixed asset is their house. After checking the sales prices of other houses in their neighborhood and consulting a real estate agent, they arrived at what they thought would be a realistic market value for their home. To determine the value of their four-year-old car, they asked an automobile dealer or lending institution to quote them the "blue book" value. They decided to increase the figure slightly because of the excellent appearance of their particular car.

Arriving at the market value of their household furnishings and personal belongings was much more difficult for the Morgans. They knew what they had paid for most large items, and they had a good idea of what it would cost to buy those items in today's market—the so-called *replacement cost*. But they had no idea of what someone else might be willing to pay for them. In fact, they were not sure whether some items had any value at all beyond a sentimental one. In making their determination, they used a recommendation of a financial adviser: furnishings and personal belongings are worth about 5 percent of the value of the house itself.[7] The value of Phyllis's jewelry was determined by a professional appraiser.

LIABILITIES

To arrive at their current debts, the Morgans added up the bills that had come in but had not been paid. Their telephone bill, a gasoline credit-card charge, and a bill from the dentist amounted to $322. A balance sheet is intended to show a person's financial condition at a given point in time, so bills that will come due after the date on which the balance sheet is prepared should also be included.

Installment loans should include the total amount on any loans other than those for house or car. The Morgans still owe Visa $635 for their stereo equipment, $276 on their MasterCard, and a $2,348 on a home-improvement loan with the bank. They are paying these debts off with monthly payments.

---

liquid assets: cash or assets that can be easily converted into cash (also called quick assets).

fixed assets: assets that are not easily converted to cash.

replacement cost: how much an item would cost if it were replaced in today's market.

A Hard-Times Scorecard

Robert L. Block, who heads the Seattle office of Laventhol & Horwath (a certified public accounting firm), has developed a recession scorecard to use in determining how well you can weather tough economic times. We can see how it works in the example below. First calculate your quick assets—cash or those assets you can convert into cash promptly, such as stocks, money-market funds, and the cash value of life insurance policies, and bonds. Then compute your current debts. Consider only those that are now due, not long-term debts such as mortgage balances. Your *quick net worth* equals your quick assets minus your current debts.

Block then suggests classifying your expenses as essential and nonessential. Essential expenses include food, housing, and the other necessities. Nonessential expenses are those that do not have a major impact on your basic style of living. Dividing your quick net worth by your essential monthly expenses yields a *survival score*—the length of time you could cover basic living expenses if you suddenly lost your ongoing income. Block figures that six months should be the minimum score, although a year is more appropriate.

Similarly, a *lifestyle score* can be obtained by dividing your quick net worth by your total monthly expenses (both essential and nonessential). The lifestyle score indicates how long you could maintain your current spending level if your income stream stopped.

quick net worth: the figure that results from subtracting current debts from quick assets.

survival score: a ratio (quick net worth divided by essential monthly expenses) that shows how long one could cover basic living expenses if one lost one's ongoing income.

lifestyle score: a ratio (quick net worth divided by total monthly expenses) that shows how long one could maintain one's current spending level if one's income stream stopped.

HOW TO CALCULATE YOUR SURVIVAL AND LIFESTYLE SCORES

A.	Quick Assets	$19,800
B.	Current Debts	3,200
C.	Quick Net Worth (A − B)	$16,600
D.	Essential Monthly Expenses	2,100
E.	Survival Score (C ÷ D)	7.9 months
F.	Nonessential Monthly Expenses	1,000
G.	Total Monthly Expenses	$ 3,100
H.	Lifestyle Score (C ÷ G)	5.4 months

Source: Richard Buck, "It's Test Time: How Recession-Proof Are You?" *Seattle Times*, January 7, 1982, p. D1. Used by permission of The Associated Press.

Any outstanding loans for cars should be entered on the balance sheet. Since the Morgans' car is paid off, they did not include this line in their statement.

The Morgans' largest liability is their home mortgage. By checking their payment records, they were able to determine how much they still owe on their house.

NET WORTH

By subtracting their liabilities from their assets, the Morgans discovered that they have a net worth of $48,092. It should be noted, however, that in the case of an emergency, the forced sale of assets would probably yield less than the estimated value reported here. Moreover, in emergency circumstances, the Morgans would have only $11,923 to draw on. Their quick net worth was $11,601 ($11,923 − $322). A rough approximation of their essential monthly expenses would be $2,357. So their survival score would be 4.9 months ($11,601 ÷ $2,357). Nonessential monthly expenses come to $320, making their lifestyle score 4.3 months ($11,601 ÷ $2,677). Clearly, increased savings ought to be a primary goal in the Morgans' financial planning.

Married couples typically prepare joint rather than separate net-worth statements, as has been done for the hypothetical couple featured in this chapter. In other instances, separate statements might be developed. Another approach might be used for couples living in *community property states* (states that consider all properties acquired after marriage other than by gift or bequest to be owned equally by both spouses). Here a combined net-worth statement might be used to show both the property of the married couple and the separate property of each spouse.[8] The community property states are Arizona, California, Idaho, Louisiana, Nevada, New Mexico, Texas, and Washington.[9]

Up-to-date financial statements are the starting point of all problem-solving efforts in the area of personal finance. But nothing is possible unless the people involved maintain adequate records on which these statements and other financial analyses can be based.

community property states: *states of Arizona, California, Idaho, Louisiana, Nevada, New Mexico, Texas, and Washington consider all property secured after marriage to be owned equally by both spouses.*

RECORD KEEPING

Stephen Lewis of Dean Witter Reynolds, a stock-brokerage firm, considers the "failure to keep careful records" one of the seven most serious mistakes we make with our money.[10] Lewis suggests that adequate records be kept of checking and savings accounts, time deposits, brokerage accounts, securities, money-market funds, Keogh plans and individual retirement accounts (IRAs), wills and trusts, real estate deeds, real estate investments, hard assets, safe-deposit boxes, attorney, accountant, executor, trustees, stockbroker, insurance agent, life insurance policies, letter of instruction (see Chapter 20 for details), employee benefits, net-worth statement, credit cards, current taxes, and tax records. The details necessary for each of these records are outlined in Figure 3-1.

WHERE SHOULD RECORDS BE KEPT?

Where you keep your records really depends on the specific record. Lewis suggests using a file card to handle simple information like the name, address,

Figure 3-1
RECORDS ESSENTIAL FOR PERSONAL FINANCIAL PLANNING

Checking and Savings Accounts:
name of bank, address, account number, where bankbook or checkbook is kept

Time Deposits:
name of bank, address, principal, interest rate, maturity date, account number, where certificate or bankbook is kept

Brokerage Accounts:
name of broker, address, account number

Securities:
name, number of shares or units, serial numbers, purchase date, gross price, sale date, net proceeds, where certificates and transaction slips are kept

Money-Market Funds:
name of fund, address, toll-free number, account number, where statements are kept

Keogh Plans and IRAs:
where invested, address, account number

Wills and Trusts:
where originals and copies are kept

Real Estate Deeds:
address of property, register number, where kept

Real Estate Investments:
type of property, address, purchase date, gross price, depreciation schedule, when sold, net proceeds, where maintenance and tax receipts, tax forms and income records are kept

Hard Assets (Precious Metals, Gems, Collectibles, etc.):
type, quality, quantity, when bought, gross price, when sold, net proceeds, where asset and transaction slips are kept

Safe-Deposit Box:
location, number, where inventory of contents and key are kept

Attorney, Accountant, Executor, Trustees:
name, address, phone

Stockbroker, Insurance Agent:
name, address, phone

Life Insurance Policies:
company, amount, beneficiaries, policy number, where kept

Letter of Instructions in Case of Death:
where kept

Employee Benefits:
description, where latest statement of benefits is kept, person to call at company

Net Worth Statement:
latest annual appraisal of assets and liabilities

Credit Cards:
company name, card number, phone number for reporting lost cards

Current Taxes:
where canceled checks or receipts for deductibles, earnings slips, record of capital gains and losses, quarterly estimated-tax forms are kept

Tax Records:
where copies of returns, schedules and documentation for the previous seven years are kept

Source: Stephen W. Lewis, "Seven Serious Mistakes with Your Money," *Money*, November 1981, p. 102. Reprinted by permission.

*"OK, which one of you erased Daddy's
investment portfolio program and replaced it
with 'Space Invaders'?"*

Investment Records Should Be Kept Safe from Children.
Source: From the *Wall Street Journal*. Permission, Cartoon Features Syndicate.

and telephone number of an attorney. The file card can also note where the other records are kept. One option is to put significant information into a home computer (see the boxed item). Voluminous but less important records can be kept in a home filing cabinet. But probably the most popular choice is a safe-deposit box. Of course, information about the safe-deposit box's location should be kept elsewhere. Stock certificates, home insurance policies, real estate deeds, birth certificates, passports, and so on are typically held in safe-deposit boxes. If these documents are substantial, a home safe might be considered. One word of caution: Chapter 20 will note that wills should not be kept in safe-deposit boxes because many states seal the box upon the leasee's death.

HOW LONG SHOULD RECORDS BE KEPT?

Effective record keeping does not mean excessive record keeping. So the general rule should be to keep what is truly important and discard the rest. All records should be reviewed periodically to determine which are still essential, and which are not. Before discarding a record, you need to consider whether the record is available elsewhere—for instance, in an accountant's, lawyer's, or escrow company's files. If it is not, you should reconsider a decision to throw the material out. There is also one very specific rule about records: keep anything pertaining to tax returns (actual returns, supporting documents, worksheets, and cancelled checks) for seven years.[11]

Once your records are in proper order and your financial statements up to date, you can turn to the question of how best to budget the money you have available. This issue is dealt with in the next chapter.

Buying a Personal Computer

By 1985, almost 10 percent of the nation's households were equipped with a personal computer. These small-sized, relatively low-priced, highly versatile machines are rapidly taking their place as a common household furnishing.

Since personal computers range in price from less than $100 to more than $10,000, the decision of which one to choose is a major one. Moreover, new systems are being introduced on a regular basis; once-popular systems frequently disappear from the market; prepared software for handling specific computer tasks is becoming less expensive and increasingly available; and prices change continually. Consequently, the computer purchase decision should be made with care.

Questions and Answers about Personal Computers

The rapid development of the computer industry and the complexity of computer technology make the decisions concerning the most appropriate personal computer much more difficult than those for most household purchases. It is not necessary, however, to be a computer science major to decide on the right one for you or how to learn how to operate it. The following paragraphs supply answers to the most commonly asked computer questions.

How Do I Buy a Personal Computer for My Home?

First, says Merl Miller, chairman of Dilithium Press, a publisher of books on computers, determine what you

Many Americans are now taking advantage of the personal computer to keep track of and update their household budgets and other personal financial records.

want to do with it. For use in the home a computer matched up with the right software—application programs—can play games, keep track of budgets and diets, prepare income taxes and help educate children. A professional or business person can, among many other things, use a computer to write reports, make financial forecasts, keep files, and monitor inventory and accounts.

Then, go to a computer or software store and see if programs to accomplish your goals exist. With thousands of programs available for everything from horse-race handicapping to soil analysis, chances are you'll find what you need.

What's the Next Step?

Find out what specific computers the software will run on. Different machines use different operating systems, so software that runs on one computer won't necessarily run on others. Today most software is written for IBM's personal computer, the Apple II series, and machines using the CP/M operating system. Nearly all computers using these systems cost more than $1,000.

What If I Don't Have a Lot of Money?

Then you should look at less expensive computers made by such companies as Commodore, Coleco, and Atari.

Just How Much Do I Have to Spend to Get a Useful System?

As little as $700, as much as $5,000, perhaps more. System is the key word. You can buy a computer—the microprocessor and keyboard—for $100 or even less. But you may quickly become frustrated by its limitations. To do much more than play games will require a memory-storage device—either a cassette tape recorder or, preferably, a disc drive—adding $50 to $500 to the total price. You also want to make sure that the computer has enough temporary, or internal, memory. For home use, 16,000 bytes, or characters, will suffice, though 64,000—equivalent to about 32 double-spaced type-written pages—is preferable. For business use at least 128,000 may be necessary.

Will I Need Anything Else?

If games and education are your primary purposes, you'll want color graphics and joysticks. If it's writing, you'll want a comfortable keyboard and, probably, a printer, plus a monitor instead of a television set. And if you want your computer to "talk" to outside information services, such as CompuServe, over telephone lines, you'll need a modem.

It Sounds More and More Like I Can't Afford a Computer

The point is not to expect too much from a computer minus its accessories. Still, if you are an astute shopper, you can get a Commodore 64 with a disc drive for less than $400 and hook it up to your TV set. You may find a monitor and printer for $400 more. Coleco sells Adam, which includes a tape data-storage device, a letter-quality printer, and built-in writing software, for about $700. A complete IBM PC package, with two disc drives, printer, and monitor, costs about $4,000. Software generally costs between $10 and $500.

With So Many Computers on the Market, How Do I Figure Out Which One to Purchase?

First, talk to people who own computers. Ask what they use them for and if they are satisfied. Or locate a local users' group that brings together people who own the same make. Read reviews of products in the computer magazines. There are numerous books with descriptions of and recommendations on computers.

Where Should I Buy My Computer?

A novice would be advised to shop in computer specialty stores, where the salespeople are generally knowledgeable and helpful. However, since mass-market retailers began selling home computers, many specialty shops have stopped carrying the lower-priced machines. Mail-order houses may have the lowest prices, but offer little or no counseling. Beware: The same pitfalls exist as in buying any consumer product through the mail.

Why Not Wait for Prices of Computers to Come Down Even More?

If you need a computer, waiting may be pointless. Among home computers, the days of cutthroat price slashing appear to be over, and several manufacturers raised prices recently. Price cutting never has been severe among the more expensive machines.

Software for Personal Finance

A number of the thousands of different software packages offered for sale are particularly applicable to personal finance matters. Although they typically sell for $100 or more, they may be particularly appropriate for many specific tax, investment, or household budgeting problems.

Home Accountant, developed by Continental Software (11223 South Hindry Ave., Los Angeles, Calif. 90045), is one of the most popular budgeting programs. It can accommodate as many as five separate checking accounts and 200 separate budget categories. Its flexibility has led a number of small-business users to purchase it, at prices ranging from $75 for the Apple, Atari, and Commodore 64 computers to $150 for the IBM, Kaypro, TRS-80, and Texas Instruments professional computer.

Two special programs designed to assist consumers with tax decisions and the preparation of annual tax forms are *Tax Manager* (Micro Lab, Inc., 2699 Skokie Valley Rd., Highland Park, Ill. 60035) and *Hometax* (Learning Source, 17791 Fitch St., Irvine, Calif. 92714). A number of specialized programs focusing on securities investing are currently being marketed. Since new personal-finance-oriented software is continually being developed, personal computer users should check computer magazines and computer retailers periodically to stay abreast of available materials.

Source: Reprinted from *U.S. News & World Report* issue of February 6, 1984. Copyright, 1984, U.S. News & World Report, Inc.

SUMMARY

Financial statements are assessments of a person's current finances. The two primary statements are the income statement (which traces the flow of income and expenses) and the balance sheet (which determines net worth by subtracting liabilities from assets). Financial statements are important in planning for loan applications and in estate planning, investments, and so on. Personal financial statements should be revised annually.

The income statement traces the individual's or family's annual income, expenditures, and savings. It subtracts expenditures from the total income after taxes to determine how much is available for saving and investment. A personal income statement provides the basic data needed for effective budgeting, the topic of Chapter 4.

The balance sheet lists the person's assets (what is owned) and liabilities (what is owed). Its purpose is to determine one's net worth, the amount you would have left if you liquidated all your assets and paid off all debts. The balance sheet or statement of net worth is the primary tool used to determine a person's economic well-being.

All personal financial statements are based on effective record keeping. Chapter 3 ends with a brief discussion of where to keep valuable financial records and how long this information should be retained.

REVIEW QUESTIONS

1. Briefly define the following terms:
   - financial statements
   - income statement
   - balance sheet
   - assets
   - liabilities
   - net worth
   - liquid assets
   - quick assets
   - fixed assets
   - replacement cost
   - quick net worth
   - survival score
   - lifestyle score
   - community property states

2. How are financial statements used in personal financial planning?

3. How often should financial statements be revised?

4. Identify the major items included in a personal income statement.

5. Why do Americans have a low rate of savings?

6. Discuss the major elements of a balance sheet.

7. How is a person's net worth calculated?

8. How should net worth be adapted for community property states?

9. What records are important to personal financial planning?

10. Where should personal financial records be kept, and for how long?

CASES AND EXERCISES

1. Critically evaluate the late Nelson Rockefeller's net-worth statement at the beginning of the chapter. What strengths and weaknesses are evident?

2. Prepare your own personal income statement. What have you learned from this exercise?

3. Prepare your own balance sheet. What have you learned from this exercise?

4. Using the data developed above, calculate your survival score and your lifestyle score. What does this information tell you about your personal finances?

5. Listed below is President Reagan's balance sheet. The information was gathered from financial-disclosure statements made public in May 1984. Review the balance sheet and decide whether the Reagans are well positioned for inflationary times. How about a recession? Discuss both possibilities.

President Reagan's Balance Sheet

Assets (minimum amounts)
California ranch assets	$ 669,000
Blind trusts	$ 500,000
Payments due on house sale	$ 100,000
Savings, checking accounts	$ 66,000
Life-insurance policies	$ 61,000
Total assets	**$1,396,000**

Liabilities (minimum amounts)
Loans on insurance, ranch	$160,000

1983 Income (exact amounts)
Presidential salary	$ 200,000
Interest, dividends	$ 192,659
California state pension	$ 26,538
Other net income	$ 3,637
Total adjusted gross income	**$422,834**

ANSWERS TO PERSONAL FINANCE I.Q. TEST

1. Fiction. 2. Fiction. 3. Fiction. 4. Fiction. 5. Fact. 6. Fiction.

HOW SHERRI THOMPSON REACHED HER PERSONAL FINANCIAL DECISION

"I believe you have the hole-in-the-pocket syndrome," commented Mr. Worosz. "You need to develop an income statement to determine how you are spending your money."

Here are the steps Mr. Worosz recommended:

1. Begin by keeping a log of every penny you spend for four to six weeks.

2. Then, as patterns emerge, divide your expenditures into six or ten categories like entertainment, housing, whatever.

3. These categories should then fit under three basic headings: necessary expenses, items you can do without, and purchases you can postpone.

"Now you have the information you need for your income statement," Mr. Worosz indicated, "and you can set up a budget for yourself. Once you see where your money's going, you can eliminate some of the nonessentials and make a priority list for the items you can postpone. Your spending should then be limited to paying for necessities and for whichever of the postponable things you can afford at the time."

"But there is *another* step you need to take," Mr. Worosz emphasized. "As a top priority, set some money aside in a savings account. Knowing where your money is being spent should help you to avoid overspending, but a savings account is what will help you get ahead."

After dutifully recording all this in her notebook, Sherri remarked that it sounded like a lot of work. Still, she'd give it a go. Mr. Worosz assured her, "Although it takes some discipline in the beginning, it soon gets easier. You become almost automatically aware of how you're spending your money. Plus—don't forget the savings account. Once that begins to grow, you'll have a tangible reward for your efforts."

LEARNING OBJECTIVES

1. To define the concepts of financial planning and budgeting. / *2.* To explain why adequate emergency funds and insurance are important to financial planning. / *3.* To discuss the development of a personal financial plan. / *4.* To describe how budgeting is related to financial planning. / *5.* To construct an actual budget for an individual or a family. / *6.* To identify the actions creditors take in the event of a default on a loan. / *7.* To explain the concept of bankruptcy and its alternative forms.

TESTING YOUR PERSONAL FINANCE I.Q.

	FACT	FICTION
1. CFP is a type of budget recommended by bankers and insurance agents.	☐	☐
2. Budgeting is a short-term version of financial planning.	☐	☐
3. Cash flow is an irrelevant concept in personal financial budgeting.	☐	☐
4. Emergency funds should equal at least six months of income.	☐	☐
5. Many top executives are financially insecure.	☐	☐

The materials in this chapter assist in separating fact from fiction. Your answers can be checked on page 83.

CHAPTER FOUR

FINANCIAL PLANNING AND BUDGETING

SHARING A PERSONAL FINANCIAL DECISION WITH PROFESSOR ETHEL C. MALLOY OF SUFFOLK COUNTY COMMUNITY COLLEGE

Professor Ethel Malloy asks all her students to prepare budgets, personal income statements, and balance sheets early in the course. The students agree: this is a useful exercise, because it makes them think about their spending habits. They get a general idea of where they stand financially and can see how this compares with their financial aspirations.

One student who took this exercise very seriously was Tom Lee. Tom went to school during the day and worked evenings. He lived at home, so he always had plenty of spending money. What Tom really wanted to do was to move out and live on his own. The extra money in his pocket certainly made this seem possible. But after preparing his income statement, Tom felt less sure. Looking at his income and expenditures in black and white, Tom realized that there wasn't all that much money left over. "In New York the cost of living is just too high," he grumbled.

The next day Tom raised his hand in class. "What's the good of financial record keeping if all you find out is that you don't have enough money for anything?" he asked. "I don't see how I'll ever be able to move away from home."

If you were Professor Malloy, how would you respond?

To find out how Professor Malloy helped Tom with his personal financial decision, turn to page 83.

"Income $1,000 a year, outgo $1,050 a year; result, misery. Income $1,000 a year, outgo $995 a year; result, happiness."
Benjamin Franklin[1]

Marrily Applewhite is an expert at balancing her family's budget. Marrily is the wife of a Congregational minister and the mother of five. When her husband decided he wanted to leave his Washington, D.C., post for a church on the West Coast, Marrily decided she would give up full-time employment. She thought that she would like to work in her own business on a part-time basis. This is when the Applewhites discovered the virtues of a family budget (she prefers to call it a "family spending plan").

Tough decisions had to be made if both spouses were to achieve their objectives. As a result, the Applewhites decided to:

1. Buy a less expensive house.
2. Send their two college-age children to public rather than private schools.
3. Set up a family budget to control their expenses.

Things have worked well for the Applewhites. The minister has the new assignment he sought, and Marrily can spend every Wednesday (a minister's day off) with her husband. She is also very happy with her own part-time business venture—setting up personal budgets for others.[2]

SOME BASIC CONCEPTS

financial planning: the process by which financial goals and related courses of action are developed.

budgeting: the process of monitoring and controlling expenditures in order to achieve financial planning goals.

Financial planning is the process by which financial goals and related courses of action are developed. It involves the determination of both objectives and strategies (which are clearly reflected in the actions taken by the Applewhites).

Budgeting entails monitoring and controlling expenditures in order to achieve the goals set in financial planning. All consumers have limited economic resources. Budgeting deals with the process of allocating these scarce resources. This chapter will describe how budgeting is interrelated with the overall process of financial planning.

Financial planning and budgeting vary according to a person's age, family status, and income group. A household head involved in a skilled trade, for example, might want to increase savings at a younger age than a middle-income executive would, since this person's income peak will occur earlier. A couple with several children at home is more concerned about life insurance than is a retired couple. Financial goals should never be set once and for all; they must be adjusted as one grows older. When goals are reached, new ones that are appropriate to a person's stage in life should be established. Table 4-1 outlines the major financial tasks that a person faces in different age brackets. Many of the terms may be unfamiliar at this point in your study of personal finance, so you will want to refer back to this table once you have finished reading the text.

FINANCIAL PLANNING

An income statement and balance sheet show where you are financially at a given point in time (see Chapter 3). A financial plan, on the other hand, is a guide to help you reach a targeted goal in the future. Many people assume that if they can meet their monthly payments they are doing all right financially. Often it takes a dramatic jolt to make people realize that they should make plans for handling their money. Consider the case of Tom and Kim Alcala.

> Tom Alcala . . . is a free-lance filmmaker in the Dallas area; and his wife, Kim, . . . works for Southwest Airlines. Together the Alcalas . . . earn about $48,000 a year. By rights, they should have it made.
> What they have instead is . . . a checkbook that doesn't always balance and a nagging feeling that all is not right with their financial world.
> That feeling came to a head shortly after they were married, when Kim took a look at their checking account and found they had gone through $15,000 in two months. A lot of that went toward closing the deal on their house, but the numbers still gave the Alcalas a jolt. "It kind of shook us up," says Tom. "In my business there are lots of people who have nothing but the last paycheck they made. I don't want that to happen to me."[3]

DEVELOPING A FINANCIAL PLAN

A starting point for financial planning is to determine where you want to be at some later date—perhaps five or ten years from now. This goal will probably be stated in terms of net worth for financial planning purposes. But it should be noted that financial plans are usually intertwined with lifestyle decisions. A high-level executive who aspires to a business administration teaching position in a college or university will have to moderate his or her net-worth projection to coincide with the career decision. The salary of a professor will not match that of an executive.

Financial goals should be based on a realistic estimate of future income. If your financial goals cannot be reached through your present career path, you may want to switch careers or obtain additional qualifications, such as an advanced degree in business.

People with substantial net worth and future income might enlist the help

FINANCIAL PLANNING

Table 4-1
YOUR LIFETIME FINANCIAL TASKS AND HOW TO GET THEM DONE

Age Group		Your Lifetime Financial Tasks	and How to Get Them Done
22 to 35	Without children	Establish credit. Buy or improve home. Set up emergency fund. Get adequate insurance. Start investment program. Begin retirement planning. Draw up will.	Meet monthly credit payments promptly. Use money-market fund, certificates of deposit or blue-chip stocks to build up savings. Buy disability, health, homeowners and auto policies; liability insurance on car and house should cover full net worth. Invest in moderate-risk mutual funds. Establish IRA or Keogh plan. Consult a lawyer.
	With children	Same as above PLUS: Purchase adequate life insurance. Begin saving for children's education. Provide for children in will.	Increase coverage with the birth of each child. For education, invest funds for long-term growth. Name guardian and executor.
35 to 50	Without children	Keep property insurance current. Protect increasing income and assets from taxes. Continue retirement savings. Revise will.	Make an inventory of possessions and update homeowners insurance. Secure replacement value insurance for valuables. Update liability insurance. Consider tax-exempt and tax-deferred investments. Invest also for long-term capital gains. Contribute maximum amount to IRA and/or Keogh. Take full advantage of employee profit-sharing and stock-purchase plans. Include recently acquired assets.
	With children	Same as above PLUS: Increase savings for children's education. Begin planning estate.	Consider tax-free gifts and interest-free loans to children to reduce taxes and pay college costs. Consult attorney to determine how assets, insurance and real estate should be distributed in case of death to avoid taxes. Update will.
50 to 55	Without children	Continue saving for retirement. Protect income from taxes. Review homeowners insurance.	Keep up contributions to IRA or Keogh. Increase tax-sheltered holdings; also continue investing for long-term capital gains. Make fresh inventory of home and include newly acquired assets.
	With children	Same as above PLUS: Protect children in case of parents' death. Provide additional funds for children's education.	Set up trusts for each child. Consider income-producing assets for children.
55–60		Plan retirement. Consolidate investments. Continue estate planning.	Estimate income needed to live comfortably. Buy retirement home if relocation is contemplated. Consider selling house to invest proceeds. Sell illiquid investments such as tax shelters. Reinvest cash in tax-deferred annuity. Update will and letter of last instructions.
60>		Provide stable monthly income from investments. Plan for future cash needs. Secure insurance coverage. Complete estate planning.	Switch investments for low-risk fixed income. Retain some growth investments as inflation hedge. Maintain health and disability insurance. Alter will for changing circumstances.

Source: Marlys Harris, "How to Make Yourself Financially Secure," *Money,* October 1983, p. 69. Reprinted by permission.

of a professional financial planner. Financial planning assistance is available from diverse advisers: accountants, attorneys, stockbrokers, bankers, insurance agents, and financial planning specialists.[4] Since the nature and quality of their advice can vary widely, it is important to spend adequate time and effort checking the qualifications of the financial planners you are considering hiring.

Once your financial goals are established, your attention should shift to developing an action plan for achieving these objectives. How are the necessary funds going to be obtained? By savings? By sale of another asset? And how much time will you need to accomplish these goals?

All financial plans should be on paper so they can be reviewed periodically. Financial planning is not a one-time task; it is a continuing process. Financial plans should be reassessed at least once a year. The general format for a written financial plan appears in Table 4-2. This particular plan is designed for a hypothetical student taking a personal finance course.

Table 4-2
THE FINANCIAL PLAN OF A HYPOTHETICAL PERSONAL FINANCE STUDENT

Financial Plan	Time Frame	Action Plan
Purchase a Porsche	By age 23	Borrow against the million the student expects to earn by age 25
Become a millionaire	By age 25	Open a new business that . . .
Establish an annuity for parents	By age 26	Use part of the first million
Pay back a student loan	By age 27	Make regular payments out of the petty-cash fund of the business

The financial plans outlined above might be considered aspirations, or long-run objectives. But what about the present? How does one plan to handle immediate financial needs and priorities?

PRELIMINARY BUDGET CONCERNS

Before you begin the actual process of developing a budget and setting long-range goals, you must take care of several preliminary matters essential to sound financial planning. Establishing an emergency fund and acquiring adequate insurance are important steps in financial planning. They are initial priorities because they provide the necessary protection upon which effective financial decisions can be made.

SETTING UP AN EMERGENCY FUND

Everyone—whether married, single, divorced, or widowed—should have an *emergency fund* to cover unexpected expenditures. This fund should be kept readily available, or liquid, so one can have easy access to it in an emergency. An account that pays some interest is a good alternative, since it provides both liquidity and a modest return. Another popular option is the money-market fund, discussed in Chapter 6. Most financial experts recommend that you have an emergency fund equal to at least six months of income. So a person making $1,500 a month should have a $9,000 emergency fund.

Like all savings plans, the establishment of an emergency fund may require some self-denial until the desired amount is built up. If the fund is tapped to meet an unexpected expenditure, it should be replenished as quickly as possible. Savings (and particularly the accumulation of an emergency fund) should be the first expenditure in anyone's budget. The old adage is to pay yourself first.

emergency fund: a fund set up to handle unexpected expenses; it should amount to six months of income.

ACQUIRING ADEQUATE INSURANCE

Purchasing insurance poses a dilemma for a lot of people—particularly those who are young, single, or divorced. In some cases their disdain may be justified, but for most people, insurance plays a critical role in their financial plans.

It is important to determine how much insurance is adequate. Full coverage is usually recommended for homes and automobiles, and good health care protection is a must. Liability coverage is relatively cheap and is essential in today's litigation-prone society. The amount of insurance coverage needed, therefore, depends on what financial responsibilities and obligations a person has. These may include the support of a family, mortgages, and debts. Couples often think of insurance protection only for the breadwinner in the household. They should, however, consider the costs that would be incurred if this income were eliminated because one spouse became disabled or died. For example, if they had children, they might have to consider the cost of childcare. Many insurance companies now actively promote policies for nonworking spouses as well as for two-career families.

Contemporary Personal Finance provides a complete discussion of each aspect of insurance. Life insurance is the topic of Chapter 12. Health care protection is outlined in Chapter 13, and Chapter 14 deals with automobile, property, and liability coverage.

FINANCIAL PLANNING AND BUDGETING

BUDGETING

A budget is a short-term financial plan. It is designed to monitor and control expenditures so that long-term objectives can be met. A budget permits a person to track past and current expenditures and plan future ones. A budget also helps people avoid impulse purchases by pointing out monthly obligations. All members of the household should be involved in the preparation of the budget since this will make implementation easier.

A budget should not deprive people of what they need; instead, it should support long-term goals. If a person's financial plans call for saving $200 per month in order to reach a ten-year financial goal, then a monthly budget that includes savings as a *fixed expense* (an obligation that does not vary from month to month) is appropriate.

fixed expenses: expenses that do not vary from month to month.

BUDGET COMPONENTS

A budget consists of two major components: income and expenses. Income should include all money that is expected to come in during the month: net salary (salary minus deductions for taxes, Social Security, and retirement fund contribution), stock dividends, interest, bonuses or commissions, and the like. Expenses are divided into two categories: fixed and *variable expenses* (those that vary from month to month). Fixed expenses include mortgage payments, although some of these are now variable (see Chapter 9); loans; insurance; and savings. Variable expenses include all other monthly obligations: food, electricity, telephone, entertainment, transportation, and so forth. Because these amounts vary, they have to be estimated each month. One should try to remain within these estimates.

variable expenses: expenses that vary from month to month.

The concept of *cash flow* (the timing of money coming in and going out) is important to budgeting. Even if you know that there will be sufficient funds over the year to cover all expenses, it might still be difficult to come up with enough cash in any given month. If, for example, you know that there will be adequate stock dividends to cover life insurance and auto insurance payments during the year, but the quarterly dividend payments do not coincide with the due date of the insurance payments, you have a cash-flow problem. You

cash flow: the timing of money inflows and outflows.

Your Financial Plans Should Also Account for the Increased Cost in Paying Your Bills Each Month.

should chart your cash flow and set aside enough money in some type of readily available interest-earning account to pay the large bills that will fall due at a later date.

CONSUMER SPENDING PATTERNS

When constructing a personal budget, it is useful to look at the way others in similar circumstances spend their money. Major categories of consumer spending include food, housing, transportation, clothing, personal care items, fees for doctors' and dentists' services, and medications. What percentage of their income do people typically spend on each of these categories?

Spending patterns in the United States vary depending on level of income. The U.S. Bureau of Labor Statistics has established three typical budgets for four-person families. These budgets are classified as lower, intermediate, and higher. Table 4-3 indicates that a low-income family of four spends 29.7 percent of its income on food, 18.4 percent on housing, and 8.6 percent on transportation. Middle-income families spend 23 percent on food, 21.8 percent on housing, and 9.3 percent on transportation, whereas those in the upper-income bracket spend 19.4 percent on food, 22.1 percent on housing, and 8.1 percent on transportation. People preparing personal budgets can select the situation most similar to their own and use the percentages listed in Table 4-3 for comparative purposes.

Table 4-3
DISTRIBUTION OF CONSUMER EXPENDITURES IN 1981

	Percent Distribution		
Budget Category	Lower Budget	Intermediate Budget	Higher Budget
Food	29.7	23.0	19.4
Housing	18.4	21.8	22.1
Transportation	8.6	9.3	8.1
Clothing, personal care	8.6	7.2	7.0
Medical care	9.4	5.7	4.0
Other	8.3	8.7	9.7
Social Security	6.8	6.7	5.2
Personal income taxes	10.4	17.5	24.5

Source: Adapted from U.S. Bureau of the Census, *Statistical Abstract of the United States: 1982–1983* (Washington, D.C.: U.S. Government Printing Office, 1983), p. 467.

SAMPLE BUDGET ALLOCATIONS

Although it is important to study average figures for different budget categories, a variety of factors can affect the ideal budget allocations in your particular situation. Age, income, marital status, children, and stage in the family cycle are some of the more important factors.

Money magazine—in cooperation with Financial Strategies, a financial planning firm in Washington, D.C.—has published some ideal budgets for four distinctly different situations. These suggested budgets allocations are shown in Figure 4-1 on page 74.

TYPES OF BUDGETS

Various types of budget forms are available from insurance companies, the government, personal finance books, and office supply stores. In general, however, all budget forms provide for the same basic information: estimated income, actual income, estimated expenses, actual expenses, surplus or deficit (sometimes called *variance*), and monthly totals. If there are problems with a specific category in the budget, you can track expenditures within only that category and then construct a separate budget for that particular category. If, for example, your food budget fluctuates wildly from month to month, you might want to set up a system for analyzing all grocery store expenditures. Maybe toiletries and even some clothing items are being purchased at the grocery store. If this is the case, then estimates for all three categories—food, toiletries, and clothing—will be off.

variance: *the difference between actual and projected budget items.*

Budgets should be kept as simple as possible. The elimination of cents is often a good idea since rounding to the nearest dollar is adequate for household budget purposes. Budget record keeping should not become a chore.

It is important to find a budgeting system that works for you. Let's look at a standard budget form for a hypothetical couple, Phil and June Goodman.

COMPLETING THE BUDGET FORM

Table 4-4 shows Phil and June Goodman's actual budget for August and September 1985. They have used a basic form that provides estimates, actual figures, and monthly outcomes. The following discussion shows how the Goodmans use their budget and make adjustments in it.

Income. The Goodmans' net salary is the amount of their take-home pay. Their stock dividends are paid quarterly, so they show no dividend income during August and September. They expect to receive $40 per month in repayment of a loan to June's brother. In August, however, he failed to make the payment. Phil had expected that his annual bonus would be about $1,000, and he was pleasantly surprised to receive $100 more than he had expected.

FINANCIAL PLANNING

Figure 4-1
SAMPLE BUDGET ALLOCATIONS

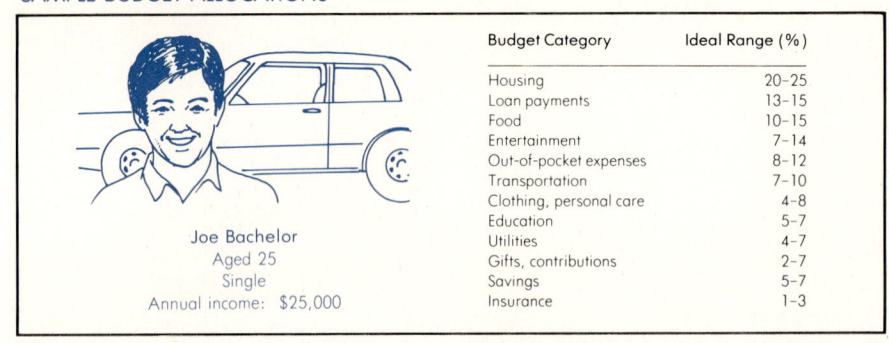

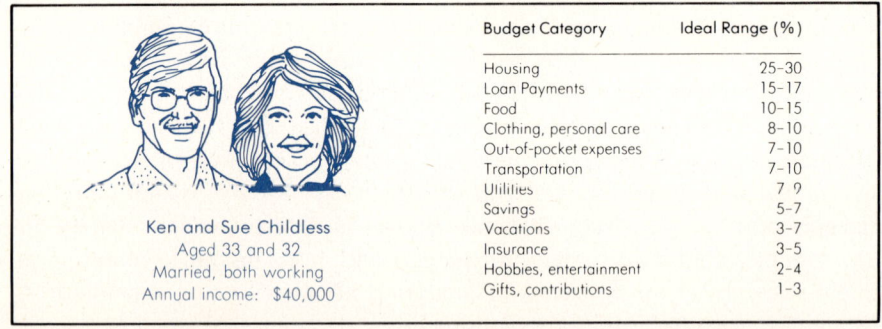

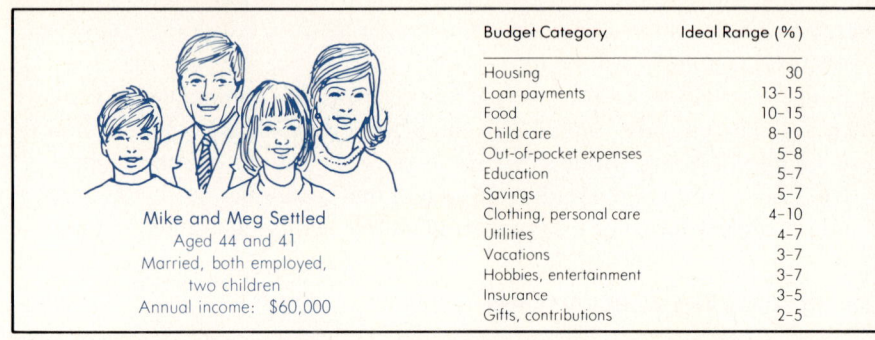

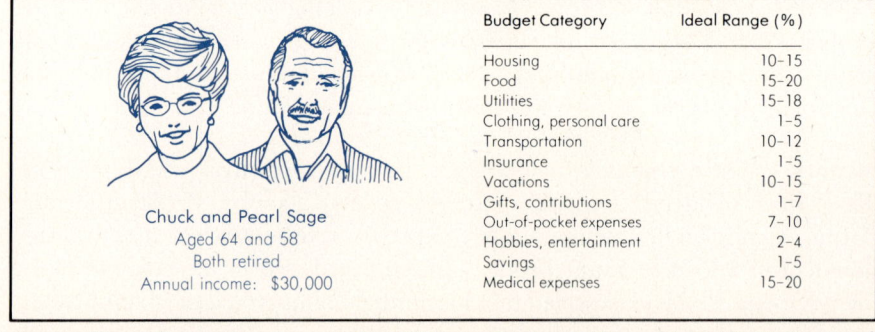

Joe Bachelor
Aged 25
Single
Annual income: $25,000

Budget Category	Ideal Range (%)
Housing	20–25
Loan payments	13–15
Food	10–15
Entertainment	7–14
Out-of-pocket expenses	8–12
Transportation	7–10
Clothing, personal care	4–8
Education	5–7
Utilities	4–7
Gifts, contributions	2–7
Savings	5–7
Insurance	1–3

Ken and Sue Childless
Aged 33 and 32
Married, both working
Annual income: $40,000

Budget Category	Ideal Range (%)
Housing	25–30
Loan Payments	15–17
Food	10–15
Clothing, personal care	8–10
Out-of-pocket expenses	7–10
Transportation	7–10
Utilities	7–9
Savings	5–7
Vacations	3–7
Insurance	3–5
Hobbies, entertainment	2–4
Gifts, contributions	1–3

Mike and Meg Settled
Aged 44 and 41
Married, both employed,
two children
Annual income: $60,000

Budget Category	Ideal Range (%)
Housing	30
Loan payments	13–15
Food	10–15
Child care	8–10
Out-of-pocket expenses	5–8
Education	5–7
Savings	5–7
Clothing, personal care	4–10
Utilities	4–7
Vacations	3–7
Hobbies, entertainment	3–7
Insurance	3–5
Gifts, contributions	2–5

Chuck and Pearl Sage
Aged 64 and 58
Both retired
Annual income: $30,000

Budget Category	Ideal Range (%)
Housing	10–15
Food	15–20
Utilities	15–18
Clothing, personal care	1–5
Transportation	10–12
Insurance	1–5
Vacations	10–15
Gifts, contributions	1–7
Out-of-pocket expenses	7–10
Hobbies, entertainment	2–4
Savings	1–5
Medical expenses	15–20

Source: Marlys Harris, "Creating a Budget," *Money*, October 1983, pp. 71–72, 74, 76. Reprinted, as adapted, by permission.

Table 4-4
THE GOODMANS' BUDGET FOR AUGUST AND SEPTEMBER 1985

	August			September		
Income	Estimated	Actual		Estimated	Actual	
Net salary	$ 2,486	$ 2,486		$ 2,486	$ 2,486	
Stock dividends	0	0		0	0	
Bonus	1,000	1,100		0	0	
Loan repayment	40	0		40	40	
TOTAL	$ 3,526	$ 3,586		$ 2,526	$ 2,526	

Expenses	Estimated	Actual	Balance	Estimated	Actual	Balance
FIXED						
Mortgage and property tax	$ 578	$ 578	$ 0	$ 578	$ 578	$ 0
Auto loan	123	123	0	123	123	0
Insurance						
Life	0	0	0	0	0	0
Auto	0	0	0	0	0	0
Homeowner's	350	350	0	0	0	0
Savings	200	200	0	200	200	0
VARIABLE						
Food	400	370	+30	400	415	−15
Electric	80	94	−14	80	82	− 2
Heating oil	0	0	0	0	0	0
Water	0	0	0	60	56	+ 4
Telephone	60	55	+ 5	60	61	− 1
Medical and dental (unreimbursed)	100	110	−10	50	20	+30
Clothing	200	175	+25	40	35	+ 5
Recreation	50	50	0	50	50	0
Entertainment	125	95	+30	125	120	+ 5
Vacation	500	650	−150	0	0	0
Gas and oil for auto	90	110	−20	90	87	+ 3
Music lessons	60	60	0	60	60	0
Toiletries and cosmetics	20	18	+ 2	20	12	+ 8
Haircuts and beauty salon	50	50	0	50	50	0
Veterinarian	0	0	0	25	22	+ 3
Household maintenance	0	15	−15	300	300	0
Contributions	25	25	0	0	0	0
Gifts	0	0	0	0	0	0
Personal spending money	125	125	0	125	140	−15
TOTAL	$ 3,136	$ 3,253	$ −117	$ 2,436	$ 2,411	$ +25

Month-End Outcome

	August	September
Total income	$ 3,586	$ 2,526
Total expenses	3,253	2,411
Surplus (deficit)	$ 333	$ 115

In September, June's brother made his loan payment, but of course there was no bonus; therefore, their September income was considerably lower than their August income.

Fixed Expenses. There are seldom any surprises in the category labeled *fixed expenses*. Fixed expenses are set; they do not vary over time. However, there are usually some large annual, semiannual, or quarterly expenses that must be anticipated. The Goodmans' homeowner's insurance, for example, comes due every August.

Variable Expenses. Most imbalances occur under variable expenses. Here one has to be particularly concerned with deficits.

At the end of each month, the Goodmans sit down and review their budget and try to determine the reasons for major differences between their estimated expenses and their actual costs. In August they decided that their food expenses were lower than anticipated because they had been away on vacation for ten days and had included the cost of food during that period in their vacation budget. June Goodman felt that their actual expenses for food for August should have been even lower than they were. When September's food expenses ran over their estimates, the Goodmans decided to track this budget item more carefully.

Except for the August electric bill, their other utilities were very close to the original estimates. The Goodmans are aware that their electric bills are higher during the months that they use air conditioning, and they plan to increase their estimated expenses during the summer months next year. They are also considering installing a ceiling fan to cut their use of the air conditioner. Their estimates and actual expenses for heating oil are zero for August and September, but they know that October will bring a large expense for

---

The Martsens' Dilemma

With a combined income of $41,000, Will and Kathryn Martsen of Seattle would be considered well-off by most standards. They have one daughter, live in a nice home, and have good jobs. After taxes and basic living expenses, the Martsens have an annual surplus of $14,000 for savings and investment. Yet their savings are minimal; the Martsens' $14,000 surplus has simply slipped away. In fact, Kathryn Martsen has observed:

Our problem is that we don't seem to be able to save for the future, although we realize that we must have a plan for college and retirement goals. You would think that with both of us working, we would be able to put money aside and even begin investing on a small scale, but we don't seem [to be able to]. Where are we going wrong?

What would you suggest to the Martsens?

Source: Elizabeth Rhodes, "Couple's Money Sifts through Fingers," *Seattle Times*, June 22, 1981, p. B1.

heating oil in anticipation of winter. They intend to talk with their heating-oil supplier about going on a budget plan that will enable them to pay a consistent, prorated amount each month throughout the year. In that case they would list heating oil under fixed expenses and avoid the occasional budget shock that occurs after an oil delivery. This kind of plan makes budgeting easier, but it has a disadvantage in that the oil company has use of the Goodmans' money, which could have drawn interest during the zero-expense months.

The Goodmans' estimates for medical, dental, and clothing expenses were considerably higher in August because they were anticipating preschool checkups and school clothing. Their vacation expenses were also higher than their estimated figure. But the increased bonus cushioned some of this added expense.

The August bonus also provided a cushion that enabled the Goodmans to pay for repairs to their roof in September. They had received a written estimate for these repairs and knew that they would have to show a surplus of $300 in August in order to avoid dipping into their emergency fund.

Month-end Outcome. The Goodmans appear to be managing their money well. Perhaps, given their income, they should be trying to save more, but they are in a stage of family development where variable expenses are relatively high. But the family clearly has its expenditures under control through an effective budgeting system. This hypothetical family illustrates how a personal budget can be used to reach financial goals—in this case, goals based on an active lifestyle.

Life at the Top—Not as Easy as It Seems?

A recent *Wall Street Journal*/Gallup Poll of 824 chief executives reveals a startling fact—many of these business leaders are financially insecure. Only about 60 percent of the respondents from medium- and large-sized firms are satisfied with their progress toward their own financial goals. And this figure drops to 40 percent for the heads of smaller companies.

Housing is a major concern. Those executives who report the least satisfaction with their financial progress are usually the ones spending the most on housing. Inflation is another factor. One aerospace company head puts it this way: "I can afford it, but I resent it." High tax brackets are another common concern expressed in the survey.

As a group, these top executives do not have excessive spending habits. Over 80 percent of them say they do not spend a lot of money on personal expenditures, primarily because of a lack of time. When questioned about what they would like to buy more of, the responses tend to fall into categories like travel, recreation, and personal pursuits. This study suggests that improved financial planning can assist everyone—even those at the top.

Source: Frank Allen, "Top Executives, Though Well-Paid, Still Worry about Personal Wealth," *Wall Street Journal*, October 15, 1981. Sec. 2. p. 25.

CREDIT ABUSE: A COMMON CHARACTERISTIC OF INDIVIDUALS WHO IGNORE FINANCIAL PLANNING

Too many consumers fail to engage in financial planning. All too often they find themselves with mounting debts and rapidly growing monthly payments. What happens when they cannot meet such monthly payments? Missed payments will not be ignored by creditors, who are likely to send written inquiries concerning your failure to make a scheduled repayment. Unless you make the payment or contact them and make other arrangements agreeable to all parties, your creditors are likely to take further action, ranging from garnishing your wages to repossessing your property or sending you into bankruptcy. As a result, it might be virtually impossible for you to obtain credit during the next seven to ten years.

WAGE GARNISHMENT

default: failure of a borrower to make required principal and interest payments on a loan.

garnishment: a repayment arrangement resulting from a court order requiring that a specified portion of the borrower's wages be paid directly to a lender or lenders by the employer.

The failure of a borrower to make required principal and interest payments on a loan is called *default*. In such instances, the lender has the legal right to take a number of actions in an attempt to recover all or part of the funds (or merchandise) provided to the credit purchaser. Garnishment of the borrower's wages is one of the strongest actions a creditor can take. *Garnishment* is a repayment arrangement resulting from a court order requiring that a specified portion of the borrower's wages be paid directly by the employer to the lender. The amount, which is specified by the court, is deducted directly from the borrower's paycheck, just as income tax and Social Security payments are. The garnishment continues until the total debt is paid.

Garnishment is a formal, legal process that begins with a court proceeding. The individual who has defaulted on a loan is given an opportunity to offer a defense in court and can bring an attorney. Persons in default who do not appear at the hearing automatically lose the case and, in many instances, learn that their wages have been garnished only when they discover the deductions from their paychecks.

The size of the garnishment is limited by the federal Consumer Credit Protection Act. This law, discussed in detail in Chapter 7, also prohibits employers from dismissing employees whose wages are subject to a single garnishment. However, if two or more creditors succeed in garnishing a borrower's wages, the law no longer prohibits the employer from dismissing the employee.

REPOSSESSION

repossession: the act of seizing property pledged against a loan when the buyer defaults.

In some cases of default, the creditor will secure legal permission to seize the property sold on credit or other property offered as collateral to secure the loan. This return of property sold on credit is termed *repossession*.

FINANCIAL PLANNING AND BUDGETING

"It says it's our final notice."

Some Lenders Send Dramatic Notices about Past-Due Bills.
Source: From the *Wall Street Journal*. Permission, Cartoon Features Syndicate.

Although repossession puts the property—or the property of value used as collateral—back in the creditor's hands, it frequently does not settle the debt. If the property purchased on credit has declined in value to the point where its market value is less than the outstanding loan, the remaining balance is still subject to collection. If the used-car dealer who sold you the automobile for $5,000 two months ago on credit repossesses the auto and resells it for $4,000, you still owe the $1,000 difference, despite the fact that you no longer have possession of the car. In addition, you are responsible for the creditor's court costs and legal fees. The debt that remains after the property has been repossessed is called a *deficiency judgment*.

In many instances, deficiency judgments add up to more than the borrower paid for the original item, particularly with such products as furniture or appliances, for which no strong resale market exists. In order to protect low-income credit purchasers, a number of states no longer allow deficiency judgments. Still others prohibit deficiency judgments on amounts of less than $1,000.

Credit purchasers who are unable to make monthly payments on merchandise purchased on credit and have little expectation of improved financial conditions should arrange to return the property to the merchant or lender voluntarily. Although they may still owe the creditor additional money, this action will have less of an adverse impact on the borrower's credit rating than would a forced repossession.

deficiency judgment: *the residual claim of lenders in instances where the value of repossessed property is less than the outstanding debt.*

BANKRUPTCY

This was not the way the fairy tale was supposed to end. The couple, married for four years and with two children, found themselves in severe financial difficulties. With a total household income of $22,000, no savings, and $35,000 in debts, the monthly nightmare of stretching too little income to cover too many expenses was growing worse. The telephone had already been disconnected, the power company was threatening to cut off the electricity, and a parade of bill collectors marched to the front door each week. Faced with these seemingly unsolvable problems, the couple chose bankruptcy.

Bankruptcy is a legal procedure by which an individual, household, or business firm that cannot meet its financial obligations is relieved of these obligations by having the court divide the assets and/or income among creditors. Bankruptcy has traditionally been an action of last resort, since it carried a stigma for the bankrupt individual and virtually eliminated the chances of securing future credit.

The *Federal Bankruptcy Reform Act of 1978* is the latest in a series of federal laws designed to assist people with excessive debts through a three-year debt repayment plan or through a plan for liquidating assets. Individuals choosing bankruptcy pay a $60 filing fee in the federal district court and have two alternatives. The first, Chapter 13 of the bankruptcy law, allows individuals to establish a three-year debt repayment plan, known as a wage-earner plan. Debtors who choose this plan are allowed to retain possession of their property and to repay specified monthly amounts to their creditors over a three-year period. Although this plan may result in payments as low as 10 cents per dollar owed, the typical Chapter 13 bankruptcy agreement calls for debts to be repaid at a rate of 60 to 70 cents per dollar owed.

The second bankruptcy alternative is to use Chapter 7 of the law. Chapter 7 is a liquidation plan in which the debtor's assets are seized by the court and are sold. Any funds remaining after court costs and legal fees are paid are then prorated among the various creditors. Since Chapter 7 does not contain repayment provisions other than through funds generated by the sale of the bankrupt party's assets, creditors typically receive only a small portion of the funds owed them.

Chapter 7 of the bankruptcy law allows individuals to exempt the following items from the claims of creditors:

1. Home equity of $7,500.

2. Automobile or other motor vehicle equity of up to $1,200.

3. Work tools or prescribed health items of up to $750.

4. Personal jewelry up to $500.

---

bankruptcy: *general procedures by which an individual, household, or business firm that cannot meet its financial obligations is relieved of these obligations by having the court divide the assets and/or income among creditors.*

Federal Bankruptcy Reform Act of 1978: *a federal law designed to assist individuals, households, and business firms with excessive debts through a three-year repayment plan or through a plan for liquidating assets.*

5. Personal items such as household furnishings and clothes up to $200 each.

6. Other personal property with total value of up to $400.

When husbands and wives file jointly, these exemptions are doubled.

The latest bankruptcy law greatly eased people's ability to use bankruptcy as a way out of excessive debt. Although bankruptcy does not relieve the individual of the obligation to pay taxes, alimony, or child support, it is in marked contrast to the pattern that existed from the 1100s through the late 1800s, when people were put in debtors' prisons until their family or friends could repay their creditors. In fact, the new law has been criticized by lenders as overly permissive in allowing people to avoid repaying loans.

Clearly the number of persons filing for personal bankruptcy has increased dramatically in the years since the passage of the law. In 1982, some 450,000 people filed for personal bankruptcy, more than twice the number who filed before this law was passed. However, a General Accounting Office study of those who filed for bankruptcy revealed that the typical bankruptcy resulted from economic factors such as cost-of-living increases, unemployment, easy credit availability, and unprecedented medical bills. The study also developed a profile of the typical person filing for bankruptcy: a blue-collar worker who earns $13,000 a year and is $30,000 in debt.[5]

Bankruptcy should never be considered a quick fix for an individual's financial problems. In some ways, once the person files for bankruptcy, his or her financial problems have just begun. Individual credit ratings will list the bankruptcy judgment for the next ten years—a fact that is likely to make it extremely difficult to secure future credit. Indeed, a declaration of bankruptcy may result in the withdrawal of all the credit the individual currently has.

Every person considering bankruptcy should first seek the advice of a credit counselor, who will work with the individual in developing a financial plan. It may be possible to develop a plan that, with the cooperation of creditors, will allow the individual to meet basic expenses and slowly repay outstanding debts. Credit counselors are described in detail in Chapter 7.

SUMMARY

Financial planning is the process by which financial goals and related courses of action are developed. Although financial plans are based on the financial statements discussed in Chapter 3, they go beyond this to account for where the person wants to be at some specific point in the future. All financial plans assume that an adequate base has been established in terms of an emergency fund and appropriate insurance protection. For some people—particularly those with significant wealth—the services of a financial planner are helpful.

Budgeting is a short-term financial plan. Its purpose is to monitor and control expenditures so that long-term obligations can be met. The major budget components are income and expenses. The budget should track the various sources of income and then allocate this money to either a fixed or variable expense category. Cash flow, or the timing of when money is received and when it goes out, is important to budgeting since inflow and outflow must coincide.

The U.S. Bureau of Labor Statistics has constructed three typical household budgets at lower, intermediate, and higher levels. Spending patterns differ markedly among these various budgets. The case of a hypothetical family—the Goodmans—shows how an actual budget should be constructed and the various components involved.

Consumers who fail to engage in financial planning sometimes abuse their credit. This can have a disastrous effect on an individual's financial situation. If there is a default on a loan, creditors may be able to garnish the borrower's wages—that is, to obtain a court order requiring the borrower's employer to pay a portion of the borrower's wages directly to the creditor. Repossession of the property purchased on credit or pledged against the loan is another possibility. Bankruptcy may be the ultimate consequence of credit abuse.

REVIEW QUESTIONS

1. Briefly define the following terms:
   financial planning
   budgeting
   emergency fund
   fixed expenses
   variable expenses
   cash flow
   variance
   default
   garnishment
   repossession
   deficiency judgment
   bankruptcy
   Federal Bankruptcy Reform Act of 1978

2. How are financial planning and budgeting related?
3. Identify the demographic variables that influence financial planning and budgeting.
4. Why are emergency funds and insurance programs important to financial planning?
5. How does one develop a personal financial plan?
6. What are the major components of a personal budget?
7. Why is the concept of cash flow important to budgeting?
8. How do U.S. spending patterns vary with the level of income?
9. Identify the possible actions a creditor might take in the event of default on a loan.
10. Differentiate between Chapters 7 and 13 of the Federal Bankruptcy Reform Act of 1978.

CASES AND EXERCISES

1. Jim Graham has come a long way since he left California $6,000 in debt. Today Jim, a handsome bachelor, drives around Seattle in a BMW. Jim adopted a financial plan to improve his financial circumstances once he arrived in Seattle. He began working in a wholesaler's showroom and rented a house with an option to buy (along with another party). Within three years Jim's financial planning paid off. He was out of debt and had become manager of the showroom; he had also bought out his partner, purchased the house, and acquired the BMW. By most standards Jim Graham is a success, yet he admits that he still feels he is an underachiever. Now Jim needs to develop a new financial plan. As he explains his thinking:

   - "It's really hard for me to define [monetary] goals. I'm accountable to no one, I'm not saving to put kids through school, I have everything I really need."
   - "I'd like to feel that if I lost my job tomorrow I wouldn't be in a mess. I'd like to have an emergency fund so I wouldn't have to sell the house or my car if I got in a jam."
   - "I want to build my net worth and become a self-made person. I'd like to be able to do what I want to do and not have a 9-to-5 job by the time I'm 55."
   - "My philosophy has been if I get a large sum, I put it in my savings account till I decide what to do with it."[6]

   How can financial planning and budgeting help Jim Graham?

2. What can be learned from the Gallup poll of the personal financial opinions of top executives? Discuss.
3. Interview a financial planner in your area. Find out how he or she works with clients. What services are offered? How is the financial planner paid? Report your findings to the class.
4. Construct an actual budget for your own expenditures. What have you learned from this exercise?
5. Consider the Goodmans' hypothetical budget presented in Table 4-4 on page 75. What suggestions would you offer the Goodmans about their personal finances?

ANSWERS TO PERSONAL FINANCE I.Q. TEST

1. Fiction. 2. Fact. 3. Fiction. 4. Fact. 5. Fact.

HOW TOM LEE REACHED HIS PERSONAL FINANCIAL DECISION

"It's important to understand that *you* control your money; your money doesn't control you," replied Professor Malloy. "That's why you need to keep records, set financial goals, and make realistic plans to achieve them.

"To understand what this means," she continued, "let's look at your situation, Tom. Your goal is moving away from home. First, do a little research and find out what your expenditures would actually be for rent, food, transportation, etc. Prepare a budget including these additional expenses. If expenses now outweigh income, review your expenses to see which ones you can live without. Suppose that you still do not have enough income—how much more work would you have to do to earn enough?

"At this point," Professor Malloy explained, "you need to evaluate what's right for *you*. How important is leaving home to you? Would an increased workload interfere with your studies? How much longer do you have before you graduate and work full time? All these factors will guide you to your decision. Maybe you can't afford to move out now, but don't stop there. Ask yourself what steps you should take to make it a reality in the future. This is a time to daydream about what you want—and to figure out how to get it."

Tom went home and thought about this. He worked through some more numbers. Envisioning all the things he wanted to do in his life, he decided that any extra money he had now should be used to build a solid financial foundation for himself.

The next day when he came to class, Tom felt a lot better. After class he approached Professor Malloy to let her know he had taken her advice. He had determined that it was impossible to move out this year. However, he planned to open a savings account so that he could move out after graduation, when he began working full time. "At least," he said, "I feel better about staying at home. In fact, I feel grateful to have the opportunity to start saving for what I really want."

LEARNING OBJECTIVES

1. To identify the major categories of taxes paid by U.S. taxpayers. / *2.* To contrast the ability-to-pay philosophy of taxation with the benefits-received philosophy and compare progressive with regressive taxes. / *3.* To describe the role of the Internal Revenue Service. / *4.* To discriminate between tax avoidance and tax evasion. / *5.* To explain how to determine which income tax form an individual should choose. / *6.* To distinguish taxable income from nontaxable income, gross income from adjusted gross income, capital gains from ordinary income, marginal tax rates from effective tax rates, and tax deductions from tax credits. / *7.* To discuss the major provisions of the Economic Recovery Tax Act (ERTA) of 1981.

TESTING YOUR PERSONAL FINANCE I.Q.

	FACT	FICTION
1. The salaries of the president of the United States and members of the U.S. Senate and House of Representatives are exempt from federal, state, and local income taxes.	☐	☐
2. A city sales tax enacted to raise funds for revitalizing the central business district is an example of a progressive tax.	☐	☐
3. The IRS—not the FBI—was responsible for sending Al Capone to federal prison.	☐	☐
4. Although several states, such as Florida, New Hampshire, Texas, and Washington have no state income taxes, all states impose sales taxes on the sale of goods and services.	☐	☐
5. George Washington never completed a Virginia state income tax form, nor did he pay federal income taxes.	☐	☐
6. The marriage penalty is an example of a state and local licensing tax.	☐	☐
7. Capital gains taxes are lower than taxes on ordinary income.	☐	☐
8. New York has both a state and local income tax and a sales tax; Texas has a sales tax but no state income tax; New Hampshire has neither.	☐	☐
9. Managers and employees of tax preparation agencies are required to complete a special course and then pass state licensing exams before offering their services to the public.	☐	☐

The materials in this chapter assist in separating fact from fiction. Your answers can be checked on page 121.

CHAPTER FIVE

TAXES

SHARING A PERSONAL FINANCIAL DECISION WITH PROFESSOR CLYDE D. WESTWOOD OF UTAH TECHNICAL COLLEGE AT PROVO

Burt and Sally James, a young married couple, are part-time students at Utah Technical College at Provo. They decided to take Professor Clyde Westwood's personal finance course together, in hopes that they'd get some ideas on how to better manage their money. One of their main concerns is their tax situation. They've heard their friends talk about tax deductions, but they're not sure how to make this work for them.

Burt and Sally have already picked up some practical tips on budgeting and planning from Professor Westwood, who seems genuinely interested in how personal financial decisions affect his students. On the day he lectures on taxes, they wait until the rest of the class leaves and then ask for his opinion on how they can legally reduce their tax burden.

"Together we earn about $2,000 per month," Burt explains, "but we end up paying very high taxes because our only exemption is for ourselves. We can't, for instance, claim deductions for a house because we live rent-free in an apartment owned by my parents."

"We *have* been able to save some money," Sally adds. "The cost of living isn't high here, and we're careful about our spending. But if we could cut our taxes, we'd have a better chance of getting ahead."

If you were Professor Westwood, what would you propose?

To find out how Professor Westwood helped Burt and Sally make their personal financial decision, turn to page 121.

"I'm proud to pay taxes in the United States. The only thing is, I could be just as proud for half the money."
Arthur Godfrey[1]

Even presidents must file tax returns and pay taxes. Just twelve days before the April 15 deadline, President Ronald W. Reagan and his wife Nancy filed their joint tax return. By withholding from the president's $200,000 annual salary and by quarterly estimated tax payments, the Reagans overpaid their income tax by $70,526. They asked the government to refund all but $20,000 and to apply the balance to the following year's tax bill.

The summary of the Reagans' tax return, shown in Figure 5-1, reveals a total income of $422,834 and payment of $128,639 (30 percent) in federal income taxes. This income placed the first family in the top one-half of 1 percent of the nation's taxpayers. In fact, less than 50,000 of the approximately 95 million U.S. taxpayers report incomes of more than $400,000 a year.

The Reagans are by no means the largest taxpayers in the United States. In 1980, for example, the Internal Revenue Service received 4,112 tax returns with adjusted gross incomes of $1 million or more. Of course, this figure does not accurately reflect the number of millionaires in this country, since many ultra-wealthy people reduce their income by investing in tax-exempt municipal bonds, using tax shelters, and taking other legal deductions.

Of the 4,112 reported millionaires, about a dozen paid no federal income taxes at all. A bigger surprise, however, is the number who took the standard deduction of $3,400 for a joint return and $2,300 for an individual return. Forty-one millionaires fell into this group in 1980.[2]

Tax payments—income taxes, sales taxes, property taxes, and seemingly dozens of other types—are a fact of life for most consumers. They represent a significant portion of total household expenditures. An understanding of taxes is important for anyone who is to meet the legal obligation of paying them. But of equal importance is the possibility of reducing taxes by understanding the rules concerning deductions, special credits, and varying treatments of different types of income and purchases. Careful tax planning is essential to modern personal finance.

tax: a payment that individuals and organizations having income or property, or engaging in various types of activities, must make to a government agency at either the local, state, or federal level.

WHAT ARE TAXES?

A *tax* is a payment a local, state, or federal government requires of individuals and organizations that have property, receive income, or engage in various forms of activities. Property taxes, capital gains taxes, and estate taxes are all

Figure 5-1
THE REAGANS' FEDERAL INCOME TAX RETURN

Form 1040 Department of the Treasury—Internal Revenue Service
U.S. Individual Income Tax Return 1983 (2)

For the year January 1-December 31, 1983, or other tax year beginning , 1983, ending , 19 | OMB No. 1545-0074

Use IRS label. Otherwise, please print or type.
FT 480-07-7456 322-18-0676 S89 -002
RONALD W & NANCY REAGAN
ROY MILLER ESQ
333 SO GRAND 4723
LOS ANGELES CA 90071

IRS

Your social security number: 480 07 7456
Spouse's social security number: 322 18 0676
Your occupation: U.S. PRESIDENT
Spouse's occupation: FIRST LADY

Presidential Election Campaign ▶ Do you want $1 to go to this fund? . . . . . Yes X No
If joint return, does your spouse want $1 to go to this fund? Yes X No
Note: Checking Yes will not increase your tax or reduce your refund

First Family's Income-Tax Return for 1983

Income

Wages as President	$200,000
Interest	$164,029
Dividends	$ 28,630
Capital loss, transactions in blind trust	–$ 3,000
Pension from California governorship	$ 26,538
Rent from radio repeater station at ranch	$ 3,600
Other income, including Nancy's book advance	$ 3,037
Adjusted gross income	**$422,834**

Deductions

Medical	$ 0
Taxes	$ 63,293
Interest	$ 14,840
Contributions	$ 15,307
Legal fees (taxes, financial planning and audit)	$ 32,200
Other deductions, including union dues ($102)	$ 8,321
Total itemized deductions over $3,400	**$130,561**
Personal exemptions	$ 3,000
Taxable income	**$289,273**
1983 federal income tax	**$128,639**

Source: "The Reagans Get a Refund," *U.S. News & World Report*, April 23, 1984, p. 11. Reprinted by permission.

related to the property of individuals; the first two types of taxes also apply to the property of organizations. Taxes related to income include personal and corporate income taxes and Social Security taxes. Sales taxes, excise taxes, and import and export duties are all related to activities in which individuals and organizations engage.

Most types of taxes are levied by governments in order to raise money to cover operating costs and to pay for such products and services as streets and highways, police and fire protection, the national park system, national defense, and educational and social services. In some instances, taxes are

FINANCIAL PLANNING

designed to influence and regulate activities in the economy. Higher taxes on gasoline, for example, may be levied in an attempt to reduce gasoline consumption. Higher taxes on imports may result in increased purchases of domestic goods.

PHILOSOPHIES OF TAXATION

How should a government determine the appropriate share of taxes for each citizen? In general, there are two philosophies of taxation. The first, the *benefits-received philosophy*, argues that those citizens who receive the benefits of a particular expenditure should pay the cost of this expenditure. If the citizens of a community benefit from the installation of a municipal water system, they should share in the cost of its installation. This philosophy is frequently used by tax authorities. Toll roads levy tolls to users; property taxes are used to fund public schools, police and fire protection, and streets and highways used by persons paying these taxes; and gasoline taxes generate revenue for highway repairs and new construction.

The second philosophy argues that taxes should be based on the *ability to pay*. The philosopher Adam Smith summarized this philosophy more than 200 years ago in his book *Wealth of Nations*: "The subjects of every state ought to contribute towards the support of the government, as nearly as possible, in proportion to their respective abilities."[3] This argument—that the rich should be responsible for a greater share of the tax burden than the poor—has been incorporated into state and federal income taxes. By taxing a disproportionately small percentage of the first dollars earned by either the rich or poor, tax collectors leave people with the lion's share of these funds so they can feed, clothe, and provide themselves with adequate housing. Such an approach focuses on the discretionary income of individuals and households as the primary source of tax revenues.

PROGRESSIVE AND REGRESSIVE TAXES

It is possible to categorize taxes based on their impact on individuals and households in different income brackets. The two major categories are progressive and regressive taxes.

Taxes paid on income are usually *progressive taxes*. A progressive tax takes larger and larger shares of each additional increment of personal income. Figure 5-2 reflects the impact of progressive taxes on different income levels. As the figure reveals, a family of four with an adjusted gross income of $10,000 will pay 3 percent of its total income in taxes. By contrast, an affluent family of four with an adjusted gross income of $200,000 will pay 41 percent of its total income in taxes.

The percentages shown in Figure 5-2 reflect average tax payments by

---

benefits-received philosophy: the idea that taxes should be levied on those individuals and households who benefit from expenditures made with tax revenues; for instance, turnpike tolls should be paid by people who drive on those turnpikes.

ability-to-pay philosophy: the idea that relatively greater amounts of taxes should be levied on higher-income taxpayers and less on lower-income individuals and households.

progressive tax: a tax that takes increasing percentages of each increment of income.

Figure 5-2
IMPACT OF PROGRESSIVE TAXATION ON DIFFERENT INCOME LEVELS

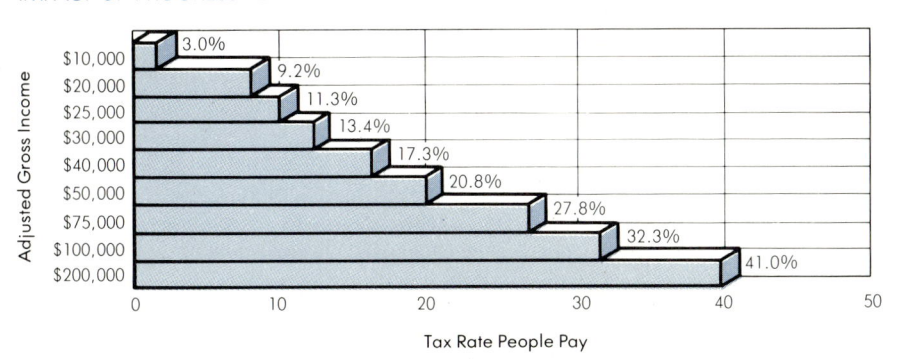

Adjusted Gross Income	Tax Rate People Pay
$10,000	3.0%
$20,000	9.2%
$25,000	11.3%
$30,000	13.4%
$40,000	17.3%
$50,000	20.8%
$75,000	27.8%
$100,000	32.3%
$200,000	41.0%

Note: Figures assume family of four filing jointly, with one wage earner and no itemized deductions, at 1983 tax rates.

Source: "Do We Really Need an Income Tax?" Reprinted from *U.S. News & World Report*, April 18, 1983, p. 41 Copyright 1983, U.S. News & World Report, Inc.

households in the various income brackets. The specific impact of progressive taxes can be analyzed through an example. Consider the tax impact when an individual receives a $5,000 salary increase. The federal government's share of that added $5,000 depends on the individual's income level. A $10,000-per-year wage earner who receives a $5,000 raise will pay additional federal income taxes of $718, or 14.4 percent of the raise. On the other hand, if the recipient of the $5,000 raise was earning $100,000 before the raise, the federal government's share of the salary increase will be $2,400, or 48 percent.

A *regressive tax* affects low-income persons more than high-income persons. In contrast to a progressive tax, it takes a smaller and smaller percentage of income as income rises. Sales taxes and property taxes are considered regressive, since less affluent people often use a higher percentage of their income to pay them than do the rich. While more-affluent households may pay more in sales taxes and property taxes in absolute terms, their relative expenditures as a proportion of total income are usually less than those of lower-income households. The household earning $80,000 and paying $2,200 in property taxes spends more in absolute dollars on property taxes than does the family with a total income of $20,000 and a property tax bill of $800. As a percentage of total income, however, the $80,000-per-year household spends only 2.75 percent of total household income on property taxes, while the less affluent household pays property taxes equal to 4 percent of its total income.

regressive tax: a tax that takes a larger percentage of the total income of low-income taxpayers than of higher income taxpayers.

TYPES OF TAXES

Personal finance decisions are affected by a variety of taxes—both progressive and regressive—that reduce available funds. The amount of taxes paid and the types of taxes affecting individual consumers depend on such factors as where they live, what they buy, what government services they use, and whether they own or rent their homes. The major types of taxes include income taxes, Social Security taxes, property taxes, sales taxes, excise taxes, and a variety of state and local licensing taxes.

INCOME TAXES

income tax: *a tax levied by the local, state, or federal government on the incomes of individuals and/or businesses.*

Income taxes are levied by the federal government; by all state governments except Alaska, Connecticut, Florida, Nevada, New Hampshire, South Dakota, Tennessee, Texas, Washington, and Wyoming; and by many local governments. Such taxes apply to the incomes of individuals, married couples, and business firms. Since income tax rates increase as income rises, they are categorized as progressive taxes. In 1982, $298 billion was collected in federal income taxes. That same year, $46 billion in state income taxes was collected.[4]

Federal Income Tax. The first nationwide income tax was a temporary levy used over 120 years ago during the American Civil War. When Congress attempted to use this method of generating funds again in 1894, the Supreme Court declared the income tax unconstitutional. The Court's ruling was based on a constitutional requirement that taxes be apportioned among states according to their populations. This constitutional barrier was removed in 1913 with the passage of the Sixteenth Amendment to the U.S. Constitution.

During the nearly three-quarters of a century the federal income tax has been in effect, both the number of taxpayers and the size of tax revenues have increased dramatically. In 1914, fewer than one out of every 200 men, women, and children even filed an income tax return; today returns are filed annually by two out of every five Americans—children and adults. Today, the federal government collects an average of $3,000 for each return submitted, compared with about $75 per return in 1914.

State and Local Income Taxes. Although important, income taxes play a far less critical role in state and local government budgets than in the federal budget. Individual income taxes provide 17 cents out of every dollar raised by state governments and 3 cents out of every dollar raised by local governments.[5] The bulk of state and local government financing is generated from property and sales taxes.

Much of the revenue collected by state and local governments is spent to provide services similar to those provided by the federal government from income taxes. These taxes support such important functions as public education, welfare, and health care. The priorities, however, are different. Whereas most of the federal government's tax revenues are spent on income security payments and national defense, state and local governments spend most of their tax revenues on education, public welfare, and highways. The states and municipalities also pay for such vital services as police and fire protection and public sanitation.

SOCIAL SECURITY TAXES

A second major tax deducted from the salaries and wages of consumers is for Social Security. This deduction is listed on a pay stub under the heading FICA, an acronym for the Federal Insurance Contributions Act. Social Security taxes and benefits are discussed in detail in Chapter 19.

PROPERTY TAXES

Approximately three of every four tax dollars collected by local governments come from property taxes. Property can be divided into two categories: real and personal. *Personal property* is movable and includes furniture, boats, machinery, inventory, automobiles, and airplanes. *Real property* includes such immovable property as homes, land, condominiums, factories, shopping centers, and other buildings.

Property taxes—both real and personal—are typically based on market value of the property involved. The fair market value is determined by a physical inspection of the property by a representative of the county tax assessor and by a comparison of the property's description with the values of similar properties. Although fair market value is defined as the price the property would bring if it were sold, the typical valuation for taxation purposes is considerably less than the true market value.

In order to determine the exact property taxes to be levied, the fair market value is multiplied by the effective tax rate—the percentage of the property's market value that is equal to the tax liability. This serves as the assessed value that is placed on the property by local tax authorities for tax purposes.

As Table 5-1 indicates, the average effective tax rate in the United States is $1.28 per $100 of assessed value. This translates into an average property assessment of $1,280 for a $100,000 home. The lowest effective tax rate is in Hawaii, where the owner of the $100,000 home would pay $420 in taxes. The highest is in New York, where taxes on the same property are $2,750. Table 5-1 also indicates the percentage of local government revenues derived from property taxes in each state.

personal property: such movable items of value as machinery, inventory, automobiles, boats, and airplanes.

real property: such immovable items of value as factories, homes, condominiums, land, shopping centers, and other buildings.

SALES TAXES

Forty-five states and thousands of municipalities across the United States have imposed *sales taxes* on the retail prices of goods and services. These taxes, which range from 4 to 8.25 percent of the value of the purchase, accounted for $79 billion in state income and $13 billion in local income during 1982.[6]

sales taxes: payments levied by a state or local government in the form of a percentage of the sales price of products and services purchased by individuals and business firms.

Table 5-1
1980 PROPERTY TAXES BY REGION AND STATE

Region and State	Tax Rates*	% of Local Taxes	Region and State	Tax Rates	% of Local Taxes
United States	1.28	75.9	**Southeast**		71.7
			Virginia	1.26	67.5
New England		99.0	W. Virginia	0.43	80.1
Maine	1.25	99.4	Kentucky	1.19	56.5
N. Hampshire	1.73	98.3	Tennessee	1.27	64.3
Vermont	1.60	99.3	N. Carolina	0.95	81.1
Massachusetts	2.51	99.3	S. Carolina	0.81	92.6
Rhode Island	1.93	99.0	Georgia	1.24	72.9
Connecticut	1.55	98.9	Florida	1.02	81.4
			Alabama	0.56	39.0
Mideast		72.6	Mississippi	0.93	94.1
New York	2.75	64.9	Louisiana	0.26	41.0
New Jersey	2.60	87.5	Arkansas	1.53	90.1
Pennsylvania	1.57	63.6			
Delaware	0.85	87.2	**Southwest**		75.0
Maryland	1.61	59.8	Oklahoma	0.91	63.2
District of Columbia	1.30	23.3	Texas	1.57	83.5
			New Mexico	1.12	74.0
			Arizona	1.16	79.1
Great Lakes		87.1			
Michigan	2.54	92.3	**Rocky Mountain**		85.5
Ohio	1.08	72.7	Montana	1.11	96.9
Indiana	1.19	95.0	Idaho	0.96	96.3
Illinois	1.50	77.1	Wyoming	0.50	87.3
Wisconsin	1.67	98.4	Colorado	1.05	69.3
			Utah	1.02	77.7
Plains		89.1			
Minnesota	0.93	95.3	**Far West**		70.6
Iowa	1.48	97.9	Washington	1.06	62.4
Missouri	1.00	64.2	Oregon	1.72	89.7
N. Dakota	1.00	95.7	Nevada	1.22	61.1
S. Dakota	1.70	88.5	California	0.98	69.2
Nebraska	2.37	90.1	Alaska	1.35	80.3
Kansas	0.94	92.0	Hawaii	0.42	79.4

*Per $100 of assessed value.

Source: Samuel T. Barash, "How to Shrink These Inflated Property Taxes," *Consumers Digest,* July/August 1982, p. 21. Copyright © 1982 by Consumers Digest. Reprinted by permission.

Sales taxes are typically levied on what the tax authority considers discretionary purchases—toys; cosmetics; such household goods as furniture, linens, and dishes; clothing; automobiles; and jewelry, for example. Most states provide exemptions from sales taxes for such necessities as food, medication, and medical care. However, it is often difficult to determine exactly where the line ends between necessities and discretionary purchases. In New York, for example, prepared sandwiches purchased at a delicatessen are taxable, but the ingredients purchased separately are not. Thus, a $2 roast beef sandwich costs $2.17 in New York City—where the sales tax is 8.25 percent—17 cents more than the sandwich's ingredients would cost if purchased separately.

Although residents of most states pay both sales taxes and state income taxes, New Hampshire's citizens pay neither. Figure 5-3 indicates the states with no sales taxes and those with no state income taxes.

VALUE-ADDED TAXES—THE EUROPEAN SALES TAX TWIST

In many European countries a special kind of sales tax called a *value-added tax,* or *VAT,* is used. Whereas conventional sales taxes are levied on the total retail value of a product or service being sold and are paid directly by consumers,

value-added tax (VAT): a special form of national sales tax, popular in many European countries, in which taxes are imposed at each stage of the production process on the value added to the item at that stage.

Figure 5-3
STATES WITH NO INCOME TAX AND NO STATE SALES TAX

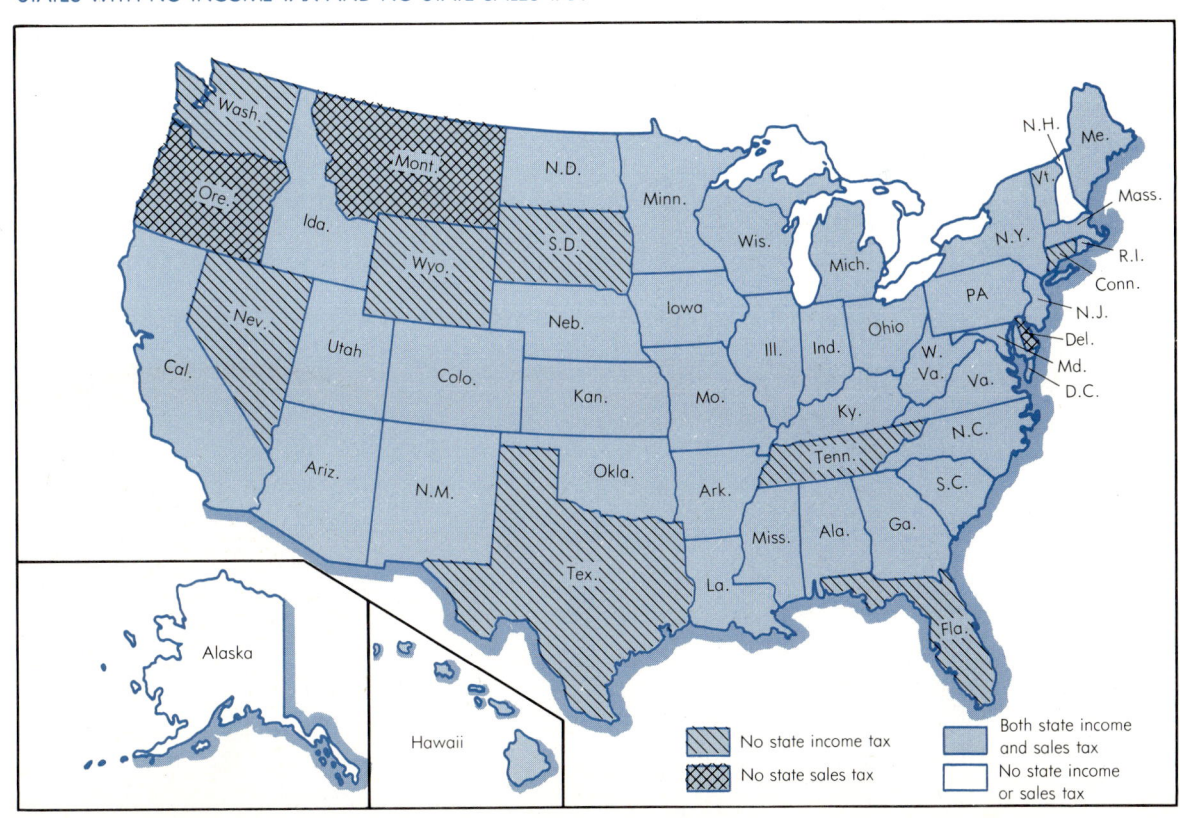

the VAT is imposed at each stage of the production and distribution process on the value added to the item during that stage. The aggregate amount of these taxes is then typically passed on to the consumer as part of the item's retail price instead of a separate surcharge.

Value-added taxes work in the following manner: a fabric maker who turns raw cotton into finished cloth pays a tax on the increased value of the cloth. A shirt manufacturer who then turns the cloth into shirts pays a tax on the increased value that results between the cloth stage and its transformation into a shirt. The wholesaler who represents the manufacturer in marketing the shirt to retail stores pays a tax based on the difference between the manufacturer's selling price and the price the retailer pays for it. Finally, the retailer pays a tax on the markup charged to consumers—the difference between the wholesale and the final retail price.

U.S. tourists who make large purchases in Europe can arrange a refund of any value-added taxes paid by obtaining special forms available from the stores at which the purchases were made. These forms must be completed and turned in at the airport upon departure for the United States. The VAT refund is then processed and mailed to the purchaser's U.S. address.

Although the value-added tax is not used in the United States, it has been proposed as a form of national sales tax—either as a means of reducing federal income taxes or as a means of standardizing the varying sales taxes of individual states. To reduce the burden of the VAT on the poor, such a tax would probably exclude food, medicine, and rent payments.

EXCISE TAXES

Consumers who drive into an Exxon station for gasoline, purchase a package of cigarettes, a bottle of vodka, or a six-pack of Stroh's beer, or obtain an airline ticket to Papeete, Tahiti, spend part of the purchase price in payment of an *excise tax*. This is a tax levied by all levels of government on the consumption or purchase of so-called luxury items. In addition to the items listed above, excise taxes are levied on sporting goods, such as fishing equipment, on gambling wagers, and on firearms and ammunition. Perhaps the major federal excise tax affecting consumers is the gasoline tax, which currently totals 9 cents per gallon. This is in addition to the gasoline taxes levied by the state. Excise taxes, unlike sales taxes and property taxes, are not deductible from your federal income tax.

excise tax: a payment levied by all levels of government on the consumption or purchase of such so-called luxury items as gasoline, sporting goods, liquor, and tobacco.

licensing taxes: special fees levied by state and local governments on persons engaged in such activities as hunting or fishing or conducting certain types of businesses.

STATE AND LOCAL LICENSING TAXES

A number of special *licensing taxes* are levied by state and local governments. These include licensing fees for the use of an automobile; for hunting, fishing,

Taxing Crime

"They never got Al Capone on murder—they got him on tax fraud" was the way a state senator summed up a new antinarcotics law in Arizona. The law, which went into effect [in July 1983], requires illicit dealers to buy a $100 license and to pay ultra-high taxes on their illegal sales.

Tax stamps, available for affixing to the narcotics, cost $10 an ounce for marijuana and $125 an ounce for cocaine, heroin, and other drugs. Unlicensed pushers who were arrested faced not only criminal narcotics charges; they also had to pay the taxes immediately on all contraband in their possession.

"Nobody has been licensed yet," reports Greg V. Smith, a spokesman for the Arizona Department of Revenue. But so far there have been two marijuana arrests in which the law has been invoked, he says.

In one case two young men in southern Arizona have been assessed $39,520. "They were pretty worried about it; they're a little short on assets," Mr. Smith notes. In the other case a $4,320 tax lien has been filed against a house owned by a Lake Havasu City couple.

"So far it is working," Mr. Smith says of the new law. "When a couple of big cases come along, we could be in for some big money. If someone gets caught with 10,000 pounds of marijuana, you're looking at an assessment of $1.6 million."

Source: Richard Haitch, "Pushing Pushers," *New York Times*, August 28, 1983, p. 49. Copyright © 1982/83 by the New York Times Company. Reprinted by permission.

"They never got Al Capone on murder—they got him on tax fraud." Here, the notorious gangster is led from Chicago Federal Court after being sentenced for income tax evasion.

or conducting certain types of businesses; for getting married or owning a dog. Although these fees can prove costly, they are not deductible for federal income tax purposes.

THE COLLECTION OF TAXES

Mark Twain summarized the sentiments of millions of taxpayers:

What is the difference between a taxidermist and a tax collector?
The taxidermist takes only your skin.

At the heart of any system of taxation is a system for tax collection. In the United States this system is run on the federal level by a branch of the U.S. Treasury Department, the *Internal Revenue Service,* or IRS as it is known to every American taxpayer. On the state and local levels, collection is done by state and local tax agencies. Because the operations of the federal tax collection agency affect every U.S. taxpayer, the following sections focus on how the IRS works. Similar operations are utilized on a smaller scale for state and local tax collection agencies.

The Internal Revenue Service is responsible for collecting the billions of dollars owed the government each year by the nation's 95.5 million individual and 3 million corporate taxpayers. It is a job that the nation's approximately 80,000 IRS agents do well. But it is also a task that generates at least some anxiety for honest taxpayers and makes the IRS the nemesis of both small-time and big-time tax dodgers.

Every April 15, IRS employees must sort through mountains of tax forms. This process begins as soon as each tax form is received by one of the IRS's ten regional service centers. Clerks scan each return for completeness, enter into a computer the figures contained on the return, gather and deposit checks, and sort into separate piles returns claiming refunds.

During this process, nearly 9 percent of all tax returns are found to contain mathematical errors. In a recent year, the IRS reduced the taxes of millions of Americans, who had made mathematical errors totaling $814 million. This unexpected bonanza was more than offset, however, by the mistakes taxpayers made in their own favor. In the same year, the IRS informed taxpayers of mistakes that, when corrected, increased their taxes by a total of $1.3 billion. At some point during this initial analysis, every return is examined briefly by IRS personnel who attempt to weed out such glaring errors as deductions for having Fido's teeth cleaned or for purchasing a wardrobe of maternity clothes.

During the next stage of investigation, the information on your return is subjected to a more rigorous and detailed analysis. It is compared with income statements submitted by employers, banks, and others to determine whether all income has been reported. Deductions are evaluated to ensure they are consistent with income. Figures are checked once more to make certain that they are based on the correct tax tables. The IRS uses a complex computer-scoring system to weed out those returns that need further investigation. A return, for example, that claims the cost of building a $10,000 swimming pool as a medical expense would receive a high score, as would one showing

---

Internal Revenue Service (IRS): *the federal agency responsible for managing the federal income tax system, collecting taxes, and enforcing compliance with the tax laws.*

TAXES

"Other folks have to pay taxes, too, Mr. Herndon, so would you please spare us the dramatics!"

Most Tax Audits Are Handled at the Local IRS Office.
Source: Drawing by Booth; © 1972 The New Yorker Magazine, Inc.

$25,000 worth of income and a deduction of $12,000 for charitable contributions. Returns with high scores are generally audited.

TAX AUDITS

Despite Americans' reputation as the most honest taxpayers in the world, hundreds of thousands of taxpayers each year face additional tax assessments, interest charges, and penalties. These result from situations ranging from mistakes in arithmetic and inappropriate deductions to failure to report income or even outright tax fraud. Most arithmetic mistakes are uncovered during the initial computer analysis of returns, but the more serious problems are typically uncovered as a result of a tax audit. An IRS *tax audit* is a thorough examination of a taxpayer's return—either specific portions or the entire return—to determine whether the return is accurate. In some cases, the audit is completed through written correspondence, with the IRS examiner requesting documentation to support claimed deductions. In other instances, the audit may be conducted in person at either the home or office of the taxpayer or at a local IRS office. Tax audits—and the possibility of an audit—are an effective mechanism for keeping millions of taxpayers honest.

In its most extreme form, an audit can require that a taxpayer justify every single statement on his or her tax return. Every three years, approximately

tax audit: a thorough examination of a taxpayer's return by an IRS agent to determine whether it is accurate.

Following Your Return Through the IRS

1. Federal income tax returns flood Internal Revenue Service centers as April 15, the filing deadline, approaches. These workers weigh returns to estimate the amount of attention they are likely to need. Then the envelopes are slit open and sorted by a high-speed machine.

2. This worker removes returns from envelopes, makes sure nothing is left inside the envelopes, and separates returns into general categories—for example, those with checks enclosed and those without.

3. Returns then wait to be processed. They are reviewed to make sure that they are complete, assigned an individual number, and briefly skimmed for mistakes. At this point, checks are removed from returns and deposited.

TAXES 99

4. The information on each tax return is then fed into a computer, which checks for mathematical and other potential errors. The optical scanner shown here reads the simple type of return, the 1040 EZ, automatically, though human workers must be on hand to read illegible entries.

5. The data from tax returns are then transferred to computer tape and forwarded to the central IRS computer in Martinsburg, West Virginia. There, records for each taxpayer are updated, and certain returns are chosen to be audited or pulled for follow-up queries.

Source: "What Happens to Your Return Now," *U.S. News & World Report*, March 26, 1984, pp. 40–41. Photos by Gary L. Kieffer, *U.S. News & World Report*.

FINANCIAL PLANNING

50,000 individual taxpayers, chosen at random, are subjected to this rigorous, fine-toothed-comb audit. IRS officials use the information they gather from these audits to improve their general auditing techniques.

In 1983 the IRS audited the returns of about 1.3 million taxpayers. As Figure 5-4 indicates, a taxpayer's chances of being audited increase with income. Only about 1 in 250 taxpayers with income of less than $10,000 is audited, but the number increases to almost 5 in 100 of all taxpayers earning $50,000 or more.

Although individual taxpayers with relatively high incomes are still more likely to be audited than those with lower incomes, the overall number of audits has declined in recent years, from 2.59 percent in 1976 to 1.38 percent in 1983.[7] However, the average additional tax income received by the federal

Figure 5-4
CHANGES OF AN IRS AUDIT

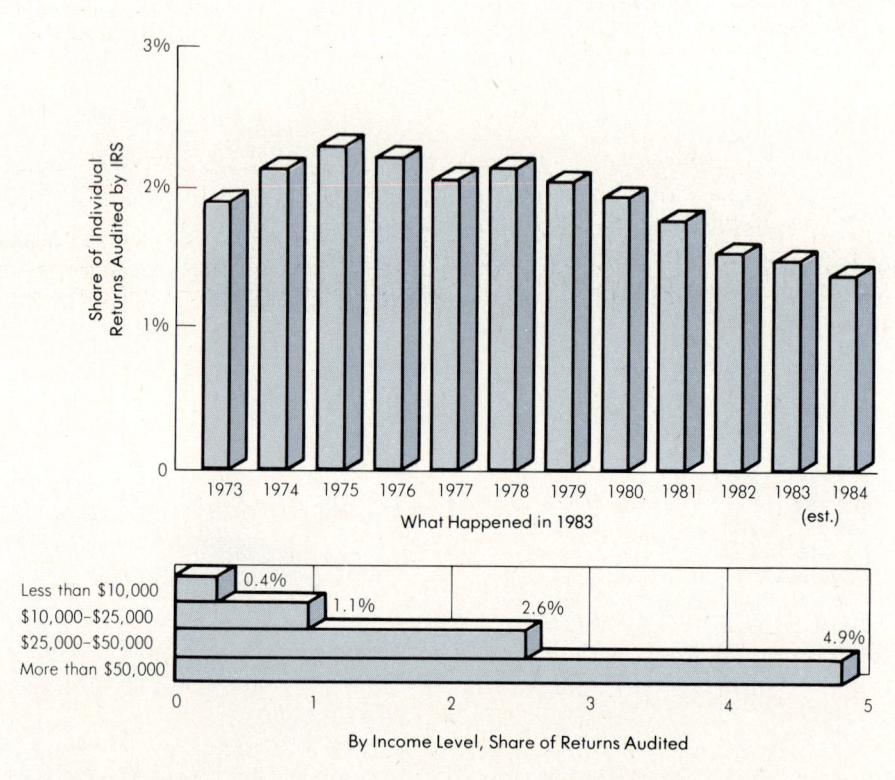

What Happened in 1983

By Income Level, Share of Returns Audited:
- Less than $10,000: 0.4%
- $10,000–$25,000: 1.1%
- $25,000–$50,000: 2.6%
- More than $50,000: 4.9%

Note: Incomes do not include investment or other losses. Audit year is usually one year after return is filed.

Source: "Odds of an Audit," *U.S. News & World Report*, March 26, 1984, p. 39 ; Copyright 1984, U.S. News & World Report Inc. Reprinted by permission.

government as a result of these audits has more than offset the decline in the number of audits. In 1968 more than 4 of every 19 audits produced no additional income for the federal government; today, fewer than 2 of 10 audits are fruitless. Since 1968 the amount of additional taxes per audited return has increased from $359 to $2,045.[8]

What to Do When the IRS Calls

There are few worse feelings in the world than finding the notification of an official IRS audit in your mailbox. News that the IRS wants to know more about your tax return can ruin your day, if not your week. While your immediate response may be panic, it is important to keep a clear head, for what you do from that moment on will influence how successful or disastrous the audit will be.

Here are the experts' recommendations for handling yourself at an IRS audit:

1. The letter you receive from the IRS will list the various items to be examined, such as medical expenses, charitable contributions, and exemptions for dependents. (As has already been pointed out, few audits examine your entire return.) Your first step is to collect and organize the records of these items so that you can support your deductions. (These are the only records that you *must* bring to the audit.) While you are examining your records, you can also check for any deductions you overlooked when you filed your returns. Did you forget to deduct last year's accounting fees or the rental fee on your safe-deposit box? You can use these newly discovered deductions to offset any additional taxes owed.

2. Insist that the audit be conducted at your local IRS office, not in your home or office. Conducting the audit on your home ground often gives the IRS agent more information about you than you might want him or her to have.

3. If you feel at all uneasy about the audit, ask your accountant to come along. You may not need professional help if the IRS simply asks you to substantiate a deduction and you have the receipt on hand. But if the issue is more ambiguous, a professional representative is frequently comforting. Another alternative is to stay home and ask your accountant to represent you at the audit.

4. If you decide to go to the audit, be polite but firm when you get there. Make certain you understand *exactly* what is being asked of you before you give the auditor any information.

5. The cardinal rule of conduct is *never* volunteer any information. Focus only on the specific question the examiner asks. Talking about anything else can only open a Pandora's box of problems for you. Although auditors are supposed to focus only on the specific items mentioned in your audit notice, topics arising during the audit may be pursued. At the other extreme, should you decide not to cooperate and refuse to provide requested information, the auditor will simply disallow all the disputed items on your tax form and present you with a new tax bill.

Your tax return can generally be audited any time during the first three years after it was filed. For example, your 1984 return, filed on April 15, 1985, can be audited until April 15, 1988. In the case of fraud, the IRS has an even longer period to examine your return.

How can you avoid being audited in the first place? Experts agree that the best way is to keep your itemized deductions in line with those taken by others in your income bracket. If your deductions are much larger than the average, your return is likely to be identified by the IRS computer for examination by an agent. Such an examination may lead to an audit. Of course, the possibility of an audit should not discourage you from taking legitimate deductions—even if they are much higher than the average. However, you should be prepared to defend them should you receive a letter from the IRS.

Sources: IRS audits are discussed in Peter Kadzis, "Audits: Avoidable, Appealable," *Money*, February 1982, p. 42; and "If the IRS Calls You In for an Audit," *U.S. News & World Report*, June 1, 1981, pp. 72–73.

APPEALING THE RESULTS OF A TAX AUDIT

What happens when the IRS agent disallows what you consider to be a legitimate deduction and insists you owe more than you have already paid in taxes? A series of appeals of the audit results are possible, starting with a request for a second opinion from the auditor's supervisor. If you are still not satisfied, you can request a formal IRS appeals hearing to plead your case. In 1983 more than 76,000 disgruntled taxpayers demanded and received an IRS hearing. A survey conducted by the General Accounting Office revealed that settlements resulting from these hearings favored taxpayers in more than eight out of ten cases—a reflection in part of how well prepared taxpayers are who undertake such appeals.

The federal appeals mechanism allows taxpayers to take their cases even further. They can appeal IRS rulings in tax court, federal district court, or the U.S. Court of Claims. Tax court, which holds hearings in some 100 cities throughout the United States, is especially convenient for those taxpayers with disputed amounts of less than $5,000 in one tax year. Filing fees are as low as $10 and attorneys are not required for the proceedings. This easy access encouraged some 31,000 taxpayers to bring their cases to tax court in 1982—an 80 percent increase over the number of cases filed in 1979. The growing popularity of tax courts has produced a substantial backlog of cases, resulting in delays of as long as one year.

Even when cases are finally heard in tax court, taxpayers achieve a clear victory in only 8 percent of the rulings. In about 56 percent of all tax court cases, the rulings represent a clear IRS victory. Some compromise is reached in the remaining cases. Regardless of the outcome, the ruling of the tax court judge is final.

TAX EVASION

Despite all the efforts of the IRS to collect taxes, tax cheating occurs on both large and small scales. Humorist Will Rogers once commented that the income tax "has made more liars out of the American people than golf."

Tax evasion is the illegal reduction of tax liability through activities ranging from fraudulent acts designed to create tax deductions, to the nonreporting of income. The IRS estimates the cost in uncollected taxes from tax evasion at $120 billion for 1985, compared with only $29 billion in 1973.[9] The uncollected taxes from tax evasion become an additional burden for honest taxpayers to cover.

Tax evaders range from common criminals, corrupt politicians, and the rich and famous to seemingly ordinary citizens. In 1931 the federal government sentenced mobster Al Capone to 11 years in federal prison for failing to pay $1.2 million in taxes. In 1973 President Carter's brother had his home and business seized and sold by the IRS as a result of his failure to pay

---

tax evasion: the illegal reduction of tax liability through nonreporting of taxable income and/or fraudulent acts designed to create or overstate tax deductions.

$105,000 in taxes. Similar actions were taken against singer Jerry Lee Lewis in 1981. And in 1982 the Reverend Sun Myung Moon was fined $25,000 and sentenced to 18 months in prison for failing to report $162,000 in personal income. An IRS investigation revealed that 360 of 400 private-duty nurses in New York City failed to report all their income and that the average nurse owed the government $3,500 in back taxes.

THE UNDERGROUND ECONOMY

For thousands of persons in every segment of society, tax evasion has become an accepted way of life. The term *underground economy* has been coined to refer to the billions of dollars in unreported income that result from cash payments for products and services, barter exchanges of one good or service for another, or services rendered by business firms and independent contractors that are not recorded in the firms' accounting statements. When waiters and taxi drivers fail to report their tips, when doctors and dentists do not report cash payments, when an independent contractor does business off the books, and when street vendors fail to even file an income tax return, they are part of the underground economy. Estimates of the size of the underground economy run as high as 15 percent of the nation's gross national product and involve as many as one in four members of the nation's work force.

In recent years the IRS has taken a number of steps designed to reduce the size of the underground economy. Amid a chorus of protests, it began requiring employers of people receiving tips—taxi drivers, waiters, and waitresses, among others—to withhold taxes on estimated tip income. In addition, it began to scrutinize the membership lists of barter clubs. Finally, it effectively used news releases to publicize the illegality of the underground economy and the IRS penalties for wrongdoers.

underground economy: unreported and untaxed income resulting from cash payments for products and services, barter exchanges of one good or service for another, or unreported business transactions and activities.

TAX AVOIDANCE

In contrast with the illegal activity of tax evasion, *tax avoidance* refers to a taxpayer's legitimate efforts to minimize the government's tax bite. According to former Supreme Court Justice Learned Hand, every citizen has the right to pay as low a tax as he or she legally can. Wrote Justice Hand a half-century ago: "Nobody owes any public duty to pay more than the law demands: taxes are enforced exactions, not voluntary contributions." Deductions for interest on mortgage payments and other loans, qualified retirement programs, depreciation on rental property, medical expenses, and accounting fees are all legitimate ways to reduce your taxes. These deductions are always open to question and scrutiny by the IRS and may be the subject of an IRS audit. However, they differ in kind from such illegal activities as failure to report income, and when they are legitimate, they will not be disallowed.

tax avoidance: the legal reduction of taxes through deferring taxable income and/or taking advantage of maximum deductions and tax credits.

Street vendors who do not file an income tax return are only one component of the huge and illegal underground economy in the United States today.

It is important to remember that tax-avoidance techniques have been built into the tax code by Congress. Financial writer Jerry Edgerton explains why: These techniques "encourage Americans to save, invest, and become homeowners, which in turn enables businesses to start, to grow, and to expand employment."[10]

PREPARING YOUR FEDERAL TAX RETURN

Even Albert Einstein complained about the difficulty in meeting his annual obligation of calculating and paying income taxes. As he put it, "The hardest thing in the world to understand is the income tax." Anyone who has ever tried to understand the difference between a tax deduction and a tax credit, an income adjustment and an exclusion, a short and a long form knows how difficult tax preparation can be. But even Einstein would have to admit that as difficult as tax preparation may seem—and truly is on occasion—understanding the basics is not an impossible task. Moreover, by taking at least part of the responsibility for preparing your own tax return, you will be sure that it is prepared correctly and that you pay the government the minimum amount of taxes due. Handing over a stack of receipts and other papers to a tax preparer a few days before the April 15 filing deadline guarantees you very little beyond getting your taxes in on time. It does not ensure that your return will save you valuable tax dollars or that the framework for saving money on next year's return is in place.

By understanding the basics of tax preparation, you will understand the importance of tax planning all year round. Paying your state income tax in December instead of January, setting up a tax-deferred retirement program, retaining the records of all the improvements you make to your home—these are year-round activities that will pay off when you file your taxes. Learning your rights under the system and how to manipulate the system to minimize your taxes should be your goal. As you are going through the different stages of tax preparation, it is important to remember once more the words of Justice Learned Hand: "Nobody owes any public duty to pay more than the law demands."

WHO MUST FILE?

Few households can avoid the requirement of filing an income tax form. In general, filing is required if you have paid taxes during the year; if you are self-employed; if you are a U.S. citizen living abroad, a resident of Puerto Rico, or a surviving spouse or legal representative of someone who died during the tax year. Even the president of the United States must file, as we saw with Ronald Reagan. For most taxpayers, the following conditions apply:

- Single persons who earn a gross income of $3,300 or more for the year must file.
- Single persons 65 years or older who earn a gross income of $4,300 or more for the year must file.
- Persons with a combined gross income of $5,400 or more who are married and living together at the end of the tax year must file.
- Persons with a combined gross income of $6,400 or more who are married and living together at the end of the tax year must file if one spouse is 65 years or older.
- Persons with a combined gross income of $7,400 or more who are married and living together at the end of the tax year must file if both persons have reached 65.

Gross income refers to all the income subject to taxes that has been received during the year, whether in the form of money, property, or services.

gross income: *all income received by a taxpayer in a single year—in the form of cash, property, and/or services—that is subject to taxes.*

WHICH FORM TO USE?

The government offers a choice of three forms on which to file your income tax return: Form 1040EZ, Form 1040A, and Form 1040. All of these forms enable you to calculate your *taxable income*—the amount subject to taxes. In each case you are allowed certain exemptions—deductions from the taxable income—that are based on the number of persons supported by the taxpayer's income.

taxable income: *the amount of income that is subject to taxes.*

Form 1040EZ

As its name implies, *Form 1040EZ* is the simplest, most straightforward method for filing taxes. With only 11 lines of figures to complete, it is designed for people with uncomplicated tax returns. In order to use Form 1040EZ, you must be single, claim no exemptions for age or blindness, take no tax credits, have no dependents, and earn less than $50,000 a year from wages and $400 from interest income. If you do not meet these requirements, you must use either Form 1040A or Form 1040.

Form 1040EZ: *the shortest, simplest, and most straightforward federal income tax form to use by single filers with no dependents.*

EXAMPLE Pat R. Brown, age 24, is employed as an office manager at a local insurance agency. She earned $14,801 in salary last year and an additional $55 in interest on her interest-earning checking account at her bank. Since Pat is single and meets the other requirements listed above, she decides to use Form 1040EZ in filing her taxes. Figure 5-5 shows her completed tax form.

After recording her salary and interest income on lines 1 and 2, Pat totals them on line 3 to determine her adjusted gross income of $14,856. She subtracts her $1,000 personal exemption from this total to determine her taxable income of $13,856 on line 7. The W-2 form supplied to Pat by her employer indicates that the total federal income tax withheld during the previous year was $2,065. This amount is recorded on line 8. Pat then refers to the tax table in her packet of forms supplied by the

Figure 5-5

COMPLETED FORM 1040EZ INCOME TAX RETURN

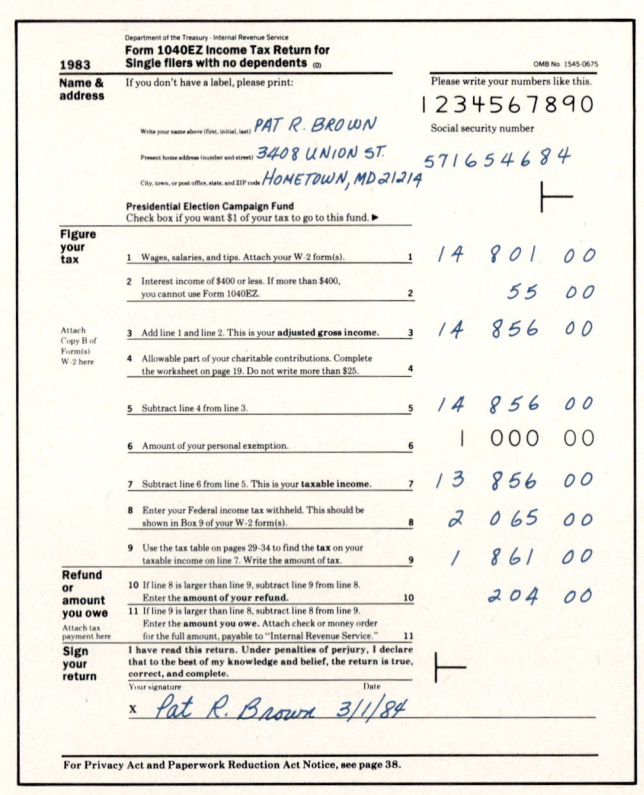

```
                Department of the Treasury - Internal Revenue Service
                Form 1040EZ Income Tax Return for
   1983         Single filers with no dependents (o)          OMB No 1545-0675
Name &    If you don't have a label, please print:      Please write your numbers like this.
address                                                 1234567890
          Write your name above (first, initial, last) PAT R. BROWN
                                                        Social security number
          Present home address (number and street) 3408 UNION ST.   571 65 4684
          City, town, or post office, state, and ZIP code HOMETOWN, MD 21214

          Presidential Election Campaign Fund
          Check box if you want $1 of your tax to go to this fund. ▶
Figure
your
tax       1  Wages, salaries, and tips. Attach your W-2 form(s).     1   14 801 00
          2  Interest income of $400 or less. If more than $400,
             you cannot use Form 1040EZ.                              2        55 00
Attach    3  Add line 1 and line 2. This is your adjusted gross income. 3  14 856 00
Copy B of
Form(s)   4  Allowable part of your charitable contributions. Complete
W-2 here     the worksheet on page 19. Do not write more than $25.    4
          5  Subtract line 4 from line 3.                              5   14 856 00
          6  Amount of your personal exemption.                        6    1 000 00
          7  Subtract line 6 from line 5. This is your taxable income. 7   13 856 00
          8  Enter your Federal income tax withheld. This should be
             shown in Box 9 of your W-2 form(s).                       8    2 065 00
          9  Use the tax table on pages 29-34 to find the tax on your
             taxable income on line 7. Write the amount of tax.        9    1 861 00
Refund
or        10 If line 8 is larger than line 9, subtract line 9 from line 8.
amount       Enter the amount of your refund.                         10      204 00
you owe   11 If line 9 is larger than line 8, subtract line 8 from line 9.
Attach tax   Enter the amount you owe. Attach check or money order
payment here for the full amount, payable to "Internal Revenue Service." 11
Sign      I have read this return. Under penalties of perjury, I declare
your      that to the best of my knowledge and belief, the return is true,
return    correct, and complete.
          Your signature                        Date
          X  Pat R. Brown                       3/1/84

For Privacy Act and Paperwork Reduction Act Notice, see page 38.
```

Source: Forms Courtesy of U.S. Department of the Treasury, Internal Revenue Service, *Publication 17: Your Federal Income Tax* (Washington, D.C.: U.S. Government Printing Office, 1983), p. 9.

Internal Revenue Service and determines that the tax owed on her taxable income of $13,856 is $1,861. She records this amount on line 9.

By comparing the amount of taxes withheld against the amount actually owed, Pat can determine whether she will receive a refund or will have to pay additional taxes. In this case, her taxes withheld ($2,065) exceed taxes owed ($1,861) by $204. She records the $204 on line 10, signs and dates the return, and mails the completed form to the regional IRS office. Her $204 refund check should arrive within eight to twelve weeks following the date of filing.

Form 1040A

Also known as the short form (only 27 lines long), *Form 1040A* is designed for taxpayers who earn no more than $50,000 and whose income comes exclusively from wages, interest, dividends, or unemployment compensation.

Form 1040A: the "short form," a relatively simple tax form for use by taxpayers with no complex tax deductions or credits who do not wish to use the longer form, but who do not qualify for use of Form 1040EZ.

TAXES 107

Figure 5-6
COMPLETED FORM 1040A INCOME TAX RETURN

[Figure shows a completed 1983 Form 1040A US Individual Income Tax Return for Don B. and Jean B. Smith, 2210 Midland St., Hometown, MI 48001. SSN 329-65-1000 / 410-65-1111. Filing status: Married filing joint return. Exemptions: 2. Line 6 wages $13,200; line 7 interest $300; line 10 total income $13,500; line 11a IRA deduction $1,000; line 13 adjustments $1,000; line 14 adjusted gross income $12,500; line 15 $12,500; line 17 $12,500; line 18 exemptions $2,000; line 19 taxable income $10,500; line 20 tax $943; line 23 $943; line 24a federal income tax withheld $900; line 25 total payments $900; line 27 amount you owe $43. Signed Don B. Smith (Salesperson) and Jean B. Smith (Student), 3/31/84.]

Source: Forms Courtesy of U.S. Department of the Treasury, Internal Revenue Service, *Publication 17: Your Federal Income Tax* (Washington, D.C.: U.S. Government Printing Office, 1983), p. 158.

EXAMPLE Since Don and Jean Smith are married, they cannot use Form 1040EZ. In addition, they contributed $1,000 to an IRA account during the year. As a result, they decide to use Form 1040A. Figure 5-6 shows their completed form.

Jean is a full-time student, so she has no income to report. Don's salary as salesperson for a local industrial distribution firm totaled $13,200. This figure is recorded on line 6. The Smiths' $300 interest income for the year is recorded on line 7, and the total income of $13,500 is shown on line 10. The $1,000 IRA contribution is recorded on line 11a, reducing the Smiths' total adjusted gross income to $12,500 (line 14). Jean and Don each receive a $1,000 exemption, so $2,000 is recorded on line 18. This reduces their taxable income to $10,500 (line 19).

They refer to tax tables provided in their tax packet to determine taxes owed based on their taxable income and filing status. The amount of the tax, $943, is then recorded on line 20.

By checking the W-2 form supplied by Don's employer, they record on line 24a the amount of federal income tax withheld during the year. Since the amount withheld is $43 less than the amount of taxes owed, they record the $43 difference on line 27 as the amount of additional taxes owed. They sign and date the return and forward it to the regional office with a check or money order for $43 made payable to Internal Revenue Service.

Forms 1040A and 1040EZ are intended specifically for taxpayers who do not *itemize their deductions*—the process in which taxpayers list the amount of each item to be subtracted from their adjusted gross income. *Adjusted gross income* refers to the total income minus any special adjustments, such as tax-deferred retirement contributions and deductions for alimony, long-term capital gains, and certain business expenses. If total deductions are less than the *zero-bracket amount*—the standard deduction (not subject to taxes) that the government gives every taxpayer—the short form should be used. In 1984 the zero-bracket amount was $2,300 for a single person and $3,400 for taxpayers filing a joint return. If total deductions are more than this amount or if you otherwise do not qualify, Form 1040 should be used.

Form 1040

Form 1040 permits taxpayers to itemize their deductions. They can list large, uninsured medical and dental expenses; interest and taxes paid on their home; charitable contributions; and major uninsured casualty losses. Form 1040 also gives taxpayers the option of making adjustments to income for certain disability pensions, moving expenses, alimony, and employee business expenses. In addition, taxpayers may take advantage of specified tax credits, such as those for childcare, for the elderly, and for making your home energy-efficient. Because of its length—68 lines—and relative complexity, Form 1040 is known as the long form. Figure 5-7 shows a completed Form 1040.

Taxpayers using Form 1040 often have to file associated tax schedules as well. These schedules provide the specific facts and figures to justify the deductions taken in Form 1040. Schedule A, which explains the taxpayer's itemized deductions, is one of the most frequently used. As Figure 5-8 indicates, many of the deductions shown on Figure 5-7's Form 1040 are explained on Schedule A.

✶ CAPITAL GAINS AND LOSSES

Sale of property—stocks, bonds, and real estate—may produce profits or losses for the seller. If the property has been owned for longer than one year prior to its sale, the gain or loss resulting from the sale is considered a long-term *capital gain* or *capital loss*. For instance, the profit or loss resulting from the sale of stock you owned for longer than six months is considered a long-term capital gain. On the other hand, had you held the stock for only a few months, the sale would have produced a short-term gain or loss.

The importance in the distinction between long-term and short-term gains and losses lies in how they are taxed. If you sell at a profit stocks, bonds, or real estate that you owned for longer than six months, taxes are paid on only 40 percent of the gain. By contrast, short-term profits are fully taxable. Whenever possible, persons who plan to sell stocks, bonds, or real estate should hold

---

adjusted gross income: the amount of income remaining after subtracting allowable deductions from gross income.

zero-bracket amount: the standard deduction—an amount of money not subject to taxes—that the government gives every taxpayer.

Form 1040: the "long form" used by taxpayers who itemize deductions, use tax credits, and have relatively complex tax situations.

capital gain: profit earned from the sale of an asset such as a home, shares of stock, or other property owned for longer than six months.

capital loss: loss incurred when the sale price of an asset such as a home, shares of stock, or other property owned for longer than six months is sold for less than its acquisition cost.

Figure 5-7
COMPLETED FORM 1040 INCOME TAX RETURN

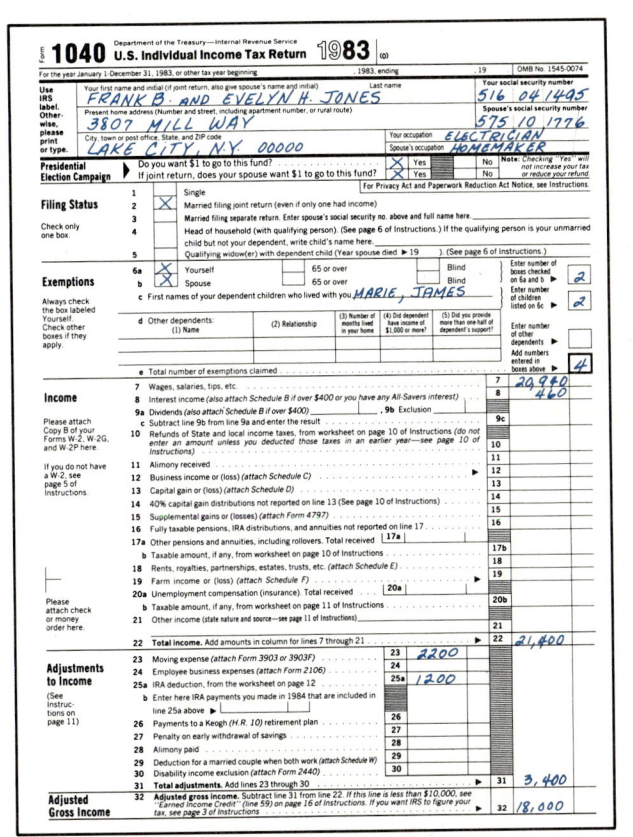

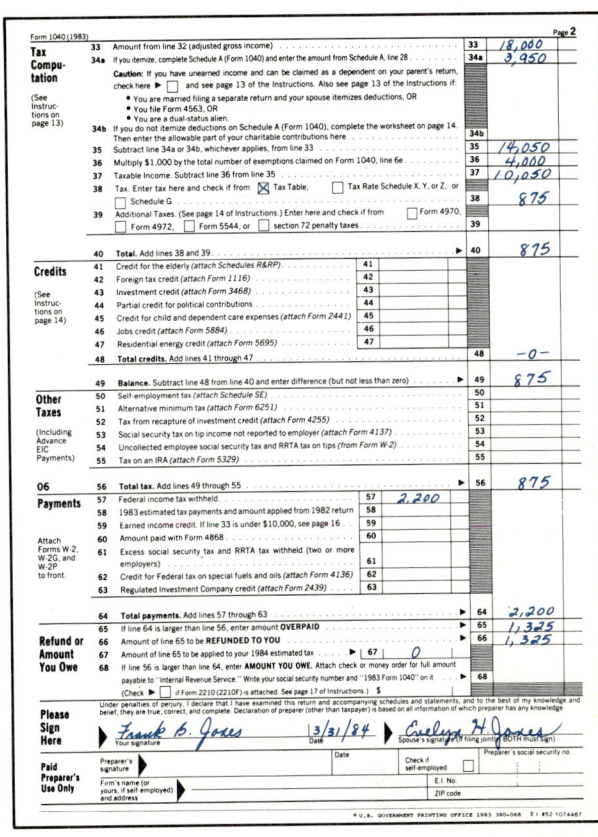

Source: Forms Courtesy of U.S. Department of the Treasury, Internal Revenue Service, *Publication 17: Your Federal Income Tax* (Washington, D.C.: U.S. Government Printing Office, 1983).

them for more than six months prior to their sale. This positive approach to tax planning produces significant tax savings.

What happens in the case of losses resulting from the sale of stocks, bonds, and real estate? Such losses can be used to offset other income received during the year. For every dollar you lose on a short-term basis, you can deduct $1 from your income. If your loss is long-term, it takes $2 in long-term losses to offset $1 of ordinary income.

TAX CREDITS AS A METHOD OF REDUCING TAXES

Tax credits—acknowledgments given for certain specified expenses—are more valuable to taxpayers than tax deductions because the amount of each credit is directly subtracted from the taxes owed. In other words, a $100 tax credit will

tax credits: acknowledgments for such items as being elderly, making political contributions, hiring child and dependent care, and making energy-saving residential improvements that are subtracted directly from taxes owed.

Figure 5-8

COMPLETED SCHEDULE A SHOWING ITEMIZED DEDUCTIONS

SCHEDULES A&B (Form 1040) Department of the Treasury Internal Revenue Service (0)

Schedule A—Itemized Deductions (Schedule B is on back) ▶ Attach to Form 1040. ▶ See Instructions for Schedules A and B (Form 1040).

OMB No. 1545-0074 **1983** 07

Name(s) as shown on Form 1040: FRANK B. AND EVELYN H. JONES — Your social security number: 516 04 1492

Section	Line	Description				
Medical and Dental Expenses (Do not include expenses reimbursed or paid by others.) (See page 18 of Instructions.)	1	Medicines and drugs	1	570		
	2	Write 1% of Form 1040, line 33	2	180		
	3	Subtract line 2 from line 1. If line 2 is more than line 1, write zero	3	390		
	4	Other medical and dental expenses:				
	a	Doctors, dentists, nurses, hospitals, insurance premiums you paid for medical and dental care, etc.	4a	950		
	b	Transportation	4b	50		
	c	Other (list—include hearing aids, dentures, eyeglasses, etc.) ▶	4c			
	5	Add lines 3 through 4c	5	1,390		
	6	Multiply amount on Form 1040, line 33, by 5% (.05)	6	900		
	7	Subtract line 6 from line 5. If line 6 is more than line 5, write zero ▶			7	490
Taxes (See page 19 of Instructions.)	8	State and local income	8	1,201		
	9	Real estate	9	1,440		
	10 a	General sales (see sales tax tables)	10a	299		
	b	General sales on motor vehicles	10b			
	11	Other (list—include personal property) ▶	11			
	12	Add lines 8 through 11. Write your answer here ▶			12	2,940
Interest Expense (See page 20 of Instructions.)	13 a	Home mortgage interest paid to financial institutions	13a	2,860		
	b	Home mortgage interest paid to individuals (show that person's name and address) ▶	13b			
	14	Credit cards and charge accounts	14			
	15	Other (list) ▶	15			
	16	Add lines 13a through 15. Write your answer here ▶			16	2,860
Contributions (See page 20 of Instructions.)	17 a	Cash contributions. (If you gave $3,000 or more to any one organization, report those contributions on line 17b.)	17a	910		
	b	Cash contributions totaling $3,000 or more to any one organization. (Show to whom you gave and how much you gave.) ▶	17b			
	18	Other than cash (attach required statement)	18			
	19	Carryover from prior year	19			
	20	Add lines 17a through 19. Write your answer here ▶			20	910
Casualty and Theft Losses	21	Total casualty or theft loss(es) (attach Form 4684) (see page 20 of Instructions) ▶			21	-0-
Miscellaneous Deductions (See page 21 of Instructions.)	22	Union and professional dues	22	150		
	23	Tax return preparation fee	23			
	24	Other (list) ▶	24			
	25	Add lines 22 through 24. Write your answer here ▶			25	150
Summary of Itemized Deductions (See page 21 of Instructions.)	26	Add lines 7, 12, 16, 20, 21, and 25			26	7,350
	27	If you checked Form 1040 { Filing Status box 2 or 5, write $3,400; Filing Status box 1 or 4, write $2,300; Filing Status box 3, write $1,700 }			27	3,400
	28	Subtract line 27 from line 26. Write your answer here and on Form 1040, line 34a. (If line 27 is more than line 26, see the Instructions for line 28 on page 21.) ▶			28	3,950

For Paperwork Reduction Act Notice, see Form 1040 Instructions. **Schedule A (Form 1040) 1983**

Source: Form Courtesy of U.S. Department of the Treasury, Internal Revenue Service, *Publication 17: Your Federal Income Tax* (Washington, D.C.: U.S. Government Printing Office, 1983).

reduce income taxes by $100, whereas a tax deduction only reduces your taxable income. Among the most important tax credits affecting individual taxpayers are those for the elderly, for political contributions, for child and dependent care, and for residential energy saving.

MARGINAL VERSUS EFFECTIVE TAX RATES

Regardless of the size of a taxpayer's income, his or her maximum tax rate is 50 percent. Many taxpayers might argue that this rate is too high, but consider the Norwegian taxpayer. Norway has no upper limit, so it is possible for high-income taxpayers to pay more than 100 percent of their income in marginal taxes. One Norwegian shipping magnate was reportedly taxed at 491 percent of his income in a single year.[11]

How Much Is Too Much?

The U.S. system of federal income taxation depends to a large extent on voluntary reporting by taxpayers. Although the IRS has the authority to seek fines and even prison terms for criminal tax evasion, these harsh measures are used only in unusual situations involving clear instances of illegality. For the other 99 of every 100 taxpayers, the IRS uses tax audits—and the fear of audits—to motivate taxpayers to file honest, accurate tax returns. In fact, the IRS is frequently accused of using news releases concerning severe penalties levied against tax offenders as a publicity technique to make taxpayers think twice about taking questionable deductions or failing to report income received in the form of cash.

The rules are simple: every taxpayer should both report all income and claim every deduction for which he or she is eligible. But since most taxpayers know that many audits are triggered by unusually high deductions, they frequently wonder just what an "unusually high" deduction is. The table below indicates the average deductions claimed by taxpayers with various adjusted gross incomes for a recent year.

AVERAGE ITEMIZED DEDUCTIONS*

Adjusted Gross Income	State and Local Taxes	Interest Paid	Charitable Contributions
$ 10,000–12,000	$ 1,063	$ 2,589	$ 595
12,000–16,000	1,263	2,455	753
16,000–20,000	1,478	2,549	662
20,000–25,000	1,831	2,966	721
25,000–30,000	2,058	3,195	732
30,000–40,000	2,576	3,596	859
40,000–50,000	3,238	4,483	1,149
50,000–75,000	4,575	6,242	1,551
75,000–100,000	6,919	8,719	2,523
100,000–200,000	10,120	13,915	4,647

* These are average deductions on itemized tax returns for 1982 filed in 1983.
Source: Internal Revenue Service

The 50-percent tax rate does not mean that every dollar of the high-income taxpayer's earnings is taxed at that rate. The rate applies only to those dollars in the highest bracket.

As Table 5-2 indicates, there is a difference between the tax you pay in your marginal tax bracket and your effective tax rate. The *marginal tax rate* refers to the top rate at which your income is taxed, while the *effective tax rate* refers to the actual percentage of each taxable dollar you pay in taxes. Your effective tax rate is almost always lower than your marginal tax rate.

marginal tax rate: the highest tax rate at which the taxpayer's income is taxed.

effective tax rate: average percentage of taxes paid by an individual on total taxable income.

RECENT CHANGES IN THE FEDERAL TAX SYSTEM

A number of sweeping changes in the federal tax system have occurred recently. In general, they reflect the Reagan administration's attempts to reduce

Table 5-2
MARGINAL AND EFFECTIVE TAX RATES FOR DIFFERENT CATEGORIES OF TAXPAYERS EARNING $40,000

$40,000 Taxable Income—1982

Status	Tax	Marginal Bracket	Effective Rate
Married, joint returns	$ 9,195	39%	23%
Surviving spouse	9,195	39%	23%
Head of household	10,571	41%	26%
Single	11,408	44%	29%
Married, filing separately	13,752	49%	34%

Source: Reprinted from *The Only Tax Book You'll Ever Need* by Robert Gardner. Copyright © 1983 by Robert A. Gardner. Used by permission of Harmony Books, a division of Crown Publishers, Inc.

government regulation and to reverse the severe recession of the early 1980s by reducing taxes. These changes resulted from the passage of the Economic Recovery Tax Act in 1981.

THE ECONOMIC RECOVERY TAX ACT OF 1981

Economic Recovery Tax Act (ERTA) of 1981: a federal act designed to reduce federal income taxes, rectify such inequities as the marriage penalty, and lessen some problems resulting from inflation.

In 1981, with the *Economic Recovery Tax Act (ERTA)*, Congress passed the largest tax cuts in U.S. history. These cuts, which occurred sequentially over three years, have reduced individual federal income taxes by 23 percent. Table 5-3 shows how the tax cut translates into savings for different groups of taxpayers.

Table 5-3
TAX SAVINGS FOR DIFFERENT HOUSEHOLDS RESULTING FROM ERTA*

Gross Income	Single Person with No Dependents 1984 Taxes	Tax Savings	Single Parent with Two Children 1984 Taxes	Tax Savings	One-Earner Couple with Two Children 1984 Taxes	Tax Savings	Two-Earner Couple with No Children 1984 Taxes	Tax Savings
$ 20,000	$ 2,292	$ 113	$ 1,840	$ 564	$ 1,549	$ 93	$ 1,795	$ 108
30,000	4,385	252	3,542	180	3,003	170	3,278	183
50,000	9,673	560	8,281	424	7,165	404	7,413	419
100,000	27,155	1,468	24,439	1,351	22,056	1,174	21,846	1,164

* It is assumed that deductions equal 23 percent of income, which is typical, and that all income is earned.
Source: Adapted from Richard Eisenberg, "Now What Do I Do?" *Money*, September 1981, p. 63.

In addition to across-the-board tax reductions, ERTA also attempts to eliminate certain inequities in the tax laws, to give specific reductions in order to stimulate business investment, and to reduce the problem that arises when inflation pushes taxpayers into higher tax categories. In many instances, these changes have an even greater impact on individual taxpayers than do the overall tax cuts. Moreover, ERTA includes changes that affect estate and gift taxes, childcare expenses, retirement planning, capital gains taxes, and taxes on home-sale profits.

Reducing the Marriage Penalty. Before the passage of ERTA, most two-income married couples paid a higher tax bill than they would have had they remained single and simply lived together. The new tax law attempts to reduce this penalty by granting working spouses who file a joint tax return a 10-percent deduction against the income of the lower-paid spouse, up to a maximum of $3,000. Table 5-4 shows how the marriage penalty reduction affects married couples in different tax brackets and with different income combinations.

Indexing Tax Rates. One of the most important provisions of ERTA is tax *indexing*—a mechanism designed to reduce the effect of inflation on the amount of taxes paid. Effective in 1985, indexing focuses on the problem of *bracket creep*, whereby inflation pushes taxpayers into higher tax brackets even though their purchasing power has not increased.

Indexing counters bracket creep by keying income tax brackets to the rate of inflation. If, for example, during 1984 a taxpayer earned between $28,801 and $34,100, he or she would be taxed at a marginal rate of 34 percent. Should inflation, as measured by the Consumer Price Index, occur in the amount of 5 percent during 1984, the 34-percent tax bracket would automatically be raised

indexing: a mechanism for reducing the effect of inflation on the amount of taxes paid by relating tax bracket amounts to changes in inflation.

bracket creep: a phenomenon in which increased household incomes place consumers in higher income tax brackets even though overall purchasing power may remain the same or even decline.

Table 5-4
IMPACT OF ERTA ON REDUCING THE MARRIAGE PENALTY*

Combined Earned Income of Couple with No Children	Amount of Bonus (+) or Penalty (−)**		
	80/20 Income Split	60/40 Income Split	50/50 Income Split
$ 30,000	+ $162	+ $ 20	+ $ 31
50,000	+ 247	− 388	− 304
70,000	+ 128	− 1,018	− 1,162
100,000	+ 99	− 1,970	− 2,290

* It is assumed that deductions equal 23 percent of income.
** Bonus (+) indicates that married couples end up owing less in taxes than single people do.
  Penalty (−) indicates that married couples end up owing more in taxes than single people do.
Source: Adapted from Richard Eisenberg, "Now What Do I Do?" *Money*, September 1981, p. 57.

Table 5-5
IMPACT OF INDEXING ON TAXES PAID ASSUMING PRICES AND WAGES RISE 5 PERCENT

Adjusted Gross Income		Federal Income Tax			Saving with Indexing
1984	1985 with 5-Percent Increase	1984	1985 without Indexing	1985 with 5-Percent Indexing	
$ 10,000	$ 10,500	$ 291	$ 351	$ 305	$ 46
20,000	21,000	1,741	1,921	1,827	94
25,000	26,250	2,673	2,948	2,807	141
30,000	31,500	3,815	4,190	4,006	184
40,000	42,000	6,538	7,198	6,865	333
50,000	52,500	9,848	10,798	10,341	457
75,000	78,750	19,788	21,363	20,777	586
100,000	105,000	30,600	32,850	32,130	720

Note: Assumes a one-earner married couple with two children and no itemized deductions.
Source: "What's Wrong with the System." Reprinted from *U.S. News & World Report*, April 18, 1983, p. 57; Copyright 1983, U.S. News & World Report, Inc. Reprinted by permission.

5 percent, to $30,241 to $35,805, for 1985. This type of adjustment is made every year for each tax bracket in order to eliminate bracket creep resulting from inflation. Of course, taxpayers whose *real* income increases are likely to pay higher marginal tax rates as they move into higher income tax brackets. On the other hand, taxpayers whose income fails to keep up with the inflation rate may find that they are placed in a lower marginal tax bracket as a result of inflation. Table 5-5 shows how indexing will save money for taxpayers at various income levels should both prices and wages rise at a rate of 5 percent.

Although indexing affects taxpayers at every income level, it is especially important for lower income households due to the smaller income ranges in the lower tax brackets. In addition, two other features of indexing are likely to affect lower income taxpayers greatly. The $1,000 exemption allowed for each dependent is adjusted for inflation, as is the standard deduction taken by taxpayers who do not itemize their deductions when calculating their federal income taxes. These changes are important because lower income taxpayers typically use exemptions and the standard deduction as the primary means of reducing the amount of their income that is subject to taxes.

SECURING COMPETENT TAX ADVICE

Many Americans consider filing their taxes a yearly nightmare. Either their returns are too complicated for them to complete on their own, or they are concerned about the consequences of a major error. The simple solution for such people is professional tax advice: they need an expert who knows the ins and outs of tax regulations to assist them in tax preparation and in developing a plan to minimize future taxes.

WHO NEEDS A TAX PROFESSIONAL?

With IRS forms and regulations becoming more and more complex, professional tax advice is an absolute necessity for millions of American taxpayers. (In fact, many experts have accused the IRS of spawning the tax preparation industry.) In these times of numerous supplementary tax schedules and special credits, millions of taxpayers completing Form 1040 and itemizing their deductions are turning to tax experts to ensure that they take advantage of every possible legal method for reducing their taxes.

A taxpayer with the following characteristics typically does not need outside professional assistance: a salaried employee earning less than $30,000 a year with few, if any, extraordinary deductions, no outside income other than interest on a savings account, and no complicated investments or life situations. As there is no reason to itemize, such a taxpayer is likely to use the short form and take the standard deduction.

Self-employed persons and other taxpayers whose finances are more complex are likely to obtain the services of a tax professional. They can find one at the IRS, at a tax preparation agency, or at the office of an accountant who specializes in taxes.

HELP FROM THE IRS

Even though many people think of the IRS as an adversary, the agency is actually a source of invaluable information for taxpayers with questions or problems. By calling a toll-free IRS telephone number, visiting the local IRS office, or sending your inquiry by mail, you can find agents who will answer your questions and assist you with the tax forms.

Unless you are disabled or show some other extraordinary need, however, the IRS will not complete your form *for* you. Rather, an agent will work *with* you so that you can complete the task on your own. The goal of the IRS is to help you understand your taxes so that in the future you can complete your returns without assistance.

Clearly, the tax advice obtained from the IRS will be straightforward and conservative. You should not expect the IRS to assist you in taking "creative" deductions. If you need more detailed advice, which, you should remember, is completely legal, you should seek another source of assistance.

USING A TAX PREPARATION AGENCY

One source of advice is a *tax preparation agency*. Such agencies spring up like mushrooms around tax time, offering taxpayers last-minute tax preparation assistance. The best-known and largest of these services is H&R Block. With

---

tax preparation agency: a business firm, such as H&R Block, which provides taxpayer assistance in completing tax reports.

Tax preparation agencies, like the one pictured above, offer taxpayers the advantages of speed, convenience, and a relatively inexpensive fee. The drawbacks of using such agencies, however, include the chance of having an inexperienced tax preparer handle your return, and the emphasis on tax preparation instead of tax counseling.

over 9,000 offices throughout the country, H&R Block completed 8.6 million returns in 1983 at an average price of $39.25 per return. Other companies, such as Beneficial Finance, offer similar tax preparation services on a national level. In addition, many independent, local tax preparation services open in shopping centers and storefronts throughout the nation during the tax season.

Although these agencies offer such advantages as speed, convenience, and a relatively inexpensive fee, they also have some serious limitations. Because of the sheer volume of returns the large companies handle during tax season, they must hire an army of tax preparers, some of whom have little tax preparation experience. Although these employees typically complete an extensive training program, they may not be skilled at handling a complicated return.

At local storefront operations, taxpayers have no assurance that the preparer has had any training at all. Tax preparers are not required to meet any national licensing requirements or pass any national examinations to offer their services to the public. Taxpayers who use these services should examine the credentials of the preparer assigned to their case and, if dissatisfied, should request a replacement or go elsewhere.

Moreover, these agencies specialize in tax preparation, not tax counseling. They are not likely to analyze your situation with a fine-toothed comb to maximize your deductions and minimize your taxes. They may point out such obvious deductions as opening a tax-deferred retirement account or waiting until you are at least 55 to sell your house, but they will do little more to reduce your taxes. It is important to keep in mind that they are not set up to analyze complex financial situations. For these reasons, many experts believe that tax preparation agencies offer few if any services you could not provide yourself.

Tax preparation agencies may also be overconservative at times; as a result, they are often unwilling to take slightly questionable but legal deductions. Agencies that say they will pay any penalties or interest charges if they make an error are not likely to take the smallest risk, even when you have a convincing argument to justify your deductions.

THE ADVANTAGES OF A TAX ACCOUNTANT

If you sold or purchased property during the previous tax year, are involved in tax shelters, own rental property, earn outside income, pay quarterly estimated taxes, deduct part of your home as an office, use your car for business, are involved in a divorce, or just earn a lot of money, you will probably want to consult a *certified public accountant (CPA)*—a specialized tax accountant, who will advise you and prepare your tax forms. Considered tax experts, CPAs must pass a rigorous set of exams covering accounting theory and practice to gain their title. Since most CPAs charge by the hour ($50 to $100 an hour is common), it is important to have all your receipts and other papers organized and all your questions listed before you set foot in your accountant's office. (This same advice is applicable when dealing with any tax adviser.)

certified public accountant (CPA): a person who has passed a rigorous standardized examination covering accounting theory and practice.

A good accountant is an invaluable financial adviser throughout the year, not just at tax time. He or she can assist you in deciding how to minimize your taxes through investments and business decisions and counsel you on the kinds of tax records you will need to justify your deductions. An accountant performing this advisory function will probably suggest an end-of-year tax-planning session in October or November in addition to your meeting before April 15.

If you are audited, your accountant will accompany you to your local IRS office or go in your place. Although you will have to pay for this service, it is well worth the money if you are at all uncomfortable about representing yourself. (Many tax preparation agencies also offer this service.)

TAX INFORMATION SOURCES

Each year dozens of volumes are published on how to reduce your taxes. All contain valuable tips that can save you money if you follow their advice.

Every year, for instance, the Internal Revenue Service publishes *Publication 17: Your Federal Income Tax.* This free, 176-page booklet helps you prepare your own return by taking you step by step through each part of the return. In addition, it explains the tax code and provides illustrative examples to clarify the law.

Valuable tips are also included in such books as *Tax Saving: A Year-Round Guide* by Julian Block; *All You Need to Know about the IRS* by Paul Strassels and Robert Wool; *How You Can Profit from the New Tax Law: 101 Plans to Pay Less Taxes,* and *How to Avoid a Tax Audit* by the J. K. Lasser Tax Institute; *Everything You Always Wanted to Know about Taxes But Didn't Know How to Ask* by Michael Savage; and *How to Get Free Tax Help* by Matthew Lesko.

SOME TAX-SAVINGS TIPS

Here are some general tax-saving tips on which all the books agree:

- *Take advantage of the reduced marriage penalty.* If you file a joint return, you may be able to deduct from your gross income 10 percent of the income of the lower-paid spouse up to a maximum of $3,000.

- *Start an IRA.* You can shelter up to $2,000 a year in taxes by opening an individual retirement account, even if you are covered by your employer's pension plan.

- *Deduct for charitable contributions.* You can deduct 25 percent of the first $100 you contribute to a qualified organized charity even if you do not itemize your deductions.

- *Pay all your state and local taxes before the year's end.* These tax payments are deductible on the tax form you file on April 15. Include any income, property, and sales taxes you paid during the year.

- *Deduct all interest payments.* The interest you pay on your home mortgage, car loan, department store charge cards, and installment loans is deductible.

- *Take a dividend exclusion.* If you receive dividends on stocks, you can exclude at least part of the amount you receive from taxes. You can exclude up to $100 for an individual return and $200 for a joint return.

- *Deduct legitimate medical expenses.* If your medical bills are high (they must exceed 5 percent of your adjusted gross income), you can deduct them from your income taxes. Legitimate medical expenses include doctors' and dentists' bills; medicine; treatment for drug and alcohol addiction; cosmetic surgery, including hair transplants; and so on. The government will also absorb the cost of special equipment for your car if you are physically handicapped, the cost of special telephones if you are hard of hearing, and the purchase price and maintenance cost of a seeing eye dog if your sight is impaired. You can deduct your travel expenses to and from doctor, dentist, and medical facilities as well.

- *Deduct the cost of finding a job.* You can deduct all of your job search expenses, including résumés and employment agency fees, if you are attempting to find a new job in the same line of work.
- *Exclude scholarships and fellowships from your taxable income.* If you receive financial assistance other than that from an employer and you are seeking a degree, the total award is exempt from taxes. Nondegree candidates can exclude $300 a month up to 36 months.
- *Make estimated tax payments.* If you owe the government $300 or more in taxes that will not be withheld from your income, you are required to make quarterly tax payments. In general, you must pay at least 80 percent of your tax bill in order to avoid stiff penalties.

SUMMARY

Since taxes consume a large share of the income of virtually every employed adult, understanding the various types of taxes and methods of minimizing their impact is essential to effective personal finance planning. In some instances taxes are progressive, taking a larger share of each increment of personal income — as in the case of income taxes. In other cases, taxes are regressive, consuming a larger proportion of low incomes than of higher incomes — as in the case of the sales tax.

Individuals and business firms pay a variety of taxes. These include income taxes levied by the federal government, most state governments, and a number of local governments; Social Security taxes paid by employers, employees, and the self-employed; property taxes; sales taxes; excise taxes; and various types of state and local licensing taxes. The tax with the dominant impact on most consumers is the federal income tax.

Each state and most municipalities operate tax collection agencies. Tax collecting on the federal level is run by the Internal Revenue Service (IRS). The IRS, a branch of the U.S. Treasury Department, is responsible for enforcement of federal tax laws, providing taxpayers with information and documents for the preparation of their income tax reports, and collecting taxes owed by individual and business taxpayers. Much of the process is handled through a withholding system, whereby employers deduct estimated taxes from their employees' payroll checks. Self-employed persons and individuals with a substantial income that is not subject to withholding are required to make quarterly estimated tax payments directly to the IRS.

In most instances, taxpayers are required to file tax returns by April 15 of the year following the tax year. The accuracy of each return is checked when it is received at one of the ten IRS regional service centers. Approximately 1.4 percent of all returns are examined thoroughly in the form of a tax audit in order to substantiate income reported and deductions or tax credits claimed and to enforce compliance with tax laws. Dissatisfied taxpayers may appeal the results of an IRS audit by requesting a formal appeals hearing or through hearings in tax court, federal district court, or the U.S. Court of Claims.

Tax returns and the necessary information for completing them are mailed to taxpayers by the IRS several months before the April 15 deadline. Taxpayers may use one of three forms — Form 1040EZ, Form 1040A, or Form 1040 — to complete their returns. The IRS will also provide assistance in the preparation of tax returns. Taxpayers with sizable income; numerous, complicated deductions; or special investments or life situations may utilize tax preparation agencies or the services of a certified public accountant who specializes in taxes. Tax accountants can also provide useful tax-planning assistance for taxpayers.

REVIEW QUESTIONS

1. Briefly define the following terms:

   tax
   benefits-received philosophy
   ability-to-pay philosophy
   progressive tax
   regressive tax
   income tax
   personal property
   real property
   sales taxes
   value-added tax
   excise tax
   licensing taxes
   Internal Revenue Service (IRS)
   tax audit
   tax evasion
   underground economy
   tax avoidance
   gross income
   taxable income
   Form 1040EZ
   Form 1040A
   adjusted gross income
   zero-bracket amount
   Form 1040
   capital gain
   capital loss
   tax credits
   marginal tax rate
   effective tax rate
   Economic Recovery Tax Act (ERTA) of 1981
   indexing
   bracket creep
   tax preparation agency
   certified public accountant (CPA)

2. Contrast the ability-to-pay philosophy of taxation with the benefits-received philosophy. Why are sales taxes considered to be regressive taxes? Give an example of a progressive tax.

3. Distinguish between a sales tax and a value-added tax. Why is the value-added tax likely to be used more often than sales taxes in European countries?

4. Outline the review and audit process used by the Internal Revenue Service. What remedies are available for taxpayers who disagree with the ruling of an IRS examiner?

5. Distinguish between tax avoidance and tax evasion. With which is the underground economy related?

6. Identify the three forms available to taxpayers for filing their income tax returns. Under what circumstances should each be used?

7. Distinguish between capital gains and ordinary income. Suggest reasons why a government might levy lower taxes on capital gains than on ordinary income.

8. Identify the major tax credits that taxpayers can claim on their tax returns. Explain why tax credits are preferable to tax deductions in reducing income taxes.

9. Explain the major provisions of the Economic Recovery Tax Act (ERTA) of 1981. What are the benefits of indexing taxes? How can this be accomplished?

10. Which taxpayers are most likely to use specialized tax preparation firms? Who is likely to use a tax accountant such as a certified public accountant?

CASES AND EXERCISES

1. In a recent attempt to generate additional tax revenues and provide a more equitable tax treatment for renters, the Congressional Budget Office suggested the following changes:

   a. limit the interest deduction for mortgage interest to $5,000.
   b. allow only a 75-percent deduction for property taxes paid.
   c. allow a 7-percent tax credit.

   Do you agree with these suggestions? Defend your answer.

2. Jennifer Sexton earns $14,000 annually as a salesperson. She is attempting to convince her fiancé, a full-time student with no earned income, to change the wedding date from January 15 to Christmas Day of this year. Prepare a tax-based argument for accelerating the wedding date.

3. Explain the concept of a marriage penalty. What factors in the U.S. system of taxation cause it to occur? How can it be reduced or eliminated?

4. Gloria Palmyra is in the 25-percent tax bracket and has a $2,000 tax credit. Cynthia Swift is in the same tax bracket and has a $2,000 deduction.

Explain the distinction between deductions and credits and the impact of each on the tax returns of the two women.

5. Jamal Jabbar is in the 40-percent tax bracket. Explain the federal income taxes owed on each of these transactions:

   a. He sold for $8,000 shares of stock purchased for $6,000 30 days ago.

   b. He sold for $15,000 shares of stock purchased for $10,000 18 months ago.

   c. He sold for $18,000 bonds purchased for $20,000 4 months ago.

   d. He sold for $9,000 bonds purchased for $10,000 2 years ago.

ANSWERS TO PERSONAL FINANCE I.Q. TEST

1. Fiction. 2. Fiction. 3. Fact. 4. Fiction. 5. Fact. 6. Fiction. 7. Fact. 8. Fact. 9. Fiction.

HOW BURT AND SALLY JAMES REACHED THEIR PERSONAL FINANCIAL DECISION

Professor Westwood was glad to offer advice. He determined that the simplest and best way for them to start their tax planning was with three basic steps:

1. First Burt and Sally should take advantage of the reduced marriage penalty, which they had not been aware existed.

2. They should invest the maximum allowable amount in IRAs for each of them. This could give them a great tax break, with the added benefit of an early start on their retirement planning.

3. The next best investment would be real estate* so they could deduct for depreciation, property taxes, interest on the mortgage, and upkeep expenses. But, because Burt and Sally paid no rent, they weren't ready to move. As an alternative, Professor Westwood suggested that they join in a real estate limited partnership so they could acquire similar deductions.

With just these few steps, he indicated, Burt and Sally could greatly reduce their tax burden.

While still mulling over these ideas, Burt and Sally chanced on the opportunity to buy a friend's two-bedroom condominium. The down payment was only $3,000, with a mortgage of $400 per month and maintenance fee of $100 per month. Here Burt and Sally were lucky. Because the condominium is near the school, they were able to rent it to two students and collect the mortgage and maintenance costs in rent. Even with the added rent income, they gained in deductions because a large percentage of the mortgage payment is for interest in the early years of a loan and their property tax is high. They deduct for depreciation and have had many upkeep expenses because they have made many repairs and improvements.

*must be real estate for investment; NOT live in it.

- brokerage fee is deductible

PART THREE
MANAGING YOUR MONEY

LEARNING OBJECTIVES

1. **To outline the role of savings and money management in modern personal finance.** / *2.* **To identify and compare the various types of savings instruments.** / *3.* **To discuss the impact of deregulation on the banking industry.** / *4.* **To define and differentiate the various types of financial institutions that serve consumers.** / *5.* **To explain the accounts and services offered by commercial banks and thrifts.** / *6.* **To describe the electronic revolution in banking.** / *7.* **To evaluate the relative safety of money invested with various financial institutions.** / *8.* **To list the factors that go into selecting a place to put your money.** / *9.* **To explain how to use checking, NOW, and Super-NOW accounts.**

TESTING YOUR PERSONAL FINANCE I.Q.

	FACT	FICTION
1. NOW accounts were developed for feminists who were not well served by traditional savings instruments.	☐	☐
2. The Bank of America has more assets than all the credit unions in the United States put together.	☐	☐
3. Services obtained through barter have the advantage of being nontaxable to their recipients.	☐	☐
4. A treasury bill has a longer term than a treasury note.	☐	☐
5. Sears has been called a financial supermarket because of the wide range of financial, real estate, and insurance services it offers.	☐	☐
6. A thief would encounter more difficulty cashing a check with a blank endorsement than with a restrictive endorsement.	☐	☐

The materials in this chapter assist in separating fact from fiction. Your answers can be checked on page 169.

CHAPTER SIX

MONEY MANAGEMENT

SHARING A PERSONAL FINANCIAL DECISION WITH PROFESSOR ROBERT BOHN OF GOLDEN GATE UNIVERSITY

After class one day Marcie Stillwell approached Professor Robert Bohn. "Something seems to be wrong with my bank account," she began. "I can't figure out why."

At the beginning of the semester Marcie had proudly opened her first checking account, and at first there was no problem. But now she complained, "The bank bounces every check I write." Just the day before her landlord had called, annoyed because the check she'd given him was no good. It was embarrassing. "And it doesn't make sense," Marcie added, taking out her checkbook to confirm her point. "See, I still have lots of checks left."

If you were Professor Bohn, how would you advise Marcie?

To find out how Professor Bohn helped Marcie with her personal financial problem, turn to page 169.

"The secret and the difference between winners and losers is in discipline. The winners manage their money. The loser lets the money manage him."
Nick the Greek[1]

money: *an accepted and conventional medium of exchange.*

barter: *trading goods and services instead of using cash.*

Many Americans find it difficult to decide whether to keep their money in checking accounts, savings accounts, money-market funds, or in their wallets. Marietta Dzoitek, however, has a somewhat different problem. Marietta, a hospital switchboard operator, realizes that her currency—the zloty—is nearly worthless. Such is the case in present-day Poland!

So, like many Poles, Marietta spends long hours in lines so that she can trade ration coupons and zlotys for Poland's real mediums of exchange (the traditional definition of *money*)—cigarettes and vodka. She rarely uses these products, but they are how one *barters* (trades) in Poland in the 1980s. As Marietta Dzoitek puts it: "Tobacco and alcohol are the best currencies nowadays. Money no longer matters."[2]

Americans may not have to deal with the complex financial system that confronts Marietta Dzoitek, but the concept of money management is playing an increasingly important role in modern personal finance. Inflation, expanded cash management alternatives, tax legislation, and other factors have made money management one of the prime determinants of one's financial health.

Today's consumers must understand exactly what money is, how it functions in our financial lives, and how savings are the key to money accumulation. In addition, consumers must comprehend the various savings and money management choices available from an expanded set of financial institutions and decide exactly where to put their money. This is no small choice now that Sears, J. C. Penney, and other nonfinancial giants are competing for savings and checking dollars. Finally, consumers must be able to handle the practical details of a checking account and learn what to do and whom to contact when they have a banking problem.

WHY MAINTAIN MONEY BALANCES?

It is expensive to maintain a supply of readily available money. The currency stored in your wallet or the deposits in a checking account are costly because of the loss of potential interest. Depositing the same money in a certificate of deposit, money-market fund, NOW account, Super-NOW account, treasury bill, or other savings instrument will generate additional funds in the form of interest. In fact, one begins to wonder why a person should maintain a money balance at all.

There is one major reason why money is important: convenience. If you have to make a purchase or pay a bill, it is more convenient to pay with currency or issue a check than it is to go through the trouble, time, and expense of converting such noncash holdings as art, real estate, or even savings bonds or certificates of deposit into money. A ready supply of money provides the funds needed to pay bills for rent, electricity, the phone, tuition, and the dentist. Money on hand is a critical part of personal finance, and one of your most important financial goals should be to increase the amount of funds you have available to convert into money. The most effective way to do this is through savings.

WHY SAVING IS SO IMPORTANT

People save money for a variety of reasons. First, savings ensure that they have funds on hand to convert to cash. Deposits can be transferred from a savings to a checking account to meet a large bill that exceeds available funds. In this way savings can provide the money needed to balance one's monthly budget.

The money accumulated in savings also provides an emergency fund, which can be tapped if you are ill or out of work. Having money in the bank enables you to continue your life without resorting to banks, family, or friends for a loan. This is especially important if your job is uncertain or if you are in an industry known for sudden layoffs. Said one senior executive in such an industry, "In this business your bank book is your best friend."[3]

Many people save for a specific purpose—a vacation, a new home, a bigger car, college tuition. Retirement is another reason for saving (see Chapter 20). Savings can also be earmarked for investments that require large sums of money. As investment advisers point out, "You must save in order to invest."[4]

SETTING SAVINGS GOALS

How much savings do you actually need? The answer to this question is tied to the amount of money you must put in an emergency fund. Most financial experts agree that you should aim for between three and six months of after-tax income to pay medical bills, replace lost income, and meet monthly expenses if your income is cut off. It is important to keep in mind that medical and disability insurance and unemployment compensation will help reduce the burden on savings if you are ill or unemployed.

Any savings accumulated that exceed these needs should be viewed as discretionary. That is, you may want to save for a cabin cruiser, but you certainly do not have to.

Barter: An Alternative to Money

History books tell us that bartering is as American as apple pie—and maybe more so. However, although we all remember tales of the Dutch buying Manhattan Island from the Indians for a mere $24 worth of beads, the bartering tradition has faded from the American scene—until now. In the last few years there has been a renewed interest in bartering and barter clubs. Today there are some 400 barter clubs scattered across the country through which goods and services can be acquired without even opening your wallet. These clubs traded some $350 million worth of goods and services in 1981—a volume twice the size of that only three years earlier.

Barter clubs have prospered, in part, because of recent high interest rates. Instead of charging a purchase on a credit card, in a barter club you can trade your skills as a carpenter, doctor, computer programmer, or financial consultant for dental care, scuba-diving lessons, a weekend in a Florida condominium, a restaurant meal, or a new fur coat.

Laura Rohmann, writing in *Forbes*, describes how the barter system works at Pfeister Barter, one of the country's largest barter exchanges:

As a new member you are given a trade credit card with a 500 trade credit limit. You spend 400 credits to have your back adjusted by a chiropractor. . . . Now you owe Pfeister 400 credits, so you offer your services as a hang-gliding instructor (which is why you needed your back adjusted). You give the lessons at 50 credits per lesson to any exchange member, earning 500 trade credits. You pay an 8 percent service fee of $40 to Pfeister, and settle your 500 credit debt. And you still have 100 credits left over to be spent later. All 500 of these credits you earned count as taxable income now.

The Internal Revenue Service, as well as state and city tax collectors, keep close tabs on barter clubs to make sure that these cashless swaps do not cheat them of their tax bite.

The benefits of this system are clear, says Marvin Grafton, president of Pfeister Barter. "You can get $1,000 of value in a purchase that would cost you maybe five hours' work on a Friday night when you have nothing to do anyway." You can also improve your cash flow and attract new customers to your business. But there are problems as well. If there are too many other barter club members offering your service, you may find yourself unable to pay the club back. (Pfeister limits the number of chiropractors and podiatrists it allows in the club for this reason.) And an auto mechanic who accepted your card last month may turn it down because he or she already has substantial credits built up. You also may not be able to get the gold necklace you promised yourself because the jeweler you hoped to deal with went out of business, or you may find that the printer you hoped to use to print your wedding invitations deals only in bulk orders of 1,000 copies or more.

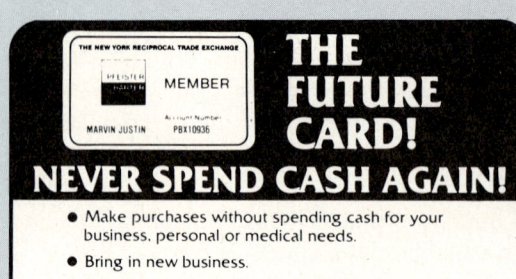

Sources: Rohmann and Grafton quotes from Laura Rohmann, "Cashing in on Cashless Swaps," *Forbes*, March 29, 1982, pp. 120–121. See also "Beware the Hidden Risks of Bartering," *Business Week*, April 19, 1982, p. 110.

The "Future Card" enables Pfeister Barter members to pay for one another's professional services by barter exchange, without using cash or conventional credit cards.

If you have little or no money in the bank and are just starting out, it may take years before you reach your savings goal. The best way to begin is to put 5 percent of your after-tax income into a savings account. Consider this money as a required expenditure, much like a regular monthly payment.

DETERMINING INTEREST ON SAVINGS

Savings grow through regular deposits and through the interest the money earns while it is in a savings account. Interest is computed by multiplying the principal (your savings) by the rate of interest by the time period. An investment of $10,000 in an account paying 5 percent compounded annually will be worth $10,500 at the end of the year. The same amount of money at the same rate of interest compounded quarterly will earn $10,509.

It is important to remember that the more frequently interest is compounded, the higher the rate of return. Consequently, savers are particularly interested in not only the annual interest rate on savings but also the effective rate. The *effective rate of interest* is the interest actually earned for a period of time, based on both the annual interest rate and the number of times it is computed annually. If interest is computed daily, each day the balance in the savings account will increase by the amount of interest earned that day. The result is that the annual rate is higher than it would be if the interest were computed only four times a year (quarterly).

Figure 6-1 shows how the frequency of compounding interest influences the effective rate. When $1,000 is compounded annually at a nominal rate of 6 percent, it earns only 6 percent interest. When it is compounded daily, the effective interest rate jumps to 6.27 percent.

Savings-account interest rates are also differentiated on the basis of the treatment of deposits and withdrawals. There are four different methods.

FIFO. In the first-in, first-out method (FIFO, for short), withdrawals are subtracted from the opening balance of the interest period before interest is computed. Suppose that on January 2 you deposit $500 in an account in which interest is compounded quarterly. If you make no deposits but withdraw $100 from the account on March 26, just a few days before the end of the quarter, the interest credited to the account will be based on only $400, not on the $500 that was in the account for almost the entire three-month period.

> **effective rate of interest:** the interest actually earned for a period of time, based on both the annual interest rate and the number of times it is compounded annually.

Figure 6-1
NOMINAL AND EFFECTIVE RATES OF INTEREST

Beginning Balance: $1,000 + Nominal Rate of Interest: 6%

Compounding Period	End Balance	Effective Rate of Interest
Annual	$1,060.00	6.00%
Semiannual	$1,060.90	6.09%
Quarterly	$1,061.36	6.14%
Daily	$1,062.70	6.27%

LIFO. In the last-in, first-out method (LIFO), withdrawals are deducted not from the opening balance, but from the most recent deposit. For example, if in January you deposit $500 in a savings account, then deposit $100 at the end of February and withdraw $50 at the end of March, the $50 withdrawal is charged against the deposit made in February (last in, first out), not against the opening balance in January (as is done in the FIFO method).

Low Balance. As its name suggests, the low-balance method calls for the payment of interest on the lowest balance in the account for the entire interest period. Even if you make a $350 deposit to a $500 account on January 14, interest is paid only on $500 because that was the lowest balance during the quarter. Although the balance was $850 for most of the quarter, interest is not earned on the $350 deposit until the next quarter, and then only if the balance never falls below $850.

Day of Deposit to Day of Withdrawal. This method of computing interest is the most favorable of the four for depositors because it allows savers to deposit and withdraw money in the account without penalty. If $100 of the $500 principal is withdrawn on January 20, and $150 deposited on February 1, the interest earned by the account will be paid daily on the exact current balance. Savers may benefit by seeking this type of account, since it pays the highest effective rate of interest.

TYPES OF SAVINGS INSTRUMENTS

Which savings instruments best suit your financial needs? This question has become difficult to answer as the number of savings options has increased during the past several years. But even though the decision is harder, the basic decision-making process is the same: a consumer can make an intelligent choice only if he or she knows exactly what is being offered.

PASSBOOK SAVINGS ACCOUNTS

Until recently, the passbook savings account was the place most savers put their money. This account—offered by commercial banks, savings and loan associations, mutual savings banks, and credit unions—pays between 5.25 and 5.5 percent interest.*Commercial banks are restricted by government regulation from offering more than 5.25 percent interest, while the *thrifts* (the remaining savings institutions mentioned above) can offer 5.5 percent.

Savers' allegiance to passbook savings accounts began to fade when banks, thrifts, and money-market funds began offering savings instruments that yielded much higher interest rates. In 1978, for example, passbook savings

thrifts: savings and loan associations, mutual savings banks, and credit unions.

*deregulation laws have changed that - now can set own competitive rates.

deposits totaled more than $490 billion; three years later this figure had declined more than 25 percent.[5]

Although the amount of money in passbook accounts is rapidly shrinking, a substantial cache still remains. Why do savers tie up money in such low-interest-bearing accounts when they can earn far more elsewhere?

There are several reasons. First, many people—especially older people who were scarred by the more than 9,000 bank failures that occurred during the Great Depression—are afraid to change their savings habits. They automatically reject money-market mutual funds because of their lack of government insurance and steer away from insured bank certificates of deposit and money-market accounts because of their novelty. Second, many people cannot afford to tie up their money for three, six, or eighteen months, as they are required to do with a certificate of deposit. Third, many savers cannot afford the minimum deposits required by bank money-market funds and money-market mutual funds. Fourth, many savers use passbook accounts as a kind of holding bin between investments. They value the fact that they can get their money on a moment's notice. Finally, many people earmark their passbook accounts for special purposes, such as buying a new car or taking a vacation. In their minds, the purpose is more important than the amount of money they earn in interest.

CHRISTMAS CLUB ACCOUNTS

Christmas (or holiday) club accounts pay passbook-savings-account rates for money that is put into holiday savings programs. These programs require savers to pay anywhere from $2.50 to $20 a week or more into a passbook-type account that is earmarked for a Christmas nest egg. In 1982, approximately 15 million Americans participated in Christmas club programs offered by commercial banks and thrifts. Each of these depositors saved a little more than $300. Christmas clubs do not have the total flexibility of passbook savings accounts. If money is withdrawn before the end of the holiday savings period, interest is generally not paid, and one cannot borrow on these savings. However, no money is lost if the savings schedule is not maintained.

CERTIFICATES OF DEPOSIT

Commercial banks, savings and loan associations, savings banks, and credit unions offer a higher rate of interest than that for passbook accounts if money on deposit is left for a specified period of time. By investing money in a federally insured *certificate of deposit*, or *CD* (also known as a savings certificate or term account), savers can earn considerably more interest than is possible with a passbook account. There are drawbacks, however. To lock into the highest interest rates (the longer the maturity, the higher the interest), liquidity

certificate of deposit: a federally insured deposit that offers higher interest rates than passbook accounts but requires that the money remain on deposit for a specified period of time.

"I'm afraid that with this kind of account you can't withdraw your money for another three months. However, I can take you into our vault and let you visit it for a few minutes."

Illiquidity Is a Major Disadvantage of Certificates of Deposit.

Source: Drawing by Levin; © 1981 The New Yorker Magazine, Inc.

is sacrificed. Money withdrawn before the end of the certificate term, which may be as short as 7 days or as long as 8 years, results in a substantial interest penalty. This condition creates problems for savers when interest rates are on the rise. If, for example, interest rates are now 10 percent and rising, the 30-month CD purchased a few months ago, which pays only 8.5 percent, is not a good deal. However, before cashing in a certificate and taking the penalty, calculate exactly how much money will be gained by such an action.

Certificates of deposit are available at both fixed and variable rates. Interest may be simple or compounded and may be paid monthly, quarterly, yearly, or at the CD's maturity.

Here are some of the certificates of deposit that banks and thrifts offer:

- *Seven- to 31-day certificates:* their interest is tied to the 3-month treasury bill rate, although under certain conditions the rate is completely unregulated.
- *Three-month certificates:* their interest is tied to 3-month treasury bills. If the money is withdrawn before the end of the period, all the interest is lost.
- *Six-month certificates:* the most popular savings certificates, their interest rate is linked to 26-week treasury bills.

- *Small-saver certificates:* these require savers to lock their money in for 18 months. They are especially attractive to savers because there is no minimum purchase requirement; in many cases, they can be purchased for as little as $100. Interest rates are tied to the average yield on 2½-year treasury notes.
- *Wild-card certificates:* these pay whatever interest rate the bank or thrift wants to offer on time deposits of 3½ years or more. They may be purchased for as little as $500, and in many cases, money can be added to the certificate during the first year.

Although bank certificates of deposit have enjoyed great popularity in recent years, their attraction may decline as a result of the introduction in 1982 of bank money-market accounts, with their high interest rates. These accounts have taken away much of the incentive to buy CDs because, although CDs offer approximately the same rate of interest, they are less liquid.

Insured certificates of deposit are also available through major brokerage houses. These CDs are the same as those offered by banks, but the brokerage houses offer customers one important advantage. They will help find buyers for investors who want to sell their certificates before they mature, and they will arrange a sale that involves no interest penalty. Of course, savers who hold low-interest CDs in a high-interest market may have to sell at a loss.

BANK MONEY-MARKET ACCOUNTS

At the end of 1982, banks and thrifts were given the authority to offer money-market accounts, which tie interest rates to market conditions. Now savers can receive unregulated bank interest rates on deposits that can be withdrawn at their discretion. In most cases, these rates are tied to average interest rates paid by the money-market mutual funds.

A minimum $2,500 balance must be maintained in order to receive these high interest rates. Transfers are restricted to six withdrawals a month, three checks, and three preauthorized or automatic transactions. There are no interest penalties for withdrawals. Bank money-market accounts are insured up to $100,000.

MONEY-MARKET MUTUAL FUNDS

As Chapter 17 explains, money-market mutual funds invest in short-term money-market instruments such as bank certificates of deposit, government securities, and corporate commercial paper. Although originally intended for investors who needed a temporary repository for surplus funds between investments, money funds became a haven for savers during the explosive interest-rate period of the late 1970s and early 1980s. Savers found a safe, although uninsured, instrument through which they could earn higher interest

Keep Your Eye on the Real Rate

The interest rate paid on a bond or bank account actually doesn't tell you how much you're making. That nominal rate has to be matched against the inflation rate to compute the real rate. If the bank is paying 10% and prices are going up 5% a year, the real rate is 5%. If those figures are reversed, the real rate is −5%, meaning that you are losing purchasing power each year. Real rates also affect your status as a borrower. If you get a loan for 5% while prices are increasing 10% a year, you're 5% ahead of the game. You're paying off the loan with dollars that are becoming progressively cheaper in terms of purchasing power. If the rates are reversed, you're at a disadvantage. Real rates have fluctuated wildly over the past several years, as the accompanying table demonstrates. Recently, real rates have strongly favored investors and savers.

Source: Reprinted with permission from *Changing Times* Magazine, © Kiplinger Washington Editors, Inc., 1984.

REAL RATES

	Inflation Rate	High-grade Municipal Bonds	Aaa Corporate Bonds	Mortgages
1977	6.8%	−1.24%	1.22%	2.22%
1978	9.0	−3.10	−0.27	0.56
1979	13.3	−6.91	−0.67	−2.52
1980	12.4	−3.89	−0.46	0.26
1981	8.9	2.33	5.27	5.80
1982	3.9	7.67	9.89	11.24
1983*	3.3	6.07	8.62	9.50

*Estimate.
Source: Council of Economic Advisers (U.S. Government)

---

rates on their money. As a result, the size and number of money funds grew at an astronomical rate. Starting with fewer than a dozen funds managing a few billion dollars' worth of assets in the mid-1970s, the number of money funds mushroomed to 250 by 1983 and their assets skyrocketed to $232 billion.

Most money funds require an initial deposit of at least $500 and limit checks to amounts of $250 or more (some funds have even higher limits). These restrictions, as well as the lack of federal insurance on money-market deposits, have spurred many depositors to shift their money to bank money-market accounts. In the first week after these bank accounts were introduced at the end of 1982, deposits in money-market mutual funds dropped by a record $8.3 billion. Analysts believed that the bulk of this money was transferred to bank money-market accounts.[6]

To attract depositors back, many of the money-market funds are considering private insurance and the elimination of check-writing restrictions. They may also draw depositors by offering higher yields than the bank money-market funds.

MONEY MANAGEMENT 135

TREASURY BILLS, NOTES, AND BONDS

If you have $10,000 or more to save, consider a *treasury bill,* or T-bill—a short-term security backed by the full faith and credit of the U.S. Government. T-bills, which are available at maturities of 3, 6, and 12 months, have a number of positive features. First, they pay attractive rates that are competitive with those of money-market funds. Second, although they are subject to federal income tax, they are not taxable on a state or local level. Third, they may be sold at any time. Fourth, T-bills pay off shortly after purchase rather than at the end of the period. Instead of receiving interest when the instrument matures (as with a CD), savers receive a discount from the face value in the amount of the interest to be earned on the T-bill. To purchase a $10,000 T-bill, for example, you would pay the full $10,000 face value. Shortly after the purchase the government will send you a check representing the discount on the T-bill. If, for example, the discount is $360, the actual purchase price is $9,640 ($10,000 − $360). Receiving this discount at the beginning of the period provides an important interest-rate advantage since the amount of the interest payment can be re-deposited to earn even more interest.

Treasury notes, which are available in 2- to 10-year maturities, can be purchased in denominations of $1,000 to $5,000. *Treasury bonds,* which may be purchased for as little as $1,000, have a much longer term than the other treasury securities. They take 10 to 30 years to mature, although they can be sold on a secondary market before reaching maturity. Unlike treasury bills, which are sold weekly, treasury notes and bonds are available less frequently—generally once every 3 months.

Treasury bills, notes, and bonds can be bought directly from any branch of the Federal Reserve or you can obtain a purchase form by writing to the Bureau of the Public Debt, Securities Transaction Branch, Main Treasury Building, Room 2134, Washington, D.C. 20226. Treasury bills are also available through banks or brokers, who will charge a commission of $20 to $50 for each purchase.

How do treasury bills compare with certificates of deposit? There are several important differences. Treasury bills generally have higher interest rates than bank CDs. As indicated, unlike CDs, they carry no penalties for early withdrawal. However, CDs are federally insured while treasury bills are not (although they are backed by the full faith and credit of the U.S. Government). In addition, you do not know exactly how much interest will be received on a treasury bill until after it is purchased (T-bills are auctioned—offered for sale to the highest bidder—every Monday by the Federal Reserve, while the exact interest rate to be paid on a CD is known before the purchase).

U.S. SAVINGS BONDS

Until recently U.S. savings bonds were virtually ignored by savers because of their low yield compared with money-market funds. This undesirable status

treasury bill: *a short-term security backed by the full faith and credit of the United States Government.*

treasury note: *a security backed by the U.S. Government that is available in 2- to 10-year maturities and denominations of $1,000 to $5,000.*

treasury bonds: *long-term (10- to 30-year) securities backed by the U.S. Government; they may be purchased for as little as $1,000.*

changed in 1982 when the Treasury Department linked the interest rate on Series EE bonds to the average yield on treasury bonds. Now the EE bonds you buy at your bank will yield 85 percent of the treasury-bond rate if held to maturity. That means that if treasury bonds earn 10 percent, an EE bond will return 8.5 percent, compounded annually. The Treasury Department also protects savers from a sharp decline in interest rates by putting a floor on the percentage below which the rates cannot drop.

Holders of EE bonds are required to pay federal taxes on the interest earned (they are exempt from state and local income taxes, as well as from property taxes). The federal taxes, however, are not due until you cash in the bond or until its final maturity, which is equal to the original maturity plus three 10-year extensions. Thus, on a 10-year bond, the tax bite need not come until 40 years after the original purchase. This feature makes EE bonds ideal for retirement planning since taxes on the bond interest can be paid after retirement, when you may be in a lower tax bracket.

EE bonds may be purchased through a payroll deduction; through commercial banks, savings and loan associations, mutual savings banks, or credit unions; from a Federal Reserve Bank; or from the Bureau of Public Debt, Securities Transaction Branch, Main Treasury Building, Room 2134, Washington, D.C. 20226. Consumers desiring the safety of government bonds as well as regular interest payments may prefer Series HH bonds. Unlike EE bonds, HH bonds are sold at their face value and pay interest to their owner as current income.

There is never a fee to buy, convert, or redeem a U.S. savings bond. Since they are guaranteed by the federal government, they are considered among the safest investments in the world.

EVALUATING THE SAVINGS ALTERNATIVES

Choosing the best savings instrument for your purposes is obviously a complex decision. The following criteria should be considered:

- *Minimum investment:* What is the smallest acceptable investment?
- *Liquidity:* What must you do to withdraw money from your account? Are there any penalties for early withdrawal?
- *Yield:* What will the investment earn? What fees and bank charges are associated with the account?
- *Safety:* What risk am I taking with my savings? Are they federally insured?
- *Taxation:* Is the interest taxable on the federal, state, and local levels, or is the interest totally or partially tax-exempt?
- *Suitability:* Is the savings account compatible with my lifestyle and other investments? Is it easy to manage?

Table 6-1 (pp. 138–139) allows you to compare these criteria in the different savings instruments, some of which are not discussed until later in the chapter.

FINANCIAL INSTITUTIONS OF THE 1980s: HOW THEY'VE CHANGED

It wasn't that long ago that there were only two places to deposit currency: commercial banks and thrifts. Times have changed, and so have today's financial institutions. Banks and thrifts must now compete with the likes of Sears and Merrill Lynch. The result is a bonanza for consumers.

This bonanza has been fueled by the *Depository Institutions Deregulation Committee*—a federal body charged with the task of phasing out interest-rate ceilings on all accounts by 1986. The committee's deregulation moves have lifted many restrictive banking regulations and left banks and thrifts to compete for consumers' banking dollars just as retailers are free to compete for the dollars consumers spend on clothing, food, and other purchases. This competition has spawned a variety of high-interest savings and money management instruments, which have changed the face of banking.

With so much choice available in financial instruments and services, it is important to define exactly where Americans are banking now and where they can expect to bank in the years ahead.

COMMERCIAL BANKS

To millions of Americans, banking means doing business with one of the nation's 14,000 commercial banks. Known as full-service banks, *commercial banks* offer more than 100 financial services, including checking and savings accounts, personal and business loans, trust services, and mortgages.

Although commercial banks were originally founded to serve businesses, they are now perceived by the American public as *the* place to bank. There are three main reasons for this: convenience, service, and financial advice. People choose commercial banks over thrift institutions simply because there are more of them. In fact, there are three times as many commercial bank branches as there are thrifts in the United States. According to an American Bankers Association survey, people also value the wide range of services available at commercial banks. Moreover, they believe that commercial bankers have the experience to help them with their financial problems, that they can trust this financial advice, and that, indeed, their bankers are open to giving advice.[7]

commercial banks: full-service banks that offer a wide range of accounts and services.

SAVINGS AND LOAN ASSOCIATIONS

Savings and loan associations (S&Ls) have traditionally been in business to serve people—not businesses—and to handle small as well as large sums of money.

savings and loan associations (S&Ls): originally chartered to provide mortgage money, these financial institutions concentrate on serving consumers—not businesses.

Table 6-1
MAJOR SAVINGS AND CASH MANAGEMENT INSTRUMENTS*

Type of Instrument

Criteria	Passbook, Statement Savings, & NOW Accounts	Bank CDs	U.S. Treasury Issues
Minimum Investment	Some banks have minimum opening deposits. Some banks have minimum balance requirements to avoid charges &/or loss of interest.	Varies from bank to bank. Some as low as $500, or less.	T-bills: $10,000 minimum, with $5,000 additional increments. T-notes: $1,000 minimum. T-bonds: $1,000 minimum.
Liquidity	Can withdraw money at any time without penalty.	Specified maturities. Penalties for early withdrawal.	T-bills: 3-, 6-, 12-month maturities. T-notes: 2- to 10-year maturities. T-bonds: 10- to 30-year maturities. Continually traded on secondary market, but no guarantee at what price.
Yield	Passbook or Statement: • Fixed rates. • 5.5% at thrift institutions. • 5.25% at commercial banks. NOW Accounts: • 5.25% at all institutions.	Fixed & variable rates. Interest can be simple or compounded. Interest can be paid at month-end, quarter-end, year-end, &/or at maturity.	Generally competitive with other money-market instruments. Service fee charged by banks, but no fee if bought directly from Federal Reserve bank.
Safety	Federally insured up to $100,000.	Federally insured up to $100,000.	Issued & backed by U.S. government.
Taxation	Interest taxable on federal, state, & local levels.	Interest taxable on federal, state, & local levels.	Interest tax-free on state & local levels; taxable on federal level.
Suitability	Safe. Instant liquidity. Fixed rate. Convenient to get at local bank.	Safe. Fixed & variable rates. Flexible in choice of maturities. Convenient to get at local bank.	Safe. Flexible in choice of maturities.

*Information in this table is subject to change and may differ by institution. It is advisable to contact tax and financial consultants when evaluating investments.

Before deregulation of financial institutions began, savings and loans attracted savers seeking slightly higher interest rates on passbook savings accounts than they could obtain at commercial banks. (On these accounts commercial banks offer only 5.25 percent interest, while savings and loans offer 5.5 percent.) They also attracted people in search of home mortgages. Chartered

Criteria	Money-Market Mutual Funds	Bank Money-Market Accounts	Super-NOW Accounts
Minimum Investment	Varies greatly according to fund. Some as low as $500, some as high as $10,000.	$2,500 (or higher at some banks).	$2,500 (or higher at some banks).
Liquidity	Can withdraw money without penalty. Some funds have 15-day waiting period after deposit of noncash items.	Limited third-party transfers. Unlimited in-bank or ATM transactions. Some banks may have minimum transaction amounts.	Unlimited check writing. Unlimited in-bank or ATM transactions. Some banks may have minimum transaction amounts.
Yield	Yield fluctuates according to market rates.	Set at bank's discretion. Rate varies; can be guaranteed no longer than 30 days.	Set at bank's discretion. Rate varies; can be guaranteed no longer than 30 days.
Safety	Good safety to date but not federally insured.	Federally insured up to $100,000.	Federally insured up to $100,000.
Taxation	Varies according to the type of investments the fund purchases.	Interest taxable on federal, state, & local levels.	Interest taxable on federal, state, & local levels.
Suitability	Money market yield. Easy access to funds. Some funds offer joint stock & money market funds.	High yield. Convenience of branch network. Limited access to funds.	High yield. Convenience of branch network. Limited access to funds.

Type of Instrument

by Congress or individual states to provide mortgage money, savings and loans have traditionally been in business to make long-term, fixed-rate mortgages at prevailing interest rates. Fifty-one percent of all home mortgages are held by savings and loan associations and mutual savings banks (described below).

Savings and loans prospered until deregulation allowed interest rates to rise on many savings instruments. They then found themselves in the position of having to pay out more for money than they were taking in on their mortgage loans. Commercial banks did not experience this problem to the same extent since they concentrated on short-term loans that were attuned to current interest rates. As interest rates on various certificates of deposit topped 14, 15, and even 16 percent in 1980 and 1981, 60 percent of all the mortgages held by the thrifts yielded less than 10 percent.[8]

In 1982, when the crisis was most severe, savings and loans paid an average of 11.49 percent on their deposits while they earned only 10.41 percent on their loans.[9] Depositors shifted their money from passbook accounts yielding 5.5 percent to certificates of deposit paying more than twice that much—with the result that a major source of relatively inexpensive funds almost dried up. This caused the most serious crisis in the American banking system since the Great Depression. More than 2,000 savings and loans experienced huge losses and about 1,100 of them closed their doors between 1979 and 1983.[10]

Despite these problems, the nation's 3,500 savings and loans continue to be an important part of the American banking system; indeed, they hold more than $600 billion in assets, so Americans' expression of confidence in them is still strong. Deregulation has given the thrifts the power to offer many of the services traditionally reserved for commercial banks at competitive rates. As thrifts begin to offer consumer loans, issue credit cards, and buy corporate bonds to finance businesses, they will become indistinguishable from commercial banks and better able to compete in the marketplace.

MUTUAL SAVINGS BANKS

The names of some of the nation's mutual savings banks conjure up thoughts of an American economy that was once far simpler than it is today. Names like the Union Dime Savings Bank, the Seamen's Bank for Savings, and the Emigrant Savings Bank tell us a lot about the original mission of the mutual savings bank: to meet the needs of ordinary people and to handle small amounts of money.

mutual savings banks: thrift institutions authorized by 17 states; like savings and loans, they concentrate on consumer deposits and mortgages.

Like savings and loans, the nation's 424 *mutual savings banks* are in business primarily to accept consumer deposits and make home mortgage loans. They exist in only 17 states and are clustered in New York and New England. Considered thrift institutions, mutual savings banks offer savings, NOW, and money-market accounts as well as long-term certificates—all similar to those of savings and loans. They also give consumers the same slightly higher rate on passbook savings accounts. Although in 1981 mutual savings banks had $176 billion in assets, they suffered severe losses because of the interest-rate squeeze. Thirty-nine mutual savings banks went out of business.

CREDIT UNIONS

In the world of high finance, where profit is the only bottom line that matters, *credit unions* are unique: they are not-for-profit cooperative ventures that are owned and operated by their depositors and borrowers. Although credit unions are used by 47 million Americans and have assets totaling $75 billion, they are much smaller than commercial banks. By comparison, the Bank of America alone had $44 billion more in assets than all U.S. credit unions combined.

Credit unions have a limited mission. They are organized to serve specific groups of people who work at certain jobs, belong to certain religious or fraternal organizations, or live in certain neighborhoods. Eight out of ten credit union members belong to occupational-based associations. The largest credit union in the United States is the Navy Federal Credit Union, located in Washington, D.C. Its 500,000 members are bound together by their affiliation with the U.S. Navy or Marines.

Credit unions offer the same range of services as the other thrifts, including savings and certificate of deposit accounts, interest-earning checking accounts (called share-draft accounts), individual retirement accounts, home mortgages, life insurance, and line-of-credit loans. One of the most important

credit unions: not-for-profit cooperative ventures owned and operated by their depositors and borrowers; they are designed to service specific groups of people like a certain occupational group.

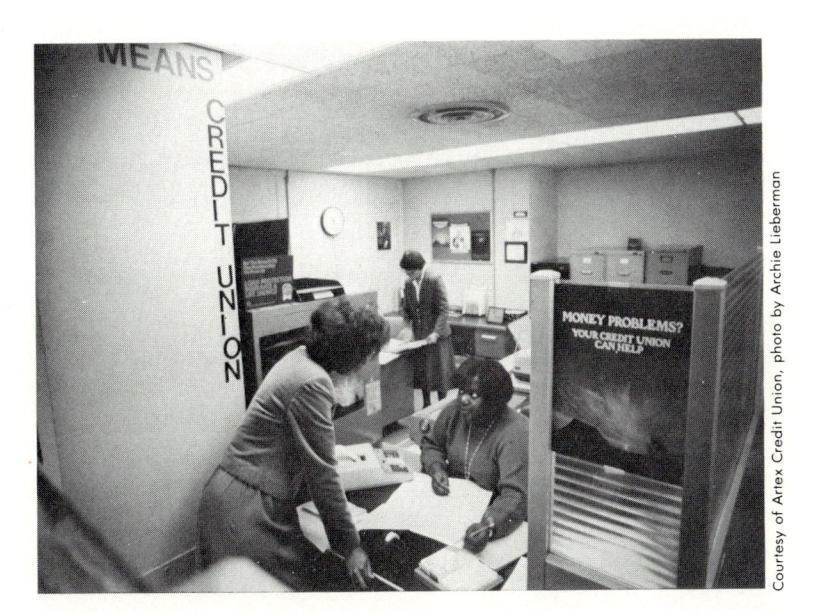

Credit unions provide financial services to groups of people who share a common occupation, residential area, or religious or fraternal affiliation. Because credit unions are nonprofit organizations, they are frequently able to offer their members more favorable terms than other financial institutions do.

services that credit unions offer their members is financial counseling. They also encourage savings through payroll deduction plans.

Because credit unions operate on a nonprofit basis, they often provide services at terms that are better than those of other financial institutions. Any income that the credit union earns after meeting expenses and reserve requirements is returned to members in the form of higher interest on savings or lower consumer loan rates. In 1982, for example, consumers taking out short-term personal loans from a credit union were charged interest rates averaging 3.7 percentage points below what they would have paid in a commercial bank and 7.5 points below what they would have paid with a finance company.[11] This interest-rate savings is especially significant because of the huge number of personal loans made by credit unions. Only commercial banks and finance companies issue more consumer installment loans.

MONEY-MARKET MUTUAL FUNDS

The astronomical rise in interest rates at the beginning of the 1980s benefited money-market funds more than any other financial institution. Depositors, eager to earn the high interest rates offered by these funds, transferred their savings from thrifts to money-market accounts.

Investors were also attracted to the funds' liquidity. Most funds permit depositors to write checks over a stated amount (such as $500) against their investments. In addition, since most money funds are just one part of a large mutual fund organization, investors have the option of moving their deposits from one fund to another as conditions change. (Mutual funds, including money-market funds, are examined in greater detail in Chapter 17.)

FINANCIAL SUPERMARKETS

financial supermarkets: nonbanks that offer consumers a wide range of financial services and the convenience of banking, borrowing, investing, buying insurance, as well as shopping, in just one place.

Until a few years ago, shopping at Sears meant buying clothing and appliances, not certificates of deposit or money-market funds. That changed when Sears became one of a growing number of *financial supermarkets*—nonbanks that offer consumers a wide range of financial services and the convenience of banking, borrowing, investing, buying or selling a home, purchasing insurance, as well as shopping, in just one place. Unencumbered by government regulations that have limited the access of banks and thrifts to financial markets and will continue to limit their activity in varying degrees until 1986, companies like Sears, Merrill Lynch, and J. C. Penney have moved into traditional banking realms.

Sears Leads the Way. The more than 36 million families who regularly shop at Sears are able to deposit their spare cash in money-market mutual funds, which are invested in federal government securities, as well as purchase

Figure 6-2
THE SEARS FINANCIAL NETWORK

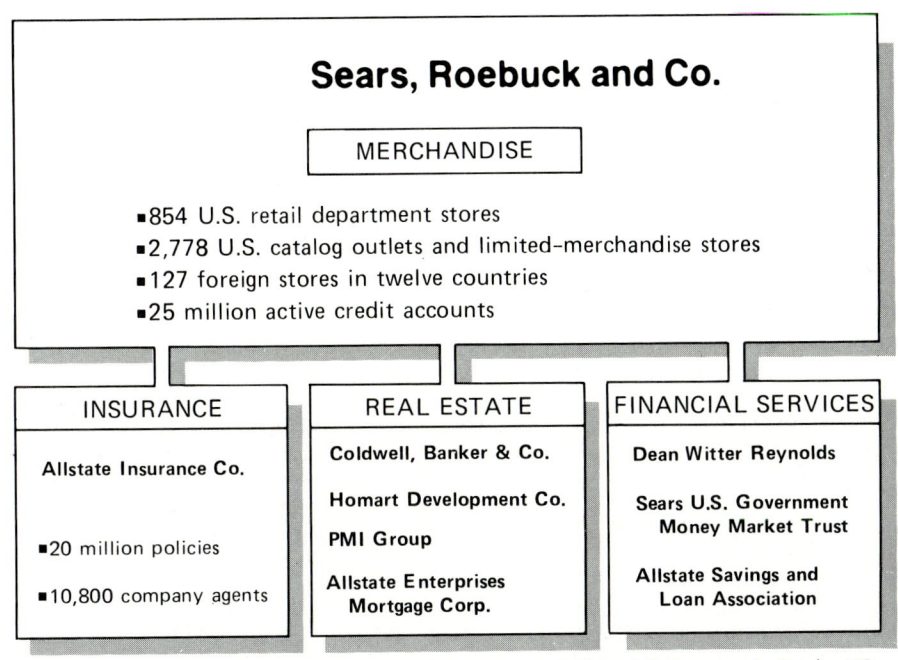

Sears, Roebuck and Co.

MERCHANDISE

- 854 U.S. retail department stores
- 2,778 U.S. catalog outlets and limited-merchandise stores
- 127 foreign stores in twelve countries
- 25 million active credit accounts

INSURANCE

Allstate Insurance Co.

- 20 million policies
- 10,800 company agents

REAL ESTATE

Coldwell, Banker & Co.

Homart Development Co.

PMI Group

Allstate Enterprises Mortgage Corp.

FINANCIAL SERVICES

Dean Witter Reynolds

Sears U.S. Government Money Market Trust

Allstate Savings and Loan Association

Source: Marta Norman and Claire Nivola, "Where America Will Bank," *Newsweek*, October 19, 1981, p. 80. Copyright 1981, by Newsweek, Inc. All rights reserved, reprinted by permission.

stocks, bonds, IRAs, insurance, and real estate. In addition, customers in Sears' California stores can actually do their banking at a branch of Allstate Savings & Loan. In the future all Sears shoppers may be offered a universal credit card, which they can use for their retail purchases and their banking transactions in their Sears savings and loan and money fund accounts as well as in an account that provides a prearranged line of credit. Figure 6-2 shows the individual companies that make up the Sears financial empire. According to Edward Telling, chairman of Sears, Sears' goal is to become "the premier provider of financial services in the country."[12]

Merrill Lynch. Merrill Lynch, the nation's largest securities brokerage firm, is paving its own path in the rush to attract consumer banking dollars. After its highly successful introduction of the cash management account (CMA), Merrill Lynch began selling certificates of deposit at its 450 brokerage branches throughout the United States. The sales effort was enormously successful; approximately $200 million worth of CDs were sold in the first four days after their introduction in 1982. To avoid being classified as a bank and becoming subject to banking regulations, Merrill Lynch transfers customers' money to

The Asset Management Account

As money management needs have become more sophisticated, so have the money management services offered by the nation's major brokerage houses. One of the most comprehensive plans offered in recent years is the asset management account, which combines into one plan a range of financial services that includes check writing, money-market funds, brokerage services, and credit cards.

Attractive as this may sound, asset management accounts are not for everyone. With a typical initial investment requirement of $10,000 to $25,000 in cash or securities, they are out of the reach of many small investors.

The cash deposited in an asset management account is placed in one of the brokerage firm's money-market accounts—usually a regular money fund, a tax-free fund, or a U.S. Treasury security fund. The client has immediate access to the account through a checking system that allows the writing of as many checks as he or she wants, no matter the amount of the check. This is a major advantage over money-market accounts, which restrict checks to amounts of at least $250 or $500. The asset management account eliminates the need for more than one checking account.

Clients also have access to their money through the credit card that comes with the account. Some brokerage houses, like E. F. Hutton and Shearson/American Express, offer the American Express Gold card—a card with no set credit limit. However, the vast majority of brokerage houses, including Merrill Lynch, Dean Witter, and Bache, use a debit card issued by Visa. This card directly charges your account for the amount of your purchases. Instead of receiving a monthly bill, as you do with the American Express Gold card, there is a monthly statement advising you how much was automatically withdrawn from the account. The debit card can also be used to issue yourself an instant loan at a participating bank. The stocks held by the brokerage house serve as collateral for the loan.

The asset management account concept began in 1977 with the Merrill Lynch cash management account (CMA). The concept caught on very quickly and by 1982 more than 650,000 people were CMA customers. The success of Merrill Lynch encouraged other brokers to offer this service.

Although there are some differences among these accounts (Bache's annual fee is $50, while Dean Witter's is $30; E. F. Hutton requires a minimum investment of $10,000 in cash or $20,000 in securities, while Shearson/American Express requires $25,000), the basic cash management services are nearly the same no matter which account is chosen.

Sources: Pete Kadzis, "Here Come Those Financial Supermarkets," *Money*, July 1982, pp. 108–112; and "News You Can Use in Your Personal Planning," *U.S. News & World Report*, November 16, 1981, p. 95.

---

either a bank or a thrift. (Merrill Lynch would be classified as a bank if it accepted and held consumers' time deposits.) But many bankers are still critical: "Merrill Lynch is getting to the point where it can tell people they don't need to go to a bank anymore, and that concerns us," said Thomas S. Brainerd, a vice-president at Crocker National Bank of San Francisco.[13] Other banks fear that it is only a matter of time before government regulations permit Merrill Lynch to become a true bank and before they eagerly take on that role.

MONEY MANAGEMENT

Merrill Lynch introduced the concept of the asset management account in 1977, when it offered its customers the cash management account. The concept caught on quickly, as can be seen by the focus of this 1984 CMA advertisement. The ad suggests that there are now a "galaxy" of asset management accounts to choose from.

(Ad reprinted by permission of Merrill Lynch, Pierce, Fenner & Smith, Inc. © 1984 by Merrill Lynch, Pierce, Fenner & Smith, Inc.)

J. C. Penney. The financial supermarket trend is also being followed by J. C. Penney, the nation's third largest retailer. Penney has joined forces with a major savings and loan association to offer its northern California customers the opportunity to bank and shop at any of five local Penney stores; its credit card customers can obtain the same financial services through the mail. Penney customers have access to checking accounts, money-market funds, mortgages, consumer loans, retirement accounts, and other financial services.

The Kroger Company, a chain of groceries, dairies, bakeries, and drug stores, has also joined the financial services bandwagon, making it as easy to bank as it is to shop for the family's dinner.

A DIFFERENT FUTURE

How will these changes affect consumer banking? Experts predict that by the early 1990s banks, thrifts, and semibanks will provide the same financial services. Unless the *Pepper-McFadden Act* forbidding banks and thrifts to engage in interstate banking is repealed, however, the new nontraditional banks will have an enormous competitive edge. While Sears can set up a nationwide network of financial services, banks and thrifts generally cannot. However, as the chief executive of American Express points out, traditional financial institutions have a promising future because of the personalized service they offer: "The local bank is the expert when it comes to its clients and its community. It can provide far better insight into its customers than can a national organization."[14]

What services can consumers expect from the major financial institutions? The next section focuses on the services offered by commercial banks and thrifts—the institutions where most people do their banking.

> **Pepper-McFadden Act:** *legislation that forbids banks or thrifts to engage in interstate banking.*

BANKING SERVICES

NOW, Super-NOW, IRA, overdraft checking, special checking: these are only some of the vast array of services offered by commercial banks and thrift institutions to their noncommercial customers. Checking and NOW accounts are particularly important as they are primary keys to effective money management.

CHECKING ACCOUNTS

Nine out of ten payments in the United States are made by check, and three out of four American families have at least one checking account. Aside from coins and currency, checks are the most familiar form of money. Almost all of us rely on them to pay regular monthly bills as well as unexpected expenses.

Even though checking accounts have different names at different banks, there are really only two types of accounts: regular checking and special checking. These accounts share one important characteristic: for nearly 50 years, between 1933 and 1981, banks and thrifts were prohibited by law from paying depositors interest on their money. Whatever checking account you choose, it is important to remember to ask for a list of all fees before opening an account. Charges do vary, and some comparison shopping is in order.

MONEY MANAGEMENT

Regular Checking Accounts. These accounts typically require that depositors maintain a specified minimum balance in order to avoid monthly service charges. If you maintain this balance—say, $500—you are given unlimited check-writing privileges at no cost. If funds fall below this balance, some banks charge a small service fee. Other banks simply tack on an account maintenance fee, which you must pay even if your balance exceeds the minimum requirement. Still other banks impose no fee until the number of checks you write exceeds a given number.

Special Checking Accounts. Unlike regular checking accounts, special checking accounts require no minimum balance. To make up for this lost revenue most banks charge a per-check fee (typically 10 or 15 cents per check) as well as a monthly maintenance fee. This type of account is ideal for people who write very few checks each month, since the relatively small per-check fees and maintenance charges cost less than the interest lost by maintaining a minimum balance.

Overdraft Checking Accounts. Some banks allow people to write checks for amounts that are greater than their account balances. In effect, they are insuring loans for overdrafts. These loans are often issued at lower interest rates than regular bank personal loans since they cost less to process than do conventional loans. But the bank may also charge for each overdraft check written.

NOW ACCOUNTS

The *NOW,* or negotiable-order-of-withdrawal, *account* combines checking and savings into a single financial instrument. Developed in the mid-1970s in the New England states, NOW accounts were authorized for use in all 50 states in 1981. They are now offered by thousands of commercial banks, savings and loan associations, mutual savings banks, and credit unions (in the form of share-draft accounts).

NOW account: *a negotiable-order-of-withdrawal account that combines a savings and checking account and pays interest on deposits.*

How NOW Accounts Work. NOW accounts act as a savings and checking account combined. As a savings account, NOW accounts pay 5.25 percent interest on the account balance. As a checking account, they allow you to write negotiable orders of withdrawal—authorizations to take money out of your savings account. These authorizations look and act like checks and are accepted as checks by all who receive them.

The Cost of a NOW Account. The fees associated with the NOW account are tied to the minimum-balance requirement. If you keep more money in the account than needed, you will not be charged. But, at most banks, if the account falls below the minimum for even one day, a service charge—ranging

NOW Accounts: Compare How You'd Fare

If the low balance in your checking account for most months resembles any of those shown below, the table will give you some idea of how you'd come out with two hypothetical NOW accounts, a share-draft account, and a typical checking account. In each case the table shows your monthly gain (+) or loss (−). The gain or loss figure is found by subtracting the monthly cost of the checking account from the interest earned on the average balance in the account each month. Check charges are figured on 15 checks per month.

COMPARING NOW ACCOUNTS

Monthly Gain (+) or Loss (−)

Low Balance	Average Balance	NOW Account #1 $1,500 minimum balance needed to avoid all charges; otherwise $3 monthly charge and 15-cent charge per check; 5% interest	NOW Account #2 $500 minimum balance needed to avoid all charges; otherwise $3 monthly charge; no charge per check; 5% interest	Share-Draft Account no minimum balance needed; no monthly charge; no charge per check; 6% interest rate on minimum balance	Checking Account $300 minimum balance needed to avoid all charges; otherwise 10-cent charge per check; no monthly charge; no interest
$ 90	$ 250	−$ 4.21	−$ 1.96	+$0.45	−$1.50
225	450	− 3.37	− 1.12	+ 1.13	− 1.50
425	750	− 2.12	+ 0.13	+ 2.13	0
785	1,250	− 0.04	+ 5.21	+ 3.93	0
1,350	2,250	+ 4.13	+ 9.38	+ 6.75	0
1,500	2,750	+ 11.46	+ 11.46	+ 7.50	0

Source: "The Strings Attached to Checking Accounts That Pay Interest," *Changing Times*, November 1980, p. 61. Reprinted with permission from *Changing Times* Magazine, © Kiplinger Washington Editors, Inc., 1980.

from $2 to $6 or more—will be assessed. There may also be an interest penalty. Some banks charge a fee only if the month's average balance falls below the minimum.

To avoid fees associated with falling below a minimum balance, it may pay to transfer a few hundred dollars from a passbook savings account to a NOW account. Even if you lose .25 percent interest on the transfer (the difference between the interest on a passbook savings account and a NOW account in a thrift), it is worth doing in order to avoid costly service charges.

The table above comparing NOW accounts shows how various minimum-balance requirements, monthly charges, and per-check fees affect the amount earned on two different NOW accounts, a share-draft account, and a regular checking account. A $2,750 balance can earn as much as $11.46 a month or as little as no interest at all, while a $250 average balance can cost $4.21 in monthly charges or earn 45 cents interest. These figures give an idea of why it is so important to analyze various checking, NOW, and share-draft accounts and to shop around for the best deal.

Share-Draft Accounts. Credit unions have their own version of the NOW account, called the *share-draft account*. Credit-union members issue share drafts against an interest-bearing account. The share-draft account has two major advantages over the NOW account. First, it usually pays a higher rate of interest than the NOW account (6 to 7 percent is common), and second, it rarely requires a minimum balance or charges per-check fees.

share-draft account: a credit union's version of a NOW account.

SUPER-NOW ACCOUNTS

The *Super-NOW account*, first offered in 1983, is a checking-type account that offers a higher yield than the regular NOW account. Whereas the NOW account pays interest up to a maximum of 5.25 percent, the super-NOW account yielded between 7 and 9 percent at its introduction. This interest rate is tied to money-market rates and is free of interest-rate ceilings. In return for higher interest rates, consumers are expected to keep at least $2,500 in their accounts. If the balance dips below that level, it will earn a maximum of 5.25 percent interest. In addition, hefty monthly maintenance and per-check fees are often charged.

Super-NOW account: a checking-type account that offers a higher yield than a regular NOW account.

SAVINGS INSTRUMENTS

As noted earlier, commercial banks and thrifts are where most Americans save. The primary reason for this is the variety of accounts these institutions offer, including passbook accounts, certificates of deposit, bank money-market accounts, U.S. savings bonds, and Christmas club accounts. In addition, insurance protection is offered to depositors.

CONSUMER LOANS

Commercial banks and thrifts are also important sources of consumer credit. Commercial banks offer the widest variety of loans, including automobile loans, mortgage loans, tuition loans, and unsecured personal loans. Savings and loan associations and mutual savings banks specialize in mortgage loans but also lend money for home improvements, education, and so on. Credit unions offer a full range of loan services and often provide the most attractive credit terms.

A unique consumer loan offered by commercial banks and thrifts is the passbook loan—an arrangement that uses a passbook savings account as collateral. The interest charge on this loan is relatively low since you are really borrowing money from yourself. This loan is especially useful to people who need to establish a credit rating. It is also useful for people who occasionally borrow from accumulated savings but find it difficult to replenish their savings account. Many banks and thrifts also offer debt-consolidation loans, which replace many monthly payments to various creditors with one consolidated payment. These and other loans offered by commercial banks and thrifts are examined in detail in Chapter 7.

BANK CREDIT CARDS

The MasterCard and Visa cards found in the wallets of millions of Americans are bank credit cards. These cards are recognized all over the world. Bank credit cards also provide the option of obtaining a cash advance at any bank or thrift across the country that issues the card—an option that is indispensable if a problem arises while traveling.

LIFE INSURANCE

Residents of New York, New Jersey, and Connecticut can purchase a limited amount of term or straight life insurance from their savings banks. In New York, for example, the limit per person is $30,000. Life insurance from a savings bank pays dividends and is one of the cheapest forms of insurance available. For more information on life insurance, see Chapter 12.

PENSION PLANS

Since individual retirement accounts (IRAs) became available to all working people and their spouses, banks and thrifts have played a major role in pension planning. These financial institutions also offer Keogh retirement accounts and Simplified Employee Pension (SEP) plans. For more details on these plans, see Chapter 20.

MISCELLANEOUS SERVICES

In addition to the services just mentioned, banks and thrifts also offer trustee services, safe-deposit boxes, and bank wire transfers.

Trustee Services. The trustee services of banks generally handle only large individual trusts. Some banks, however, pool and manage the funds of small trusts. Trustee services are examined in greater detail in Chapter 20.

Safe-Deposit Boxes. For an average annual fee of $15 to $25, banks and thrifts rent safe-deposit boxes, in which valuable papers and possessions can be placed. Safe-deposit boxes protect valuables from loss due to fire, theft, or negligence. A box is an especially good place to store such items as stock and bond certificates, insurance policies (excluding life insurance policies), property records, and personal documents.

Bank Wire Transfers. A bank wire service can be used to send money to someone in another city. Even though most transfers are done for businesses and involve large sums of money, small sums can be sent to individuals as well. Money can be electronically transferred to another bank where a cashier's check is issued. The charge for this service varies from bank to bank.

THE ELECTRONIC REVOLUTION IN BANKING

On New Year's Day 1983, a 69-year-old man was kidnapped in Los Angeles, California, by two would-be robbers who instructed the man to drive to his bank. When they got there, the bandits forced the man to hand over his bank card and reveal his personal identification number. One bandit then left the car and punched the information into the automated teller machine. The machine refused to cooperate. The second bandit tried as well but could not make the machine hand over the kidnapped man's money.[15]

This somewhat unusual example of banking in the computer age provides an appropriate opening to a discussion of electronic banking—an unmistakable trend. In the future more and more banking will be done electronically.

ELECTRONIC FUNDS TRANSFER

A few years from now cash, checks, and bank passbooks may be as passé as the nickel candy bar. In their place may be an electronic system that makes bank transactions through sophisticated computer technology. This system—known as *electronic funds transfer,* or *EFT*—relies on such tools as automated teller machines, telephones, personal computers, and even televisions.

Automated Teller Machines. Almost before anyone knew it, the automated teller machine, or *ATM,* was a fact of life. After a poor showing at the end of the 1970s, ATMs surprised nearly everyone when their sales nearly doubled between 1980 and 1982 to their current level of 26,000 units. The reason for their success, however, is no surprise: banks like ATMs and so do their customers.[16]

To the delight of cost-conscious bankers, automated teller machines have reduced the need for bank tellers and may soon even replace bank branches. Despite their cost of $20,000 and up, they are far cheaper to operate than a fully-staffed bank and can be set up in airports and shopping centers, where bank branches often cannot be. Moreover, they are tireless: most ATMs are open 24 hours a day, 7 days a week.

Consumers benefit because they are simple, fast, and convenient to operate. By simply inserting a special debit card, which acts as the key to the ATM, and punching in a personal identity code, consumers can make deposits and withdrawals, transfer money from one account to another, make

---

electronic funds transfer (EFT): *an electronic system that makes bank transactions through sophisticated computer technology.*

ATM: *an abbreviation for automatic teller machine—electronic banking machine permitting bank customers to make deposits, cash withdrawals, and funds transfers at any time by using a special coded access card.*

payments on certain loans and credit card accounts, borrow money from a credit card, and check a current balance. Even though most ATMs are located in bank branches, an increasing number are found in supermarkets, shops, and other point-of-sale locations—places where people are most likely to run out of money.

The Telephone. Thousands of people across the country pay their bills by phone. That is, their bank or thrift pays directly whatever bills they list ($1,385 to the college bursar, $40 to the telephone company, $150 to the ophthalmologist) after receiving a phone call from them. Many of these systems permit electronic payments by using a push-button phone. Such a system eliminates the need to write checks and saves the bank the cost of clearing checks. At the end of each month, the individual's bank statement lists all the telephone transactions made.

The Personal Computer and the Television. In New York City, some of Chemical Bank's customers bank at home by way of a television and an Atari home computer. In Columbus, Ohio, selected customers of Bank One are experimenting with a system that connects their TV set to their bank accounts by way of a telephone hookup. When customers want to pay bills and analyze their most recent checking and savings account statements, they simply tap out signals on a special key pad. Revolutionary as these banking systems seem today, experts predict that they will be commonplace within this decade.

A typical electronic banking system works in the following manner. When it is time to pay the monthly bills, you call up the bank's channel on your TV monitor and then insert a personal identification code, which gives access to your personal account. As each bill appears on the screen, you punch out instructions on the computer, which tells the bank how to handle the bill (pay the telephone company in full; pay $500 to the bursar; no payment to the ophthalmologist). The account balance is reduced by the amount of each payment so that at the end of the bill-paying session, you can see how much money still remains.

HOW EFT IS USED TODAY

Even though banking at home—the real EFT revolution—is still ahead of us, electronic transfers are already used for the automatic transfer of funds and payment of bills, direct deposit of paychecks and dividends, and direct deposit of Social Security checks and other retirement payments. Many people who are concerned about the safety or inconvenience of receiving their Social Security payment by mail request that the funds be transferred electronically to their financial institution. After this electronic transfer is made, many banks and thrifts send Social Security recipients a deposit notice. All institutions note the deposit on the customer's monthly statement.[17]

Chemical Bank's PRONTO System of Electronic Banking

Banking at home is already a reality for thousands of checking account customers of New York's Chemical Bank. In 1983, the bank made PRONTO available commercially: the first major electronic banking system that enables customers to carry out all their banking activities at home. Bank customers can pay their bills to more than 1,000 merchants, transfer funds from one account to another, check their current balance, budget, receive local and national news, and more, all by way of an Atari, IBM, Apple, or Commodore personal computer and PRONTO software linked to the bank's computer by way of a modem.

Consumers need not know anything about computer language to operate the PRONTO system since all questions and answers are made in plain English. The fee for this service is $12 per month.

With computer terminals becoming a common fixture of the American workplace and with children learning how to operate computer terminals at school, more and more people are becoming "terminal-literate"—knowledgeable enough to operate a terminal in their home. For these millions of people, operating an electronic banking system like PRONTO is only one step away from playing a winning game of PAC MAN—and certainly a lot easier.

Source: Chemical Bank news release on PRONTO.

FLAWS IN THE SYSTEM

A major problem with the electronic banking system occurs when something goes wrong—and occasionally it does. This can be an extremely frustrating process, since you have no cancelled checks and no deposit or withdrawal slips.

Electronic banking also takes away certain options. You can no longer stop payment on a check since the funds transfer is instantaneous. And you can no longer indulge in the practice of writing checks before you deposit money to cover them—banking, so to speak, "on the *float*" (the time it takes a check to clear).

float: the time it takes a check to clear.

When Errors Occur. To protect consumers from electronic fund transfer abuse, Congress passed a law in 1978 setting up the following safeguards:[18]

1. Cash machines must provide a record of cash transactions.

2. Consumers must receive a regular statement from their banks that includes EFT transactions.

3. There must be notification that preauthorized deposits are made.

4. You must be allowed to stop a preauthorized payment up to 3 business days before the payment is scheduled.

5. If a preauthorized payment is missed, the bank must prove that it made the payment. If it cannot, it is responsible for any late charges that result from the mistake.

6. If your EFT card is lost or stolen, your liability is limited to $50 if you notify the bank within 2 business days and $500 if you notify that bank

Figure 6-3
CITIBANK CORRECTION-OF-ERROR STATEMENT

In case of errors or questions about your electronic transfers.

Contact us as soon as you can, if you think your statement or receipt is wrong or if you need more information about a transfer listed on the statement or receipt. We must hear from you no later than 60 days after we sent the FIRST statement on which the problem or error appeared.

1 Tell us your name and account number (if any).
2 Describe the error or the transfer you are unsure about, and explain as clearly as you can why you believe it is an error or why you need more information.
3 Tell us the dollar amount of the suspected error.

If you tell us orally, we may require that you send us your complaint or question in writing within 10 business days.

We will tell you the results of our investigation within 10 business days after we hear from you and will correct any error promptly. If we need more time, however, we may take up to 45 days to investigate your complaint or question. If we decide to do this, we will recredit your account within 10 business days for the amount you think is in error, so that you will have the use of the money during the time it takes us to complete our investigation. If we ask you to put your complaint or question in writing and we do not receive it within 10 business days, we may not recredit your account.

If we decide that there was no error, we will send you a written explanation within 3 business days after we finish our investigation. You may ask for copies of the documents that we used in our investigation.

See back panel for more information.

Source: Citibank, N.A.

after the 2-day deadline has passed. If you wait longer than 60 days after receiving your first statement that shows the mistake, your loss might be unlimited.

7. If you receive an unsolicited debit card in the mail, it must be invalid. It becomes usable only after you open the account with the bank and indicate your personal identification code.

8. The financial institution must tell you its procedure to investigate errors. (See Figure 6-3 for the correction-of-error statement sent to customers by New York's Citibank.)

9. Finally, all these terms must be disclosed to you in writing when you open an account.

HOW SAFE IS YOUR MONEY?

The American banking system is a trusted element of the United States economy. Since the Great Depression, when the U.S. government established the Federal Deposit Insurance Corporation (FDIC) and the Federal Savings and Loan Insurance Corporation (FSLIC), Americans have had their faith repaid in full: no depositor has lost money in an insured account.

But America's perception of the stability of the American banking system is changing—and so is Americans' trust that their money is absolutely safe. Indeed, trust has turned to anxiety for many Americans. According to a recent survey, nine out of ten people questioned expressed some concern about the stability of the U.S. banking system.[19]

Much of this concern centers on the nation's approximately 3,600 savings and loan associations and mutual savings banks, 80 percent of which lost money in 1981. In addition, during 1983, 48 commercial banks failed—the largest number in 46 years. The problems faced by the nation's banks and thrifts focused attention for the first time in years on the FDIC and the FSLIC and their role in safeguarding the $1.9 trillion deposited by individuals and businesses.

THE FEDERAL DEPOSIT INSURANCE CORPORATION (FDIC)

Established in 1934, the *FDIC* safeguards deposits in more than 14,000 commercial banks as well as in 424 mutual savings banks. These deposits are guaranteed by the federal government for up to $100,000 for each account.

To assure yourself of full insurance coverage, you must be aware of certain FDIC rules. If you have two or more accounts in your name, these accounts are covered to a maximum of $100,000, even if the accounts are at different branches of the same bank. Thus, if you have $75,000 in one account and $50,000 in another, $25,000 of your money is unprotected. This problem can be avoided by opening a joint account with a family member. In this case, the FDIC fully protects the money in the joint account as well as deposits made by each individual into individual accounts. Still another option is to open individual accounts in different banks or thrifts.

FDIC insurance covers all kinds of accounts, including checking, savings, trust, bank money-market, and Christmas club as well as certificates of deposit, and so on. IRA and Keogh plans are also guaranteed up to $100,000.

FDIC: *the Federal Deposit Insurance Corporation, which regulates banking practices and insures deposits in most commercial banks and mutual savings banks up to $100,000.*

THE FEDERAL SAVINGS AND LOAN INSURANCE CORPORATION (FSLIC)

The *FSLIC* insures deposits in almost all of the nation's savings and loan associations. Operating under the same rules as the FDIC, the FSLIC is obligated to begin repaying insured deposits within ten days of a bank closing. If any money remains after these accounts are paid, the FSLIC will attempt to pay back uninsured accounts as well.

Both the FSLIC and the FDIC are self-sufficient bodies, drawing funds from their own special reserve accounts in case of bank failure. In 1981, for example, the FSLIC had approximately $6.5 billion in reserve and had access to an additional $750 million from the U.S. Treasury. Although this money covers only a fraction of the $500 billion deposited in savings accounts, federal officials consider it sufficient, for at worst they envision that only a few savings and loans will fail at any one time.[20]

FSLIC: *the Federal Savings and Loan Insurance Corporation, which regulates savings and loans and insures deposits in most savings and loan associations up to $100,000.*

The Federal Deposit Insurance Corporation was founded during the Great Depression of the 1930s to protect the public against bank failures. Previously, hard-earned savings could be wiped out overnight if a bank could not remain in operation. In this August 1931 photograph, for example, depositors flock—too late—to withdraw their money from a New York City bank that has been closed by the state.

Part of the reason so few banks and thrifts fail is the watchdog role played by the FDIC and the FSLIC. When either body suspects trouble, it quickly steps in and arranges a merger, and the floundering institution simply becomes part of a healthier one.

CREDIT UNION INSURANCE

Credit unions have their own insurance system. All credit unions chartered by the federal government and the majority of state-chartered credit unions are insured for up to $100,000 by the National Credit Union Administration.

MONEY-MARKET MUTUAL FUNDS: AN UNINSURED OPTION

"No investor has ever lost a penny in a modern money fund," says money-market analyst William E. Donoghue. "There is really nothing to worry about."[21] Although money-market funds are uninsured, most experts share the view that the system is nearly 100-percent safe. The main reason for this confidence is the investments chosen by money-fund managers. Money funds invest in the "money market," which includes short-term loans to the federal government, large corporations, and banks. During a recession, these investments are extremely conservative. According to William C. Melton, money-market economist at Irving Trust Company, "When the money fund managers now say they are 'lending long' they mean 52 days; when they say 'risky' they mean General Motors."[22]

CHOOSING THE RIGHT PLACE FOR YOUR MONEY

There are a lot of reasons for choosing one financial institution over another. Some of the reasons are good while others are not. Most people would agree that the following factors should make some difference in your choice—even though the importance of each factor varies from person to person.

CONVENIENCE

Many people choose a financial institution simply because it is conveniently located—perhaps just around the corner or in the local shopping center. Although convenience of this kind cannot be minimized, it is becoming less important as the financial institution arena grows. Today millions of people mail deposits into money-market mutual funds whose main offices are located thousands of miles from their homes. Countless others use the mail to transact business with the brokerage house that handles their certificate of deposit or cash management accounts. And still others use commercial banks or thrifts located on the other side of town for some services, such as long-term CDs.

Consumers should consider maintaining at least a small savings, checking, or NOW account in a commercial bank or thrift close to home so that they can conveniently cash checks. A bank or thrift with several branches or automated teller machines is especially convenient.

SERVICES

By all means, bank where you get most of the financial services you need. It is inefficient to go from one institution to another to do your day-to-day checking and saving or to use the safe-deposit box of one bank and the electronic banking facilities of another. However, in these times of competitive services and rates, it may be a mistake to have an exclusive relationship with one institution.

Personal Attention. Many consumers judge the services a financial institution offers by the kind of service its personnel offers. Put off by computers, computerized letters, and bank officers who move in and out of a branch before customers get to know them, many people choose to do business with small banks and familiar bankers, whom they learn to trust and to whom they listen. Some banks now use a personal banking system that assigns a specific bank employee to each account.

Today's bankers understand the need to maintain personal relationships in an age of impersonal technology. At the Burke & Herbert Bank in Alexandria, Virginia, for example, bank vice-president Edward F. Johnson sits by the door of the main office ready to answer customers' questions about the confusing array of savings instruments and loans the bank offers.[23]

FEES

Before deregulation, financial institutions offered a number of free services for depositors. These services included free checks and checking, checkbook-balancing assistance, and token charges for a bounced check. These services were paid for by the money that the banks and thrifts earned on passbook savings accounts paying 5.25 and 5.5 percent interest. By lending this money at higher rates, they were guaranteed a large enough profit to afford to provide these services.

When interest rates rose, however, many of these free services disappeared. Many financial institutions revised their consumer fee structures and instituted charges where there were none before. In New York, for example, Chemical Bank, the nation's sixth largest bank, now charges a quarterly fee of $4 on savings accounts that fall below an average of $400. The Arizona Bank in Phoenix requires that customers keep $1,500 in their interest-bearing checking accounts—$500 more than the bank required before interest rates rose—to avoid service charges.

Although they are becoming more popular, these fees are by no means universal. According to a recent study, for example, only 20 percent of all U.S. banks charge fees on small savings accounts, while 48 percent impose maintenance charges on credit cards and only 25 percent charge senior citizens for their checking services.[24] So, with banks and thrifts competing aggressively, it pays to shop for the institution with the lowest fees. Similarly, the fees charged by money-market funds, brokerage houses, and such financial supermarkets as Sears vary on such items as new checks, bounced checks, and minimum-balance violations. Comparative shopping is again in order.

INSURANCE

Millions of Americans still do not trust money funds because they are uninsured. This attitude is as valid as any other, for the willingness to take a risk—even a small risk—is highly individual. It is important to understand your own need for security before putting your money in anything but a fully insured bank or thrift account. Whatever the first choice, you should understand and feel comfortable with the risks involved.

HOW TO USE CHECKING, NOW, AND SUPER-NOW ACCOUNTS

Checking, NOW, and super-NOW accounts are almost indispensable in these complex financial times. Aside from their convenience, they enable you to keep track of your money just by looking at your check records. Moreover, a cancelled check or a listing of each written check offers proof that a bill has been paid. Let's look at how these accounts should be used.

CHOOSING AN INDIVIDUAL OR JOINT ACCOUNT

As their names imply, an individual checking account is in the name of one person and a joint checking account is in the names of two or more persons. Each type of account has advantages and disadvantages.

An individual checking account gives you complete control over the money in the account. It guarantees that there will be no surprises: you will never find too little money in the account because your spouse, roommate, parent, or child wrote a check without telling you. However, an individual account seriously limits the use of your checking account, especially if you are married. Whenever a check must be written, you must write it.

For joint accounts, it is best to establish certain rules. Keep just one checkbook in a convenient place—the desk drawer, for example—where the monthly bills can be written. Every time you take a blank check, you can initial the stub to indicate that it is your responsibility to record the amount. Your checking partner follows the same procedure. This system ensures that you will have an accurate checking record when you reconcile the monthly statement.

OPENING AN ACCOUNT

Whether you choose a joint or an individual checking account, you must follow certain simple procedures to open the account. All accounts start with an application form on which you are asked to provide your name, address, employment background, and other personal data. You must also sign signature cards so that the bank can verify that the signatures on the checks are actually yours. Your signature safeguards the money in your account, for the bank will honor only those checks bearing it.

Once an account number is issued, you must deposit money into the account. As we have seen, regular checking accounts require that you maintain a minimum balance, while special checking accounts do not. NOW and

Super-NOW accounts also require a minimum balance to avoid penalties and the loss of interest.

Next you will receive a small supply of checks and deposit slips printed with your account number. Within a few weeks you will receive a large supply of personalized checks and deposit slips printed not only with the account number but also with your name and address. Most banks charge a small fee for these items.

MAINTAINING AN ACCOUNT

The key to maintaining an accurate checking account is record keeping. The only way to keep track of the account is to record diligently every check and deposit in the check register.

MAKING DEPOSITS

When you deposit money into your checking account, you must fill out a deposit slip. If you hand the deposit to a bank teller, you will receive a carbon copy, usually stamped with the time and date of the transaction. If the deposit is mailed to the bank, you will receive a receipt a few days later. If you use an automated teller, the receipt is subject to verification by bank personnel, who open your deposit envelope at the end of the business day. In all these cases, you should keep the deposit receipt until the deposit shows up on the monthly statement.

WAITING FOR CHECKS TO CLEAR

Unlike a cash deposit, which is immediately available for use, a check deposited in your account may take anywhere from several days to several weeks to clear. (Checks drawn on out-of-town banks and thrifts take longer to clear than those drawn on local institutions.)

It is important not to write checks against the deposit until you are sure the check has cleared. If you write a check prematurely, before the deposit has been credited to your account, the bank will not honor it.

OVERDRAFTS

overdraft: *a check written for more than is in an account; also known as a bounced check.*

An *overdraft*, commonly known as a bounced check, is a check written for more money than is in an account. The check will be marked "insufficient funds" and returned to the person to whom it was written. Banks will bounce a check even if you have enough money in your account to cover it partially.

As soon as an overdraft is received, the bank will mail a notification. You will then have to deposit enough money to cover the check (most banks allow the check to be redeposited once), and you must pay a fee, which may be $5, $10, or more. The company or person to whom the check was written may also charge you for the inconvenience.

To protect yourself against overdrafts, a line of credit can be added to your checking account. Every time you write a check for more money than you have in your account, an automatic loan is issued to cover the amount of the overdraft. Some banks withdraw money for the exact sum of the overdraft, while others withdraw only even $100 sums. These overdraft privileges are limited to a prearranged credit line.

STOPPING A CHECK

There are some situations in which you write a check but do not want the payment to be made. Suppose, for example, a check you mail to a company in payment of a bill is never received. After waiting a few weeks to see if the check is delivered, you issue a new check to take the place of the first. At this point your only protection against the first check being cashed at some later date is to issue a stop-check order. You may also want to stop a check if you are unhappy with someone's services.

The mechanics of stopping a check are simple. The bank must be notified within a reasonable time after the check is issued that you do not want it to be paid. Most states allow you to issue a stop-order by telephone as long as it is followed up by a written authorization. In general, should the bank cash your check after you have issued a stop-order, it must reimburse you for any loss.

HOW TO WRITE AND ENDORSE A CHECK

If you have an active checking account, you may write and endorse dozens of checks a month. Therefore, it is important to know the proper check-writing and endorsement procedures.

Writing a Check. Be sure to complete the check stub or check register *before* you write your check. This simple habit will prevent you from forgetting the amount of the check—an omission that makes it impossible to balance the checkbook. Always keep in mind the possibility of check alteration. By following the rules listed in Figure 6-4, you will make it extremely difficult for anyone to change what you have written: always write checks in ink, and if you make a mistake, write "void" across the face of the check before you tear it up and throw it away. It is always a mistake to sign a blank check even if you are giving it to a trusted relative or friend. If the check is lost or stolen, it can be cashed.

Endorsing a Check. Once written, a check must be endorsed, or signed by the person to whom it is made out. There are three types of check endorsement: blank, restrictive, and special.

Figure 6-4
PROPER CHECK-WRITING PROCEDURE

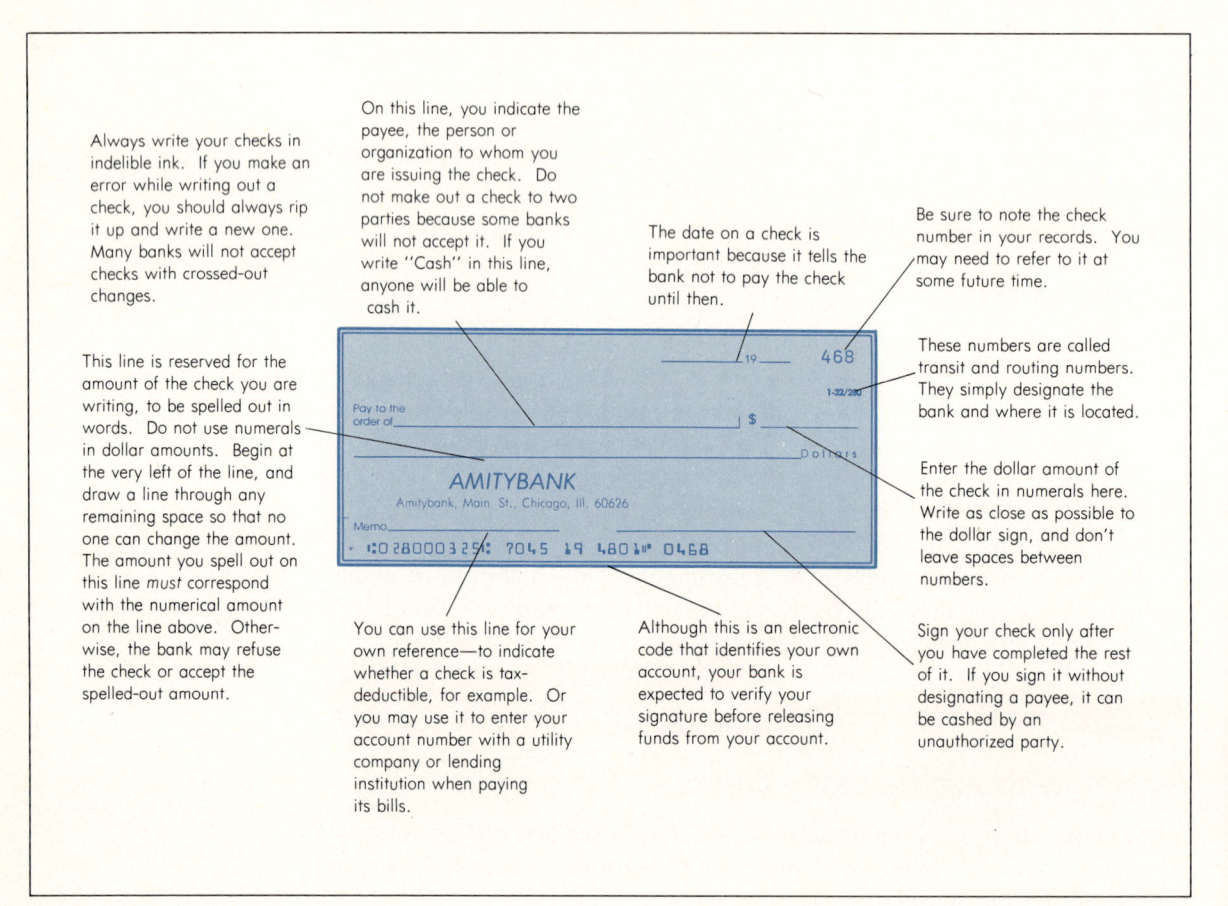

Always write your checks in indelible ink. If you make an error while writing out a check, you should always rip it up and write a new one. Many banks will not accept checks with crossed-out changes.

On this line, you indicate the payee, the person or organization to whom you are issuing the check. Do not make out a check to two parties because some banks will not accept it. If you write "Cash" in this line, anyone will be able to cash it.

The date on a check is important because it tells the bank not to pay the check until then.

Be sure to note the check number in your records. You may need to refer to it at some future time.

This line is reserved for the amount of the check you are writing, to be spelled out in words. Do not use numerals in dollar amounts. Begin at the very left of the line, and draw a line through any remaining space so that no one can change the amount. The amount you spell out on this line *must* correspond with the numerical amount on the line above. Otherwise, the bank may refuse the check or accept the spelled-out amount.

These numbers are called transit and routing numbers. They simply designate the bank and where it is located.

Enter the dollar amount of the check in numerals here. Write as close as possible to the dollar sign, and don't leave spaces between numbers.

You can use this line for your own reference—to indicate whether a check is tax-deductible, for example. Or you may use it to enter your account number with a utility company or lending institution when paying its bills.

Although this is an electronic code that identifies your own account, your bank is expected to verify your signature before releasing funds from your account.

Sign your check only after you have completed the rest of it. If you sign it without designating a payee, it can be cashed by an unauthorized party.

---

blank endorsement: the most common type of endorsement, in which the person to whom a check is made out usually signs his or her name on the back.

restrictive endorsement: an endorsement that limits further negotiation of a check, such as "For Deposit Only."

The *blank endorsement* is the most common type of endorsement. The person to whom the check is made out merely signs his or her name on the back of the check. For example, if Sandy McCormick makes out a check to Jane Freelander and then Jane signs her name on the back of the check, the check is as good as cash.

The *restrictive endorsement* limits further negotiation of a check. For example, no one except the bank can cash the check if Jane endorses it as follows:

> For Deposit Only
> Account #247-5668
> Jane Freelander

Always use a restrictive endorsement when mailing checks to the bank for deposit.

A *special endorsement* names a third party who can cash the check. For example, Jane can take the check from Sandy and sign it over to Stanley Hargrove. The special endorsement should read:

>Pay to the order of Stanley Hargrove
>Jane Freelander

special endorsement: an endorsement that names a third party who can cash the check.

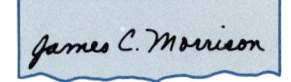

James C. Morrison
blank endorsement

*For deposit only to account #12-3456789
James C. Morrison*
restrictive endorsement

*Pay to the order of
James Hughes
James C. Morrison*
special endorsement

RECONCILING THE MONTHLY BANK STATEMENT

Consumers should reconcile their bank statements every month. This statement shows deposits to the account, deductions from the account for checks and various service charges, dividends (in the case of NOW and Super-NOW accounts), and the current balance. Start by placing your cancelled checks in numerical order and then note in your checkbook that they have been processed by the bank (some banks automatically list cancelled checks in numerical order).

Compare the computer marking in the lower right-hand corner of the check to make certain that it agrees with the amount of the check, for it is this computer read-out that will be listed on the statement and deducted from the account. Next, compare your record of deposits with the deposits shown on the bank statement. Then subtract any service fees charged by the bank from the balance shown in your checkbook.

Now total all the checks you have written that are not included on the bank statement. Subtract this amount from the balance shown on the bank statement. In addition, if you have made deposits to the account that have not yet been processed by the bank, add them to the balance shown on the account statement. Most banks provide a handy form on the back of your bank statement for balancing your checkbook. Figure 6-5 shows how this form is used. If the final amount does not agree with the checkbook balance, then check the arithmetic for a possible error.

Here are two helpful hints for locating errors:

1. If the difference in the two totals is $1, $10, or $100, the error is probably a subtraction or addition error in the check register.

2. If the difference between the bank statement and the check register is exactly divisible by nine, a transposition error is likely to have occurred. Such an error results from the reversal of two digits in any position, such as $34.67 entered in the check register and $43.67 written on the check.

SPECIAL TYPES OF CHECKS

On some occasions a check drawn on a personal account is not the best way to transfer funds. Certified checks, cashier's checks, and traveler's checks are alternatives to personal checks.

Figure 6-5
BALANCING YOUR CHECKBOOK

This form is provided for your convenience to help you verify the balance listed on this statement.

Please report any discrepancies on this statement to your Branch immediately!
Send inquiries to: The East New York Savings Bank
P.O. Box 2087
N.Y., N.Y. 10117

OUTSTANDING DRAFTS NOT CHARGED TO ACCOUNT

No.	$	
	66	
	50	
	348	32
	70	93
	74	81
	769	03
	209	79
	438	
	69	67
	676	20
	228	
TOTAL	$ 3000	75

ACCOUNT BALANCE SHOWN ON STATEMENT $ 2,124.55

ADD (+) DEPOSITS NOT CREDITED TO THIS STATEMENT $ 1,799.37
....
....
....
....

TOTAL $ 3,923.92

SUBTRACT (−) OUTSTANDING DRAFTS (FROM COLUMN AT LEFT) $ 3,000.75

BALANCE $ 923.17

This should agree with your records after you have deducted Miscellaneous Charges, if any, shown on reverse side from your account.

NOTE: Please notify us immediately of any Name or Address change on this account.

IMPORTANT INFORMATION CONCERNING CASH RESERVE
(if Applicable)

− Line of credit in use.

A In lieu of returning this draft for uncollected funds we have applied it against your cash reserve.

The amount of the FINANCE CHARGE may be determined by multiplying the DAILY AVERAGE BALANCE by the number of days in the current statement period and then multiplying the product by the DAILY PERIODIC RATE.

A negative balance (−XXX.XX) in the BALANCE column represents the amount of the cash reserve in use and a positive balance (XXX.XX) represents the balance of your funds in this account.

Source: Form courtesy of The East New York Savings Bank.

CERTIFIED CHECKS AND CASHIER'S CHECKS

Receiving a personal check for $100 is no guarantee that you will receive $100 in cash. If there is not $100 in the account, the check will bounce, and you may have difficulty getting your money. So, in some instances, you might insist on a *certified check*. A certified check is a personal check that the writer of the check presents to his or her bank for certification, which amounts to guaranteed payment. When the bank certifies the check, the funds are immediately withdrawn from the check-writer's account and placed in a special account of the bank. Payment of funds to the check's recipient then becomes the bank's responsibility. A certified check looks like any other check drawn on a personal account but has the word *certified* stamped on its face. Most banks charge a small fee for certifying a check.

A *cashier's check* is another type of guaranteed check, but it is not drawn on a personal account. Instead, a customer purchases a check drawn on the bank's general funds. Naturally, the bank will not issue a cashier's check unless it is paid for. A small fee is typically charged by banks for issuing a cashier's check.

If either a certified or a cashier's check is not used for the purpose for which it was intended, it should not be destroyed. A certified check should be taken to the bank, endorsed "not used for purpose intended," and signed by the depositor. A cashier's check should also be returned to the bank and endorsed in a similar manner; the funds will then be returned to the customer. If either instrument is lost, stolen, or destroyed, the customer will have to post a bond, usually for twice the check's amount, in order to recover the funds. There may be a substantial delay in receiving these funds.

certified check: a personal check for which a bank transfers the amount of the check to a special account of its own, thus making payment the bank's responsibility and so guaranteeing that the check is good.

cashier's check: a guaranteed check that is drawn on a bank's general funds after the bank has received funds and a fee from the person purchasing the check.

TRAVELER'S CHECKS

Like other special checks, *traveler's checks* are guaranteed by their issuer. As a means of ensuring the purchaser's identification, they are signed once when purchased and again when cashed. These checks are prepaid in specific denominations, such as $10, $20, $50, and $100. Purchasers of traveler's checks should keep the record of the checks' serial numbers separate from the checks themselves because most issuers will make immediate refunds of lost or stolen checks if the proper identification is provided. In most cases fees for traveler's checks are about $1 for every $100 worth of checks purchased. Although they provide no return on their purchase price, they are good forever.

traveler's check: a guaranteed check used by travelers; it is also insured.

HOW TO RESOLVE BANKING PROBLEMS

What do you do if a deposit is not credited to your account, if a fraudulent check is cashed against the account, or if a stop-check order is not honored?

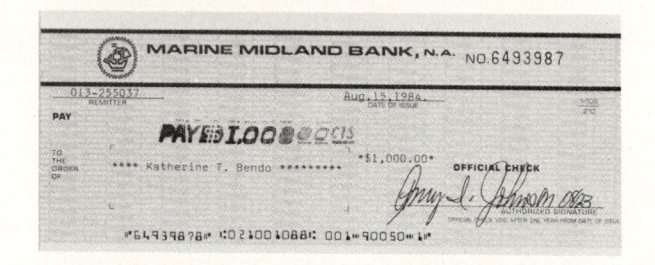

Top: certified check; middle: cashier's check; bottom: traveler's check.

Your first step is to contact the manager of your bank. Give the manager your name, address, and account number and explain what happened. He or she may insist on documentation—a deposit slip that shows the discrepancy, for example, or an incorrectly coded check.

If after you have presented these documents the bank does not correct the error, you will have to move beyond the branch-manager level. Write to the bank's consumer relations department, including photocopies of all the relevant documents with the letter. If this does not work, write to the bank president. As one industry spokesperson remarked, "When the president starts asking why he or she is being bothered with a consumer complaint, you're going to get action fast."[25]

If the problem is still not resolved, you can send your complaint to the agency that regulates the bank. Table 6-2 lists these agencies, their identifying symbols, and their addresses.

Table 6-2
WHERE TO COMPLAIN

Type of Bank	Identification Marks	Where to Complain
National bank	The word "national" appears in the bank's name, or the initials N.A. appear after the bank's name.	Comptroller of the Currency, 490 L'Enfant Plaza East, S.W., Washington, D.C. 20219.
State bank, member Federal Reserve, FDIC-insured	Look for two signs at the bank: "Member, Federal Reserve System," and "Deposits Insured by Federal Deposit Insurance Corporation."	Board of Governors, Federal Reserve System, 20th Street & Constitution Avenue, N.W., Washington, D.C. 20551.
State nonmember bank or state-chartered mutual savings bank	FDIC sign will be displayed; Federal Reserve sign will not.	Office of Consumer and Compliance Programs, Federal Deposit Insurance Corporation, 550 17th Street, N.W., Washington, D.C. 20429.
Federal savings and loan association	The word "federal" appears in the name. A sign on the door or in the lobby says: "Deposits Insured by FSLIC," or Federal Savings and Loan Insurance Corporation.	Federal Home Loan Bank Board, Office of Community and Consumer Division, 17th & G Streets, N.W., Washington, D.C. 20552.
Federally chartered credit union	Look for this sign: Member, National Credit Union Administration.	National Credit Union Administration, Office of the Administrator, 1776 G Street, N.W., Washington, D.C. 20456.

Source: Adapted from "News You Can Use in Your Personal Planning: Bank Complaints," *U.S. News & World Report,* March 9, 1981, p. 69.

SUMMARY

Money consists of currency and any funds that can be converted easily into checks, paper money, and coins. Everyone needs to keep some cash or other readily available funds on hand to pay both regular and unexpected expenses. Savings is the way that additional money is accumulated. Chapter 6 points out the importance of setting savings goals.

Various types of savings instruments are available to consumers. These include passbook savings accounts, Christmas or holiday club accounts, certificates of deposit, bank money-market accounts, money-market mutual funds, treasury bills, and U.S. savings bonds. All have specific features that should be evaluated when deciding where to place your savings dollars.

There are a variety of financial institutions available to serve customers. The deregulation trend has meant that there is increased competition among such financial institutions as commercial banks, savings and loan associations, mutual savings banks, credit unions, money-market mutual funds, and financial supermarkets like Sears and Merrill Lynch.

Among the new services today's banks offer are the NOW (a negotiable-order-of-withdrawal) account, which combines savings and checking accounts and pays interest on deposits, and the Super-NOW account, a checking-type account that offers a higher yield than the regular NOW account. In addition, banks provide such financial services as a variety of savings instruments, consumer loans, bank credit cards, pension plans, trustee services, safe-deposit boxes, and bank wire transfers.

The electronic revolution has also had an impact on financial institutions. Automated teller machines (ATMs) are now commonplace. Telephone transfer services and even computer-linked banking services are available in some cases.

Either the Federal Deposit Insurance Corporation (FDIC) or the Federal Savings and Loan Insurance Corporation (FSLIC) protects the accounts (up to $100,000) of most commercial banks, mutual savings banks, and savings and loan associations. Money-market mutual funds are uninsured, but they are invested in conservative securities, which are considered to be safe. Insurance along with convenience, service, personal attention, and fees are factors to consider when selecting a financial institution.

Chapter 6 concludes with discussion of how to use checking, NOW, Super-NOW accounts, and special types of checks and how to resolve banking problems.

REVIEW QUESTIONS

1. Briefly define the following terms:

   money
   barter
   effective rate of interest
   thrifts
   certificates of deposit
   treasury bill
   treasury note
   treasury bonds
   commercial banks
   savings and loan associations
   mutual savings banks
   credit unions
   financial supermarkets
   Pepper-McFadden Act
   NOW account
   share-draft account
   Super-NOW account
   electronic funds transfer (EFT)
   ATM
   float
   FDIC
   FSLIC
   overdraft
   blank endorsement
   restrictive endorsement
   special endorsement
   certified check
   cashier's check
   traveler's check

2. What is the role of savings and money management in modern personal finance?

3. Identify and compare the various types of savings instruments.

4. Discuss the impact of deregulation on the banking industry.

5. Identify and compare the various types of financial institutions that serve consumers.

6. What are the various types of accounts and services offered by commercial banks and thrifts?

7. Comment on the electronic revolution in banking.

8. How safe is money invested in the various financial institutions?

9. What factors should be considered when selecting a place to put your money?

10. Explain how to use a checking account, NOW account, and Super-NOW account.

CASES AND EXERCISES

1. Consider the case of two banks. First Mutual used the LIFO technique for calculating interest. By contrast, Second Federal used the day-of-deposit-to-day-of-withdrawal approach. Suppose a person deposited $1,000 on May 2 and another $500 on June 30 but withdrew $400 on July 28. Which of these banks would pay the depositor the most interest for this period?

MONEY MANAGEMENT   **169**

2. Norm Simpkins recently sold his condominium and earned a profit of $10,000. Since he has decided to rent a townhouse in the near future, he is interested in earning maximum returns from his $10,000. Norm is currently considering savings deposits at four local financial institutions. First State Bank will pay 12 percent compounded annually, while Consumer Finance offers 12 percent compounded on a daily basis. The credit union at the firm where Norm is employed offers 12 percent compounded quarterly. Norm's final alternative, a local savings and loan association, will match the 12-percent annual rate compounded on a semiannual basis.

    What interest would Norm earn for a one-year deposit at each of these four financial institutions? What is the effective interest rate at each institution? What additional factors should Norm consider prior to making a choice?

3. Distinguish between a bank's money-market account and a money-market mutual fund. Give a general profile of the type of saver who is likely to be most attracted to a money-market mutual fund. Describe a typical depositor in a bank's money-market account.

4. Why would a firm such as Sears be interested in expanding into financial services? What special advantages can the firm offer potential clients? What disadvantages are present in such an arrangement?

5. Suppose an investor wanted to deposit $200,000 received from the sale of a commercial property in Third Commercial Bank. Could the investor secure FDIC coverage for the entire amount by setting up two separate accounts—one labeled Edward M. Jameson, and the other, E. M. Jameson? Explain. What alternatives exist for securing such coverage?

ANSWERS TO PERSONAL FINANCE I.Q. TEST

1. Fiction. 2. Fact. 3. Fiction. 4. Fiction. 5. Fact. 6. Fiction.

HOW MARCIE STILLWELL REACHED HER PERSONAL FINANCIAL DECISION

Professor Bohn explained to Marcie that it is the amount of money currently available in a bank account that determines whether or not a check will bounce. Each time she wrote a check, she needed to subtract that amount from her running balance. And, of course, she should add in any deposits or deduct bank service charges.

Then, when her bank statement came each month, she should make sure it agreed with her accounting. This was important not only to ensure that the bank hadn't made an error, but also to double-check her own arithmetic. To give an example, Professor Bohn commented, "Imagine that one day you're distracted and absent-mindedly add in a check you wrote for $100—it happens to all of us. How would you know you needed to correct this mistake? That's what the bank statement is for."

The two then sat down to put Marcie's checkbook in order. Professor Bohn also showed Marcie how to use her checking account as a tool to help her establish—and stick to—a budget. At the end Marcie, chagrined at not having understood the obvious, vowed never to bounce a check again.

LEARNING OBJECTIVES

1. To explain the three C's of credit. / *2.* To compare the alternative sources of consumer credit. / *3.* To distinguish between open-end installment credit and closed-end installment credit. / *4.* To classify the types of consumer credit on the bases of form and method of repayment. / *5.* To identify several appropriate reasons for borrowing money. / *6.* To explain the role of credit counselors in personal finance. / *7.* To identify and briefly explain the features of each of the major federal laws affecting consumer credit and borrowing.

TESTING YOUR PERSONAL FINANCE I.Q.

	FACT	FICTION
1. One of the best ways to use credit is for impulse purchases.	☐	☐
2. No more than 10 to 20 percent of an individual's take-home pay should be used to repay installment debt.	☐	☐
3. Financial deregulation has ended state usury laws.	☐	☐
4. The Bankruptcy Reform Act of 1978 is commonly referred to as the Rule of 78s.	☐	☐
5. The three C's of credit are customers, cash, and cosigners.	☐	☐
6. People who borrow on their life insurance policies do not have to repay the loan.	☐	☐

The materials in this chapter assist in separating fact from fiction. Your answers can be checked on page 204.

CHAPTER SEVEN

BORROWING: OBTAINING CONSUMER CREDIT

SHARING A PERSONAL FINANCIAL DECISION WITH PROFESSOR CLYDE D. WESTWOOD OF UTAH TECHNICAL COLLEGE AT PROVO

When Professor Clyde D. Westwood's neighbor, Clark Boyd, enrolled for his class on personal finance, they got a chance to know each other better. Often they rode to school together.

On the way to class one day, Clark expressed his enthusiasm for a terrific stereo system he'd seen. "It's just what I want," he exclaimed. "Sure, it's expensive. It'll take me awhile to save for it. But I don't care—it'll be worth it. Besides, I'm used to saving. It took me over two years of tight budgeting and hard work, but I got this car that way." Clark chuckled. "The dealer sure seemed surprised when I walked in with the full cash amount."

Professor Westwood asked if Clark had considered buying the stereo on credit. That way he wouldn't have to wait to enjoy it.

"I don't think I can," Clark replied. "I've never bought anything on credit. How would I qualify for credit?"

If you were Professor Westwood, what would you tell Clark?

To find out how Professor Westwood helped Clark with his personal financial decision, turn to page 204.

"Credit buying is much like being drunk. The buzz happens immediately, and it gives you a lift. . . . The hangover comes on the day after."
Dr. Joyce Brothers[1]

In 1852 a young army officer was assigned as regimental quartermaster for the U.S. Army's Fourth Infantry at Vancouver Barracks, Washington. Since an Indian uprising was expected, the lieutenant expected a lengthy tour of duty. A junior officer's pay was barely sufficient to support a family, so he began looking for an investment that would provide the necessary funds to bring his wife and children out West. The lieutenant managed to borrow his investment funds—at 2 percent interest—from his superior officer, Lieutenant Colonel Benjamin Louis Eulalie de Bonneville (for whom the Bonneville Dam was later named). The young officer then invested with a partner in a potato-growing venture near the Columbia River. The partners planted the crop themselves, and the investment appeared promising until a flood destroyed the entire crop.

The officer then came under intense pressure from Bonneville to repay the debt. Eventually, the lieutenant used another loan—this time from a sergeant—to pay off Bonneville. Two additional business ventures were to end in failure for the young officer. An attempt to ship 100 tons of rice to San Francisco for resale failed when the schooner was delayed. Another venture involving chickens flopped when all the birds died en route to their intended market.

Although the young officer never did become a successful businessperson, things finally took a turn for the better for him. He was promoted, eventually became a general, and later entered political life. Who was this debtor and failed businessperson? Ulysses S. Grant![2]

Although Grant's efforts with borrowed funds were far from triumphant, millions of others have converted credit into both immediate pleasure and business success. Today, for most people, life revolves around credit. As the average retail price of a new car exceeds $10,500 and the price of a new home approaches $100,000, few consumers can afford either without resorting to borrowed funds. Indeed, it's hard to imagine life without credit. Complete reliance on cash payments would convert home telephones into coin-operated machines, and would require advance payments for such utilities as electricity and water. Would-be entrepreneurs could not take advantage of financial opportunities that required more money than they had on deposit at their bank. And, of course, credit card purchases would become only a memory.

If all forms of credit simply disappeared, modern financial life as we know

Figure 7-1
THE CONSUMER INSTALLMENT CREDIT DOLLAR

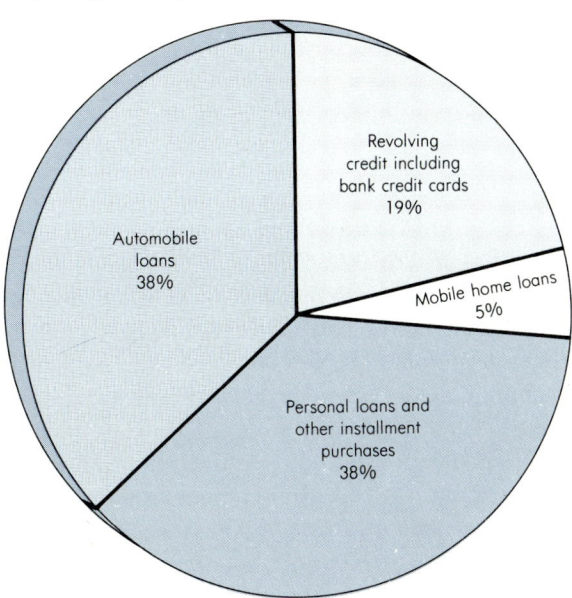

- Automobile loans 38%
- Revolving credit including bank credit cards 19%
- Mobile home loans 5%
- Personal loans and other installment purchases 38%

Source: Federal Reserve Board.

it would be drastically changed. Our nation's economic system depends on the availability of credit, and so do most people's personal financial budgets. In fact, our dependence on credit is growing every year. In 1982, total consumer installment credit in the United States was $330 billion. As Figure 7-1 indicates, auto loans, personal loans, and other installment credit purchases accounted for over three-fourths of this total. Approximately one in five dollars went for revolving credit, including bank credit cards, and the remainder was used in purchasing mobile homes.

WHAT IS CREDIT?

Borrowing may involve a specialized financial institution such as a commercial bank, savings and loan association, savings bank, or credit union; a specialized consumer lending company such as Household Finance or Beneficial Finance; or a neighborhood pawnbroker. On the other hand, borrowed funds may be obtained from a friend, a relative, or the person from whom you purchase a product, whether it is an automobile, furniture, or a condominium. In each case, the borrower receives credit. *Credit* can be defined as the receiving of money, products, or services based on an agreement between the lender and the borrower that the loan is for a specified period of time with a specified

credit: receiving of money, products, or services based on an agreement between the lender and the borrower concerning such terms of the loan as amount, interest rate, method of repayment, and time period of the loan.

rate of interest. In some instances, the loan is secured by a claim against your property should you fail to repay it. In other instances, no specific security is involved. In the latter case, the lender typically investigates the previous credit history of the borrower and makes the loan based on faith in the borrower's ability to repay it.

SECURING CREDIT

After winning the New Jersey lottery, which assured him an annual income of $71,000 for the next 20 years, 60-year-old Tom DeBari, a Hoboken, New Jersey, longshoreman, applied for an American Express Gold Card and a Visa card. Tom had never had a credit card before, since he had always preferred to pay cash for everything he purchased. Now, however, the publicity that surrounded his lottery winnings made him reluctant to carry too much cash around.

To Tom's surprise, his credit request was rejected by both credit card companies. Despite his huge winnings, Tom was considered a poor credit risk because he had no credit record at all. Without active checking and savings accounts, existing charge accounts with local merchants, and a history of buying items on installment loans, the lenders had no way of knowing whether or not Tom was a good credit risk. After all, they reasoned, a big income was no guarantee of credit worthiness since it could be spent almost as quickly as it was received.[3]

WHAT CREDITORS LOOK FOR

If a large annual income is no guarantee of a loan, then what is? In essence, creditors try to protect themselves from loss by looking for evidence that you are both able and willing to repay the loan. They base their judgment on what are called the three C's of credit—capacity, character, and collateral.

capacity: the ability of a potential borrower to repay the debt; one of the three C's of credit.

Capacity. The creditor wants to know your *capacity* for credit—whether you can afford to repay the debt. To determine capacity, a potential lender compares your current income with your current expenses. He or she asks for employment information: what you do, how much you earn, length of time on the job. In addition, the creditor will require a complete list of your current debts, number of dependents, and alimony and child-support obligations.

character: the willingness of a potential borrower to repay the debt as determined by his or her credit history; one of the three C's of credit.

Character. While capacity judges your ability to repay your debt, *character* judges your willingness. By checking your past credit history, creditors can quickly determine whether you have always lived within your means or have overextended yourself; whether you have paid your bills on time or been delinquent; whether you have provided accurate, honest information about your employment, income, and current and past debts. Most creditors judge character at least in part by stability: the number of years you have lived at your present address and worked at your present job.

+ capital
conditions
cash flow
(6 c's)

Collateral. Since creditors can never fully protect themselves against their loss should you fail to repay the loan, they often require *collateral* in the form of property in order to secure the loan. In essence, the creditor requires the borrower to pledge something of value to secure his or her promise to repay the loan.

collateral: an item or items of value pledged as security in case of a loan default; one of the three C's of credit.

Creditors obtain many of the details they need to judge an applicant's credit worthiness by analyzing his or her credit file, which they obtain through a local credit bureau.

THE ROLE OF CREDIT BUREAUS

When you apply for credit, most prospective lenders request information about your credit history from a *credit bureau*, which serves as a clearinghouse of consumer credit information. The credit file they receive contains the following details:

credit bureau: a local, regional, or national organization that collects and stores credit information and disseminates it to clients who request it.

1. *Identifying information,* including your name, address, employer, date of birth, spouse's employer, number of dependents, monthly income, former address, former employer, and whether you own or rent your home.

2. *A credit history,* giving a summary of your credit experiences with specific granters. This informs the prospective creditor whether or not you have paid your bills on time.

3. *Public-record information,* which may include such items of public record as civil suits, judgments, bankruptcies, and criminal convictions, any of which may affect your credit application.

Credit bureaus do not collect or store information about your personal lifestyle, friends, relatives, medical history, religious beliefs, or political activities. Nor do they make judgments about whether you are a good or poor credit risk. They merely list information on your credit history, enabling lenders to make up their own minds about your credit worthiness.

The information on your credit file is obtained from the credit applications you have submitted to lenders in the past, from lenders' records of loan payments, and from such sources of public records as the courts. This objective information is updated regularly to ensure that it is both current and accurate. It is weighed by each lender, who uses his or her own standards to decide whether or not to grant you a loan. The information in a credit file may not be judged in the same way by all lenders. Although some lenders have extremely strict standards, others are willing to take small risks. Some lenders use sophisticated scoring systems to determine whether you are a good credit risk.

HOW TO APPLY FOR CREDIT FOR THE FIRST TIME

If, like lottery-winner Tom DeBari, you have never built up a credit history, there are several steps you can take to establish credit.

1. **Open checking and savings accounts to show that you have a system for managing your money.** Although these accounts are not included in your credit file, they add a sense of permanence and stability to your financial history.

2. **Apply for a department store credit card or purchase a large item such as furniture on installment credit.** In most cases, it is easier to qualify for a credit card from a local retailer than from a major national lender.

3. **If you are moving to a new city, ask the credit bureau for a copy of your file and then submit it to the credit bureau in your new location.**

4. **Ask a relative or close friend to cosign your loan.** A cosigner is responsible for repaying the loan should you default. However, if you repay the loan on your own, you will receive full credit for it in your credit file.

5. **Apply for a secured loan, such as an auto loan, so that you can add to your credit history.**

By taking each of these steps in a responsible way, you will begin to establish an impressive credit record.

WHAT TO DO WHEN YOU'RE DENIED CREDIT

Lenders may deny credit for a number of reasons. These fall into the following categories:

- You may already be overextended. Your income simply may not be sufficient to repay additional loans.
- You may have negative factors on your credit rating, such as a wage garnishment, foreclosure, repossession, or bankruptcy.
- You may appear unstable to the lender as a result of recent job changes or several recent addresses. Some lenders are reluctant to approve loans for applicants who have made any move within the last two or three years.
- Your credit background may be incomplete or contain unverifiable information.

If after being turned down for credit, you discover an error in your credit file, you can demand that the incorrect information be changed and that all

How to Read a Credit Report

If you're one of the 90 million consumers whose bill-paying habits are cataloged by TRW computers, your credit report looks like the one below.

When you check your credit history, an employee at the local credit bureau will explain how to read it, or if you get your report by mail, it should be accompanied by a detailed explanation.

The . . . account profile columns at the left on the TRW report are designed to give a credit grantor a quick feel for what's in the file. A letter (A or M, depending on whether the data was received via an automated or manual report) in the POS column means most creditors would look positively on the way the consumer has handled this account; NON, for non-evaluated, means this account history might be considered favorably, unfavorably or indifferently, depending on the creditor's policy; NEG suggests most creditors would frown at the handling of this account. As a convenience to the creditors, TRW handles the clerical function of placing individuals into appropriate categories, which have been determined and defined by the creditors. TRW sticks an account that's up to 60 days overdue in the nonevaluated column, for ex-ample, whereas one that's 90 days late gets a negative mark.

For each account, the report shows the creditor and a current status. TRW uses codes for 73 different status comments, ranging from "paid satisfactorily" and "current account in good standing" to "debt discharged through bankruptcy" and "credit grantor cannot locate consumer." Under TYPE and TERMS of account, this report shows a 36-month auto loan from Citibank (paid off in January), revolving charge accounts at three department stores, and a bank credit card from the ABC Bank. AMOUNT shows the size of the original debt or the credit limit on a revolving amount. BALANCE shows debt outstanding on the most recent report.

The payment profile section at the far right shows the payment history for the previous 12 months. C means the borrower paid as agreed that month; a number shows how many months the consumer fell behind on the payments.

Although there is no public record information in this hypothetical file, such reports—about a bankruptcy or court judgment, for example—would be printed below the account information.

Updated Credit Profile

INQUIRY INFORMATION

TCR2

DFD2 9999999ABC CONSUMER JANE Q..,1825 H 90027,P-2234 W 92667,
S-548926847,M-1825 HILL STREET?LOS ANGELES CA 90027   IDENTIFICATION NO.

PAGE	DATE	TIME	PORT	KEY	CONSUMER	TCA1	02-999999/99
1	04-09-83	15:19:14	AL11	A14			

JANE Q CONSUMER   1-80 A & B SALES   SS#548926847
1825 HILL STREET   1350 4TH STREET
LOS ANGELES CA 90027   3100900 LOS ANGELES CA 90067   YOB-1952

| ACCOUNT PROFILE | SUBSCRIBER NAME/COURT NAME | SUBSCRIBER COURT CODE | ASSN CODE | AMOUNT | ACCOUNT/DOCKET NUMBER | PAYMENT PROFILE NUMBER OF MONTHS PRIOR TO BALANCE DATE |
| POS NON | STATUS COMMENT | DATE REPORTED/INQUIRY | DATE OPENED | TYPE | TERMS | BALANCE | BALANCE DATE | AMOUNT PAST DUE | 1 2 3 4 5 6 7 8 9 10 11 |

A	CITIBANK		3100900	1			892939495969		
	PAID SATIS	1-83	1-80	AUT	36	$5000			
A	ABC BANK		3200500	1			40245566789		21CCCCCCCC
	DELINQ 60	3-83	6-77	CRC REV		$1000 $242	3-31-83	$40	
A	SEARS		3347586	2			838485868777		CCCCCCCCCC
	CURR ACCT	3-83	3-75	CHG REV		$500 $0	3-15-83		
A	MAY CO		3388338	2			770004122333		CC
	CUR ACCT	3-83	1-83	CHG REV		$200 $54	3-28-83		
A	JC PENNEY		3394959	1			596979493922		CCCCCCCCCC
	CURR ACCT	3-83	2-79	CHG REV		$200 $149	3-21-83		
A	MAY CO		3388338						
	INQUIRY	12-10-82							
A	B OF A		3192212						
	INQUIRY	4-09-83		CHG REV					

Source: "What the Credit Bureau Is Saying about You," *Changing Times*, July 1983, p. 58. Reprinted with permission from *Changing Times* Magazine, © Kiplinger Washington Editors, Inc., 1983.

Buying a major item—a large piece of furniture, for example—from a local retailer on installment credit is an important step toward building a sound credit rating.

lenders receive your revised file. Persistence pays off even when you are denied credit, and so does shopping around.

AGREEMENTS FOR REGULAR AND REVOLVING CHARGE ACCOUNTS

Shoppers who open a charge account with a retailer sign an agreement that binds all future credit purchases and cash advances to its terms. This agreement is in force for as long as the account continues. In addition to the annual percentage rate and finance charge, the agreement lists the time the purchaser has to pay a bill before finance charges are levied and the maximum amount due on each payment. Similar written agreements are signed when you acquire a bank credit card or a national credit card such as American Express, Diners Club, or Carte Blanche.

SOURCES OF CREDIT

Money is a commodity just like jelly beans and Pac Man cartridges. It is important to remember this when you are shopping for credit, for the price you pay for credit—in the form of interest—frequently varies from lender to lender. Just as the same pound of coffee might cost $3 at a local grocer and $6 at an exclusive gourmet food store, the same unsecured loan may cost 15 percent per year at a local bank and 25 percent at a finance company. Clearly, spending time to comparison-shop among lenders is the only way to locate the best credit deal. To do this, borrowers must be familiar with the major sources of available credit.

BORROWING: OBTAINING CONSUMER CREDIT

BANKS, THRIFTS, AND CREDIT UNIONS

As noted in the previous chapter, commercial banks, thrifts (savings and loan associations and mutual savings banks), and credit unions are the primary sources of most consumer and business loans. However, a number of other sources of borrowed funds exist.

CONSUMER FINANCE COMPANIES

Many would-be borrowers who are unable to obtain a loan from a commercial bank or savings and loan association discover that they can secure financing at a *consumer finance company*. Often called small-loan companies, these firms, such as Household Finance and Beneficial Finance, are willing to assume more risk by making relatively small, short-term individual loans, but they frequently charge higher interest rates than banks charge.

Most consumer finance company loans are unsecured, and many are issued in amounts as small as $100. Often the maximum loan a consumer finance company can make is set by state law. Many borrowers find that consumer finance companies are easier to deal with than commercial banks and savings and loan associations. Application forms tend to be less formidable, and loan approvals and funds are frequently handled in a single day. Indeed, because of the convenience of securing such loans, many borrowers fail to consider the interest costs involved. In general, borrowers who are able to qualify for loans from credit unions, commercial banks, savings and loan associations, or mutual savings banks should compare their interest rates with those of a small loan company before deciding where to borrow needed funds.

consumer finance company: sometimes called a small-loan company, this financial institution makes relatively small loans to qualified borrowers.

SALES FINANCE COMPANIES

A second type of finance company assists credit purchasers of more expensive, major purchases, such as automobiles, appliances, and furniture—products that frequently require financing for customers. Since many retailers are unable to tie up their funds in installment contracts, they "sell paper." That is, they sell an installment purchase agreement to a *sales finance company*. The retailer receives the full amount of the purchase (unless it is discounted, as is the case when the sales finance company feels that the likelihood of default is relatively high), and the sales finance company earns the interest paid on the agreement. When such a sale occurs, the customer is typically advised to make payments directly to the sales finance company.

A number of manufacturers have now established their own "captive" finance companies. Consumers who purchase a Chevrolet directly from a General Motors dealer are eligible to apply for financing from General Motors Acceptance Corporation—GM's captive finance company. General Electric Credit Corporation provides similar financing for qualified purchasers of GE appliances.

sales finance company: a financial institution that purchases installment notes from retailers of major consumer products such as automobiles, furniture, and appliances.

LIFE INSURANCE COMPANIES

Life insurance policyholders may be able to obtain loans from their insurance company. People who have certain types of policies and have been paying premiums for a number of years will have built up a substantial cash value as well as protection. An amount equal to this cash value can be borrowed in the form of a policy loan. These loans are discussed in more detail in Chapter 12.

An especially attractive feature of an insurance-policy loan is that there is no maturity date on it and it does not have to be paid back. However, it is important to realize that failure to repay the loan reduces life insurance coverage by the amount of the loan.

GOVERNMENT LOANS

As noted in Chapter 2, a number of loans are available for students seeking to finance their education. Although a drastic reduction of individual loans has occurred during the 1980s, funds are still available under the federal Guaranteed Student Loan Program and the National Direct Student Loan Program. In addition, the federal- and state-sponsored Parent Loans for Undergraduate Students program also offers loan assistance.

The U.S. Small Business Administration provides loans for small-business owners in many instances—either by providing government funds or by guaranteeing loans. The interest rates on these loans are usually slightly lower than those which the businessperson would pay on the open market.

RETAILERS

Credit purchases from retailers represent a sizable source of consumer borrowing. Whenever a shopper purchases an item and charges it on a store credit card, a loan has been made by the store for the sales price of the item. Like bank credit cards and national credit cards, retail credit cards carry substantial interest rates unless the shopper repays the outstanding credit balance at the end of each month.

PERSONAL LOANS FROM FAMILY AND FRIENDS

A frequent source of borrowed funds involves a loan from a relative or close friend. Such loans are frequently attractive since relatives and friends are not likely to require complicated loan applications and credit checks or charge excessive interest rates. However, the cynic's definition of a friend in need as a pain in the neck often applies. The potential for misunderstandings, disagreements, and conflicts is minimized with a written agreement that specifies the terms of the loan and the obligations of both borrower and lender. Even with such a document, the potential for disagreement continues to exist, and such borrowing is advisable only if funds are not available from traditional lenders at comparable terms.

LENDERS OF LAST RESORT

Pawnbrokers. People who desire credit and have personal possessions of value may decide to pawn them in order to qualify for a loan. *Pawnbrokers* accept such valuables as jewelry, small musical instruments, guns, electronic equipment, and typewriters as collateral for loans. After appraising each item, the pawnbroker will issue a loan for a fraction (typically 35 to 40 percent) of the item's value. The item is then held as security until the loan is repaid in full, including interest.

Although the federal Truth in Lending Act requires pawnbrokers to inform borrowers in writing of both the dollar amount and the annual percentage rate of interest to be charged for the loan, in most cases, the debt is never repaid and the item is resold. Most pawnbrokers demand repayment within 60 to 90 days, and most charge annual interest rates ranging from 20 to 40 percent. In some states, interest rates as high as 100 percent are charged.

Pawnbrokers are a lender of last resort. Borrowers who do not plan to reclaim pawned items should consider potential outlets for outright sale of the items, since they will almost always be able to obtain more money from such sales than from a pawnbroker.

> **pawnbrokers:** financing source for small personal loans, these lenders accept such goods as jewelry, guns, stereos, and typewriters as collateral and make loans equal to 35 to 40 percent of the value of the goods.

Loan Sharks. *Loan sharks* are aptly named, since they provide illegal credit services and prey on people who are desperate for money and willing to pay as much as 2,000-percent interest a year for loans. Physical violence is sometimes associated with such operations, and the loan-shark victim is virtually assured of compounding his or her financial problems. If the services of a loan shark seem to be the only available source of funds to solve a financial emergency, personal bankruptcy is likely to be a preferred alternative.

> **loan sharks:** persons who make loans at usurious interest rates.

TYPES OF CONSUMER CREDIT

Consumer credit can be classified according to two broad categories: form of payment and method of payment. As Figure 7-2 indicates, credit may be in the form of cash provided by a lender, or it may be in the form of a product or service purchased with credit that is provided by a merchant or other lender. A borrower is required to repay the credit in a single, lump-sum payment or in periodic payments of principal and interest that continue until the entire debt is repaid.

Figure 7-2

CLASSIFYING CONSUMER CREDIT

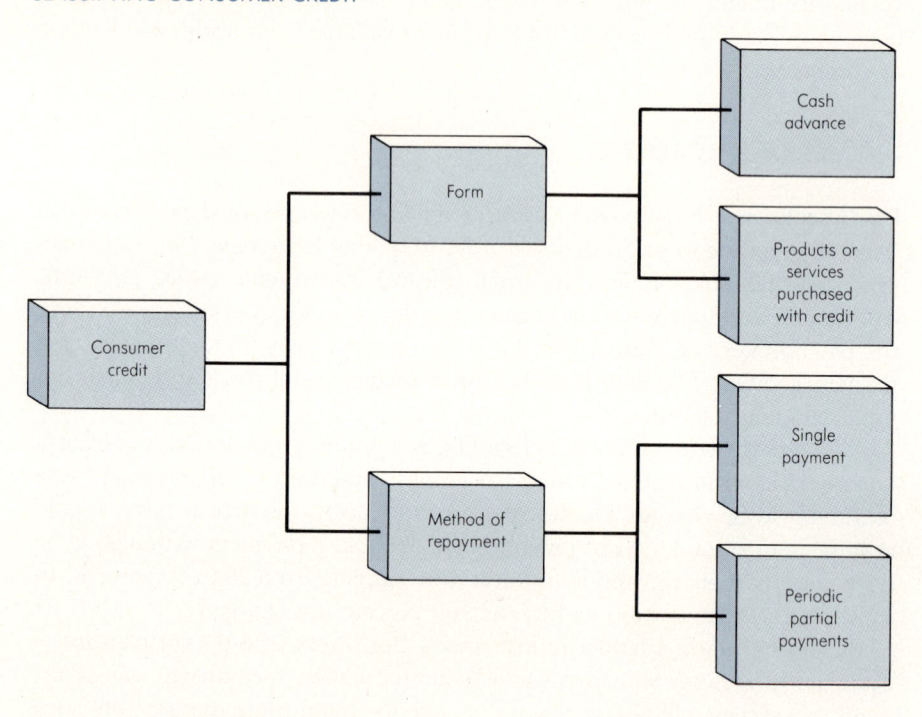

Consumer credit
- Form
  - Cash advance
  - Products or services purchased with credit
- Method of repayment
  - Single payment
  - Periodic partial payments

CONSUMER INSTALLMENT CREDIT

installment credit: a loan that is repaid over a period of time through a series of payments rather than in a single lump sum.

Consumers who utilize *installment credit* as a source of funds agree to repay the loan plus interest on a regular basis for a specified time period. Loan repayments are typically made on a monthly basis, and the length of the installment loan may be as short as several weeks or as long as several years. Installment loans include revolving, or open-end, charge accounts; closed-end installment purchase plans; and regular, or 30-day, charge accounts. Mortgages are actually a form of installment credit, although they are typically treated as a separate category due to their importance to consumers.

revolving charge account: a form of credit frequently used by retail stores that permits consumers to continue to purchase goods and services so long as they do not exceed their maximum credit limit and so long as they continue to make specified minimum payments on the account.

Revolving (Open-End) Charge Accounts. (Credit cards) The *revolving charge account* is a form of installment credit that enables shoppers to make a number of different purchases up to a specified credit limit, which is set by the lender when the account is opened. If, for example, your limit on such credit cards as Visa and MasterCard is $1,500, you can charge no more than that amount on your account.

Each month the lender sends a statement to the cardholder listing all credit transactions occurring during the previous billing period, including all pur-

NOT an Auto overdraft — checking account

chases, payments, and finance charges. Most revolving charge accounts levy a finance charge on the unpaid balance. This charge is expressed in terms of the periodic rate used to calculate the annual percentage rate. For example, the finance charge may be computed at a monthly rate of 1.5 or 2 percent, which translates into annual percentage rates of 18 and 24 percent, respectively. It is not possible to list these finance charges in dollars at the time the account is opened since they depend on the amount of credit used and how quickly it is repaid.

In 1982 the total outstanding revolving credit in the United States amounted to $63 billion. Commercial banks held $33 billion of this amount, retailers another $26 billion, and gasoline companies the remaining $4 billion.

A recent Federal Reserve Board study revealed that credit cards are used in approximately 15 percent of all general merchandise transactions. An estimated 600 million credit card accounts—retail charge cards, bank cards, gasoline credit cards, and others—currently exist in the United States.[4] Visa and MasterCard alone had nearly 190 million cards in circulation in 1983.[5]

An *automatic overdraft account* operates in much the same manner as a revolving charge account. This account—which is available from such financial institutions as commercial banks, savings and loan associations, and mutual savings banks—permits a depositor to overdraw his or her checking account up to a predetermined limit. The depositor then repays these funds advanced by the lender plus interest according to a set monthly installment schedule.

A bank *line of credit* is similar to an automatic overdraft account in providing the depositor with access to additional funds when needed. After signing an agreement with the lender, who approves the credit line, the depositor can borrow up to a predetermined amount of money without requiring further approval from bank officials. The borrowed funds are repaid at an interest rate and within time periods specified in the original agreement.

Closed-End Installment Purchase Plans. Unlike open-end plans, *closed-end installment purchase plans* require a written agreement for each credit purchase. The agreement specifies the annual percentage rate, the total finance charge, the length of the repayment period, and the exact amount to be paid in each installment. It may also specify collateral used to secure the loan. In most cases, the seller holds title to the merchandise until the borrower makes the final loan payment.

Closed-end installment loans are frequently used for automobile loans and personal loans. An automobile loan—used to pay for the cost of a new or used car—is secured by title to the car itself, which is held as collateral in case of default. A personal loan—used for such varied expenses as a vacation, converting a garage to a playroom, replacing a furnace, or obtaining braces for a child's teeth—is often a cash loan that is secured only by the borrower's character and capacity to pay.

automatic overdraft account: a feature of some checking accounts that permits the depositor to overdraw his or her account up to a predetermined limit; available at commercial banks, savings and loan associations, and mutual savings banks.

line of credit: a prearranged loan agreement between a financial institution, such as a commercial bank, and a customer that permits the customer to borrow up to a predetermined limit without requiring further approval from bank officials.

closed-end installment purchase plans: a form of installment purchasing that requires separate written agreements for each credit purchase specifying such terms as length and timing of the repayment period, total finance charges, and annual percentage interest rate.

regular (30-day) charge accounts: credit agreements requiring total repayment of all outstanding credit purchases within a specified period (normally 30 days); interest is not charged on such accounts.

Regular (30-Day) Charge Accounts. (*most charge cards*) While installment loans allow the borrower to spread payments over a predetermined period of time, *regular (30-day) charge accounts* require that the loan be repaid in full in 30 or fewer days. If you meet this requirement, there is no finance charge.

Noninstallment loans, as these loans are frequently called, are issued by retailers and service providers as varied as physicians, dentists, and repairers as a convenience for their customers and clients. National credit cards such as American Express, which require cardholders to repay in full the amount of the outstanding balance each month, represent a form of noninstallment loan. In addition, many shoppers utilize retail credit cards and bank cards in the same manner. As long as they repay the total amount of their outstanding credit purchases within the time period specified on the monthly transaction summary, no interest charges are levied on these accounts. In 1982 noninstallment credit totaled $78 billion.

MORTGAGE LOANS

As noted earlier, mortgage loans are actually a form of installment credit. They are treated as a separate category due to their importance to both borrowers and lenders and their impact on the overall economy. A *mortgage* is simply an installment loan secured by real estate or other real property. It is typically written for 20 to 30 years and requires a substantial down payment, usually ranging from 10 to 30 percent of the value of the property.

mortgage: an installment loan secured by real estate or other real property.

Two types of documents are signed by the borrower (or mortgagor). The first document, called the *mortgage note,* specifies the terms of the loan and includes the total amount borrowed, the number of installments, the amount of each installment, and the time each installment is due. The second document, the *mortgage deed,* is security for the lender (or mortgagee) since it pledges the house or other specified property as collateral in case of default by the borrower.

The unprecedented interest rates of the early 1980s and the recent fluctuations in mortgage rates have led to the development of a number of unique mortgage arrangements. These are discussed in detail in Chapter 9.

TYPES OF CONSUMER CREDIT AGREEMENTS

Each time you enter into a credit agreement, you sign a written contract, which outlines the specific terms of the agreement. Although this agreement binds you as well as the lender to specific repayment and penalty terms, it also protects both parties in the event that one party fails to carry out his or her part of the agreement. Should this occur, the wronged party can seek a remedy in a court of law.

According to the federal Truth in Lending Act (discussed in detail later in this chapter), every credit contract must contain the following information:

the amount financed; the total finance charge in dollars; the annual percentage rate; the total number of payments and the amount of each payment; the date the finance charges begin if it is different from the contract date; charges not included in the finance charge; the number, amounts, and due dates of payments; late-payment or default charges; prepayment refund or penalty statement; and a description of the security held by the creditor. You should analyze each of these terms before you sign any credit agreement.

A major way in which consumer credit agreements vary is according to the credit source and the type and amount of credit requested. The two basic categories of agreements are (1) for cash loans or installment purchases and (2) for regular or revolving charge accounts.

AGREEMENTS FOR CASH LOANS AND INSTALLMENT PURCHASES

If you make an installment purchase, or take out a cash loan for an extended period of time, you will be required to sign a promissory note or a retail installment contract and security agreement. These documents spell out terms that are binding on both the creditor and the borrower.

Promissory Note. Used mainly by commercial banks, savings and loan associations, mutual savings banks, credit unions, and consumer financial companies, a *promissory note* defines the terms of a cash loan, including its length and annual percentage rate. The note also outlines what actions the lender can take if the borrower defaults. Figure 7-3 is an example of a promissory note. In this case, the promissory note is a secured agreement guaranteed by specific property.

Retail Installment Contract. Consumers who make installment purchases through a retail store are typically required to sign a *retail installment contract*, also known as a conditional sales contract. This agreement contains most of the information included on a promissory note, but it is used for credit purchases of goods and services rather than for a cash loan. The agreement defines the annual percentage rate and finance charge as well as the seller's rights if the purchaser fails to meet payment obligations. This agreement enables the purchaser to take possession of the merchandise at the time of the purchase.

promissory note: a written agreement between a cash lender and borrower stating the terms of the loan, including its date of repayment and interest rate and the rights of the lender in case of default.

retail installment contract: a written agreement between a retail store and a credit purchaser stating the terms of the agreement and the accompanying security agreement; also called a conditional sales contract.

THE COST OF BORROWING

Since the late 1970s, interest rates have been on nearly everyone's mind. No longer can consumers depend on paying annual interest rates of 10 percent or less for their loans. During the early 1980s, interest rates skyrocketed to 20 percent and higher, causing consumers to consider the cost of borrowing almost as important as the cost of their purchases. Although interest rates on

Figure 7-3

PROMISSORY NOTE AND SECURITY AGREEMENT

Source: Courtesy of Citibank, N.A.

consumer loans have gone down in recent years, they are still relatively high. In February 1982, for instance, the annual interest rate on a $6,000 five-year loan was 21 percent. By 1984 rates of 12 percent were available. This nine-point decline saved consumers $45 per month in interest charges.

Although the rate of inflation had declined to 3.8 percent by 1984, interest rates on consumer loans have remained relatively high. As Chapter 6 pointed out, a major factor affecting interest rates has been the deregulation of financial institutions. Since financial institutions are required to pay higher interest rates in order to attract deposits, they also charge higher interest rates on borrowed funds. In addition, since the interest rates they pay to depositors frequently fluctuate, they are likely to charge slightly higher rates on fixed-interest-rate loans with maturities longer than one year in order to protect themselves against the risk of an increase in the cost of money over the life of the loan.

Despite deregulation, the interest rate on a loan cannot be greater than that allowed by state *usury laws*. In some states these laws, which regulate the maximum interest charged on loans, have been in effect since the eighteenth century. The earliest usury laws typically established a single maximum rate for all kinds of loans. Today, however, each state has a variety of specific laws stating the maximum finance charge for retail installment loans; auto loans; and loans from commercial banks, savings and loan associations, mutual savings banks, credit unions, and other sources of consumer credit.

Usury ceilings vary considerably from state to state. In New York, for example, credit card companies can charge their customers no more than 18 percent per year on their unpaid balances, while in South Dakota the rate is 23 percent. In order to take advantage of these higher permitted rates, New York–based Citibank moved its MasterCard operations to South Dakota. Although the parent bank continues to operate in New York, it can now charge its New York customers South Dakota rates.

usury laws: *state laws establishing maximum interest rates on various types of consumer loans and other types of credit.*

CALCULATING FINANCE CHARGES AND THE ANNUAL PERCENTAGE INTEREST RATE

Although today's borrower must be informed in writing of all finance charges and the interest rates charged on loans, it was not always so simple. Before the passage of the federal Truth in Lending Act in 1968, lenders could use a number of different methods for calculating interest. Loans issued at a stated interest rate of 6 percent might actually cost the borrower 12 percent.

The 1968 law changed this by requiring all loans to clearly state the finance charge and annual percentage rate. The *finance charge* is the total dollar amount charged for credit. It includes the total interest charge and all other costs, including service charges, finder's fees, and the cost for any credit, life, health,

finance charge: *the total dollar amount charged for credit; it must be disclosed on the credit application form.*

annual percentage rate (APR): *the interest rate paid per dollar per year for credit; it must be disclosed on the credit application form.*

or property insurance incurred during the life of the loan. The *annual percentage rate (APR)* is the interest rate paid per dollar per year for credit. Like the unit-pricing approach in listing the price per pound or gallon of products purchased at a supermarket, it allows the borrower to compare value. With the 1968 law, for the first time one could compare the terms of several loans and decide which loan offered the best credit buy.

As Table 7-1 reveals, using this information to choose a loan can save you a great deal of money over the life of the loan. If you borrow $5,000 for four years at a 14-percent annual interest rate, your total finance charge will equal $1,559. That same loan with an annual interest rate of 20 percent will cost you an additional $737 over the life of the loan.

Table 7-1 also reveals how much more expensive it is to extend the life of a loan over additional years rather than repay it in one year or less. A $6,000 loan with a 14-percent annual interest rate will result in total payments of $6,465 if the lender repays it within a one-year period. If, however, payments are spread over four years, the borrower will make total principal and interest payments of $7,870—more than four times as much in interest payments.

ALTERNATIVE METHODS OF CALCULATING INTEREST ON CASH LOANS AND INSTALLMENT SALES

Unfortunately, determining the best interest rate on cash loans and installment purchases is not as simple as reading the annual percentage rate listed on the loan agreement. Confusion frequently arises as a result of the variety of methods lenders may use to compute basic charges. Three methods used in such calculations are the add-on method, the discount method, and the

Table 7-1
COMPARISON OF MONTHLY PAYMENTS AND TOTAL FINANCE CHARGES ON LOANS WITH ANNUAL INTEREST RATES OF 14 AND 20 PERCENT

	14% Annual Percentage Rate				20% Annual Percentage Rate			
	2 Years		4 Years			2 Years		4 Years	
Amount Financed	Monthly Payment	Total Finance Charge	Monthly Payment	Total Finance Charge	Amount Financed	Monthly Payment	Total Finance Charge	Monthly Payment	Total Finance Charge
$1,000	48	152	27	312	$1,000	51	222	30	459
2,000	96	305	55	624	2,000	102	443	61	918
3,000	144	457	82	935	3,000	153	665	91	1,378
4,000	192	609	109	1,247	4,000	204	886	122	1,837
5,000	240	762	137	1,559	5,000	255	1,108	152	2,296

Source: Federal Trade Commission, *Credit Shopping Guide* (Washington, D.C.: U.S. Government Printing Office, 1979), pp. 15, 21.

declining balance method. Borrowers who are planning to pay off their loan early should understand two other methods: the actuarial and the Rule of 78s.

Add-On Method. The *add-on method* involves calculating the total finance charge and then adding it to the principal of the loan. The combined amount is the amount to be repaid. Thus, if an individual borrows $1,000 at a 15-percent annual add-on, the finance charge will total $150 for one year and $300 for two years ($1,000 × .15 × 2). Monthly payments are then determined by dividing the total amount of the loan (principal plus interest) by the total number of payments. The add-on method is used extensively by banks and other savings institutions, finance companies, and retail merchants.

add-on method: a method of calculating interest according to which the amount of the loan and the total finance charge are totaled and then divided by the number of payments to be made.

Discount Method. By the *discount method,* total interest and other finance charges are deducted from the face value of the loan before the borrower receives any money. In other words, the amount of money the borrower receives is equal to the difference between the face value of the loan (say, $1,000) and the total finance charge (say, $150). When you repay the loan, you repay the entire $1,000 even though you received only $850. The discount method is used extensively by financial institutions that make consumer loans.

discount method: a method of calculating interest according to which total interest and other finance charges are calculated and subtracted from the face value of the loan before the borrower receives the funds.

Declining-Balance Method. The *declining-balance method* of computing finance charges is used by department stores, credit-card companies, and other financial institutions offering revolving credit plans. These lenders calculate your monthly finance charge as a percentage of your total outstanding balance, which can be computed in one of three ways:

1. Using the *adjusted balance,* the finance charge is based on the unpaid balance at the end of the current billing period.

2. Using the *previous balance,* the current finance charge is based on the balance on the closing date of the previous month. Any payments, credit, or charges made after that date are not considered in this calculation.

3. Using the *average daily balance,* the finance charge is determined by dividing the sum of the balance outstanding for each day in the billing period by the number of days in the period.

declining-balance method: a method of determining total finance charges on installment credit according to which monthly finance charges are computed as a percentage of total outstanding balances.

Actuarial Method. Lenders who believe that you should be charged for your loan only for the period you use the money base their interest charges on the *actuarial method.* The advantage of this method is that it does not penalize borrowers who pay off their loans early. Interest charges are calculated in the following way:

$$\text{interest due} = \text{outstanding balance} \times \frac{\text{annual interest rate}}{365} \times \text{number of days since last payment}$$

actuarial method: a method of determining interest according to which interest charges are levied only on the outstanding balance due for the period in which the loan is in effect.

In essence, you are charged $\frac{1}{12}$ of the annual interest for each month the loan is outstanding. If you prepay a one-year loan after 6 months, you are charged $\frac{6}{12}$, or 50 percent, of the year's total interest fee. This method is both the simplest and the fairest way to calculate interest.

Rule of 78s. This interest-calculation method loads most of your interest payments onto the early installments, with less on the later installments. The name *rule of 78s* derives from the fact that the sum of the number of months in a one-year loan equals 78. Thus, you pay $\frac{12}{78}$ of the total interest charge the first month, $\frac{11}{78}$ the second month, $\frac{10}{78}$ the third month, and so on until you reach the final payment, which is equal to $\frac{1}{78}$ of the loan. If you total all these payments, you get $\frac{78}{78}$, which is equal to the total interest charge of your loan.

This method penalizes borrowers in two ways. First, if you repay your loan early — after 6 months — you will have paid 73 percent of the total interest bill for the entire year. Second, even when no early payment is involved, loans calculated under the Rule of 78s cost you more than those calculated under the actuarial method.

Rule of 78s method: a method of determining interest charges according to which relatively high interest is charged during the early period of the loan.

– been mostly outlawed

DECIDING HOW MUCH TO BORROW

An important prerequisite of successful borrowing is determining in advance the limits of borrowing. A common characteristic of persons who overextend their credit is that they never set debt limits for themselves. Even though the determination of a precise credit maximum is an individual decision affected by numerous personal, financial, and other considerations, general guidelines do exist.

A common rule of thumb is that no more than 10 to 20 percent of an individual's take-home pay should be used to repay installment debt. This rule does not include mortgage debt, which is typically considered a portion of a household's total expenditure for shelter rather than debt. Persons who spend less than 10 percent of their net income on debt repayments are taking a conservative, safe approach to installment buying. Those who exceed 20 percent are likely to encounter difficulties in both repaying outstanding debts and finding sufficient funds for necessary monthly expenditures.

Table 7-2 indicates the amount of debt repayment an individual can afford at various income levels. For example, if your total take-home pay is $30,000 per year, you can spend $250 per month on debt repayments if you adopt the 10-percent guideline; $375 if you use the 15-percent guideline; and $500 if you apply the 20-percent rule. The last rule appears to be followed by most households. In 1981 consumer debt equaled 20.2 percent of total disposable personal income. This amount was considerably less than in 1978, when the consumer debt was 22.9 percent of overall disposable personal income.[6]

Table 7-2
GENERAL DEBT REPAYMENT GUIDELINES

Annual Take-Home Income	Monthly Installment Maximums		
	10 percent	15 percent	20 percent
$ 8,000	$ 67	$ 100	$ 133
12,000	100	150	200
16,000	133	200	267
20,000	167	250	333
24,000	200	300	400
35,000	292	438	583
40,000	333	500	667
50,000	417	625	833
75,000	625	938	1,250
100,000	833	1,250	1,667

Source: Adapted from Frederick Amling and William G. Droms, *The Dow Jones–Irwin Guide to Personal Finance Planning* (Homewood, Ill.: Dow Jones–Irwin, 1982), p. 154.

By completing Figure 7-4 (on page 192), you will be able to determine whether your current amount of outstanding debt falls within the acceptable range. In addition to revealing the total amount of debt, Figure 7-4 will allow you to see at a glance to whom you owe money, the amount of the original loan, your current balance, the annual interest rate charged on each loan, your monthly payments, the number of months remaining on each loan, and the total amount remaining to be paid. By updating this figure on a regular basis, you will have an accurate statement of your current obligations.

RIGHT—AND WRONG—REASONS FOR BORROWING

People borrow for a number of reasons. Making credit purchases for the right reasons can help to improve your lifestyle; the wrong reasons can lead to financial ruin.

THE RIGHT REASONS FOR BORROWING

There are several reasons an individual might obtain credit to finance a purchase instead of paying cash. These include purchasing a major item, such as a home, car, or college education; meeting emergency needs; taking advantage of an unexpected opportunity; convenience; and improving one's credit rating.

Purchasing Large, Important Products and Services. Although individuals vary greatly in their willingness to make credit purchases, few people

Figure 7-4
SUMMARY OF OUTSTANDING LOANS

HOW MUCH DO YOU OWE, AND TO WHOM?

Write your monthly take-home pay here: $

Payments on all debts should not exceed [20] percent of your take-home pay, excluding mortgage.

Annual Percentage Rate (APR) is the interest rate on each loan, as defined by the Truth in Lending Act. The act requires that a lender tell you the APR.

The "total to be paid" (right-hand column) is the monthly payment times the number of months remaining.

Type of Debt		Original Amount	Balance Remaining	Annual Percentage Rate	Monthly Payment	Months Left	Total To Be Paid
Auto loans	1.						
	2.						
Checking overdrafts							
Credit cards	1.						
	2.						
	3.						
Education loans	1.						
	2.						
Home-improvement loans							
Passbook loans							
Personal loans	1.						
	2.						
Loans from friends	1.						
	2.						
Other loans or debts	1.						
	2.						
Total							

Source: John R. Dorfman, "Do You Owe Too Much?" *Parade*, December 15, 1982, p. 16. Parade Publications Inc. © 1982. Reprinted by permission.

have the necessary funds to pay immediately, in full, for a new home or condominium, a new automobile, a college education at a high-tuition university, or the costs of starting a new business. If one has sufficient income or savings to make monthly payments involved in repaying the debt, borrowing for a credit purchase is certainly justified. Even if the purchaser has sufficient savings to cover a major purchase such as a new automobile, he or she may choose to borrow a portion of the needed funds in order to maintain a savings reserve in case of emergency. This may be particularly important for people who find it difficult to save.

Dealing with Emergencies. Borrowing may be necessary in the case of an emergency. Unexpected hospital and medical expenses may surpass insurance coverage; you may experience a temporary job loss; an illness may prevent you from working. In all these cases, financial needs may exceed savings and cash on hand.

Taking Advantage of Opportunities. Borrowed funds sometimes allow a person to take advantage of business investments that will result in economic gain. In other instances, the opportunity is a temporary price reduction of needed merchandise. When the local department store offers 50 percent off on the $3,000 bedroom suite you have always wanted but could hardly afford, a credit purchase may be appropriate. By buying the suite now at the $1,500 discount price, you improve your current lifestyle and save money at the same time.

Convenience. Since borrowing has become as simple as handing a salesperson a credit card or writing yourself a loan on your overdraft checking account, millions of Americans regularly choose to use credit instead of cash. Credit cards are especially convenient for shoppers who find unexpected bargains but do not have the necessary cash on hand or in their checking account to pay for them. Even planned shopping trips may be made less stressful through the use of credit cards, since the shopper does not have to carry large amounts of cash or endure the frequent inconvenience of having personal checks approved. One study of commercial bank credit card holders revealed that higher-income shoppers are more likely to use credit cards for their convenience as a cash substitute. Lower-income shoppers frequently use credit cards for installment purchases.[7]

Improving Your Credit Rating. Borrowing funds and repaying loans on time create a credit history for you and permit you to build and maintain a good credit rating. This rating is considered by future lenders should you apply for a loan.

THE WRONG REASONS FOR BORROWING

The reasons for borrowing discussed above are all appropriate ones—*if* the individual will generate sufficient income to repay the loans in a timely manner. Typically, the *wrong* reason for borrowing involves the use of credit to live beyond your means. Unfortunately, the more you rely on credit, the larger the problem becomes. As Chapter 4 pointed out, the economic consequences of too much debt can be garnishment of wages, repossession of products, and even bankruptcy.

Reliance on credit to live beyond your means becomes a vicious circle. The more you overspend, the more credit you use and the less you have available to meet your regular needs. This results in more overspending, more future income committed to repaying current overspending, and so on.

Consumers who think of credit purchases as a series of small monthly payments face the dilemma of these payments quickly adding up. The $7,461 automobile advertised for $499 down plus 48 monthly payments of $199 actually includes the additional cost of $2,590 in interest payments over the life of the loan. Thus, the purchaser will ultimately pay over $10,000 for the car. Although the consumer may still be justified in purchasing the automobile with credit, it is essential that he or she consider both the cost of the borrowed funds and whether the monthly payments will be an unwieldy burden on the household financial budget.

What are the warning signs of credit abuse? The major danger signals include the use of credit to meet basic expenses, to substitute for savings, to improve your social standing, to make impulse purchases, to gamble, and to make short-lived purchases.

Using Credit to Meet Basic Expenses. The clearest signal of credit abuse is when borrowed funds are necessary to pay your basic monthly living expenses. If you cannot cover the routine costs of food, clothing, and rent payments without borrowing, your lifestyle is excessive. Although there are several methods for improving your lifestyle, reliance on borrowed funds is not a long-term solution. Methods for determining how much you can afford were discussed earlier in this chapter.

Using Credit to Improve Your Social Standing. A danger facing the financial stability of many households—and particularly those of younger adults who have not yet secured the raises that come with promotions—is the desire to impress friends, neighbors, business associates, and other acquaintances through visible symbols of affluence and success. Over three-quarters of a century ago, the economist Thorstein Veblen coined the term *conspicuous consumption.* He applied this label to the actions of status seekers in joining prestigious country clubs, driving luxury cars, wearing expensive designer clothes,

conspicuous consumption: the purchase of products and services designed to communicate to others the purchaser's lifestyle, income, or tastes.

"My goodness, man, you don't need a loan granted, you need three wishes granted."

Using Borrowed Funds to Pay for Basic Expenses Is a Sign of Credit Abuse.

Source: From the *Wall Street Journal*—Permission, Cartoon Features Syndicate.

and living in high-status neighborhoods. While such spending decisions represent fulfillment of individual needs and desires, they can result in financial ruin if they are supported largely by borrowed funds.

Using Credit to Make Impulse Purchases. Too often, unplanned, *impulse purchases,* triggered by a desire for immediate gratification, are ill-advised. Readily available credit compounds the problem for impulsive shoppers. Their purchases frequently disappoint them for two reasons: (1) a better alternative might have been chosen had he or she taken the time to compare quality, price, and service; and (2) the cost of the unplanned purchase usually lingers in the form of principal and interest payments long after the pleasure of the new product or service has disappeared.

Using Credit to Gamble. Whether your gambling takes place at the race track or in response to the latest stock-market tip, financing the venture with borrowed funds almost always spells trouble. As financial writer Sylvia Porter

impulse purchases: unplanned purchases triggered by a desire for immediate gratification.

points out, "Borrowing to buy stocks or real estate or invest in a small business deal is entirely in order, particularly if you are young enough to recoup if you lose. But borrowing to gamble is begging for trouble and the very fact that you have to borrow means that this is not extra money you can afford to lose."[8]

Using Credit to Purchase Short-Lived Products and Services. Purchasing a $600 baby carriage on credit may mean that you will still be paying for the carriage long after your child is walking. Similarly, paying for this year's vacation in 24 monthly installments may mean monthly vacation bills—but no vacation—for the next two years. In essence, certain purchases should be paid in cash, postponed until sufficient savings are available, or forgone. They simply are not worth the debt they create. The decision concerning what these goods are is an individual one and depends, to a great extent, on your personal priorities. If this year's vacation represents a once-in-a-lifetime trip to Europe, you might decide to borrow the necessary funds despite the financial consequences.

buy s-term assets w/ s-term debt

CREDIT COUNSELING: A WAY BACK

Borrowers who find themselves too deeply in debt to manage their finances on their own should consult a consumer *credit counselor*—a professional trained to assist in developing personal financial budgets and arranging programs of debt repayment. An excellent source of free credit assistance is the nonprofit Consumer Credit Counseling Service, which is affiliated with the National Foundation for Consumer Credit and has offices in over 200 U.S. cities. For the location of the nearest office, write the National Foundation for Consumer Credit, Inc., Suite 601, 8701 Georgia Avenue, Silver Springs, Md. 20910.

Typically, the counselor's first actions will involve creditors who may be threatening to repossess the debtor's property or garnish his or her wages. After calculating the funds necessary to cover basic living expenses, the counselor will allocate the remainder of the debtor's income among the various creditors. In some instances, the counselor will make direct payments to creditors; in other instances, the debtor will make such payments. In either case, creditors are likely to agree to the plan—especially since they know they will receive much less should the individual declare bankruptcy. Their cooperation is even more likely if the debtor can explain the problems in repayment as resulting from an unexpected emergency, such as job loss or illness, and if the debtor and financial counselor have developed a workable budget and are sincere about repaying the debt.

Once the credit emergency is over, the credit counselor should be able to assist the individual in learning the basic budgeting skills discussed in Chapter 4. A counselor can be helpful in pinpointing the difference between necessities and luxuries and offering methods for weeding out unnecessary expenditures.

---

credit counselor: *a professional financial counselor trained to assist debt-ridden individuals and households in developing a budget and in arranging a program of debt repayment.*

Most important, the credit counselor will aid, not judge, the individual in escaping from the credit trap.

LEGISLATION GOVERNING CONSUMER CREDIT AND BORROWING

Since 1968, the federal government has played an important and growing role in protecting your rights as a borrower. These rights have been guaranteed by such laws as the Consumer Credit Protection Act of 1968, the Fair Credit Reporting Act of 1970, the Fair Credit Billing Act of 1974, the Equal Credit Opportunity Act of 1975, and the Fair Debt Collection Practices Act of 1978.

TRUTH IN LENDING

The grandparent of all federal consumer credit legislation is the Consumer Credit Protection Act of 1968. The *Truth in Lending Act,* as it immediately became known, produced major changes in the relationship between creditors and borrowers.

For the first time creditors were required to state the full cost of credit in plain language on credit purchase agreements and loan applications. As pointed out earlier, borrowers must be informed in writing of the total finance charge and the annual percentage rate (APR). They thus have a specific method for comparing the cost of credit offered by different lenders.

The Truth in Lending Act also contains a number of other important provisions. In some instances, creditors may levy a prepayment charge on loans that are repaid before their specified repayment date. In most cases, late payment charges are assessed. Although Truth in Lending does not prohibit these practices, it does require creditors to disclose these charges on the loan documents. In addition, lenders must:

1. Describe the property that can be seized or repossessed if the borrower does not meet repayment requirements.

2. Specify the borrower's right of recision—the conditions under which a borrower can change his or her mind and cancel the contract.

3. Label all "balloon" clauses, which require that the last payment be much higher than all previous payments.

4. Accurately and fairly advertise credit terms.

The Truth in Lending Act was revised in 1971 and again in 1982 to protect credit card holders. Under this new legislation, credit card companies are prohibited from sending consumers cards they never requested. The law also protects consumers whose credit cards have been lost or stolen by limiting their liability to $50 when an unauthorized person uses their card. This penalty

Truth in Lending Act: a major consumer credit protection law that requires lenders to inform borrowers in writing of the total finance charges and the annual percentage rates to be charged.

is levied only if you fail to report that the card has been lost. The credit card company also loses its right to collect the $50 from you if it has not informed you in writing of this liability; personalized the card with your signature, photograph, or fingerprints; and sent you a stamped, self-addressed envelope in which to report the loss.

The 1982 revision of Truth in Lending also requires all installment credit contracts to be written in plain English. This plain-language contract must be mailed to borrowers separately from all other forms so that they can take time to read it carefully.

FAIR CREDIT REPORTING ACT

Fair Credit Reporting Act: federal legislation that regulates credit-information practices and allows consumers to have access to their own credit files.

Passed in 1970, the *Fair Credit Reporting Act* gives consumers a mechanism by which to remove obsolete or inaccurate information from their credit file. The act ensures that credit bureaus obtain, maintain, and give out information

Protecting Yourself Against Credit-Card Fraud

Credit-card fraud is one of the most serious problems facing retailers and consumers. Losses in 1982 totaled $265 billion. Visa, MasterCard, and other bank cards alone lost about one-third of this amount. To protect yourself against the unauthorized use of your credit card or card number, the following steps should be taken:

1. Never let your card out of your sight. Watch it carefully while the sales clerk makes an impression for a credit purchase. A blank sales slip with your card information on it can be used to charge items you never bought.
2. Always check the amounts before you sign a sales slip.
3. Never discard sales slips until you compare them with your monthly statement. If your statement includes charges you did not make or incorrect charges, notify the credit-card company immediately in writing.
4. Carefully dispose of all old bills, receipts, and credit cards. Make certain that they are thoroughly shredded before placing them in a public trash receptacle.
5. Be especially wary about revealing your credit-card number over the telephone. Such information should be provided only in instances where you wish to charge a specific item, not when you request general information such as a catalog.
6. Never give your credit-card number to a company that solicits your business over the telephone. If the telephone offer is of interest, call the main office of the firm on your own and ask whether the offer is legitimate. In addition, you can contact the local Better Business Bureau to request information about the company.
7. Keep & destroy all carbons!

Merchants are taking a number of steps to spot credit-card thieves before the damage occurs. They concentrate on customers who buy indiscriminately without asking for a specific size, style, or color; never compare values; and inquire about the maximum amount that can be charged at one time and then make purchases of slightly less than the maximum. They also focus on people who try to take merchandise from the store as quickly as possible even though it might mean refusing free alterations or having to carry heavy or bulky items to their cars without the assistance of a store employee. Another suspect is the person who enters a store immediately before closing time and makes major, rushed purchases. In these cases, a thief may be trying to purchase the merchandise and leave the store before the stolen card number is revealed by the store's computer.

about your credit background in a fair and equitable way. This act is important because, as noted earlier, most prospective creditors will review your credit file before granting a loan.

The main provisions of the Fair Credit Reporting Act include the following:

1. If you are denied credit, insurance, or a job or must pay an added premium to purchase credit or insurance, you must be told the name and address of the consumer-reporting agency that prepared your credit file.

2. The consumer-reporting agency must tell you exactly what your credit file contains and where the information came from.

3. If you find incomplete or inaccurate information, you have the right to an investigation. If the consumer-reporting agency verifies your charges or cannot determine the accuracy of the credit file statement, you can have this information removed from your file.* At your request the credit bureau must then notify individuals and businesses who have received the incorrect or incomplete information that this information is no longer part of your file.

*only inaccurate info.

4. When no resolution is possible on a credit dispute, or when there are extenuating circumstances that explain a credit problem, you have the right to include your version of the dispute in your credit file.

5. If you are denied credit, insurance, or employment because of negative information in your credit report, you have the right to obtain a copy of the report at no charge from the credit bureau. When no negative information is involved, you can receive a copy for a small fee.

6. Consumer-reporting agencies are required to withhold the details of your credit file from all individuals and businesses who do not have a legitimate right to them.

7. Any negative information about you can be part of your file for no longer than 7 years. The only exception is bankruptcy, which may be reported for 10 years.

FAIR CREDIT BILLING ACT

In 1974 the *Fair Credit Billing Act* established procedures for dealing with billing errors and billing disputes. These procedures are binding for both lenders and borrowers.

According to the law, a billing error may involve a charge for something you never purchased or for a purchase made by an unauthorized person. It may also involve an incorrect price or date of purchase, an item that was never delivered, failure to record a payment on your account, arithmetic errors, and more. If you discover any of these errors on your account, you can take the following steps to correct the problem. A statement of these procedures is sent periodically to consumers.

Fair Credit Billing Act: federal legislation that establishes procedures for dealing with billing errors and disputes and creating time limits within which bills must be mailed and complaints and disputes addressed.

1. Inform the creditor in writing that you have a problem. This notification must be mailed within 60 days after the original bill was mailed. Your letter must include your name and account number, the amount of the error, and the reasons you believe the bill was wrong.

2. You can withhold payment for this disputed amount as well as for any finance charges that apply to it while the problem is being resolved. However, you must pay the undisputed part of the bill on schedule.

3. You can expect to receive an acknowledgment of your letter within 30 days. Within 90 days, the creditor must either correct your bill or tell you why your claim is in error. If your claim is incorrect, you will have to pay all finance charges and minimum payments that accumulated while you were questioning the bill. No matter how the dispute is resolved, you must receive a complete accounting of the amount you still owe.

4. If you continue to have questions or problems, you can notify the creditor once more within the billing period.

The Fair Credit Billing Act also allows you to withhold payment when the goods you receive are damaged or shoddy or the service is inadequate if you purchased these items with a credit card. Finally, it requires that your payments be promptly credited to your account, that you receive prompt bills, and that overpayments be credited to your account or, if you request, be returned to you in cash.

EQUAL CREDIT OPPORTUNITY ACT

Equal Credit Opportunity Act (ECOA): *federal legislation that prohibits discrimination based on race, sex, national origin, religion, age, or receipt of public assistance when considering credit applications.*

Originally passed in 1975, the *Equal Credit Opportunity Act (ECOA)* is considered a landmark in removing discriminatory credit practices. For the first time, creditors were required to treat women and men equally when granting credit. Creditors are also prohibited from discriminating because of race, national origin, religion, age, or the receipt of public assistance.

The primary beneficiaries of the Equal Credit Opportunity Act are women. Traditionally considered appendages to men and in no need of credit of their own, women had frequently been denied credit simply because of their sex and marital status. The Equal Credit Opportunity Act changed this situation in the following ways:

1. To qualify for credit, a woman can now establish her own credit history, separate and apart from that of her husband. Before the passage of ECOA, a woman's credit history was typically linked to her husband's in a joint credit bureau file under the husband's name even when she was totally responsible for repaying a loan.

The new law establishes two separate credit files for husband and wife. If a woman signs a contract to repay a debt along with her husband, the payment history is recorded in both names. If the woman divorces or if her husband dies, her personal credit history is still intact; it does not end with the death of her marriage or husband, forcing her to start anew in building her credit rating.

2. The ECOA also prohibits discriminatory questions and practices on credit applications. Creditors can no longer ask applicants their sex or child-bearing plans. They must include all sources of income, such as alimony and child-support payments, as well as income from part-time work. In addition, when women apply for credit on their own, creditors cannot ask about their husband's or former husband's financial situation.

3. Mortgage lenders can no longer take into account only the husband's income when calculating whether a couple can afford a mortgage.

4. Creditors can no longer force women to apply for loans with their husbands or have their husbands or father cosign the agreement if they can meet the loan requirements on their own.

FAIR DEBT COLLECTION PRACTICES ACT

To protect harassed consumers from the widespread abuses of debt collection agencies, Congress passed the *Fair Debt Collection Practices Act* in 1978. This act requires collection agencies to act in an ethical way when dealing with debtors. It specifically prohibits the following practices:

1. Debt collectors can no longer call debtors in the middle of the night demanding payment. They cannot use abusive language, make threats, impersonate government officials or attorneys, or misrepresent a consumer's legal rights.

2. Debt collectors may not inform your employer or any third party of a debt without your direct consent. Credit bureaus are the only exceptions to this rule.

3. If you owe money to several creditors, the law guarantees you the right to decide how your repayment will be distributed.

4. Once a debt collector is informed that you are represented by an attorney, the collector can no longer contact you directly.

Fair Debt Collection Practices Act: federal legislation that prohibits harassment and other unethical collection practices by debt collectors.

SUMMARY

Borrowed funds are an important component of most people's financial plans. Shopping for the best credit deal is likely to produce savings for the careful personal financial manager. Factors to consider include total cost of merchandise and total cost of credit, time period for repayment, requirements of collateral, and other factors, such as service provided by the merchant or financial institution.

Creditors evaluate the three C's—capacity, character, and collateral—in reviewing loan applications.

Credit bureaus assist the review process by providing the lender with information about the applicant's credit history and other public record information. Consumers who plan to apply for credit for the first time should consider (1) opening a checking account and a savings account; (2) applying for a retail credit card and/or bank credit cards; (3) requesting that the credit bureau in their former city of residence forward their file to the credit bureau in their new city if they have moved recently; and (4) asking a relative or close friend to cosign a loan agreement.

Sources of credit may differ considerably in such characteristics as selectivity in approving loan applicants and interest rates charged. Consumers seeking to borrow funds can investigate such sources as commercial banks, savings and loan associations, mutual savings banks, credit unions, the government, and small loan companies. In addition, consumers with certain types of life insurance policies may be able to borrow money from their insurance companies. They may also obtain credit purchases from retailers and loans from family members and close friends.

Consumer credit can be categorized by form (as a cash advance or as a product or service purchased with credit) and by method of repayment (in a single lump-sum or in partial periodic installments over a longer time period). Open-end consumer installment credit includes revolving charge accounts, bank credit cards, automatic overdraft accounts, and bank lines of credit. Closed-end payment plans require a separate written agreement for each credit purchase specifying the length of the repayment period as well as the amount and timing of each partial payment. Mortgage loans are a form of installment loan.

Cash loans typically require the borrower to sign a promissory note detailing the terms of the agreement and the rights and obligations of both lender and borrower. Credit purchases involve a similar loan document, called a retail installment contract and security agreement.

While interest rates vary for different types of loans, different financial institutions, and different borrowers, the maximum rates are typically specified by state usury laws. Loan applications must inform borrowers of the cost of credit using two measures: (1) the finance charge, the total dollar amount charged for credit; and (2) the annual percentage rate (APR), the interest paid per dollar of credit per year. Alternative methods for calculating interest on cash loans and installment sales include the add-on method, discount method, and the declining-balance method. Some lenders use the actuarial method of figuring interest, which is based on the exact number of days the loan is unpaid; others use the Rule of 78s, which tends to allocate greater percentages of early payments to interest rather than to principal reduction, thereby penalizing borrowers who repay their loans early.

Credit is typically used for major purchases, to deal with emergencies, for convenience, to improve credit ratings, and to take advantage of opportunities. These are all proper uses of credit provided the borrower has sufficient excess funds to cover the additional costs involved in repaying these credit purchases. The following are examples of inappropriate uses of credit: to meet basic expenses, to improve one's social standing, to buy impulsively, to gamble, and to purchase short-lived products and services.

Credit abuse frequently results in the inability to make scheduled payments when they are due. In an attempt to prevent credit abuse and improve consumer financial planning, the Consumer Counseling Service provides professional credit counselors to debt-ridden people. Their professionals are trained to assist in the development of personal financial budgets and arranging programs of debt repayment. Although determination of borrowing limits is an individual decision, most credit counselors recommend that no more than 10 to 20 percent of an individual's take-home pay be used in repaying installment debt.

A number of significant federal laws have been enacted within the past 20 years to provide information on credit costs, provide consumers with access to their credit files, correct billing errors, end discrimination in lending, and prohibit harassment by, and the unethical practices of, some bill collectors. These laws include the Truth in Lending Act, the Fair Credit Reporting Act, the Fair Credit Billing Act, the Equal Credit Opportunity Act, and the Fair Debt Collection Practices Act.

REVIEW QUESTIONS

1. Briefly define the following:
   - credit
   - capacity
   - character
   - collateral
   - credit bureau
   - consumer finance company
   - sales finance company
   - pawnbrokers
   - loan sharks
   - installment credit
   - revolving charge account
   - automatic overdraft account
   - line of credit
   - closed-end installment purchase plans
   - mortgage
   - promissory note
   - retail installment contract
   - usury laws
   - finance charge
   - annual percentage rate (APR)
   - add-on method
   - discount method
   - declining-balance method
   - actuarial method
   - Rule of 78s method
   - conspicuous consumption
   - impulse purchases
   - credit counselor
   - Truth in Lending Act
   - Fair Credit Reporting Act
   - Fair Credit Billing Act
   - Equal Credit Opportunity Act
   - Fair Debt Collection Practices Act

2. Explain each of the three C's of credit and the role played by credit bureaus in consumer loans.

3. What are the major alternative sources of consumer credit?

4. Distinguish between open-end and closed-end installment credit.

5. Classify the types of consumer credit on the basis of form and method of repayment.

6. What is the difference between the finance charge on a consumer loan and the annual percentage rate? Give an example of each.

7. Contrast the following methods of calculating interest:
   a. add-on method and discount method
   b. actuarial method and Rule of 78s

8. What are several appropriate reasons for borrowing? What are some wrong reasons for relying on credit?

9. Explain the role of credit counselors in personal finance.

10. Identify and briefly explain the chief features of the major federal legislation affecting consumer credit and borrowing.

CASES AND EXERCISES

1. Explain the appropriate uses of bank credit cards and national credit cards such as American Express, Diners Club, and Carte Blanche.

2. Match the following consumer credit-related laws with the features listed in the column on the right:
   a. Truth in Lending Act
   b. Fair Credit Reporting Act
   c. Fair Credit Billing Act
   d. Equal Credit Opportunity Act
   e. Fair Debt Collection Practices Act

   ___ loss of credit card
   ___ bankruptcy
   ___ disclosure of credit information
   ___ credit discrimination
   ___ protection from harassment by creditors

3. Anna Hargrove borrowed $2,000 and agreed to repay the loan in 12 installments. The Rule of 78s applied on the loan, and total finance charges were $160. What is the total amount received by the lender if Anna decides to repay the entire loan in 6 months?

4. Write a brief profile of a person using each of the following sources of credit:
   a. credit union
   b. life insurance company
   c. consumer finance company
   d. pawnbroker
   e. loan shark

5. After a day of comparison shopping, Jerry Weinstein has located three retail stores that are offering the same model television set and are willing to allow him to purchase the set for a $25 down payment with the remaining balance to be paid

one year later. Albertson's Electronics offers the lowest price ($290), but will charge interest on the unpaid balance at 18 percent annually. Connelley's has the highest price ($330), but will finance the unpaid balance for one year at no interest. Baker's television set is priced at $315, and they will finance the unpaid balance at an annual percentage rate of 10 percent. From which retailer will Jerry receive the lowest total price?

ANSWERS TO PERSONAL FINANCE I.Q. TEST
1. Fiction. 2. Fact. 3. Fiction. 4. Fiction. 5. Fiction. 6. Fact.

HOW CLARK BOYD REACHED HIS PERSONAL FINANCIAL DECISION

"Many people have credit references, even though they may not know it," Professor Westwood noted. "Think about it for a minute—have you ever purchased something and then paid for it later?"

"Well," began Clark, "I do know the owner of the gas station around the corner from my house. A couple of times when I've asked if I could write a check, he's told me just to pay him the next time. I always do."

"That's one reference for you," Professor Westwood agreed. "Can you think of any others?"

"I hate to admit this," Clark hesitated, and then grinned. "You see, when I bought my car, I thought I'd saved up everything. But I forgot to include the costs of taxes and licensing. The dealer carried the extra cost for me for a month. Oh, yes—and then there was last Christmas. I borrowed $200 from the credit union at my job. I paid them back, too, right after Christmas."

"Those are all sources you can use for your references," Professor Westwood pointed out. "Plus buying a stereo on time would give you an established credit line, which would help you later on if you wanted to get a national credit card or any kind of loan."

Clark took Professor Westwood's advice. He bought the stereo and used the gas station owner, car dealer, and credit union as references. Now he enjoys both a growing credit rating and a state-of-the-art stereo.

PART FOUR

EFFECTIVE BUYING

LEARNING OBJECTIVES

1. To identify the major stages of the family life cycle and their influence on consumer purchase behavior. / *2.* To enumerate the steps in the consumer decision-making process. / *3.* To list the major categories of consumer fraud and abuse. / *4.* To define the concept of consumerism and relate it to President Kennedy's statement of consumer rights. / *5.* To outline the major federal regulatory agencies and their consumer-related responsibilities. / *6.* To highlight the most important forms of business self-regulation. / *7.* To describe the primary private sources of consumer assistance and the services each provides. / *8.* To explain the use of small-claims courts in solving consumer problems.

TESTING YOUR PERSONAL FINANCE I.Q.

	FACT	FICTION
1. "Bracket creep" is a form of bait-and-switch advertising.	☐	☐
2. Over 50 percent of all U.S. families can be classified as two-income families.	☐	☐
3. The largest family-life-cycle category is middle-aged married with children.	☐	☐
4. The average total cost of raising a child in the United States is now estimated at $375,000.	☐	☐
5. The *Good Housekeeping* seal is awarded to all products meeting a published set of standards by the magazine.	☐	☐
6. President Kennedy's statement of consumer rights includes the right to an attorney or one appointed by the court.	☐	☐
7. It is not necessary to have a lawyer for cases in small-claims court.	☐	☐

The materials in this chapter assist in separating fact from fiction. Your answers can be checked on page 241.

CHAPTER EIGHT

THE INFORMED CONSUMER

**SHARING A PERSONAL FINANCIAL DECISION WITH
PROFESSOR IRA WILSKER OF LAMAR UNIVERSITY**

A few days after his lecture on what consumers should know, Professor Ira Wilsker was approached by Floyd Campbell, one of his students. As Floyd explained, his mother was having trouble with the local branch of a large national chain store. It all began when her old air conditioner broke down and couldn't be fixed anymore. After some comparison shopping, she decided that the chain store offered both the best price and the fastest installation service. The salesman even visited her house and assured her that there would be no problem in installing the new system.

"You wouldn't believe what happened then," exclaimed Floyd. "She told me that two inexperienced 'kids' arrived in a rusty pickup truck. They spent *hours* trying to install the air conditioner, with frequent calls to the shop for advice. They did—to their relief, I bet—get it going. But shortly after they left it stopped."

"And now it gets even worse," Floyd added. "My mom called the store to complain, and the next day another repairman came. He discovered that not only had the 'kids' failed to install the air conditioner properly, but they'd managed to damage my mom's perfectly good furnace. To make a long story short, he couldn't get the parts to fix the furnace and told my mom to call the chain store back again. You won't believe it, but the salesman offered to sell her a new furnace. And only a few days before, he'd told her what excellent condition her old one was in!"

"By now my mom was totally fed up," Floyd continued. "I offered to go directly to the store manager and complain. After almost a 45-minute wait, he saw me. The best he could do, he said, was to sell my mom a new furnace at cost and install it free. But why should we have to spend several hundred dollars replacing something that wasn't broken to begin with?"

If you were Professor Wilsker, what additional steps would you recommend that Floyd take?

To find out how Professor Wilsker helped Floyd with his personal financial problem, turn to page 241.

"Is there such a thing as Shoppers Anonymous?"
President John F. Kennedy
(on receiving a $40,000 bill for his wife's clothes)[1]

Delta Airlines advertises that "Delta is ready when you are." But Delta was not ready for a retired Illinois Supreme Court justice and his wife when they were *bumped* (denied seats) from a Florida-bound flight. The couple had been invited to spend the weekend at the ranch of Alberto-Culver's chairman and watch the birth of a horse.

Delta bumped the couple because the flight was oversold but offered another flight two hours later. The retired judge and his wife refused, and decided to sue instead. The couple claimed that they suffered "humiliation, indignity, and outrage." The jury's decision? The judge and his wife were each awarded $100,000 in punitive damages and $4,000 in compensating damages. The $208,000 award was more than twice what the original suit requested. Delta's lawyer called the decision "absurd" and appealed.[2]

Most consumer grievances concerning services that are paid for and then denied are resolved without a lawsuit. But as consumers we all rely on other individuals and organizations to provide us with satisfactory goods and services. Although today's consumers are typically better informed than their counterparts in earlier eras, the economic pressures on consumers have increased rather than decreased in recent years. These pressures make mastering consumer skills a dollars-and-cents necessity for the majority of Americans.

THE CONSUMER OF THE 1980s

Three major problems have confronted the consumer in recent years: inflation, recession, and unemployment. As a consequence, consumers have experienced difficulties in their attempts to maintain a decent standard of living.

- Despite the fact that the median income for a family with one wage earner and two dependent children rose from $11,165 to approximately $23,895 between 1972 and 1982—a 114-percent increase over the 10-year period—its purchasing power declined due to increased taxes and, until 1982, very high inflation. A doubling of family income could not offset the tripling of federal income taxes and the effects of inflation, which turned an increase of $10,159 in after-tax income during the 10-year period into a loss of $1,159 in terms of 1972 purchasing power.[3]

THE INFORMED CONSUMER 209

- A 7-percent unemployment rate in 1984 left almost 8 million Americans struggling to pay their basic monthly expenses. Census Bureau statistics reveal that median family income declines 31 percent when the husband becomes unemployed and 24 percent when the wife is out of work. (This discrepancy reflects the lower earning power of women.)[4]
- Even though the 3.8-percent inflation rate in 1983 represented the lowest inflation rate in more than 10 years, consumer buying power continued to suffer from years of runaway inflation. Consumer prices have risen approximately 579 percent since 1939, with the result that a 1939 dollar is worth only 15 cents today. → After taxes: 5.78¢.

CONSUMER RESPONSES

Economic pressures have caused many consumers to change their buying patterns in significant ways. Tired of products that sometimes fall apart after a few uses, consumers are now demanding more for their money. "People are very concerned with quality," says Ellen Metcalf, representing the consulting firm of Arthur D. Little. "And manufacturers won't be able to ride on past reputations. They'll have to keep proving themselves."[5]

Millions of Americans have postponed numerous purchases. According to a recent survey, nearly 22 percent of washing machines, 28 percent of freezers, and 33 percent of ranges are more than 10 years old. Another study revealed that one-third of the respondents plan to keep their cars for more than a decade—up 12 percent from only three years earlier.[6]

The result of these postponed purchases is pent-up consumer demand, which will inevitably bring consumers back into the marketplace. Their purchases, however, may be far different from those made 10 years ago, for today's consumers tend to be more sophisticated and cost-conscious than their predecessors. They have realized, for instance, that the energy efficiency of home appliances is often just as important as the purchase price.

These decisions are of crucial importance to business and to the entire American economy, for two out of every three dollars spent in the United States can be traced back to consumers. On a daily basis, more than $5 billion passes from consumers' wallets to the cash registers of merchants, manufacturers, and other suppliers. That translates to about $23 for every man, woman, and child. Thus, businesses must be responsive to consumer demand if they are to survive.

BUYING ON CREDIT

Double-digit inflation, which was a fact of life for several years, changed American attitudes toward spending and saving. During the first half of the twentieth century, most consumers deciding on a purchase—especially a major one, such as a new car or a house—planned for it well in advance. They knew how much the item cost and how much they could—or wanted to—spend. They often postponed purchases until they felt able to afford them or chose something for the interim, until they could afford something better. If prices increased, people usually waited for them to come down again before buying. Most families deposited surplus funds into their savings account, which served as both an emergency reserve for the present and a source of funds for future expenses—college education for children, money for the retirement years, funds for a special vacation.

Once inflation took hold, however, consumers began to realize that saving was being penalized rather than rewarded. Their money lost rather than gained value, since passbook savings accounts earned a rate of interest that was less than the inflation rate. Borrowing money to make purchases, on the other hand, brought consumers some advantages: all the interest paid on a debt was tax-deductible, whereas interest earned on a savings account was taxed. In addition, the money used to repay a debt was usually worth less than the money that was borrowed, because inflation had eroded its value. As a consequence, during the late 1970s and early 1980s, many consumers decided to buy now rather than later and to borrow rather than save.

These consumer spending and saving patterns quickly changed when interest rates began to outpace the inflation rate. Many consumers who could afford it returned to savings—this time at higher yields than ever before. Millions of others, unable to save because of the recession and unemployment, postponed making major purchases. As a result, consumer and mortgage debt declined in 1981, after having set record levels in 1979. By 1982 Americans were using only 15.1 percent of their disposable income to repay their debts, down from 18 percent in 1979.

TWO-INCOME FAMILIES

An increasingly common response to declining purchasing power is the two-income family. For those husbands and wives fortunate enough to be working at the same time, two incomes often mean that consumer purchases are possible, even though in many cases these purchases strain the family budget.

Two incomes have become a fact of life for the majority of American families in the mid-1980s. In 1950 only one-fourth of all married women were employed outside the home. By 1984 almost 65 percent of all married women held outside jobs.[7] The percentage of working wives increases as children grow older. At the present time, over half of all married women with school-age children hold jobs outside the home.[8] The most recent U.S. census revealed that the 32 million U.S. families with at least two working members earn far more than one-income families. The median household income for families with two or more wage earners exceeded $34,560 in 1981, while the income for families with a single wage earner was $26,710.

Two-income families fall into two distinct groups: those relatively affluent households with sufficient funds for essential purchases and discretionary purchases of luxuries and those who are working as hard as they can to pay their bills and stay financially afloat.

The Haves. The *haves* make up a large percentage of the top tier of the consumer market. Many of these two-income families are relatively young and affluent, and a large part of their $50,000, $60,000, $70,000, and $80,000-plus income is spent on such consumer luxuries as stereo systems, videotape recorders, personal computers, and microwave ovens. Even during recessionary times, childless working couples earning $50,000 or more continue to purchase luxury consumer goods and services. Indeed, they spend so much that they have disproportionately weighted retail sales in their favor: the richest 40 percent of consumer households account for 60 percent of retail sales.

Steve and Nancy Sayer, recently profiled by *U.S. News & World Report*, match the income, age, and spending patterns of the haves.

> "We lead a good life, but not an extravagant life," says Steve, 29, a marketing representative for IBM.
>
> He and Nancy, a 28-year-old specialist in international hiring for General Electric, have no children, so they can each work 60 hours a week at jobs they consider a vital part of their lives.
>
> The sense of achievement work brings, they say, is as important as the income. "It is the process of doing something really well and being recognized for it that matters most," says Nancy. "I'm ambitious. I set high standards, even outside of work."
>
> Despite dedication to their jobs, the couple manages to spend most evenings together, in suburban Ossining, New York, where they are restoring a spacious four-bedroom home. The one-hour commute by train to their jobs in New York City gives them added time with each other.
>
> Though their income puts them in the top one percent of U.S. families, the money does not stretch as far as the Sayers would like. "When you add up our fixed expenses, our discretionary income isn't near what you'd think it would be," observes Nancy.
>
> Eating into their earnings are household expenses, taxes, monthly commuting costs of about $200, hefty clothing bills and upkeep on two cars. But they still manage to save about 20 percent of their gross income . . . and to spend most of their weekends away from home, visiting friends and family or skiing and hiking in Vermont. The savings might eventually go for a weekend house or a boat.[9]

The Have-Nots. Two-families at the bottom of the consumer market are in a very different position. Both husband and wife must work just to make ends meet, and unnecessary expenses of any kind are avoided. For Teresa and Mike Hiland, whose $19,000 total annual income is barely enough to pay bills and meet the costs of necessary monthly purchases, two incomes are a matter of survival.

EFFECTIVE BUYING

Total Financial Planning.

Two incomes need it twice as much.

With more income at your disposal, you have more opportunities to build capital through a broader range of investments. Yet that very buildup is slowed, often stopped, by the higher tax penalty generated by two incomes. You're well aware of the problem. But what's the most sensible answer?

A financial strategy built for two.

Prudential-Bache can help you make more and keep more, with Total Financial Planning. It's an investment strategy designed to help two incomes produce maximum returns, while you minimize risk by diversifying.

You control your strategy. And you can change it, as your own situation or the economy changes.

Our Account Executives are specially trained in the Total Financial Planning process, and equipped with technology unique in the financial world. So they have an unsurpassed capability to evaluate more than one hundred financial opportunities, and choose those that best meet the needs of your two-income household.

We can help raise your income, lower your taxes...

We'll help you select from a variety of investments structured to keep two incomes earning even more money. Among them: high-yielding stocks, discount corporate bonds, growth stock funds, and zero coupon bonds. And to protect those earnings from the tax invasion: municipals, annuities, tax-advantaged mutual funds, utilities with dividend reinvestment plans, and gifting strategies.

...and make the American Dream happen for both of you.

With Total Financial Planning, two incomes can realize their fullest potential. The two of you can better meet your needs, maintain your lifestyle, and retire comfortably. Even in this difficult economy of ours, Total Financial Planning can help you attain the American Dream.

We're the ones your money needs.

Discover how Total Financial Planning can turn two incomes into a lifetime of investment opportunity and financial security. Call us: 800-654-5454.

We're Prudential-Bache Securities. Day or night, we'll be there.

Bring us your future.

Prudential-Bache Securities

© 1984 Prudential-Bache Securities. Member SIPC

Courtesy of Prudential-Bache. Photo by Nancy Brown.

The above advertisement stresses that with the extra money that two incomes bring, the *haves*, or relatively young and affluent two-income families, need to give more thought to financial planning. On the other hand, *have-nots*, or couples who work out of necessity, need two incomes just to make ends meet.

For Teresa and Mike Hiland, it was just another typically hectic day. They awoke at 5:30 A.M. and 15 minutes later nudged their two young boys from sleep. Then they had to find a substitute sitter because Teresa's mother, who normally cares for 18-month-old Christopher, was ill.

That accomplished, Teresa dropped 4-year-old Daniel at a day-care center on the way to her job as a clerk-typist at an insurance firm. Mike, meanwhile, left Christopher at the substitute sitter's and headed for the hospital where he is employed as a groundskeeper.

At day's end, there was enough time for a quick dinner and an hour or so of family time before the children went off to bed. Then Teresa and Mike, both in their mid-20s, began to gear up for a repeat performance on the next morning.

The Hilands keep this breakneck pace out of necessity. Says Mike: "Any family that's going to make a living these days has to have two people working."

Between them, the couple earns $19,000 a year, just enough to cover rent on their modest three-bedroom house, food, car payments, child-care costs and medical bills. Thoughts of buying a house have been pushed far into the future as inflation wreaks havoc with their budget. Says Mike: "We do not have enough saved to even make a down payment."

There is no room for frills in their lives. TV and an occasional dinner with friends are the main sources of recreation. On weekends, they have little time to relax, being busy with cleaning, running errands and shopping.

Vacations are out of the question: they haven't had one since they were married almost five years ago. Teresa uses most of her vacation time to care for the boys when they are ill.[10]

Even though the Hilands are having a much harder time than the Sayers, the couples have several things in common. At both consumer levels, the presence of two incomes makes it less likely that unemployment will eliminate all family income. Even if one member loses his or her job, the other is likely to continue working. This fact has eased the effects of economic hard times on millions of American families.

Two People Working Means Added Expenses. Nevertheless, as both profiles reveal, when both a husband and wife work, new consumer expenses are added to the family budget. Costs of commuting typically rise; both partners may need a work wardrobe; both may now eat lunch and other meals separately and away from home. Because time is a precious commodity for a working couple, they may hire someone to help with household chores. If there are children, funds must be spent on childcare—babysitters, special after-school programs, summer schools, camps, and daycare programs. And working wives, short of time and energy after a long day, are more likely to choose more expensive convenience foods or opt for more family dinners outside the home at fast-food restaurants.

In addition, as working couples increase their income, taxes take a larger and larger share of the income pie. This tax bite grows even larger when it is placed in the context of an inflationary dollar. For example, in 1981 a married

EFFECTIVE BUYING

Downward Mobility

Rising costs, unemployment fears, and climbing taxes have combined to give some consumers the distinct impression that they are worse off than their parents and that the future seems gloomier than they ever expected.

Since the turn of the century, every generation has achieved more at a faster rate than the generation that preceded it—at least until now. "There's still upward mobility, but the rate appears to be leveling off," says Robert Hauser, professor of sociology at the University of Wisconsin. This trend is even reflected in a statement in a recent federal budget: "The baby boom generation may never achieve the economic success of the generations immediately preceding it or following it."

Why is this trend toward downward mobility occurring? The primary reason is the sustained inflation of the late 1970s and early 1980s. Although many families—especially those with two incomes—earn $50,000, $60,000, $70,000, and more, they often have less buying power than their parents did. This problem is especially severe in the area of housing, where property costs have far outstripped the incomes of many young people. It is easy to understand the difficulties facing young couples in attempting to beat inflation when you realize that a couple needed $101,000 in 1982 to buy as much as their parents could with $28,000 in 1952.

Joseph Bensman, a sociology professor at the City University of New York, sums up this attitude:

The ethic for most middle-class adults in the fifties was to pay bills on time, shop during sales, and save for a house. The rest was gravy. For their offspring, it's just the reverse. Many of them buy what they feel they must have, and if there's anything left, they pay the bills. Unable to buy a house, some discard the notion of saving altogether. It's the middle-class version of buying Cadillacs when you're poor. If you're stuck in an apartment because you can't afford a house, you might as well buy a Betamax and a stereo.

Source: Hauser's and Bensman's quotations from Fran R. Schumer, "Downward Mobility," *New York Magazine*, August 16, 1982, pp. 20, 23. Copyright © 1984 by News Group Publications, Inc. Reprinted with permission of *New York Magazine*.

New York City couple with a combined income of $66,000 paid about 40 percent of its income in taxes; 20 years earlier, the same married couple earning an equivalent amount (approximately $22,000 in 1962 dollars) would have paid only 27 percent of its income in taxes. This 13-percent difference was referred to in Chapter 5 as *bracket creep*. Bracket creep and other factors affecting family purchasing power have led to what is called *downward mobility*.[11]

But even with all these extra costs, the two-income household is better off financially than the typical single-wage-earner household. In many cases the two-income family has some discretionary funds remaining after the necessities are paid for; it is better able to plan for the future and to work toward goals. The nature of these goals depends on the stage of the family life cycle.

THE CHANGING FAMILY LIFE CYCLE

family life cycle: the stages a household goes through over time based on such characteristics as marital status, age, presence or absence of children, and ages of children.

The *family life cycle* refers to the process of household formation and dissolution, the stages an individual household goes through over time. It is based on such family characteristics as marital status, age, presence or absence of children in the household, and the age of any children present. The various stages of the family life cycle are shown in Table 8-1.

Table 8-1
STAGES OF THE FAMILY LIFE CYCLE

Stage	Percentage of Total U.S. Population
1. Young single (age under 35)	8.2
2. Young married without children	2.9
3. Other young	
Married with children	17.1
Divorced with children	1.9
Divorced without children	0.1
4. Middle-aged (age 35–64)	
Married with children	33.0
Married without dependent children	5.5
Married without children	4.7
Divorced with children	1.8
Divorced without children	0.3
Divorced without dependent children	0.1
5. Older (age 65 and older)	
Married	5.2
Unmarried (divorced, widowed)	2.0
6. Other (all adults and children not accounted for by the above life-cycle stages)	17.2

Source: Patrick E. Murphy and William A. Staples, "A Modernized Family Life Cycle," *Journal of Consumer Research*, June 1979, p. 16. Adapted with permission of *Journal of Consumer Research*.

Purchase patterns vary according to stages in the family life cycle. One study reports the following behavioral characteristics and buying patterns:[12]

1. *Young singles:* these individuals have few financial burdens; they are fashion leaders and tend to be recreation-oriented. Purchases include basic kitchen equipment, basic furniture, cars, and vacations.

2. *Newly married without children:* these couples, who are better off financially than those with children, have the highest purchasing rate of durable consumer goods. Purchases include cars, kitchen appliances, furniture, vacations, dinners, and entertainment.

3. *Young married with youngest child under six:* in this group home purchasing is at a peak and liquid assets at a low. They tend to be dissatisfied with their financial position and the amount of money saved. Television viewing is higher than in previous stages. Purchases include washer and dryer, television, baby food, baby products, diaper services, and toys.

4. *Young married with youngest child over six:* the financial position of this group is better, with more wives working than in the previous stage. They buy larger-sized items. Purchases include food, cleaning materials, bicycles, home computers, and pianos.

5. *Middle-aged married without dependent children:* here home ownership is at a peak. This group is the most satisfied with financial position and is interested in travel, recreation, and self-education. Purchases include new, more tasteful furniture; travel; dental services; and magazines.

Newly married couples in the 1980s tend to be older than the newlyweds of the 1960s and 1970s. As a consequence, both husband and wife are likely to be working and both have probably already made many of the "big-ticket" household purchases. If both are working and they choose to postpone having children or decide not to have children, their purchasing patterns may be different from those of young married couples with children. They are likely to have more money to spend, and their goals may not include a home in the suburbs or saving for children's education.

When a couple does have children, the wife will not necessarily leave her job to stay at home and care for them. The number of children is likely to be low and the timing of their births carefully planned. It is also increasingly likely that these children may not grow up in a household with both parents: in the 1980s one in every three couples who marry can expect to be divorced at least once. Often this results in financial hardships for both partners and a radical change in consumption patterns. Children usually stay with the mother, who often has to work outside the home in order to supplement child support or alimony. The father, who must maintain a separate household in addition to contributing to the support of his children and former wife, may also experience financial difficulties.

Such families, however, are not yet the majority; most households of the 1980s still consist of couples with young or adolescent children who may find themselves living comfortably because of two incomes. These couples, along with two-income childless couples, are most likely to be able to afford the "good things" of life. Older couples with at least one partner still working also fall in this category, but many older, retired couples and widowed often do not—in part because inflation has severely penalized households on fixed incomes.

Every household, regardless of its life cycle stage, needs the knowledge and skills to use its funds wisely. One of the most important set of skills household members can learn is that of making careful consumer purchases.

THE CONSUMER DECISION-MAKING PROCESS

Suppose you want to purchase a major item like a new car, a piece of furniture, or a stereo. Most of us begin by thinking about the purchase: we look at our own lives and circumstances to form an idea of what we would like to have; we look at ads; we check *Consumer Reports*; we talk to parents, friends, and acquaintances; we begin to get an idea of the range of price and quality available. We soon determine whether the item is about the same price everywhere, or whether there is considerable price variation among competitive retail outlets. The products, manufacturers, and retail stores we consider in our deliberations are affected by our individual attitudes and personalities, as well as by our previous experiences.

What we have done is set a goal for ourselves and begun to collect the information that will help us reach it. Once we have a clear idea of what we want, we usually gather additional information. We visit stores and showrooms to see the item; we check prices and repayment methods; we compare what we would like to have with what we can afford; we collect brochures and check newspaper ads. Then we consider all the alternatives available to us. We calculate costs and benefits; we look at whether the extra cost of highest quality will ultimately pay off; we consider the impact of this purchase on our other goals. We study all the possible combinations until we find the one that is the best match for our needs and pocketbook. At that point we buy the item. Our degree of satisfaction with the product becomes a part of our accumulated experience and will greatly affect our likelihood of purchasing the same product or service again when similar needs arise. Figure 8-1 outlines the steps in the consumer decision-making process.

A STEP-BY-STEP APPROACH

Buying a product or service appears to be a long and complicated process, and sometimes it is. How elaborate and formal our decision making is depends on many things: what we are going to buy, how important it is to us, how often we buy it, and how greatly it will affect our finances.

In instances where major purchase decisions such as clothing, furniture, a place to live, household appliances, telephone service, personal computers, furniture, and leisure and recreational activities and equipment are involved, the decision process is likely to be relatively complex. Your preliminary decisions involve the choice of specific items under consideration, including price range and preferred styles. Unless you have an unlimited budget, you will spend a great deal of time on comparison shopping before you purchase an item. *Comparison shopping* is the process of comparing the products, prices, and services offered by different stores in order to get the best values.

Of course, we all buy items on impulse, and sometimes our decisions are changed somewhat by a persuasive salesperson. But we all go through some sort of decision-making process most of the time—in fact, taking the time to make a choice is an important part of being an informed, satisfied consumer.

Consumers who follow a deliberate, step-by-step approach to purchasing are able to take control of an important facet in their lives. By making conscious choices in an organized way, they frequently are able to extend the

comparison shopping: *the process of identifying alternative products, prices, and services offered by different retail stores, evaluating each alternative, and selecting the preferred alternative.*

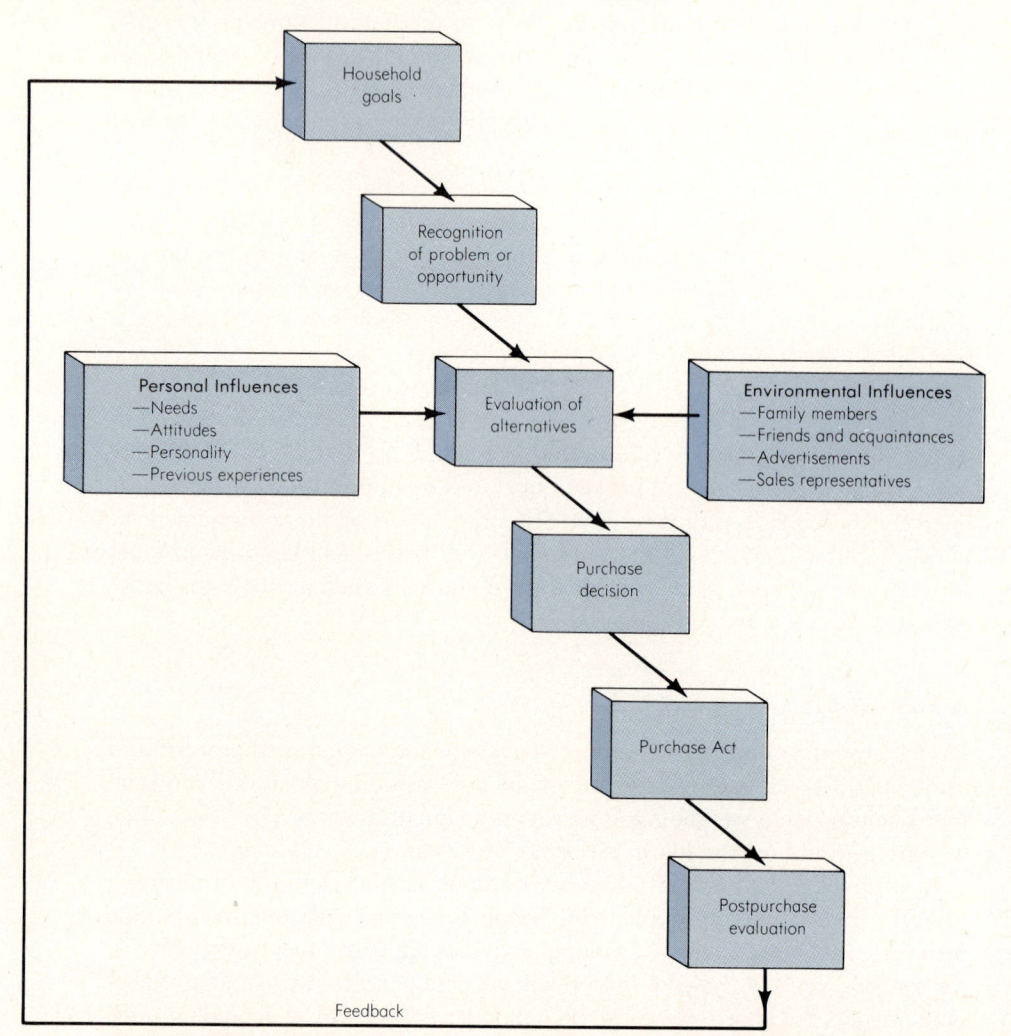

Figure 8-1
STEPS IN THE CONSUMER DECISION-MAKING PROCESS

```
Household goals
      ↓
Recognition of problem or opportunity
      ↓
Personal Influences  →  Evaluation of  ←  Environmental Influences
—Needs                   alternatives      —Family members
—Attitudes                                 —Friends and acquaintances
—Personality                               —Advertisements
—Previous experiences                      —Sales representatives
      ↓
Purchase decision
      ↓
Purchase Act
      ↓
Postpurchase evaluation
      ↓
   Feedback (loops back to Household goals)
```

Source: Adapted from John Dewey, *How We Think* (Boston: Heath, 1910), pp. 101–105.

purchasing power of their limited funds. Consumers who set goals, keep informed, budget carefully, and leave enough time for reasoned decisions benefit in many ways:

- They are able to take advantage of sales, bargains, and sudden opportunities.
- By planning their purchases over long time periods, they can often pay for them in the most convenient and least expensive way.

- By controlling their expenditures for food and everyday items, they avoid impulse buying and the frequent mistakes that accompany such purchases.

INDIVIDUAL VERSUS FAMILY DECISION MAKING

Consumer decisions become more complex when a number of household members are involved. Each member has his or her own idea of what to buy and where and when to buy it. These differences must be resolved before a purchase can be made.

Household decision making tends to evolve over time, and individual members begin to assume primary responsibility for purchasing certain products. Newly married couples tend to make numerous *joint* decisions, since each member is still learning the other's preferences and because of the social nature of shopping. After a short time, however, more individual decisions are likely to occur. For some purchases (such as kitchen products and food), the adult female household member is likely to exert the greatest influence. The male household member is likely to exercise the dominant influence in the purchase of such products as life insurance. Major purchases such as furniture, housing, vacation, and schooling for children tend to involve the joint influence of both the adult male and female. Figure 8-2 illustrates the roles played by married couples in 25 decisions.

THE INFLUENCE OF CHILDREN ON CONSUMER DECISIONS

When children are part of a household, they also exert considerable influence on the family's purchasing behavior. In large part this results from the cost of raising them. As Figure 8-3 indicates, parents in moderate circumstances spend $142,700 to raise a child from birth to age 18. College costs are extra.

In addition, children have strong likes and dislikes that influence what the family buys. The choice of the family's vacation, car, home, stereo, food, sporting equipment, and more is influenced by what children want. When children reach adolescence, their influence soars. The money they receive from their parents or earn from part-time jobs results in a huge consumer market, which experts estimate runs into the tens of billions of dollars. This is reflected in the results of a survey taken by the University of Michigan's Institute for Social Research. The survey found that half of all high school graduates not bound for college as well as 40 percent of those who planned to attend college already owned cars. In most cases, the purchase of the car was a family consumer decision.

CONSUMER FRAUD AND ABUSE

Making a wise purchase is one thing; being aware of pitfalls is another. The days of county fairs, where snake-oil salesmen made pitches for the virtue of a

Figure 8-2
MARITAL ROLES IN DECISION MAKING

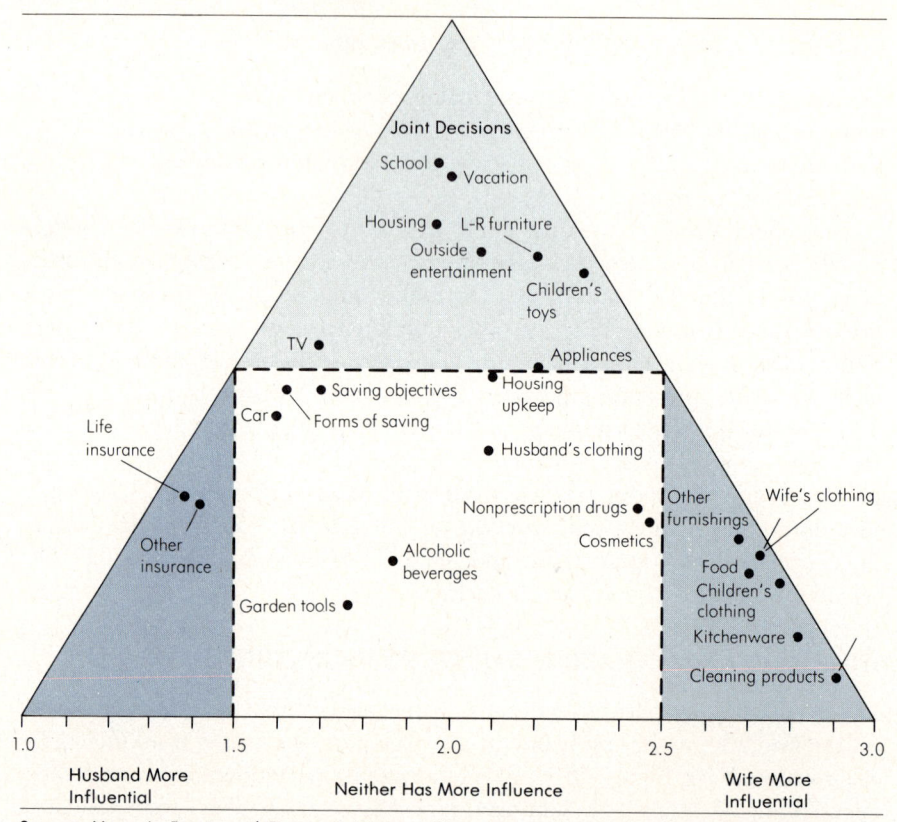

Source: Harry L. Davis and Benny P. Rigaux, "Perception of Marital Roles in Decision Process," *Journal of Consumer Research*, June 1974, p. 57. Adapted with permission of *Journal of Consumer Research*.

particular cure, are largely history; today there are more sophisticated ways to fleece the gullible, the careless, and the ignorant. Consumer fraud is big business, and it ranges from the ad that promises more than the product can deliver or the photograph that makes a small product appear to be two or three times its real size to the contractor who does half the work and takes all the money or a land scheme that defrauds people of millions of dollars. Some warranties use fine print to destroy virtually all guarantees, and some guarantees seem to exist for about as long as it takes to bring the product home and plug it in.

Unfortunately, consumer abuse and fraud increase as economic times worsen. Out-of-work consumers are more susceptible to seemingly inexpensive auto and home repairs, imitation products carrying brand names and bargain prices, employment services that charge a fee for nothing, and other

Figure 8-3
THE COST OF RAISING A CHILD

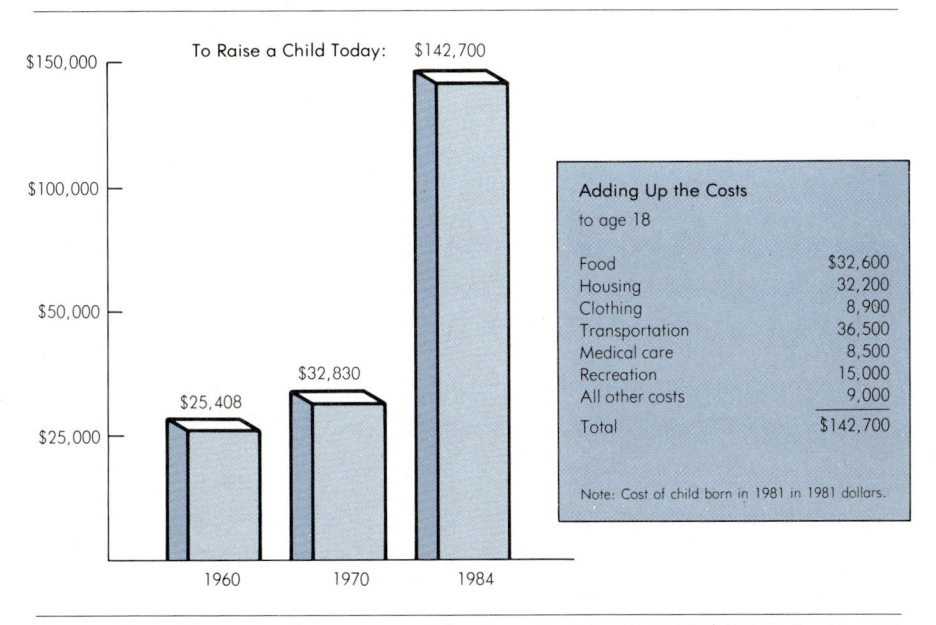

To Raise a Child Today: $142,700

1960	1970	1984
$25,408	$32,830	

Adding Up the Costs
to age 18

Food	$32,600
Housing	32,200
Clothing	8,900
Transportation	36,500
Medical care	8,500
Recreation	15,000
All other costs	9,000
Total	$142,700

Note: Cost of child born in 1981 in 1981 dollars.

Source: Adapted from Tim Schreiner, "Your Bill to Bring Up Baby: $142,700," *USA Today*, May 31, 1984, p. A1. 1960 and 1970 data from U.S. Department of Agriculture.

swindles that take money and dash hopes. Table 8-2 lists the 10 businesses that draw the most consumer complaints to Better Business Bureaus across the country.

Table 8-2
TARGETS OF CONSUMER COMPLAINTS

Ranking	Business	Number of Complaints to Better Business Bureaus
1	Mail-order firms	76,076
2	Franchised auto dealers	16,461
3	Home-furnishings stores	11,832
4	Magazines ordered by mail	10,437
5	Home-maintenance companies	10,230
6	Independent auto repairs	9,713
7	Department stores	9,262
8	Miscellaneous automotive	8,276
9	Television servicing	7,028
10	Insurance companies	6,797

Source: "Tis the Season to Be Wary of Crooks." Reprinted from *U.S. News & World Report*, December 6, 1982, p. 79 ; Copyright 1982, U.S. News & World Report, Inc.

MAIL AND TELEPHONE FRAUDS

Mail fraud is by far the leading cause of consumer complaints. According to the Council of Better Business Bureaus, during 1982, consumers made more than 76,000 complaints about mail-order companies that delivered misrepresented, poor-quality, or damaged merchandise; delivered merchandise long after it was expected; or never delivered any merchandise at all. In addition, the U.S. Postal Service receives about 200,000 complaints about mail fraud a year.[13] These complaints are growing as fast as the mail-order business itself. In 1982 consumers spent nearly $26 billion on mail-order purchases.

Mail frauds involve fake bargains, fake contests, chain letters and pyramid schemes, all kinds of get-rich-quick proposals, franchise and investment swindles, and much, much more. Consumers may be asksed to send money to charities that do not exist — except to help the receiver of the cash. They can also buy an endless array of self-improvement products promising miracles for $9.98. Sometimes the product never arrives; sometimes what does arrive is a far cry from what the ad promised. These abuses have been going on for years. An early example was the direct-mail brochure promising a guaranteed method of eliminating all roaches for only $5. The person sending the $5 received by return mail two square wooden blocks and a brief set of instructions: "First, place roach on top of first block. Then hit roach with second block."

Another common mail trick — at least until recently, when publicity alerted most recipients that they could treat such mailings as a gift — is to send consumers unordered merchandise accompanied or followed by a bill and then followed by threats of action for nonpayment of debt if the consumer protests. A variant of this gimmick is to entice the recipient to accept and pay for merchandise supposedly ordered by a neighbor who just happens not to be at home.

Mail-order insurance is an especially risky venture for the buyer, for often the low premiums mean little or nonexistent coverage, many fine-print limitations, and trap-door clauses that exempt the company for liability in many of the situations for which the purchaser expects to be covered.

Selling schemes by telephone can also trap the unwary consumer or the person who still believes in something for nothing. There is the familiar magazine-subscription scheme, where the offer is made in such a way that the unwary fail to add up the 82 cents a week for 208 weeks plus a small handling charge and are stunned by the bill for nearly $200 that accompanies the first delivery and must be paid within 30 days. There are the phony-prize schemes, in which the person is told that he or she has won some sort of free prize. A salesperson soon visits to deliver the prize — and to sell.

REPAIRS: THE RIPOFF BONANZA

In recent years, two of the most fertile fields for fraud and abuse have been auto and appliance repairs. Auto repairs have long been a source of consumer complaints, but in years past cars were simpler and people more frequently purchased and installed replacement parts on their own. As a result, the need for major repairs occurred less frequently. Repair frauds have multiplied and become more expensive in recent years. Transmissions have sometimes been overhauled or replaced with rebuilt, rather than new, parts; tune-ups, oil changes, and lubrication jobs are simply not done; the same part is supposedly fixed over and over again, until finally it must be replaced at considerable cost. The list is almost endless since the kinds of fraud are limited only by the imagination of the dishonest mechanic.

Appliance repairs, particularly of televisions and air-conditioners, have become another relatively easy method of defrauding the consumer, since most consumers lack the mechanical knowledge that would enable them to identify likely problems, whether major or minor, or the extent of the repair job. Thus, for example, TV sets may be given new color assemblies (or other more expensive components) when only a small adjustment was needed.

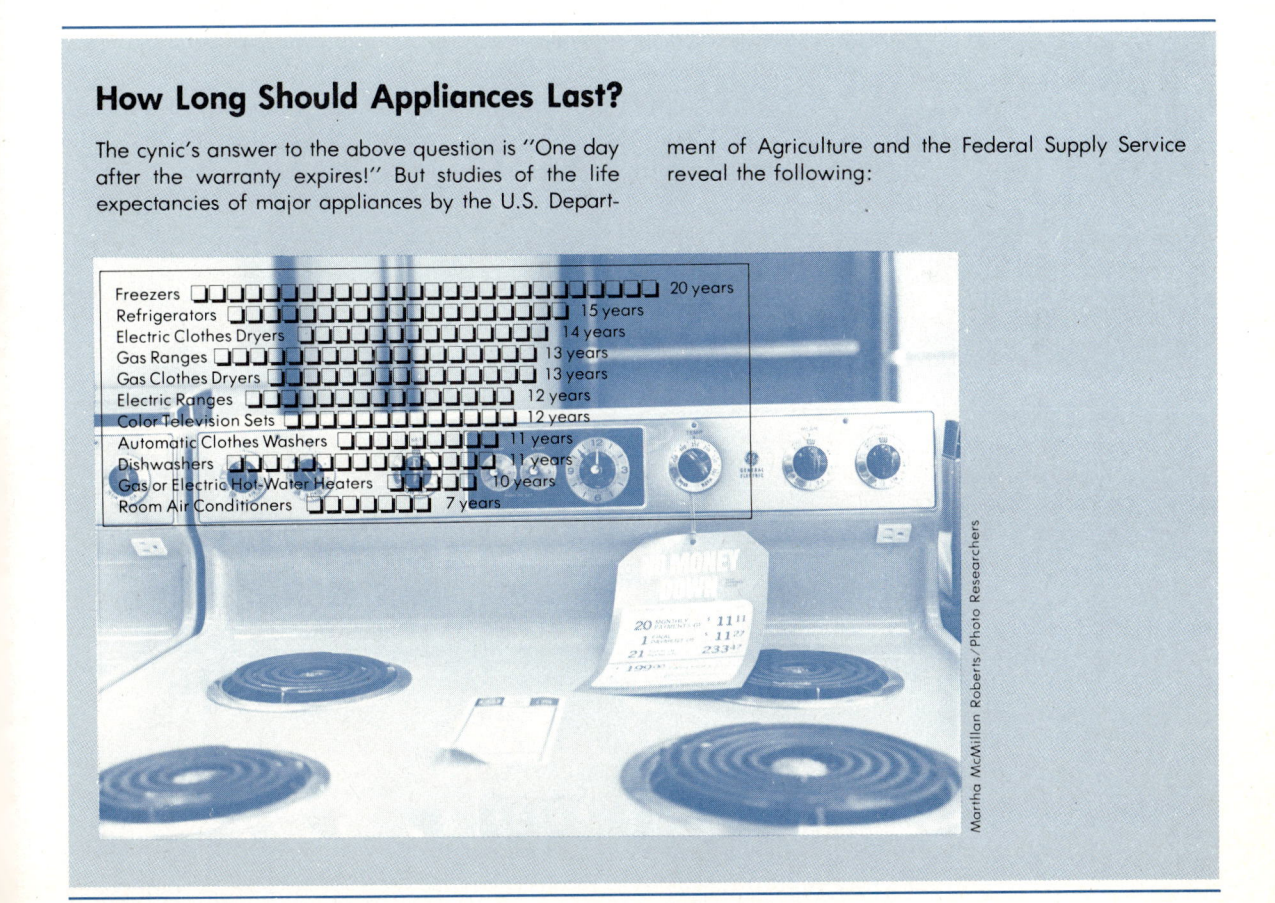

How Long Should Appliances Last?

The cynic's answer to the above question is "One day after the warranty expires!" But studies of the life expectancies of major appliances by the U.S. Department of Agriculture and the Federal Supply Service reveal the following:

Freezers	20 years
Refrigerators	15 years
Electric Clothes Dryers	14 years
Gas Ranges	13 years
Gas Clothes Dryers	13 years
Electric Ranges	12 years
Color Television Sets	12 years
Automatic Clothes Washers	11 years
Dishwashers	11 years
Gas or Electric Hot-Water Heaters	10 years
Room Air Conditioners	7 years

LAND SALES AND DOOR-TO-DOOR SELLING SCHEMES

As the value of land has escalated in recent years, and as Americans have streamed to the Sunbelt or the country for a second home, land-sale abuses have become common complaints. Most of the schemes involve long-distance sales, with prospective buyers being wined and dined by high-pressure salespeople in their home cities in the Northeast or Midwest. They are shown photographs or slides of the land for sale, told how the area will develop, and asked to sign a purchase agreement.

If, however, they travel to see their purchase first-hand, they may discover that it is located far from cities and that development will be delayed for years. Attempts to resell the land may prove fruitless, since the individual is now competing with the land-development firm in the sale of future homesites.

Door-to-door selling schemes are as sophisticated as land sales, with well-dressed, fast-talking salespeople offering expensive repair and improvement contracts. One scheme involved two men in a truck driving around a suburban neighborhood offering to resurface driveways cheaply "since they happened to be there on a job anyway." The price was appealing but the materials were inferior and the work unsatisfactory.

Deceptive practices by sellers of goods are as old as the history of trade. In 1481, King Louis XI of France issued a warning to food sellers specifying the punishment for attempting to increase the weight of butter:

> Anyone who sells butter containing stones or other things [to add to the weight] will be put into our pillory, then said butter will be placed on his head until entirely melted by the sun.
>
> Dogs may lick him and people offend him with whatever defamatory epithets they please without offense to God or King.
>
> If the sun is not warm enough, the accused will be exposed in the great hall of the gaol in front of a roaring fire, where everyone will see him.

Source: Adapted from Roger Leroy Miller, *Economic Issues for Consumers* (St. Paul, Minn.: West, 1975), p. 180.

DECEPTIVE ADVERTISING

In 1981 American businesses spent $61 billion on television, radio, newspaper, magazine, billboard, and direct-mail advertising—or about $270 per American consumer. Procter and Gamble alone spent $672 million to promote its products that year. The vast majority of these ads were neither deceptive nor unscrupulous. Each year, however, a certain number of advertisements fail to meet government and industry standards of ethics.

How is deception in advertising defined? According to James C. Miller III, chairman of the Federal Trade Commission (FTC), whose mission is to guard against advertising abuses, an ad is deceptive if reasonable consumers are deceived by its claims. In addition, ads that are intended for certain vulnerable groups, like children and the terminally ill, must meet specific FTC standards.[14]

Perhaps the most famous case of deceptive advertising was that for Listerine, which advertised for decades that it helped prevent colds and was an effective sore-throat remedy. In the early 1970s, the FTC determined that the "helps prevent colds" slogan was false. Not only did Warner-Lambert, the maker of Listerine, have to stop making this claim, but the firm was also required to sponsor corrective advertising. Ten million dollars in future ads had to include the statement that the product had no effect on colds or sore throats.

DECEPTIVE SALES PRACTICES AND PRICING

Someone once pointed out that the two words most likely to gain consumers' attention in an advertisement are *New* and *Free*. The word *new* has been used so often that the FTC finally placed a six-month limit on its use on product labels and other offers. While the term *free* continues to be used, special sales on consumer goods and services are almost as effective in stimulating consumer interest. In uncertain economic times, sales attract consumers to retail stores and represent prudent use of limited funds.

Sales are often a bargain, but they also may be a source of consumer abuse. Sometimes the sales merchandise, which looked so attractive in the newspaper ad or on the TV screen, appears to be worn or dirty. Sometimes the store has only a minimal quantity of the item in stock. One of the oldest tricks is *bait and switch*. The seller advertises a real bargain on an item: brand-name merchandise, all attachments, full warranty. But when the customer comes to the store, only a shopworn floor model is available. Sometimes the item is rigged to perform poorly or is deliberately damaged by salespeople. The disappointed customer is immediately led to a more expensive model. Instead of purchasing a portable TV at a 40-percent discount, the customer winds up with a more expensive, regular-priced model.

Then there are the price abuses: wholesale prices and specials. "Wholesale" prices are obviously a ploy. Retailers do not sell at a loss and must add an additional fee to their costs in order to pay for the service rendered and earn a profit. Although the amount of the markup may vary, it must be sufficient to cover the retailer's costs. In some instances, prices are raised so that they can be dramatically "slashed" for special sales. A comparison of prices for the same

bait and switch: a deceptive sales technique in which the retail seller lures customers to retail stores by advertising low-priced merchandise and then attempts to induce them to purchase regular-priced merchandise after demonstrating the advertised products as damaged, shopworn, or otherwise inferior.

amount, model, or quality of merchandise at other stores will prevent the consumer from being deceived by such inflated "specials."

REGULATION: A ROUTE TO CONSUMER PROTECTION

Given all these opportunities for fraud and abuse, the birth of the consumer movement was inevitable. American consumers and their advocates became angry and frustrated at wasting time and money on fraud and abuse; at times, even their well-being was threatened by shoddy and dangerous products. So they began to fight back with publicity and with pressure on federal, state, and local governments. These proved to be potent weapons. Government and private agencies have appeared at all levels—national, state, and local—with the aim of correcting fraud and abuse and protecting the consumer. In their dealings with mail and point-of-sale frauds, product labeling, defective products, and thousands of other consumer concerns, both large and small, these government and private agencies have changed the face of the American marketplace.

Consumerism is a social force within our environment designed to aid and protect the consumer by exerting legal, moral, and economic pressure on business.[15] Before the consumerism movement emerged in the late 1960s and early 1970s, laws at the local, state, and federal levels sought to maintain a competitive environment among businesses under the assumption that such an environment would best protect consumer interests. In more recent years, however, specific consumer protection laws have been enacted to provide safeguards against abuses.

In 1962 President John F. Kennedy expressed what has proved to be the most frequently quoted statement of consumer rights. American consumers, he declared, should possess the following:

- The right to choose freely.
- The right to be informed.
- The right to be heard.
- The right to be safe.

These *consumer rights* have served as the conceptual framework for much of the consumer legislation enacted during the late 1960s and 1970s. It started with Ralph Nader's successful campaign for auto safety and the passage of the National Traffic and Motor Vehicle Safety Act of 1966. In the same year came the Fair Packaging and Labeling Act, followed in 1968 by the Consumer Credit Protection Act, the Truth in Lending Act, and the Interstate Land Sales Full Disclosure Act and in 1970 by the Fair Credit Reporting Act. The Consumer Product Safety Act, which created the Consumer Product Safety Commission, was passed in 1972. In 1974 a significant amendment—the

---

consumerism: *a social force within the environment designed to aid and protect the consumer by exerting legal, moral, and economic pressure on business.*

consumer rights: *according to President John F. Kennedy, these include the right to choose freely, to be informed, to be heard, and to be safe.*

THE INFORMED CONSUMER

President John F. Kennedy stressed that American consumers should have the right to choose freely, to be informed, to be heard, and to be safe. His support for the average shopper helped to trigger the consumer legislation enacted in the late 1960s and early 1970s.

Equal Credit Opportunity Act (discussed in Chapter 7)—was added to the Consumer Credit Protection Act, and in 1975 the Magnuson-Moss Warranty Act was passed.

FEDERAL REGULATORY AGENCIES

The enforcement of these laws, as well as others that regulate trade and set safe standards for foods, drugs, and cosmetics, is the responsibility of several agencies. The primary federal agencies involved in consumer affairs are the Consumer Product Safety Commission, the Federal Trade Commission, the Food and Drug Administration, the Department of Agriculture, the National Highway Traffic Safety Administration, and the U.S. Office of Consumer Affairs.

Consumer Product Safety Commission (CPSC): a federal commission with the authority to specify safety standards for most consumer products, except those already regulated by other federal agencies.

Consumer Product Safety Commission.

The safety and performance of nonfood products is under the jurisdiction of the *Consumer Product Safety Commission (CPSC),* which has broad powers to set standards, evaluate products, and order the cessation of sale or manufacture of those products it deems dangerous. Its primary aim is to protect consumers against injury or unreasonable risk of injury. It tests products, works on developing uniform safety standards, maintains a nationwide network for the collection of information on product-related deaths, illnesses, and injuries, and conducts informational and educational programs.

The CPSC pays special attention to those products that are responsible for large numbers of injuries. In recent years the agency has focused on chain saws and lawn mowers, which cause about 100,000 injuries a year; baby toys and equipment, whose small parts may be swallowed by young children; and such possible cancer-causing materials as formaldehyde, asbestos, and benzidine dyes.

Federal Trade Commission (FTC): an administrative agency created to prohibit unfair methods of competition and to oversee the various laws affecting businesses and their relations with consumers.

Federal Trade Commission.

The *Federal Trade Commission,* established by the Federal Trade Commission Act of 1914 to regulate and promote competition, concentrates on such practices as truth in advertising, fair credit arrangements, and product reliability and standards (warranties and guarantees). It also guards against antitrust violations that restrain the competitiveness and efficiency of the economy to the detriment of consumers.

The FTC does not act on behalf of an individual but will accumulate individual complaints and then take action against a company or an industry to stop a practice it determines is unfair under the laws it is empowered to enforce or the rules it is empowered to make. For example, the FTC has played a major role in forcing advertisers to substantiate their claims and in taking obviously false, deceptive, or misleading ads off the market. In recent years it has also attempted to eliminate the anticompetitive business practices of doctors, lawyers, opticians, and other professionals—practices that include price fixing, boycotts, and restraints on truth in advertising.

Food and Drug Administration (FDA): an administrative agency authorized to regulate such areas as product development, branding, and advertising for drug and food products.

Food and Drug Administration.

The *Food and Drug Administration (FDA)* focuses on product performance. It is responsible for licensing drugs for sale and use within the United States; for testing food and cosmetic products for possible harmful effects; for setting and enforcing preparation, packaging, and labeling standards; and for enforcing radiation safety standards for color television, microwave ovens, and other products that emit X-rays. In recent years the FDA has been involved in protecting the public from such quack cures as the wearing of copper bracelets to cure arthritis and the use of potentially dangerous diet pills to lose weight. It has also put into effect new food-labeling rules that specify nutritional content. Figure 8-4 shows a food product label listing the product's ingredients.

THE INFORMED CONSUMER

Figure 8-4
PRODUCT LABEL LISTING NUTRITIONAL CONTENTS

Source: Reprinted by permission of Campbell Soup Company.

Department of Agriculture. The *Department of Agriculture* inspects and maintains standards for meat, poultry, fruit, and vegetables and requires nutrition-information labels on processed versions of these products. The department also provides nutritional information and programs to consumers throughout the country.

National Highway Traffic Safety Administration. The *National Highway Traffic Safety Administration (NHTSA)* sets safety standards for all moving vehicles, including cars, trucks, buses, motorcycles, bicycles, mopeds, and recreational vehicles. It also sets the standards for automotive equipment and in recent years has been at the heart of the controversy over the installation of air bags and involuntary seat belts as standard equipment in all new cars. The NHTSA has required manufacturers to recall vehicles with serious safety problems. (Product recalls are discussed in greater detail in Chapter 10.)

U.S. Office of Consumer Affairs. The *U.S. Office of Consumer Affairs* grew out of the White House Consumer Advisor Office established by President Richard Nixon in 1971. Although the Office of Consumer Affairs does not enforce any laws, it does coordinate federal consumer efforts and is active in consumer education and in information gathering through surveys, investigations,

Department of Agriculture: *the federal department responsible for developing and maintaining standards for meats and meat products, fruits, and vegetables.*

National Highway Traffic Safety Administration (NHTSA): *the federal agency responsible for establishing safety standards for moving vehicles on the nation's highways.*

U.S. Office of Consumer Affairs: *the White House agency responsible for coordinating federal consumer efforts, consumer education, and consumer information-gathering activities.*

EFFECTIVE BUYING

and conferences. In addition, department spokespersons appear before federal agencies as representatives of consumers and keep consumers abreast of consumer-related issues pending before these agencies. It is also an information source of last resort. Consumers who do not know where to turn can contact the U.S. Office of Consumer Affairs for guidance.

REGULATING PRODUCT WARRANTIES

Another area of federal regulation concerns durable products, such as automobiles, appliances, and watches, which are usually accompanied by a manufacturer's or service company's warranty. A *warranty* is a promise to repair or replace defective merchandise. Figure 8-5 shows an advertisement that describes the product warranty provided to purchasers of Midas automobile brake shoes and disc brake pads. Such warranties have become much more precise in recent years as a result of government actions.

warranty: *a manufacturer's or seller's promise to replace defective merchandise or to repair it within a stated time period following its purchase.*

Figure 8-5

ADVERTISEMENT DESCRIBING PRODUCT WARRANTY FOR AUTOMOBILE BRAKE SHOES AND DISC BRAKE PADS

Source: Copyright 1984 Midas International Corporation.

An important piece of federal consumer legislation is the *Magnuson-Moss Warranty Act* of 1975, which protects consumers by empowering the FTC to develop regulations affecting warranty practices for any product that costs more than $15 and is covered by a written warranty. Although the law does not force manufacturers to give warranties, it does require that warranties be made easy to read and understand and that mechanisms for processing consumer complaints be established.

The Magnuson-Moss Warranty Act also requires that a warranty be labeled *full* or *limited*. A product carrying a *full warranty* must be repaired without charge within a reasonable period of time. If it cannot be repaired, the purchaser is entitled to a replacement or a refund. A *limited warranty* specifies those parts that are covered and those that are not. It also states exactly how long the warranty lasts. Even when no warranty is included with a product, an implied warranty guarantees that the product will do what it was intended to do. Thus a lamp that does not light must be taken back by the store that sold it even if it carried no written warranty.

STATE AND LOCAL GOVERNMENT CONSUMER PROTECTION SERVICES

All states have some type of consumer protection or consumer information office. In some states, this office forms a separate department of consumer affairs; in others, it is included in the office of the governor or the attorney general or in both.

These consumer affairs offices have broad powers, including the regulation of public utilities, insurance practices, health care delivery, and business and professional licensing. In addition, state and local consumer affairs programs often provide an information service, which offers the public a wide range of consumer-oriented educational materials.

Municipal consumer affairs agencies, particularly in the larger cities and metropolitan areas, work in conjunction with state agencies to educate consumers and protect them from fraud and abuse. New York City's Department of Consumer Affairs, for example, has been particularly visible and active. In a recent year, the department's 275 staff members investigated more than 12,000 complaints.[16]

As a general rule, state and local consumer affairs departments have jurisdiction over only those consumer issues not addressed by federal laws. Many local consumer leaders are convinced that state and local consumer protection laws are more capable of addressing consumer issues than those enacted in Washington, D.C. Moreover, in many cases, state and local consumer leaders are in a better position to make things happen. This was shown in Dade County, Florida, when consumer leaders convinced the state insurance commissioner to approve some major insurance reforms at a time when federal insurance protection was lacking.

Magnuson-Moss Warranty Act: federal legislation granting the Federal Trade Commission the authority to develop regulations affecting warranties for any product costing more than $15 that is covered by a written warranty.

full warranty: a guarantee to purchasers that the product will be repaired at no cost within a reasonable time period or the purchase price will be refunded should it prove defective.

limited warranty: a guarantee to purchasers that specified parts of the product will be repaired or replaced at no additional cost.

BUSINESS SELF-REGULATION

Business self-regulation had its start about 70 years ago with the formation of the first *Better Business Bureau*. In more recent years, self-regulation has increased, as evidenced by a variety of consumer action panels and occupational and professional licensing boards.

Better Business Bureaus. The 160 Better Business Bureaus (BBBs) and their nationwide branches seek to prevent consumer problems rather than cure them. Each Better Business Bureau serves as an informational source, giving information about companies and charities, supplying general information to help consumers make intelligent purchases, monitoring local advertising, and providing help—including the option of binding arbitration—to settle any complaints consumers have against a company.

By contacting the local Better Business Bureau, consumers can learn about a company's record of handling consumer complaints and details about many products or services. Although many Better Business Bureaus will not reveal the exact nature of the complaints they have on file, all will inform consumers about a company's record of dealing with its customers. Better Business Bureaus do not provide legal advice, give ratings of individual products or brands, or assist in complaints solely about pricing practices.

The National Advertising Division of the Council of Better Business Bureaus monitors national television, radio, and print ads and makes recommendations to businesses about correcting or withdrawing unsubstantiated advertisements. Disputes that cannot be solved at this level are referred for further action to the National Advertising Review Board, sponsored in part by the Council of Better Business Bureaus.

Consumer Action Panels. In response to consumer pressure and in an attempt to build consumer goodwill, many industries have established special offices to settle complaints between individual business firms and consumers. These offices, known as *consumer action panels (CAPs)*, investigate the specific problems consumers have with a manufacturer or retailer. Currently operating programs for resolving disputes include FICAP (Furniture Industry Consumer Advisory Panel), ThanaCAP (Funeral Service Consumer Action Program), Household Goods Settlement Program, the Ford Motor Consumer Appeals Board, the Chrysler Corporation Customer Satisfaction Arbitration Board, AUTOCAP, the Home Owners Warranty (HOW) Program, and the Major Appliance Consumer Action Panel (MACAP).

After receiving a complaint, the consumer action panel asks the manufacturer or retailer to reconsider the case and report its findings. If the consumer is still dissatisfied, a panel of consumer and business representatives hears the case and recommends a settlement.

According to the National Automobile Dealers Association's AUTOCAP,

---

Better Business Bureau: a nonprofit organization of business firms that join together to protect consumers from unfair business practices.

consumer action panels: special organizations established in many industries to settle complaints between individual consumers and businesses operating in those industries.

which is made up of approximately 11,000 new- and used-car dealers, many consumers are satisfied with this system of settling disputes. The results indicate why. AUTOCAP's ten-member panel (five consumerists and five auto dealer representatives) has decided in favor of the consumer in nearly one out of two cases.

Another consumer action panel—the Home Owners Warranty (HOW) Program—is considered one of the most successful alternatives to government action. HOW guarantees that the nearly 13,000 builders that issue new-home warranties will live up to their agreement for a period of ten years. In 1982 nearly one million homes were covered by HOW, a figure that represents 42 percent of all new homes built. (In 1978, only 18 percent of new homes were part of this program.) HOW funds this new-home coverage through a system of premiums based on the purchase price of the home, its location, and the builder's reputation. In 1982 coverage on a $64,000 house could be purchased for $166 to $250.[17]

The Major Appliance Consumer Action Panel (MACAP) has handled more than 32,000 complaints since its founding in 1971 by the manufacturers of washers, dryers, refrigerators, ranges, and other major appliances. The funeral, moving, and furniture industries also have consumer action panels, and a number of other industries are considering the program.

Predictably, consumer, business, and government leaders have somewhat different views concerning consumer action panels. Consumer leaders express some skepticism about their unbiased nature. Business spokespersons point to the panels' accomplishments and look to an even more promising future of handling consumer complaints without the need for government interference or court action. Reagan administration officials view CAPs as a mechanism that frees the marketplace from government regulations. Said James C. Miller III, chairman of the Federal Trade Commission: "Business in America should not be the captive handmaiden of government. It should be an institution responding efficiently to consumers in a free market."[18]

OCCUPATIONAL AND PROFESSIONAL LICENSING BOARDS

If you have a problem with your doctor, dentist, pharmacist, electrician, plumber, employment agent, or another professional or occupational group member, you can turn to any of the 1,500 state licensing or regulatory boards for assistance. These boards set professional and occupational standards for the nation's 550 professions and occupations. They also deny or revoke licenses, bring disciplinary actions, and handle consumer complaints.

These state boards follow up the complaints they receive by reviewing the matter with the licensee. If they cannot resolve specific problems in this way, they conduct a formal investigation that may result in a temporary or permanent loss of license. Additional information concerning the jurisdiction, activities, and methods of seeking remedies from licensing boards in specific states can be obtained by contacting the local or state office of consumer affairs.

GETTING HELP: ADDITIONAL SOURCES OF CONSUMER ASSISTANCE

If you encounter a problem with a product or service or are contemplating a purchase and do not know which brand or manufacturer to choose, the sources of information are seemingly endless. Many have been mentioned in the last section. Securing assistance is mostly a matter of time and patience. Obtaining satisfaction or restitution in the case of faulty products or unsatisfactory service is much more likely today than it was even a decade ago.

PRIVATE SOURCES OF CONSUMER ASSISTANCE

Private consumer organizations are frequently the best source for product information and complaint procedures. Some of these organizations are familiar to several generations of American consumers; others grew out of the consumer movement of the 1960s.

Better Business Bureau Arbitration Program. The national consumer mediation/arbitration program operated through 180 Better Business Bureaus is an important means of resolving disputes throughout the United States and Canada. The system is the largest out-of-court forum in the nation, and the cost is underwritten entirely by the businesses that use it. The consumer pays nothing.

BBB arbitration is available if a bureau's informal mediation efforts fail. While a wide variety of products and services are the subject of arbitrations, the largest number involve automobile problems. Manufacturers currently using the program on a nationwide basis include General Motors, Nissan, Volkswagen, Porsche, Audi, and Honda.

BBB arbitrators are unpaid community volunteers from all walks of life. In nonautomobile cases, the arbitrator's decision is binding on both parties. In automobile cases the consumer may accept or reject the decision. If accepted, the decision is legally binding on all; if rejected, it is binding on no one.

Consumers Union: a private, nonprofit, product-testing organization that publishes results in its monthly magazine Consumer Reports.

Consumers Union. *Consumers Union* tests a wide range of products in its own laboratories and publishes its results in the form of product evaluations in its monthly magazine *Consumer Reports.* These evaluations are a "bible" to many shoppers, particularly for those making major purchases, such as automobiles. Shoppers have learned to trust *Consumer Reports'* evaluations because of the policies of Consumers Union. Since it was established in 1936, Consumers Union has accepted no advertising and has no relationship with any commercial interest. It buys on the open market all the products it tests, and

"And now listen to what 'Consumer Reports' has to say about your Model 1211 Electric Train: 'Extremely noisy, poor rail grip on curves at even moderate speeds, offers only fair protection against shock, and displays an utter lack of historical accuracy in re-creating B. & O. circa 1890.'"

Consumer Reports Is Widely Used in Making Comparisons of Competing Products.
Source: Drawing by Dedini; © 1974 The New Yorker Magazine, Inc.

its carefully controlled laboratory tests are often supported by the opinions of recognized experts.

Consumers' Research Magazine. Published by Consumers' Research, Inc., *Consumers' Research* magazine was the first consumer publication involved in product testing and comparisons. Since its founding in 1928, *Consumers' Research* has conducted scientific studies on a range of controversial subjects, such as the health hazards of marijuana, the safety of nuclear energy, and the problems with air bags. In addition, like *Consumer Reports,* the magazine tests and rates brand-name products. Both magazines inform their readers of the latest developments in consumer legislation and regulation.

Underwriters Laboratories. The *Underwriters Laboratories (UL)* is a nonprofit testing organization that issues the UL seal to products or parts of products it has tested and deemed safe. When the UL seal is attached to an electrical product, it tells consumers that the part to which it is attached is of adequate quality for performing the intended function and that the wire connections are designed to avoid short-circuiting. Gas or refrigeration products that carry the UL seal are recognized as being leak-free and able to withstand stress.

Underwriters Laboratories (UL): a nonprofit organization that grants the UL seal to electrical products that have been successfully tested for safety.

Suing the Product Raters

Evaluations by independent organizations such as Consumers Union and Consumers' Research, Inc., that condemn products as dangerous or useless put consumers on guard and often result in dramatic sales declines for those products. On five separate occasions, these negative evaluations have also put Consumers Union in a courtroom defending itself against huge damage suits.

In 1982, Kero-Sun, Inc., a manufacturer of portable, fuel-efficient kerosene heaters, filed a $41-million damage suit against Consumers Union. The lawsuit resulted from an article in *Consumer Reports* that called kerosene heaters a serious health hazard, capable of endangering the well-being of such high-risk groups as pregnant women and the elderly. As a result of the Consumers Union report, the Consumer Product Safety Commission investigated the matter and issued its own report, which generally supported the Consumer Union's conclusion that kerosene heaters are a serious health hazard.

Source: "A Chill over Kerosene Heat," Newsweek, November 8, 1982, p. 62.

American Gas Association Laboratories Seal of Approval: a seal granted to gas appliances that have been successfully tested for safety, durability, and performance.

American Gas Association Laboratories Seal of Approval. A blue star—the *American Gas Association Laboratories Seal of Approval*—is issued to those gas appliances that meet its standards of safety, durability, and performance. The star informs consumers that the range, clothes dryer, heater, furnace, or other appliance meets the American Gas Association Laboratories' stringent standards. Participation by gas appliance and accessory manufacturers is voluntary.

Good Housekeeping Seal of Approval: a seal pledging that Good Housekeeping magazine will replace or provide a refund for any product advertised in the magazine should it prove defective within a four-year period following purchase.

Good Housekeeping Seal of Approval. The *Good Housekeeping Seal of Approval* is a unique provision of a limited warranty for all products advertised in the monthly magazine. The seal is a promise to *Good Housekeeping*'s readers that the publisher will replace the product or provide a refund if it proves to be defective.

Additional Consumer Protection Organizations. Consumers can also seek help from a number of other private consumer protection groups. These organizations range in scope and size from huge national groups like the Consumer Federation of America, the Council on Consumer Interests, the Conference of Consumer Organizations, and the National Consumer Congress to the local street or neighborhood association that takes on small-scale problems that are amenable to small-group pressure.

Although these organizations vary in focus and activities, all have traditionally been geared to getting attention for consumer complaints, to focusing on common or prevalent problems and possible solutions, to promoting consumer education, and to directing individuals to sources of help if the organization itself does not provide the service.

USING THE MEDIA

Sometimes the quickest and simplest method to get action is bringing the problem or complaint to the consumer affairs or action-line departments of local media. Most companies and businesses are prepared to make some adjustment or take some action rather than face the adverse effect of public exposure in the local paper or on the TV evening news. Having a defective or shoddy product or an unfair contract shown to thousands or even millions of potential customers can undo the goodwill of years of advertising and public relations efforts.

PUBLIC SOURCES OF CONSUMER AID

In addition to the federal, state, and local consumer affairs programs already discussed, the government provides consumer assistance in the form of ongoing consumer education programs for children and adults in many public schools throughout the country.

One of the consumer's most valuable resources can be obtained through the federal government: the *Consumer's Resource Handbook*, published annually by the U.S. Office of Consumer Affairs, is a what-to-do, where-to-go manual for resolving consumer problems. It contains a primer on how to make a consumer complaint and whom to see to resolve consumer problems. It also contains a comprehensive consumer assistance directory, which lists the names, addresses, and phone numbers of various federal, state, and business organizations that consumers can contact in case of a problem. A copy of the *Consumer's Resource Handbook* can be obtained by writing to Handbook, Consumer Information Center, Pueblo, Col. 81009.

Consumer's Resource Handbook: *an annual publication by the U.S. Office of Consumer Affairs providing specific information and suggestions for resolving consumer problems.*

HOW TO COMPLAIN AND GET ACTION

Suppose the new $500 personal computer you purchased never worked correctly from the first day you brought it home. After reading your rights under the warranty, you know what you want from the manufacturer—a machine that works. Whether the company repairs this one or gives you a replacement matters little. You simply want a functioning computer as quickly as possible. According to the *Consumer's Resource Handbook*, you should take the following steps when you complain:

1. Decide exactly what the problem is and what you want as a settlement. Do you want your money back, or will a new or repaired machine do? Make certain that you have all the necessary documents on hand to substantiate your claims, including sales receipts, repair orders, warranties, or canceled checks. *The more documentation you have, the better off you are. Do homework!*

2. **Contact the person who sold you the item or performed the service and tell him or her exactly what is wrong and what you want done.** If this contact fails to resolve the problem, ask to see the supervisor or manager. Nearly nine out of ten consumer complaints are resolved at the salesperson or supervisor level.

3. **If you are still not satisfied, write a letter to the company.** You can write directly to the consumer affairs director or the company president. The president's name can be found by consulting *Standard & Poor's Register of Corporation Directors and Executives.* Available at most libraries, this source book lists the top executives in over 37,000 American business firms. The names of many corporate consumer contacts can be found in the *Consumer's Resource Handbook.* If you know the name of the product but not the manufacturer, consult the *Thomas Registry,* which is also in your library. Figure 8-6 shows what form your letter should take and what points of information it should contain.

Figure 8-6
SAMPLE COMPLAINT LETTER

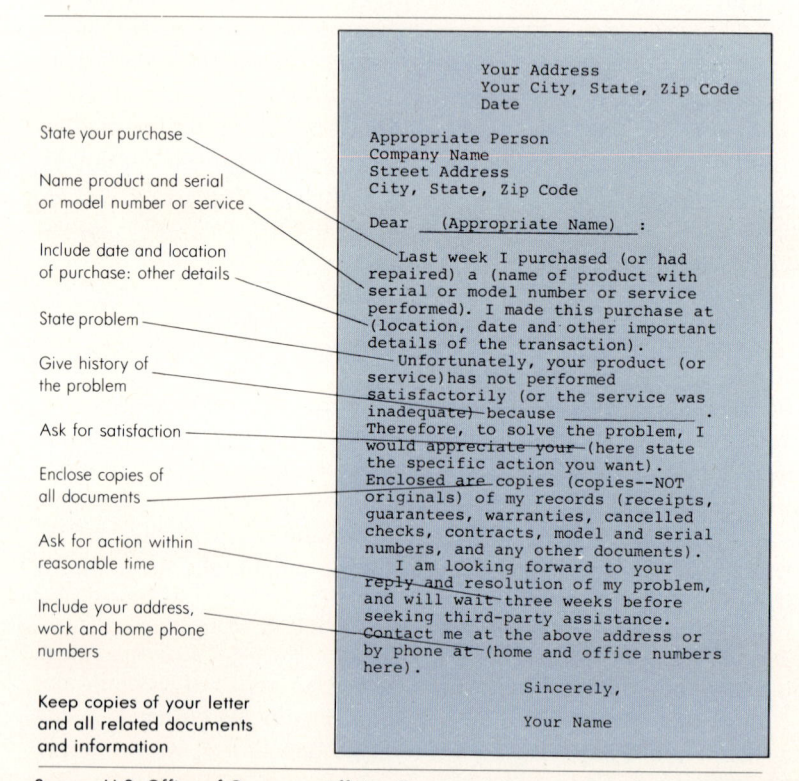

```
                                    Your Address
                                    Your City, State, Zip Code
                                    Date

Appropriate Person
Company Name
Street Address
City, State, Zip Code

Dear    (Appropriate Name)   :

    Last week I purchased (or had
repaired) a (name of product with
serial or model number or service
performed). I made this purchase at
(location, date and other important
details of the transaction).
    Unfortunately, your product (or
service) has not performed
satisfactorily (or the service was
inadequate) because _____.
Therefore, to solve the problem, I
would appreciate your (here state
the specific action you want).
Enclosed are copies (copies--NOT
originals) of my records (receipts,
guarantees, warranties, cancelled
checks, contracts, model and serial
numbers, and any other documents).
    I am looking forward to your
reply and resolution of my problem,
and will wait three weeks before
seeking third-party assistance.
Contact me at the above address or
by phone at (home and office numbers
here).
                        Sincerely,

                        Your Name
```

Callouts:
- State your purchase
- Name product and serial or model number or service
- Include date and location of purchase; other details
- State problem
- Give history of the problem
- Ask for satisfaction
- Enclose copies of all documents
- Ask for action within reasonable time
- Include your address, work and home phone numbers
- Keep copies of your letter and all related documents and information

Source: U.S. Office of Consumer Affairs, *Consumer's Resource Handbook* (Washington, D.C.: U.S. Government Printing Office, 1982), p. 2.

Keep temper down! Don't cuss in letter. Calmly state case.

THE INFORMED CONSUMER

TAKING THIRD-PARTY ACTION

The third-party action referred to in Figure 8-6 can take several forms. First, it can involve contacting any of the federal, state, or local consumer affairs or regulatory offices described earlier. Second, it can involve contacting the Better Business Bureau, a consumer action panel, or an occupational or professional licensing board, whose functions we also examined.

If your problem is still unresolved after going to one or more of these sources, you may have only one option left. You may be forced to take your complaint to court.

GOING TO SMALL-CLAIMS COURT

Most states have set up special *small-claims courts* to handle disputes involving small amounts of money—typically under $500. These courts hear 3.5 million complaints each year involving such grievances as dry cleaners who ruin clothing, home-improvement contractors who perform unsatisfactory work, and retailers who refuse to exchange or repair a defective product. Proceedings are informal: a judge or arbitrator listens directly to the two parties and makes a decision. The amount of awards varies. In some states the maximum judgment is as low as $300; in others, as high as $5,000. The average maximum judgment awarded in small-claims court is $750 or less.

The small-claims court remedy is relatively inexpensive since attorneys are not necessary (and in some states are forbidden). Only a small filing fee, ranging from $2 to $20, is charged. The procedure for filing is simple. Complaints are filed on a special form available at your local courthouse at the same time as the filing fee is paid. Approximately two weeks later, a court time is scheduled (evening and weekend hours are often available). Documentation supporting the complaint should be available for the judge to inspect. After hearing both sides of the issue, the court will order that the claim be settled in favor of one of the parties.

small-claims courts: specialized courts established to handle disputes involving limited amounts of money.

SUMMARY

The consumer of the mid-1980s has been affected by recent economic problems of inflation, recession, and unemployment. As inflation has eroded the purchasing power of the dollar, consumer purchasing patterns have frequently changed. In addition, more and more U.S. families have become two-income households, with both adult members working outside the home to generate added purchasing power.

Household purchasing varies with the stage of the family life cycle and according to the presence or absence of children in the household. The steps of the consumer decision-making process include:

1. Formation of household goals.
2. Recognition of problem or opportunity.
3. Evaluation of alternatives.
4. Purchase decision.
5. Purchase act.
6. Postpurchase evaluation.

The consumer of the 1980s may be victimized by a variety of consumer frauds and abuses. Abuses include mail and telephone frauds, automobile and appliance repair schemes, land-sale offers, and door-to-door selling tactics. Other problems arise from misleading advertising and deceptive sales practices, such as the bait-and-switch technique.

Consumer protection, however, is available from a variety of sources: specific federal, state, and local agencies, self-regulation by businesses, occupational and professional licensing boards, private consumer agencies and organizations, the media, and legal action. Important federal agencies include the Consumer Product Safety Commission, the Federal Trade Commission, the Food and Drug Administration, the Department of Agriculture, and the National Highway Traffic Safety Administration. Some type of consumer protection agency or consumer information service exists in all states and in many large cities.

Business self-regulation has taken the form of Better Business Bureaus located throughout the United States, as well as consumer action panels. Private sources of consumer assistance include such organizations as Consumers Union, *Consumers' Research* magazine, Underwriters Laboratories, the American Gas Association, *Good Housekeeping* magazine, and such private organizations as the Consumer Federation of America, the Council on Consumer Interest, the Conference of Consumer Organizations, and the National Consumer Congress. Media hotlines and investigative reporting by newspapers and radio and television stations are other potential sources of consumer aid. Systematic approaches to consumer complaints are often effective in obtaining redress for defective or inferior products or services. Legal action is a final avenue of consumer assistance.

REVIEW QUESTIONS

1. Briefly define the following terms:

   family life cycle
   comparison shopping
   bait and switch
   consumerism
   consumer rights
   Consumer Product Safety Commission
   Federal Trade Commission
   Food and Drug Administration
   Magnuson-Moss Warranty Act
   Better Business Bureau
   consumer action panels
   Consumers Union
   Underwriters Laboratories
   American Gas Association Seal of Approval
   Good Housekeeping Seal of Approval
   Consumer's Resource Handbook
   small-claims courts

2. Explain the most frequent consumer responses to recent economic problems of inflation, unemployment, and recession.

3. What are the major stages of the family life cycle? How might consumer purchases vary for each life cycle stage?

4. Briefly describe the steps in the consumer decision-making process. Does this model apply to small purchases as well as major decisions?

5. What are the major categories of consumer fraud and abuse?

6. Explain the concept of consumerism and relate it to President Kennedy's statement of consumer rights.

7. Distinguish the major consumer-related responsibilities of the following:

   a. Federal Trade Commission
   b. Consumer Product Safety Commission
   c. Food and Drug Administration
   d. Department of Agriculture
   e. National Highway Traffic Safety Administration
   f. U.S. Office of Consumer Affairs

8. Identify and briefly explain the most important forms of business self-regulation.

9. What are the primary private sources of consumer assistance?

10. How may consumers use small-claims court?

CASES AND EXERCISES

1. Discuss the impact that the growth of two-income households has had on the typical household budget.
2. Identify the household member who is likely to exert the greatest influence on the purchase of the following:
   a. breakfast cereal
   b. husband's clothing
   c. kitchenware
   d. life insurance
   e. housing
   f. choice of restaurant

   Make any assumptions necessary, but defend your answer.
3. Outline an effective approach to the art of complaining as a means of seeking consumer redress.
4. In recent years, proposals have been made by the Federal Trade Commission to require used-car dealers to issue warranties, to control advertising directed at children, and to regulate nonprescription drugs. Discuss the advantages and shortcomings of implementing such proposals.
5. Business self-regulation is hailed as an important step in minimizing consumer abuse and fraud. What are the limitations of relying on business self-regulation as the primary source of consumer protection?

ANSWERS TO PERSONAL FINANCE I.Q. TEST

1. Fiction. 2. Fact. 3. Fact. 4. Fiction. 5. Fiction. 6. Fiction. 7. Fact.

HOW FLOYD CAMPBELL REACHED HIS PERSONAL FINANCIAL DECISION

During his break Professor Wilsker went over to the library with Floyd and showed him some of the corporate directories in the business reference section. Together, they looked up the name and address of the chairman of the board of the chain store. After a quick check in the out-of-town phone books, they had a phone number. "Call him," Professor Wilsker suggested, "and see what he can do for you."

On the following class day, Floyd came in just beaming. "I did as you said," he announced, "and tried to call the chairman of the board. I didn't get him, but his secretary gave me the vice-president for consumer affairs. When I explained the situation to him, he said that he would call the local store right away, check into the situation, and call me right back. He never did."

Floyd paused, then grinned, "But the store manager did. 'I'm so sorry,' he said, 'but I did not understand the situation. When can we come by and install your new furnace at no charge?'"

Some time later, at graduation, Professor Wilsker met Floyd's mother. Shaking his hand with a vengeance, she enthused, "You just don't know what a help you've been. Last month I took my car to the auto center of that chain store for their complete $99.95 brake job, as advertised."

Chuckling, she continued, "When I went to pick up the car, the bill was over $250. I refused to pay. I ran to the store manager's office and demanded to see him right away. He called the auto service manager, who explained that my car had needed additional work plus parts. Then I asked the store manager if he remembered what happened when his store ruined my furnace and my son called corporate headquarters. His eyes widened—'Give the lady her car for $99.95!' he ordered the auto service manager."

LEARNING OBJECTIVES

1. To outline the factors that should be considered in making a personal housing decision. / *2.* To discuss the rent-or-buy decision and other housing options, such as manufactured homes, condominiums, and cooperative apartments. / *3.* To explain the two major parts of every home-buying decision. / *4.* To examine how houses are financed. / *5.* To describe how someone goes about building a new home. / *6.* To identify the issues involved in selling a house. / *7.* To list the special concerns involved in buying a second home.

TESTING YOUR PERSONAL FINANCE I.Q.

	FACT	FICTION
1. A landlord cannot legally prohibit you from having a waterbed in your apartment.	☐	☐
2. Lenders are authorized to issue only 10-year loans on manufactured housing.	☐	☐
3. Many Hawaiian condominiums are sold without the land.	☐	☐
4. The size of the average U.S. house has declined in recent years.	☐	☐
5. A cooperative apartment is another name for a condominium.	☐	☐
6. A quit-claim deed is preferable to a warranty deed.	☐	☐

The materials in this chapter assist in separating fact from fiction. Your answers can be checked on page 269.

CHAPTER NINE

THE HOUSING DECISION

**SHARING A PERSONAL FINANCIAL DECISION WITH
PROFESSOR WILLIAM BURR OF THE UNIVERSITY OF OREGON**

Professor William Burr had just finished his lecture on the housing decision. As he was erasing the blackboard, Alan Markus came up to him to discuss the lecture. "Everything you said about the pluses and minuses of renting versus buying was interesting," Alan commented, "but the emphasis seemed to be on the future—when we've graduated and are in a better position to buy a house. Most students don't think they have much of a choice right now. I've thought of a way to buy a house now, and I think it makes sense, but maybe I haven't considered everything."

Alan explained that he'd seen a house for sale not too far from campus. His parents were willing to lend him the money for the down payment. It's a four-bedroom house, so he could live in one room and rent out the other three. With the rent money, he'd be able to cover the monthly mortgage payments. Then, when he graduated, he'd sell the house. With the money from the sale, he'd pay back his parents. And even if he didn't make a profit, he'd have lived rent-free for several years. Plus he'd be able to deduct the mortgage payments and depreciation from his taxes. "It doesn't seem like I can lose," Alan concluded.

If you were Professor Burr, would you agree with Alan?

To find out how Professor Burr helped Alan with his personal financial decision, turn to page 269.

"Obviously, the property is not worth as much as it was this time last year."

Florida appraiser after the earth opened up in the town of Winter Park, creating a huge sinkhole that swallowed trees, cars, and buildings.[1]

Mar-a-Lago, a 118-room mansion in Palm Beach, Florida, that once belonged to heiress Marjorie Merriweather Post, is one of the most expensive houses in the United States today.

The home was so expensive that not even the United States government could afford it. Mar-a-Lago—Marjorie Merriweather Post's estate in Palm Beach—has 118 rooms, including 58 bedrooms and 32 bathrooms. It is situated on 17 acres. When Post, the cereal company heiress, died in 1973, the mansion went to the Post Foundation, which decided to give it to the federal government as a winter retreat for presidents and foreign leaders visiting the United States. But by 1980 the government had to give Mar-a-Lago back to the foundation because of its annual $1 million operating costs and because its proximity to airstrips made it a security risk.

The property was listed for $20 million. In 1984, two Florida developers announced that they had bought the property and planned to live in the mansion. The selling price? $13.5 million. But because of "financing problems" the sale did not go through and the property is still on the market.[2]

Although most of us will never acquire a property like Mar-a-Lago, home ownership has been the American dream for generations. Unfortunately, high housing prices and mortgage interest rates have made it a difficult goal for many younger people in the 1980s. Still, good values are always available if one knows where and how to look. This chapter provides the information you need to make the right housing decision and the one that is most economical. The first step is to determine what your housing requirements are.

PERSONAL HOUSING REQUIREMENTS

For some people, choosing the perfect home to buy is a purely emotional decision. Young people often say that they are looking for a home they can love—a dream house. But like dreams, this emotional approach does not clearly define or describe the best house to buy. The home-buying decision requires careful analysis and thought. To succeed, you must begin with a careful appraisal of your housing requirements: where you want to live, the kind of home you need, and how much you can spend on housing.

WHERE DO YOU WANT TO LIVE?

No factor influences the housing decision more than location. People usually choose a general area—or even a specific neighborhood—before they select a house or apartment. To make the best choice, the following factors should be considered.

Lifestyle. Your home should reflect your lifestyle. It should allow you to pursue your leisure-time activities as well as being convenient to your work. For example, if you enjoy cultural activities and are employed in a downtown office, you would probably want to purchase a house near the metropolitan area. A home should also reflect your personality and temperament. Therefore, if you like the back-to-nature lifestyle, you would probably be unhappy living in a "sidewalk" city home and would want a home in the suburbs or even in the country. On the other hand, the excitement of the city and the almost-maintenance-free living provided by high-rise apartments may better suit your lifestyle.

Commuting Distance and Time. An important aspect of lifestyle is the amount of time it takes to get to and from work. The most idyllic house becomes an albatross if one has to leave for work at five in the morning and cannot return home until eight at night. Therefore, it is important to consider access and availability of transportation facilities when choosing a place to live.

Taxes. Taxes vary tremendously from state to state and among local communities within the state. Housing decisions are often based on tax factors. Many residents of the New York City metropolitan area, for example, live in Connecticut or New Jersey because income, sales, and property taxes in these states are much lower than they are in New York.

Public Service. Public service may also be a consideration. Health care, police and fire protection, libraries, and parks and recreation facilities are often decision factors. San Antonio, for instance, is a popular retirement area for former military personnel because they can take advantage of military health care and other base facilities.

Schools. Parents often pick a location because of its school system. One might look for a school district with a high annual expenditure per pupil, a favorable student–teacher ratio, special programs for the gifted and handicapped, modern facilities, a compatible educational philosophy, a high percentage of high school graduates who go on to college, high achievement scores, and so on. But good school systems cost money, and this may mean higher local real estate taxes.

WHAT KIND OF HOME DO YOU WANT?

The housing decision involves choices between a single-family detached home on its own lot; a single-family attached home; a condominium or cooperative

A real estate agent shows a house to prospective buyers. Important factors in the housing decision include the neighborhood to live in and the size and design of the house.

apartment in a high-rise tower or garden-apartment setting; a mobile home; or a rental apartment. To a large extent, the area you choose will determine the kind of dwellings available. For example, in the heart of the city, where land values are high, you will find fewer detached homes.

Other decisions concern the style and design of the house, as well as the types and number of rooms needed. Smaller families, more single people in the population, and rising costs have shrunk the average U.S. home remarkably. U.S. home size peaked in 1978 at 1,650 square feet.[3] Today, 1,000-square-foot homes are becoming commonplace.[4] These modern homes often feature "great rooms," which combine the traditional living and family rooms. Built-ins provide an aura of spaciousness in today's smaller units.

More homes are also being purchased by unmarried people who pool their funds. The real estate industry has responded to this trend by building homes and condominiums with two or more separate and equally sized bedrooms, baths, and sitting area combinations. These new housing configurations are often referred to as *tandem units*.

WHAT ARE YOUR MONTHLY PAYMENT LIMITATIONS?

Monthly payment limitations may be the most important consideration of all. High interest rates have had a profound effect on today's home buyer. A $50,000, 30-year mortgage costs $349.61 per month in principal and interest

Profile of the New Home Buyer

The typical buyer of a new home in 1983 was 32.8 years old, married, had an income of $35,226, and made a 10 percent down payment on a new $73,000 home 27 minutes away from work.

That's according to a nationwide survey conducted by NAHB [National Association of Home Builders] of people buying new homes and condominiums from July 1982 to June 1983. The survey also revealed:

- Traditional households (a husband, wife, and children) accounted for 51 percent of the single family buyers.
- Single parents and groups of unrelated individuals living together accounted for 16.4 percent of the buyers.
- 56 percent of the households had two incomes.
- 91 percent of the single family buyers and 88 percent of the condominium buyers were "somewhat to very satisfied" with their new homes.
- 55 percent of the condo buyers and 47.5 percent of the single family buyers were purchasing their first home.
- Median household income was $35,226 for single family buyers and $31,217 for condo buyers.
- Fixed-rate mortgage loans remain the most popular, accounting for 63 percent of the single family sales and 48 percent of the condo sales.
- 74 percent of the buyers ranked the energy efficiency of the unit a very important consideration in deciding which home to purchase.
- Anticipated appreciation of the home was another major incentive to buy, according to 89 percent of the single family buyers and 83 percent of the condo buyers.
- The monthly bill, including principal, interest, taxes, insurance and utilities, was $841 for single family buyers and $651 for condo buyers.

Source: "Profile of the New Home Buyer," *USA Today*, January 19, 1984, p. 5C. Reprinted with permission of *USA Today*.

---

at 7.5 percent, a common rate just a decade or so ago. But at 13.25 percent, the monthly payment is $562.89. That is before insurance, utilities, taxes, and the like. The net result is that many Americans cannot afford to buy a home in today's marketplace. First-time buyers must be careful to restrain their enthusiasm for a home if the monthly payments will wreck their budget.

SHOULD YOU RENT OR BUY?

An important housing decision is whether to rent or buy. Each option offers unique advantages for both long-term and short-term personal interests and financial situations.

The primary advantages of renting are liquidity, mobility, and certain cost savings. Because renters do not have to make a sizable upfront investment in their living units, they can deploy their funds to high-yielding investments like money-market funds. Renters also have a mobility advantage over homeowners: they can quickly pursue new career opportunities elsewhere without being concerned about selling a home. Moreover, renters are spared the bulk of home-repair and maintenance expenses, such as lawnmowers and the cost of having the plumbing fixed.

appreciation: *the growth in value of an asset such as a home.*

equity: *the personal funds that accumulate in a home as the years pass.*

mortgage table: *a schedule showing the relationship between the interest and equity portions of each mortgage payment.*

The accepted number of apartment vacancies is 5 percent in many areas. When the local rate exceeds this figure, apartment owners offer premiums to lure renters. For example, in the recession of the early 1980s, Seattle's Mueller Group offered *equity rents* on its 2,300 apartments. Under this plan, a renter could apply a maximum of $250 per month up to $3,000 in rent toward the purchase of any of the firm's 300 condominiums.[5]

After a decline in the early 1980s, housing prices have started to rise again. So purchasing a house now allows a person to avoid anticipated future price increases. In other words, purchasing a home may provide *appreciation,* or growth in value.

In addition to this benefit, home ownership provides a mechanism for saving that renters do not have. An ever-increasing part of the monthly mortgage payment translates into *equity*—the personal funds that accumulate in a home as the years pass. Since payments in the early years of the mortgage are almost all interest, equity builds slowly. But in the later years, almost all payments are applied to the principal. The relationship between the interest and the equity portions of a mortgage payment at different points in time are shown in a *mortgage table* (see Table 9-1).

The federal income tax system provides another incentive to owning your own home. Mortgage interest and real estate taxes are deductible from your federal income taxes—a fact that makes home ownership cheaper than most rental situations. A person in the 32-percent income tax bracket with a $1,000-per-month mortgage actually has an after-tax cost of about $680 in the first year of home ownership, since nearly all of the mortgage payment is interest and thus is deductible.

As Chapter 5 indicated, there are other tax benefits associated with home ownership. If a person lives in a home for longer than a year, profits from its sale are taxed at capital-gains rates rather than the tax rates for ordinary income. The maximum rate at which those profits are taxed is then 20 percent rather than 50 percent. In addition, homeowners who are 55 years old or over and sell their homes can exclude up to $125,000 in profits from the federal income tax bite.

Another traditional advantage of home ownership is that housing costs remain stable over the years. Renters can expect regular increases. Although fixed-rate mortgages are not as commonplace as they were a few years ago, even today's adjustable-rate mortgages go up less drastically than do rent hikes.

THE RENTAL OPTION

Rental units are found in urban, suburban, and even rural areas. One can find rental apartments in high-rise buildings, garden apartments, and townhouses. Single-family homes can also be rented from owners who, for any

Table 9-1
SLICES FROM THE LIFE OF A REPAYMENT SCHEDULE

Here are portions from an amortization schedule for a $60,000 mortgage at 14% repayable in 360 monthly installments of $711. As the years go by, more of each month's payment is for principal, less for interest. In the earlier years a relatively small prepayment moves you ahead on the schedule.

	PYMT #	PRINCIPAL	INTEREST	BALANCE
YEAR 1	1	$10.93	$700.00	$59,989.07
	2	11.06	699.87	59,978.01
	3	11.19	699.74	59,966.82
	4	11.32	699.61	59,955.50
	5	11.45	699.48	59,944.05
	6	11.58	699.35	59,932.47
	7	11.72	699.21	59,920.75
	8	11.85	699.08	59,908.90
	9	11.99	698.94	
	10	12.13		
	11			
	21	$13.78	$697.15	$59,741.61
	22	13.94	696.99	59,727.67
	23	14.11	696.82	59,713.56
	24	14.27	696.66	59,699.29
SUBTOTAL		$160.80	$8,370.36	$59,699.29
YEAR 3	25	14.44	696.49	59,684.85
	26	14.61	696.32	59,670.24
	27	14.78	696.15	59,655.46
	28	14.95	695.98	59,640.51
	29	15.12	695.81	59,625.39
	30	15.30	695.63	59,610.09
	31	15.48	695.45	59,594.61
	32	15.66	695.27	59,578.95
	33	15.84	695.09	59,563.11
	34	16.03	694.90	59,547.08
	35	16.21	694.72	59,530.87
	36	16.40	694.53	59,514.47
SUBTOTAL		$184.82	$8,346.34	$59,514.47
YEAR 4	37	16.59	694.34	59,497.88
	38	16.79	694.14	59,481.09
	39	16.98	693.95	59,464.11
	40	17.18	693.75	59,446.93
	41	17.38	693.55	59,429.55
	42	17.59	693.34	59,411.96
YEAR 10	113	$40.07	$670.86	$57,462.25
	114	40.54	670.39	57,421.71
	115	41.01	669.92	57,380.70
	116	41.49	669.44	57,339.21
	117	41.97	668.96	57,297.24
	118	42.46	668.47	57,254.78
	119	42.96	667.97	57,211.82
	120	43.46	667.47	57,168.36
SUBTOTAL		$489.67	$8,041.49	$57,168.36
YEAR 11	121	43.97	666.96	57,124.39
	122	44.48	666.45	57,079.91
	123	45.00	665.93	57,034.91
	124	45.52	665.41	56,989.39
	125	46.05	664.88	56,943.34
	126	46.59	664.34	56,896.75
	127	47.13	663.80	56,849.62
	128	47.68	663.25	56,801.94
	129	48.24	662.69	56,753.70
	130	48.80	662.13	56,704.90
	131	49.37	661.56	56,655.53
	132	49.95	660.98	56,605.58
SUBTOTAL		$562.78	$7,968.38	$56,605.58
YEAR 12	133	50.53	660.40	56,555.05
	134	51.12	659.81	56,503.93
	135	51.72	659.21	56,452.21
	136	52.32	658.61	56,399.89
	137	52.93	658.00	56,346.96
	138	53.55	657.38	56,293.41
	139	54.17	656.76	56,239.24
	140	54.81	656.12	56,184.43
	141	55.44	655.49	56,128.99
	142	56.09	654.84	56,072.90
	143	56.75	654.18	56,016.15
	144	57.41	653.52	55,958.74
SUBTOTAL		$646.84	$7,884.32	$55,958.74
	145	58.08	652.85	55,900.66
	146	58.76	652.17	55,841.90
	147	59.44	651.49	
	148	60.13		

Source: "Does It Pay to Pay Ahead on Your Mortgage?" Reprinted with permission from *Changing Times Magazine*, November 1983, p. 106. © Kiplinger Washington Editors, Inc., 1983.

lease: a legal document defining the rights and obligations of both the landlord and the tenant.

number of reasons, want to hold on to their property. For example, transferred executives on temporary assignment in another part of the country often rent instead of sell their homes. High interest rates have forced other potential home sellers to become landlords. Unable to find buyers who can meet their price, homeowners rent their property until market conditions change.

Whatever kind of rental property is chosen, renters have rights that are protected by a legal document known as a lease. The *lease* defines the rights and obligations of both the landlord and tenant; it tells both parties what can and cannot be done, the services that can be expected, and those the renter must provide.

Major Provisions of the Lease. The lease agreement specifies many important areas of responsibility for the renter and landlord, including:

1. The monthly rent and the date on which it is due: Fees for late payment are sometimes specified.

2. The period during which the lease is in force: This may range anywhere from six months to three years.

3. The security deposit that is required: If the renter damages the apartment, the cost of repairs is deductible from this deposit.

sublease clause: a clause in some leases that gives a renter the right to rent the unit to another party if he or she leaves.

4. A *sublease clause*: Such a clause allows the tenant to rent the apartment to another party if he or she leaves temporarily.

5. Repairs that are required before a renter moves in: If no repairs are to be made, the lease simply specifies that the apartment is available "as is."

6. The occupants: The lease usually defines who will live in the apartment.

7. What is included in the rental price: The lease specifies whether the tenant pays the utility bills, whether a garage space is included, and whether there is access to a pool or other recreational facilities.

8. Allowable alterations: The lease defines what can and cannot be done to the apartment and whether improvements are to be left behind when the tenant leaves. Many leases require that a renter secure the landlord's approval before altering the apartment in any way.

9. Access to the apartment: The lease specifies the conditions under which the landlord can enter the apartment when the renter is not at home.

10. Additional rules: These are set by the landlord and might include no pets, no waterbeds, no loud music after 10 P.M., and/or no running of a business from the apartment.

Uniform Residential Landlord and Tenant Act: adopted by several states and cities, this law provides important safeguards for tenants.

The Uniform Residential Landlord and Tenant Act. To protect tenants from landlord abuse, several states and cities have adopted the *Uniform Residential Landlord and Tenant Act,* which sets the following standards:

1. The fit housing requirement: if an apartment does not meet minimum housing code standards, tenants have the right to break their lease, reduce their rent, sue for damages, or deduct from their rent the cost of any repairs they have made.

2. Protection against landlord retaliation: a landlord is prohibited from evicting, as well as raising the rent or cutting the services of, a renter who organizes a tenants' union or files a complaint with a local housing authority.

3. Protection against seizure of personal property: the landlord cannot seize a renter's property or lock a tenant out of the apartment.

4. Limitation on the amount of security deposit required: landlords cannot ask for more than one month's rent as a security deposit, and they must return the deposit within two weeks of the time the lease expires. Needed repairs and the amount deducted from the deposit must be itemized.

5. Elimination of the landlord's right to shut off utilities.

6. Consistently applied rules and regulations: the rules regarding renters' behavior must be reasonable and applied equally to everyone. If 20 tenants in a 22-tenant building have dogs, the landlord cannot single out one particular dog owner for eviction.

These and other provisions are law in some states but not in others. Check with your local housing agency to see just what your rights are.[6]

OTHER HOUSING OPTIONS

If a person decides to buy rather than rent, but a conventional single-family dwelling seems inappropriate, there are still other housing options. The prospective buyer might want to consider a manufactured home, a condominium, or a cooperative apartment.

Manufactured Homes. The name change from mobile home to *manufactured home* reflects the fact that only 4 percent of these housing units are ever moved once they are delivered. The manufactured-home industry peaked in 1972, with the sale of 575,940 homes, but then came the bust of the mid-1970s, when many manufacturers dropped out of the industry. The quality of manufactured housing has improved significantly in recent years.

There are several reasons to believe that the manufactured-housing industry will increase its output in the late 1980s. Legislation and court decisions in California, Indiana, Michigan, and Vermont have removed many of the zoning restrictions that limited the use of manufactured housing. But even more important is the fact that lenders have begun to issue regular 30-year mortgages for manufactured housing instead of the short-term financing that was commonplace a few years ago.[7] Manufactured housing may not be appropriate for everyone, but it is becoming an increasingly viable option.

manufactured home: *formerly called "mobile homes," these dwellings are at least partially manufactured and then transported to the site, rather than being built on location.*

condominium: a housing unit that is composed of both individually- and commonly-owned property.

Condominiums. The term *condominium* refers to a housing unit that is composed of both individually- and commonly-owned property. As a percentage of total housing starts, condominiums almost doubled during the past decade.[8] The growth of this housing option can be attributed to the increase in the number of senior adults, single people, and working couples without children. All of these groups have been attracted to the lifestyle offered by condominiums: the economic and tax advantages of home ownership without the responsibility for exterior or grounds maintenance.

Condominiums are located throughout the country and are available in many different styles. Some are semi-attached townhouses built in clusters, while others are separate, single-family homes. Still others are apartments in high-rise buildings. They are often located in vacation communities—especially in Florida and the other Sunbelt states. Some are designed and located in such a way as to attract a certain segment of the population, such as singles or retired persons.

"Sorry, but your tree is going condo."

Many Apartment Complexes Have Been Converted into Condominiums During the 1980s.

Source: From the *Wall Street Journal*—Permission, Cartoon Features Syndicate.

Condominium owners are involved in two forms of ownership. First, they own a personal residence. Second, they own an interest in the common grounds, including the lawns, recreational areas, and clubhouses of a suburban or country condominium, and the elevators, laundry rooms, hallways, roof-top sun deck, and so on of a high-rise apartment condominium. All members of the condominium community must pay a monthly fee to maintain these common properties. Additional assessments may be made for capital improvements, like a new clubhouse roof. Owners are also responsible for maintaining and repairing the interior of their homes. If the dishwasher goes, the cost of replacing or repairing it is borne by the unit owner.

Condominiums are eligible for conventional home mortgages as well as for Federal Housing Authority and Veterans Administration loans. It is important to remember that the mortgage payment is only one part of total ownership expenses. Maintenance fees increase periodically and must be considered in this purchase decision. The Federal Trade Commission has suggested that potential buyers check maintenance fees carefully to see if there is a ceiling or an annual increase.

Cooperative Apartments. People who own a *cooperative apartment* do not actually own the unit per se. They own shares in the building's cooperative corporation, which owns each apartment in the building and all the common facilities. The larger the apartment, the larger the number of shares the person owns.

If the shares for a co-op apartment cost $100,000, the buyer must secure a mortgage for that amount (minus any down payment). The buyer must also pay a monthly maintenance charge, which covers the cost of maintaining the building, property taxes, and the building's own monthly mortgage payments.

Paying for the "master" mortgage is one of the major differences between condominium and co-op ownership. Like condominium owners, co-op owners must meet the mortgage payments for their units, but they have to meet the building's obligation as well. These payments can skyrocket if the building has a mortgage that must be refinanced at a higher rate at some time in the future.

Co-op apartments are run by a board of directors, elected by the owners. The board makes the building's operating decisions. It decides about repairs, monthly maintenance payments, and refinancing. The board can also reject a proposed apartment buyer. Cooperatives have resale restrictions and can turn down potential buyers.

Cooperative apartments, which are generally found in large cities like New York, provide all the tax advantages of home ownership. Owners can deduct from federal income taxes the interest paid on their personal mortgage and the portion of the building maintenance fee that pays for property taxes and interest on the master mortgage. Co-op apartments are often cheaper than comparable condominium apartments.

cooperative apartment: an arrangement in which the person owns shares in a building's cooperative association, with the number of shares reflecting the relative size of the apartment.

Sometimes It Is Tough to Buy a $1.8 Million Apartment

The retired executive had a beautiful 15-room house in Saddle River, New Jersey. But he felt it was best to go back to being a city dweller because of his wife's poor health. The executive picked out a $1.8 million cooperative apartment on Manhattan's Park Avenue. The 12-room unit was one of a dozen in the building. It seemed perfect—until a hitch developed in the real estate negotiations.

Cooperative apartments are not like other homes. Their dwellers own a pro-rata share of the total building and so have a say in the buying and selling of its apartments. In this case, a 96-year-old resident sued to prevent the New Jersey couple from buying the apartment. He argued that the celebrity status of the proposed buyer would attract undesirable elements to the building. The 96-year-old also contended that the security people protecting the executive would clog the building's one elevator.

The suit was eventually dropped and cooperative members approved the sale by a three-to-one margin. But Richard and Pat Nixon had the last say in the matter. They decided to remain in Saddle River.

Source: "Tenant Tries to Keep Nixon Out of Co-op," *Journal-American* (Bellevue, Wash.), January 21, 1984, p. A8; "Nixon Not Wanted as Condo Neighbor," *Seattle Times*, January 21, 1984, p. A3; "Nixon: The Long Climb Back," *Newsweek*, February 20, 1984, pp. 53–54; "Nixon Gives up on Apartment," *Seattle Times*, March 2, 1984, p. A3; "Money and Fame Can't Get You a Home Here," *Journal-American* (Bellevue, Wash.), March 4, 1984, p. B8.

BUYING A HOUSE

There are two major parts to every home-buying decision: the first involves evaluating how much you can afford to pay, and the second focuses on finding the house that is right for your situation and agreeing on the terms of the sale.

HOW MUCH CAN YOU AFFORD?

Most home ownership costs are predictable, so you can evaluate them before the actual purchase. The basic costs of home ownership include the down payment, mortgage payments, taxes, insurance, and maintenance expenses.

down payment: *the initial cash investment in a major purchase such as a home.*

The Down Payment. The *down payment* is the initial cash investment in the home. First-time buyers need to save or borrow this amount before they can consider buying.

mortgage: *a real estate loan that is repaid over several years; the property involved is pledged as collateral for the loan.*

Mortgage Payments. Most people finance their homes through a *mortgage*, a real estate loan that is repaid in installments over several years and for which the property involved is pledged as collateral. The size of the mortgage payment depends on the amount of money borrowed from the bank or other lending institution, the interest rate that determines the cost of the money, and the term of the mortgage.

The Federal Housing Administration and the Veterans Administration set their eligibility standards for mortgages on the basis of residual income, which is defined as gross income minus taxes, Social Security payments (see

Chapter 19), long-term bills, mortgage payment, and home maintenance. The standard for a family of three is a minimum monthly residual income of $700.

Taxes and Insurance. Property taxes are the second largest home ownership cost after mortgage payments. These taxes are based on an official valuation of the property, which tends to increase over the years along with increases in the price of the home. As Chapter 5 described, property taxes vary significantly in different localities. Minnesota, for instance, has high property taxes, while those in Alabama are low.

The cost of homeowners insurance must also be considered. Lending institutions often require adequate insurance coverage to safeguard their investment. The cost of homeowners insurance depends on the type and amount of coverage chosen, the structure of the house and the materials it is made of, and its proximity to a good fire department. (For a complete discussion of homeowners insurance see Chapter 14.) In addition to homeowners insurance, a buyer will probably also purchase title insurance to protect against other claims on the house or the land. Title insurance is required by most lending institutions.

Taxes and insurance are typically paid on a monthly basis as part of the regular mortgage payment. In real estate jargon, these monies are said to be held *in escrow.* That is, the holder of the mortgage keeps the money and then uses it to pay the tax and insurance bills when they come due.

in escrow: *the holding of monies (for payment of tax and insurance bills) by a third party (the mortgage holder) until some specified time when payment of the bills is due.*

Maintenance and Operating Expenses. The unknown in monthly housing costs is the expense of maintaining and operating the home. A starting point is to study the costs of the previous owner or those of similar homes in the area. Energy costs, water and sewer charges, lighting, landscaping, and normal repairs should be considered in such an assessment.

WHERE DO YOU START TO LOOK?

Searching for a house is a tedious process, requiring considerable effort and patience. It can be done by either working with one or more real estate agents or examining "For Sale by Owner" homes.

Real Estate Agents. A *real estate agent* is a salesperson who works on commission and attempts to match buyers with sellers. Buyers should always remember that real estate agents are working for the seller. But since agents can select from extensive inventories of available homes, they also serve the buyer's needs. Agents have access to *multiple listing services,* cooperative arrangements among various real estate firms to share *listings* (homes for sale through these firms). As a prospective buyer, your task is to tell the agent exactly what type of home you are seeking.

real estate agent: *a salesperson who works on commission and attempts to match home buyers and sellers.*

multiple listing services: *cooperative arrangements among various real estate firms to share listings.*

listings: *the homes offered for sale by a real estate firm.*

EFFECTIVE BUYING

For Sale by Owner. Homes sold privately now account for a sizable portion of the real estate market in most areas. Buyers should check comparable prices in the area to be sure that the owners have not set an unrealistic price. Real estate agents are particularly successful at getting their listings set at close to market value. So the primary advantages of a "For Sale by Owner" are that a given house may be underpriced, and that the owner may be more flexible in negotiating the price or terms.

Asking Prices and Counteroffers. Most asking prices are set relatively high so that the owner has room to negotiate the final price. In most cases, the prospective buyer starts the negotiation process by offering a price considerably lower than what is asked. The compromise offers of sale and purchase, by the owner and buyer, are referred to in real estate parlance as *counteroffers*.

Offers and counteroffers will vary. Some buyers are very anxious to sell because of a job transfer, divorce, or financial setbacks. Others—especially those in active real estate areas—may be just "testing the market" by offering to sell at relatively high prices. Buyers should set the highest price they are willing to accept and then offer a lower figure. Most offers to purchase real estate include an *earnest money provision*, whereby the buyer makes a deposit to show his or her good faith. In some places, personal notes can be substituted for part or all of the earnest money deposit. These provisions typically include language that makes the deposit subject to the buyer's ability to receive acceptable financing and inspection reports on the property.

The Final Sale Price. The buyer and seller will eventually settle on a mutually agreeable price for the home. In 1984 the estimated median price was $83,400 for a new home and $76,500 for an existing home,[9] but prices vary widely from one location to another.

counteroffers: the compromise offers of sale and purchase, by the owner and buyer, in a housing transaction.

earnest money provision: a prospective purchaser's deposit showing good faith that he or she will complete a real estate transaction.

Have I Got a Deal for You!

Sometimes houses are offered with additional incentives or in an interesting fashion. Consider the following examples:

- General Motors was carrying an inventory of $10 million worth of houses acquired from transferred employees. So the auto manufacturer decided to offer free cars with the purchase of one of its homes. A $78,000 house came equipped with a Chevette, and a $204,000 dwelling with a Cadillac Seville.

- A seller in Peoria, Illinois, offered a trip to Hawaii as a premium. But the purchaser chose to deduct the trip's cost from the price indicated.

- In Ferryville, Wisconsin, a $79,000 farmhouse and 51 acres were offered as the prize in a contest that asked entrants to tell why "I want to own a farm in Wisconsin." The contest format got around Wisconsin's prohibition of lotteries since skill, not luck, decided the winner.

THE HOUSING DECISION

The Purchase Contract. The *purchase contract*—also known as a sales contract or agreement of sale—specifies the legal description of the property; the selling price; when and how the money will be paid; the date the property will change hands; all the items that will be included in the sale, such as draperies and appliances; the portion of property taxes, insurance, and other charges that each party must pay; an assurance that the seller will pass the title and deed on to the buyer at the time of closing; details of owner financing; and so on. Buyers sometimes make the purchase contingent on obtaining a mortgage that is below a certain interest rate. The contract must be signed by both the buyer and the seller.

purchase contract: the sales contract involved in a real estate transaction.

The Title and Deed. The *title* is a document that gives the buyer the right to use the property as he or she desires, subject to the zoning restrictions of the local community. The buyer is assured the right to sell the property at any time. To be sure that the title is free and clear, a title search is usually conducted to reveal liens or easements on the property that restrict its use. An *easement* is the right granted by a property owner to another property owner or company to use part of the land for a specific purpose. An example would be a utility company's right to run underground cables across part of the property.

A *deed* is an instrument for transferring ownership from the seller to the buyer. Deeds are usually recorded at the county courthouse. There are two major types of deed. A *warranty deed* guarantees that the seller will defend the title of the property against anyone who makes a claim on it. In the *quit-claim deed,* the seller makes no promises that the title is clear of claims, but merely hands over whatever rights he or she has to the property.[10] So, from a buyer's perspective, warranty deeds are generally preferable.

title: a document that gives the buyer the right to use certain property subject to relevant zoning restrictions.

deed: an instrument for transferring ownership from seller to buyer.

warranty deed: a guarantee that a seller will defend the title of a piece of property against anyone who makes a claim on it.

quit-claim deed: a document by which the seller simply surrenders any rights he or she might have in a piece of property.

Land Leases. One exception to the above discussion should be noted: in some areas, only the actual building is sold; the land is leased to the buyer for an extended period, typically 99 years. *Land leases* have been used in Baltimore for years, and today they are common in Hawaiian condominium developments. In areas where land leases exist, real estate is either sold *fee simple* (meaning that the buyer is purchasing both the building and the land) or as a *leasehold* (meaning the buyer is purchasing the building and leasing the land). Land leases usually escalate over their 99-year lives and are subject to renegotiation at the end of the leasehold period. Sometimes leaseholds are sold with an option to buy the property.[11]

land lease: a situation in which only the building is sold, and the land is leased for an extended period of time.

fee simple: a situation in which both building and land are included in a real estate transaction.

leasehold: a situation in which a buyer purchases the building but leases the land in a real estate transaction.

FINANCING A HOME

As indicated, the primary method of financing a home is through a mortgage. Only 3 percent of all house purchases are paid for in cash. Mortgages usually require that a modest percentage of the selling price, sometimes as low as 5 or

Johnson 4: Texas 1

Jessie and Malissie Johnson of Leon County, Texas, know the importance of a clear deed to real estate. Jessie used much of the 26 cents an hour that he earned from the railroad to buy a 120-acre farm during the Depression. He did not know it at the time, but the title was defective.

It all began after the Texas War of Independence, when a soldier named Thornton P. Kuykendall was awarded 640 acres of land for his military service. But the three parcels that Kuykendall selected exceeded 640 acres. The former soldier later sold the acreage with its improper titles. No one noticed it from 1836 to the mid-1960s, when oil company surveyors spotted the problem. In 1978 the state land office advised the Johnsons that the State of Texas was the legal owner of their farm.

Finally, in 1981, Johnson got legal title to the farm he bought more than 50 years earlier. This required a statewide vote to approve an amendment giving the Johnsons clear title by a 4-1 margin.

Source: "Texas Couple Finally Wins Deed from State for Farm They Purchased 50 Years Ago," *Seattle Times*, November 5, 1981, p. A3. Reprinted by permission of the Associated Press.

---

10 percent, be put into a down payment. This is a far cry from the Roaring Twenties, when 50 percent down, five-year financing, and a big "balloon payment" at the end of five years was the rule.[12] Or is it? Half a century ago, the five-year balloon payments caused many people to lose their homes. But today some people argue that the "creative" financing arrangements common in the early 1980s may lead to the same outcome. Before considering this problem, however, let's look more closely at down payments, closing costs, and more conventional mortgage arrangements.

DOWN PAYMENT

private mortgage insurance: *insurance that guarantees the payments of a mortgage up to the point where the buyer has a given amount of equity in a home; this insurance allows buyers to purchase homes with a lower down payment since the lender's risks are decreased.*

One of the most critical home-financing factors is the *down payment,* or initial cash investment, which can range from 5 percent of the purchase price on up. People willing to make relatively large down payments are usually considered more desirable from the lender's perspective and may even be offered a lower mortgage rate. And of course the monthly payments will be smaller. By contrast, a low down payment increases one's tax deduction for interest income, liquidity, and potential profit upon resale.

Down payments can be reduced by purchasing *private mortgage insurance* (often called a MAGIC loan), which guarantees the payments of the mortgage up to the point where the buyer has a given amount of equity in the home, perhaps 20 percent. This reduces the lender's risk since buyers are less likely to walk away from a home in which they have substantial equity. Down payments of only 5 percent are possible under private mortgage insurance plans. The premium is added to the buyer's mortgage interest rate.[13]

CLOSING COSTS

Closing costs are the costs associated with the transfer of ownership from seller to buyer. These costs are paid when contracts are signed and title is passed. Lenders are required by federal law to provide an estimate of settlement costs within three days of the date of the mortgage application.

Sellers are required to pay the real estate commission (if any) at the time of closing. They also have to buy title insurance and pay escrow fees and transfer taxes. In the case of mortgages issued by the Veterans Administration, they have to pay a *points* charge as well. Most other closing costs are charged to the buyer. The buyer, for instance, may have to pay a *loan origination fee* (a fee that lenders charge borrowers for arranging financing; sometimes called a loan placement fee). Other charges include appraisal fees, attorney's fees, survey fees, pro-rated property taxes, title search, insurance and related expenses, recording and documents fees, fire insurance, private mortgage insurance, and adjustments for utilities, fuel, and other expenses. Many first-time buyers are shocked at the number and amount of closing costs involved in a home purchase.

closing costs: all the costs associated with a real estate transfer; also known as settlement costs.

points: a closing cost expressed as a percentage of the sales price.

loan origination fee: a fee that lenders charge borrowers for arranging financing; sometimes called a loan placement fee.

SOURCES OF MORTGAGES

Three traditional types of mortgage are available for home financing: the conventional mortgage, the Federal Housing Administration (FHA) mortgage, and the Veterans Administration (VA) mortgage.[14]

The Conventional Mortgage. Conventional mortgages usually have a term of up to 30 years. They are made up of a mortgage (which pledges the property to the lender if the buyer fails to meet the payments) and a bond or note (which holds the buyer personally responsible for the debt). Thus, if the property is sold for a lesser amount than the lender is owed, the borrower is obligated to repay the rest out of other assets. Most conventional mortgages are based on a fixed-payment schedule. In other words, the monthly payments are the same throughout the life of the loan, even though the amounts going to interest and principal vary over time.

Lenders have the right of mortgage *foreclosure*—the legal process of taking the property back if certain conditions are not met. These conditions include the borrower's failure to meet the monthly payments, to provide appropriate fire insurance to protect the lender, or to pay taxes. If the lender forecloses, the property is sold to pay off the debt.

foreclosure: the legal process of taking a property back if certain conditions are not met.

The FHA Mortgage. The Federal Housing Administration (now part of the Department of Housing and Urban Development) was established to insure long-term loans as a result of the housing collapse of the 1930s.[15] Lenders can offer borrowers more favorable terms—such as lower down payments—if the loan is guaranteed by the FHA.

FHA loans are subject to an appraisal of the property and ceilings set by the agency. In 1984, for example, the FHA loan maximum was $82,500 in King County, Washington. Buyers are required to pay an insurance premium to finance the FHA program.

The VA Mortgage. Veterans Administration loan guarantees are available to those who served in the armed forces. They can be used to buy a single-family house, a condominium, or a mobile home or to build, repair, or improve a home. The great advantage of the VA mortgage is that it requires no down payment if the amount borrowed is below the allowable mortgage ceiling. In 1984 the maximum guarantee was $27,500. This means that if you default and the house is sold after repossession for less than the amount of the outstanding mortgage, the lender will be reimbursed for the amount of the loss but not to exceed $27,500.

Program applicants must provide information regarding their eligibility, financial status, credit and employment history, and the like. The approval process is relatively lengthy.

MORTGAGE RATES 1980s STYLE

For years, home ownership was the best buy in town. People who were fortunate enough to take out a 20- or 30-year mortgage when interest rates were 6, 7, or even 10 percent not only got homes at affordable prices but also paid back the debt with increasingly cheaper dollars. In other words, as inflation eroded the dollar's buying power and increased take-home salaries, mortgage holders, paying at fixed rates, reaped enormous benefits. These benefits, however, came at the expense of the savings and loan associations and other lending institutions. Their lending portfolios were filled with low-interest mortgages at a time when, to attract savings deposits, they had to pay market interest rates. The net effect was a huge increase in the rates they charged for new mortgages.

What effect did this changed mortgage climate have on homeowners' ability to borrow? As mortgage rates increased, fewer and fewer families could afford a home. Table 9-2 shows that nearly 21 percent of all American families can afford a 30-year, $60,000 mortgage when interest rates are 9 percent. But at 13-percent mortgage rates, nearly half of these families can no longer afford to purchase a home with a $60,000 mortgage.

With fluctuating interest rates, both buyers and sellers have had to adapt to a changed mortgage environment. A variety of innovative mortgage payment plans are now available, involving floating rates, graduated payments, and shared appreciation.

THE HOUSING DECISION

Table 9-2
AFFORDABILITY OF A 30-YEAR, $60,000 MORTGAGE AT DIFFERENT INTEREST RATES

Interest Rate	Payment	Expense*	Annual Income Needed to Afford**	Number of Families Who Can Afford	Percent of Families Who Can Afford
9	$483	$215	$33,504	11,786,000	20.6
10	527	215	35,616	10,528,000	18.4
11	572	215	37,776	9,212,000	16.1
12	617	215	39,936	7,896,000	13.8
13	664	215	42,192	6,553,000	11.8
14	711	215	44,448	5,207,000	9.1
15	758	215	46,704	3,833,000	6.7
16	807	215	49,056	2,403,000	4.2
17	856	215	51,408		less than
18	904	215	53,712	1,831,000	3.2

* Insurance, taxes, utilities.
** Assumes ¼ of income goes toward total housing payment.
Source: "Who Can Afford What?" *Sentinel Star*, May 13, 1981, p. 10A.

Fixed-Rate Versus Floating-Rate Mortgages. Until the 1980s, the only mortgage available to potential homeowners was the long-term, fixed-rate mortgage in which payments were made in equal monthly installments. Today, however, floating-rate mortgages are popular. These plans offer borrowers some form of floating rate, which ties mortgage payments to current interest rates based on some preselected index.[16]

There are three basic types of floating-rate mortgages:

1. The *variable-rate mortgage,* which places restrictions on how often and how much interest rates can increase during the term of the mortgage.

2. The *adjustable-rate mortgage,* which allows interest rates to fluctuate more often; even monthly changes are possible.

3. The *renegotiable-rate mortgage,* which adjusts mortgage rates every one to five years with a set maximum-allowable mortgage-rate swing over the life of the mortgage.

Graduated-Payment Mortgages. The *graduated-payment mortgage* is designed to attract young buyers who expect their income to rise significantly in the future—for instance, young professionals. Under this plan, the payments rise over time until they reach a designated leveling-off point. The mortgage rate remains constant after that point is reached.

---

variable-rate mortgage: a mortgage that allows the interest rate to change (within limits) over its term.

adjustable-rate mortgage: a floating-rate mortgage that allows interest rates to change more frequently than with a variable-rate mortgage.

renegotiable-rate mortgage: a floating-rate mortgage that permits the interest rate to change every three to five years.

graduated-payment mortgage: a mortgage that features low initial payments but higher ones during later stages of the term of the loan.

EFFECTIVE BUYING

shared-appreciation mortgage: *a mortgage that features lower-than-average interest rates, but requires the borrower to give up a certain share of any appreciation in the property (even if it is not sold).*

Shared-Appreciation Mortgages. Another option is the *shared-appreciation mortgage*, which offers a lower-than-market interest rate if the buyer agrees to give the lender a share of the increased value of the home when it is sold. A typical shared-appreciation agreement gives one-third of the capital gain earned on a house to the lending institution that provided the mortgage. Some lenders require that if the buyer has not resold the home within five years from the date when the mortgage was taken out, the property must be appraised and the lender paid one-third of its increased value.

MORTGAGE PROVISIONS

In addition to interest-rate and payment specifications, mortgages often include certain clauses covering prepayment, delinquency, assumption of the existing mortgage, and second mortgages.[17]

prepayment clause: *a mortgage clause that restricts prepayment of the debt in some fashion.*

Prepayment. A *prepayment clause* restricts prepayment of the mortgage debt in some fashion. Lenders sometimes charge a fee if the borrower pays off the mortgage before it matures or pays more than a specified amount. They may also charge for any first-year prepayment. Although once common in mortgages, prepayment clauses no longer appear in FHA and VA mortgages. These clauses have also been eliminated in 80 percent of conventional mortgages.

Delinquency. Late payments are penalized by most lenders. If they do not receive payment before the due date or within a specified grace period, they may tack a charge of 4 to 6 percent of the late payment onto the month's bill. This charge is specified in the *delinquency clause*.

delinquency clause: *a mortgage clause setting up a late charge on past due monthly charges.*

assumable-mortgage clause: *a mortgage clause allowing the mortgage holder to transfer the unpaid balance on the mortgage to another party.*

Assumable Mortgage. An *assumable-mortgage clause* allows the borrower to transfer the unpaid balance on the mortgage to someone who buys the home. This is an important advantage when interest rates are high. If someone has a 9-percent mortgage in a 13-percent mortgage market, an assumable-mortgage clause would significantly lower the cost of the home to any prospective buyer and would make it a more attractive housing value.

second mortgage: *a mortgage that takes a secondary position to the first, or primary, mortgage.*

Second Mortgages. A *second mortgage* is one that takes a secondary position to the first, or primary, mortgage. In other words, the first-mortgage holder has first claim on your property in the case of foreclosure. Homeowners often use "seconds" to tap the equity they have built up in their homes. The proceeds can be used for any purpose the homeowner chooses.

Many first-mortgage lenders believe that homeowners who carry second mortgages may become overwhelmed by their debts and default on their first mortgage. To protect their interests, these lenders may prohibit second

THE HOUSING DECISION

mortgages or require the homeowner to clear the lender and the terms of the second mortgage with them first.

Because second-mortgage lenders take a greater risk than first-mortgage lenders, they generally charge higher interest rates. There will also be additional closing costs and fees. Most second mortgages are marketed through companies that specialize in them. *[handwritten: Not usually lending institutions]*

SOURCES OF MORTGAGE MONEY

Mortgages may be obtained through a variety of sources, including lending institutions, commercial banks, mortgage companies, and insurance companies. Another option is through the seller—an alternative referred to below as Creative Financing.

Lending Institutions and Commercial Banks. Lending institutions are by far the greatest source of mortgage money for home buyers. These institutions include savings and loan associations, building and loan associations, and mutual savings banks. Commercial banks also offer mortgage loans, although in recent years there has been a shortage of loan money from these sources because depositors have sought higher-yield investments. FHA and VA mortgages are available through both lending institutions and commercial banks.

Mortgage and Insurance Companies. Mortgage companies, also known as mortgage bankers, often have more available money at better rates than lending institutions and commercial banks, since they have access to capital from a variety of places, not just depositors' accounts. Although insurance companies sometimes make mortgage loans, they generally favor large investment properties, such as shopping centers and hotels.

Creative Financing. High interest rates have priced many buyers out of the mortgage market—would-be buyers simply cannot qualify for the loans under existing conditions. As a result, the owners have been required to provide all or part of the financing. This situation is often referred to as *creative financing* (a term that applies to any home-financing plan other than the traditional fixed-payment plan). Sometimes buyers assume the existing mortgage and wrap around a seller-carried second mortgage. In other words, the seller agrees to finance the remaining portion of the purchase price. When the seller owns the property outright, he or she may finance the amount of the purchase price after a down payment. The terminology for all this varies from state to state—land contract, deed of trust, contracts for deed, and so on—but the bottom line is that the seller is carrying at least part of the financing for the transaction.

Most creative financing schemes provide a below-market interest rate—often in line with existing or earlier state usury laws. For example, most contracts in Washington State are 12 percent, while 11 percent is commonplace in

creative financing: any home-financing plan other than the traditional fixed-payment plan; in most cases, it refers to some form of seller financing.

cash-out period: the time limit set for owner financing.

balloon payment: a large loan balance due at a specified time.

Michigan. The contract with the owner is typically for a short period of time (the *cash-out period*; usually 3 to 5 years), but the monthly payments are calculated on the basis of a 30-year mortgage. Thus, at the end of the contract period, a large balance is due—a *balloon payment,* which usually forces the buyer to obtain alternative financing.

Buyers who opt for this arrangement assume that interest rates will be lower before the cash-out period is over, so that long-term financing will be available. Today, however, many experts believe that this may not always be the case. If the balloon payments cannot be met, foreclosure may follow. As indicated earlier, this prospect may be an unfortunate consequence of creative financing in the late 1980s.[18]

BUILDING A HOME

Many people prefer to build their own home rather than buy an existing one. The building option allows people to select the location, housing style, type of construction, and fixtures that best suit their lifestyles. But building your own home is also costly, and it can be troublesome.[19]

BUILDING ANALYSIS

Building a house involves a careful study of four major steps: choosing a location, picking an architect, financing the construction, and supervising the actual construction.

Choosing a Location. To find the right building site, you must first narrow down the general area to a specific neighborhood and then locate a suitable building lot. The lot should be compatible with the house you want to build. You must also make sure the proposed new home is available to utilities and public services and in accordance with local zoning and building codes and so on. Some localities, such as in California, have placed severe restrictions on new housing starts.

Picking an Architect. Many people who build a home use an architect to design the residence. Others design their homes themselves or use prepared plans. The architect plays many roles during the building process—from analyzing the family's housing requirements, designing a suitable house, and drawing appropriate structural plans to helping to pick the building site, building materials, and building contractor. The architect also supervises construction, authorizes periodic payments to the contractor, and inspects the completed home.

Building a home is an exciting but difficult and costly project that involves selecting a location and an architect and financing and overseeing the construction.

Financing the Construction. It is necessary to secure financing before construction starts. Once a lender has approved the financing, a construction contract can be negotiated with a builder. This contract specifies what is to be done and when as well as the payments the builder will receive during the construction period. A typical schedule gives the builder 10 percent upon completion of the foundation; 30 percent when the rough enclosure is done; another 30 percent when the rough plumbing, heating, and electrical work is finished and the drywall is up, and the final 25 percent when the job is done.

Supervising the Construction. Supervising the actual construction is one aspect of home building that cannot be neglected. Although building inspectors and architects play major roles, the owner should also be personally involved in this stage of construction.

SELLING A HOUSE

So far we have approached housing from the buyer's point of view. Selling is the other side of the housing decision. How does one go about selling a home?

REAL ESTATE BROKERS VERSUS "SALE BY OWNER"

Using a real estate firm to sell a home is as advantageous to the seller as it is to the buyer. These specialists use advertising to bring in a steady flow of potential buyers. They also verify that potential buyers are able to conclude the purchase, and they guide both seller and buyer through the negotiations and closing.

Although selling a home yourself can be time-consuming and taxing, the saving on the real estate commission is a sizable reward. If you decide to sell the property yourself, however, be careful not to misprice it. A professional appraiser might be used to make sure the price is on target.

Still another option is to use a so-called discount broker. These firms do not provide all the services of traditional real estate sellers. They may ask that you handle the showings of the house to prospective buyers. Some discount brokers also require the homeowner to pay for advertising. The bargain for these reduced services is a lower real estate commission.

- Find out who's good & who's not.

SELLING COSTS

Selling costs involve home repairs and professional fees. By undertaking minor cosmetic improvements, you may be able to add thousands of dollars to the selling price. Invest in a paint job; fix cracked plaster, broken bathroom tiles, leaky faucets, and the like. A seller may also want to make such major changes as putting on a new roof and adding insulation.

In terms of fees, the real estate broker's commission is the largest. But this charge is well worth it if he or she arranges the sale. Legal and other professional fees can also be sizable.

PURCHASING A SECOND HOME

As leisure time has increased over the years so has the urge to buy second, or vacation, homes. Today, several million American families own second homes. Located in ski and sun resorts, in the back woods, or on the ocean, these vacation homes have many of the pluses and minuses of primary residences. Yet they also bring special concerns to two areas: (1) financing and (2) maintenance.

When money is tight and mortgage rates are high, many lenders simply stop financing vacation homes. And when mortgages are available, rates may be higher than they are for primary residences. It may also cost more to maintain a vacation home than a primary home. Many vacation homes—especially country homes—are older and in need of repair. These repairs can be costly if the buyer has to contract the work out. Since vacation homes are vacant for long periods of time, they are often targets of vandalism and theft.

Time Shares

If real estate is a good investment, the argument goes, then a time share in a vacation condominium is a good investment too. This can be seductive reasoning for a small investor who believes real estate *is* a good investment but can't afford a $100,000 condo of his own. With only a few thousand dollars, he can buy a time share—ownership of a unit for a week out of every year.

It's most unlikely, however, that a time share will produce returns comparable with those of other real estate investments. The problem is price. A time-share developer may have to find as many as 50 buyers for a unit. To cover his high selling costs, the developer may charge the 50 buyers a total of $300,000 for a unit that he could sell profitably to a single buyer for $100,000.

When you go to sell, the hype—and the price—probably will have settled down. In any case, time shares have no track record; the industry is only about a decade old, and no one has kept resale price data. Says Maryanne Kane, a Federal Trade Commission attorney who specializes in time shares: "I have seen no evidence that time-share units have good resale potential. It's much more likely that people who want to sell won't be able to find a buyer."

If you're figuring on rental income from a time share, it's doubtful that you'll cover your costs. Time-share units compete for rental business with the owners of regular condos, who on a per-week basis pay lower prices for their units and can thus charge lower rents. Your tenant, or you for that matter, probably would do better to rent a single-owner condo.

Source: "Temptations That You Should Resist," Money, December 1983, p. 100. Reprinted by permission.

SUMMARY

The housing decision should be based on a rational analysis of such factors as where you want to live, what kind of home you want, and your monthly payment limitations. Careful thought must be given to the "rent or buy" decision. Renting offers the advantages of liquidity, mobility, and certain cost savings. Home ownership, however, provides equity buildup, possible appreciation, tax savings, and relatively stable housing costs. Other housing options include manufactured homes, condominiums, and cooperative apartments.

There are two major aspects of the decision to buy a home. The first is how much to spend on a home—including the down payment, mortgage payments, taxes, insurance, and maintenance and operating expenses. The second issue concerns evaluating alternative homes. In looking for a home, you might go to a real estate agent, who uses multiple listing services. Another possibility is contacting "for sale by owner" offerings. Discount brokers now provide a third option.

The original asking price for a home is usually negotiated to a lower figure through a series of counteroffers. When the final sale price is determined, the purchase or sales contract that is signed usually includes an earnest money provision, requiring a deposit by the prospective buyer. Two other important documents in home buying are the title, giving the buyer the right to use the property subject to zoning restrictions, and the deed, which transfers the ownership of the residence.

Most houses are financed through mortgages on the balance of the purchase price remaining after a down payment. Traditional types of mortgages include conventional mortgages, which are granted by private lenders, and the Federal Housing Administration (FHA) and Veterans Administration (VA) mortgages, which also come from private lenders but with certain guarantees from the respective government agencies. In the 1980s additional financing options have become popular. Fixed-rate mortgages have been replaced by floating-rate mortgages with variable, adjustable, or renegotiable rates. Graduated-payment and shared-appreciation mortgages are also available.

In addition to these financial arrangements, mortgages may include provisions for prepayment, delinquency, assumable mortgages, and second mortgages. Among the sources of mortgage money are lending institutions, commercial banks, mortgage companies, insurance companies, and the sellers themselves. Owner financing has led to the risks of creative financing with a short cash-out period followed by a balloon payment.

Building a home—another housing option—requires careful analyses of such factors as the location, the architect, construction financing, and supervision of the actual construction.

Two other aspects of the housing decision are selling a house and purchasing a second home.

REVIEW QUESTIONS

1. Briefly define the following terms:
   - appreciation
   - equity
   - mortgage table
   - lease
   - sublease clause
   - Uniform Residential Landlord and Tenant Act
   - manufactured home
   - condominium
   - cooperative apartment
   - down payment mortgage
   - real estate agent
   - multiple listing services
   - listings
   - counteroffers
   - earnest money provision
   - purchase contract
   - title
   - deed
   - warranty deed
   - quit-claim deed
   - land lease
   - fee simple
   - leasehold
   - private mortgage insurance
   - foreclosure
   - closing costs
   - points
   - loan origination fee
   - variable-rate mortgage
   - adjustable-rate mortgage
   - renegotiable-rate mortgage
   - graduated-payment mortgage
   - shared-appreciation mortgage
   - prepayment clause
   - delinquency clause
   - assumable-mortgage clause
   - second mortgage
   - creative financing
   - cash-out period
   - balloon payment

2. What factors should be considered in making a personal housing decision?

3. Outline the factors to consider in a rent or buy decision.

4. What are the advantages and disadvantages of the following home purchase options: a single family residence, manufactured home, condominium, or cooperative apartment?

5. List the major costs of home ownership.

6. Many sources have reported that the size of the American home is shrinking. What are the reasons for this trend?

7. What is the function of titles and deeds in the real estate industry?

8. Discuss the major types of mortgages available today.

9. What is meant by "creative financing"? How is it used in today's housing market?

10. What are the major issues involved in building a home?

CASES AND EXERCISES

1. Some Canadian home buyers are making weekly rather than monthly mortgage payments. So a $600 a month payment would be broken down into four weekly payments of $150. The weekly interest rate is set equal to the annual rate for monthly payments. In the case of a 13-percent mortgage, the weekly rate comes out to 9.25 percent on an annual basis. What are the advantages of such a mortgage? The lender benefits by improved cash flow since the loan is paid off 12.2 years earlier. The borrower saves some $70,942 in interest over the mortgage period. This is

particularly important to Canadians since they cannot deduct interest for tax purposes.[20] Would you prefer to pay weekly mortgage payments rather than monthly ones? Why or why not? Do you think the Canadian system could be implemented in the United States? Discuss.

2. Analyze your own personal housing requirements. Where do you want to live and why? What kind of home do you want and why? Do you want to rent or buy and why?

3. Obtain a copy of the lease agreement used by a local apartment complex. What are the most significant parts of this lease? As a renter, would you find the lease acceptable? Discuss.

4. If you were looking for a house, would you go to a real estate firm or contact "for sale by owner" offerings? Why? Discuss.

5. Interview a housing lender. What types of mortgages are available in your area? What rates are being charged? What down payments are required?

ANSWERS TO PERSONAL FINANCE I.Q. TEST

1. Fiction. 2. Fiction. 3. Fact. 4. Fact. 5. Fiction. 6. Fiction.

HOW ALAN MARKUS REACHED HIS PERSONAL FINANCIAL DECISION

"Well, you've certainly come up with an intriguing alternative," Professor Burr remarked. He then sat down with Alan to go over a few additional considerations.

Although Alan liked the look of the house, he still needed to have it inspected to make sure there weren't any structural problems or major repairs in the offing. If he had to replace the roof or repair the boiler, for instance, it would really set him back. Alan hadn't thought about possible maintenance costs.

Another aspect Alan hadn't considered was his role as landlord. What would he do if a tenant who was also a friend failed to pay the rent on time? A lease can help to avoid misunderstandings.

Overall, though, Alan had already thought through many of the financial details. Both the asking price and the mortgage terms were reasonable. Professor Burr praised Alan for his enterprise. "Let me know how you make out," he said as they parted. "I'd like to use your situation as an example in one of my lectures."

LEARNING OBJECTIVES

1. To discuss the major transportation alternatives available to consumers. / ***2.*** To list the alternative methods of purchasing used cars and the relative importance of each in total sales. / ***3.*** To describe the advantages and disadvantages of leasing rather than purchasing an automobile. / ***4.*** To enumerate the steps in deciding to purchase an automobile. / ***5.*** To explain the roles played by car-buying services. / ***6.*** To identify the major sources of funds for financing automobile purchases. / ***7.*** To distinguish between fixed and variable expenses of automobile ownership and to give examples of each expense category.

TESTING YOUR PERSONAL FINANCE I.Q.

	FACT	FICTION
1. Two-thirds of all Americans over the age of 18 have never flown.	☐	☐
2. Intercity buses are more important than passenger rail service and commercial airlines, in terms of both passengers transported and number of places served.	☐	☐
3. The average automobile on the road today is 4.8 years old.	☐	☐
4. Most used cars are bought and sold through private transactions rather than through auto dealers.	☐	☐
5. Commercial banks and savings and loan associations are usually the cheapest source of automobile financing.	☐	☐
6. An automobile recall is actually an indication of the auto manufacturer's high standards, since it shows that the manufacturer has identified a potential safety defect and is willing to correct it at no charge.	☐	☐

The materials in this chapter assist in separating fact from fiction. Your answers can be checked on page 301.

CHAPTER TEN

THE TRANSPORTATION DECISION

SHARING A PERSONAL FINANCIAL DECISION WITH
PROFESSOR MICHAEL J. AHERN, III, OF THE UNIVERSITY OF TOLEDO

In a recent lecture, Professor Michael Ahern stressed the importance of understanding all the facets of financing the purchase of an automobile, especially the effects of high interest rates. In addition, he discussed the various sources for financing: a credit union; commercial banks; savings and loan associations; mutual savings banks; and the automobile manufacturer's financing subsidiary. Professor Ahern emphasized that it is always wise to shop around for interest rates and other financing terms.

After class, Bill Mikelson asked Professor Ahern to take a look at what he considered to be a good offer on financing from the local dealer. He pulled out an unsigned contract that quoted an 11.5 percent annual percentage rate for the financing of the new car he was interested in buying. Closer examination of the contract revealed that he was required to secure credit life insurance and credit disability insurance for the term of the loan. In addition to the finance charges on the money borrowed for the purchase of the car, the insurance premium payments were also assessed finance charges. The cost of the insurance was $141.37 for credit life and $286.84 for credit disability. The cash price of the automobile was $6,000, and Bill had $1,000 available for a down payment. He asked Professor Ahern if he thought that this would be a good deal.

If you were Professor Ahern, how would you advise Bill?

To find out how Professor Ahern helped Bill with his personal financial decision, turn to page 301.

"If you think nobody cares if you're alive, try missing a couple of car payments."
Earl Wilson[1]

Janet Guthrie, the first woman to compete in the Indianapolis 500 auto race, knows more about buying, driving, and servicing cars than almost any American—man or woman. We decided to seek her automotive advice for a would-be automobile purchaser.

BOONE & KURTZ: *For most of us, a car is the second or third most important purchase of our lives. What advice would you give someone who is making this purchase for the first time?*

GUTHRIE: Before you even begin looking, you must first define in your own mind exactly how you intend to use the car. Ask yourself how much regular driving you will do and how many people will travel along with you. Your answers will tell you how large a car you need, whether you can afford a low-gas mileage model, and the accessories you should purchase. For example, if you drive several hours each day along with three other people, you will probably need a full-sized car that offers good gas mileage. If you do this amount of driving on your own, you will probably want to add a radio or tape deck to keep you alert. Image may also be important. If you're a real estate agent, a fairly expensive, good-looking car is necessary for your job. If you're a college professor, you'll probably want a ten-year-old Volkswagen.

By the time you've defined your needs, you will probably have a few choices in mind. Ask all your friends about their experiences with these cars. Those who rent cars on business should be especially helpful. Then check *Consumer Reports* and car-buff books like *Car and Driver*, *Motor Trend*, and *Road and Track* for their analyses. Since the buff books derive a large part of their revenue from automobile advertising, their reviews are generally favorable. But you can generally read between the lines to figure out what they really mean.

BOONE & KURTZ: *Does the new-car dealer you choose make a difference?*

GUTHRIE: Absolutely. The best way to check out a dealer's reputation is to ask your friends. Strangers can be helpful too. If you're thinking about buying a car from a particular dealer and you see a car with that dealer's tag on the back, ask the owner what kind of experience he's had. You'll be surprised how much information you'll get. You can also find out a lot about a dealer by checking with your local consumer protection agency or Better Business Bureau.

In each case, what you're really asking is whether you can get good service under warranty. You can almost always find a mechanic who will charge you less for your regular maintenance than a dealer. But if anything covered by the warranty goes wrong, having a dependable, honest dealer can make all the difference in the world.

BOONE & KURTZ: *Do most drivers understand how to service their cars?*

GUTHRIE: Definitely not. A lot of young people don't have the foggiest notion that their cars need regular oil changes. And in these days of do-it-yourself service stations, there are simply no neighborhood service station attendants to remind drivers to look under their cars' hoods.

The regular maintenance intervals suggested by the manufacturers don't help either. It's very common for manufacturers to recommend changing the oil every 7,500 miles. That's nonsense. If I had $10,000 invested in an automobile, you can be sure I would have the oil changed every 3,000 miles at most. That's two and one-half oil changes in the same interval the manufacturer suggested one oil change.

Frequent oil changes are a very cheap way of avoiding expensive repair costs. Mechanical problems may not crop up right away, but if you expect to keep your car for a long time—and most people do—infrequent oil changes can mean trouble.

BOONE & KURTZ: *Would you ever buy a used car?*

GUTHRIE: Sure. I bought just one new car in my life and that was the car I was going to turn into a race car. I drove it just 80 miles and then tore it apart down to the last nut and bolt. My street cars have always been used. Right now I'm driving a 1968 Barracuda that I bought when it was a year old. It has 174,000 miles on it and is still going strong.

BOONE & KURTZ: *Where did you buy it?*

GUTHRIE: I bought it through a private sale. Of course, this route will take you a lot longer than buying through a dealer—you'll have to look at a lot of cars before you find a good one—but it can save you a lot of money.

When you finally find a car you like, have a mechanic check it out before you buy. You'll have to pay for this service, so it's important to make some preliminary judgments yourself. Look under the car for wet spots, and if you see any, find out where they're coming from. Be wary of accelerator and brake pedals that look worn. Check the tires for uneven wear and check the tailpipe when the car is started for any sign of oil smoke. Listen to the motor for any sounds that don't belong and operate all the controls to make sure they're working. These are only some of the things to look for. For a full list, the best source I know is Deanna Sclar's *Auto Repair for Dummies.*

BOONE & KURTZ: *When should you sell a car?*

GUTHRIE: It's a tough decision. You should consider how expensive it is to repair and how important it is to have a car you can always depend on—no matter what. You can tolerate more failures in a second family car than in a car you must use every day. In the end you have to sit down with pencil and paper and figure out the cost of each repair and what the car might be worth if you tried to sell it.²

THE TRANSPORTATION ALTERNATIVES

If the consumer dollar were divided into pieces, allotting portions for various expenditures—transportation, food, recreation, and so on—almost 15 cents of it would go for transportation. In 1981, for example, Americans spent $143 billion on the costs of purchasing, repairing, and insuring their automobiles; an additional $97 billion went to gas and oil; and over $20 billion was spent on airlines, buses, commuter trains, taxicabs, and other forms of public transportation.³

The American love affair with the car and other forms of transportation is no accident. The United States is a huge nation with a 3,000-mile cross-country expanse. Recent Census Bureau data revealed that in a single year, Americans took 141 million recreational, entertainment, and sightseeing trips involving 94 billion miles of travel by car, bus, train, and plane. These statistics prompted one cynic to define tourists as people who drive thousands of miles so they can be photographed standing in front of their car. Consider the following:

- American passenger cars are driven about 9,000 miles annually, with new passenger cars now averaging 25.6 miles per gallon.⁴
- There is a car or truck for nearly every American adult. Approximately 142 million vehicles are now on the road.
- Since 1972, the first full year of Amtrak's service, railroad passenger miles have increased by 50 percent (each passenger mile equals one passenger carried one mile).⁵
- Intercity buses, which serve approximately 272,000 miles of highway across the nation, transported 375 million passengers in 1981.⁶

DO YOU NEED A CAR?

For most consumers, a car is the second or third largest purchase they will make, after a home and a college education. An important first decision is to determine whether an automobile is really needed or whether public transportation is a more practical and less expensive alternative. Statistics provide a good idea of why the vast majority of Americans choose the automobile above all other forms of transportation. Americans drive because they have to. Four of every five miles driven each year by passenger cars are for commuting to and from work, business travel, and important family errands, including trips to and from the grocery, school, doctor's office, and so on. Only about 20 percent of American driving is nonessential. When we travel on vacation, go for a drive in the country, or take a trip to the ballpark, automobiles become a discretionary product rather than an absolute necessity.

In most cases, suburban and rural Americans have no choice: the only way to get where they want to go is by car. But many city residents find a car the least attractive way to get around and choose other options instead. In large cities where the cost of owning a car is prohibitive (garaging a car in the heart of New York City can cost $200 a month or more) and where traffic jams and no-parking signs make driving more pain than pleasure, people have taken to trains, buses, subways, bicycles, and even walking.

Obviously, the transportation alternatives facing individuals are greatly affected by location. Mass transit may be a preferred alternative for many commuters, but quality, flexibility, and even availability vary greatly. For intercity travelers, an array of options may be available, including passenger rail transportation, air travel, and bus transportation.

MASS TRANSIT

Commuting within a city or between a city and its surrounding areas without a car is possible on subway and elevated rail lines, city buses and trolley coaches, ferry boats, cable cars, commuter railroads, and other forms of *mass transit*. The percentage of people using public transportation in various major metropolitan areas ranges from 1 percent in the Riverside–San Bernadino–Ontario area in California to 44 percent in the New York metropolitan area.[7]

In total, over 1,000 separate transit systems serve the transportation needs of both large and small cities and towns throughout the nation. Over 75 percent of all Americans live in areas served by mass transit, and millions of Americans take advantage of the opportunity to leave their cars at home every chance they can. The approximately 8.5 billion passengers who use mass transit systems every year to travel to their jobs, to shops, schools, and recreational facilities attest to the public acceptance of mass transit.

Buses are by far the most common form of mass transit. Serving 75 percent of the American public, bus transit systems range from the huge to the tiny. The largest systems operate more than 2,000 buses 24 hours a day. In these systems, rush-hour passengers need wait only a minute or two before the next bus arrives. At the other extreme are systems with only one or two buses, which operate only during morning and evening rush hours. In addition to buses, many large systems are served by several other forms of mass transit. In New York City, for example, people can travel by bus, subway, commuter railroad, ferryboat, or aerial tramway. New Orleans residents have the options of ferryboat, bus, and streetcar.

The various mass transit services add up to major benefits for both the traveling public and the community at large. On a personal level, mass transit

mass transit: *the use of city buses, commuter railroads, subways, and other methods by large numbers of people who commute within a city or between a city and its suburbs.*

EFFECTIVE BUYING

MARTA (Metropolitan Atlanta Rapid Transit Authority) provides Atlanta residents with a mass-transit alternative to the automobile.

provides reliable, economical service and enables nondrivers to travel from place to place. On a community level, it reduces air pollution and energy consumption, both of which are critical concerns today. This is illustrated by Figure 10-1, which compares the amounts of propulsion energy that are required to move commuters.

Mass transit also provides a number of additional benefits for the community. It can make important contributions to stimulating economic development and increasing employment opportunities. Finally, it permits concentration of urban activities into small areas and conserves urban space by reducing the amount of land needed for roads, parking garages, and highways.

Despite these considerable benefits, nearly every part of the nation's mass transit system is in serious financial trouble. By 1990, 72 percent of all transit buses and 28 percent of all subway cars will need to be replaced—a job that will cost the nation an estimated $40 billion.[8]

AMTRAK

Amtrak: the government-run National Railroad Passenger Corporation that operates passenger rail service in the United States.

The government-run National Railroad Passenger Corporation, known as *Amtrak*, serves 475 communities throughout the United States and travels over 23,000 miles of track. Amtrak's popularity as an alternative to the automobile grew during the late 1970s, when the energy shortage boosted the cost of

Figure 10-1

PROPULSION ENERGY CONSUMED PER PASSENGER MILE BY VARIOUS FORMS OF TRANSPORTATION

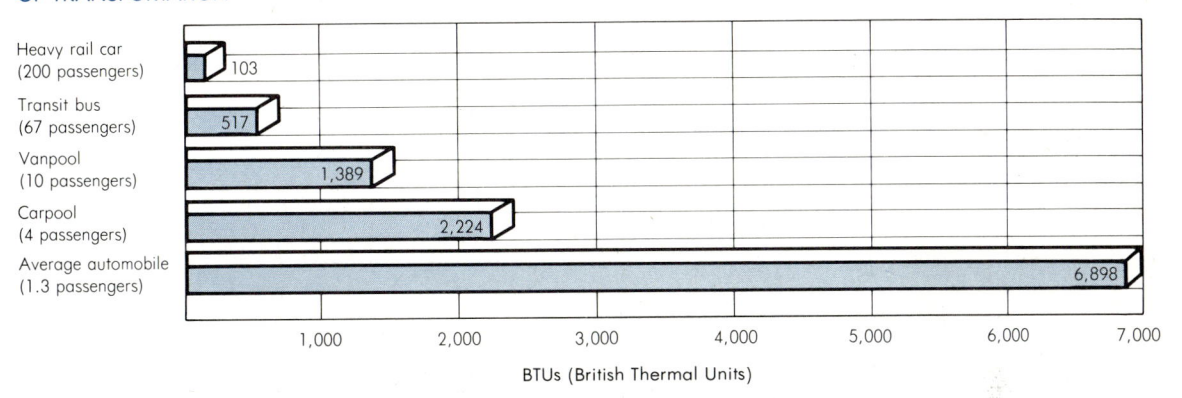

Mode	BTUs
Heavy rail car (200 passengers)	103
Transit bus (67 passengers)	517
Vanpool (10 passengers)	1,389
Carpool (4 passengers)	2,224
Average automobile (1.3 passengers)	6,898

BTUs (British Thermal Units)

Source: *Transit Fact Book* (Washington, D.C.: American Public Transit Association, 1981), p. 36.

gasoline. By 1982, almost 20 million businesses and vacation travelers had flocked to Amtrak. Recently, however, price wars among the commercial airlines have adversely affected Amtrak's ridership. Willing to operate at a loss in order to attract new passengers, the airlines have frequently offered travel fares that are better than Amtrak's. As a result, even confirmed Amtrak passengers have begun traveling by air. Still, Amtrak made substantial fiscal gains in 1984, a fact they attribute to a better reputation, better performance, and an improved U.S. economy. With an on-time record of 85 percent (higher than most airlines), Amtrak is considered one of the most dependable means of travel.

AIR TRAVEL

Travelers seeking alternatives to automobiles for medium- and long-distance trips frequently consider commercial airlines. Air travel is typically the fastest of all transportation alternatives between medium- and larger-sized cities. The number of commercial airline passengers in the United States has increased from 62 million in 1960 to approximately 300 million today. In 1971, 51 percent of the U.S. adult population had never flown in a commercial airliner. By 1984 the percentage of Americans aged 18 or over who had never used commercial air transportation had dropped to 34 percent.[9]

Recent deregulation of the airline industry has produced price competition on some routes that makes air transportation competitive with rail and bus transportation. At one point, competing airlines slashed cross-country fares to $99. In some instances, however, deregulation produced less air service and even higher prices, particularly for air travelers residing in smaller cities. Since airlines were given more leeway in choosing routes and cities, many of them abandoned their previous service to smaller, less profitable cities and focused on potentially higher-profit routes. For example, before deregulation, United Airlines flew between Bakersfield, California, and San Francisco for $28. After deregulation, Pacific Express, a commuter airline with smaller planes and fewer amenities, was the only choice available; it charged $75 for the same trip.

Because of the various rates offered, the conditions necessary to qualify for such rates, and the rapidity of changes in rates offered for different routes, air travelers should work with a knowledgeable independent travel agent. There is no charge for travel agents' services, since they are compensated by the airlines in the form of a percentage of total fares. What they can provide is current information on fares and available flights for all commercial air carriers.

BUS TRAVEL

Buses are the transportation lifeline of small-town America. For many cities too small to be served by commercial airlines and not on Amtrak routes, buses represent the only available form of public transportation. During 1981 approximately 375 million Americans traveled nearly 30 billion miles collectively on the 21,000 intercity buses that connect almost 15,000 U.S. communities.

Bus ridership is divided almost equally between scheduled services and tours and charters. Although buses have not replaced the automobile as the most widely used form of transportation, they carry more travelers and service more communities than either Amtrak or commercial airlines. Figure 10-2 compares the three intercity carriers.

Like the airlines, intercity buses were recently deregulated, and this move has already begun to change the nature of the bus industry, which had been strictly controlled for almost 50 years. Although deregulation has resulted in new bus routes and tours and in increased competition, it has also meant the end of service on less-profitable routes. Greyhound, the nation's largest carrier, has sought to end service on nearly 4,500 of its 94,000 route miles and to eliminate more than 1,300 stops in 43 states. Included in this number are many towns that have no other form of public transportation. Trailways, the nation's number-two carrier, dropped 50 stops in 7 states.[10]

Despite these industry changes, travelers are attracted to intercity buses for the same reasons they have always been. Buses are especially attractive to people too old, too young, or too infirm to drive long distances; who do not own cars; or who simply want to relax when they travel. To lure passengers away from other forms of transportation, bus lines offer a variety of fares, many of which feature single, low-price tickets to anywhere.

Figure 10-2
COMPARING INTERCITY BUSES, COMMERCIAL AIRLINES, AND AMTRAK

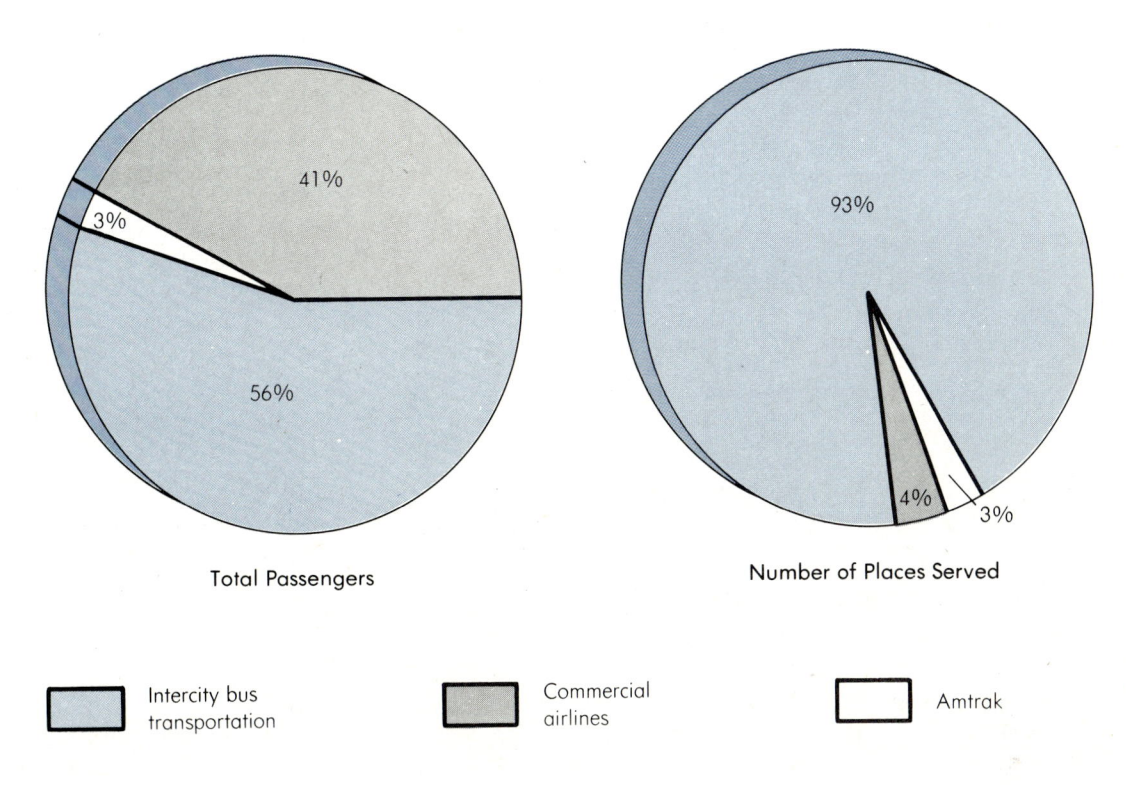

Total Passengers: 3%, 41%, 56%

Number of Places Served: 93%, 4%, 3%

☐ Intercity bus transportation   ☐ Commercial airlines   ☐ Amtrak

Source: Based on data in *Bus Facts* (Washington, D.C.: American Bus Association, 1982), p. 4.

PURCHASING AN AUTOMOBILE

Even consumers who use the alternative forms of transportation on a regular basis are likely to need an automobile. The auto purchaser faces a number of decisions in choosing the most appropriate vehicle for his or her needs. Among the questions you have to consider are what kind of car you need; whether it should be domestic or imported, new or used, purchased or leased; what financing options are available; and how much it costs, both to buy and to run.

CHOOSING THE RIGHT CAR FOR YOU

With the dizzying array of alternatives from which to choose, pinpointing the most appropriate automobile is not an easy matter. Auto shoppers should begin by narrowing their choices. This can be accomplished by making a number of preliminary decisions concerning the desired make and model, size, body style, options, and price. Completing the brief questionnaire in Figure 10-3 can help you to focus on the type of car that best matches your needs.

Make and Model. Do you want a General Motors car or a Chrysler; a Honda or a Toyota? Do you prefer a Cadillac Seville or a Chrysler LeBaron; a Honda Accord or a Toyota Celica? Most people base their decisions, at least in part, on the automaker's reputation as well as on the reputation of the specific model they want to buy. Foreign imports, for example, have acquired a reputation for quality and value while larger American cars are believed to provide greater safety. Auto shoppers should check consumer buying guides—especially *Consumers Reports* and *Money*—for in-depth reviews of specific models and ask people who currently own the car their opinion of its performance, repair record, and other important factors.

Size. Despite the variety of car-size descriptions that sometimes confuse more than clarify, there are three basic choices:

1. *Small-sized cars* (often referred to as compacts or subcompacts) seat two or four people (although rear-seat passengers are often cramped and uncomfortable). They offer better gas mileage than any other car size, generally have four-cylinder engines, and perform best with a manual rather than an automatic transmission.

2. *Medium-sized cars* (or intermediates) seat five or six people and are often used as family cars. With a four- to six-cylinder engine, they are powerful enough to handle the load of an automatic transmission and air conditioner and small enough to save on gas consumption.

3. *Large-sized cars* seat six people comfortably and have six- to eight-cylinder engines. Consumers are attracted to large cars for such reasons as increased safety, comfort, seating capacity, and status.

Although small cars have gained a permanent place in the U.S. car market as a result of the energy crisis of the 1970s, many American auto purchasers return to large cars whenever they sense a moderation in gasoline prices. Another factor affecting the willingness to buy larger-sized cars is their improved gas mileage. Many large cars now average 18 or more miles per gallon—a major improvement from the 9 or 10 miles per gallon that were common in the early 1970s.

Body Style. Most cars offer a choice of either a two-door or a four-door model. Although the two-door model offers a sporty look, it often sacrifices back-seat leg room, rear-view visibility, and ease in getting in and out of the back seat.

Some two- and four-door models are available as hatchbacks—cars that

Figure 10-3
AUTOMOBILE PREFERENCE QUESTIONNAIRE

Directions: Answer each question and place the letter in the box to the right that matches your automobile size preference.*

QUESTIONS	PREFERRED AUTOMOBILE SIZE		
	Subcompact/Compact	Intermediate Size	Full Size
1. What's the maximum you are willing to pay for a car? a) $6,000–$9,000 b) $10,000–$15,000 c) $16,000 or more	☐	☐	☐
2. What kind of car do you prefer? a) Japanese b) European c) American	☐	☐	☐
3. Are you interested in a sports car? a) yes b) undecided c) no	☐	☐	☐
4. Which body style do you prefer? a) 2-door hatchback b) 4-door sedan c) station wagon	☐	☐	☐
5. Choose which of the following you like better: a) front-wheel drive b) don't know c) rear-wheel drive	☐	☐	☐
6. How many passengers do you usually carry? a) two b) four c) six or more	☐	☐	☐
7. What's the minimum combined city-highway mpg you'll accept? a) 35 b) 23 c) 11	☐	☐	☐
8. Which is most important to you? a) acceleration b) both c) long-distance fuel economy	☐	☐	☐
9. How large an engine do you prefer? a) 4 cylinders b) doesn't matter c) 6 cylinders	☐	☐	☐
10. Which type of transmission do you prefer? a) manual b) undecided c) automatic	☐	☐	☐

*A preponderance of answers in any one of the three categories indicates your inclination to buy that size vehicle.

Source: "Finding the Right Car for You," *Changing Times*, November 1983, p. 39. Reprinted with permission from *Changing Times* Magazine, © Kiplinger Washington Editors, Inc., 1983.

have a large, hinged rear window that can be raised for easy entry into the luggage area. A hatchback accommodates large cargo when its rear seat is folded down; but because its luggage compartment is not concealed, it may present a problem in high-crime areas. (Some models come with a detachable luggage compartment cover.) Two other possible purchases include the station wagon and the van, both of which combine comfort with a large cargo capacity.

Options. The final price of a car is directly related to the options chosen. A large, powerful engine, automatic transmission, power brakes and steering, air conditioning, radial tires, deep, plush upholstered seats, and scores of other extras can drastically increase the purchase price. To avoid this added cost, purchasers should choose only those options that are absolutely necessary for safety and comfort. Table 10-1 compares factory-installed optional equipment in 1970 with that in 1981.

Price. By 1984 the average retail price paid for a new car had climbed above the $10,000 mark. By 1990 the average price is expected to increase another 70 percent, to $17,300, as a result of buyers drifting to higher-price models and continued inflationary pressures on production costs.[11] These prices have produced three reactions by U.S. automobile buyers:

Table 10-1
FACTORY-INSTALLED OPTIONAL EQUIPMENT ON AUTOMOBILES FOR 1970 AND 1981

Equipment	Percent of Cars Produced 1970	1981
Automatic transmission	91%	85%
V-8 engine	84	29
6-cylinder engine	16	36
4-cylinder engine	0	35
Power brakes	56	86
Power steering	81	87
Power windows	17	27
Air conditioning	61	78
Tinted glass	70	85

Source: U.S. Bureau of the Census, *Statistical Abstract of the United States* (Washington, D.C.: U.S. Government Printing Office, 1983), p. 618.

- Increased length of time a new automobile is kept before it is sold or traded for another car.
- Increased willingness to purchase used cars.
- Increased willingness to purchase imported automobiles, which sometimes, but not always, carry lower retail prices than American-built cars and have a reputation for quality.

DOMESTIC VERSUS IMPORTED CARS

More than one out of four cars purchased by U.S. consumers is a foreign import. Names like Nissan, Toyota, Mercedes, Volvo, Volkswagen, and Honda are as common on some American highways as are GM and Ford. In the Pacific Coast states, over 50 percent of new cars sold are foreign.

Why has this occurred? In general, foreign imports developed a reputation for offering more quality for their price than American-built cars. In addition, they were perceived to offer more fuel economy and to produce a higher resale value than their U.S. counterparts. Only after being stung severely by the rise in imports, especially from Japan, did Detroit automakers begin to produce cars designed to better match the needs of various segments of the car-buying market.

The move toward producing more fuel-efficient cars and improving product quality has led to major sales and profit gains for American car manufacturers. These gains are reflected in Chrysler's recovery from near-bankruptcy: during the past two years it has repaid its government-backed loans and gone on to earn a profit. One advantage U.S. automakers are able to offer car buyers is a network of service and repair facilities that is wider than that of their foreign competitors. In addition, they benefit from the patriotic desires of some segments of the car-buying public to "buy American," thereby protecting American jobs and strengthening the economy. Finally, the U.S. auto manufacturers have benefited from a voluntary agreement between the United States and Japan to limit the number of foreign cars coming into this country.

A NEW CAR OR A USED CAR?

New cars have the obvious advantages of being fresh out of the showroom and offering the latest comfort, fuel-economy, and safety features. The purchaser is assured that no other driver has had an accident in the car or neglected its maintenance. Of course, the new-car purchaser must pay for these assurances. In additon to the retail price of a new car being higher than that of a used car, its value depreciates more quickly.

At one time the used car was strictly a choice of last resort. Almost no one bought a used car if he or she could afford a new one. The situation changed

The Growing Popularity of "Lemon Laws"

One of the most effective pieces of consumer protection legislation ever put on the books has never been used. It is the automotive Lemon Law, which is designed to protect the new car buyer from being stuck with a lemon—a car that can't be fixed. First passed in Connecticut [in 1982], now law in [19] states and under consideration in several more, the law has yet to be tested in court. And yet, it appears to be highly effective, because car buyers with serious, supportable complaints are finding dealers and manufacturers displaying a degree of understanding and responsiveness that didn't exist before the law was passed.

John Woodcock, who sponsored the Connecticut bill, says, "We haven't had a court case, but the Lemon Law works every day. Since it went into effect, at least 20 cars have been replaced."

Why this sudden change in attitude if the law hasn't even been used in court? Simple, Woodcock says. No manufacturer wants a judge to publicly stamp one of its products a lemon. The negative publicity a court action could create is enough to encourage dealers and manufacturers to change their stance.

Although Lemon Laws vary in wording from state to state, they are all based on essentially the same guidelines. If, during the first year, four unsuccessful attempts are made to correct the same fault, or if the car is out of service for the same problem for 30 days total, the manufacturer must replace the vehicle or refund its cost, less a fair amount for the time the car was actually used. However, if the manufacturer objects, the owner must first take his or her complaint to an independent arbitration panel. Only if that fails does the case go to court.

THESE STATES DECLARE A CAR TO BE A LEMON AFTER THE FOLLOWING NUMBER OF TRIES TO CORRECT A DEFECT OR DAYS OUT OF SERVICE—

	Tries	Days Out of Service
California	4	30
Connecticut	4	30
Delaware	4	30*
Florida	4	25*
Illinois	4	30*
Maine	4	30*
Massachusetts	4	22*
Minnesota	4	30*
Montana	4	30*
Nebraska	4	40
Nevada	4	30
New Hampshire	4	30*
New Jersey	4	31*
New York	4	30
Oregon	4	30*
Texas	4	30
Washington	4	31*
Wisconsin	4	30
Wyoming	4	30*

*Business days.
Source: USN&WR—Basic data: Center for Auto Safety

Source: Mike Knepper, "Auto Lemon Laws Now on the Books in 16 States," *Consumers Digest*, September/October 1983, p. 5. Copyright © 1983 by *Consumers Digest*, reprinted by permission. Table reprinted from *U.S. News & World Report* issue of December 12, 1983. Copyright, 1983, U.S. News & World Report, Inc.

---

as new-car prices rose. Today, used-car dealers have difficulty maintaining adequate inventories of the most popular used-car models. But the price gap between new and used cars has been closing in recent years. One survey revealed that the average 1983 price of a used car was $5,460, compared with an average of $8,358 for a typically equipped new compact car.[12]

The increased prices for used cars are attributable to three factors. First, the higher prices for new cars eventually filter to the used-car market. Second, declines in new-car purchases during the early 1980s reduced the number of late-model used cars. Finally, Americans are choosing to run their cars longer

Figure 10-4
METHODS OF PURCHASING USED CARS

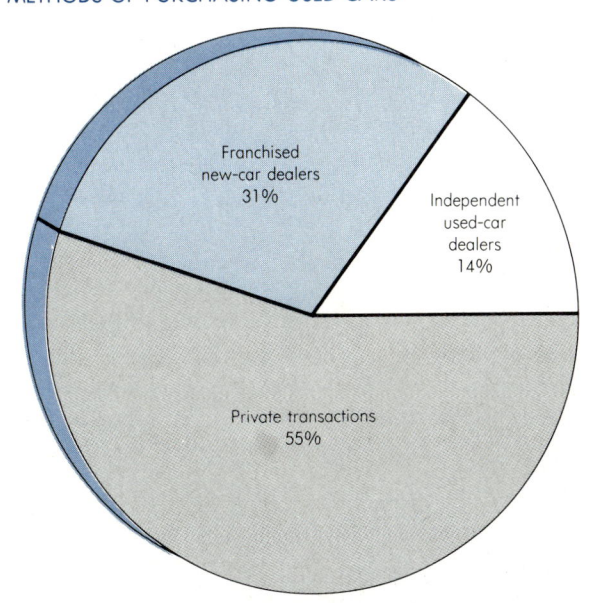

- Franchised new-car dealers 31%
- Independent used-car dealers 14%
- Private transactions 55%

Source: Estimates by National Automobile Dealers Association.

rather than trade them in for new models. Today, the average car on the road is over 7 years old, compared with 5.7 years a decade ago. In general, the most sought-after and valuable used cars have been driven between 15,000 and 25,000 miles and are two to four years old. But there are other things you should look for. Be sure to check such items as tire wear, the condition of the car's interior, rust spots, ripples in the metal, which may indicate that the car has been damaged in an accident, and any other obvious features. And remember Janet Guthrie's advice: arrange for the car to be inspected by a trained mechanic. This inspection can save you from being unpleasantly surprised by problems not obvious to the untrained eye.

Where should you go to buy a used car? Figure 10-4 shows the typical methods of purchasing used cars. New-car dealers generally charge more for used cars than other sources do, but they also tend to sell only the best used cars. Most new-car dealers service their used cars completely and provide a written warranty. Real bargains are sometimes available through a private sale. By dealing directly with the seller, the middleman's profits are eliminated. But there are disadvantages. Sellers offer no warranty, and the purchaser may recover funds for a defective car only by a successful lawsuit. In addition, private sales almost invariably are cash sales, and the buyer must secure any needed financing. Finally, the buyer must handle the paperwork involved in transferring legal ownership.

EFFECTIVE BUYING

> **NADA Used Car Guide:** a monthly publication of the National Automobile Dealers Association listing current retail and trade-in prices for most domestic and foreign cars; also called the "blue book."

The NADA Official Used Car Guide. Both sellers and purchasers of used cars should consult the most recent copy of the *NADA Official Used Car Guide*, published monthly on a regional basis by the National Automobile Dealers Association. This pocket-sized "blue book" shows the current retail and trade-in prices for most domestic and foreign cars; it even includes the additions to the value of each model as a result of specific options or unusually low mileage. The *Guide* is available at your local credit union, bank, or other lender. In addition, many insurance agents have subscriptions to it.

THE LEASING ALTERNATIVE

An alternative to the purchase of a new or used car is leasing. A consumer who leases a car receives the use of the car for a specified period of time (typically two or three years) in exchange for making monthly payments, which are described in a written lease.

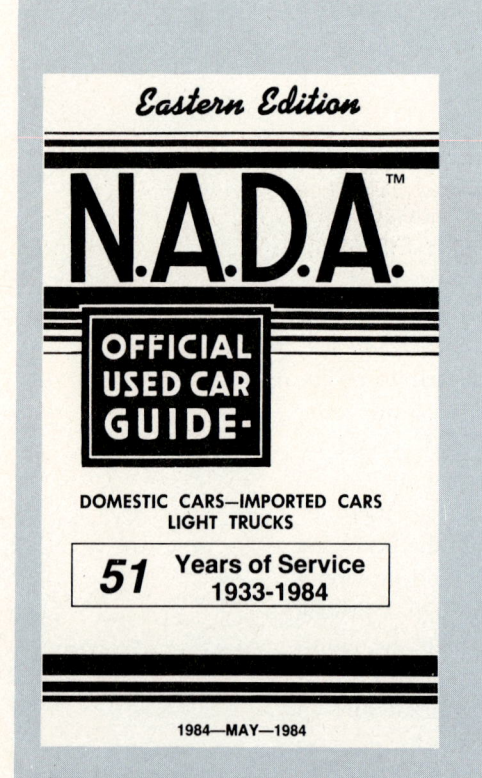

The National Automobile Dealers Association (NADA) publishes its *Official Used Car Guide* monthly in various regional editions. This "blue book" lists up-to-date retail and trade-in prices for most American and imported cars.

Source: NADA *Guide* and sample page reproduced courtesy National Automobile Dealers Association.

THE TRANSPORTATION DECISION

Lease payments are based on such factors as the cost of the automobile, the length of the lease period, and the type of lease. *Open-end leases* base the monthly payments in part on the expected resale value of the car when the lease expires. If the resale value proves to be less than expected, the person leasing the car could be liable for up to three months of additional payments. However, should the actual resale value exceed the expected resale value, the person who has leased the car receives about 90 percent of the difference from the leasing company.

Closed-end leases, by contrast, obligate the person leasing the car to make only the stated monthly payments. Although closed-end leases can cost as much as 15 percent more per month than comparable open-end leases, most people choose the closed-end contract because of the possible additional financial obligation present in open-end leases.[13]

Consumers who choose the closed-end leasing option can usually reduce their monthly payments by selecting models with particularly low depreciation rates. One Maryland dealer, for instance, recently offered a four-year lease on an AMC Spirit DL with a $6,300 retail price for $142 a month. An identically priced Nissan Sentra was available at $122 monthly. Thus, the total savings over the life of the lease amounted to $960. Favorable leasing terms can frequently be obtained for a variety of models, among them the Chevrolet Cavalier, Pontiac Firebird, and the Japanese-made Dodge Colt.[14]

Leasing is especially attractive for individuals who drive a car for business purposes, since they can deduct all or part of the lease payments and related expenditures from income taxes. Since leasing represents temporary use of a vehicle rather than ownership, monthly payments are also typically lower than those for outright purchases. In addition, people who lease do not have to make a down payment, a sizable outlay that may be as much as 25 percent for a used-car purchase. The disadvantage, of course, is that the consumer does not own the vehicle. At the end of the lease period, he or she must either lease another car or pay full price to purchase one.

Leases of automobiles and other consumer products are regulated by the *Consumer Leasing Act of 1976*. This law requires written disclosure of the required payments and payment dates; warranty coverage; repair service available; insurance costs; late payment penalties; conditions under which the lease can be terminated; available purchase options, if any; and specification of what is owed at the end of the lease period.

HOW TO PURCHASE AN AUTOMOBILE

For those consumers who wish to own rather than lease a car, the process of choosing the appropriate model, selecting a dealer, and negotiating with the salesperson on the price of the car can be a traumatic experience. They may also face the uncertainties of alternative financing options and whether to trade in an old model or attempt to sell it themselves.

---

open-end lease: an automobile lease obligating the person leasing the car to make the stated monthly payments and additional payments at the end of the lease if the resale value of the car has declined below that specified at the beginning of the lease.

closed-end lease: an automobile lease obligating the person leasing the car only to make the stated monthly payments, with no residual obligations after the lease expires.

Consumer Leasing Act of 1976: federal legislation requiring firms leasing automobiles and other consumer products to disclose in writing information about payments and payment dates, and other provisions.

EFFECTIVE BUYING

This decision, one of the more important ones faced by most consumers, involves the steps outlined in Chapter 8 for any major purchase. First, you must consider overall household goals and how the automobile affects them—both the physical car itself and its cost. The second step is problem recognition—the determination of the need for a new or used car. Next comes an evaluation of alternatives, with input from the outside environment as well as from your own needs, attitudes, personality, and previous experiences. Now you are ready for the purchase decision and the act of purchasing the car. Following a purchase, you will have several months or years to evaluate the wisdom of your choice. This postpurchase evaluation becomes part of the accumulated experience that affects subsequent auto purchase decisions.

Many of the preliminary steps in deciding to purchase an automobile have already been described: determining the desired make and model, size and body style, price limits, options, acceptability of a new car or used car, and preference for a domestic or imported make. The next step involves finding the right dealer.

CHOOSING A DEALER

Most shoppers contact a number of different dealers in making such preliminary decisions as preferred size and body style, so they are already aware of several alternatives before beginning the negotiating process. But the shopper

The "sticker price" is rarely the actual price paid by the auto purchaser.

THE TRANSPORTATION DECISION

should also contact a *car-buying service,* a business organization that, for a fee, provides listings of dealer costs for a car and desired accessories. Two of the largest car-buying services are Car/Puter International Corporation (1603 Bushwick Avenue, Brooklyn, N.Y. 11207; 800 221-4001) and Nationwide Auto Brokers, Inc. (17517 West Ten Mile Road, Southfield, Mich. 48075; 800 521-7257). The difference between the dealer costs and the sticker price posted in the window of the car represents the range for price negotiations between the shopper and the salesperson.

car-buying service: a business organization providing consumers with a listing of dealer costs for specified automobiles and options and assisting in arranging new-car purchases at discount prices.

The final price frequently reflects the relative negotiating skills of the purchaser as well as such factors as the current level of auto industry sales and whether a trade-in is involved. As overall retail automobile sales increase, there is less need for auto retailers to accept minimal markups on their models. Many industry analysts recommend that shoppers wait until the last few days of the month to shop and then go about two hours before closing, when few customers are likely to be there. If the automaker or dealer is sponsoring a sales contest, the salesperson may be more willing to negotiate in order to exceed the contest quotas. In most cases, the best price that can be negotiated is approximately $300 above the wholesale price, since some markup is needed to pay dealership expenses and earn a profit.

PURCHASING AUTOMOBILES THROUGH CAR-BUYING SERVICES

In addition to providing data on new-car costs, car-buying services such as Car/Puter and Nationwide Auto Brokers also assist in arranging new-car purchases in most parts of the United States at discount prices. Here is how the system works:

> For no additional fee, the services will also supply the name of a cooperating dealer who will deliver a domestic car to you—typically for $75 over his cost and rarely more than $150. On imported models, the markup is usually about $300. Car/Puter has lined up 500 dealers, in 243 metropolitan areas, who pay the service a marketing fee and honor the prearranged prices. If there is no Car/Puter dealer near you, the service will arrange for you to take delivery of your car from a closer, nonaffiliated dealer. You'll have to pay him an additional "courtesy fee" of 1% to 2% of the vehicle's total price. Nationwide, by contrast, has only 36 dealers. Its prices are for cars delivered to Detroit; home delivery adds $50 to $125 to the price.
>
> When they are available through a car-buying service, hot sellers like Firebirds, Camaros, Porsches, or Toyota Celica Supras have $400 to $500 markups and the wait can be as long as three months. Whatever the make, Car/Puter and Nationwide claim to save you as much as $500 to $800 over the price you could strike on your own. And you don't forfeit any warranty rights or manufacturers' rebates.[15]

Auto purchasers who use car-buying services are not likely to arrange a trade-in for their old car. In addition, they may have to arrange outside financing.

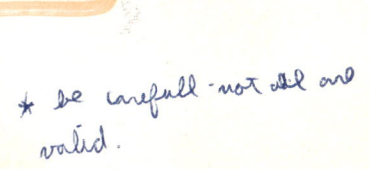

However, for some car buyers the savings possible through such arrangements may more than offset the additional inconvenience.

DO'S AND DON'TS OF NEGOTIATING

Angela Fox Dunn, a syndicated journalist writing for the Los Angeles Times Syndicate, sought the advice of former auto dealers to describe an appropriate negotiating strategy for people seeking to buy a new car. Her experts recommended that the consumer should "bargain, barter, horse trade, but remember you're dealing with an expert, a professionally trained salesman."[16] Table 10-2 summarizes their suggestions.

Table 10-2
THE CAR BUYER–SALESPERSON NEGOTIATION

Don'ts	Do's
Don't say, "I'm just looking." Marks you as a nonserious buyer not worth negotiations.	Do say, "I'm interested in seeing a ____." Tells the salesperson you at least know what kind of car you need.
Don't say, "I couldn't consider paying cash."	Do say, "I want to pay cash for this car. How much is it?" Then spring your trade on him (or her). When the price is now lower, ask for the finance terms. This way you get a price on each phase.
Don't be the first to make an offer, and don't sign the write-up sheet the salesperson prepares.	Do let the salesperson come up with a figure first.
Don't let the salesperson take his (or her) offer to the sales manager, who might redline it (draw a red line through it and insert a higher figure). The salesperson is off the hook; the sales manager is now the heavy.	Do take out your own red pencil, and draw a red line through the salesperson's figure. Insert your own lower figure and ask him to take it to the sales manager for approval, smilingly.
Don't reveal your entire budget, the amount you've computed you can comfortably afford for a car payment. Any smart salesperson will try to raise it.	Do keep your budget figure in mind, plus maintenance and insurance costs, and whatever the total, do not raise it by even $10 a month.
Don't show off, talk about your recent promotion, or volunteer any personal information. The salesperson can use it. He wants to become your buddy as quickly as possible. Stay aloof.	Do answer a question with a question, just as the salesperson is trained to do: "Will you buy this car today?" "Will you meet my deal?" "Would you consider the blue car instead of the red?" "What kind of deal will you make me on the blue?"
Don't assume similar means equal. New cars do not all drive, handle, and feel alike.	Do drive at least two of the same model and equipment. Do inspect the very same car you plan to buy.

Source: "How to Beat the Auto Dealers," Angela Fox Dunn, Syndicated Series, 1981. Copyright, 1981, Angela Fox Dunn, *Los Angeles Times Syndicate*; reprinted by permission.

WHAT ABOUT TRADE-INS?

New-car shoppers can determine the trade-in and retail values of their old cars by checking a recent issue of the *NADA Used Car Guide.* Since the retail auto dealer who accepts a used car in trade for a new car will still have to resell the trade-in, the salesperson is likely to offer the wholesale price listed in the *Guide*—or even less if the car is defective. If the used car is in good condition and less than four years old, it may be possible to negotiate a price between the *Guide*'s wholesale and retail prices. Such used cars, however, are relatively easy to sell privately, and the new-car buyer may receive more money by selling it through newspaper classifieds than by trading it in. If the car is traded in, the consumer should be careful to separate the two transactions. In many cases, an above-wholesale price offered on the trade-in is more than offset by the price charged for the new car.

FINANCING THE AUTOMOBILE PURCHASE

For most car buyers, securing funds to finance at least part of the purchase price is crucial. Even with a trade-in, there may still be several thousand dollars of additional costs. The high interest rates of recent years have led to the increased importance of choosing the best auto-financing plan.

Figure 10-5 shows the dramatic impact of the borrowing period and interest rates on monthly car payments. These payments skyrocket when the interest rates and financing period climb. A purchaser who finances $5,000 at 9 percent for three years will make monthly payments of $159 in principal and interest. By contrast, the same loan at 18 percent will result in monthly payments of about $181.

As auto prices continue to climb, many people choose to reduce their monthly payments by opting for a longer-term loan. Unfortunately, the result is that thousands of dollars are spent on financing alone—often with only a slight reduction in monthly payments and a considerably greater number of them. As Figure 10-5 indicates, a person who finances a $5,000 automobile loan over five years at 12 percent annual interest will make 60 monthly loan payments of $111. Had the purchaser chosen to finance the same loan over four years, the monthly payments would increase only $20.50, to $131.50—and the final 12 monthly payments during the fifth year could have been avoided.

SOURCES OF FINANCING

As discussed in Chapter 7, a number of financing sources exist for the automobile purchaser. In many instances, car buyers who belong to a credit union will discover that it offers the most competitive interest rates for an automobile loan. With their low down-payment requirements, interest rates that may be lower than the prevailing market rate, and frequent option of a payroll deduction

Figure 10-5

MONTHLY PAYMENTS ON A $5,000 LOAN AT DIFFERENT INTEREST RATES AND DIFFERENT LENDING PERIODS

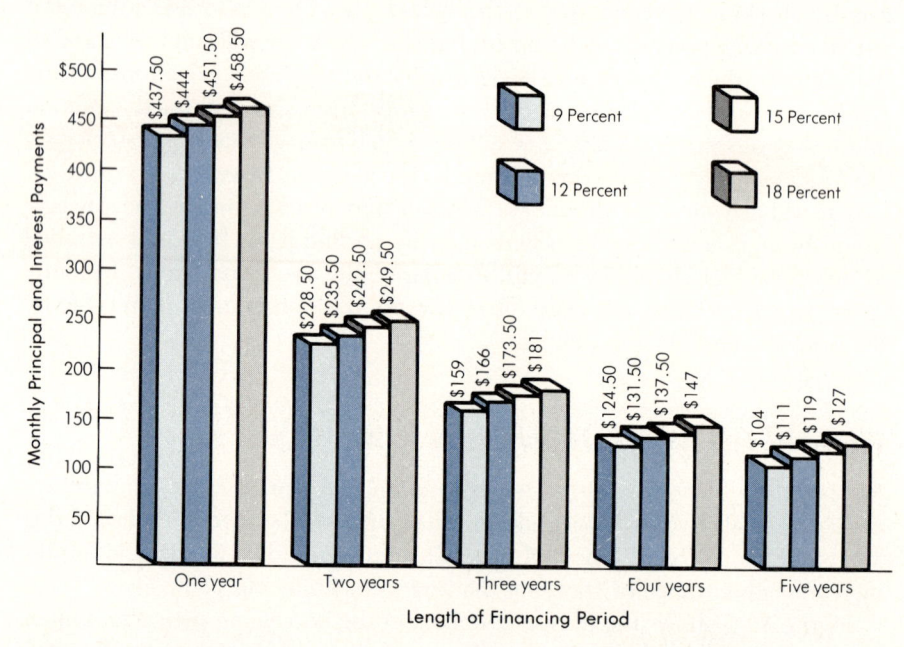

Length of Financing Period	9 Percent	12 Percent	15 Percent	18 Percent
One year	$437.50	$444	$451.50	$458.50
Two years	$228.50	$235.50	$242.50	$249.50
Three years	$159	$166	$173.50	$181
Four years	$124.50	$131.50	$137.50	$147
Five years	$104	$111	$119	$127

plan for monthly payments, credit unions often offer unsurpassed auto-financing terms.

Other possible sources include commercial banks and thrift institutions such as savings and loan associations and mutual savings banks. Still another option is the automobile manufacturer's financing subsidiary. Traditionally, this option has been relatively expensive. In recent years, however, such companies as General Motors Acceptance Corporation and Chrysler and Ford Credit have made periodic offers of financing at below-market rates in an attempt to stimulate sales. However, before taking advantage of such an incentive, you should determine whether a discount is available if you secure financing from another source and pay cash to the auto dealer. A sound purchasing strategy is to separate each element of the auto purchase—the actual purchase price of the car, the down payment, the financing cost, and the value of any trade-in. As Janet Guthrie pointed out, "You can count on the skill of the salesperson to save your dollars in one place by adding them on in another."[17] Comparison shopping for interest rates and other terms is always wise.

WHAT CAR OWNERSHIP REALLY COSTS

Although most drivers realize that the operating costs of an automobile represent sizable outlays on a regular basis, few have any idea exactly how much is

"Last time we spent this much, we got a deed."

Automobiles Are a Major Consumer Expenditure.

Source: From the *Wall Street Journal*—Permission, Cartoon Features Syndicate.

spent or where the money goes. Runzheimer and Company, a consulting firm specializing in travel and living costs, compiles data each year to determine average car ownership costs. These costs, presented in Figure 10-6, indicate that it costs 23.6 cents per mile to own and operate a compact car that is driven 15,000 miles a year and 27.3 cents per mile for an intermediate-sized car. Predictably, per-mile driving costs increase when annual mileage declines. Driving the compact only 10,000 miles increases the per-mile cost to 28.5 cents, while the costs of the intermediate-sized car increase to 33 cents per mile.

FIXED EXPENSES

As Figure 10-6 reveals, total automobile expenses are made up of a number of different factors. Some of these factors can be labeled *fixed expenses* since they remain the same regardless of how much the car is driven. Fixed expenses include such items as insurance, license and registration fees, taxes on the vehicle, depreciation, and finance charges. Other costs vary depending on usage. These *variable expenses*, which include gasoline and oil, a portion of the maintenance expenses, and tires, are discussed in the next subsection.

fixed expenses: for an automobile, the ownership expenses such as insurance, license and registration fees, taxes, depreciation, and finance charges, which remain the same regardless of the number of miles driven.

variable expenses: for an automobile, the operating expenses such as gas and oil, maintenance, and tires, which vary, depending on car usage.

Figure 10-6
WHAT IT COSTS TO OWN AND DRIVE A CAR

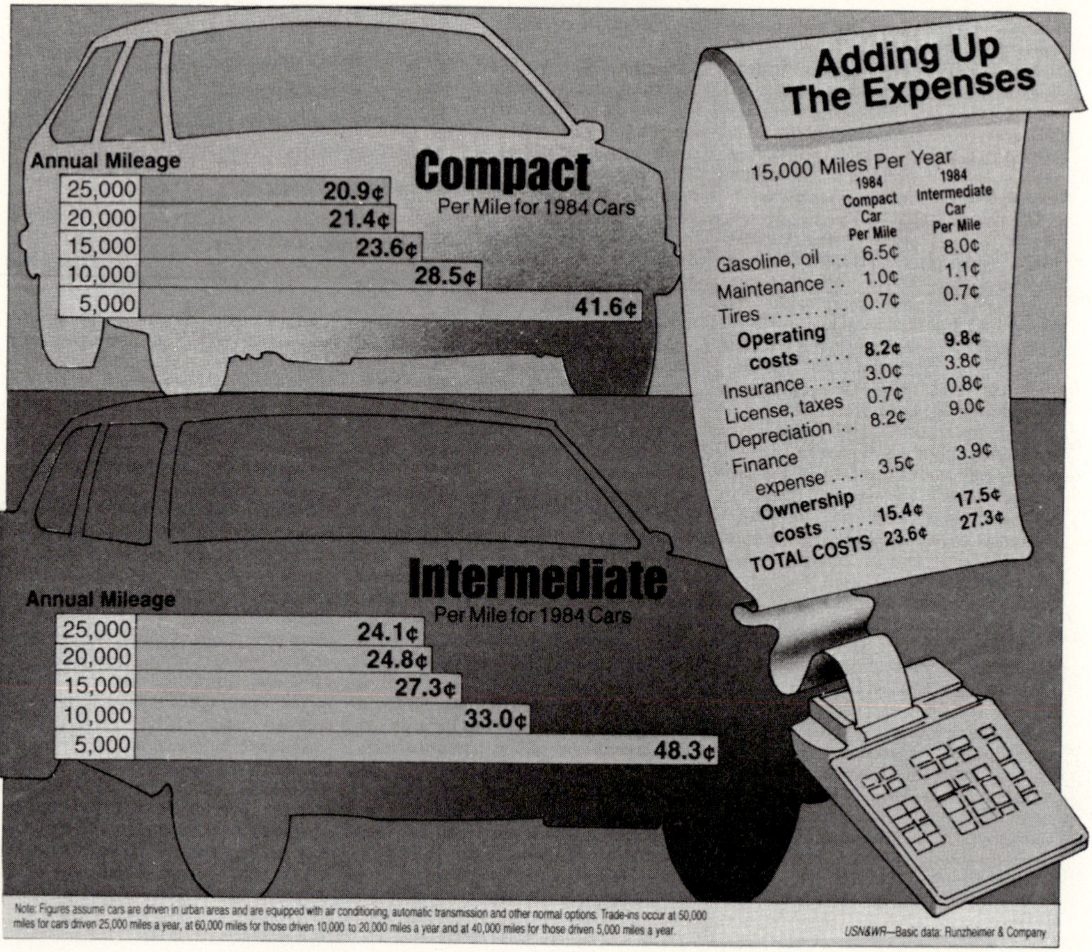

Compact — Per Mile for 1984 Cars

Annual Mileage	Cents per mile
25,000	20.9¢
20,000	21.4¢
15,000	23.6¢
10,000	28.5¢
5,000	41.6¢

Intermediate — Per Mile for 1984 Cars

Annual Mileage	Cents per mile
25,000	24.1¢
20,000	24.8¢
15,000	27.3¢
10,000	33.0¢
5,000	48.3¢

Adding Up The Expenses

15,000 Miles Per Year

	1984 Compact Car Per Mile	1984 Intermediate Car Per Mile
Gasoline, oil	6.5¢	8.0¢
Maintenance	1.0¢	1.1¢
Tires	0.7¢	0.7¢
Operating costs	**8.2¢**	**9.8¢**
Insurance	3.0¢	3.8¢
License, taxes	0.7¢	0.8¢
Depreciation	8.2¢	9.0¢
Finance expense	3.5¢	3.9¢
Ownership costs	**15.4¢**	**17.5¢**
TOTAL COSTS	**23.6¢**	**27.3¢**

Note: Figures assume cars are driven in urban areas and are equipped with air conditioning, automatic transmission and other normal options. Trade-ins occur at 50,000 miles for cars driven 25,000 miles a year, at 60,000 miles for those driven 10,000 to 20,000 miles a year and at 40,000 miles for those driven 5,000 miles a year.

USN&WR—Basic data: Runzheimer & Company

Source: Reprinted from *U.S. News & World Report*, "Autos: They Guzzle Fewer Dollars," February 20, 1984, p. 55. Copyright, 1984, U.S. News & World Report, Inc.

Depreciation. Ironically, the shock of how expensive it is to own a car often comes first when the owner tries to sell it. It is then that the person realizes that the resale price is only a fraction of the original purchase price. This loss is referred to as depreciation. A study by the Hertz Corporation indicated that depreciation reduces a car's value by 31½ percent after one year, 57 percent after two years, 76 percent after three, 83 percent after four, 87 percent after five, 90 percent after six, and 92½ percent after seven.[18] These figures emphasize the substantial depreciation expenses that occur during the first years of car ownership. Of course, depreciation varies widely from model to model. The way the car is driven, its condition, and demand for a particular model also affect how quickly the car depreciates.

To determine the exact amount of depreciation, the consumer can compare a car's current wholesale value (in the *NADA Used Car Guide*) with the car's original purchase price. Next, inflation must be considered. Even if a car purchased for $5,000 is worth $3,500 today, the owner has lost a lot more than $1,500. If a comparable new car costs $8,000, inflation has actually accounted for a considerable portion of the $4,500 difference.

Insurance. The cost of car insurance varies considerably depending on where you live, how old you are, the kind of coverage carried, and so on. One ten-area study of car operation costs reported that typical insurance rates for a full-sized car ranged from $376 in Dallas, Texas, to $1,171 in New York City. The average cost was $639.35.[19] A complete discussion of automobile insurance is included in Chapter 14.

License, Registration, Taxes, and Finance Charges. The amount paid for the car's registration, title, and inspection as well as for sales, excise, and property taxes plus your driver's license varies from state to state. According to the ALA Auto and Travel Club, owners of subcompact cars in rural New Hampshire pay $101.46 a year for these charges while similar owners in Hartford, Connecticut, and Providence, Rhode Island, pay $381.15 and $398.61, respectively.[20] Fixed expenses also include the cost of financing the car and/or the amount of interest lost on money withdrawn from your savings to pay cash.

VARIABLE EXPENSES

In addition to fixed expenses—which account for about two-thirds of the total annual cost of owning and operating a car—the driver incurs a number of variable expenses. These costs, by definition, increase or decrease depending on the number of miles driven each year.

Gas and Oil. With the price of gasoline fluctuating between $1 and $1.50 in most areas of the United States, fuel has become one of the most expensive items in the automobile budget. As Figure 10-6 indicates, gasoline and oil add 6.5 cents per mile to the annual cost of compact cars and 8 cents per mile to that of intermediate-sized cars.

296　EFFECTIVE BUYING

 The federal Environmental Protection Agency (EPA) publishes mileage estimates for new cars that provide an indication of the relative fuel efficiency of different models. These estimates must be disclosed to purchasers of new cars. The actual automobile gas mileage achieved is likely to be less than the EPA estimates. As *Consumer Reports* points out, "In our judgment, the EPA

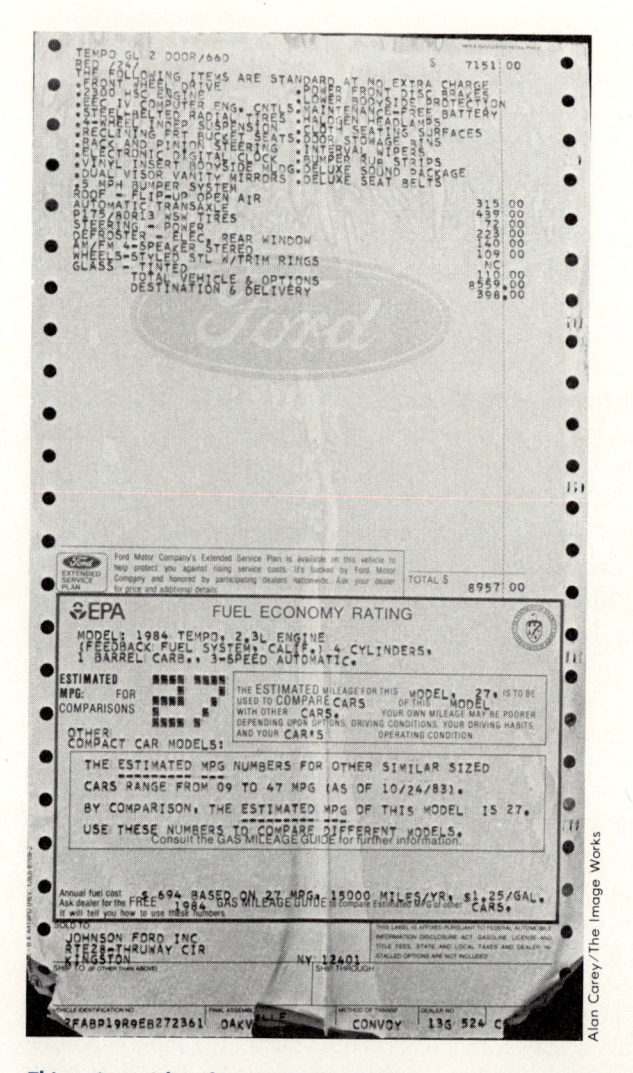

This price sticker for a new Ford Tempo contains an EPA Fuel Economy Rating, stating that this car is expected to get about 27 miles per gallon. The range of MPGs that similar-sized cars achieve is included for the consumer's reference.

mileage estimates are useful primarily when comparing cars of similar size and transmission type. We've found that the EPA figures are less reliable when comparing small cars with large cars or when comparing cars that have a manual transmission with cars that have an automatic transmission."[21] When the EPA states that "your mileage may differ" from its estimates, it means it.

Maintenance. The amount it costs to maintain a car depends on one's driving habits, the auto mechanic chosen, and the general rise in maintenance costs. In general, 22 cents out of every dollar you spend on your car over its lifetime goes toward keeping it in shape.[22] To avoid costly repair problems, a car should have regular servicing, and the car's operating instructions should be followed very carefully. Money saved by neglecting needed service and repairs all too often shows up in the form of increased depreciation.

Tire wear is such an important part of car maintenance that the American Automobile Association lists it as a separate cost category. The cost of maintaining tires increases if the wheels are not properly aligned; if the tires are underinflated; or if one travels at high speeds, stops and starts rapidly, and corners hard.

If you add up all these costs over the lifetime of a car, they make a substantial dent in a personal budget. For a four-door sedan purchased in 1981 for $9,232 and driven for 12 years, the car's operating costs would total $32,000. This includes $9,232 for depreciation (at the end of the period the car would be worth almost nothing), $8,600 for gasoline, $6,200 for repairs and maintenance, $4,000 for insurance, and so on.[23] Although more than 12 years may sound like a long time during which to own the same car, millions of Americans are keeping their cars for just that length of time. Over 13 percent of all cars on the road are at least 12 years old.[24]

AUTO WARRANTIES

An automobile warranty can save a consumer considerable auto repair costs. All new cars come with factory warranties that usually cover the cost to repair or replace defective parts for 12 months or 12,000 miles, whichever comes first, although some warranties cover much longer periods. The Chrysler Corporation, for example, offers a five-year or 50,000-mile warranty.

Warranties differ considerably from one automaker to another. Purchasers should look specifically for parts and service that are not covered and for such items as the battery that are still covered when the general warranty runs out. Keep in mind that the more service provided by a warranty, the less money that has to be spent for car repairs.

In addition to basic warranties, some dealers also offer extended service

EFFECTIVE BUYING

How to Find a Reliable Mechanic

The story is all too familiar: you pay a mechanic $80 for new spark plugs and plug wires. The car still runs like a lame nag, and after several return trips, the mechanic recommends a complete engine overhaul. Wary now, you get a second opinion. The new repairman finds some wires connected to the wrong plugs, corrects the error, and quickly has your car purring properly.

How do you avoid incompetent or—worse—dishonest mechanics? The best way is through a growing network of reputable service stations identified and thoroughly vetted by the Automobile Association of America through its Approved Auto Repair Services program. This is the first nationwide effort to separate good repair shops from bad, and it covers every kind from franchised dealers and tire-company chains to independent neighborhood garages. Started in 1977, the AAA's program now includes more than 2,000 garages in 24 states and is adding hundreds more each year.

Inspectors from the AAA apply rigorous standards to shops seeking its approval. The repair bays, tools, and mechanics' qualifications must be up to snuff; then the AAA queries customers whose names the inspector has taken from the shop's files. More garages fail than pass the first inspection. Once approved and under contract, the proprietors give each customer an evaluation form to fill out and send to AAA.

You don't have to join AAA to take advantage of the program; simply look for the . . . sign below. Non-members can phone the local affiliated auto club for names of approved shops in the area or write to AAA headquarters (8111 Gatehouse Rd., Falls Church, Va. 22047). By no means all garages that answer auto club members' calls for emergency road service have this AAA pedigree, but membership (at about $30 a year) does include the right to binding arbitration of irreconcilable disputes with AAA garages.

One of the AAA's measures of a worthy shop is whether or not its mechanics are certified by the National Institute of Auto Service Excellence. Founded 10 years ago with grants from the auto manufacturers, the institute now supports itself entirely from examination fees. To earn a certificate of competence in any of eight specialties—brakes, automatic transmissions, engine repair, rear-axle and manual transmissions, front ends, heating and air conditioning, electrical systems and engine performance—a mechanic has to pass a 2½-hour test. He also must have two years of hands-on experience.

Shops lacking AAA approval may still do first-rate work. Ask whether the mechanics are NIASE certified. Barry McNulty, the testing agency's director of industry relations, suggests a further step: "Make sure a mechanic shows you an ID card or certificate that says he can repair the system that needs fixing."

Still another ally of the car owner seeking repairs is the new generation of diagnostic equipment that prints out its findings for the customer as well as for the mechanic to see. One of the newest devices, the Smart Scope made by Allen Test Products Inc., puts its diagnosis in terms that the most mechanically illiterate motorist can understand and trust. Let's hope it says you need only a new $15 alternator belt and not, as an unscrupulous mechanic might have suggested, a whole new $100 alternator.

Source: "How to Find a Reliable Mechanic," *Money*, December 1982, p. 110. Reprinted by permission.

---

contracts, which pay for selected repairs after the warranty expires. For example, an extended service contract may cover the engine or drive train for five years or 50,000 miles. Service contracts are issued by the manufacturer in the form of a factory-backed extended warranty, by the dealer, and by independent service contract companies. They are a good value for consumers who drive long distances each year (36,000 miles or more) or for those who simply feel more secure having insurance for an extended period of time.

AUTO RECALLS

An *auto recall* is a request by an automobile manufacturer that purchasers of a specific make return it to a local dealer in order to correct a potential safety defect. In 1981, 9.4 million car owners received manufacturers' recall notices warning them to bring their cars in for immediate repair. Involved were 128 different domestic recalls as well as 28 separate foreign recalls. In addition, between 1979 and 1981 over 22 million motor vehicle tires were recalled because of hazardous defects.[25]

When a car is recalled by the manufacturer for a major or minor repair, it is the original owner who receives the recall notice. Unfortunately, if you are not the original owner, the manufacturer may have difficulty alerting you to the problem. On the average, only about 60 percent of the recalled vehicles are ever brought in for repair.[26] (Many of these no-shows have been notified but decide not to make the repair.) The Auto Safety Hotline of the National Highway Traffic Safety Administration (800 424-9393) can provide information on recalls. Manufacturers are required to make safety defect recalls without charge.

auto recall: a request by an automobile manufacturer that purchasers of a specific automobile return it to a local dealer in order to correct a potential safety defect.

SUMMARY

One of the major purchase decisions confronting consumers involves transportation alternatives. Although approximately four of five Americans feel that a private automobile is a necessity, a number of transportation alternatives exist. For urban dwellers, mass transit in such forms as city buses, commuter railroads, and subways provides a relatively inexpensive means of commuting within a city or between a city and its suburbs. People traveling longer distances between cities may choose commercial air transportation, Amtrak, or intercity buses.

A number of factors enter into the decision to purchase an automobile. Automobile shoppers should first attempt to narrow their choices by making decisions about make and model, size, body style, price, a new or used car, and a domestic or imported car. The *NADA Used Car Guide,* the "blue book" published by the National Automobile Dealers Association, provides current retail and trade-in prices for most domestic and foreign cars.

In some instances, consumers may decide to lease a car rather than resorting to an outright purchase. Leases permit the consumer to avoid the typically high down payment required for most auto purchases. In addition, use of leased cars allows the consumer to periodically exchange the old model for a newer model. On the other hand, at the end of the lease the person who chooses the leasing option has no car. He or she has rented the car—not purchased it.

The steps in the auto purchase process include determination of household goals, problem recognition, evaluation of alternatives, purchase decision, purchase act, and postpurchase evaluation. Once the preliminary steps are completed, the shopper must find the appropriate dealer and negotiate the terms of sale. An alternative is to arrange for the purchase through a specialized car-buying service such as Car/Puter and Nationwide Auto Brokers.

Since automobile purchases involve large dollar outlays, most consumers require borrowed funds to finance the purchase. Frequently used sources of such funds include credit unions, commercial banks and thrift institutions, and specialized financing subsidiaries of the automobile manufacturers. Whenever possible, auto purchasers should separate the three typical elements of the purchase—the actual purchase price of the car, the financing cost, and the value of any trade-in—in order to achieve the optimum total value.

Automobile ownership involves significant costs. The fixed expenses of owning an automobile are those that remain relatively static regardless of the number of miles driven. They include such items as insurance, license and registration fees, taxes, depreciation, and finance charges. Operating expenses are frequently called variable expenses since they tend to rise as the number of miles driven increases. These variable expenses include gasoline and oil, maintenance expenses, and tires.

Warranties are provided by the manufacturer to new-car purchasers. They obligate the auto dealer to repair or replace any defect or problem within a specified time period or before a specified number of miles have been driven, typically 12 months or 12,000 miles, whichever occurs sooner. Some manufacturers provide warranties for longer periods, and others permit the new-car purchaser to obtain extended service contracts. Auto recalls are used to ensure correction of potential safety defects in an automobile. The original owner of the automobile is notified of the recall, and the repairs or corrections are performed at a local dealership at no cost to the auto owner.

REVIEW QUESTIONS

1. Briefly define the following terms:

   mass transit
   Amtrak
   NADA Used Car Guide
   open-end lease
   closed-end lease
   Consumer Leasing Act of 1976
   car-buying service
   fixed expenses
   variable expenses
   auto recall

2. Rank the nonautomobile intercity transportation alternatives on the basis of the number of passengers transported and the number of locations served.

3. Why have the prices of used cars been increasing at a faster rate than the prices of new cars in recent years?

4. Identify the alternative methods of purchasing and selling used cars. What are the major advantages and disadvantages of each method?

5. Distinguish between an open-end automobile lease and a closed-end lease. Which is preferable? Why?

6. What are car-buying services? What roles can they play in the automobile purchase process?

7. What are the primary sources of automobile loans? Which sources are preferable? Explain your answer.

8. Distinguish between the fixed and variable expenses of car ownership and operation. Which category of expenses represents the largest portion of total automobile expenses?

9. Explain the purpose of EPA mileage estimates. What problems are consumers likely to experience when using them in actual driving? How should they be used by consumers?

10. Distinguish between an automobile warranty and an extended service contract. Describe the types of drivers most likely to express a need for extended service contracts.

CASES AND EXERCISES

1. Describe how deregulation has affected intercity transportation. Include in your answer the impact of deregulation on both small towns and larger cities.

2. Describe the typical auto shopper who is most likely to choose the following:
   a. each of the three automobile body sizes.
   b. each of the major alternative body styles.
   c. each of the major options.
   d. a used car rather than a new car.

3. Assume that you are in the market for a new car. Explain your selection of a particular model by relating each step to the steps in the consumer decision-making process.

4. Develop an argument for outright sale of an old car when purchasing a newer model. Under what circumstances should a consumer trade in the old car to the new-car dealer?

5. Since the average price of a new car exceeds the $10,000 mark, a number of auto-financing firms offer 60-month terms in order to reduce the purchaser's monthly payments. What are the major disadvantages of these longer-term loans? Relate your answer to data included in Figure 10-5.

ANSWERS TO PERSONAL FINANCE I.Q. TEST

1. Fiction. 2. Fact. 3. Fiction. 4. Fact. 5. Fiction. 6. Fiction.

HOW BILL MIKELSON REACHED HIS PERSONAL FINANCIAL DECISION

Professor Ahern sat down with Bill and helped him analyze the costs of financing the car with the dealer's terms. They came up with the figures below. The cost of the insurance plus financing would add $828.48 to the cost of the car. Professor Ahern suggested that Bill shop around a bit more to see if he could get an equally attractive rate without the insurance requirements.

FINANCING AN AUTOMOBILE (11½% FOR 48 MONTHS)

	With Credit Life & Disability Insurance	Without Credit Insurance
Cash Price of Automobile	$6,000.00	$6,000.00
Less Down Payment	1,000.00	1,000.00
Unpaid Balance	$5,000.00	$5,000.00
Insurance:		
Credit Life $141.37		
Credit Disability $286.84	428.21	
Amount Financed	$5,428.21	$5,000.00
Finance Charge @ 11½%	1,401.23	1,000.96
	$6,829.44	$6,000.96
Payment Schedule		
48 payments @	$ 142.28	$ 125.02

COST OF FINANCING

Total Sale Price	$6,829.44	$6,000.96
Less Cost of Insurance	428.21	0
	$6,401.23	$6,000.96
Less Cost of Financing Unpaid Balance of $5,000 @ 11½%	1,000.96	1,000.96
	$5,400.27	$5,000.00
Less Unpaid Balance of $5,000	5,000.00	5,000.00
Cost of Financing Insurance Premiums of $428.21	$ 400.27	$ 0

PART FIVE

PURCHASING PROTECTION

LEARNING OBJECTIVES

1. To define the two types of risk and the methods of dealing with risk. / *2.* To list the characteristics of an insurable risk. / *3.* To explain the three major types of insurance. / *4.* To distinguish between mutual insurance companies and stock insurance companies. / *5.* To identify the questions that must be answered in purchasing insurance.

TESTING YOUR PERSONAL FINANCE I.Q.

	FACT	FICTION
1. Insurance is a method of reducing speculative risk.	☐	☐
2. Insurance companies can predict how many people of any given age will die each year.	☐	☐
3. Insurance companies are not required to pay insurance proceeds to beneficiaries if the insured commits suicide within two years after the insurance policy is issued.	☐	☐
4. In general, women spend more time in the hospital and collect more disability benefits than men.	☐	☐
5. Because mutual insurance companies operate as nonprofit organizations, their insurance premiums are almost always lower than those of stock insurance companies.	☐	☐
6. Some insurance agents represent more than one directly competing insurance company.	☐	☐

The materials in this chapter assist in separating fact from fiction. Your answers can be checked on page 327.

CHAPTER ELEVEN

THE INSURANCE DECISION

SHARING A PERSONAL FINANCIAL DECISION WITH
PROFESSOR RUSSELL OGDEN OF EASTERN MICHIGAN UNIVERSITY

When Greg Berger enrolled in Professor Russell Ogden's personal finance course, he was interested in finding out how to go about making financial decisions. One area that particularly puzzled him was insurance. As a student, he wondered whether he really had to worry about insurance protection. Wasn't that just something for older, "established" people like his parents?

One day in class, after Professor Ogden had outlined the different kinds of insurance available, Greg raised his hand. "I appreciate that what you're saying about insurance may be useful to me later," he began, "but I don't quite see how it applies to me now. It seems a waste to put my hard-earned money into insurance payments rather than invest it somewhere and increase my savings."

Greg added, "Right now I don't have many possessions—nothing I couldn't easily replace if it got stolen or something. And I don't have a family dependent on me. Besides, I'm healthy and willing to work. Maybe it's a gamble to go without insurance, but the risks don't seem that great. I can't imagine anything really bad happening to me now. If it did—well, I'd just work harder."

If you were Professor Ogden, would you agree with Greg's assessment, or would you bring up other factors that he should consider?

To find out how Professor Ogden helped Greg with his personal financial decision, turn to page 327.

"Thanks to jogging, today more people collapse in perfect health than ever before."
Anonymous

Expectant father Butch Medwed thought something was unusual when his pregnant wife became very, very large early in her pregnancy. "Friends of ours kept teasing us about how we were going to have twins, how we were going to have triplets," said Medwed, "and told us we should take out insurance against it."

Medwed approached Fireman's Fund Insurance Company who, for $125, offered a policy that would pay $2,000 to cover the additional expense involved should a policyholder have multiple births. With the way his wife looked, Medwed decided the premium was a good risk. "I said to myself it was worth spending $125 not to have twins, and if fate would have it that we should have twins, the $2,000 [the amount he would collect if his wife had twins] would have been worth the cost."

When Mrs. Medwed gave birth to twin sons, the family received the full amount from Fireman's Fund. According to a company spokesperson, the Medweds were the first couple to collect on their policy in the 21 years the policy had been offered.[1]

WHAT IS INSURANCE?

Insurance plays an important role in the financial plans of most households. Since the future is, to some extent, uncertain, unexpected crises can upset even the most carefully designed financial plans. Illness may result in reduced income and sharply increased medical expenses. An accident may bring liability, damage to an automobile, and the possibility of lawsuits. And death of a household member is devastating to the household — not only in emotional terms, but also in changes in the household's income and expenses. Because of these uncertainties, many households add insurance coverage as a part of their personal financial planning. *Insurance* is the process by which a firm (the insurance company) for a fee (the premium) agrees to pay another individual or firm (the insured, the insured's beneficiary, or a third party) a sum of money stated in a written contract (the policy) if a loss occurs. The Travelers Indemnity Company, for instance, provides home insurance coverage that will cover the cost of the window and other property that is destroyed or damaged by the errant baseball, as their advertisement indicates (see Figure 11-1).

insurance: *the process by which a firm (the insurance company) for a fee (the premium) agrees to pay another individual or firm (the insured) a sum of money stated in a written contract (the policy) if a loss occurs.*

THE INSURANCE DECISION   **307**

Figure 11-1
THE CONCEPT OF INSURANCE

> **There are larger claims we've settled. But none more important.**
>
> Last year, The Travelers settled the largest single claim in its history: 14 million dollars because of the collapse of the roof of the Hartford Coliseum.
> Naturally, it got a lot of public attention.
> But a very small settlement, such as pictured above, gets a lot of personal attention from us, too.
> To discuss your needs with an independent Travelers agent, check your Yellow Pages.
> The Travelers is one of the world's largest insurance companies, a size that doesn't diminish our big concern for the individual.
>
> **THE TRAVELERS**
>
> We offer life, health, auto, and homeowners insurance, and mutual funds and variable annuities for individuals, and virtually all forms of insurance for businesses. The Travelers Insurance Company, The Travelers Indemnity Company, Travelers Equities Sales Inc., and other Affiliated Companies of The Travelers Corporation, Hartford, Connecticut 06115.

Source: Courtesy of the Travelers Indemnity Company.

   The relationship between the Medweds and Fireman's Fund is a good example of what insurance is all about. Insurance enables individual consumers to share economic risks with others; they protect themselves from economic loss by joining with other people who face similar risks. In exchange for protection, insurance companies receive carefully calculated premiums from policyholders that enable the companies to pay for their losses and administer the plan. The Medweds shared their risk of twins with other expectant families who faced a similar risk through the premiums they paid to Fireman's Fund.

Similarly, life, health, automobile, and property insurance are designed to spread the risk of economic loss among large groups of people, all of whom share a similar risk. No one knows which members of the group will actually experience a loss, but the insurance company's past experience gives it a good idea how many losses will occur.

THE CONCEPT OF RISK

risk: *the uncertainty of injury or loss.*

Risk—the uncertainty of injury or loss—plays an important part in our everyday lives. The household head who purchases a $100,000 life insurance policy to protect his or her family against economic loss in the case of death is concerned with risk. So is the family who buys a homeowners policy to provide replacement funds in case of fire, flood, and other damage; an automobile liability policy to pay the medical and auto repair bills in the event of a car accident; and a health insurance policy to pay for any expensive medical care they might need.

All of these risks have two key elements in common: (1) *possibility* of loss and (2) *uncertainty* about when (or if) a loss will happen. The family who purchases homeowners insurance does not expect a fire or tornado to destroy its home but knows that it could happen at any future time. There are two major types of risk: speculative and pure.

No one can avoid risk totally, but even people in high-risk occupations—such as this man working on the San Francisco Bay Bridge—can minimize risk by taking safety precautions.

The gambler who bets $1,000 on the Kentucky Derby favorite and the businessperson who buys 300 shares of a promising stock are involved in *speculative risk*. They have the chance of winning a great deal of money or losing it all. Speculative risks are not insurable. The businessperson who makes decisions about markets, store location, products to offer, and prices to charge faces the possibility of rewards for wise decisions and losses should the decisions prove wrong.

In *pure risk,* there is a threat of loss without the possibility of gain. If a husband dies he will leave his wife and children without his income-producing abilities and with no legitimate possibility of gain. Pure risk is the only kind of risk with which insurance is concerned.

speculative risk: *accepting the possibility of losing money in order to make money.*

pure risk: *the threat of loss without the possibility of gain.*

DEALING WITH RISK

Because risk is part of life—you can get hit by a car while crossing the street or choke on a chicken bone while eating a leisurely dinner—you must find ways of dealing with it. As Figure 11-2 indicates, there are four basic methods for managing risk.

Avoiding Risk. You can avoid risk by taking a conservative approach to life. You might, for instance, avoid such high-risk occupations as race-car driving, aerial crop dusting, and bridge building. You can avoid cigarette smoking, try

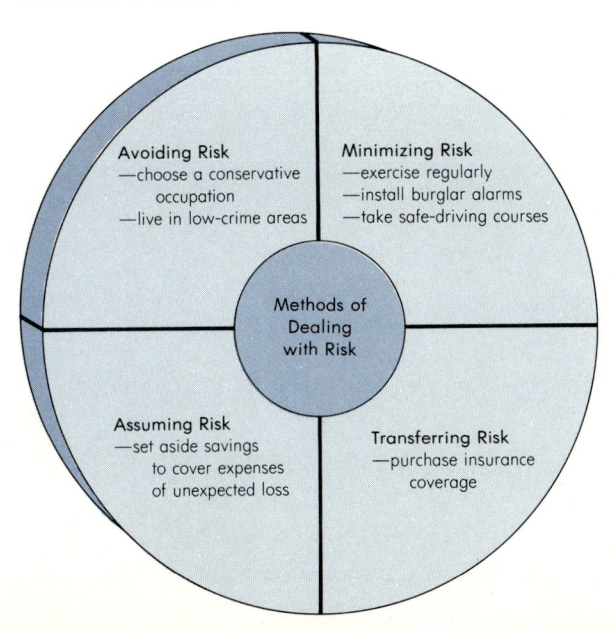

Figure 11-2
METHODS OF DEALING WITH RISK

Avoiding Risk
—choose a conservative occupation
—live in low-crime areas

Minimizing Risk
—exercise regularly
—install burglar alarms
—take safe-driving courses

Assuming Risk
—set aside savings to cover expenses of unexpected loss

Transferring Risk
—purchase insurance coverage

Methods of Dealing with Risk

to keep yourself in good health, and exercise such common-sense precautions as not driving in blizzards.

Minimizing Risk. You can attempt to reduce or eliminate risk by equipping your home with a fire detector and burglar alarms and by eating properly, going for regular medical checkups, and exercising regularly.

Assuming Risk. A third way of dealing with risk is to assume the risk through self-insurance. Knowing, for example, that your house might burn down some time in the future, you can set up a contingency fund to use in case the worst happens. But this fund must be large enough to rebuild your entire house, if necessary, so self-insurance is an impractical alternative for most people. Even people who can afford one economic loss would not be able to meet a second loss if it came immediately after the first. With costs rising, people look to insurance as the only feasible answer to the risk of financial loss.

Transferring the Risk. Transferring the risk to others in the form of insurance is the most common method of dealing with risk. Through the purchase of insurance, consumers substitute a small known loss—the amount of money they pay in premiums—for the possibility of the larger economic losses should they die, get sick, experience property damage, or suffer other catastrophes. Figure 11-3 indicates the kinds of insurance that are available to help individuals and families deal with pure risk.

Consumers Can Reduce Many Health Risks by Eating Nutritious Foods.

Source: Drawing by Koren; © 1982 The New Yorker Magazine, Inc.

Figure 11-3
TYPES OF INSURANCE AVAILABLE FOR CERTAIN RISKS

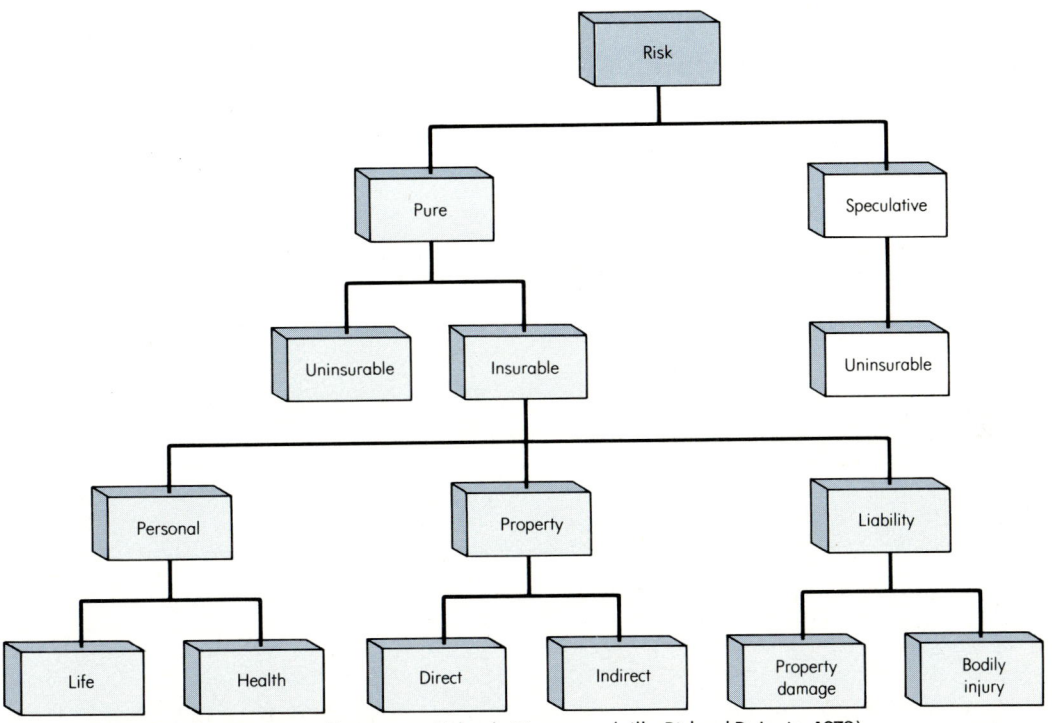

```
                        Risk
                    /          \
                 Pure         Speculative
               /     \              \
         Uninsurable  Insurable    Uninsurable
                   /     |      \
             Personal  Property  Liability
              /   \     /   \     /     \
           Life Health Direct Indirect Property  Bodily
                                       damage   injury
```

Source: David L. Bickelhaupt, *General Insurance*, 11th ed. (Homewood, Ill.: Richard D. Irwin, 1979), p. 11. Copyright, 1983, Richard D. Irwin, Inc.

CHARACTERISTICS OF INSURABLE RISK

Before an insurance company assumes the risk of insuring you, it must be certain that your risk meets a number of requirements—that it is, in essence, an *insurable risk*. Even though in theory any pure risk can be considered insurable, insurance companies insist that the following standards be met:

1. *An insurable risk must be common to a large number of people.* Insurance companies operate under the *law of large numbers,* which states that even seemingly haphazard events will follow a predictable pattern if enough events are observed. In other words, that which is not forecastable for the individual *is* forecastable for the group if the group is large enough. This pattern enables the insurance company to predict its losses during any given year and determine how much each insured person must pay in premiums.

   Life insurance companies use mortality tables to make these predictions. Table 11-1, which combines three separate mortality tables, shows the predicted number of deaths per thousand people that will occur in each age

insurable risk: a risk for which it is possible to buy insurance from some insurance company.

law of large numbers: the statistical calculation of the likelihood of the occurrence of injury or loss on which insurance premiums are based.

Table 11-1
MORTALITY TABLES

| | Commissioners 1980 Standard Ordinary (1970-1975) |||| 1983 Individual Annuity Table (1971-1976) |||| United States Population (1969-1971) ||
| | Male || Female || Male || Female || ||
Age	Deaths per 1,000	Expectation of Life (Years)	Deaths per 1,000	Expectation of Life (Years)	Deaths per 1,000	Expectation of Life (Years)	Deaths per 1,000	Expectation of Life (Years)	Deaths per 1,000	Expectation of Life (Years)
0	4.18	70.83	2.89	75.83	—	—	—	—	20.02	70.75
1	1.07	70.13	.87	75.04	—	—	—	—	1.25	71.19
2	.99	69.20	.81	74.11	—	—	—	—	.86	70.28
3	.98	68.27	.79	73.17	—	—	—	—	.69	69.34
4	.95	67.34	.77	72.23	—	—	—	—	.57	68.39
5	.90	66.40	.76	71.28	.38	74.10	.19	79.36	.51	67.43
6	.86	65.46	.73	70.34	.35	73.12	.16	78.37	.46	66.46
7	.80	64.52	.72	69.39	.33	72.15	.13	77.39	.43	65.49
8	.76	63.57	.70	68.44	.35	71.17	.13	76.40	.39	64.52
9	.74	62.62	.69	67.48	.37	70.20	.14	75.41	.34	63.54
10	.73	61.66	.68	66.53	.38	69.22	.14	74.42	.31	62.57
11	.77	60.71	.69	65.58	.39	68.25	.15	73.43	.30	61.58
12	.85	59.75	.72	64.62	.41	67.28	.16	72.44	.35	60.60
13	.99	58.80	.75	63.67	.42	66.30	.17	71.45	.46	59.62
14	1.15	57.86	.80	62.71	.43	65.33	.18	70.46	.63	58.65
15	1.33	56.93	.85	61.76	.44	64.36	.19	69.47	.82	57.69
16	1.51	56.00	.90	60.82	.45	63.39	.20	68.49	1.01	56.73
17	1.67	55.09	.95	59.87	.46	62.42	.21	67.50	1.17	55.79
18	1.78	54.18	.98	58.93	.47	61.44	.23	66.51	1.28	54.86
19	1.86	53.27	1.02	57.98	.49	60.47	.24	65.53	1.34	53.93
20	1.90	52.37	1.05	57.04	.51	59.50	.26	64.55	1.40	53.00
21	1.91	51.47	1.07	56.10	.53	58.53	.28	63.56	1.47	52.07
22	1.89	50.57	1.09	55.16	.55	57.56	.29	62.58	1.52	51.15
23	1.86	49.66	1.11	54.22	.57	56.59	.31	61.60	1.53	50.22
24	1.82	48.75	1.14	53.28	.60	55.63	.33	60.62	1.51	49.30
25	1.77	47.84	1.16	52.34	.62	54.66	.35	59.64	1.47	48.37
26	1.73	46.93	1.19	51.40	.65	53.69	.37	58.66	1.43	47.44
27	1.71	46.01	1.22	50.46	.68	52.73	.39	57.68	1.42	46.51
28	1.70	45.09	1.26	49.52	.70	51.76	.41	56.70	1.44	45.58
29	1.71	44.16	1.30	48.59	.73	50.80	.42	55.72	1.49	44.64

Source: *Life Insurance Fact Book* (New York: American Council of Life Insurance, 1983), p. 108. Authorization to reproduce granted.

group and the average number of years men and women in each age group can expect to live.

If a company ignored the law of large numbers and insured only a few people against the risk of death, it would be in no better position than

| | Commissioners 1980 Standard Ordinary (1970-1975) |||| 1983 Individual Annuity Table (1971-1976) |||| United States Population (1969-1971) ||
| | Male || Female || Male || Female || ||
Age	Deaths per 1,000	Expectation of Life (Years)	Deaths per 1,000	Expectation of Life (Years)	Deaths per 1,000	Expectation of Life (Years)	Deaths per 1,000	Expectation of Life (Years)	Deaths per 1,000	Expectation of Life (Years)
30	1.73	43.24	1.35	47.65	.76	49.83	.44	54.75	1.55	43.71
31	1.78	42.31	1.40	46.71	79	48.87	.46	53.77	1.63	42.77
32	1.83	41.38	1.45	45.78	.81	47.91	.48	52.80	1.72	41.84
33	1.91	40.46	1.50	44.84	.84	46.95	.50	51.82	1.83	40.92
34	2.00	39.54	1.58	43.91	.88	45.99	.52	50.85	1.95	39.99
35	2.11	38.61	1.65	42.98	.92	45.03	.55	49.87	2.09	39.07
36	2.24	37.69	1.76	42.05	.97	44.07	.57	48.90	2.25	38.15
37	2.40	36.78	1.89	41.12	1.03	43.11	.61	47.93	2.44	37.23
38	2.58	35.87	2.04	40.20	1.11	42.15	.65	46.96	2.66	36.32
39	2.79	34.96	2.22	39.28	1.22	41.20	.69	45.99	2.90	35.42
40	3.02	34.05	2.42	38.36	1.34	40.25	.74	45.02	3.14	34.52
41	3.29	33.16	2.64	37.46	1.49	39.30	.80	44.05	3.41	33.63
42	3.56	32.26	2.87	36.55	1.67	38.36	.87	43.09	3.70	32.74
43	3.87	31.38	3.09	35.66	1.89	37.43	.94	42.12	4.04	31.86
44	4.19	30.50	3.32	34.77	2.13	36.50	1.03	41.16	4.43	30.99
45	4.55	29.62	3.56	33.88	2.40	35.57	1.12	40.20	4.84	30.12
46	4.92	28.76	3.80	33.00	2.69	34.66	1.23	39.25	5.28	29.27
47	5.32	27.90	4.05	32.12	3.01	33.75	1.36	38.30	5.74	28.42
48	5.74	27.04	4.33	31.25	3.34	32.85	1.50	37.35	6.24	27.58
49	6.21	26.20	4.63	30.39	3.69	31.96	1.66	36.40	6.78	26.75
50	6.71	25.36	4.96	29.53	4.06	31.07	1.83	35.46	7.38	25.93
51	7.30	24.52	5.31	28.67	4.43	30.20	2.02	34.53	8.04	25.12
52	7.96	23.70	5.70	27.82	4.81	29.33	2.22	33.59	8.76	24.32
53	8.71	22.89	6.15	26.98	5.20	28.47	2.43	32.67	9.57	23.53
54	9.56	22.08	6.61	26.14	5.59	27.62	2.65	31.75	10.43	22.75
55	10.47	21.29	7.09	25.31	5.99	26.77	2.89	30.83	11.36	21.99
56	11.46	20.51	7.57	24.49	6.41	25.93	3.15	29.92	12.36	21.23
57	12.49	19.74	8.03	23.67	6.84	25.09	3.43	29.01	13.41	20.49
58	13.59	18.99	8.47	22.86	7.29	24.26	3.74	28.11	14.52	19.76
59	14.77	18.24	8.94	22.05	7.78	23.44	4.08	27.21	15.70	19.05

the individuals it insured. It could not reliably predict future losses or set premiums.

2. *An insurable interest in the life or property insured must be present.* In order to take out insurance, a policyholder must be able to demonstrate that he or

insurable interest: the concept that a policyholder must stand to suffer a financial loss before he or she is allowed to purchase insurance on a given risk.

she stands to suffer a loss due to the occurrence of a fire, an accident, death, or a lawsuit. An *insurable interest* is present in the case of homeowners insurance purchased on a family home, a $50,000 life insurance policy purchased by a husband for his wife, or flood insurance purchased for one's business. On the other hand, an individual cannot, for example, collect on a life insurance policy written on the governor of the state. In this case, an insurable interest is not present.

3. *The loss should be fortuitous, or accidental.* It cannot be expected or deliberately brought about by the insured. Suicide that occurs within the first two years after a life insurance policy is issued is not considered a fortuitous event (based on the assumption that the victim planned it), and the insurance company is not required to pay for the loss. Similarly, a policyholder who deliberately sets his or her house on fire to collect the insurance money will receive no benefits from the company—and risks a prison sentence for committing arson.

4. *The loss must be definite.* Each risk the insurance company assumes is measured in terms of the insured's financial loss: the cost of replacing a wife's earnings if she dies, of rebuilding a house destroyed by fire, or of undergoing emergency surgery. Even though it is often difficult to define precisely the dollar amount of a loss, especially in the case of death, insurance policies are always issued for specific financial losses.

5. *The cost of insurance should be low enough for a large number of people to afford it.* Providing insurance to a 95-year-old person, for example, even though theoretically possible, would be prohibitively expensive since approximately one-third of all 95-year-olds die before they reach 96. With so few people able to afford this insurance, the law of large numbers would not work and the insurance company would lose money.

6. *The loss must be unexpected.* For a risk to be insurable it must occur by chance at an unpredicted time. Even though death is inevitable for all of us, life insurance companies insure against the uncertainty of death; the time of death is unknown and therefore the loss is unexpected. People who have terminal illnesses or plan suicide are uninsurable because their deaths are no longer unexpected.

7. *The risk should be spread over a wide geographic area.* In order to avoid an excessive exposure to catastrophic loss, insurance companies try to spread their coverage over wide geographic areas. Companies providing homeowners insurance avoid concentrating their holdings along the same river if floods are possible or even in the same area if it is subject to such unusual natural catastrophes as tornadoes and earthquakes.

> ## The Boone and Kurtz List of Accidents and Disasters
>
> Although the *Guinness Book of World Records* has sold millions of copies to readers interested in learning of unusual feats, the library shelves are devoid of similar books devoted to unusual accidents, deaths, disasters, injuries, and other predicaments that might have been the subject of insurance coverage. The following examples, grouped by type of risk, represent our candidates for inclusion in such a book:
>
> 1. *Death*
>   a. More than half a million Americans died of Spanish influenza in 1918—nearly 10 times the number who died fighting World War I. The flu, which actually originated in China, killed an estimated 21.6 million people worldwide.
>   b. The eruption of Krakatoa in Indonesia in 1883, the largest volcanic explosion in recorded history, killed 36,000 people, mostly as a result of tidal waves up to 120 feet high. It was heard 3,000 miles away. Fire alarms were pulled in Connecticut, so intense were the sunsets that ensued.
>   c. A 90-foot storage tank in Boston's North End burst on January 15, 1919, releasing 2 million gallons of molasses in a 20-foot tidal wave. Buildings were knocked from their foundations; 21 people drowned. Horses, mired in molasses, had to be shot.
> 2. *Property Damage and Personal Injury*
>   a. In 1896, when there were only four automobiles in the United States, two were in St. Louis. They collided. Both drivers were hurt, one seriously.
>   b. Aetna Insurance reports that a policyholder, tormented by mosquitoes, finally "leaped out of bed and sprayed the little winged devils into oblivion." In the morning he realized he had grabbed a cannister filled with red enamel paint.
> 3. *Malpractice*
>   a. A West German surgeon removed the only kidney of a 16-year-old boy, mistaking it for a tumor.
>
> Source: Andrew Tobias, *The Invisible Bankers: Everything the Insurance Industry Never Wanted You to Know* (New York: Simon and Schuster, 1982), pp. 303–304.

Insurers apply these criteria of insurable risk to three basic forms of insurance protection: property and casualty insurance, health insurance, and life insurance.

SEX AND INSURANCE

Perhaps more than any other business, the insurance business is concerned with the differences between men and women. Its concern is economic. How long men and women live, how sick they get, and how carefully they drive affect the amount of money insurers make. Ultimately these concerns also affect every insured person's pocketbook.

As Table 11-1 points out, men and women have different life expectancies at each age. Because women, on average, live longer than men, they pay smaller premiums for a given amount of life insurance coverage. For example, at age 60 a woman in the United States can expect to live an additional 22.1 years, while a 60-year-old man can expect to live only 17.1 years. In dollars and cents, this means that a typical $50,000 life insurance policy purchased at age 50 would cost a woman about $1,180 and a man $1,430 a year.

Sex also affects the amount of money men and women have traditionally been charged for health and disability insurance. Because insurance company experience shows that women spend more time in the hospital and collect more disability benefits than men do (including pregnancy and maternity benefits), their insurance rates may be higher. Thus, a 22-year-old woman purchasing a major medical policy might pay about $300 a year—$70 more than a 22-year-old man.

Finally, auto insurance rates are also based on sex differences. Young men have far more accidents than young women, so they pay more for their insurance protection.

The use of sex to determine insurance costs has been attacked by women's groups, congressional leaders, and even President Ronald Reagan. Charging sex discrimination, critics have demanded federal legislation requiring unisex insurance rates. Mary Gray, president of the Women's Equity Action League, summed up this view when she said: "I have one life expectancy as an American, a longer one as a woman, a shorter one as a worker in Washington, a longer one as a nonsmoker, and a shorter one as an overweight person. Why use just my sex?"[2]

As Table 11-2 shows, under a unisex insurance system women would pay more for life and auto insurance than they have traditionally paid. At the same time, they would pay less for health and disability coverage and receive larger retirement payments. Industry critics maintain that these extra costs are a small price to pay to guarantee that women receive the same treatment under the law as men receive.[3]

Table 11-2
IMPACT OF UNISEX INSURANCE RATES ON CURRENT INSURANCE RATES FOR MEN AND WOMEN

Type of Insurance	Men Age 20	Men Age 40	Women Age 20	Women Age 40
Auto	Down 20%	None	Up 20%	None
Life	Down 2%	Down 3%	Up 6%	Up 11%
Medical	Up 18%	Up 13%	Down 12%	Down 7%
Disability	Up 4%	Up 2%	Down 26%	Down 21%
Individual annuities	Up 6%	Up 6%	Down 6%	Down 6%

Source: "The Price Women Would Pay for Unisex Pensions." Reprinted from U.S. News & World Report May 9, 1983, p. 169; Copyright, 1983, U.S. News & World Report, Inc.

TYPES OF INSURANCE

Insurance companies offer hundreds of different types of insurance policies, covering such uncommon risks as that of unexpected added expenses for parents who have twins (remember the Medweds) and losing weight (a serious risk for a circus Fat Lady). Most policies, however, are written for a relatively few major types of insurance protection.

The three major categories of insurance are (1) life insurance, (2) health insurance, and (3) property and casualty insurance. Life insurance is discussed in detail in Chapter 12; Chapter 13 focuses on health care protection; and Chapter 14 examines property and casualty insurance. Each of the three major types is briefly described below.

LIFE INSURANCE

Life insurance protects people against the economic losses that occur with death. Two out of three Americans and 86 percent of all American families own some form of life insurance protection. The main reason people buy life insurance is to provide financial security for their families should they die prematurely. With assets totaling over $500 billion, life insurance is one of the nation's largest businesses.

HEALTH INSURANCE

Eighty-four percent of all Americans—over 188 million people—have some form of private health insurance to cover potential economic losses due to sickness or accident. There are two basic types of health insurance: for medical expenses and for disability income. Medical expense insurance covers the expenses connected with hospital and medical care and related services. Disability income insurance provides payments when the insured is unable to work because of injury or illness.

PROPERTY AND CASUALTY INSURANCE

Property insurance covers physical damage to or destruction of property resulting from unavoidable perils. Under the category of property and casualty insurance are some of the most important forms of insurance for individuals and businesses—fire insurance; automobile insurance; burglary, robbery, and theft insurance; and liability insurance.

Fire Insurance. Every home and business is vulnerable to fire. A carelessly discarded cigarette, faulty electrical wiring, or a child playing with matches—these situations cause more than $5.6 billion in property damage each year. In

property insurance: *insurance coverage for physical damage to or destruction of property resulting from unavoidable perils.*

The risk of losses from fire prompts millions of homeowners and renters to purchase insurance protection.

order to protect themselves against such devastating losses, most property owners purchase fire insurance as part of their homeowners insurance policy.

Standard fire insurance policies protect against losses due to fire and lightning. Rates vary considerably depending on the location of the structure and the construction materials used. Buildings in cities with adequate fire departments, which can quickly respond to emergencies, have lower rates than buildings in isolated rural communities. Similarly, the rates for buildings constructed of such fire-resistant materials as brick or metal are lower than those for wood-framed structures.

Automobile Insurance. With approximately $50 billion in annual premiums, automobile insurance is the country's largest single type of property and casualty insurance. These grim statistics tell why: some 28 million auto accidents occurred in 1983, resulting in over 5 million injuries and 43,000 deaths. The economic loss associated with these accidents totaled $59 billion.[4] Most automobile insurance policies cover losses due to automobile accidents, including personal and property claims that result from accident, fire, or theft.

Burglary, Robbery, and Theft Insurance. *Burglary insurance* protects against losses due to the taking of property by forcible entry. In a recent year, there were approximately 4 million burglaries, resulting in $3.5 billion of property loss. *Robbery insurance* covers losses that result from the unlawful taking of property from another person by force or the threat of force. The 574,130 reported

---

burglary insurance: insurance coverage for losses due to the taking of property by forcible entry.

robbery insurance: insurance coverage for losses due to the unlawful taking of property.

THE INSURANCE DECISION 319

robberies in 1981 led to $382 million of property loss. *Theft,* or larceny, *insurance* provides the broadest insurance protection, as it covers losses due to the unlawful taking of property whether by force or other means. More than 7 million thefts occurred in 1981, with $2.4 billion of property losses.[5]

theft insurance: *insurance coverage for losses due to the unlawful taking of property, whether by force or other means.*

BASIC INSURANCE ELEMENTS

No matter what form of insurance protection you choose, certain basic insurance concepts will be involved. These include the insurance premium, the insurance policy, the insurance agent, and the insurance company.

THE INSURANCE PREMIUM

Insurance companies keep accurate statistics concerning how much money they will need to pay claims and administer expenses during a given period. This amount, minus the interest the company expects to earn on its investments, is divided among the policyholders according to the amount of risk each faces. Because a 50-year-old man with a $100,000 life insurance policy faces a much greater risk of death than a 25-year-old man with the same type and amount of insurance protection, the older man's costs will be higher. These costs are expressed in the *insurance premium*—the payments the insured person makes for insurance protection.

insurance premium: *payments made by the insured for insurance protection.*

A number of variations in the risks faced by different insurance applicants affect insurance premiums. As we saw, the difference in life expectancies between men and women has resulted in women paying smaller premiums than men for similar coverage. Risk variations are particularly noticeable in automobile accident statistics. Although only one-third of all drivers are under age 30, this age group accounts for 50 percent of all drivers involved in accidents. A disproportionate number of these drivers involved in accidents are males. Consequently, insurance companies charge higher premiums for young, male drivers.

Insurance companies also attempt to reduce the number of accidents and deaths among high-risk individuals by rewarding attempts to reduce the risk involved. Nonsmokers, for instance, may be able to purchase comparable amounts of life insurance coverage at lower rates than smokers. Youthful male drivers who complete a driver's education course usually qualify for lower insurance premiums. On the other hand, drivers who receive a specified number of traffic citations within a given time period may discover a premium increase when their auto insurance policies are renewed. Figure 11-4 describes the premium savings available from the Allstate Insurance Company for persons who act to reduce risk. Most insurance companies offer similar savings.

Figure 11-4

ADVERTISEMENT EMPHASIZING METHODS OF REDUCING RISK—
AND INSURANCE PREMIUMS

Source: Courtesy of Allstate Insurance Company, Northbrook, Ill.

THE INSURANCE POLICY

insurance policy: a written contract between the insurer and the person or organization covered specifying the amount and type of insurance, amount of premiums and due dates, beneficiaries, and any applicable restrictions.

An *insurance policy* is a legally binding contract between the policyholder and the insurance company. It contains all the provisions of your insurance coverage, including the amount and type of insurance, the amount and dates on which premiums are due, beneficiaries, and any applicable restrictions. An insurance policy is issued as soon as the application is approved by the company.

THE INSURANCE AGENT

insurance agent: the legal representative of the insurance company.

The *insurance agent* is the legal representative of the insurance company. The actions insurance agents take that are within the bounds of their authority are considered the actions of the insurance company itself. In most cases, agents do not have the authority to bind their company to an insurance agreement; they can only solicit applications and accept initial premiums. Agents are an integral part of the marketing system through which most forms of insurance are sold.

THE INSURANCE COMPANY

insurance company: the business that provides protection for policyholders in return for the payment of premiums.

The *insurance company* is the business that provides protection for policyholders in return for the payment of premiums. There are two basic kinds of insurance

Removing the Gobbledygook from Insurance Policies

Since insurance policies represent a formal contract between the insurance company and the insured, they tend to be relatively complex. In the past, the contract's obtuse language all too often baffled the policyholder seeking to compare the coverage of alternative policies. In recent years, however, insurance companies have reacted to criticisms of unnecessary complexity by attempting to use more straightforward, understandable language to explain insurance provisions, policyholder coverage, and all applicable restrictions. These efforts should greatly assist consumers in comparing policies, as well as enable them to discover in advance potentially problematic exclusions.

At least one policyholder has recommended that insurance companies extend this attempt of clarifying insurance coverage to their written communications. This policyholder began receiving disability benefits from Social Security and then discovered that his private disability insurer, Old Republic Life Insurance of Chicago, had reduced his private disability payments. When he wrote to inquire about this reduction, he received the following one-sentence reply:

The contract stipulates if the total monthly amount of loss of time benefits promised for the same loss under all valid loss of time coverage upon the insured person, whether payable on a weekly or monthly basis shall exceed the monthly earnings of the insured person at the time disability commenced or his average monthly earnings for the period of two years immediately proceeding [sic] a disability for which claim is made, which ever is greater, the Company shall be liable only for such portion and amount of such benefits under the certificate as the amount of such monthly earnings or such monthly earnings of the insured person bears to the total amount of monthly benefits with the same loss under all such coverage upon the insured person at the time of [sic] such disability commences and for the return of such part of the premiums paid during such two years as shall exceed the pro-rated amount of premiums for the benefits and repaid hereunder but this shall no [sic] operate the reduced total monthly amount of benefits payable under all such coverage upon the insured person below the sum of $200.00, or the sum of the monthly benefits specified in such coverage, which ever is the lesser nor shall it operate to reduce benefits other then [sic] those payable for loss of time.

Source: Quotation from Milton Moskowitz, Michael Katz, and Robert Levering, *Everybody's Business Scoreboard* (New York: Harper & Row, 1983), p. 12.

---

companies: mutual companies and stock companies. They can be distinguished by their form of ownership. Figure 11-5 identifies several major mutual and stock insurance companies.

Mutual Insurance Companies. A *mutual insurance company* is owned by its policyholders and governed by a board of directors elected by the policyholders. Operating as nonprofit organizations, mutual insurance companies issue participating policies, which return to the policyholders the funds that remain after the payment of claims, operating expenses, and the maintenance of a reserve fund; refunds are in the form of direct cash payments or premium reductions for future policy periods.

Most mutual insurance companies specialize in life insurance. They provide about 45 percent of the total life insurance in force today.

Stock Insurance Companies. A *stock insurance company* is owned by stockholders, who elect a board of directors to oversee management of the company.

mutual insurance company: an insurance company that exists as a nonprofit cooperative owned by policyholders.

stock insurance company: an insurance company owned by stockholders and operated for profit.

Figure 11-5
MAJOR U.S. INSURANCE COMPANIES CLASSIFIED BY FORM OF OWNERSHIP

Mutual Insurance Companies **Stock Insurance Companies**

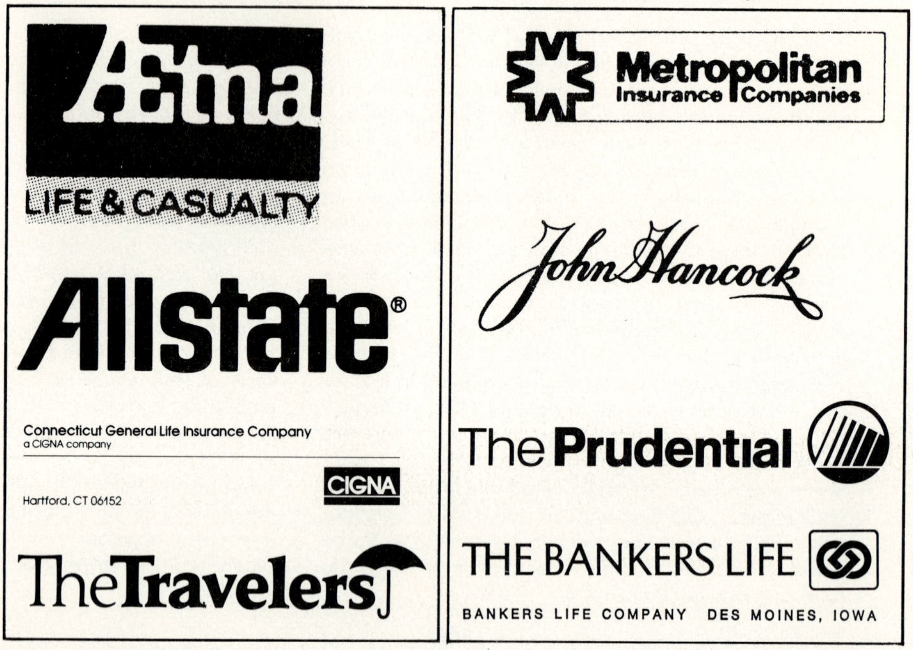

Source: Reprinted with permission, the Bankers Life of Des Moines; Metropolitan Insurance Companies; John Hancock Insurance Company; Prudential Insurance; Aetna Life & Casualty; Allstate Insurance Company, Northbrook, Ill.; Connecticut General Life (Hartford); Travelers Insurance Company.

Unlike the mutual insurance company, the stock insurance company operates on a profit-seeking basis. It may earn profits from two sources: (1) insurance premiums in excess of paid-out insurance benefits and (2) earnings from company investments. Some of these earnings are used to build company reserves, but some are also used to generate a return to company stockholders in the form of dividends. Most—but not all—stock insurance companies issue nonparticipating policies, which distribute surplus funds to stockholders rather than to policyholders.

How Does the Type of Insurance Company Affect Insurance Rates? Because stock insurance companies attempt to earn profits for their stockholders, many people think that nonprofit mutual insurance companies will be able to offer the lowest premiums for similar insurance coverage. However, direct comparisons of premiums charged typically reveal that the two types of insurance companies are highly price-competitive. In shopping for the best insurance value, you may discover that as a result of operating efficiencies, some stock companies offer lower-cost insurance than their mutual company competitors.

Although mutual insurance companies are supposed to rebate excess premiums to their policyholders in the form of dividends, many of them use a substantial portion of the excess funds to build larger reserves. One insurance industry critic offered three reasons why mutual insurers have not always felt compelled to deliver low prices and high dividends:

1. Because of the complexity of alternative insurance policies and difficulty in making direct comparisons of precisely the exact coverage, many purchasers cannot tell a low price from a high price;
2. Dissatisfied customers cannot easily switch to a competitor. Once locked into a life insurance contract, it costs dearly to cancel;
3. The management of mutual insurers are in a very real sense responsible to no one but themselves. Ownership of mutual life insurers is so broad, so dispersed, so atomized and anonymous, that for all practical purposes, *it doesn't exist.* Technically, the policyholders own the mutuals. Practically speaking, *no one does.*[6]

The moral for insurance purchasers is simple and straightforward. Compare the costs of competing insurance companies—both stock and mutual insurers—before making your purchase decision.

THE INSURANCE PURCHASE PROCESS

Many people who know they need insurance avoid buying it because the process of purchasing insurance can be a traumatic experience. They feel lost in what they expect to be a muddle of insurance jargon and high-pressure sales. In order to make the right purchase decision, the consumer must know what to insure, how much insurance to buy, for how long to buy it, and how to choose the right policy.

WHAT TO INSURE

However much you love your pet gerbil, it would make no sense to buy life insurance to protect you from economic loss in the event of its death. Similarly, insuring your favorite sports jacket against loss would waste your consumer dollars. Insurance should be purchased only for those items that if lost or destroyed would cause you, or someone dependent on you, a monetary loss. Insuring a house against fire and property damage makes sense since the burden of rebuilding it would fall on you and your family.

Choosing and Talking to an Insurance Agent

In her years of experience as a practicing attorney and estate planner, Adriane G. Berg, author of *Moneythink: Financial Planning Finally Made Easy*, has dealt with the mistakes of poor insurance planning more times than she cares to remember. In Berg's opinion, two ways to get the insurance coverage you need—and want—are to find a good insurance agent and to learn how to talk to your agent before and after you buy. Here are her views on choosing and talking to an agent:

To begin with, remember that insurance salespersons are human beings too. I am talking here of course about highly skilled professional salespeople. They have great integrity and vast knowledge. They can advise you and help you. They will knock themselves out to give you extra service and comfort. They will actually be there when the death benefit is needed. But if you don't buy insurance from them they don't eat. While one of their goals is to give you good service, their major goal is selling. They can't help it, it's their business. Because of that, never believe that their only agenda is advising you. It couldn't be or they would not be in the business. They would be paid advisors.

Of the many insurance salespersons' cards you will get, some will say C.L.U. after the name. This means that this particular person has been certified as a Chartered Life Underwriter—C.L.U. Certification takes place by the American College of Life Underwriters. Certification is given only after the individual passes ten comprehensive examinations, fulfills ethical requirements, and has experience in the field. The exams include life insurance, law, taxation, trusts, accounting, social and governmental insurance, and economics. C.L.U. means that your salesperson has taken the time to be a professional in the field, to be thoroughly educated in it. He or she is not selling insurance while marking time until something better comes along.

Inquire about the services of the various insurance companies. It is not just the amount of your coverage, but the ease in collecting that's important. The best insurance salesperson is one [who] represents many companies and is not wedded to just one. Salespeople are usually honest in telling you which is the most responsive company. After all, the worst thing that could happen to insurance salespersons other than not making a sale is making a sale with a company that doesn't deliver; if they want to keep their reputation, they will have to work overtime to make sure you get your money. There are big differences among companies in the speed of payment and, very important, in the number and complexity of the forms that have to be filled out in order to get coverage. Remember, to collect benefits, all your heirs need is the policy, a death certificate and the name and number of the salesperson. If a company asks for more, it is giving you a hard time.

Two key steps in buying insurance are choosing an agent and learning how to talk to him or her before and after you buy.

Source: Quotation reprinted by permission of the publisher from *Moneythink: Financial Planning Finally Made Easy* by Adriane G. Berg. Copyright © 1982. The Pilgrim Press.

HOW MUCH INSURANCE IS ENOUGH?

Determining how much insurance to buy depends on how large an economic loss you face and how much money you can afford to pay in insurance premiums. In addition, insurance needs vary as households move through the various stages of the family life cycle. A husband may want to guarantee that his wife and three young children will not face economic pressures should he die, but he may be unable to afford enough insurance to protect his family for the rest of their lives. Instead, he may purchase life insurance for four to five times the amount of his annual salary with the knowledge that although this is not enough to carry his family forever, it will at least provide a cushion.

FOR HOW LONG?

· for as long as the risk exists.

Purchase as much insurance as you can comfortably afford for as long as you need it. If, for example, you want to provide your family with enough money to pay off the mortgage on your home should you die, your need for life insurance ends when your mortgage is paid. Similarly, carrying enough life and health insurance for a young family is foolish once your children are grown and on their own. Periodic reviews of insurance coverage should be conducted to determine whether your insurance coverage matches your current needs.

HOW TO BUY THE POLICY

Would-be insurance purchasers should begin by learning as much as they can about the form of insurance under consideration. Information can be obtained from friends and associates with similar insurance needs. Publications such as *Consumer Reports* and *Money* provide detailed analyses of insurance alternatives. The goal is to feel comfortable with insurance terminology and with your purchasing options.

The next step is to identify companies that offer the insurance you are interested in and ask them for the name of a local agent. An excellent source of data on insurance companies is the *Best's Insurance Guide*, which can be found in local libraries. You can also solicit agent recommendations from friends and ask the agent to obtain policy costs from companies you specify.

The insurance agent is likely to be your direct line to the insurance company, so it is important to choose an agent carefully. However, you must always remember that agents are salespeople first and advisers second. You may want to check the agent's credentials (look for the letters C.L.U. after the life insurance agent's name, for example). Regardless of the agent chosen, the ultimate responsibility for buying insurance is yours, since you know best what protection you need and how much coverage you can afford.

WHAT TYPES OF INSURANCE ARE NECESSARY?

Most consumers choose several different forms of insurance coverage. The remaining chapters in Part Five provide thorough descriptions of the major types. Perhaps the most important insurance decision many consumers make is their choice of life insurance, which is explored in the next chapter.

SUMMARY

Insurance is a crucial component of a sound personal finance strategy. Although individuals may take speculative risks to make money, only pure risk, involving a threat of loss without the possibility of gain, can be insured. Some people may choose to avoid, minimize, or assume the uncertainty concerning injury or loss. In many instances, however, individuals will also choose to transfer the risk to insurance companies in the form of insurance coverage.

In order to be an insurable risk, the chance of loss must meet several requirements: (1) the loss must be common to a large number of people; (2) an insurable interest must be present; (3) the loss must be fortuitous, or accidental; (4) the loss must be definite; (5) the cost of insurance must be low enough for a large number of people to afford; (6) the loss must be unexpected; and (7) the risk should be spread over a wide geographic area.

Three major types of insurance are available: life insurance, health insurance, and property and casualty insurance. Certain basic elements are found in all types of insurance: the premium, the policy, the agent, and the company. Insurance can be purchased from profit-seeking stock insurance companies or nonprofit mutual insurance companies. Their rates tend to be highly competitive, so comparison shopping is advised.

The insurance purchase includes determination of what to insure, how much insurance to purchase, for how long to purchase it, and which is the right policy. In addition to choosing the most appropriate insurance company, insurance purchasers should select their insurance agent with care. Recommendations of friends and associates and personal interviews with a number of agents should aid in this process.

REVIEW QUESTIONS

1. Briefly define the following terms:

    insurance
    risk
    speculative risk
    pure risk
    insurable risk
    law of large numbers
    insurable interest
    property insurance
    burglary insurance
    robbery insurance
    theft insurance
    insurance premium
    insurance policy
    insurance agent
    insurance company
    mutual insurance company
    stock insurance company

2. What are the major types of risk? Give an example of each. With which type is insurance concerned?

3. Identify and briefly describe each of the alternative methods for dealing with risk.

4. Briefly explain each of the characteristics of an insurable risk.

5. Why must risks be spread over a wide geographic area in order for them to be insurable by private insurance companies?

6. Present the primary arguments favoring and opposing the use of sex as a factor in determining insurance premiums and benefits.

7. Identify and briefly explain the major categories of insurance.

8. Distinguish between each of the following:
    a. insurance premium and insurance policy
    b. insurance agent and insurance company
    c. participating policy and nonparticipating policy

9. Differentiate mutual from stock insurance companies.

10. What questions must be answered during the insurance purchase process?

CASES AND EXERCISES

1. "Because mutual insurance companies operate as nonprofit organizations, their premiums naturally are lower than those of stock insurance companies." Do you agree with this statement? Defend your answer.

2. When Paul Davis was being fitted for contact lenses for the first time, his optometrist told him about the availability of a special insurance policy that would pay 80 percent of the cost of replacement lenses for a $20 annual premium. The cost of a replacement lens is $40. The optometrist estimated that the average lens wearer loses a lens every 18 months. Should Paul purchase the insurance? Under what conditions might you make the opposite recommendation?

3. Classify the following as either speculative or pure risk:

    a. You decide to change jobs, hoping for more advancement opportunities and wage increases.
    b. You are concerned about the recent rash of automobile thefts in the neighborhood where you park your car.
    c. Your state has more tornadoes than average.
    d. You travel to Atlantic City because of your faith in a new "system" for winning at the blackjack tables.

4. Arrange the following persons in order of life expectancies based on the data in Table 11-1:

    a. 25-year-old male
    b. 25-year-old female
    c. 30-year-old female
    d. 56-year-old female
    e. 51-year-old male

5. Would you recommend that insurance purchasers limit their choice of insurance agents to those who represent a number of different companies offering competitive coverage rather than considering agents who represent a single company? Why or why not?

ANSWERS TO PERSONAL FINANCE I.Q. TEST

1. Fiction. 2. Fact. 3. Fact. 4. Fact. 5. Fiction. 6. Fact.

HOW GREG BERGER REACHED HIS PERSONAL FINANCIAL DECISION

"Let me turn your question about the need for insurance around," Professor Ogden replied to Greg. "Have you ever considered that you may be insurance-*poor*? It's easy to see insurance payments as a drain on your income, but a major crisis could totally wipe out your earnings. What would you do, for instance, if you were injured and couldn't work? Even if you'd made good investments, how long would your savings last?"

To help Greg and the rest of the class figure out whether insurance was important for them now, Professor Ogden suggested that they look at it from two viewpoints: (1) What kind of insurance is required by society? and (2) what risk might sink their professional ship?

"Automobile insurance is a good example of protection that may be required by law," Professor Ogden explained. "Here in Michigan, for instance, there's a 'semi-no-fault' provision in the law. So if you own a car, you *have* to buy insurance. It's a way of making sure that both you and other people on the road are covered if there's an accident."

As Professor Ogden pointed out, the second question is more difficult. Like any purchase decision, buying insurance involves a careful analysis of your personal financial needs and goals. "Certainly," Professor Ogden remarked, "your needs will be different if you're married, with a family, or if you're single; if you own a house or rent an apartment. But one thing you should all seriously consider is health insurance, particularly disability protection. For some reason, a lot of people think: 'Whatever happens, I'll get my paycheck.' Unfortunately, that's not true. Accidents can happen at any age, and you may not be able to work for a while. What would you do then? That's the kind of question you need to ask yourself in making the insurance purchase decision."

LEARNING OBJECTIVES

1. **To identify the reasons an individual may need life insurance.** / *2.* **To explain how to determine appropriate amounts of life insurance.** / *3.* **To contrast whole life and term insurance.** / *4.* **To explain the purpose of endowment insurance.** / *5.* **To classify credit life insurance, industrial life insurance, group life insurance, variable life insurance, and universal life insurance as either whole life or term insurance.** / *6.* **To describe the major provisions of the life insurance contract.**

TESTING YOUR PERSONAL FINANCE I.Q.

	FACT	FICTION
1. People who live alone tend to live longer than those living with a spouse or a friend.	☐	☐
2. Whole life insurance offers both protection and savings features for policyholders.	☐	☐
3. People who borrow against the cash value of their insurance policies must repay the loan or face cancellation of the policy.	☐	☐
4. Endowment insurance represents about one-third of all life insurance in force in the United States.	☐	☐
5. Group life insurance is typically a better buy than individual life insurance.	☐	☐
6. Industrial life insurance is another name for group life insurance.	☐	☐
7. Credit life insurance guarantees the right of your spouse to receive credit cards should you die.	☐	☐

The materials in this chapter assist in separating fact from fiction. Your answers can be checked on page 365.

CHAPTER TWELVE
LIFE INSURANCE

SHARING A PERSONAL FINANCIAL DECISION WITH
PROFESSOR ROBERT BOHN OF GOLDEN GATE UNIVERSITY

Seniors in particular often come to Professor Robert Bohn for advice on life insurance. Luis Sanchez presented a rather typical case. He and his girlfriend Rosa planned to get married soon after graduation. They both wanted a family, but they thought they would wait a bit first, save some money, and see how their careers shaped up.

Luis was contacted by an insurance agent about a good deal on a whole life insurance policy. The offer assured low premium rates for college graduates, who are considered good risks because they are generally young and healthy. Under a special option, Luis could even defer the first premium payment by signing a promissory note which the company would redeem by deducting from the policy's cash value growth during the first five years of the policy.

All in all, the terms sounded attractive to Luis. Life insurance would be important for a family, and, if he waited, he might not get such a good deal. Before making his decision, however, Luis decided to ask Professor Bohn for his opinion.

If you were Professor Bohn, what would you recommend?

To find out how Professor Bohn helped Luis with his personal financial decision, turn to page 365.

"Insurance is death on the installment plan."
Philip Slater[1]

The jovial insurance salesman who appeared at the homemaker's door in Plymouth, Massachusetts, had a grim message. Pointing toward a nearby nuclear power plant, he said, "Living so close to a reactor, you really ought to do something to protect your family." The product he was pitching: an insurance policy to cover her loved ones in case they got cancer. The woman turned the salesman away, but the implications of his pitch left her in tears.

Cancer insurance has become a controversial and growing enterprise. The number of Americans who have bought this special protection has risen from under 2 million in 1974 to about 15 million in 1979. The impetus behind the brisk sales is obvious: most people dread cancer and are also worried about rising health-care costs and the adequacy of their regular insurance coverage. But state and federal authorities charge that some insurance companies use scare tactics to sell such policies and that the coverage they offer isn't worth the price. "When you buy these policies," says former Pennsylvania insurance commissioner Herbert S. Denenberg, "you're not insuring, you're gambling."

Critics contend that some firms skillfully use cancer statistics to exploit the customer's fear. Last year, an undercover agent for a congressional committee sat in on a seminar for cancer insurance agents representing American Family Life Assurance Company of Columbus, Georgia, the largest underwriter of such coverage. The agents, she testified, were instructed to begin their spiels with, "When you get cancer"—not, "If you get cancer." They were told to stress that one out of four Americans will get the disease.

The dire statistics, critics note, are bandied about without qualification. Salesmen, they say, neglect to mention that the risk of cancer varies widely in different areas of the country and within different age groups. To lend authority to their sales pitches, some agents cite the American Cancer Society as the source of their data, but they don't mention the fact that the ACS officially opposes cancer insurance.[2]

Cancer insurance is one type of life and health insurance that most insurance authorities recommend that the general public avoid. In fact, sales of such policies have been banned or severely restricted in New York, New Jersey, New Hampshire, Connecticut, and Massachusetts. As one writer points out, "Although cancer is admittedly the most financially devastating of the primary diseases afflicting Americans, cancer policies pay only a small portion of the expenses likely to be incurred. *It is inherently inefficient to sell . . . insurance one disease at a time.*"[3]

Narrowly defined policies covering specific diseases or covering air passengers for a single trip typically cost much more in premiums than other, more general, policies. Two out of every three Americans have some form of life insurance. This chapter examines the role played by life insurance in the overall financial plans of many households.

THE LIFE INSURANCE DECISION

Life insurance is the payment of a specified amount of money to a beneficiary specified on the insurance policy in the event of the policyholder's death. It is intended to provide protection against the possible financial problems resulting from the death of the insured person. Unlike health care insurance and property and liability insurance—the subjects of Chapters 13 and 14—life insurance deals with a risk that is certain: the death of the insured. The uncertainty involves the time of its occurrence.

Life insurance is typically purchased to provide funds for other members of the insured's household in the event of unexpectedly early death. Although a 30-year-old father of two can refer to the mortality table in Chapter 11 and determine that he is expected, on average, to live for another 50 years, 13 of every 1,000 men will die before their thirtieth birthday. Even if such a premature death is unlikely, it is certainly possible—and the death could have devastating consequences for the man's widow and two children. Without life insurance, the burden of burial expenses, maintaining a minimal household income, and providing for the education of the children might be too great.

It is this risk that prompts U.S. households to purchase an average of $53,200 of life insurance per insured family. To obtain this protection they spend over $47 billion a year in premiums.[4] Yet as financial writer Jane Bryant Quinn points out, "We spend more money on life insurance, and know less about it, than almost any other consumer purchase."[5]

Part of the reason for this is the popular notion that life insurance is too complex for the average person to understand. Just the names of the different types of life insurance—whole life, endowment, term, credit, industrial, and variable—make many people rely almost completely on the advice of their insurance agent, thereby ignoring their responsibility to inform themselves.

Understanding the role of life insurance in personal financial planning is necessary before an individual can make rational decisions concerning whether insurance is needed, the most appropriate type of insurance, and the appropriate amount. A good place to begin is with an explanation of the various reasons people purchase it.

life insurance: *the payment of a specified amount of money to a beneficiary specified on the insurance policy in the event of the policyholder's death.*

DETERMINING THE NEED FOR LIFE INSURANCE

How much life insurance—if any—does a person need? Not surprisingly, the answer must be "It depends." The age of the individual, stage in the family life cycle, and the ratio of assets to debts are just three of the factors that affect the life insurance decision. Consider, for example, the case of a 30-year-old man or woman with a full-time job and two young children. Why would he or she need life insurance? The reasons are clear.

Cash for Immediate Needs. In addition to the expenses incurred during a final illness and for burial, other outstanding debts and taxes may be payable within a short time after a family member's death. You need to leave your spouse sufficient money to pay these immediate expenses.

Readjustment Funds. After your death, especially if you are the primary wage earner, your spouse is likely to need time to consider whether to relocate the family, return to school for vocational training, or take an immediate job offer. He or she needs insurance money to pay the bills during this interim period.

Replacement Income. Even if your spouse already has a job, the family will suffer the loss of your income, which may be a substantial portion of the total household budget. Your insurance money will help replace your lost paycheck.

Special Situations. In many households special situations unique to that household affect both the need for life insurance and the amount. In the case of a household with school-age children, life insurance may be a means of guaranteeing sufficient funds to finance their college education. In some instances, such insurance coverage may provide continuation of a current standard of living for a handicapped spouse who is not capable of holding a full-time job outside the home. In still other households, life insurance may be a means of making certain that an aged parent, relative, or other dependent is cared for should the insured die.

HOW MUCH LIFE INSURANCE IS ENOUGH?

Although many rules of thumb are commonly cited in answer to the question of how much life insurance is appropriate, in truth the needs are highly individual. Some economists and attorneys suggest a *human life value approach,* attempting to forecast the value of the income a person would earn if he or she lived as long as the actuarial tables predicted. Others recommend a *multiple earnings approach,* arguing that sufficient insurance must be available to replace the earnings of the insured for three, five, ten, or even more years. Many life

Figure 12-1

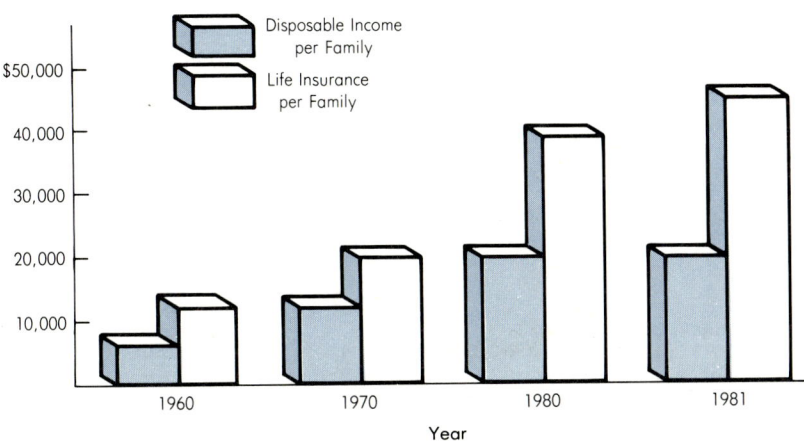

COMPARISON OF LIFE INSURANCE AND DISPOSABLE PERSONAL INCOME PER FAMILY, 1960–1981

Source: U.S. Bureau of the Census, *Statistical Abstract of the United States* (Washington, D.C.: U.S. Government Printing Office, 1983), p. 521.

insurance salespeople suggest that a person should have enough life insurance to cover four to five times his or her annual income. As Figure 12-1 reveals, however, the typical household has only enough life insurance to cover annual income for two years.

In general, determination of the appropriate amount of life insurance must be based on individual household *needs*. Fortunately, there is a specific method for calculating these needs:

1. Estimate how much money your family will need for immediate needs, readjustment funds, replacement income, and any special situations.

2. Subtract from the above total the financial resources already available for your survivors.

The difference between the two amounts is the amount of insurance needed.

Figure 12-2 is a worksheet that can help you determine your insurance needs. The figure shows a worked-out example—the case of 34-year-old Michael Fulco. Fulco is married, has a 2-year-old son, and he and his wife are expecting another child. How did the Fulcos calculate their needs?

To determine the funds needed should Michael die, the Fulcos recorded Michael's total annual income and then multiplied it by the number of years money would be needed for child rearing. They added an estimated $40,000 in college expenses for each child, plus $20,000 for funeral costs, estate costs, and other debts. Had any special situations existed in the Fulco household

Figure 12-2
WORKSHEET FOR DETERMINING LIFE INSURANCE NEEDS

	MICHAEL FULCO	YOU
Funds Needed		
1. Annual contribution to household	$ 16,000	$
2. Remaining years of child rearing	x 18	x
3. Multiply line 1 by line 2	$ 288,000	$
4. College contribution per child	$ 40,000	$
5. Number of children	x 2	x
6. Multiply line 4 by line 5	$ 80,000	$
7. Funeral and estate costs and debts (excluding mortgage)	$ 20,000	$
8. Total needed now: add lines 3, 6 and 7	$ 388,000	$
Existing Resources		
9. Life insurance	$ 85,000	$
10. Savings and investments	$ 2,000	$
11. Wife's earning power per year	$ 12,000	$
12. Years she'd work during child rearing	x 10	x
13. Multiply line 11 by line 12	$ 120,000	$
14. Social Security (per year):		
14a. Benefit for each survivor	$ 3,912	$
14b. Maximum family benefit	$ 9,720	$
14c. Benefit for three or more survivors: enter amount on line 14b	$ 9,720	$
14d. Years of eligibility	x 6	x
14e. Multiply line 14c by line 14d	$ 58,320	$
14f. Benefit for two survivors: multiply line 14a by 2	$ 7,824	$
14g. Years of eligibility	x 10	x
14h. Multiply line 14f by line 14g	$ 78,240	$
14i. Benefit for one survivor: enter amount on line 14a	$ 3,912	$
14j. Years of eligibility	x 2	x
14k. Multiply line 14i by line 14j	$ 7,824	$
15. Total resources: add lines 9, 10, 13, 14e, 14h and 14k	$ 351,384	$
Insurance Needed		
16. Subtract line 15 from line 8	$ 36,616	$

Source: Malcolm N. Carter, "How Much Do You Really Need?" Money, April 1982, p. 134. Reprinted by permission.

requiring additional funds, these needs would have been included in this section. For the Fulcos, the anticipated total of funds needed came to $388,000.

The next step involves an evaluation of existing financial resources. The Fulcos, for instance, already had $85,000 life insurance coverage for Michael (line 9) and $2,000 in savings and investments (line 10). They estimated Mrs. Fulco's current annual earning power at $12,000 and recorded this amount on line 11. Other data may require contacting the local Social Security office.

> You can work out all the entries for yourself except Social Security payments. Those amounts are based on a parent's age at death—you should assume that it occurs this year—and on his earnings history. Your nearest Social Security office can find out for you what your survivors would get. Ask for your maximum monthly benefit per survivor and your maximum family benefit. Multiply these amounts by 12 to get annual income and enter the results on lines 14a and 14b of the worksheet.
>
> To determine the years of eligibility for various levels of survivors' benefits, start with line 14c, 14f, or 14i, depending on your family size, and fill in each subsequent blank. Keep in mind that children are eligible until they are 18, and that while any child is still under 16, a parent who earns less than $4,440 a year is also eligible. (Benefits start to diminish above that earnings level.)
>
> The Fulcos counted Mrs. Fulco as a Social Security beneficiary for only six years because after that she would go back to work. But while she stayed home, three survivors would be eligible, so the Fulcos started computing Social Security on line 14c. Both children would remain eligible for 10 more years (line 14g). The younger child, then 16, would collect for a final two years (line 14j).[6]

The calculations indicate that Michael Fulco needs an additional $36,616 in life insurance.

Such calculations should be made every few years to ensure that life insurance coverage matches current needs. Changing conditions, such as the birth of additional children, increased income, variations in the rate of inflation, or availability of additional insurance from an employer at no cost, may require substantial adjustments to current insurance coverage.

Even though the worksheet forces an individual to consider both needs and available financial resources, many questions remain unanswered that make a precise determination of insurance needs extremely difficult. Several important factors—inflation rates, the amount of money your spouse will earn, the cost of your children's college education, and the amount of Social Security income your survivors will receive five years from now—must be estimated. At best, your estimates are informed ones, based on current available information. Consequently, some life insurance purchasers may choose to add another 5 or 10 percent to their calculations as a kind of uncertainty cushion.

BASIC VARIABLES IN LIFE INSURANCE POLICIES

The life insurance policy you purchase should be designed to meet your specific insurance needs. Each of the following factors can be varied in order to secure the precise kind of coverage you need.

Protection. All life insurance policies offer protection against economic loss in case of death. The amount of protection you receive depends on the type and amount of insurance you buy. As the next section points out, term insurance offers the most protection for a specified amount of money, followed by whole life and endowment insurance.

Savings. If your goal is to use your life insurance as a method of saving, only certain types of policies will be appropriate. Whole life and endowment insurance build a cash value that can be borrowed and used as a "living benefit" of your life insurance policy.

Face Amount. The size of your insurance coverage is determined by the face amount of the policy—the sum of money to be paid to a named beneficiary in the event of your death. The larger the face amount, the greater the possible benefit—and the more costly the policy.

Policy Period. You can buy a standard life insurance policy for a specific term as short as one year or as long as your entire life. The rate you pay will depend in part on the policy period you choose.

Premium. As Chapter 11 pointed out, the annual cost of your insurance protection is expressed in your premium. Premiums remain the same in whole life and endowment insurance but change at the end of the policy period in the case of term insurance. You can choose to pay your premium monthly, quarterly, semiannually, or annually.

TYPES OF LIFE INSURANCE POLICIES

Three major types of life insurance policies are offered to consumers: term insurance, whole life insurance (either straight or limited-payment), and endowment insurance. Although a number of subcategories exist, all types of life insurance can be included in one of the three categories. Both whole life and endowment insurance combine savings with protection. By contrast, term insurance is solely concerned with protection.

LIFE INSURANCE

TERM INSURANCE

As its name implies, *term insurance* offers insurance protection for a specified term, or period of time, in the life of the insured, but it has no value at the end of that term. Term insurance is considered pure protection. Like homeowners, auto, and fire insurance, it offers protection for the period of time the policy is in force and nothing more. If you die while your term policy is in effect, your claim is paid. If you live and your policy expires, the insurance company is free of any further obligation to you. You are left with the assurance that had you died, the financial loss caused by your death would have been reduced by the amount of the policy.

The earliest life insurance agreement on record was a term policy taken out on the life of William Gybbons on June 18, 1583, for a period of 12 months. Gybbons died on May 28, 1584—well within the covered period—but the insurers refused to pay, claiming that 12 months meant 12 lunar months of 28 days each. The courts settled the claim in favor of Gybbons's estate and the first term life insurance policy paid off. In 1981 more than 38 percent of all individual life insurance purchases were for term insurance—up from 28 percent in 1970.

Level Term and Decreasing Term Insurance. Two different types of term insurance have been developed for persons with different types of needs. In some instances, a purchaser of life insurance may desire a fixed amount of insurance coverage at a premium that remains constant throughout the term of the policy. Such policies, called *level term insurance,* are commonly issued for periods of 1 year, 5 to 10 years, and to age 65 or 70. A person who purchases a 10-year level term policy will pay the same premiums for 10 years. After that, the premiums will increase to reflect the insured's age and increased likelihood of death. By contrast, premiums on a 1-year level term policy will remain constant for 12 months and then increase. Thus in every instance level term insurance provides a specific amount of insurance protection during the term of the policy. Should you die 1 day or 9½ years after purchasing a 10-year term policy with a face value of $25,000, your beneficiary will receive the full $25,000 death benefit.

In some instances, the amount of term insurance required by a family declines over a period of time. When a family has children to put through college or a home mortgage to pay off, their need for insurance protection decreases as time goes by. When the mortgage is paid off and the children are grown, educated, and on their own, these temporary life insurance needs are gone. An appropriate form of insurance protection for this family may be *decreasing term insurance.*

Here is how decreasing term insurance works. Assume that you purchase $70,000 worth of decreasing term insurance to cover a 30-year, $70,000

---

term insurance: *insurance coverage protecting the individual for a specified period of time, with no value at the end of that period.*

level term insurance: *term insurance whose face value remains constant throughout the coverage period.*

decreasing term insurance: *term insurance whose face value declines according to a predetermined schedule throughout the coverage period.*

mortgage on a new home. As you repay the mortgage, your insurance protection is reduced an equal amount. Should you die after 15 years, leaving $40,000 still to be paid, your beneficiary will receive that amount as a death benefit.

Decreasing term policies lack some of the flexibility of straight term insurance. If your debts increase and you want to maintain the same level of insurance protection, you are forced to purchase another policy and to once again show evidence of your insurability. Ordinary straight term insurance gives you the option of keeping a constant level of insurance protection or reducing it as the years pass.

Even though the amount of insurance protection decreases, the premiums of a decreasing term policy remain the same. The reason for these constant premiums is simple. A $40,000 decreasing term policy in effect for 10 years provides the insured with average coverage of $20,000 over the 10-year period. The premium is calculated based on this average. Despite this, decreasing term is one of the cheapest forms of term insurance.

Conversion and Renewable Features. Most term insurance policies (other than decreasing term) include two key provisions for the insured. The first provision permits renewal of the policy every time the term expires. The second provision allows the insurance policy to be converted, at the option of the insured, to another form of life insurance.

The first feature gives you the option of renewing your insurance protection for at least one additional period without having to pass another physical exam. In most cases, the additional period is the same length as the original term. Thus, you can renew a 5-year policy for at least 5 years, a 10-year policy for 10 years, and so on.

Many insurance companies permit renewal of 5-year term policies as many times as you wish until you meet a specified limit, which is usually age 65 or 70. Ten-year policies offer less flexibility. The renewable privilege, if it is permitted at all, is usually limited to one 10-year term.

During the life of your term policy, your premiums remain constant; a 5-year term policy will cost you the same the fifth year as it did the first. However, every time you renew your insurance, your premiums rise. That is because as an older person, your risk of dying and the insurance company's risk of loss are greater. Before the age of 45, the premiums rise slowly and are a manageable part of most people's budgets. During the middle and later years, when the probability of death increases, premiums are considerably higher.

Even though guaranteed renewable policies are somewhat more expensive than nonrenewable term policies, the extra cost is a small price to pay for this right. The ability to secure continuing insurance protection at standard rates, regardless of changing health conditions over time, can be invaluable should health problems prevent a policyholder from otherwise qualifying for insurance coverage.

Life Insurance for Homemakers?

Life insurance advertising campaigns aimed at women often feature the successful career woman, usually single, sometimes married to another high earner. Mostly ignored are women whose lives revolve around home and family.

A housewife doesn't bring in a paycheck, but she contributes thousands of dollars' worth of service to her household. Financially, her disability or death involves far more than medical or burial costs.

"I've run into many men who were astounded by what it costs them to run the house," says Ann Benson, an investor information specialist at Merrill Lynch, Pierce, Fenner & Smith, who gives seminars on financial affairs for women and families.

The cash from insurance can relieve scores of unexpected financial worries when a wife dies. More and more, financial planners advise one-paycheck families to insure both spouses.

How much do you need?

The first thing to consider when shopping for life insurance for a wife and mother is how much money the father and children would need if she should die.

The consumer science department at the University of Alabama estimates that a 24-year-old mother of two who stays home with the children will perform $11,797 worth of labor this year—from cooking, cleaning and childcare to decorating and gardening.

Those services must be maintained to keep the family functioning. A family should also be insured for funeral and burial costs and a possible loss of income if the husband has trouble coping with his wife's death for an extended period.

Income taxes could rise, too. The tax law permits a widowed spouse to pay taxes at joint rates for the year the other spouse died. You can continue to use the joint tax schedules for the following two years if you have a dependent child.

After that, you may qualify as a head of household. A head of household with taxable income of $35,000 last year paid $9,392 in federal income taxes—$700 less than a single person but $1,396 more than a married taxpayer filing a joint return.

How do you decide how much insurance to buy? First compute immediate and future cash needs following these steps:

- Estimate the costs of settling the wife's estate, including all burial expenses.
- Calculate the needs for housekeeping and childcare. This will be the greatest problem, particularly for a father with very young children. The University of Alabama estimate of about $12,000 a year could be right for the father of two preschoolers; less than half that amount could suffice if teenagers are around to care for younger siblings and to help with the cooking and cleaning.
- Figure out how much income the wife contributes in other ways, such as tending the garden or making the kids' clothes. Include an estimate of how much she could earn outside the home if she plans to return to the job market later.

In addition to estimating the average monthly loss in dollars, you must calculate how many years you'll need to draw that income. Suppose you estimate the loss to be an average of $833 a month over 20 years. That's a total of almost $200,000, but you don't need it all at once. Death benefits of $86,318, invested at 10% and compounded monthly, would give you $833 a month for 20 years.

It may be as important for a homemaker to have an adequate life insurance policy as for a head of household.

Source: "Life Insurance for Homemakers," *Changing Times*, June 1982, p. 62. Reprinted with permission from *Changing Times* Magazine, © Kiplinger Washington Editors, Inc., 1982.

The Conversion Option. The second feature found in many term policies is the option of converting the policy to whole life or endowment plan at standard rates without having to pass a physical exam or show other proof of insurability. The conversion privilege is usually limited to purchasing an amount of insurance equal to or less than the coverage you already have. There is also a limit to the time period during which you can convert the policy. Most policies require you to convert well before your term insurance expires. For example, you may lose the right to convert your policy during the last year of a 5-year term plan and during the last 2 years of a 10-year plan. Insurance companies impose this restriction in order to discourage people who develop health problems or take on hazardous occupations during the last years of their term coverage from switching to permanent insurance at the last minute.

Deposit Term Insurance. *Deposit term insurance* is a relatively new form of term protection designed to reward policyholders who keep their insurance in force for a long period of time. When you purchase deposit term insurance for 10 years, you must pay a deposit (typically $10 per $1,000 of coverage) on top of your regular premium. This first-year deposit is placed in a high-rate interest-bearing account. If you maintain your insurance coverage for the full 10 years, you will receive your deposit back plus interest. If you let your policy lapse at any time during the 10 years, you will forfeit the deposit and the interest. If you die during the term of the policy, your beneficiary will receive the face amount of the policy plus the deposit and the interest earned on it.

Deposit insurance is one of the cheapest forms of term insurance if you maintain your policy for its full length. A 10-year, convertible deposit term policy is cheaper than any other 10-year policy—if you hold on to it. If you do not, it can be one of the most expensive term insurance purchases.

The Cost of Term Insurance. Term insurance is typically the least expensive kind of insurance protection primarily because it offers pure protection. As we shall see, the cash value of straight life, limited-payment life, and endowment policies is accumulated through larger premiums than those charged for term insurance. Table 12-1 compares the cost of these forms of insurance for $1,000 of protection at various ages.

WHOLE LIFE INSURANCE

There are two basic differences between whole life insurance and term insurance. Whereas term insurance covers you for a specified period of years, *whole life insurance* is purchased for your entire life. No matter when you die, if your policy is still in force, the company will pay the face amount of your policy to your beneficiary. In addition, the premium dollars spent on whole life insurance are divided between insurance protection and savings. Although this

---

deposit term insurance: term insurance designed to reward policyholders who maintain insurance coverage for long time periods.

whole life insurance: insurance providing both protection and savings for the policyholder, who pays premiums throughout life and builds up a cash value in the policy.

LIFE INSURANCE

Table 12-1
COMPARISON OF SAMPLE ANNUAL PREMIUMS PER $1,000 IN INSURANCE ON A $50,000 POLICY

Male Age at Issue	Straight Life	Annual Premium* Limited-Payment 20-Year	Endowment 20-Year	5-Year Term**
18	$ 7.32	$21.07	$44.07	$ 2.93
20	7.86	22.07	44.21	3.05
25	9.24	24.73	44.56	3.36
30	11.15	27.72	45.10	3.96
40	17.62	34.92	47.04	5.78
50	29.29	44.89	51.86	11.13

*Nonsmoker classification.
**Rates for initial 5-year term. Policy is renewable for additional 5-year terms, at applicable premium rate for then-attained age.
Source: Courtesy of Metropolitan Life Insurance Company, May 9, 1983.

savings element provides flexibility not present in a term insurance policy, it also makes the policy more costly to maintain.

According to the insurance industry, the cost of whole life insurance in the early years of a policyholder's life exceeds the actual cost of insurance protection, and the cost in later years is far lower than needed. Companies invest the excess amount they collect in premiums paid during the early years and hold these funds in reserve to cover the increasing risk of death as the policyholder grows older. When these reserve funds are combined with the policyholder premiums, the cost of permanent insurance protection becomes manageable throughout the policyholder's life. The vast majority of whole life policies fall into two categories: straight life and limited-payment life.

Straight Life Insurance. When you buy *straight life insurance* (also known as continuous-premium whole life insurance and ordinary life insurance), your premiums remain the same throughout the life of the policy. The amount you pay at age 25 when you buy the policy will be the same 40 years later. Your premiums are determined primarily by your initial age at enrolling (the older you are the higher the premiums) and health (physical problems affecting your life expectancy increase the cost). In 1981, 47 percent of the face value of all life insurance policies in force were straight life policies.

Within the first three years your straight life policy is in effect, it begins to build *cash value*—accumulated savings that grow steadily as the years go by. A table specifying the amount of cash value accumulated at the end of each year is included in the policy. One major life insurance company offers a $10,000 straight life policy that would cost a 25-year-old man annual premiums of

straight life insurance: whole life insurance in which the insured continues to pay the same premiums throughout the life of the policy.

cash value: the savings portion of a whole life insurance policy that can be borrowed by the policyholder at relatively low interest rates or paid to the policyholder if the policy is canceled.

"According to actuarial statistics, we shouldn't even be here, let alone be sitting here sipping Piper Heidsieck '59."

Mortality Tables Are the Starting Point for Determining Life Insurance Premiums.
Source: Drawing by Stan Hunt; © 1972 The New Yorker Magazine, Inc.

$180. The policy will accumulate a cash value of $256.60 after 5 years, $873.40 after 10 years, and $1,567.10 after 15 years. By the time the policyholder is 60, his policy will have a cash value of $4,808.50. If he lives to 100, the cash value will equal $10,000—the face amount of the policy.

Borrowing from Your Life Insurance Policy. Once your policy has accumulated cash value, you can borrow all or part of it in the form of a *policy loan*. For example, a $50,000 whole life policy purchased by a 35-year-old man may have a cash value of $19,350 when he is 55 and he can borrow that money at a low interest rate. Depending on the insurance company, you can borrow between 95 and 100 percent of the cash surrender value.

In the past the interest rates have been as low as 5 percent. Currently, however, 45 states allow insurance companies to base their policy loan rates on an index of corporate bonds—a move that ties them more closely to the general interest-rate climate. On January 1, 1983, the Metropolitan Life Insurance Company charged its customers 11.5 percent for policy loans. This was somewhat lower than the maximum percentage the law allowed at that time, which was over 13 percent. Policy loan rates can be changed as often as every three

policy loan: *a loan made to the policyholder by the insurance company based on the accumulated cash value of the whole life policy.*

months—although many companies change them less frequently in order to simplify their accounting practices. At Metropolitan Life, for example, rates are changed once a year.

With high interest rates and an uncertain economy a fact of life in the 1980s, millions of people have taken advantage of this inexpensive source of borrowed funds. By 1981, policy loans totaled nearly $48 billion—up more than $7 billion from 1980 and $32 billion from 1971.

Policyholders borrow on their life insurance for a variety of reasons, according to a study made for the life insurance industry. The money from policy loans is used to buy such tangible goods as a house or car, to meet unexpected expenses such as those due to a medical emergency or unemployment, to make business investments, to meet debts, and to pay other insurance premiums.[7]

Policy loans do not have to be paid back—a fact that makes them even more attractive to many whole life policyholders. If the loan has not been paid at the time of the policyholder's death, however, the beneficiary's death benefit is reduced by the amount of the loan plus interest. A $25,000 policy that is reduced by a $4,000 loan plus $1,280 in interest would pay only $19,720 to the beneficiary if the policyholder died without having repaid the loan.

Because it is so easy and so inexpensive to take out a policy loan and because no pressure is placed on the policyholder to pay it back, many policyholders unwittingly reduce the amount of insurance they leave their families. Moreover, a study by the Life Insurance Marketing and Research Association shows that compared with those with no outstanding loans, 2.5 times as many policyholders who have borrowed on their insurance policies let their policies lapse.[8]

Limited-Payment Whole Life Insurance. Like straight life insurance (continuous-premium) policies, *limited-payment whole life insurance* offers protection through the policyholder's life. But instead of charging a continuous premium for the insurance protection, limited-payment policies charge premiums for a limited number of years—10, 20, or 30 years or to age 65, for example. Because payments are made in a shorter period of time, premiums are higher than those charged for continuous-premium whole life policies and cash values increase more rapidly.

Limited-payment life insurance offers the insured the advantage of having paid off his or her life insurance before retirement. In addition, the policy's larger cash value provides greater flexibility during the postretirement years. The insured can choose to surrender the policy and use the money for living expenses or take out a low-interest policy loan.

To gain this flexibility, however, you give up the additional insurance protection you could have purchased had you chosen a continuous-premium policy. For example, a 35-year-old man who purchases a $10,000, 20-payment life policy will pay $340 a year—$120 more than the cost of a continuous-premium

limited-payment whole life insurance: whole life insurance in which premiums are paid for a limited number of years, but insurance protection remains throughout the policyholder's life.

policy. Had he used all his premium dollars to purchase continuous-premium insurance, he could have increased his insurance by $5,000. Critics of limited-payment life policies also question the wisdom of paying excessive premiums during earning years, when a family's need for money is greatest, so that insurance money will be available after age 65, when the need for coverage may be reduced or nonexistent.

TERM VERSUS WHOLE LIFE: THE DEBATE GOES ON

Deciding which form of insurance—term or whole life—is best for you is no easy matter; the insurance industry and its critics have debated the issue for years. Here are some of the key areas of controversy.

Arguments Against Purchasing Whole Life Insurance. Much criticism of whole life insurance centers on its cash value—the portion of the premium invested for the policyholder. For years, a segment of the insurance industry promoted the whole life policy as insurance protection combined with a savings plan, but in fact, say critics, the policy contains no separate savings account. When a policyholder dies, the beneficiary does not receive a savings account payment in addition to the face value of the policy. Whatever cash reserve the policyholder has accumulated simply becomes part of the face amount of the policy.

To understand this better, let us take a closer look at the whole life policy's system of level premiums—a system that critics claim is a myth. When a policyholder dies, the insurance company pays the policyholder's beneficiary the face value of the policy. The insurance company's liability is greatest for new policies, which have not yet accumulated significant cash values, and smallest for older policies, whose large cash values leave little for the company to pay. As your cash value builds and the insurance company's risk declines, your premium dollars—which remain the same over the years—buy less and less insurance.

As one financial writer explains:

> At age 35, as a male non-smoker, you will pay an annual premium of $1,300 for $100,000 of whole life insurance. Annual renewable term will cost you $130. At age 45, you still will pay $1,300 a year for the whole life but your term insurance will cost $370. The whole life cost will remain the same while the term goes up until at age 65 it will cost $2,300.
>
> Meanwhile, the insurance company has been collecting $1,300 from you every year on your whole life, so your policy now has a cash value of $50,000. Basically, the insurance company will have to pay only $50,000 worth of benefits if you die; the rest of the money is what you've paid in, plus interest. The term has cost you considerably less for the same protection.[9]

The *real* cost of your insurance protection increases just as it does with term insurance. Moreover, if you buy a whole life policy when you are young—

because of the attraction of guaranteed premiums for as long as you keep the insurance coverage—you will pay premiums for a longer period of time, thus increasing rather than decreasing your lifetime insurance costs.

Critics also point to the 1977 study conducted by the Federal Trade Commission, which reported that the cash reserve portion of a typical whole life policy earns on average 1.3 percent annual interest—far less than is available in banks and other equally secure investments. This, critics contend, is even more reason to buy term insurance and invest the rest. A young couple starting out with a limited household income needs a policy that will give them the most protection for the least money, say critics. With $250 to spend on insurance, the 25-year-old husband can purchase $25,000 worth of whole life insurance and four times that amount of term insurance.

Finally, statistical evidence indicates that a surprising number of insured persons change their mind concerning whole life insurance coverage. Over 20 percent of all whole life policyholders drop their policies in the first two years; more than half drop them within 20 years.

The Arguments in Favor of Purchasing Whole Life Insurance. The insurance industry paints a very different picture of the role that whole life insurance plays in a family's financial planning. Whole life insurance, the

---

Building a Case for Term Insurance

Financial counselor Venita VanCaspel is clearly no fan of whole life insurance. Although she feels that life insurance is a necessary keystone of a good investment program, her advice to insurance purchasers favors term insurance:

1. Buy your life insurance as if you were going to die tomorrow.
2. Life insurance is based on a mortality table; therefore, it should cost you more each year because you are more likely to die each year.
3. Every time the insurance companies are forced to go on a new mortality table, apply for a new policy. If you pass the physical and are granted a new policy at a lower rate, redeem or cancel the old one. A life insurance policy is no more sacred than an automobile insurance policy.
4. The purpose of life insurance is to protect those dependent on you in the event you do not live long enough to accumulate a living estate. Your goal is to become self-insured by age 65 or sooner. You've either made it by then, or you'll probably never make it. Life insurance is to protect an economic potential. After 65 your economic potential has greatly diminished. . . .
5. Life insurance is for dying. Investments are for living.
6. All life insurance is pure protection (term), or pure protection plus banking. There are no other kinds.
7. Do not bank with an insurance company under conditions you would not bank with your bank.
8. Be sure that your policies are renewable and convertible at your option without evidence of insurability. You should also consider waiver of premium provisions.

Source: Venita VanCaspel, Money Dynamics, 1975. Reprinted with permission of Reston Publishing Company, a Prentice-Hall Company, 11480 Sunset Hills Road, Reston, Va. 22090.

industry claims, provides a mechanism for long-term saving that most families cannot do without. With rising costs battering the family budget, people are willing to sell stocks, withdraw money from savings accounts, and liquidate other personal investments to pay bills. They are reluctant, however, to terminate their whole life policy for its cash value because they know that doing so will also terminate their insurance protection. Because of the "semicompulsory" nature of life insurance (once a policy is surrendered it is not easy to replace, especially if one's health has worsened), few people fail to pay their life insurance premiums when they come due. The argument that one should buy term insurance and invest the rest, counters the insurance industry, is neither realistic nor practical.

Insurance agents also point out that the overwhelming majority of term policyholders outlive their coverage. With the average life expectancy of both men and women increasing every year, term policies to age 60 or 65 leave individuals unable to provide insurance protection for their spouses in their later years. This problem is compounded by the fact that on average, men die earlier than women and marry younger women. Even if term coverage were available, says the industry, it would be too expensive for most old people to afford.

ENDOWMENT INSURANCE

endowment insurance: life insurance coverage for a specified period after which the face value is refunded to the policyholder.

Endowment insurance has two purposes: (1) to provide a specific sum of money to the policyholder when he or she reaches a given age and (2) to provide the same amount of insurance coverage during the time the policy is in force. Policyholders receive a payment equal to the face value of the policy at the end of the endowment period. If you die before then, your beneficiaries receive that amount.

Endowment policies are commonly purchased on the lives of infants for payment at the age of 18, when they are about to enter college. They are also purchased to provide for retirement needs beginning at a predetermined age—65, for example.

Endowment policies have many of the same drawbacks as limited-payment policies. Because they are much more expensive than continuous-premium whole life insurance, they offer less insurance protection for each premium dollar. Besides, a whole life policy, with its ever-increasing cash value, offers the policyholder the option of surrendering the policy and withdrawing the cash or taking a policy loan. These options, which put cash in your hands, have the same effect as receiving a matured endowment.

Because of these drawbacks, endowment insurance is purchased by very few people. In 1981, for example, endowment policies accounted for only 2.6 percent of the face value of all life insurance policies in force throughout the country. Sales are even lower at many individual companies. Of all the policies sold by Metropolitan Life Insurance Company in 1982, fewer than 1 percent were for endowment insurance. As a result of this poor showing, Metropolitan stopped offering endowment policies in 1984.

CREDIT LIFE INSURANCE

If you buy a car or a new home or take out a consumer loan, you may be asked to add a few extra dollars each month to your payments for credit life insurance. *Credit life insurance* guarantees that your debt will be repaid even if you die—thereby protecting the seller or lender from losing money and your family from having to pay the debt from your estate. In 1983, $160 billion of credit life insurance was in force in the United States—twice the amount in force a decade earlier.

> **credit life insurance:** a type of decreasing term insurance that guarantees repayment of the amount due on a loan or installment contract should the borrower die.

Credit life insurance is actually decreasing term insurance, offered for the length of the loan or mortgage. However, it is much more expensive than conventional term coverage. Maximum rates range from 39 cents for every $100 of insurance in New York to $1 per $100 in Alabama. If a 35-year-old man borrows $6,000 for four years at 13 percent interest and purchases credit life insurance from the lender at 75 cents per $100 of coverage, he will have to pay the following costs:

Loan principal	$6,000.00
Interest on loan	1,725.60
Credit life premium	241.08
Interest on premium	69.33
Total	$8,036.01

Thus, he will need insurance to cover $8,036.01—not $6,000. Premiums on a credit life policy for this amount would cost $310.41 ($241.08 + $69.33), or $6.47 a month. He could have purchased the same amount of decreasing term insurance from a major company for $4.41 a month and over twice the coverage—$16,893—for the $6.47 premium.[10]

Because of its high cost, critics recommend purchase of credit life insurance only on small, short-term loans. Borrowers may have difficulty, for example, insuring a $2,000 loan for two years through traditional insurance channels; credit life may be the only alternative. In addition, credit life may be appropriate for individuals whose age or health makes it difficult or expensive to purchase traditional insurance.

When is credit life insurance not a good buy? According to the editors of *Changing Times*:

- Not if you're in your twenties or thirties and eligible for other kinds of life insurance at better rates.
- Not if you're single with no heirs to worry about. Credit life is supposed to

protect your surviving family from claims against your estate; if you have no family, you end up protecting the creditor.
- Not if you already have enough insurance to cover the debt.
- And not if your main reason for wanting more insurance is to beef up your overall coverage. Depending on your age and health, you can usually buy long-term policies in large enough amounts for a much smaller unit cost than you can buy credit life.[11]

Individuals who determine that credit life is necessary should attempt to secure this coverage from credit unions whenever possible. CUNA Mutual, the insurance affiliate of the Credit Union National Association, charges rates of 39 cents per $100 of coverage for such policies.

INDUSTRIAL LIFE INSURANCE

Industrial life insurance — small, high-priced, whole-life policies paid for weekly to traveling collectors — has its roots in nineteenth-century industrial England. It started among factory workers who could not afford the quarterly premiums needed to purchase regular life insurance policies. Instead, they purchased industrial life policies, which were issued in small amounts with weekly premiums that were sometimes as low as 3 or 5 cents. Insurance agents, who sold the policies as burial insurance, traveled to policyholders' homes to collect premiums.

Industrial life insurance has survived in the twentieth century using the same basic principle of frequent payment for insurance policies issued in small amounts. In 1981, the average policy was $630. Weekly collections of small premiums are expensive; the typical industrial insurance agent receives 20 percent of the premium for compensation. In addition, the cost of maintaining small insurance policies contributes to pushing the cost of industrial insurance policies as much as 50 times higher than an equivalent term insurance policy.

Partially for this reason and partially because many low-income families now have access to group life insurance policies through their work, the popularity of industrial life insurance has declined over the years. In 1983, $30 billion of industrial insurance was in force in the United States — less than 1 percent of all life insurance and a decline of $6 billion since 1980. This decline is applauded by industry critics, who agree with financial writer Jane Bryant Quinn's characterization of industrial life insurance as "yet another case of 'the poor pay more.'"[12]

GROUP LIFE INSURANCE

Millions of Americans have some form of group life insurance, either as the sole source of their insurance protection or as a supplement to their individual policies. In 1950 one out of five life insurance policies in force was a group

industrial life insurance: whole life insurance policies sold in small amounts with premiums payable weekly or monthly; burial policies are an example.

Figure 12-3
GROWTH OF INDIVIDUAL, GROUP, AND CREDIT LIFE INSURANCE IN THE UNITED STATES

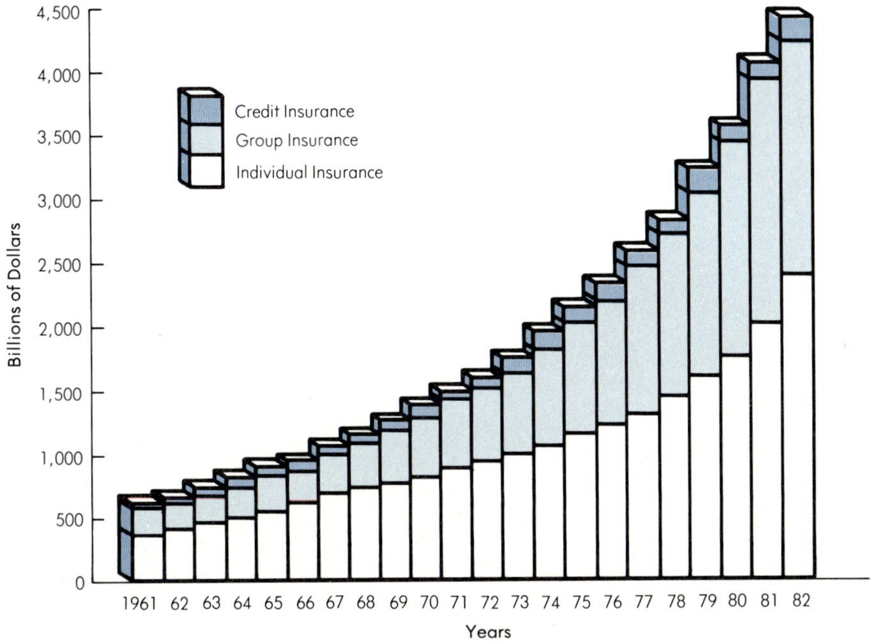

Source: *Life Insurance Fact Book* (Washington, D.C.: American Council of Life Insurance, 1983), p. 16. Authorization to reproduce granted.

policy. By 1981 that number had more than doubled with group insurance accounting for 47 percent of total insurance in force (see Figure 12-3).[13]

Most *group life insurance* policies are available through the workplace at rates that are lower than those available to most individuals. Frequently, these policies are offered as a fully paid fringe benefit, or employers may share the cost of a base amount of insurance with their employees and give them the option of purchasing additional amounts. The average amount of group life insurance available through employers is $16,753. As Table 12-2 indicates, group insurance may also be available through professional and fraternal organizations and other groups.

Group life insurance serves an important need for those workers who have little or no individual life insurance coverage. This number is steadily declining, but as recently as 1960 one out of every four workers relied solely on group life insurance to meet insurance needs. Policy amounts may be determined by the employee's salary (often the face value of the policy equals the employee's annual wage), his or her position in the company (executives receive the most extensive coverage), or length of service (those with the greatest tenure receive the largest benefits).

group life insurance: life insurance (typically term insurance) for company employees or group members; it is usually written under a single master policy.

Table 12-2
GROUP LIFE INSURANCE IN FORCE BY TYPE AND BY SIZE OF INSURED GROUP IN THE UNITED STATES 1978

Type of Group	Master Policies Number	Master Policies Percent of Total	Insurance in Force Amount (000,000 omitted)	Insurance in Force Percent of Total	Average Amount of Coverage per Member
Related to Employment or Occupation					
Employer-Employee	453,670	91.7	$ 945,891	87.8	$16,753
Union and Joint Employer-Union	5,250	1.1	35,209	3.3	5,175
Professional Society	960	.2	18,458	1.7	28,052
Employee Association	1,730	.3	19,911	1.8	13,703
Other—Related to Employee Benefit Program	3,290	.7	7,933	.7	11,497
Other—Not Related to Employee Benefit Program	130	—*	2,095	.2	22,287
Total	465,030	94.0	1,029,497	95.5	15,561
Not Related to Employment or Occupation					
Fraternal Society	340	.1	2,517	.2	12,460
Savings or Investment Group	21,380	4.3	17,764	1.7	633
Group Mortgage Insurance	5,720	1.1	24,780	2.3	17,512
Other	2,370	.5	3,170	.3	6,108
Total	29,810	6.0	48,231	4.5	1,597
Total All Groups	494,840	100.0	$1,077,728	100.0	$11,183

Note: Data exclude dependent coverage, Federal Employees' Group Life Insurance, and Servicemen's Group Life Insurance. Group credit life insurance on loans of over 10 years' duration is included.
*Less than .05 percent.

Source: Life Insurance Fact Book (Washington, D.C.: American Council of Life Insurance, 1983), p. 29. Authorization to reproduce granted.

Employees who leave their jobs are sometimes given the option of converting their group benefit insurance into individual whole life coverage (term coverage is rarely offered). Most conversion policies are less competitive than policies one might find by shopping around, so employees usually purchase the converted policy only if a health problem makes them ineligible for other, lower-priced insurance.

Astute consumers include group life insurance as only one part of their insurance package. Because group insurance is often tied to the place of work, individuals may find themselves without adequate coverage—in the right amount and at the right price—if they change jobs. By maintaining a base of individual protection and supplementing it with group coverage, they are less dependent on a single source of insurance coverage.

VARIABLE LIFE INSURANCE

Variable life insurance gives individuals the opportunity to combine a straight life policy with an investment that might increase the death benefit paid to their beneficiaries. This is accomplished by the insurance company investing part of the insurance premium and allowing the insured to participate in returns on the investment. If the company's net return on its investment increases, the death benefit also increases. An 8 percent gross annual return would turn a $40,000 policy into a $40,655 death benefit after 5 years, a $51,000 benefit after 20 years, and an $87,000 benefit after 40 years. In order to provide relatively predictable returns, many variable insurance policies invest in such fixed-return securities as bonds. If, however, the insurance company invests in corporate stocks and the stocks perform poorly, the policy may lose gains made in previous years. Unlike the death benefit, the policy's cash value has no guaranteed minimum.

In 1983 variable life insurance accounted for approximately 2 percent of total life insurance sales. In recent years, variable life insurance policies have given policyholders even greater flexibility and control over their insurance protection. Newer plans enable policyholders to switch back and forth among different types of stock funds, including aggressive, blue-chip, and income funds. According to a spokesman for the American Council of Life Insurance, the trade association of the life insurance industry, "insurance companies now recognize that a significant number of policyholders want a greater voice in controlling where and how their cash value is invested."[14] Figure 12-4 describes the variable life policy offered by one major life insurance company.

variable life insurance: a hybrid form of whole life insurance permitting policyholders to pay premium supplements that are invested by the insurance companies; the amount of the policy is then adjusted based on earnings (or losses) from these investments.

UNIVERSAL LIFE INSURANCE

In 1979 Hutton Life, an insurance subsidiary of E. F. Hutton, foresaw dim prospects for the market in whole life insurance. As interest rates soared, whole life insurance became far less attractive to policyholders, who saw the 5 or 6 percent they earned on the cash value of their policy as a poor investment. Abandoning the idea of a combined insurance and savings plan, they turned instead to term insurance, which was far cheaper than whole life. In order to lure policyholders back to more permanent forms of insurance, Hutton Life introduced a policy that combines term insurance with a tax-deferred savings account that earns interest at bond-market rates. Called *universal life insurance*, this policy has revolutionized the insurance business. Today, approximately 130 insurance companies offer some form of universal life insurance. These policies—combining term insurance with a money-market–like cash value account—made up approximately 10 percent of all new life insurance sales in 1982.[15]

A typical universal life policy works in the following way. Part of each year's

universal life insurance: a hybrid form of life insurance combining term insurance with a tax-deferred savings account that earns interest at bond-market rates.

Figure 12-4

ADVERTISEMENT FOR VARIABLE LIFE INSURANCE

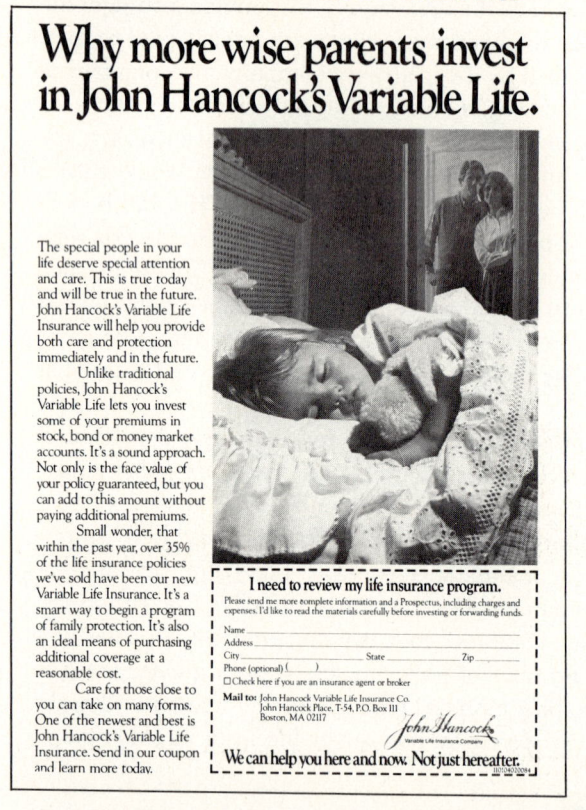

Source: Courtesy of John Hancock Variable Life Insurance Company.

premium is used to purchase low-cost term insurance while the rest, minus the company's expenses, is placed in high-yielding investments. Policyholders are not taxed on their investment earnings, which in recent years have been as high as 12 percent, since they are part of the life insurance plan. When the policyholder dies, the base policy amount and the accumulated earnings are paid to beneficiaries, free of income or capital gains tax.

Universal life insurance offers some attractive options. It enables policyholders to vary the amount they contribute to the savings portion of their insurance plans once their initial premiums are paid. It also allows them to adjust upward or downward the amount of term insurance coverage. Although increasing their insurance coverage depends on continued good health, this procedure is generally as easy as completing a simple form from the insurance company. In addition, policyholders can use their accumulating cash values to pay part or all of the annual premiums or to raise the death benefit. Also, they can make tax-free withdrawals from the investment portion of the account as long as they do not exceed the total amount already paid in premiums. Unlike loans on whole life insurance policies, these withdrawals do not have any effect on base insurance protection.

Figure 12-5 (pages 354–355) illustrates how a family might use universal life insurance to adjust the protection and cash value to its changing needs in different stages of the life cycle. Should the husband die, his dependents would receive both the insurance and the cash value, which at their peak total $244,452 in this example. The amounts shown in Figure 12-5 are projected at an 11-percent interest rate on the cash value of the insurance policy.

The return on universal life policies usually remains stable for an entire year and then varies up or down to reflect market interest rates and the success of the insurer's investments. However, this return is not paid on the entire cash value. First-year sales fees, which are higher than those for term insurance, must be deducted, as must annual fees, which range from 3 to 10 percent of each premium dollar. In addition, many companies pay only 4 percent interest on the first $1,000 of cash value in your account. These drawbacks make it even more important to shop around before buying. Different insurance companies offer slightly different sets of options, so individuals should carefully investigate alternative plans in selecting the most appropriate plan for their needs.

CHOOSING THE BEST POLICY

No universal rule of thumb exists for individuals to follow in choosing the best life insurance policy from among the hundreds of alternatives. It is an individual decision based on individual circumstances such as age, health, family responsibilities, and income.

You must decide whether you want pure protection or a savings element as well. As stated earlier, your decision will determine how much you pay for your insurance protection. Work with a qualified life insurance agent who will guide you in choosing the policy that is right for you. But always remember that the final decision is your own.

THE LIFE INSURANCE CONTRACT

The life insurance contract, which binds you and the insurance company in a legal agreement, contains several key provisions. Many of the provisions described below are common to all policies no matter the type. Others apply only to certain kinds of life insurance contracts.

THE BENEFICIARY CLAUSE

Every life insurance policy contains a clause that names the *beneficiary*—the specific individual or organization to receive the proceeds of the policy when

beneficiary: the individual or organization designated to receive the proceeds of a life insurance policy when the insured dies.

Figure 12-5

USE OF UNIVERSAL LIFE INSURANCE TO MATCH NEEDS AT DIFFERENT STAGES OF THE FAMILY LIFE CYCLE

Age 25: Marriage
Insurance: $50,000
Cash value: $365
Annual outlay: $800

Age 28: Birth of First Child
Insurance: $100,000
Cash value: $2,575
Annual outlay: $800

Age 30: Purchase of House
Insurance: $150,000
Cash value: $4,232
Annual outlay: $800

Age 32: Birth of Second Child
Insurance: $175,000
Cash value: $6,273
Annual outlay: $1,000

Source: Text from Robert Runde, "At Last—An Almost Ideal Policy," *Money*, July 1981, pp. 98–99. Reprinted by permission.

---

the insured person dies (see Figure 12-6). If no specific individual is mentioned, the insurance proceeds are paid to the estate.

The beneficiary clause contains the name of the *primary beneficiary*, who has the first, or primary, right to receive the policy proceeds. More than one primary beneficiary may be named, as is usually the case when children receive the proceeds of the policy. The clause also names *contingent*, or secondary, *beneficiaries*, who receive the insurance money if the primary beneficiary is no longer living. Life insurance purchasers should always list a contingent beneficiary, due to the possibility of an accident resulting in the death of both the insured and the primary beneficiary.

In most cases, a policy beneficiary designation can be changed as many times as you wish during your lifetime. Only when you designate an *irrevocable beneficiary*—who cannot be deprived of the policy's proceeds without his or her consent—are you bound to your choice.

Since the primary purpose of life insurance is to protect a spouse and children from financial hardship should the policyholder die, the beneficiary clause is a vital element in the life insurance contract. This protection provided $14 billion to policyholder beneficiaries during 1981 (see Figure 12-7).

SETTLEMENT OPTIONS

The life insurance contract also contains a provision specifying how the policy's death benefit will be paid. Ninety-eight out of every 100 policyholders

---

primary beneficiary: the individual or organization designated first on the insurance policy.

contingent beneficiaries: individuals or organizations who will receive the proceeds of an insurance policy if the primary beneficiary is no longer living.

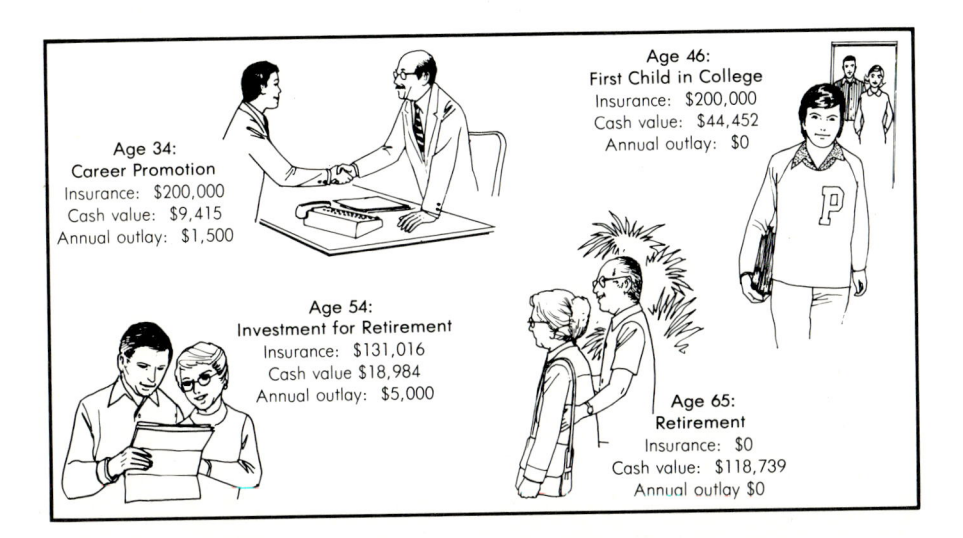

Age 34:
Career Promotion
Insurance: $200,000
Cash value: $9,415
Annual outlay: $1,500

Age 46:
First Child in College
Insurance: $200,000
Cash value: $44,452
Annual outlay: $0

Age 54:
Investment for Retirement
Insurance: $131,016
Cash value $18,984
Annual outlay: $5,000

Age 65:
Retirement
Insurance: $0
Cash value: $118,739
Annual outlay $0

choose to have their beneficiaries receive the benefit in a lump sum. The remaining policyholders choose one of the four remaining settlement options:

1. *Life income:* Under this option, the beneficiary receives a monthly installment for life. The size of the installment is determined by the age of the beneficiary; a young beneficiary, who can expect to live for many years, will receive a smaller payment than an older beneficiary. Under some plans, if the beneficiary dies within 20 years or another specified period, the life income will pass on to a secondary beneficiary, who will continue to receive it for the remainder of the 20 years.

2. *Fixed income:* Here regular payments are made to the beneficiary until the proceeds of the policy and the interest accrued on the proceeds are used up. A $20,000 policy yielding a fixed income of $100 a month would provide an income of about $41,000 and last more than 34 years. The extra $21,000 is earned through interest paid by the insurance company on the decreasing principal.

3. *Limited installments:* Under this option, the beneficiary receives benefits in regular installments for a specified number of years. These proceeds are made up of the life insurance benefit plus a guaranteed rate of interest. A $20,000 policy would pay $210 a month over a 10-year period, with the total amount paid equalling more than $25,000.

4. *Interest only:* Under this option, the beneficiary receives only the interest from the policy, which is paid at a guaranteed rate at specified intervals. The interest may be distributed in this manner until a certain date—at

Figure 12-6
EXPLANATION OF BENEFICIARIES IN A TYPICAL LIFE INSURANCE POLICY

SECTION 8. BENEFICIARIES

8.1 DESIGNATION AND CHANGE OF BENEFICIARIES

(a) **By Owner.** The Owner may designate and change direct and contingent beneficiaries and further payees of death proceeds:

(1) during the lifetime of the Insured.

(2) during the 60 days following the date of death of the Insured, if the Insured immediately before his death was not the Owner. Any such designation of direct beneficiary may not be changed. If the Owner is the direct beneficiary and elects a payment plan, any such designation of contingent beneficiaries and further payees may be changed.

(b) **By Direct Beneficiary.** The direct beneficiary may designate and change contingent beneficiaries and further payees if:

(1) the direct beneficiary is the Owner.

(2) at any time after the death of the Insured, no contingent beneficiary or further payee is living, and no designation is made by the Owner under Section 8.1 (a) (2).

(3) the direct beneficiary elects a payment plan after the death of the Insured, in which case the interest in the share of such direct beneficiary or any other payee designated by the Owner shall terminate.

(c) **By Spouse (Marital Deduction Provision).** Notwithstanding any provision of Section 8 or 9 of this policy to the contrary, if the Insured immediately before death was the Owner and if the direct beneficiary is the spouse of the Insured and survives the Insured, such direct beneficiary shall have the power to appoint all amounts payable under the policy either to the executors or administrators of the direct beneficiary's estate or to such other contingent beneficiaries and further payees as he may designate. The exercise of that power shall revoke any then existing designation of contingent beneficiaries and further payees and any election of a payment plan applying to them.

(d) **Effective Date.** Any designation or change of beneficiary shall be made by the filing and recording at the Home Office of a written request satisfactory to the Company. Unless waived by the Company, the request must be endorsed on the policy. Upon the recording, the request will take effect as of the date it was signed. The Company will not be held responsible for any payment or other action taken by it before the recording of the request.

8.2 SUCCESSION IN INTEREST OF BENEFICIARIES

(a) **Direct Beneficiaries.** The proceeds of this policy shall be payable in equal shares to the direct beneficiaries who survive to receive payment. The unpaid share of any direct beneficiary who dies while receiving payment shall be payable in equal shares to the direct beneficiaries who survive to receive payment.

(b) **Contingent Beneficiaries.** At the death of the last surviving direct beneficiary, payments due or to become due shall be payable in equal shares to the contingent beneficiaries who survive to receive payment. The unpaid share of any contingent beneficiary who dies while receiving payment shall be payable in equal shares to the contingent beneficiaries who survive to receive payment.

(c) **Further Payees.** At the death of the last to survive of the direct and contingent beneficiaries, the proceeds, or the withdrawal value of any payments due or to become due if a payment plan is in effect, shall be paid in one sum:

(1) in equal shares to the further payees who survive to receive payment; or

(2) if no further payees survive to receive payment, to the executors or administrators of the last to survive of the direct and contingent beneficiaries.

(d) **Estate of Owner.** If no direct or contingent beneficiaries or further payees survive the Insured, the proceeds shall be paid to the Owner or the executors or administrators of the Owner.

8.3 GENERAL

(a) **Transfer of Ownership.** A transfer of ownership will not change the interest of any beneficiary.

(b) **Claims of Creditors.** So far as permitted by law, no amount payable under this policy shall be subject to the claims of creditors of the payee.

(c) **Succession under Payment Plans.** A direct or contingent beneficiary succeeding to an interest in a payment plan shall continue under such plan subject to its terms, with the rights of transfer between plans and of withdrawal under plans as provided in this policy.

Source: *Sample Life Insurance Policy* (Washington, D.C.: American Council of Life Insurance), p. 7.

which time, according to the policyholder's wishes, the principal will be paid. This is often done when a parent wants to guarantee money for his or her children's college education.

PREMIUM PAYMENT CLAUSE

The amount of money paid in premiums is customarily listed on the face, or first page, of the life insurance policy. The policy also specifies where, to whom, and how often the premiums must be paid. As noted earlier, policyholders may choose to pay their premiums on an annual, semiannual, quar-

LIFE INSURANCE 357

Figure 12-7
ANALYSIS OF PAYMENTS TO BENEFICIARIES UNDER STRAIGHT LIFE INSURANCE IN THE UNITED STATES

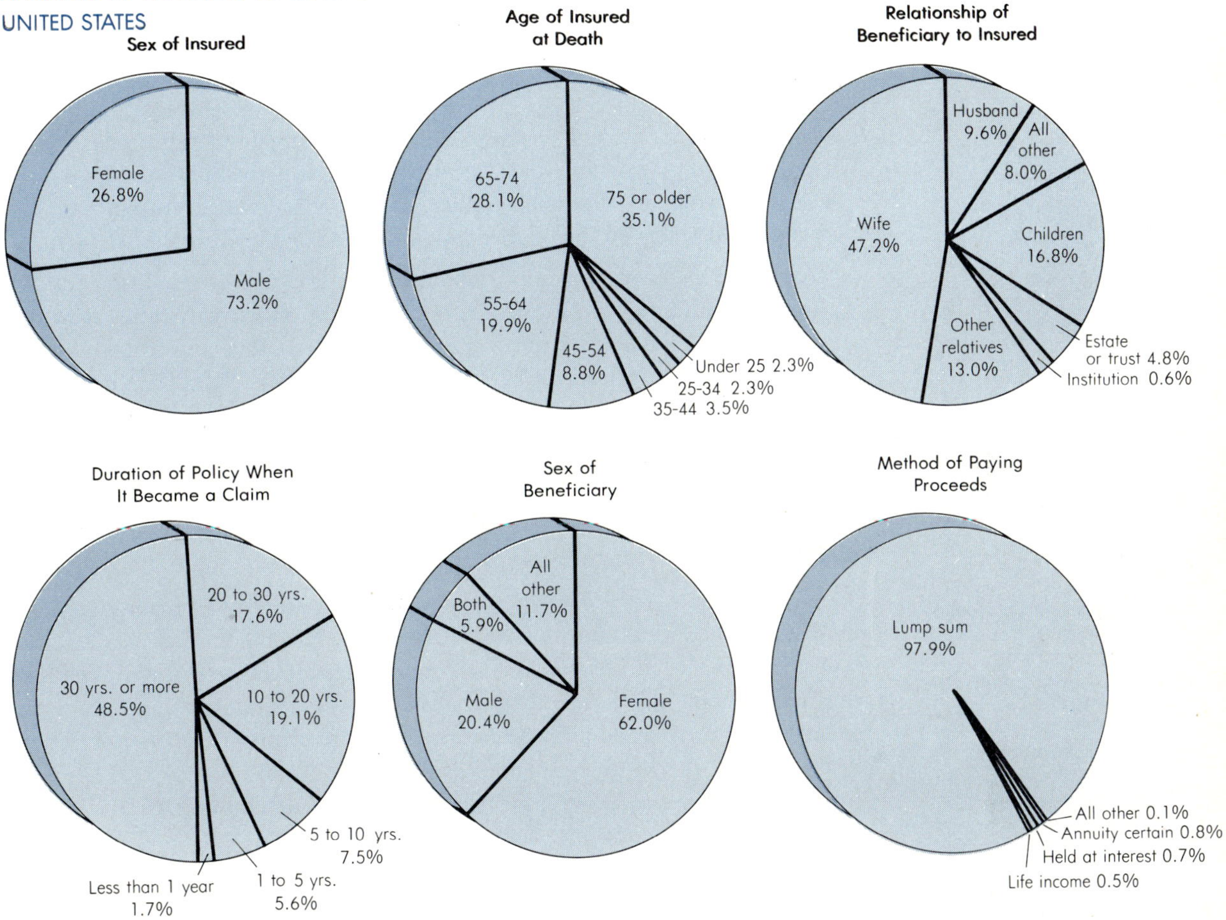

Sex of Insured
- Female 26.8%
- Male 73.2%

Age of Insured at Death
- 65-74 28.1%
- 75 or older 35.1%
- 55-64 19.9%
- 45-54 8.8%
- Under 25 2.3%
- 25-34 2.3%
- 35-44 3.5%

Relationship of Beneficiary to Insured
- Husband 9.6%
- All other 8.0%
- Wife 47.2%
- Children 16.8%
- Other relatives 13.0%
- Estate or trust 4.8%
- Institution 0.6%

Duration of Policy When It Became a Claim
- 20 to 30 yrs. 17.6%
- 30 yrs. or more 48.5%
- 10 to 20 yrs. 19.1%
- 5 to 10 yrs. 7.5%
- 1 to 5 yrs. 5.6%
- Less than 1 year 1.7%

Sex of Beneficiary
- All other 11.7%
- Both 5.9%
- Male 20.4%
- Female 62.0%

Method of Paying Proceeds
- Lump sum 97.9%
- All other 0.1%
- Annuity certain 0.8%
- Held at interest 0.7%
- Life income 0.5%

Note: Figures exclude individual credit life insurance on loans of 10 years or less duration.
Source: Adapted from *Life Insurance Fact Book* (Washington, D.C.: American Council of Life Insurance, 1982), p. 42.

terly, or monthly basis. Semiannual premiums are typically 51 percent of the annual premium; quarterly premiums, 26 percent of it; and monthly premiums, 8.8 percent. In effect, the insurance company offers discounts for annual premium payments since they reduce billing expenses and allow the insurance company to use the premium for the entire year.

DIVIDEND CLAUSE

The dividend clause is included only in participating policies issued by mutual life insurance companies. The clause gives the policyholder the following options for receiving the dividend payments:

1. *Cash payment:* Under this option, dividends are paid directly to the policyholder on an annual basis.

2. *Premium reduction:* Here the dividends are applied directly to the policyholder's premium, thereby reducing the total amount paid.

3. *Interest:* This option places the dividends with the insurance company in a special interest-bearing account. Every time a dividend payment is made, it is deposited into the insured's account, where it earns interest at a guaranteed rate or higher. The policyholder may withdraw the accumulated funds at any time or leave them to become part of the policy's final settlement.

4. *Dividend additions:* With this option, the insured can use each dividend to purchase additional life insurance on a paid-up basis. Over the years this option gives policyholders the opportunity to purchase a substantial amount of additional insurance. A 22-year-old man with a $10,000 continuous-premium whole life policy can almost double his protection by the time he is 65. Policyholders who are no longer insurable because of poor health may use this option as their only way to purchase additional insurance.

ACCIDENTAL DEATH CLAUSE

accidental death clause: a provision in the life insurance contract guaranteeing additional amounts of insurance should the policyholder die as a result of an accident; also called the "double-indemnity clause."

The *accidental death clause* guarantees an additional amount of insurance, usually equal to the face amount of the policy, if the policyholder dies as a result of an accident. Since the effect of this clause is to double the amount of insurance coverage, it is often referred to as the *double-indemnity clause.*

Certain kinds of accidental deaths are excluded from this provision. These exclusions include death by suicide, as the result of riot or insurrection, in an airplane (except as a passenger on a regularly scheduled flight), and as the result of the commission of a felony.

SUICIDE CLAUSE

suicide clause: a provision in the life insurance contract relieving insurance companies of the requirement to pay most insurance proceeds should the insured commit suicide within two years of initial insurance coverage.

As stated in Chapter 11, a risk must be fortuitous—unexpected and not purposefully brought about by the insured—in order to be insurable. Since suicide—the deliberate taking of one's life—is not fortuitous, the *suicide clause* limits the insurance company's liability in the event of death by suicide within two years of the policy's issuance to the amount the policyholder already paid in premiums.

WAIVER-OF-PREMIUM CLAUSE

waiver-of-premium clause: a provision in the life insurance contract committing the insurance company to make premium payments for policyholders who suffer disabling illnesses or injuries.

The *waiver-of-premium clause* commits the insurance company to make premium payments for you if an illness or accident prevents you from working. Policyholders who become disabled are thus protected from the possibility of losing their insurance because they cannot meet the premium payments. The benefits usually take effect six months after the policyholder becomes totally disabled.

Since the definition of *disability* varies from company to company, it is a good idea to read the waiver-of-premium clause carefully. Some companies will declare a policyholder disabled only if he or she is unfit to perform any type of work. Companies with more liberal policies define *disability* as the inability to perform the normal duties of a chosen occupation or any other occupation for which the insured's education, training, and experience make him or her reasonably suited.

GUARANTEED INSURABILITY CLAUSE

Under the *guaranteed insurability clause,* the policyholder has the right to purchase additional insurance without having to pass a physical exam in the future. Option dates on which a new policy may be purchased and the maximum amount of available coverage are listed in the policy.

The guaranteed insurability clause, which is available for a small fee and can usually be obtained through the age of 40, may be a wise investment for individuals who must limit their insurance purchases when they are young because of budget limitations.

> **guaranteed insurability clause:** a provision in some life insurance contracts enabling policyholders to purchase specified additional amounts of insurance without having to pass a physical examination.

NONFORFEITURE OPTION

A feature of both whole life and endowment policies, the *nonforfeiture option* protects you if your policy lapses. When an insurance policy with accumulated cash value is allowed to lapse (the premium is unpaid), you are offered one of three choices: you may (1) surrender the policy for a portion of the cash your premium payments have accumulated over the years; (2) use the cash value as a single premium and purchase a reduced amount of paid-up life insurance; or (3) purchase extended term insurance for as long as the single premium will provide.

> **nonforfeiture option:** a provision in some life insurance contracts permitting the policyholder to maintain some insurance coverage in the case of failure to pay the insurance premiums.

POLICY REINSTATEMENT

Every life insurance policy must include a reinstatement provision, which allows policyholders to put a lapsed policy back into effect if they can demonstrate that they are still healthy and insurable. This provision requires payment of accumulated premiums plus interest. The policyholder must also apply for reinstatement within a specified time period, usually less than one year.

POLICY LOANS

As pointed out earlier, policy loans are available on all life insurance policies that have accumulated a cash value reserve. Policy loans fall into two general categories: request loans and automatic premium loans.

The request loan permits the policyholder to borrow on request an amount of money approximately equal to the cash value of the policy. Interest is charged on the loan at a rate specified in the policy. There is no obligation to repay the loan or the interest since the loan and interest charges are secured by the cash value of the policy. If the loan is not repaid when you die, the outstanding amount is deducted from the death benefits.

The automatic premium loan authorizes the insurance company to withdraw money from the policy's cash reserve to pay the premium if it is unpaid at the end of the grace period—which is usually one month after the policy's due date. Most companies continue to do this for as long as the cash value meets the premium cost plus unpaid interest. When your cash reserve is exhausted, the company terminates the policy.

CHANGE OF POLICY

Insurance companies are required to adjust your policy at your request in the following ways:

1. You can purchase paid-up insurance with your policy's accumulated cash value. This will leave you with a smaller policy than you originally had but with no more premiums to pay.

2. You can convert your cash value into single-payment extended term insurance for the same face value as your original policy. The policy will remain in effect only as long as the cash value can pay for it.

3. You can convert an endowment or a limited-payment life policy to a straight life policy. This move will reduce your premiums since straight life is less expensive than these other forms of insurance.

4. You can also make the opposite switch and convert a straight life policy to an endowment or limited-payment life plan. In both cases, the insurance company will adjust the premiums you have paid to make them consistent with your new coverage.

SHOPPING FOR RATES

Life insurance is like any other consumer product; some companies sell it for much more than others. When you begin shopping around for the cheapest policy, you may find that some companies charge 100 percent more than others for the same insurance coverage.

In order to secure the best buy for your insurance dollar, the following guidelines are suggested:

1. Always compare prices. Resist buying from the first agent you talk to—even if he or she sounds convincing.

2. Don't assume that a company that offers you the best price on one policy will offer you the best price on all policies. Some companies, for example,

Mail-Order Life Insurance: Is It a Bargain?

There in the mailbox with bills, local advertising circulars, and this week's copy of *Sports Illustrated* is the offer that sounds almost too good to be true: $25 a year for a $10,000 life insurance policy. A check of your current policy reveals that you are paying $43 in premiums for your $5,000 policy. Have you found the answer to the life insurance selection dilemma?

Maybe . . . and maybe not. Just as the used-car buyer checks more than the asking price, so the life insurance shopper should check to make certain that the policy conditions and restrictions are the same before simply choosing the lowest-priced policy. A casual reading of the advertisement is likely to reveal that the mail-order company is offering term insurance and that the maximum coverage is relatively low. However, the mail-order insurance claims to be lower-priced because no commissions are paid to individual agents. The editors of *Changing Times* make the following recommendations for adding up the pros and cons of mail-order life insurance:

You can't bank on mail-order insurance being a bargain merely because no agent commission is involved.

The insurance companies set premium rates on the basis of sales costs as well as actuarial considerations. Only 1% to 2% of the people solicited by mail may actually buy the insurance, and that is often regarded as a good return. Therefore, the rates have to take into account the costs of mailing to the other 99% or 98% who fail to respond to the first solicitation. . . .

The lack of premium and other guarantees in many mail-order policies indicates that it is best to regard them as a supplement to your individual insurance, not as the core of a family protection program.

Plans for which there are no medical qualifications must be hedged and priced to cover the additional risks the companies assume, so there is no point in buying that kind of policy until you're sure you need it. Try first to obtain regular insurance, either by mail or through agents, at standard premiums.

Source: Quotation from "Is Mail-Order Life Insurance a Bargain?" excerpted with permission from *Changing Times*, November 1980, p. 44, © Kiplinger Washington Editors, Inc., 1980.

---

offer the best value on policies for young people; others offer special rates for large policies. Always compare prices when you add to your insurance coverage.

3. If you live in one of the 17 northeastern states offering Savings Bank Life Insurance, investigate its rates. It is generally lower-priced than comparable insurance company policies.

4. Find out about group life insurance. Check with the administrator of any club, union, or professional or fraternal organization to which you belong to learn about their low-cost group term insurance.

5. If you were employed in a dangerous occupation when you purchased your policy but have now changed the nature of your work, inform your insurance company and ask for a risk reclassification. It may save you a lot of money in premiums.

6. Similarly, if you were in poor health when you purchased a policy and your health has improved, ask to have your policy reviewed. You may be able to reduce or eliminate high-risk premiums.

THE LIFE INSURANCE BUYER'S GUIDE

In an attempt to assist insurance purchasers in making objective comparisons of alternative insurance offerings, the National Association of Insurance Commissioners (NAIC), an association of state insurance regulatory officials that aids the various state insurance departments in coordinating insurance laws for the benefit of all consumers, developed a model *Life Insurance Buyer's Guide*. Its major purpose is to provide consumers with the information they need in order to choose the most appropriate life insurance plan for their needs and to evaluate and compare the costs of similar life insurance plans. A copy of the *Guide* is available from most insurance agents.

INSURANCE COST INDEXES

The *Life Insurance Buyer's Guide* uses two types of index numbers: the surrender cost index and the net payment cost index.

The surrender cost index is useful if you consider the level of the cash value to be of primary importance to you. It helps you compare costs if at some future point in time, say, in 10 or 20 years, you were to surrender the policy and take its cash value.

The net payment cost index is useful if your main concern is the benefits that are to be paid at your death and if the level of cash value is of secondary importance. It helps you compare costs at some future point in time if you continue paying premiums on your policy and do not take its cash value.

The most important thing to remember when using cost indexes is that a policy with a low index number is generally a better buy than a comparable policy with a higher index number. The following rules are also important:

1. Cost comparisons should be made only between similar life insurance plans. Similar plans are those that provide essentially the same basic benefits and require premium payments for approximately the same period of time. The closer policies are to being identical, the more reliable the cost comparisons will be.

2. Compare index numbers only for the kind of policy, for your age, and for the amount you intend to buy. Since no single company offers the lowest cost for *all* types of insurance at *all* ages and for *all* amounts of insurance, it is important that you get the indexes for the actual policy, age, and amount you intend to buy. Just because a shopper's guide tells you that one company's policy is a good buy for a particular age and amount, you should not assume that all of that company's policies are equally good buys.

3. Small differences in index numbers may be offset by other policy features or by differences in the quality of service you may expect from the

Figure 12-8
SAMPLE POLICY SUMMARY

```
                    METROPOLITAN LIFE INSURANCE COMPANY
                            EASTERN HEAD OFFICE
                    P.O. BOX 833 MADISON SQUARE STATION
                            NEW YORK, N.Y. 10010

INSURED         JOHN DOE                    NONSMOKER    CLASSIFICATION

AGE AND SEX     25 - MALE                                AMOUNT ON
                                            $50,000      INSURANCE
POLICY NUMBER   000000000A

BASIC POLICY    WHOLE LIFE

GUARANTEED DEATH BENEFIT
    BASIC POLICY    $50,000

ANNUAL PREMIUM              FULL YEARS
                            PAYABLE
BASIC POLICY        $462.00 LIFETIME

        END OF      GUARANTEED      TERMINAL        ANNUAL
      POLICY YEAR   CASH VALUE      DIVIDEND*       DIVIDEND*- CASH
          1           $0.00           $0.00           $0.00
          2           $0.00           $0.00          $21.00
          3          $50.00           $0.00          $25.50
          4         $400.00           $0.00          $31.00
          5         $850.00           $0.00          $37.00
         10       $3,600.00           $0.00          $86.00
         20      $11,050.00         $800.00         $392.50
   AT AGE 65     $27,250.00       $1,750.00       $1,298.50

INTEREST-ADJUSTED (5%) INDEXES PER $1,000:   FOR 10 YEARS    FOR 20 YEARS
LIFE INSURANCE SURRENDER COST INDEX*            $3.03           $0.43
LIFE INSURANCE NET PAYMENT COST INDEX*          $8.48           $7.26
EQUIVALENT LEVEL ANNUAL DIVIDEND*               $0.76           $1.98

FOR POLICY LOANS, THE CURRENT INTEREST RATE IS 11.0% PAYABLE AT THE
END OF THE POLICY YEAR, SUBJECT TO CHANGE ON EACH POLICY ANNIVERSARY BUT
NOT TO EXCEED THE MAXIMUM PERMITTED BY LAW.  SUCH MAXIMUM IS BASED ON
WOODY'S CORPORATE BOND YIELDS - MONTHLY AVERAGE.

BASED ON CURRENT DIVIDEND SCALE - NOT A GUARANTEE OR ESTIMATE FOR THE FUTURE.
 EXPLANATION OF THE INTENDED USE OF THE INDEXES AND THE EQUIVALENT LEVEL
ANNUAL DIVIDEND IS INCLUDED IN THE LIFE INSURANCE BUYER'S GUIDE.

PREPARED 05/09/83
```

Source: Courtesy of Metropolitan Life Insurance Company.

company or its agent. Therefore, when you find only small differences in cost indexes, your choice should be based on something other than cost.

4. In any event, you should base your purchase decision on more than a low index number. Be sure that you can afford the premiums and that you

understand the plan's cash values, dividends, and death benefits. You should also make a judgment on how well the life insurance company or agent will provide service to you as a policyholder.

5. These life insurance cost indexes apply to new policies and should not be used to determine whether you should drop a policy you have already owned for a while in favor of a new one. If such a replacement is suggested, you should ask for information from the company that issued the old policy before you take action.

Figure 12-8 is a sample policy from Metropolitan Life Insurance Company. It provides these cost comparisons in tabular form. If your state has adopted the NAIC model, you will receive both the *Buyer's Guide* and the policy summary when you make your purchase.

SUMMARY

Life insurance may be purchased for a number of reasons: to provide cash for immediate needs following the death of the insured, to readjust funds, and to replace income. The three major types of life insurance are term, whole life, and endowment. There are several variations, including credit life, industrial life, group life, variable life, and universal life. The main differences among the policies lie in their relative emphasis on protection and savings. Term insurance stresses pure protection, while whole life and endowment insurance offer both protection and savings elements.

The life insurance contract typically stipulates the beneficiaries, settlement options, premium payments, and dividend options (where applicable). Additional provisions cover accidental death, suicide, the waiver of premiums, guaranteed insurability, and nonforfeiture options. Also usually included are provisions for policy loans, policy reinstatement, and policy changes.

Comparison shopping is important in purchasing life insurance. The *Life Insurance Buyer's Guide,* with its comparative index, attempts to simplify the policy comparison process by providing quantitative data on alternative insurance offerings. These data are available for insurance purchasers in many states.

REVIEW QUESTIONS

1. Briefly define the following terms:
    life insurance
    term insurance
    decreasing term insurance
    deposit term insurance
    whole life insurance
    straight life insurance
    cash value
    policy loan
    limited-payment whole life insurance
    endowment insurance
    credit life insurance
    industrial life insurance
    group life insurance
    variable life insurance
    universal life insurance
    beneficiary
    primary beneficiary
    contingent beneficiaries
    accidental death clause
    suicide clause
    waiver-of-premium clause
    guaranteed insurability clause
    nonforfeiture option

2. List several reasons why an individual might need life insurance.

3. Distinguish between whole life and term insurance.

4. What are the primary purposes of endowment insurance? How is it different from limited-payment whole life insurance?

5. Classify the following types of insurance as either term or whole life:

   a. credit life insurance
   b. industrial life insurance
   c. group life insurance
   d. variable life insurance
   e. universal life insurance

6. In what ways is universal life insurance different from term insurance?

7. Identify the major provisions of the life insurance contract.

8. Why should a life insurance purchaser choose policies containing a waiver-of-premium clause and a guaranteed insurability clause?

9. Explain the choices available to policyholders whose insurance policies contain a nonforfeiture option.

10. How should you use insurance cost indexes in shopping for the best insurance rates?

CASES AND EXERCISES

1. Develop an argument supporting whole life insurance in contrast to term insurance.

2. Alice McWilliams is 25, single, and employed at a local utility company, where she earns $19,500 a year. How would you go about convincing her that she needs life insurance? Make any assumptions necessary.

3. Suggest appropriate insurance coverage—both type and amount—for the following individuals:

   a. 30-year-old divorced working mother with a nine-year-old son.
   b. 25-year-old newly married husband in a two-income household.
   c. 24-year-old newly married wife in a two-income household.
   d. 50-year-old widower with two married children.

4. Make suggestions for a new-car purchaser if he or she is required by the lender to purchase credit life insurance.

5. A highly publicized form of life insurance in recent years is universal life insurance. What features does it possess that represent improvements over traditional term and whole life insurance policies?

ANSWERS TO PERSONAL FINANCE I.Q. TEST

1. Fiction. 2. Fact. 3. Fiction. 4. Fiction. 5. Fact. 6. Fiction. 7. Fiction.

HOW LUIS SANCHEZ REACHED HIS PERSONAL FINANCIAL DECISION

Professor Bohn offered Luis a glass of orange juice and the following advice: Never buy a financial product until you understand it—making sure it fits your needs not the agent's. The primary purpose of personal life insurance is to provide needed money for one's survivors should the insured die unexpectedly. Secondarily, it can also work as a savings mechanism.

Professor Bohn stressed that Luis should answer the following key questions before buying life insurance:

1. How much would his survivors need to replace his income-producing ability and pay for expenses incurred resulting from his death?

2. How much can he/they afford to pay in premiums?

3. Is he concerned about future insurability?

4. Does he want to include a "savings" feature within the policy?

5. What kind of life insurance product would best fulfill Luis' needs?

6. To what extent do his survivors want to assume the risk of his dying versus transferring that risk (for a cost) to an insurance company?

7. Which quality company can provide the most competitive premium cost for the amount of insurance needed?

"Although it is important to look toward the future," Professor Bohn added, "you shouldn't go overboard and purchase a plan that may be more than you need. A whole life policy offers some advantages, but it can be expensive for someone who is just starting out. If you decide to buy insurance, a term policy might be better for you to begin with. It would be cheaper and could suffice until you enter the work force and you and Rosa are better able to determine your family needs."

Professor Bohn went on to say that Luis, his parents, and his fiancé may conclude that the current coverage on Luis in the parents' family life insurance plan would suffice until he marries and has children. Until Luis and Rosa have children, Rosa would have sufficient flexibility in being able to provide for her financial needs should Luis die unexpectedly. The probability of a 20-year-old dying during the year is only *1.9* in *1,000.*

LEARNING OBJECTIVES

1. To discuss the size and complexity of the health care industry. / 2. To explain why health care protection is an important aspect of personal financial planning. / 3. To identify the major types of health insurance coverage. / 4. To describe the various types of health care protection plans that are available. / 5. To show how to develop a personal health care protection plan.

TESTING YOUR PERSONAL FINANCE I.Q.

	FACT	FICTION
1. The United States is one of only two industrialized nations without a national health care protection program.	☐	☐
2. Harriet Agnew's face-lift would be covered under most health insurance programs.	☐	☐
3. A 20-year-old full-time college student is probably insurable under his or her parent's group health insurance.	☐	☐
4. About 10 percent of the U.S. gross national product is spent on medical care.	☐	☐
5. Over 10 million people belong to health maintenance organizations.	☐	☐
6. A good health care program sets disability income at 110 percent of regular income because of the additional costs involved when a person suffers a serious accident or illness.	☐	☐
7. About 70 percent of the U.S. population now has dental insurance.	☐	☐

The materials in this chapter assist in separating fact from fiction. Your answers can be checked on page 388.

CHAPTER THIRTEEN

HEALTH CARE PROTECTION

SHARING A PERSONAL FINANCIAL DECISION WITH
PROFESSOR GREGORY J. WOROSZ OF SCHOOLCRAFT COLLEGE

Professor Gregory Worosz wanted to bring his lecture on health insurance home to his personal finance students. He began by posing the following question to the class: "I know we all like to think nothing will happen to us. But let's suppose that after class today you're left so deep in thought by my lecture that you forget to look where you're going. You trip and fall down the stairs, breaking your arm. Doctor, hospital, and X-ray costs would be high. How would you pay for this? Do you have health insurance?"

Professor Worosz wasn't surprised to find out that a number of students didn't know if they had health insurance. They might still be covered on their parents' policy, but they weren't sure. Amy Shore raised the question directly, "Aren't students automatically covered by their parents' policy? Is there something else I need to check into?"

If you were Professor Worosz, how would you answer Amy?

To find out how Professor Worosz helped Amy answer her personal financial question, turn to page 389.

"How much health care Americans get should depend not on how much they can afford but on how much they need."
Senator Edward Kennedy[1]

H ealth care has come a long way. Consider these recent examples:
- Patient #1 underwent surgery, radiation, and hyperthermia for treatment of cancer.
- Patient #2 was put on dialysis to treat kidney disease.
- Patient #3 had cataracts removed from his eyes.
- Patient #4 received a pacemaker to allow her to lead a normal life.

Just a few years ago, the common treatment for these ills was a fatal dose of the drug Nembutal. Who were these patients? A cat, a dog, a mockingbird, and a tiger, respectively!

Yes, veterinary medicine has come a long way. It has borrowed from many of the medical advances developed for human beings. Although many of these treatments are quite expensive—the cost of the kidney dialysis comes to some $3,500—many pet owners seem to think the treatment is worth it. A poll by a Philadelphia veterinarian indicated that 19 of 20 cat owners were glad that cancer therapy had prolonged their pets' lives. And perhaps there are some hidden benefits for pet owners. For instance, research has shown that heart attack patients who adopt pets have higher survival rates than those who do not.[2]

This chapter deals with the health care of a unique animal species—human beings. The increasing cost of health care makes health care protection a significant consideration in personal financial planning.

THE HEALTH CARE INDUSTRY

There is no mistaking it. Health care in the United States is a big and very expensive business.
- Health care costs American consumers about $1 billion a day, or 10.5 percent of our gross national product.
- Health care costs are expected to climb to $1 trillion annually by 1993.
- Per capita health care expenditures are now $1,365 annually.[3]

But these statistics say nothing about the personal anguish that goes with illness—an anguish intensified by the enormous cost of health care. A hernia

Table 13-1
THE HIGH COST OF MEDICAL CARE

Type of Operation	City			
	New York	Chicago	Los Angeles	Dallas
Triple coronary bypass	$20,740	$19,048	$17,613	$12,715
Total colectomy	15,212	13,602	12,928	8,094
Radical hysterectomy	13,514	11,518	11,459	7,097
Radical mastectomy	8,523	6,943	6,880	4,122
Gall bladder removal	8,368	7,436	7,241	4,350
Appendectomy	5,320	4,357	4,591	2,718
Hemorrhoidectomy	4,390	3,777	3,651	2,183
Inguinal hernia	3,632	2,886	3,187	2,026

Source: "Evaluating Your Medical Benefits," Business Week, August 30, 1982, p. 89. Data from Prudential Insurance Company.

operation in Dallas may cost $2,026; an appendectomy in Los Angeles, $4,591; and a triple coronary bypass in New York $20,740 (see Table 13-1).

The need for health care is widely recognized in the United States, and yet approximately 45 million Americans have inadequate health insurance or none at all.[4] This group includes many younger Americans, those in the 18- to 24-year-old age group. Many young people simply deny their own need for adequate insurance coverage. But it is important to remember that facing the risk of illness, injury, or disability without adequate insurance protection can lead to personal financial disaster as well as to inferior and inadequate health care. Today's immense health care industry requires a comprehensive insurance package.

TYPES OF HEALTH INSURANCE COVERAGE

Health insurance coverage falls into two basic categories: medical expense insurance and disability income insurance.[5] *Medical expense insurance* reimburses the insured or the service provider (the hospital or physician, for example) for almost all expenses connected with hospitalization and medical care for an illness or accident, including hospital expenses, surgery costs, physicians' charges, and the like. Insurance companies have offered this form of insurance since about 1930. The earliest medical expense insurance policies covered hospital expenses alone. Coverage was later expanded to include surgical and medical expenses. *Disability income insurance*, on the other hand, provides a regular income replacement when a wage earner cannot work due to illness or injury.

medical expense insurance: health insurance that reimburses hospital expenses, surgical expenses, physician expenses, and the like.

disability income insurance: health insurance that provides a regular income replacement when a wage earner cannot work due to illness or injury.

BASIC HEALTH INSURANCE COVERAGE

Coverage for hospital, surgical, and physicians' expenses forms the basic health insurance package. Insurance for these charges is almost always purchased together.

Hospital Expenses. Hospital expense insurance has expanded significantly in recent years, largely because of the high cost of hospital bills. The average national cost for a single day in a semiprivate hospital room is $185. This represents a 76-percent increase over a five-year period.[6] A state-by-state comparison of hospital costs is shown in Table 13-2.

To protect you against skyrocketing costs, hospital expense insurance offers a daily room benefit and a miscellaneous hospital expense benefit. The daily room benefit pays the entire hospital bill for room, board, nursing care, and other related charges. It does not, however, pay for examination or treatment by physicians. Under an *indemnity plan,* the payment of hospital expenses is expressed in terms of the maximum allowable amount for each day of hospitalization up to a maximum number of days. A *service plan,* on the other hand, covers the fee for a semiprivate hospital room for a maximum number of days without reference to the actual cost of the room.[7]

In the first case, a health insurance contract specifies the maximum daily benefit—say, $200. The insurance carrier will pay the actual hospital bill up to this stated maximum, and the insured person must pay any expenses exceeding this amount. The second form of expense reimbursement is identified with Blue Cross/Blue Shield, but it is also used by other major insurance carriers. Depending on the contract, 21 to 365 days of semiprivate hospital room care is covered regardless of the actual expense.

The miscellaneous hospital expense benefit covers fees for X-rays, drugs, laboratory tests, and special treatments incurred during a hospital stay. These may be paid either according to a schedule of payments for each service or on a blanket basis with a limit for each hospitalization. According to a schedule of payments, the fee for X-rays, for example, is paid up to one maximum and that for, say, drugs is paid up to another. According to the blanket method, there is simply a set maximum paid for all services.

Surgical expenses. Surgical expense insurance pays all or part of the cost of surgical procedures, whether they are accident- or illness-related, although cosmetic surgery is usually excluded. Since it does not cover other expenses incurred during a hospital stay, it is usually sold in combination with hospital expense insurance. Surgical expense insurance also pays for the administering of anesthesia during an operation. Benefits are paid according to a fee schedule for different types of operations or up to the "reasonable and customary" charge that is defined for each procedure.

---

indemnity plan: hospital expense insurance that sets a maximum allowable daily amount and number of days of hospitalization.

service plan: hospital expense insurance that sets only the number of days of hospitalization, not the daily charge.

Table 13-2
HOSPITAL COSTS STATE BY STATE

It takes $185 on average to stay a day in a semiprivate hospital room—and that doesn't include drugs, tests and doctors' bills.

The hospital figure, reported by the Health Insurance Association of America, is 76 percent more than the $105 daily average that was reported as recently as 1978. Consumer prices in the five-year period went up 57 percent.

Highest average room rates are in hospitals in the West and the Northeast, as seen here—

State	1-Day Cost	5-Year Increase	State	1-Day Cost	5-Year Increase
California	$248	87.9%	Arizona	$163	83.1%
Alaska	$219	37.7%	Indiana	$163	85.2%
Michigan	$219	68.5%	Utah	$162	70.5%
Illinois	$218	77.2%	Minnesota	$161	87.2%
Pennsylvania	$215	100.9%	Kansas	$160	95.1%
Hawaii	$205	97.1%	Iowa	$157	82.6%
New York	$205	45.4%	Florida	$156	71.4%
Oregon	$203	88.0%	Wisconsin	$156	81.4%
Nevada	$198	85.0%	West Virginia	$153	77.9%
Massachusetts	$197	57.6%	South Dakota	$149	104.1%
Washington	$195	87.5%	Oklahoma	$148	85.0%
Delaware	$190	108.8%	Virginia	$148	76.2%
Vermont	$189	85.3%	Wyoming	$146	82.5%
Maine	$188	82.5%	Nebraska	$144	75.6%
Colorado	$187	92.8%	Kentucky	$142	84.4%
Ohio	$187	64.0%	Alabama	$141	78.5%
U.S. average	**$185**	**76.2%**	North Dakota	$139	71.6%
Connecticut	$184	64.3%	Louisiana	$136	86.3%
New Hampshire	$183	79.4%	Texas	$133	70.5%
Rhode Island	$182	51.7%	Arkansas	$128	88.2%
New Mexico	$173	88.0%	Georgia	$128	60.0%
Idaho	$169	92.0%	North Carolina	$127	81.4%
Montana	$169	89.9%	Tennessee	$124	67.6%
Maryland	$166	66.0%	South Carolina	$121	86.2%
New Jersey	$166	38.3%	Mississippi	$101	77.2%
Missouri	$165	96.4%			

Note: In some states, hospitals in 1983 survey varied from those sampled in 1978.

Source: "Hospital Costs State by State." Reprinted from *U.S. News & World Report*, October 24, 1983, p. 13; Copyright 1983 U.S. News & World Report, Inc.

Physician Expenses. Physician expense insurance pays doctors' bills for nonsurgical care in a hospital, at home, or in a doctor's office. It may cover diagnostic X-ray and laboratory expenses. Physician expense insurance specifies the maximum fees allowed for various services. It may also limit benefits for in-hospital physician visits to a specific number.

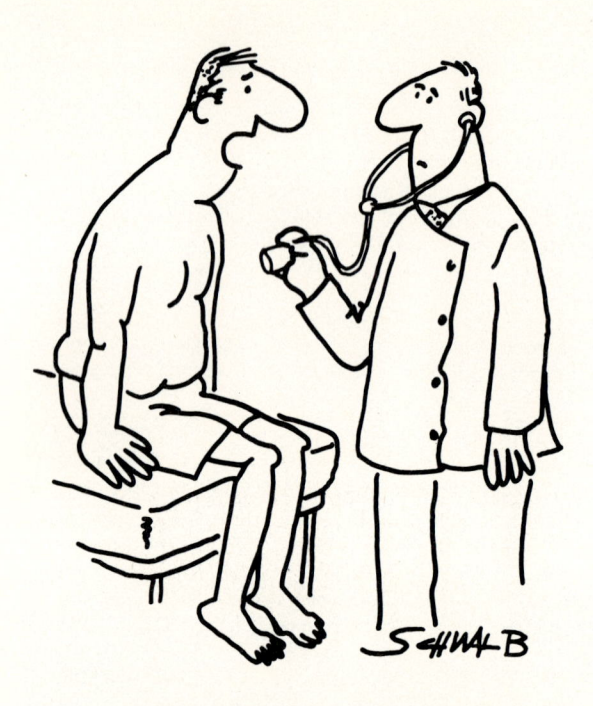

*"Why shouldn't I live on borrowed time?
Everything else I live on is borrowed!"*

Personal Financial Considerations Even Find Their Way into the Physician's Office.
Source: From the Wall Street Journal—Permission, Cartoon Features Syndicate.

MAJOR MEDICAL EXPENSE INSURANCE

Major medical expense insurance supplements basic health insurance by insuring against large health care expenses brought about by extended illness or serious injury. Maximum benefit coverage ranges from $10,000 to unlimited coverage.

Coverage. Major medical insurance covers most health care expenses in or out of the hospital, including hospital room charges; drugs and medications; doctors' bills for surgery and medical care; nursing services; artificial limbs and devices; rehabilitation; and ambulance service. With such a wide range of benefits and high coverage, major medical insurance would be unaffordable were it not for two policy features: the deductible and coinsurance.

The Deductible. The *deductible provision* requires that the policyholder pay a specified amount of medical expenses before the major medical coverage begins. An individual insurance policy may require the insured to pay the first

---

major medical expense insurance: a supplement to basic health care coverage.

deductible provision: an insurance clause that requires the insured to pay a specific amount of medical expenses before the insurance carrier pays anything.

> ### Hospice—Another Health Insurance Benefit?
>
> General Electric, RCA, and Westinghouse are among the firms offering *hospice programs*. These plans provide medical care for the terminally ill either at home or in a hospital-like setting. Sometimes these programs cover family bereavement counseling. Proponents of hospice programs argue that they save money when compared to hospitalization of the terminally ill. But so far our experience is limited. At General Electric, only seven of the 750,000 people eligible for hospice care used the benefit during a recent year.
>
> Source: Joann S. Lubin, "Labor Letter," *Wall Street Journal*, November 3, 1981, p. 1.

amounts. This provision limits the policy's benefits only to large, "major" medical expenses so that in effect the policy provides benefits only after the person's basic coverage is exhausted.

The lower the deductible, the higher the major medical insurance premiums. A policy with a $100 deductible will be far more expensive than one with a $2,500 deductible. Low deductibles make sense only if a person has no other coverage.

Coinsurance. The second policy feature that keeps down the cost of major medical coverage is *coinsurance*. Under this provision, the insured must pay a portion of the medical expenses above the deductible amount. This portion is usually 20 or 25 percent of the covered major medical expenses. Premiums are also affected by the amount of coinsurance chosen. The higher the coinsurance feature, the lower the premiums. Thus, a 75–25 arrangement is cheaper than an 80–20 plan.

coinsurance: an insurance policy feature that requires the insured to pay a certain percentage of medical costs above the deductible.

DISABILITY INCOME INSURANCE

A three-month or longer disability before age 65 is likely to occur to a third of Americans who are now 35 years old.[8] Disability income insurance, also known as salary continuation insurance, partially replaces lost income when a wage earner cannot work due to illness or injury.

The first step in assessing how much disability protection you need is the comparison of available income to monthly expenses. The amount of replacement income received under a disability income plan is usually limited to 60 or 70 percent of actual income. Many insurers also set payment ceilings that limit disability benefits to a specific amount no matter what the actual income is. Other disability income might include employee sick leave, union benefits, workers' compensation for job-related injury or illness, and so on. In addition, Social Security's disability coverage starts in the fifth month if the disability will last a year or longer. A person should generally aim for disability income protection equal to 60 to 70 percent of current income. Only this percentage is needed because most disability payments are tax-free.

Initial and Secondary Claims. Most policies divide disability claims into two parts. The *initial claim* defines disability as the inability to perform the duties of a person's occupation and pays benefits from two to five years. The *secondary claim* may remain in effect during your entire life but continues to pay benefits only if you are unable to work at any occupation for which you are reasonably suited by education, experience, and training.

Some policies include a benefit for partial disability, which is defined as the inability to perform one or more but not all job duties. This benefit is usually half of the amount paid for total disability and usually lasts from three to six months.

The Waiting Period. Most disability policies specify that payments will not be made during a *waiting period*, which may range from a week to a year. The waiting period enables insurers to substantially cut the benefits they pay policyholders and maintain manageable premium rates.

Since policies with short waiting periods cost more than those with longer waiting periods, it is important to consider this matter carefully. A person with 60 days of accumulated sick leave does not need a policy with a waiting period of less than 60 days. The extent of personal savings is directly related to the length of time for which you can continue to meet your financial obligations (and so go without disability benefits). It is therefore another important consideration in the selection of a disability policy.

Length of Payment. Disability policies can also be classified as either long-term or short-term. The length of the term determines how long benefits will be paid during the time of disability. Short-term contracts usually pay benefits for up to two years, while long-term policies may extend up to the lifetime of the insured.

Additional Disability Coverage. Life insurance policies typically include a *disability waiver*, sometimes at an additional fee. This provision waives life insurance premiums while a person is disabled. Various other types of disability coverage are available. Some accident policies, for example, pay benefits for loss of a limb or of eyesight.

---

initial claim: disability insurance for a set period of time; it is based on the inability to perform the duties of one's own occupation.

secondary claim: lifetime disability income based on an inability to perform work for which a person is reasonably suited.

waiting period: an interim period of time before disability income protection plans pay.

disability waiver: a life insurance policy feature that waives payment of premiums if the insured is disabled.

DENTAL INSURANCE

One of the most rapidly growing and popular forms of insurance is dental insurance. According to American Dental Association estimates for 1985, 41 percent of the U.S. population has dental coverage.[9]

Dental insurance, which is generally available through group insurance plans, health maintenance organizations, dental services corporations, and labor unions, covers expenses for dental services and supplies. Many employers now offer it as a fringe benefit. Depending on the plan, payments may be made for examinations (including X-rays and cleanings), fillings, extractions, inlays, bridgework, dentures, oral surgery, root-canal therapy, and orthodontics.

Reimbursement Methods. Insurers use various methods to reimburse policyholders for dental care expenses. Some plans pay the customary fee for dental work in a given area. Dentists charge their regular fees, which are verified by the insurer. A deductible is sometimes required. Other plans have a schedule of benefits listing maximum reimbursement limits for each dental service. Still others, referred to as coinsurance, or copayment, plans, require the patient to pay part of the bill.

Dental insurance encourages people to see a dentist regularly and exercise good preventive care. Regular checkups and cleanings usually cost patients little or nothing. Insurance companies benefit as well. By taking care of small dental problems before they become expensive procedures, future insurance claims are significantly reduced. For example, Seattle University's dental plan with Minneapolis-based Northwestern National Life Insurance Company pays 100 percent of all preventive and diagnostic treatments. However, employees must pay 20 percent of the cost for basic dental treatment like fillings, and half for major treatment like bridges and crowns.

A Valuable Fringe Benefit. For many millions of Americans dental insurance is a fringe benefit paid in full or in part by their employers. After the United Auto Workers won a breakthrough dental agreement in 1974, other unions quickly sought similar benefits.

With tooth decay affecting 95 percent of all Americans who still have their teeth and with more than half of all adults losing their teeth by age 65, dental insurance is a very valuable fringe benefit. However, some experts note that dental insurance may not be cost-effective if it is bought by individuals.

Health care protection is available through several means. These various insurance plans are discussed next.

HEALTH CARE PROTECTION PLANS

Two major sources of health care protection plans are private insurance companies and Blue Cross/Blue Shield, which offers both individual and group health care protection. Health maintenance organizations* also provide comprehensive health care services for their members, and Social Security and workers' compensation provide assistance to eligible individuals with health

*fastest growing

care needs. There are many different health care plans, so it is important to distinguish the plans and their features.

PRIVATE INSURANCE COMPANIES AND BLUE CROSS/BLUE SHIELD

Many private insurance companies offer medical insurance, both to individuals and to groups, such as the employees of a specific firm. By contrast, *Blue Cross* and *Blue Shield* associations are not insurance companies in a technical sense. Rather, they are non-profit hospital, surgical, and medical expense plans between groups of individuals who desire such coverage and hospitals and physicians who agree to provide these services in return for a prepaid fee. The associations are producer cooperatives, with Blue Cross paying hospital expenses—and sometimes out-patient and in-home costs—and Blue Shield providing prepaid surgical and medical services. The approximately 70 Blue Cross/Blue Shield plans currently in operation provide health care protection for almost 40 percent of the households in the United States.

Blue Cross/Blue Shield coverage differs from that offered by private insurance companies in two important ways. First, Blue Cross provides hospital benefits on a service basis. That is, each Blue Cross plan reimburses member hospitals (not all hospitals are Blue Cross–affiliated) for services the insured received during hospitalization. A Blue Cross subscriber is entitled to spend a specified number of days in certain facilities in a member hospital. Private insurance companies, on the other hand, often set a maximum amount for the cost of the hospital room or a fixed number of dollars for each day of hospitalization.

Second, Blue Cross plans pay benefits directly to the hospital, while private insurers reimburse the insured for the hospital cost. The Blue Cross/Blue Shield arrangement may provide advantages over that of the private insurers because it can negotiate with hospitals and medical specialists to determine benefits to subscribers. Thus the Blues—as Blue Cross and Blue Shield are often called—are able to use their subscribers' money more efficiently: they pay 85 to 90 percent of every premium dollar in benefits, while private, profit-making insurers pay only 60 to 70 percent.[10]

INDIVIDUAL HEALTH COVERAGE

Individual health coverage can be obtained from either Blue Cross/Blue Shield or private insurance companies. Purchasing an individual health policy is a complex process and requires comparative shopping because prices and coverage vary widely.

Individual health policies differ in one important aspect from the group policies provided by employers. Applicants must show evidence of insurability. Existing medical problems may cause the insurer to reject the application, charge higher rates, or exclude the existing problem from coverage.

Blue Cross/Blue Shield: non-profit, prepaid hospital expense and surgical and medical service plan.

Blue Cross/Blue Shield plans offer non-profit arrangements between people seeking hospital, surgical, or medical coverage and hospitals and physicians who provide these services for a prepaid fee.

GROUP HEALTH INSURANCE

Group health insurance became popular during the 1930s and 1940s when employee fringe benefits took on new importance. Forbidden by law from getting raises during the World War II wage freeze, employees received valuable group health insurance protection instead. Group health insurance became a legitimate force in labor–management negotiations when in 1947 the National Labor Relations Board declared that employers must put this issue on the bargaining table when unions requested it. Today, workers who receive their health insurance benefits on the job make up the largest single category covered by group health insurance. Group health insurance is also available through unions, fraternal and professional societies, and other organizations. Group policies include basic coverage, major medical, and disability insurance. They are offered by both private insurance companies and Blue Cross/Blue Shield.

Many employers pay the total premium bill for their employees' health care coverage, while others pay part of the bill and ask their employees to pay the difference. A major advantage is that group plans offer lower-cost and more comprehensive coverage than individual plans. And for many people who have medical problems, a group plan is the only kind of health insurance available. Unlike individual health insurance plans, previous medical problems usually do not preclude one's participation in a group policy.

Two features of group coverage are particularly important. First, most group policies require a deductible amount set either on an individual or family basis. Thus, the insured has to pay a modest portion of his or her medical expenses each year. A second significant feature is the *conversion privilege*. Although job termination for whatever reason ends group coverage, usually in about 30 days, insurance carriers are required to offer the former employee an individual plan. This offer is the conversion privilege. However, it should be noted that such conversion plans usually offer fewer benefits than does the former group insurance.

group health insurance: medical insurance available through employers, unions, professional societies, and the like.

conversion privilege: a requirement that insurance carriers offer former employees an individual policy if they lose their group insurance.

HEALTH MAINTENANCE ORGANIZATIONS

An innovative type of health care protection plan is the *health maintenance organization (HMO)* which, in exchange for a flat fee each year, provides most of the medical care you need, including hospitalization. In 1984, there were approximately 280 HMOs serving 12 million subscribers.[11]

As the name implies, health maintenance organizations emphasize preventive medical care. No matter how many doctor visits, hospital admissions, or surgical procedures a member incurs, the HMO still receives the same fee, so it is in the organization's best interest to keep the insured healthy. Regular medical checkups and immunizations are available without cost. HMOs stress checkups, health education, avoiding unnecessary operations and tests,

health maintenance organization (HMO): a prepaid medical expense plan that emphasizes preventive medical care.

in toledo "med choice".

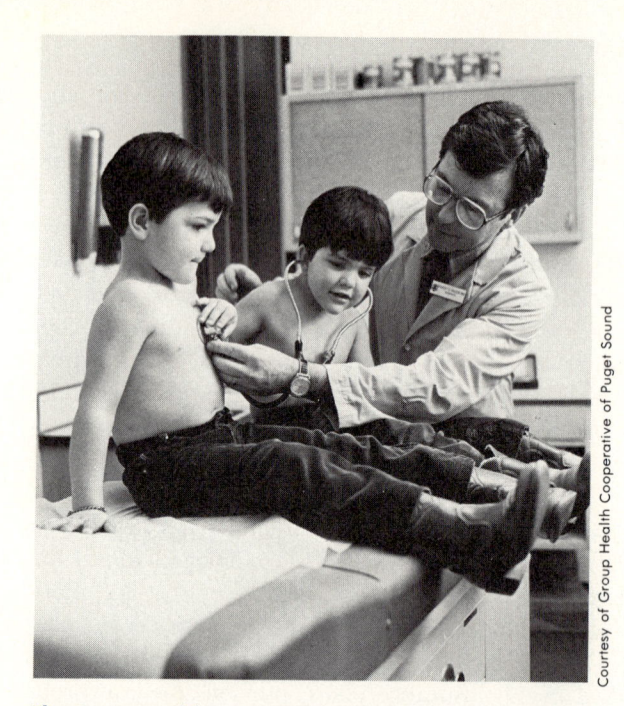

The Group Health Cooperative of Puget Sound, in Seattle, is one of the well-established health maintenance organizations (HMOs) in the United States today. Members of an HMO pay a flat annual fee that covers all of their medical needs, including hospitalization. The HMO emphasizes checkups and other forms of medical care, and it warns its members against unnecessary medications and operations.

and shortened hospital stays. The Health Maintenance Organization of Pennsylvania even offered its members a bonus of $75 a day if they cut short their hospital stay. Designed for patients who are not seriously ill, this program is just one example of how HMOs are working to reduce health care costs.[12]

Studies have shown that these efforts are paying off. The health care bills of HMO members are between 10 and 40 percent lower on an average than those of individuals who use the traditional fee-for-service system. In addition, HMO members use the hospital one-third as often and lose less time from work.[13]

Membership in a health maintenance organization is available on an individual basis or through a group. Companies with 25 or more employees that provide health insurance must offer their employees a choice of joining a qualified HMO if one exists in the area. The Kaiser-Permanente Medical Care Program in California, Group Health of Puget Sound (in Seattle, Washington), and the Health Insurance Plan of New York are some of the well-established HMOs in the United States. The Department of Health and Human Services predicts that by 1988, 442 HMOs will be in operation serving 19 million people and saving more than 20 billion dollars in hospital costs alone.[14]

SOCIAL SECURITY

Social Security—the social insurance system in the United States—is the subject of Chapter 19. But it is important to note here that Social Security provides three important health care protection plans: disability income, Medicare, and Medicaid.

Social Security: *the social insurance scheme in the United States.*

Social Security Disability Income. Insured workers who face a long-term disability can receive *Social Security disability income*. Protection is also available to the disabled worker's children and spouse, as well as to widows and widowers. The Social Security system provides considerable benefits and plays a critical role in a person's overall health care protection plan. Details of eligibility, coverage, benefits, and the like are provided in Chapter 19.

Social Security disability income: *replacement income paid to insured workers with a long-term disability.*

Medicare. A federal health insurance program designed to protect elderly and severely disabled Americans, *Medicare* is available to practically everyone who is 65 or older. It also covers disabled people under 65 who have been entitled to Social Security benefits for at least 24 months and individuals suffering from kidney disease who must have regular dialysis treatments or a kidney transplant.

The Medicare program has two parts: Part A covers inpatient hospital care plus certain follow-up care. Part B helps pay doctors' bills, outpatient hospital charges, and the cost of other services not covered under Part A. There is no fee for Medicare's Part A coverage, but there are deductible and coinsurance charges. There is a modest fee for Part B, but the benefits of this medical insurance are so extensive that most people elect to join the program.[15]

Part A Medicare enrollment is automatic for everyone receiving Social Security retirement or dependent's benefits. But you must notify the Social Security Administration if Part B coverage is desired. People who work past 65 are also eligible for both parts of Medicare.

Medicare: *a federal health insurance program designed to protect elderly and disabled Americans.*

Medicaid. In 1965 *Medicaid* became part of the Social Security program; it provides medical assistance for certain low-income individuals and families. Those who receive Aid to Families with Dependent Children and supplemental security income are also eligible for Medicaid. In addition, individual states may also provide Medicaid to those individuals who can meet their daily living expenses but cannot pay for the cost of medical care.

The disabled and elderly who are also covered by Medicare make up a disproportionately large segment of those receiving Medicaid. In New York City, for example, 26 percent of the Medicaid money was received by elderly and disabled individuals with supplemental security income although they represented only 19 percent of all Medicaid recipients. In addition, 36 percent of the funds went to nursing home care for fewer than 4 percent of the total Medicaid population.[16]

Medicaid: *a federal medical assistance program for low-income Americans.*

The Cost Containment Issue. Many senior adults complain that the government-sponsored Medicare program provides inadequate health care protection. It is true that the elderly must pay about 20 percent of their income for health care—the same as they paid before Medicare was established. The villain is runaway health care costs. As a result, cost containment has become a major issue in the health care field. In the meantime, private insurers are offering so-called Medigap policies that cover the expenses not covered by Medicare. Consumers who elect to purchase such coverage need only one Medigap policy.

The Prospective Payment System. As of October 1, 1983, the federal government set fixed prices for hospital payments under the Medicare program. This prospective payment system sets allowable charges for 468 "diagnostic-related groups" (DRGs). The schedule of fees accounts for regional differences in the cost of health care. Costs in excess of the prospective payment must be absorbed by the hospital, but health care facilities are allowed to keep any cost savings. In short, the system rewards cost-effective hospital care.[17]

WORKERS' COMPENSATION INSURANCE

Every year over 12,000 Americans are killed on the job and about 2.1 million others suffer injuries.[18] Worker injuries and death are especially common in longshoring, coal mining, roofing, sheet-metal working, meat processing, mobile home manufacturing, lumbering, wood-products manufacturing, and construction.[19]

In order to protect workers and their families from losses due to on-the-job injuries, illnesses, and deaths, all 50 state governments have passed *workers' compensation insurance* laws. These benefits are provided through private insurance, self-insurance, and state insurance funds and cost employers between 1 and 3 percent of their payroll.

Nearly all employees are covered by workers' compensation, but the exclusions vary from state to state. All programs except those for federal employees, coal miners, harbor workers, and longshoremen are administered by the individual states.

workers' compensation insurance: state-run insurance programs that pay benefits to those who suffer job-related injuries or illnesses.

Types of Benefits. Workers' compensation pays three types of benefits. Disability benefits, the largest portion of the program, are paid to workers who can no longer work because of a job-related accident or illness. Most states pay two-thirds of the workers' lost wages up to a maximum amount.

The second workers' compensation benefit pays for medical costs. In New York, medical, dental, podiatric, chiropractic, surgical, and hospital care are covered. Workers are free to choose their own physicians and surgeons for their treatment.

Finally, workers' compensation pays death benefits to the spouses and underage children of deceased workers. In New York, for example, dependents receive benefits based on a percentage of the dead worker's wages up to a maximum of $215 a week. Death benefits stop when a spouse remarries. He or she then receives two years of benefits in a lump sum as final payment. When dependent children reach 18, they too lose their benefits unless they are full-time students (whose benefits end at 23) or are fully disabled.[20]

THE DEBATE OVER NATIONAL HEALTH CARE

The debate over national health care is one of the most controversial issues facing consumers. South Africa and the United States are the only industrialized nations without a uniform national health care program. A stark comparison highlights the issue.

A California woman testified before Senator Edward Kennedy's Subcommittee on Health and Scientific Research about what had happened to her after she was involved in a head-on automobile crash with a drunk driver. Her husband had to quit his job so that the family could qualify for state aid, which would pay the more than $50,000 in medical expenses. Even with state assistance, the woman told the committee, there was no money left for the physical therapy she needed to eliminate the crippling effects of her injury.

In total contrast was the testimony of a Canadian woman who had been involved in a similar accident and had similar injuries. After hearing this report, the California woman expressed her bitterness at the U.S. system of health care that had left her unprotected. The Canadian woman's "accident was her fault and she only had to pay twenty dollars in out-of-pocket medical expenses," said the crippled California woman. "And she got all the physical therapy she needed. She walks in high heels, while I limp and have to wear special shoes."[21]

PROPOSED LEGISLATION

Various proposals have been offered for a national health care program. Senator Kennedy's "Health Care for All Americans Act" would cover virtually all medical and hospital costs with no deductions. The plan would be financed through a payroll tax on employers of 7 to 8 percent. Former President Carter once proposed a similar program in which employers would pay 75 percent of the cost up to 5 percent of their payrolls. The employee would pay the remaining 25 percent of the cost, and the federal government would make up any difference. Senator Russell Long has also suggested providing extensive coverage, but with a $3,000-individual and a $5,000-family deductible. And Senator Robert F. Dole wants to eliminate losses from catastrophic illnesses, when medical costs exceed 15 percent of a family's earnings. To date, none of this proposed legislation has been enacted.[22] Many people fear that a national health care program would worsen the federal budget deficit or would be too expensive both for businesses and individuals.

THE ARGUMENTS FOR AND AGAINST NATIONAL HEALTH CARE

A variety of arguments have been advanced in favor of some type of national health care plan. Some of the more prominent arguments are:

- Adequate health care is a basic right that should be guaranteed to all Americans.
- Some people simply cannot afford adequate health care without such a plan.
- The United States is deficient in this area since most other nations have such a program.
- National health care proposals typically include provisions that would contain the cost of medical care; thus, national health care would be cost-effective.

On the other hand, national health care proposals have been severely criticized—often by the medical profession. Some of the arguments against national health care plans are:

- National health care is just another term for socialized medicine.
- Most Americans already have adequate health insurance.
- The truly needy in our society can have their medical needs better met through other programs.
- National health care is prohibitively expensive, and Americans have shown little inclination for higher taxes.

DEVELOPING A PERSONAL HEALTH CARE PROTECTION PLAN

One out of three Americans cannot afford the cost of a catastrophic illness or a chronic disease requiring extended medical care, says the Congressional Budget Office. Among this group of underinsured Americans are millions of middle-class people who have not properly evaluated their present coverage—and many more millions who, due to unemployment, belong to no group health plan and are too poor to purchase individual coverage. During 1981 alone, more than seven million families were hit with enormous medical bills that devoured more than 15 percent of their annual income.[23]

The escalating expense of health care makes an assessment of your personal health care protection an essential part of any financial plan. A good starting point is an evaluation of the various policy features that are offered.

The Man with the Artificial Heart

A Seattle-area dentist made history in December 1982 when he became the first recipient of a permanent artificial heart. The Jarvik-7, as the heart was known, was implanted in Dr. Barney B. Clark during surgery that lasted seven and a half hours at the University of Utah Health Sciences Center. The cost of the pioneering surgery was paid for by Clark's medical insurance, his VA benefits, and private contributions to the university.

Barney Clark died 112 days later as a result of multi-organ failure and pneumonia. The air-driven Jarvik-7 was still operating effectively. Dr. Clark and the University of Utah Health Sciences Center epitomize the tremendous strides that have been made in modern health care.

Source: "The End of a Long Ordeal," Newsweek, April 4, 1983, pp. 83–84; "Feeling Much Better, Thank You," Time, March 14, 1983, p. 74; "Taking Heart from Dr. Clark," Newsweek, February 28, 1983, pp. 73–74; and "Who Owns Barney Clark's Legacy?" Time, September 12, 1983, p. 43; Department of Community Relations, University of Utah Health Sciences Center.

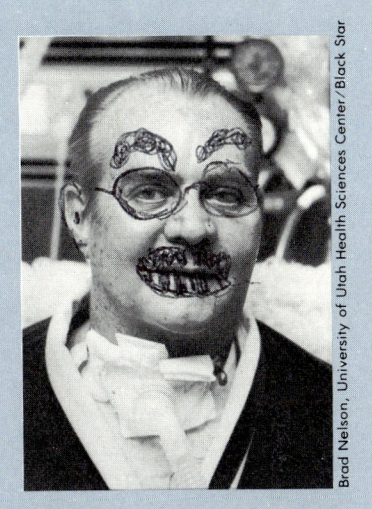

Dr. Barney Clark received the first artificial heart in December 1982. Although he died 112 days later of other illnesses, his new heart was still running well.

EVALUATING ALTERNATIVE POLICY FEATURES

In purchasing medical expense and disability income insurance, the consumer needs to ask several important questions about the exact terms of the health plan.

EVALUATING YOUR PRESENT COVERAGE

The first step is to evaluate your present coverage. Be sure to consider the role that Social Security disability income and workers' compensation might play in an extended illness. Whatever your present coverage, be sure to update and improve it as necessary. A disability income policy that provides $500 a month in benefits is inadequate for an annual income of $50,000. Similarly, a hospital expense policy that pays only $100 a day for hospital expenses fails to provide adequate protection in most states.

Which Conditions Are Covered and Which Are Excluded? Not all health insurance policies cover the same ailments, nor do they all pay the same amount for covered expenses. Information on individual policies can be obtained from an insurance agent or from a Blue Cross/Blue Shield representative. Similar information on a group policy can be obtained from the group's insurance coordinator. If group protection is poor, an individual policy can be used to supplement it.

Is There a Limitation for Preexisting Conditions? A previous medical problem may prevent you from purchasing an individual medical expense or disability income policy, or there may be a waiting period before the condition will be covered. Preexisting conditions are not a factor in most group health insurance policies since individual medical backgrounds do not affect membership in the group.

How Much Protection Is Needed? A study conducted for Roche Laboratories concluded that the "minimum adequate benefit package" should cover 15 days of hospital care; doctor services at the hospital, doctor's office, and in your home; laboratory tests and X-rays; maternity care; psychiatric care for hospitalized patients; outpatient services; and nursing home care. In general, 80 percent of these costs should be covered by your insurance plan. The study also concluded that adequate major medical insurance pays $250,000 in lifetime benefits and includes a *stop-loss feature*, which places a limit on out-of-pocket expenses. Today, however, many insurance experts would argue that 15 days of hospitalization is inadequate coverage.[24]

Who Is Covered? Both group and individual medical expense policies provide the option of covering spouses and children for an additional cost. The request for family coverage must be made at the time the application is completed. Children born after the policy is in force should be covered from the moment of birth. Policies that begin coverage 14 days after birth should be avoided since many neonatal illnesses occur during this period. Most policies insure children until the age of 19 or up to 23 if they are dependent, full-time students. Disability income policies cover only the insured.

What Is the Deductible? In general, the larger the deductible, the lower the annual premiums. The buyer should understand the terms of the deductible. Is there a new deductible for each illness, or does one deductible cover the entire year? How many family members must satisfy a deductible? Does a major medical plan require a deductible over and above the basic expenses already met? For example, a $500 major medical deductible may go into effect only after basic benefits and a $100 basic benefit deductible have been paid.

How Is Disability Defined? How the disability income policy defines *disability* is critically important. Go over this definition carefully with the insurance agent or the insurance coordinator to make sure it is adequate. If it is not, you may have to purchase additional disability income protection.

Is There a Guarantee of Renewability? The policy should not be cancelable as long as the premiums are paid. Only when all similar policies are canceled should the insurance company be allowed to cancel yours, and then you should be given the right to convert to another policy without having to pass a physical exam. Some insurance companies offer policies that can be canceled at any time. They may be cheaper, but you may find yourself without medical insurance as soon as a series of medical bills is submitted. This cannot happen in group plans, but for individuals a policy may be canceled after one year. Rates are another consideration. Buyers should look for policies that guarantee rates even if one's health changes.[25]

COMPARING COSTS

Health insurance premiums are determined by a variety of factors, including:

- A person's age and health when the policy is taken out. The older you are, the greater your chance of illness, so the higher the cost. If you already have a health problem, the insurance company may also charge higher rates.
- The type and amount of coverage chosen. To keep premium costs down, buy only what is really necessary. If, for example, you have two months of sick leave available, you probably do not need a disability income policy with only a seven-day waiting period.
- The amount of the policy's deductible.
- The length of the policy's term.
- The policy-renewal provision.

In general, try to get the most for your money. Avoid duplicating benefits since coordination-of-benefits clauses prevent you from collecting more than once for the same claim. This is a common problem in two-paycheck families. Buy a policy that covers all illnesses, not just one. Since health insurance is needed throughout your life, try to purchase a guaranteed renewable policy that will cover medical expenses until you are eligible for Medicare.

Above all, take your time and examine a policy carefully before buying it. Compare the alternatives that are available. What you learn can save you valuable premium dollars and give you better health care coverage.[26]

SUMMARY

The cost of health care and health care protection has escalated rapidly in recent years. In fact, the cost of medical care has been rising faster than the cost of living. It is now a matter of considerable importance in personal financial planning. Although the vast majority of all consumers now have health insurance, many 18- to 24-year-olds, in particular, are uninsured.

There are two basic categories of health insurance: medical expense insurance and disability income insurance. Medical coverage typically includes basic health insurance for hospital, surgical, and physician costs. Major medical expense insurance supplements basic health care packages by protecting against the costs of an extended illness or serious injury. Major medical policies include both a deductible provision (the policyholder pays some initial expenses before the policy pays) and coinsurance (the insured shares the cost of health care above the deductible amount).

Disability income insurance—the second major category of health care insurance—replaces income lost when the insured cannot work because of an illness or injury. Insurance experts consider it the most crucial part of a health insurance policy. Disability income, which is not usually taxable, should be set at 60 to 70 percent of regular income. Most disability programs require a waiting period before the replacement income is paid.

Dental insurance coverage has increased significantly in recent years. It is now one of the most popular fringe benefits offered by employers.

Health care protection plans are available through a variety of sources: private insurance companies, Blue Cross/Blue Shield, and health maintenance organizations (HMOs). Health care protection can be purchased through individual policies or under a group policy offered by one's employer, union, or professional society. Social Security plays an important role in health care protection by providing disability income insurance as well as medical insurance to the elderly and disabled through Medicare, and to the needy through Medicaid. Workers' compensation insurance provides benefits to those requiring job-related medical treatment.

To develop an adequate health care protection plan, a person must understand the various features of alternative programs. Costs and coverages should be compared, since a health care protection policy is one of the most important purchases a consumer has to make today.

REVIEW QUESTIONS

1. Briefly define the following terms:
   medical expense insurance
   disability income insurance
   indemnity plan
   service plan
   major medical expense insurance
   deductible provision
   coinsurance
   initial claim
   secondary claim
   waiting period
   disability waiver
   Blue Cross/Blue Shield
   group health insurance
   conversion privilege
   health maintenance organization
   Social Security
   Social Security disability income
   Medicare
   Medicaid
   workers' compensation insurance
2. Why is health care protection considered such an important part of personal financial planning today?
3. Describe the two major types of health insurance.
4. What specific features of major medical plans make this comprehensive coverage affordable for most Americans?
5. How much disability income protection should a person have?
6. Discuss the growing importance of dental insurance.
7. How does Blue Cross/Blue Shield differ from private insurance plans?
8. Distinguish the various features of individual and group health plans.
9. How do health maintenance organizations differ from other health insurance carriers?
10. What factors should a person consider in the development of a personal health care protection program?

CASES AND EXERCISES

1. The Boston Federal Reserve Bank converted a storage area into a physical fitness center that includes among other features a 10-station universal gym. Inter North, Inc.'s Omaha facility includes an Olympic-size pool and various testing labs. These employers are not alone; in fact, some

500 firms are now providing physical fitness centers for their employees.[27] In your opinion, is a physical fitness center a cost-effective fringe benefit for an employer to offer? How would you as a prospective employee evaluate such a benefit if it were offered by an employer?

2. It seems that everyone complains about the rising cost of health care in the United States. Outline a plan to moderate future price increases in this field. Specifically identify who should be responsible for these cost-saving actions: The government? The health care industry? Insurers? Employers? Consumers?

3. Prepare a report on the health insurance offered by your employer (alternatively you could look at the insurance that your college offers to its employees). What is covered? Hospital expenses? Surgical expenses? Physicians' fees? Major medical expenses? Disability income? Dental insurance? Eye care? How does their coverage compare with that offered by other employers?

4. Prepare a brief report tracing the history of health insurance in the United States? How does the industry's development affect its current offerings?

5. Some nations, in an effort to control costs and allocate scarce medical resources, limit the types of health care that are available to older people. Would you advocate such a program for the United States? Why or why not? Discuss.

ANSWERS TO PERSONAL FINANCE I.Q. TEST

1. Fact. 2. Fiction. 3. Fact. 4. Fact. 5. Fact. 6. Fiction. 7. Fiction.

HOW AMY SHORE REACHED HER PERSONAL FINANCIAL DECISION

Professor Worosz was glad this question came up. He knew from experience that many students didn't realize that they are usually dropped from their parents' policies at age 19 unless they are *full-time* students.

"If you don't have a policy of your own," he advised the class, "check your parents' policy. If you aren't covered because you are a part-time student, you have two basic options. You can buy your own policy —but be aware that unless you are eligible for some kind of group plan, it can cost you $1,200 to $2,400 a year. The other choice is to take more college credits to become a full-time student. Of course, you could go without insurance. But that's not something I'd recommend—it's far too risky. Just think what a relatively minor injury like a broken arm could cost."

The next day Amy approached Professor Worosz after class. As a part-time student, she'd found out she wasn't covered on her parents' plan. She agreed she should have health insurance but was confused about which option would be best. Professor Worosz learned that Amy needed only three more course credits to bring her up to twelve, which—at Schoolcraft—is full time. The cost of the extra course, he pointed out, would be far less than the cost of insurance. That made sense to Amy, and she could handle the extra workload. After thanking Professor Worosz, she went off to find the latest course schedule.

LEARNING OBJECTIVES

1. **To define the concept of liability and show how one can protect against it through insurance.** / *2.* **To identify the major forms of personal liability insurance.** / *3.* **To explain the coverage and features of homeowners insurance.** / *4.* **To outline the major types and features of automobile insurance.** / *5.* **To describe the standard sections and provisions of all personal liability, homeowners, and automobile insurance.**

TESTING YOUR PERSONAL FINANCE I.Q.

	FACT	FICTION
1. Ed Standish's collision insurance will replace his totally demolished 1985 Camaro up to the amount he originally paid for the car.	☐	☐
2. Attorneys typically collect one-third of all damage awards.	☐	☐
3. Male college students are considered better drivers than their female classmates.	☐	☐
4. Over one million motor vehicles are stolen every year in the United States.	☐	☐
5. The Chicago Bears were once found guilty of false advertising and consumer fraud as a result of a loss to the Washington Redskins.	☐	☐
6. Jennifer Evans, who was injured in an automobile accident caused by another driver, may still be able to sue for damages even though the accident occurred in a no-fault state.	☐	☐
7. Students with high grade point averages often pay lower rates for automobile insurance.	☐	☐

The materials in this chapter assist in separating fact from fiction. Your answers can be checked on page 411.

CHAPTER FOURTEEN

AUTOMOBILE, HOMEOWNERS, AND LIABILITY INSURANCE

SHARING A PERSONAL FINANCIAL DECISION WITH PROFESSOR HARVEY BRONSTEIN OF OAKLAND COMMUNITY COLLEGE

Recently Professor Harvey Bronstein donned the hat of financial detective—at least in an advisory sense. His student Shelden Brown described the scene of the crime: his two-story house was left with the drawers overturned, clothes strewn across the floor, books tumbled in a heap. Everything was in chaos after the break-in. The problem was how to track down what was missing and figure out its worth. It seemed an impossible task.

Shelden had wisely purchased homeowners insurance that covered personal property loss, but now he had to fill out his claim. "I sat down to prepare a list of the stolen articles for the insurance company," he told Professor Bronstein, "and I was stumped. How can I convey the value of what I've lost? There's some jewelry that's been passed down in my family for generations, and it has lots of sentimental value. Plus some of the pieces are so old it would be impossible to set a specific value on them today."

"Also, I can easily determine which major items were taken—my stereo and television—but it's impossible to remember all the jewelry. I hadn't looked in that old jewelry box in ages. And I think some books were taken, but my shelves weren't in any kind of order so I don't remember all the titles I had. How do I reconstruct the whole house?"

If you were Professor Bronstein, how would you solve Shelden's case?

To find out how Professor Bronstein helped Shelden with his personal financial decision, turn to page 411.

"If you're going to do something tonight that you'll be sorry for tomorrow morning, sleep late."
Henny Youngman[1]

The Chicago Bears probably never thought they needed insurance against fan dissatisfaction. But Jim Tully's unsuccessful small-claims case against the National Football League could be a forerunner for new legal concepts of financial responsibility and insurance coverage. Tully filed a claim in Winnebago County (Illinois) Circuit Court seeking the $58.40 that it cost him and his wife to see the Bears lose a game to the Washington Redskins during the 1981 season. The claim broke down as follows: $23 for tickets, $18 for gasoline, $15 for a babysitter, and $2.40 for highway tolls.

Tully's complaint alleged that the Bears were guilty of false advertising and consumer fraud since their poor performance meant they had misrepresented themselves as a professional football team. The disgruntled fan commented: "I love the Bears. I'm not angry. But we've been rebuilding for 44 years." The judge later dismissed the suit, noting that he too was a Bears fan and that the team had won twice in the three weeks preceding Tully's court appearance.[2]

Although insurance companies have not rushed to offer coverage against lawsuits by disappointed fans, this case suggests the varied interpretations of financial responsibility. A multitude of insurance policies exist to protect against those risks. Thus, the starting point in a discussion of personal liability, property, and automobile insurance is the concept of liability.

THE CONCEPT OF LIABILITY

liability: the financial responsibility one person has to another in a particular situation.

Liability refers to the financial responsibility one person has to another in a particular situation. It is an integral aspect of personal liability, property, and automobile insurance. In many instances, liability results from negligence.

NEGLIGENCE

negligence: the failure to exercise a reasonable degree of care to protect others from harm.

Negligence is the failure to exercise the necessary degree of care to protect others from harm. A negligent party is responsible for any injuries or property damage that result from a specific incident even if the incident was unintentional. The injured person is therefore entitled to collect for any suffering and damages.

An important aspect of negligence is the legal concept of *reasonable care,* defined as the action any responsible person would take in a similar position. For example, failure to repair broken driveway paving may lead to a liability lawsuit if someone falls as a result of the broken pavement. A legal judgment of negligence would suggest that the property owners did not exercise reasonable care—that is, they did not act in a responsible manner in this situation.

reasonable care: a legal concept meaning the action any responsible person would take in a similar position.

STRICT LIABILITY

Under the doctrine of *strict liability,* a person can be held financially responsible for an action even if he or she was not directly at fault. A student who keeps pet boa constrictors may be responsible if one of them hurts a neighbor even if the student had made elaborate provisions to restrain the snakes. According to the law, keeping a potentially dangerous animal as a pet puts the burden of financial responsibility on the owner despite any protective action that is taken.

strict liability: a legal doctrine whereby a person can be held financially responsible for an action even if he or she was not directly at fault.

VICARIOUS LIABILITY

The responsibility to avoid negligence sometimes extends to the negligence of others. Under the *vicarious liability* laws, automobile owners, parents, landlords, employers and others may be considered negligent even though they played no part in the negligent act. If, for example, a boy gets into an accident with his parents' car, the parents are responsible for the damages even if they were neither driving nor riding in the car. Likewise, if a ten-year-old girl throws a rock through a neighbor's window, her parents may be held liable.

vicarious liability: a legal concept whereby third parties like parents, automobile owners, and employers can be held liable for the acts of others.

THE NEED FOR LIABILITY INSURANCE

The costs of liability can be considerable. A legally liable person can be held financially responsible for property damage, medical expenses, lost wages, and the injured party's pain and suffering. *Liability insurance* is designed to protect a person (or firm) from the financial risks of legal liability.

There are many different types of liability insurance, three of which are particularly relevant to personal financial planning. They are personal liability insurance, portions of homeowners insurance coverage, and automobile liability coverage. Personal liability insurance protects a person when negligent acts cause property damage or personal injury. A portion of this protection is offered through one's homeowners insurance plan. Automobile liability coverage protects a person from financial loss when an accident caused by the insured results in injury or property damage.

liability insurance: insurance designed to protect a person (or firm) from the financial risks of legal liability.

PERSONAL LIABILITY INSURANCE

Two major forms of personal liability insurance are comprehensive personal liability and umbrella liability coverage.

The Hyatt Regency Case

Kansas City's 1981 Hyatt Regency disaster—in which the hotel's skywalks collapsed, killing 113 people—is a classic illustration of the concept of liability and the need for liability insurance. The first lawsuits were filed just days after the disaster. More than $3 billion in damages were sought. It was estimated that the defendants in the cases had about $240 million in liability insurance. The first cases were resolved four months after the disaster, when Occidental Fire and Casualty Company paid about $700,000 to the relatives of three people killed at the hotel.

The Hyatt Regency case had financial consequences for nonclaimants as well: the numerous attorneys who were hired to represent the claimants stood to receive one-third of the damages that were awarded, the typical fee charged by lawyers for handling liability cases.

Lawyers weren't the only professionals who received extra work. A few hours after the skywalks fell, the architect's attorney put in a call to a small firm in Palo Alto, California. Failure Analysis Associates went into action. The company is in the business of analyzing product failures that often end up in litigation. They have worked for such corporations as Lockheed, General Motors, Burroughs, and Exxon. Failure Analysis also provides prevention consultants to manufacturers who want to head off product liability suits before they get started.

Sources: "Relatives Get Money in Hyatt Hotel Deaths," *Seattle Times*, November 15, 1981; Jeff Blyskal, "Claim Jumpers in Three-Piece Suits," *Forbes*, December 7, 1981, pp. 40–41; and "Failure Is Success for Disaster Detectives," *Inc.*, October 1981, p. 20.

Two skywalks collapsed onto a dance floor at the Hyatt-Regency Hotel in Kansas City, Missouri, in July 1981, killing 113 people and triggering many lawsuits.

---

comprehensive personal liability insurance: part of a homeowners policy that protects against liability stemming from either inside or outside the home.

Under *comprehensive personal liability insurance*—which is part of every homeowners insurance plan and can also be purchased by nonhomeowners—the insurance company agrees to pay for any personal injuries or property losses that occur to nonmembers of the insured's household at the insured's home. It also agrees to cover the liability of most personal acts and those of one's family and pets (with certain exceptions stated in the contract) wherever they occur. If the family dog bites a letter carrier, the insurance policy will cover the damage. It will also protect the insured from personal responsibility if someone in the family accidentally backs over the neighbor's rose garden and crushes some prize-winning roses or if a guest falls down a flight of stairs and suffers a serious injury.

Standard comprehensive personal liability policies also pay the legal fees involved in such incidents. The discussion of homeowners insurance later in the chapter reviews the specific provisions found in a comprehensive personal liability policy.

Excess personal liability protection can be provided by an *umbrella policy*, which offers $1 million or more of total coverage. This policy provides more protection in more areas than the comprehensive insurance plan. In addition to bodily injury and property damage protection, it covers such liabilities as false arrest, libel, invasion of privacy, and defamation of character.

The umbrella policy should be used to supplement the liability coverage available through homeowners and auto insurance plans. Umbrella policies cover the entire family, but the insurance company will set minimum liability coverage for the insured's automobile and homeowners insurance. Umbrella policies, which also cover attorney fees, are modestly priced. American States Insurance Company, for instance, offers $1-million umbrella policies for as little as $56 per year.

umbrella policy: additional liability coverage beyond that offered by homeowners and automobile insurance.

WHO NEEDS LIABILITY INSURANCE?

According to the Insurance Information Institute, an industry trade association, "to be without personal liability insurance is to jeopardize your financial future. A large lawsuit resulting from a serious accident for which you may be held legally liable could cause you to lose your property and your savings, and even leave you with a continuing claim against your future earnings."[3]

The need for liability insurance varies according to your income, wealth, and level of activity. A professional who has considerable investments, a good future income, and is active in community life is likely to need higher-than-normal liability coverage. People in this category have greater exposure to liability suits, so greater insurance coverage is needed.

HOMEOWNERS INSURANCE

A personal residence—probably the largest single purchase anyone will ever make—requires adequate insurance protection. A variety of *homeowners insurance* plans are available to provide this coverage. Most of these policies protect against the following losses or damages:

homeowners insurance: coverage for damage to one's home, other structures on the property, trees and shrubs, personal property, additional living expenses, liability, and no-fault medical and damage payments.

Homeowners insurance usually covers damage to the policyholder's house—by fire, for example—and to other structures and greenery on his or her property. It also helps to compensate for lost personal property, additional living expenses, liability if a guest is injured, and no-fault medical payments and damages.

1. *Damage to the house:* The homeowners insurance purchased to protect a house against damage is based on the replacement cost of the house.

2. *Damage to other structures:* A homeowners policy will usually cover other structures, such as a freestanding garage, up to 10 percent of the coverage on the home. Thus a $100,000 insured home means that the other structures are covered up to $10,000.

3. *Damage to trees and shrubs:* The plants, trees, lawn, and other greenery that surround an insured home are often covered up to a specified limit.

4. *Personal property losses:* Personal property is usually insured up to an amount equal to half the coverage of the house. An $80,000 homeowners policy would insure household goods for an additional $40,000. The policy sets limits on the coverage of certain items. A typical policy may cover $500 for lost jewelry; $1,000 for valuable papers, including stocks and manuscripts; $1,000 for boats; $2,500 for theft of silverware; and so on. An off-premise theft is covered up to the policy limits. It is wise to keep an inventory of your personal property in some other location. This will assist you in case of a claim. The inventory should include photos of the items. There are several firms that now offer to provide a complete filmed inventory of your house's contents.

5. *Additional living expenses:* If the house becomes unlivable as a result of damages and the insured has to seek temporary quarters while repairs are being made, the homeowners insurance will pay expenses up to 20 percent of the coverage on the house.

6. *Liability:* The comprehensive personal liability portion of a homeowners policy protects against financial disaster if a guest is injured in the home because of the insured's negligence. Most policies offer at least $50,000 worth of liability insurance, with more protection available at an additional cost. Indeed, most people purchase $100,000 to $300,000. Increases in coverage are relatively cheap, so purchasing large amounts of this protection is feasible—and advisable.

7. *No-fault medical payments and damages:* If a visitor trips over a tree trunk on the insured property and breaks an arm—an accident that has nothing to do with the homeowners' personal negligence—the no-fault medical payment portion of the homeowners policy will cover the bills up to $1,000.[4]

STANDARD HOMEOWNERS POLICY

Most homeowners policies written today are called *all-risk policies*—they cover all perils except those specifically excluded, such as floods, earthquakes, and nuclear disasters. Flood and earthquake coverage is usually part of policies for

"Sunshine and warm breezes they take for granted, but earthquakes and hurricanes they call 'acts of God'!"

Insurance Exclusions Often Include "Acts of God."
Source: From the *Wall Street Journal*—Permission, Cartoon Features Syndicate.

Table 14-1
STANDARD FORMATS FOR HOMEOWNERS INSURANCE

Policy Type	Perils Covered*	Property Insurance — Amount on House and Attached Structures	Amount on Detached Structures	Amount on Trees, Shrubs, Plants
Basic (HO-1)	1–10	Up to 100% of replacement cost	10% of amount on house	5% of amount on house; $500 maximum per item
Broad (HO-2)	1–17	Up to 100% of replacement cost	10% of amount on house	5% of amount on house; $500 maximum per item
Special (HO-3)	1–9 and 11–17 on personal property. All risks on buildings	Up to 100% of replacement cost	10% of amount on house	5% of amount on house; $500 maximum per item
Renters (HO-4)	1–17	Covers additions and alterations only, up to 10% of amount on personal property	(Not applicable)	10% of amount on personal property; $500 maximum per item
Comprehensive (HO-5)	All risks	Up to 100% of replacement cost	10% of amount on house	5% of amount on house; $500 maximum per item
Condominium (HO-6)	1–17	$1,000 on additions and alterations	(Not applicable)	10% of amount on personal property; $500 maximum per item

*Key to Perils:
1 Fire or lightning
2 Windstorm or hail
3 Explosion
4 Riot or civil commotion
5 Aircraft
6 Vehicles
7 Smoke
8 Vandalism or malicious mischief
9 Theft

manufactured homes, however, and for a separate charge any homeowner can obtain earthquake insurance as well as other types of coverage.

The insurance industry has established four standard homeowners policies, as well as standard formats for owners of condominium units and renters. Table 14-1 outlines the different types of policies and their coverage.

THE DEDUCTIBLE

The *deductible* in a homeowners policy operates in the same way it does in any other form of insurance: the insured pays for a specified amount of damage before the insurance coverage begins. The higher the deductible, the lower the premium, since the insurance company's risk is reduced. American States, for

deductible: an insurance requirement that the insured pay for a specified amount of damage before the insurance coverage begins.

Amount on Personal Property	Loss of Use, Additional Living Expense	Liability	Liability Insurance No-Fault Property Damage	No-Fault Medical Payment
50% of amount on house	10% of amount on house	$25,000 minimum	$250	$500 per person
50% of amount on house	20% of amount on house	$25,000 minimum	$250	$500 per person
50% of amount on house	20% of amount on house	$25,000 minimum	$250	$500 per person
$4,000 minimum	20% of amount on personal property	$25,000 minimum	$250	$500 per person
50% of amount on house	20% of amount on house	$25,000 minimum	$250	$500 per person
$4,000 minimum	40% of amount on personal property	$25,000 minimum	$250	$500 per person

10 Breakage of glass
11 Falling objects
12 Weight of ice, snow, or sleet
13 Collapse of a building
14 Accidental discharge or overflow of water or steam
15 Sudden and accidental tearing apart, cracking, burning, or bulging (e.g., boiler)
16 Freezing
17 Sudden and accidental damage from artificially generated electrical current

Source: Copyright 1980 by Consumers Union of United States, Inc., Mount Vernon, N.Y. 10553. Reprinted by permission from Consumer Reports, August 1980.

instance, whose standard policy has a $100 deductible, offers a 35-percent discount for a $1,000 deductible, a 20-percent discount for a $500 deductible, and a 10-percent discount for a $250 deductible.

SUPPLEMENTING THE HOMEOWNERS POLICY

Homeowners coverage can be supplemented by policy endorsements or by floater policies. Both provide important insurance protections.

Endorsements, which are amendments to the original insurance policy, increase the standard coverages described earlier. One popular endorsement is inflation protection. An inflation protection endorsement automatically raises insurance protection to reflect the current costs of rebuilding. Similarly, a

endorsements: *amendments to homeowners policies that increase standard coverage.*

floater policies: *insurance protection for certain scheduled property.*

replacement cost coverage endorsement provides enough money to replace lost property, not just the cash value of the items lost. Cash value is equal to the item's original purchase price minus depreciation.

Floater policies provide insurance protection for certain scheduled property. Traditionally called personal articles floaters, they are designed to protect valuable personal property—such items as art works, furs, jewelry, camera equipment, antique furniture, coin and stamp collections, and silverware—against almost all risks.

Each item of property must be "scheduled" in the policy—that is, it must be completely described to the insurer's satisfaction. If the value of the property cannot be readily determined, a professional appraisal will be required.

A personal articles floater can be purchased as an endorsement to a regular homeowners policy or as a separate policy. A homeowners policy is not a prerequisite for purchasing a floater. To a large extent, the premiums depend on the crime rate in the area. This coverage is usually sold without deductibles.

MISCELLANEOUS INSURANCE PROTECTION

As was already mentioned, certain perils, like floods and earthquakes, are specifically excluded from standard homeowners policies. Insurance against these perils is available under separate policies.

Flood Insurance. The federal government, under the Federal Insurance Administration (FIA), offers low-cost flood insurance to homeowners in flood-prone areas. Only those properties located in flood-prone communities that participate in the FIA's program to minimize or eliminate future flooding can purchase flood insurance. In 1984 the FIA classified 20,000 communities as flood-prone. At the end of 1983 there were 1,960,868 flood insurance policies with a combined coverage of nearly $114 billion.

Earthquake Insurance. For those who live in areas prone to earthquakes (such as California, Oregon, Washington, and Missouri), earthquake insurance is an important financial consideration. It is generally written as an addition to a homeowners policy. In the Seattle area, such protection costs $1.45 per $1,000 of coverage.

AUTOMOBILE INSURANCE

The United States is a nation of automobile drivers and automobile insurance carriers. In fact, automobile insurance is now the single largest form of property and casualty insurance. And for good reason. In a recent year, there were nearly 29 million accidents involving motor vehicles, and the total economic loss from motor vehicle accidents was $57 billion.[5]

TYPES OF COVERAGE

There are five basic types of automobile insurance: bodily injury and property damage liability insurance, medical payment insurance, underinsured motorist insurance, collision insurance, and comprehensive physical damage insurance.

Bodily Injury and Property Damage Liability Insurance. To protect against liability for injuries and damage to others, both *bodily injury and property damage liability insurance* are necessary. Bodily injury liability insurance covers the insured if his or her car kills or injures a pedestrian or someone in the insured's car or in another car. Anyone driving the insured's car with permission is protected by this coverage, including family and others.

> **bodily injury and property damage liability insurance:** automobile insurance that protects against the liability resulting from injuries and damage to others.

Property damage liability insurance covers situations in which the insured's car damages another car or any property belonging to others. If the car skids into a utility pole in a rainstorm or knocks down shrubs in someone's front yard, the property damage liability insurance will pay the expenses. It will not, however, pay for damage to the insured's car—that is covered by collision insurance.

Both bodily injury liability insurance and property damage liability insurance cover the insured party and his or her family if they are driving someone else's car with permission. These policies also pay legal fees if there is an accident-related lawsuit and they reimburse you for lost wages while you are in court. Most important, they pay up to the policy's limits for any injury or property damage that results from the accident. Of course, these damages must be shown through court action or the agreement of both parties to be the insured's responsibility.

In the United States, most automobile liability coverage quotations take the following form: 50/100/10. The first number refers to the maximum amount in thousands of dollars that the insurance company will pay for injuries to one person in any one accident. The second number refers to the maximum amount of coverage in thousands of dollars for injuries to two or more people. And the third number sets the limit in thousands of dollars for property damage coverage. Thus a 50/100/10 policy provides $50,000 for the injuries of a single person; $100,000 for all the injuries resulting from a single accident; and $10,000 for property damage. Canadian drivers typically carry inclusive or single-limit policies that set a maximum amount of coverage for personal injury or property damage or both.

It is usually recommended that drivers carry substantial liability insurance coverage. The costs of additional coverage are comparatively small relative to the financial risks associated with an automobile accident. Insurance buyers must remember that if a judgment in excess of their insurance limit is entered against them, they will be expected to pay it from other resources. Thus, adequate automobile liability insurance is a good investment.[16]

medical payment insurance: automobile insurance that covers your own injuries and those of other passengers, without regard to liability.

Medical Payment Insurance. With *medical payment insurance,* you are covered for auto-accident-related medical expenses for yourself, your family, and any guests in the car. In addition, all family members are covered while riding in someone else's car or if they are struck by a car while walking. Coverage applies even when the insured's car is not in motion. If someone trips while getting into the insured's parked car, medical payment insurance will cover any related expenses.

Legal liability is not an issue under this form of insurance; the policy simply pays for any reasonable medical expenses up to the stated limits of the coverage. Medical payment insurance is relatively inexpensive and worthy of consideration by all drivers.

underinsured motorist insurance: automobile insurance that protects against accidents caused by people lacking adequate insurance.

Underinsured Motorist Insurance. This coverage also provides valuable inexpensive protection. *Underinsured motorist insurance* covers you if you or members of your family are hurt by an underinsured motorist or in the case of a hit-and-run or stolen-car accident. In addition, it covers immediate family even if they are passengers in someone else's car or are pedestrians.

collision insurance: automobile insurance that pays for accident damage done to the insured's automobile.

f/ new cars
& special cars
(ex. Antiques)

Collision Insurance. If the insured person's automobile is involved in an accident, *collision insurance* will pay to repair it. Or, if the damage is too extensive for repair, the insurance company will *total* it (insurance industry jargon for paying the depreciated value of the vehicle). Collision insurance does not cover the cost of repairing the other driver's car or property, nor does it pay for any personal injuries the insured or the insured's passengers suffered during the accident. Collision insurance is also subject to deductibles.

Without collision insurance, the insured would have to try to recover the damages from the driver of the other car. If the insured caused the accident, this would not be possible. But even when the other driver's negligence was clear, it would have to be proved in court, and payment could be delayed. Collision insurance eliminates the question of fault and immediately pays the insured's accident-related damages.

Collision insurance is not compulsory; one can choose to carry it or not. Collision insurance definitely makes sense if your car is new or only a few years old, because new cars often cost thousands of dollars to replace or repair. However, the need for collision insurance lessens as time goes by. Remember that the insurance company will pay no more than the depreciated value of the automobile.

Consumers are required to purchase collision insurance if they buy a car on credit. Since the car is collateral, creditors use collision insurance to protect their interest if the car is involved in a crash. This requirement has nothing to do with a state's financial responsibility requirements (discussed below) or liability and other forms of insurance coverage.

Auto Theft: A $3.27-Billion Financial Drain

Over one million motor vehicles are stolen every year in the United States. Auto thefts cost Americans $3.27 billion annually, much of it through increased insurance costs. Why are there so many auto thefts? First, there is the draw of huge returns for moderate risks. Fewer than 60 percent of all stolen vehicles are recovered. This has attracted organized crime's "chop shops," which can completely disassemble a car in 40 minutes. The parts are then sold in the black market. Many stolen vehicles also end up overseas. For example, an estimated 20,000 stolen vehicles go to Mexico every year, and recently over 100 stolen cars were found on a New York City dock. Their destination? Kuwait.

To help combat the situation, more than 500 insurance companies are funding the National Automobile Theft Bureau (NATB). This organization is engaged in training law enforcement officers, providing information services, and conducting investigations. In fact, the NATB helped identify those 100-plus cars that were headed for Kuwait.

Legislation pending in Congress would require front-end assemblies and car doors to carry identification numbers like those found on engines and transmissions. This proposal is designed to make it more difficult for the "chop shops" to operate.

Source: "Theft: Cost to Motorists Put at $3.27 Billion Annually," *Seattle Times*, October 21, 1983, p. A9.

Comprehensive Physical Damage Insurance. With *comprehensive physical damage insurance,* you are protected against financial loss if your car is stolen or damaged by earthquake, break-in, fire, flood, windstorm, vandalism, explosion, and so on. Loss of a CB radio or stereo is covered if it was screwed in or attached to the dashboard. Comprehensive insurance sometimes reimburses the insured for a rental car that is stolen.

Comprehensive physical damage insurance is less expensive than bodily injury and property damage liability coverage. The exact cost depends on the dangers the car is exposed to in an area. Insurance companies base their rates on such factors as the average number of car thefts a year or the likelihood of flooding, tornadoes, windstorms, and other environmental problems. Coverage is usually subject to deductibles.

comprehensive physical damage insurance: automobile insurance that covers losses from car thefts, earthquakes, break-ins, fires, floods, windstorms, vandalism, and the like.

FINANCIAL RESPONSIBILITY AND COMPULSORY LIABILITY LAWS

All states have *financial responsibility laws,* which require drivers involved in an accident to show proof that they will pay for accident-related damages. If the driver cannot show this proof, he or she may be required to put sufficient funds into an escrow account to cover accident-related damages. Drivers who cannot raise the money may lose their right to drive until they pay all judgments against them.

A state's financial responsibility law can be satisfied by purchasing a minimum amount of bodily injury and property damage liability insurance.

financial responsibility laws: state laws requiring drivers involved in an accident to show proof that they will pay any damages they caused.

compulsory liability insurance laws: state laws requiring drivers to purchase liability insurance before car registrations and license plates are issued.

no-fault insurance: an automobile insurance plan, operating in 25 states, that requires claims payments to be made by the policyholder's insurance company without regard to fault and limits the right of victims to sue.

Many states go one step further and require that car owners purchase liability insurance before car registration and license plates are issued. This provision is known as *compulsory liability insurance.*

NO-FAULT INSURANCE

The concept of no-fault insurance has radically changed the automobile liability insurance systems of many states. First used by Massachusetts in 1971, *no-fault insurance* eliminates the need to assign blame for certain accidents resulting in bodily injury. Like homeowners, hospitalization, and income disability insurance, it protects policyholders under their own insurance plans. Instead of going through an often-long legal process to determine who caused an accident and therefore is legally liable for damages, the no-fault auto insurance laws require policyholders to file claims with their own insurance companies for injury-related costs.

Currently, half the states and the District of Columbia have some form of no-fault insurance law, although the specific features vary from state to state. Generally, all the no-fault laws cover the following injury-related expenses: medical bills, funeral expenses, a wage earner's lost income, the cost of hiring a person to perform the essential duties of a homemaker or other non-income-producing people. No-fault laws do not exclude litigation when an accident results in death, permanent injury, or disfigurement or when medical expenses exceed a specific amount. Those who argue in favor of no-fault insurance point out that no-fault laws have shortened the time it takes to get payment for damage and injuries and that they cut the legal fees associated with accidents. Proponents also note the elimination of cases in which contributory negligence and other factors would prevent injured drivers from collecting. Moreover, they claim, no-fault laws hold down automobile insurance costs.

On the other side, opponents of no-fault insurance contend that the minimum figure for suits is so low that fault is still a factor in many cases and that no-fault insurance may deny a person's right to have his or her case heard in court. In addition, it is argued, the system has failed to keep premium costs down. Massachusetts, the original no-fault state, has extremely high insurance rates. And Nevada repealed its no-fault law after a six-year experiment.[7]

AUTO INSURANCE PREMIUMS

Gilbert Loomis of Westfield, Connecticut, paid $7.50 per $1,000 of liability coverage for his automobile insurance back in 1887. This first automobile insurance policy was an adaptation of one for a horse-powered vehicle. Today, about 40 percent of the money spent on all property and casualty insurance is for motor vehicles.[8] With the increasing costs of cars, car repairs, and medical expenses, this percentage is expected to rise even higher in future years.

The Attack on DWIs

One of the nation's most pressing traffic problems is the death, injury, and destruction caused by drunk drivers. DWIs (those who drive while intoxicated) kill 70 Americans a day. Some 5,000 of those killed each year are teenagers. It is now estimated that half of all Americans born today will be involved in an alcohol-related crash at some time.

What is being done to combat the problem? Stiffer DWI penalties have been enacted. Many states now require mandatory jail sentences for those convicted of drunk driving. Increased police efforts are aimed at targeting the drunk driver. In some communities roadblocks are used to search out DWIs. But perhaps most important, organizations like MADD (Mothers Against Drunk Drivers) have heightened the public's awareness of the problem. DWIs have not been eliminated, but the United States has clearly made considerable progress in this area. There were 43,000 traffic deaths in 1983, the lowest in 20 years. This decline was credited to the nationwide effort to get DWIs off the road.

Sources: "Send All Drunk Drivers to Jail?" *U.S. News & World Report*, January 17, 1983, p. 71; and "Traffic Deaths Hit 20 Year Low," *U.S. News & World Report*, February 20, 1984, p. 13.

A state police officer hands a pamphlet on drunk-driving laws to a motorist at a Massachusetts toll booth.

Not everyone pays the same amount of money for auto insurance protection. Premium rates are based on insurance companies' past experience with insurance claims. Companies determine how frequently accidents occur, the cost of repairs, and how such factors as inflation will affect future claims costs. A person's actual costs depend on a variety of factors, including place of residence, personal characteristics, automobile usage, driving record, the type of car driven, and eligibility for certain premium discounts.

Place of Residence. City dwellers usually pay higher rates than suburbanites. Insurance companies attempt to make the premiums they charge reflect accident, repair, and medical cost experience in different areas. According to the Insurance Information Institute, "the premium charged to an individual car owner is affected directly by the number and cost of accidents caused by drivers who live in his or her rating territory."[9] According to the National Safety Council, three out of four accidents occur within 25 miles of the driver's home.[10] So the condition of local roads, traffic volume, the effectiveness of local traffic police, the number of car thefts, and the cost of auto repairs and medical services in the community can either drive up or push down the cost of insurance.

Personal Characteristics. In most states, insurance companies can base auto insurance premiums on age, sex, and marital status. Studies have shown that age more than any other personal factor affects the likelihood of becoming involved in an accident. According to the National Safety Council, the youngest drivers, those in their teens and early twenties, have the highest risk of accident. Thirty-five out of every 100 drivers who are under 25 are involved in accidents each year. Rates quickly drop off for older drivers: 25 out of 100 drivers in the 25- to 29-year-old group and 16 out of 100 in the over-30 group are accident statistics each year. Given that nearly 40 percent of drivers involved in accidents are under age 25 and that these drivers make up only 20 percent of the total driving population, auto insurance premiums are higher for this group.[11]

Women drivers generally have fewer accidents than men and young married people have fewer accidents than young single people. Young unmarried men who own their own cars pay the highest insurance premiums. Young married women pay less insurance than their single counterparts. Elderly men and women are charged slightly reduced premiums because they drive less and have fewer accidents.

Automobile Usage. The extent and type of usage are also factors in determining automobile insurance premiums. Cars used extensively for business travel carry higher rates than those used just for a few miles of pleasure driving a week. Most automobile insurance applications contain questions concerning automobile usage.

Driving Record. Safe-driver rates are typically given to people with no accidents or serious moving violations in recent years. Drivers with past accidents or violations pay higher rates because they have proved themselves more likely to get into an accident.

People with poor driving records may not be able to purchase insurance through regular channels. Their only option may be the state's *assigned risk pool*, in which all insurers in the state are required to insure high-risk drivers on

assigned risk pool: a requirement that all insurers in a state cover high-risk drivers on a rotating basis.

a rotating basis. Coverage may be limited, and rates are usually 25 to 50 percent higher than normal.

Unfortunately, many people with good driving records are also placed in the assigned risk pool because they are young or live in high-crime areas. One should nevertheless try to secure regular coverage. Most people do so fairly quickly. At the end of one year, half the people in the high-risk plan have found a cheaper insurance source. Nine out of 10 are out of the pool at the end of three years.[12]

Type of Car Driven. The more expensive a car is to repair or replace, the more you will be charged for insurance. The higher premium charges pay for more costly collision and comprehensive coverages.

Insurance companies typically tie rates to their actual experience with specific models. For example, the Millers Casualty Insurance Company of Texas charges the standard published rate for some models and grants a 15-percent discount from the standard rate for others. The company also refuses to insure certain models.

Similarly, the rates for motorcyclists are set according to the size of the motorcycle. For example, a 21-year-old Seattle area resident with a 500 cc motorcycle can expect to pay $300 annually for liability coverage of 25/50/10, comprehensive and collision insurance with a $100 deductible, and underinsured motorist coverage.

Premium Discounts. Lower insurance rates are offered for meeting certain conditions. The following discounts are offered by many insurance companies:

1. *Driver-training discount* — for young drivers who have completed an authorized driver-training program.

2. *Good-student discount* — for students who have at least a B average and are in the top 20 percent of their class.

3. *Multicar discount* — for insuring more than one car with the same insurance company.

READING THE INSURANCE POLICY

Personal liability, homeowners, and automobile insurance policies all contain certain standard characteristics. It is important to read each section carefully.

MAJOR POLICY PROVISIONS

Most are made up of a declarations page, an insuring agreement, a statement of the policy's conditions, and a statement of exclusions.

declarations page: the part of an insurance policy that identifies the parties, type of protection, and coverage involved.

insuring agreement: the part of an insurance policy that outlines the responsibilities of each of the parties.

policy conditions: the part of the insurance policy that outlines the specific provisions of the coverage.

exclusions: the part of the insurance policy that lists the losses not covered by the policy.

1. The *declarations page* lists the policyholder, the property or liability to be insured, and the type of insurance protection purchased. It also specifies the limits of the coverage.

2. The *insuring agreement* forms the basis of the insurance contract. It details the insurer's responsibilities to the policyholder and the policyholder's responsibilities to the insurer.

3. The section on *policy conditions* outlines the specific provisions of the policy. It tells exactly what the policy will do, and it lists the actions both parties must take during the time a claim is being processed.

4. The part on *exclusions* lists the specific losses that the policy does not cover.

SPECIFIC POLICY CONDITIONS

Many liability, homeowners, and automobile policies share certain important provisions, which are detailed in the section on policy conditions. Included here are provisions concerning the following:

1. *Concealment or fraud:* This provision states that if the policyholder knowingly lies when filling out the insurance application or puts in a false claim, the insurance company may refuse to pay benefits and may void the policy.

2. *Waivers:* Provisions for waivers, also known as endorsements, detail any changes in the original terms of the policy that were agreed to by the insurance company and the insured. These changes must be written into the policy itself.

3. *Mortgagee interest and obligations:* Usually found in homeowners policies, this condition recognizes the interest of any mortgage holder in the insurance on the property. If, for example, a $120,000 house with a $60,000 mortgage is completely destroyed by fire, half of the insurance proceeds must go to the lender.

4. *Excluded perils:* Many policies specifically state that they will not cover losses that are caused by certain perils, including war, nuclear accident, floods, and earthquakes.

5. *Cancellation:* This condition sets out the terms under which the policy can be canceled by either the policyholder or the insurance company. The policyholder has the right to cancel the insurance at any time, but the company must be notified in writing. The company must then refund the unused portion of the premium.

6. *Pro rata contribution:* Because individuals may take out more than one policy on their property, this provision is included to prevent them from collecting on several policies and making a profit at the expense of the insurance companies. It states that if more than one policy exists at the time of

the loss, each insurer will pay an amount that is proportionate to the coverage provided on the property.

7. *Requirements in case of a loss:* This clause details exactly what the insured must do in the event of a loss. It requires that every effort be made to protect the property from additional loss, that the insurance company be notified immediately, that proof of the loss be submitted, and that the insured cooperate with the insurer by providing financial records relating to the loss.

8. *Appraisal:* This provision outlines the steps that must be taken if the insurance company and the insured disagree on the value of the lost or damaged property. It requires that an independent appraiser be brought in to determine the settlement.

9. *Company's options:* The insurance company's settlement options are outlined in this provision. The company can agree on a cash settlement; it can decide to take the damaged property at an agreed value after payment; or it can agree to repair or replace the damaged property.

10. *Subrogation:* This clause takes away the policyholder's right to collect damages from the person directly responsible for the loss if the policyholder receives a payment from the insurance company. Once the insurance company pays a claim, it has the right to pursue its own lawsuit against the person who caused the damage.[13]

MAKING THE PURCHASE DECISION

Liability, homeowners, and automobile insurance can be purchased from a number of different sources: an *exclusive agent,* who represents one insurance company and sells only its product; an *independent agent,* who typically represents two or more companies; and a *broker,* who deals with companies or agents to arrange coverage for clients. If coverage is bought from an exclusive agent, you will usually deal directly with the company in the case of a claim. Independent agents and brokers act as middlemen and pass claims on to the company.[14]

Whomever you choose to purchase your insurance policy from, be sure you feel comfortable with the company and its product. It is important to feel that you can call upon your agent or broker to help with a claim and that he or she will act on your behalf as well as that of the company.

exclusive agent: an insurance seller who works for just one insurance company.

independent agent: an insurance seller who represents two or more companies.

broker: someone who arranges insurance coverage for clients.

SUMMARY

The concept of liability refers to the financial responsibility one person has to another in a particular situation. In most cases liability results from negligence, the failure to exercise a reasonable degree of care to protect others from harm. But in some jurisdictions, the concept of strict liability has been adopted so that a person may be held liable even if he or she was not directly at fault. Under vicarious liability laws, automobile owners, parents, landlords, and employers may be held responsible for the actions of others.

Liability insurance is designed to protect against the financial risks of legal liability. Three types of liability insurance are particularly relevant to personal financial planning: personal liability insurance, homeowners insurance, and automobile insurance.

There are two major forms of personal liability insurance. Comprehensive personal liability insurance, which is part of a homeowners policy, protects against liability stemming from incidents either inside or outside the home. Umbrella policies provide additional liability protection beyond that offered by homeowners and automobile insurance. Like comprehensive personal liability coverage, umbrella policies cover all family members.

Homeowners insurance covers damage to a person's home, other structures on the property, trees and shrubs, and personal property; it also gives protection for additional living expenses and liability. No-fault medical payments and damages coverage is often added to these policies. Homeowners insurance may also be supplemented by endorsements or amendments to the basic policy (inflation protection is a common example) as well as by floater policies, which are designed to protect specific articles. In certain areas, flood and earthquake insurance are also important. Homeowners policies typically include deductibles.

There are five basic types of automobile insurance. Bodily injury and property damage liability insurance protects against the liability resulting from injuries and damage done to others. Medical payment insurance covers your own injuries and those of guests without regard to liability. Underinsured motorist coverage protects against accidents caused by people lacking insurance. Collision insurance pays for accident damage to the insured's automobile. Comprehensive physical damage insurance covers losses from car thefts, earthquakes, break-ins, fires, floods, windstorms, vandalism, and the like.

All states and Canadian provinces have financial responsibility laws, which require drivers involved in an accident to show proof that they can pay for any related damages. The purchase of adequate bodily injury and property damage insurance meets this legal requirement.

Automobile insurance premiums depend on a variety of factors, including the person's place of residence, physical characteristics, automobile usage, driving record, type of car driven, and eligibility for certain discounts.

All personal liability, homeowners, and automobile insurance policies contain standard characteristics. The declarations page identifies the parties, type of protection, and coverage involved. The insuring agreement outlines the responsibilities of each of these parties, while the policy conditions outline the specific provisions of the policy. A section on exclusions lists the losses not covered by the policy. Personal liability, homeowners, and automobile insurance can be purchased from either an exclusive agent, representing one company; an independent agent, representing several companies; or a broker, who arranges coverage for clients.

REVIEW QUESTIONS

1. Briefly define the following terms:

liability
negligence
reasonable care
strict liability
vicarious liability
liability insurance
comprehensive personal liability insurance
umbrella policy
homeowners insurance
deductible
endorsements
floater policies
bodily injury and property damage liability insurance
medical payment insurance
underinsured motorist insurance
collision insurance
comprehensive physical damage insurance
financial responsibility laws
compulsory liability insurance laws
no-fault insurance
assigned risk pool
declarations page
insuring agreement
policy conditions
exclusions
exclusive agent
independent agent
broker

2. What impact does the concept of liability have on personal financial planning?
3. Discuss the major types of personal liability insurance.
4. What types of losses are covered by homeowners insurance?
5. What are the typical exclusions to all-risk homeowners insurance?
6. Why is the concept of automobile insurance so important to modern personal finance?
7. Identify the five types of automobile insurance.
8. Explain financial responsibility and compulsory insurance laws.
9. What factors go into determining a person's automobile insurance premiums?
10. Identify the major policy provisions of personal liability, homeowners, and automobile insurance.

CASES AND EXERCISES

1. Most lawyers in liability cases work on a contingency fee basis; that is, if their client wins, they get a share of the damages awarded, typically 33 percent. These attorneys argue that the contingency fee system allows everyone access to good legal advice. Critics, however, argue that high contingency fees encourage too much litigation and are excessive and unfair to the injured party. What is your opinion? Discuss.
2. Obtain a copy of an insurance policy designed for apartment renters. What are the major features of this policy? What coverages are provided? What is not covered by the policy?
3. A federal grant allocated $6.50 for each of the 12,500 residents of Natchitoches, Louisiana, in an effort to get them to fasten their automobile seat belts. Prizes such as McDonald's gift certificates were passed out at the city's 23 stop lights to those who had buckled up. There was also a monthly drawing for a $25 gift certificate, and another drawing at the end of the two-year study for an overseas trip. Similar efforts were conducted in Fresno, California; Suffolk County, New York; Kalamazoo, Michigan; Dover, New Jersey; and San Antonio, Texas.[15] What is your opinion of this program? What is the best way to get people to buckle up? What are the costs associated with the approach you suggest?
4. What role should the insurance industry play in efforts to promote automobile safety? Discuss.
5. Research your state's financial responsibility law and present your findings to the class. Do you think your state's is adequate? Why or why not?

ANSWERS TO PERSONAL FINANCE I.Q. TEST

1. Fiction. 2. Fact. 3. Fiction. 4. Fact. 5. Fiction. 6. Fact. 7. Fact.

HOW SHELDEN BROWN REACHED HIS PERSONAL FINANCIAL DECISION

Professor Bronstein told Shelden that even though it would take a lot of time and work, he had to carefully reconstruct in his mind and on paper the rooms of his house as they were before the break-in, and determine as nearly as possible what was taken. Although Shelden was very wise to have personal property insurance, he had only covered himself part way by not having an up-to-date list of insurable items in the house. Without the list to verify his insurance needs, Shelden could not be sure that he had adequate coverage, as well as leaving himself open to his current bind.

In addition to coming up with the list, Shelden had to do his best to reconstruct the items' values. He would have to try to remember what he paid for any purchases in the past few years.

Insurance agents, Professor Bronstein explained,

review claims carefully. From experience, they have a good idea of how much an item is worth and can usually tell if a claim is reasonable or not. They, too, are interested in paying a fair amount, Professor Bronstein noted.

Of course, items he inherited were a different matter. One specific step Professor Bronstein suggested was for Shelden to check with a jeweler to ascertain realistically what the value of the missing pieces would be. If Shelden could describe the pieces accurately or, even better, if he had any photographs that showed them, it might help the jeweler give an opinion. Although it was always a good idea to have valuable property assessed before it disappeared, it wasn't impossible to get an estimate now.

Professor Bronstein also suggested to Shelden that he consider adding a replacement value clause to his policy. With this coverage, Shelden's settlement would be for the amount it took to replace the items lost at current prices. Shelden would still need to keep an accurate list of his belongings and make sure that he was adequately covered, but for items like televisions, personal computers, and stereos, this coverage would help assure that he was awarded an adequate amount.

Shelden took the time to itemize the articles he lost so that he felt sure his claim was fair. He included an appraisal from a jeweler, so he knew the claim was realistic. Despite inadequate planning, Shelden did have enough coverage and he was awarded the full amount of his claim with no delay.

PART SIX
INVESTMENTS

LEARNING OBJECTIVES

1. To explain why people invest in stocks and bonds and the risks of doing so. /
2. To discuss the factors that should be considered in an investment decision. /
3. To identify and explain the major features and types of common stocks. / 4. To outline the positive and negative features of preferred stocks and distinguish the major categories. / 5. To describe the major types of corporate bonds. /
6. To differentiate the major types of municipal bonds. / 7. To identify the primary characteristics of bonds and the factors that affect bond prices.

TESTING YOUR PERSONAL FINANCE I.Q.

	FACT	FICTION
1. Interest from a bond issued by the city of Louisville is exempt from federal income tax.	☐	☐
2. Blue-chip stocks got their name from the game of poker because they are considered highly speculative issues.	☐	☐
3. If interest rates rise, the value of a Westinghouse corporate bond is likely to decline.	☐	☐
4. A common stockholder with 10 shares of General Foods has just as much voting power as a person with 1,000 shares.	☐	☐
5. A bond issued by the Pennsylvania Turnpike Authority (and backed by toll revenues) is considered a general obligation bond of the Commonwealth of Pennsylvania.	☐	☐
6. Jane Doe can exempt up to $100 of dividends on her individual federal income tax return.	☐	☐

The materials in this chapter assist in separating fact from fiction. Your answers can be checked on page 450.

CHAPTER FIFTEEN

STOCKS AND BONDS

SHARING A PERSONAL FINANCIAL DECISION WITH PROFESSOR JAMES W. BAIRD OF COMMUNITY COLLEGE OF THE FINGER LAKES

Professor James Baird often helps students make investment decisions. His advice always depends on the student's current financial situation and future prospects. When Linda Griffin, a returning student in her late thirties, asks for his opinion on where to invest her money, Professor Baird first listens carefully as Linda describes her family finances.

Linda explains that John, her husband, served in the Air Force for 21 years, but then developed rheumatoid arthritis as a result of exposure to Agent Orange. Now, at long last, he can anticipate a settlement for his disability. Nevertheless, the case took several years, and there is still no guarantee of how much money he will be awarded—or when.

The Griffins have an 11-year-old daughter. At the moment, with Linda in school, their annual income is $30,000, but with John's illness, Linda's tuition fees, and the cost of living, they just make ends meet. On the other hand, they do have some savings.

In 1978, Linda tells Professor Baird, she received a $10,000 insurance settlement for a back injury she sustained while working at a local store. For years she has used the $10,000 for a six-month certificate of deposit, currently yielding 8 percent interest. Linda's CD will soon come to maturity, and she wonders if there's a way to get more money from her investment. A few nights ago a friend mentioned the profits he'd reaped on the stock market, but Linda isn't sure if that's the route she should take.

If you were Professor Baird, what would you advise?

To find out how Professor Baird helped Linda with her personal financial decision, turn to page 451.

"Now is always the most difficult time to invest."
Anonymous

common stock: units of ownership in a corporation.

Figure 15-1
THE PROSPECTUS FROM RANDOM HOUSE'S 1959 PUBLIC OFFERING

Source: Bennett Cerf, *At Random: The Reminiscences of Bennett Cerf* (New York: Random House, 1977), p. 277. Reprinted by permission.

Bennett Cerf and Donald Klopfer bought the Modern Library in 1925 and built it into a leading publisher of reprinted books. Two years later, the pair decided to publish some original works at random. Thus, Random House—the publisher of this textbook—was born.

Random House, Inc., was organized as a corporation. Cerf and Klopfer owned its *common stock,* the units of ownership interest in the corporation. But as the years went by the founders began to worry about estate taxes (see Chapter 20); so in 1959 they sold 30 percent of Random House's total outstanding shares to the public (see Figure 15-1).

This sale netted Cerf and Klopfer $1 million each. The stock soared from its issue price of $11.25 to $45, largely on the strength of two best-sellers: James Michener's *Hawaii* and Moss Hart's *Act One*. Most stock fluctuates in price over time in response to such factors as general economic conditions, company earnings, and future growth and profit prospects—and Random House's stock was no exception. At one point, the price actually declined to $9 per share.

In 1960 Cerf and Klopfer used some of their Random House stock to buy Alfred A. Knopf, Inc., a publishing house they had long admired. By 1965 Cerf and Klopfer were investigating a possible *merger* (a joining of two companies) with a larger firm (Time-Life), but this was rejected when the U.S. Justice Department opposed the combination due to the likely reduction of competition in the publishing industry.

Then RCA showed an interest. But negotiations stalled in a dispute over whether RCA would offer .6 or .62 of an RCA share for a share of Random House. RCA's David Sarnoff refused to approve the higher figure, so Cerf and his wife left town for a vacation with Frank Sinatra and Mia Farrow. When they returned, RCA agreed to the .62 to 1 stock ratio, and the sale was completed. Random House was valued at $40 million, a far cry from Cerf and Klopfer's original investment of $215,000. Random House remained part of the RCA organization until 1980, when it was acquired by the Newhouse group.[1]

The Random House story shows how important stock was in the development of this company and in the personal finances of its two principals—Bennett Cerf and Donald Klopfer. Stocks and bonds can also play a vital role in the financial health of people in the mid-1980s.

THE ROLE OF STOCKS AND BONDS IN MODERN BUSINESS

Most companies—like Random House—begin as privately owned enterprises; in other words, they are run and financed by a single family or group. If a company is successful, it will probably want to expand, but it will need additional money to finance this effort. Instead of exhausting their entire personal resources or committing the firm to substantial interest payments on borrowed funds, the owners may decide to convert their private corporation into a public one. As Cerf and Klopfer did with the ownership of Random House, the owners agree to share the company, exchanging a share in its profits for investor funds, or capital.

The company issues shares of stock, which sell for a set amount per share (the issuing price). Investors buying these shares provide the company with additional operating funds. In exchange for these funds, the company allows the shareholders to participate in its growth and may begin paying a percentage of its profits to the shareholders as dividends. Some companies do not pay dividends but instead reinvest their profits in the firm to finance further growth. Stockholders in such firms benefit from increases in the value of the shares they own.

The formation of a corporation is governed by a *charter,* a document that is registered in the state of incorporation. It describes the purpose of the firm and specifies the maximum number of shares the corporation can issue. The initial issue is usually only a small fraction of the total number of authorized shares that a company is allowed to issue. To raise additional funds in the future, firms may decide to issue more of the remaining authorized shares.

The corporation may also decide to raise money by issuing *bonds,* which are agreements to pay back a certain amount of money—the principal of the debt—in a specified period of time, with interest. In financial terms, a stock involves *equity,* or ownership, while a bond represents a *debt* repayable to the bondholder. For this reason, a bond is also known as a debt instrument.

The decision of whether to issue stocks or bonds affects the issuing corporation in different ways. Suppose a corporation with 5 million shares of outstanding stock decides to raise needed funds by issuing an additional 500,000 shares. The impact of this new stock issue is to reduce each shareholder's fractional ownership of the corporation by 10 percent. On the other hand, the firm might decide to raise money by borrowing through a bond with a 10-percent annual interest rate. Since a bond is simply an IOU, or promissory note, the interest must be paid to bondholders each year and the face value (or principal) of each bond must be repaid on the date specified on the bond. The face value is typically $1,000.

Bonds may be issued by corporations, the federal government, or state and city governments and agencies. In the same way that banks pay interest for

charter: *a document that governs the formation of a corporation, describing the purpose of the firm and the number of shares to be issued.*

bonds: *agreements to pay back a certain amount of borrowed money plus interest in a specified period of time.*

the use of funds kept in savings accounts, a corporation or government body also pays interest on the bonds they issue to raise capital. In contrast to stocks and savings accounts, however, the term of the loan is specified: 10, 20, 30, or more years. In addition, the interest rate is typically set for the life, or term, of the bond, although a growing number of firms are now offering adjustable-rate bonds.

Thus, a company's reason for issuing stocks and bonds is clear: to attract investors and raise needed capital. But why do ordinary people, who have no personal stake in a business, decide to take on this risk? The answer lies in the definition of an investment.

WHAT IS AN INVESTMENT?

Investing can be defined as follows:

> The use of one's ability to attract scarce economic resources for purposes other than current consumption with the intention of receiving future financial gain through income and/or appreciation of value.[2]

investing: the use of one's ability to attract scarce economic resources for purposes other than current consumption with the intention of receiving future financial gain through income and/or appreciation of value.

This chapter takes a closer look at this definition to learn exactly why people invest in stocks and bonds.

ATTRACTING SCARCE RESOURCES

When we "attract scarce resources," we gather together the money we have saved or borrowed to make an investment. This money cannot be used for "current consumption": it cannot be spent on food, clothing, shelter, or other necessities. Nor can it be used for such luxuries as a new stereo or videotape recorder. These luxuries are a powerful lure that can wipe out the money put aside for investments. As author Richard P. Halverson states, "most of us are constantly faced with the decision not between investing and basics, but between investing for the future and consuming some luxury today."[3]

THE INVESTOR'S INTENTIONS

The "intentions" mentioned in the definition of investing are a key investment ingredient. Investing means that we put money in stocks, bonds, real estate, collectibles, or other instruments that we one day hope to sell for a profit. Antique furniture in your home is not an investment unless you plan to sell it some time in the future. Nor are the $2 bills and silver dollars you have collected since childhood. Thus, the intention must be to make money through the future sale of something of value. Even if a loss results, an investment has been made if making money was the goal.

FUTURE FINANCIAL GAIN

The desired outcome of any investment is "future financial gain." You want to earn dividends or interest and see your holdings grow in value. Simply preserving what you started out with is not enough. As one investor puts it, "When your main concern is to preserve and protect your money, you are simply saving, not investing."[4]

Since future financial gain is the primary reason people invest, let's take a closer look at what this investment goal is all about.

WHY PEOPLE INVEST

Most investors are interested in one of two things: they want to see their investment grow in value, or they want to receive a steady, substantial income. While both objectives are desirable—and some investors seek a compromise position of some income and some growth—there is generally a trade-off between growth potential and current income.

CAPITAL GROWTH

The most important goal of most investors is capital growth, or *appreciation*—which refers to an investment's increase in value over time. In most cases, this increase does not make the investor rich overnight; rather, it steadily grows in value as the years go by. Of course, everybody dreams of buying shares of stock in new firms that will become the IBMs and General Motors of the twenty-first century. In 1940 a share of IBM could be purchased for about 35 cents. Today, IBM stock—which has split several times—changes ownership at prices that are well over $100 per share. Similarly, General Motors' stockholders who bought 10 shares in 1940 for $468 had parlayed their investment to 60 shares worth $2,200 in 1981 as a result of stock splits. Each of these stockholders also received $6,200 in dividends.

Although growth of this kind reveals previous strengths and possible growth prospects for a firm, it does not guarantee that the corporation will continue to grow or grow at the same pace in the future. Just think about companies like Auburn Motors, DeLorean, and Pierce Arrow—all of which failed—both in the marketplace and as investments for the stockholder.

appreciation: capital growth, or an investment's increase in value over time.

INCOME

Some investors—especially those with limited funds—purchase stocks and bonds for income rather than growth. They seek bonds, preferred stock, and high-quality common stocks, which offer steady, dependable interest or dividends.

Table 15-1
COMPANIES PAYING DIVIDENDS FOR MORE THAN 100 YEARS

Company	Year Dividend Payment Began
Bank of New York Co., Inc.	1784
First National Boston Corp.	1784
Fleet Financial Group, Inc.	1791
Norstar Bancorp Inc.	1804
Citicorp	1813
First National State Bancorporation	1813
Chemical New York Corp.	1827
Morgan (J. P.) & Co., Inc.	1840
Chase Manhattan Corp.	1848
Connecticut Energy Corp.	1850
Connecticut Natural Gas Corp.	1851
Manhattan National Corp.	1851
Bay State Gas. Co.	1852
Manufacturers Hanover Corp.	1852
Washington Gas Light Co.	1852
Cincinnati Gas & Electric Co.	1853
Continental Corporation	1853
Scovill Inc.	1856
Pennwalt Corporation	1863
Singer Company	1863
Irving Bank Corp.	1865
First Atlanta Corporation	1866
Travelers Corporation	1866
CIGNA Corporation	1867
American Express Co.	1868
InterFirst Corporation	1875
Stanley Works	1877
Cincinnati Bell Inc.	1879
Bancal Tri-State Corp.	1880
American Telephone & Telegraph Co.	1881
Corning Glass Works	1881
Security Pacific Corp.	1881
Bell Canada	1882
Carter-Wallace, Inc.	1883
Chesebrough-Pond's Inc.	1883
Exxon Corporation	1883
Consolidated Edison Co.	1885
Eli Lilly and Company	1885
UGI Corporation	1885

Source: 1983 New York Stock Exchange Fact Book, p. 30. Reprinted by permission of the New York Stock Exchange.

These investments are not difficult to find. More than half of the 1,499 companies with shares listed on the New York Stock Exchange have common stock on which dividends are currently being paid. As Table 15-1 shows, 35 companies have been issuing annual dividend payments for over 100 years.

In recent years, bonds have also yielded high, steady income for investors. Unfortunately, neither stock nor bond income is guaranteed. Companies can choose at any time to reinvest their earnings into the business instead of issuing dividend payments to stockholders. Or they can reduce or eliminate a payment if earnings are down.

Similarly, interest payments on bonds, which represent a debt obligation, are more assured than stock dividends. Although Chrysler Corporation omitted its preferred stock dividend for two trouble-plagued years during the early 1980s, it never missed a bond interest payment. However, bond holders, like holders of common or preferred stocks, may receive little or no return if the organization issuing the bond goes bankrupt.

THE RISK OF INVESTING

Regardless of whether the investor's primary objectives are growth or income, investing in stocks and bonds involves risk. For this reason, financial writer William G. Shepherd, Jr., calls investing a form of gambling. "Ceaseless effort goes into cloaking investment in reassuring terms," says Shepherd. "But it is and always will be a form of gambling; for it is a placing of one's chips on something that cannot be seen or touched, a game played against an infinitely imaginative opponent: the future. It is, in bookies' lingo, how we as a nation 'lay off the bets'."[5] Shepherd's conclusion is simple and direct: individuals should not invest funds they cannot afford to lose.

SPECULATORS VERSUS INVESTORS

In evaluating the risk involved in investing, it is useful to distinguish between investors and speculators. *Speculators* purchase securities with the goal of making a quick profit by reselling them within a short time period at a higher price. They purchase stock on the basis of "hot tips"—rumors of a merger, a new mineral discovery, increased prices as a result of weather conditions adversely affecting the profits of competitors, or unexpected higher company earnings. The risks taken by the speculator are typically high, but the payoffs can also be high—if the "hot tip" materializes.

By contrast, *investors* purchase stocks, bonds, and other commodities based on expectations that their earnings and values will increase gradually over a longer period of time. The stocks and bonds they buy provide them with at least some assurance of the safety of the initial investment and promise of appreciation.

Of course, the distinction between speculators and investors is not always clear-cut. Some investors are comfortable with assuming more risk than others. For this reason, investors must consider the risk-return ratio in determining the type of investment vehicles they are most comfortable with.

RISK-RETURN RATIO (Lack of Knowledge)

Risk involves uncertainty about the future. As any investor knows, risk enters the picture in varying degrees for any investment. The future is always uncertain, so no potentially profitable venture is entirely free of risk.

Although the typical investor attempts to minimize risk, additional enticements must be present to prompt investment in higher-risk securities or other business ventures. The risk-return ratio is the relationship between the expected return from an investment and the amount of risk the investor is willing to assume. The ratio is a positive one: the greater the risk, the higher the expected return must be. Figure 15-2 diagrams the trade-offs between risk and expected returns and shows several examples with different risk-return ratios.

Investors unwilling to accept the risk of losing their initial investment may choose a smaller—but virtually risk-free—return by placing their funds in government bonds. Those willing to accept more risk in return for higher expected returns will probably choose to invest in corporate stocks and bonds. Extremely risky investments such as so-called penny stocks (whose shares typically sell for less than a dollar) offer the possibility of very large payoffs for success as well as the risk of losing most or all of the initial investment in the event of failure.

Investment risks are real and potentially dangerous. They can sabotage even well-thought-out investment plans and consume profits and investment capital. Only by understanding the nature of these risks can a person attempt to reduce their effect on an investment program.

Figure 15-2

THE RISK-RETURN RATIO

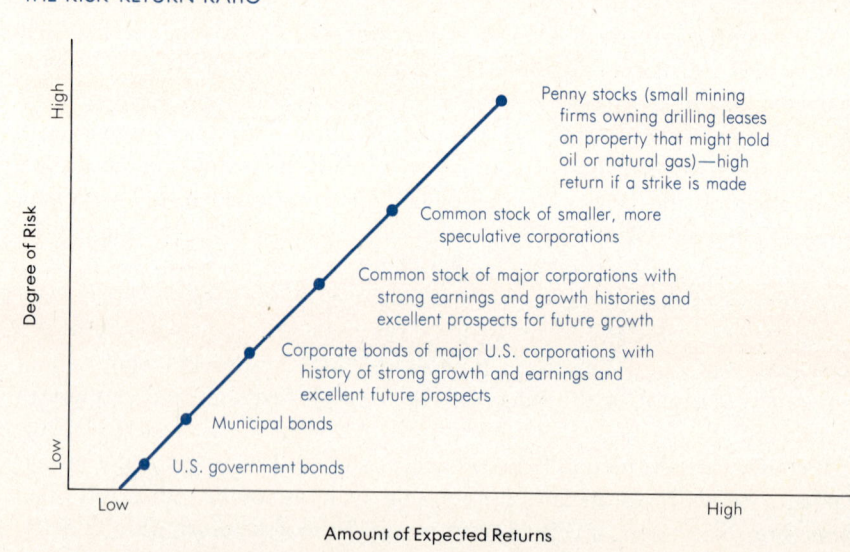

- Penny stocks (small mining firms owning drilling leases on property that might hold oil or natural gas)—high return if a strike is made
- Common stock of smaller, more speculative corporations
- Common stock of major corporations with strong earnings and growth histories and excellent prospects for future growth
- Corporate bonds of major U.S. corporations with history of strong growth and earnings and excellent future prospects
- Municipal bonds
- U.S. government bonds

(Axes: Degree of Risk (Low to High) vs. Amount of Expected Returns (Low to High))

STOCKS AND BONDS

TYPES OF RISK

Several types of risks exist for the investor. They include purchasing-power risk, market risk, business risk, and interest-rate risk.

Purchasing-Power Risk. Every investor's goal at the very least is to earn more on his or her investments than the rate of inflation. When investments fall short of this goal and earn a lower rate of return than the current inflation rate, purchasing power is lost.

[margin note: req r.o.r. > infl. rate]

The purchasing-power risk makes choosing a low-risk but profitable investment difficult, for safety and security usually imply a low rate of return. Your money may be secure, for example, if you purchase a highly rated bond yielding 6 percent interest from a solid corporation. But your purchasing power will take a beating if the inflation rate exceeds 6 percent. If the return on your investments simply matches the inflation rate, you have not made a profit.

Market Risk. Fluctuations in the prices of common stock and other securities may not be related to events taking place in a company or to the size of company earnings or dividends. They may result from such seemingly unrelated factors as the threat of conflict in the Middle East, a rumor that the Federal Reserve Board is about to tighten the money supply, the death of a world leader, or a blizzard that paralyzes New York and Washington. It is often impossible to predict even sharp changes in the market value of investments.

"Corporate Triumph, Then Death in a Ferrari"

The grim headline in the normally staid *New York Times* told of the tragic death of 40-year-old Dennis R. Barnhart, the president and chief executive officer of Eagle Computer. Only hours earlier, he had sold his company's stock to the public for the first time and become a multimillionaire.

Eagle's 2.75 million share offering had been made in order to raise needed funds for expansion. The firm's Eagle PC had proven to be competitive with the IBM personal computer, and additional new products were planned. The shares were quickly snapped up by investors at $13 each, generating $37 million in funds. Demand was so high that the stock rose in price to $17 before closing at $15.50.

But these first-day profits were short-lived. Upon learning of Barnhart's death, Eagle's board of directors rescinded the stock offer. This meant that purchasers would be refunded their purchase price and any market transactions occurring after the stock issue would also be canceled. The consequence was that those who profited during the first day's trading activity had to return their earnings as well.

Although this human tragedy shows how even the securities markets are vulnerable to issues of life and death, it also reveals the tie corporations have with these markets in raising funds. The following day Eagle's board of directors announced that a new offering would take place later the same month.

Source: The Eagle stock issue is described in Isadore Barmash, "Corporate Triumph, Then Death in a Ferrari," *New York Times*, June 10, 1983, pp. A1, D3.

Market risk can wipe out an investment if the market moves in an unexpected direction. If investors find it necessary to sell all of their stocks or bonds when market prices have declined temporarily, they can lose all the accumulated profits as well as the original investment capital. This risk is part of the investment gamble, and one must be prepared to accept it.

Business Risk. The risk of business failure is a threat to every stock and bond investor. As stockholders of Braniff, W. T. Grant, and Korvette's can attest, such a failure can result in bankruptcy. In such instances, little or no value remains in the investor's holdings of the failed firm's securities.

Business risk can also occur without an earning decline. If common stock investors expect higher earnings than are actually achieved, they may decide to sell their stock and in so doing cause the price of the stock to decline. Even a slight reduction in earnings or a maintenance of the status quo in the face of expectations for higher earnings can cause a decline in the price of a firm's shares.

The regulation of big business by the federal government can create business risk as well. The stockholders of American Telephone and Telegraph spent most of 1983 wondering what would happen to the value of their holdings after the court-ordered breakup of AT&T the following year.

Interest-Rate Risk. Interest-rate fluctuations are a major influence on stock and bond prices. Bond prices are directly linked to the rate of interest. A person who pays $1,000 for a corporate bond paying 9 percent interest will be unable to sell the bond for $1,000 before maturity should interest rates rise to 10 percent. Unless the bond is held until maturity (at which time the full $1,000 face value will be paid by the issuing corporation), he or she will suffer a loss in selling the bond. Since investors have similar alternatives offering higher interest rates, they will be willing to purchase the bond only if the price is reduced to compensate for the 9 percent interest rate.

Common-stock prices are also affected by interest rates, but in a less direct way. When interest rates rise, investors are able to secure higher returns from other investments, such as certificates of deposit, Treasury bills, and money-market accounts. Thus, their risk-return ratio shifts in the direction of the investments offering greater returns at no additional risk. The result of this increase in interest rates may be to reduce the attractiveness of common stock, thereby triggering a decline in their market prices.

WHAT RISKS CAN YOU AFFORD?

How much risk you can afford depends on your investment goals. You must know exactly what you want to accomplish from your investment program in order to assess the amount of risk you are willing to take. This knowledge can come only through analysis of your current and future financial status.

How the AT&T Breakup Affected Stockholders

What happens to shares of common stock in a major corporation when the federal government orders the breakup of the company? This question was raised recently in the face of the largest such breakup in U.S. history. Instead of owning shares in the largest communications company in the world, American Telephone and Telegraph's 3.2 million shareholders found themselves owning eight separate companies in 1984: a "new" AT&T, whose primary business is to operate Bell Laboratories, and produce and sell equipment, and seven regional holding companies that provide local and long-distance telephone service. The eight new firms (and the old... "Ma Bell") are shown below.

Under the agreement, AT&T stockholders were assigned 1 new share in each of these seven companies for every 10 shares of AT&T stock they held. They retained their shares in the parent company as well. The plan involved the creation of 610 million shares of common stock in the seven regional companies. Owners of fractional shares received cash for the partial shares.

The result of this breakup is to increase investment flexibility and uncertainty. Flexibility is created by the ability to invest in a specific segment of the "old" AT&T, rather than the entire company. Uncertainty results from the variations in strengths among the regional companies. Future investors must consider such factors as quality of management, degree of competition, and age of equipment before investing funds in these smaller companies.

A GUIDE TO THE TELEPHONE STOCKS

	Stock Table Abbreviation	Ticker Symbol
AT&T "old"	ATT	T
AT&T "new"	ATT	T
Ameritech	Amrtc	AIT
Bell Atlantic	BellAt	BEL
Bell South	BellSo	BLS
NYNEX	NYNX	NYN
Pacific Telesis Group	PcTel	PAC
Southwestern Bell Corp.	SwBell	SBC
US West	USWst	USW

Source: "Guide to Telephone Stocks" from *New York Times*, November 18, 1983, p. D17. Copyright © 1982/83 by The New York Times Company. Reprinted by permission.

AGE AND RISK

If you are young and have more than enough money to pay current bills and save for future needs, you can afford investments that promise a large potential payoff at some unknown time in the future. As you grow older and need your investments to provide steady income rather than growth, you can afford fewer risks. This movement from high-risk to low-risk investments should take place gradually as the years pass. When people reach retirement age, the great bulk of their investments should be income-producing. If you are still in good health, at least some of your investment funds should remain in securities that should grow in value over time. Since people have every reason to expect to live for quite a few years after retirement, they can afford to take some risks in the hope of making a long-term gain.

LIFE SITUATION AND RISK

Personal circumstances—your health, the amount of money in the bank, earnings, the age and educational needs of your children, the size of your family debt, the stability of your marriage—all affect how much money you can afford to risk on investments. If, for example, you have three children in college, you probably cannot afford the risk of a big investment loss. Similarly, if you are earning too little to replace the money received from a life insurance or divorce settlement, you should take as few risks with these funds as possible. The appropriate investment goal is income, not speculative growth.

PERSONALITY AND RISK

Some people are better risk-takers than others. Those who can take risk in stride can handle the occasional fluctuations in the investment markets. Those who cannot do so should not be investors. It is not unusual for some people to lie awake at night thinking about the money they might lose if stock or bond prices dropped. Others are so upset by a loss that they refuse to sell even though their stock or bond shows every sign of continuing its downward course. If you would react to risk in this way, the stock and bond markets are not for you.[6]

CLARIFYING INVESTMENT GOALS

Your self-assessment will help determine your investment goals. This information can be used to decide whether you need current income or desire future growth. Investors can choose from a number of different types of securities: common stock, preferred stock, and bonds. Figure 15-3 shows how these types of securities compare in meeting three specific investor objectives: growth in the value of the investment, income, and safety. This figure serves as a useful summary of the relative strengths and weaknesses of each type of security.

INVESTING IN COMMON STOCKS

What does it mean to own 100 shares of Monsanto or 200 shares of Texaco common stock? In its simplest terms, stock ownership represents equity; you actually own a small share of the corporation.

Figure 15-3
COMPARING SECURITIES WITH INVESTMENT GOALS

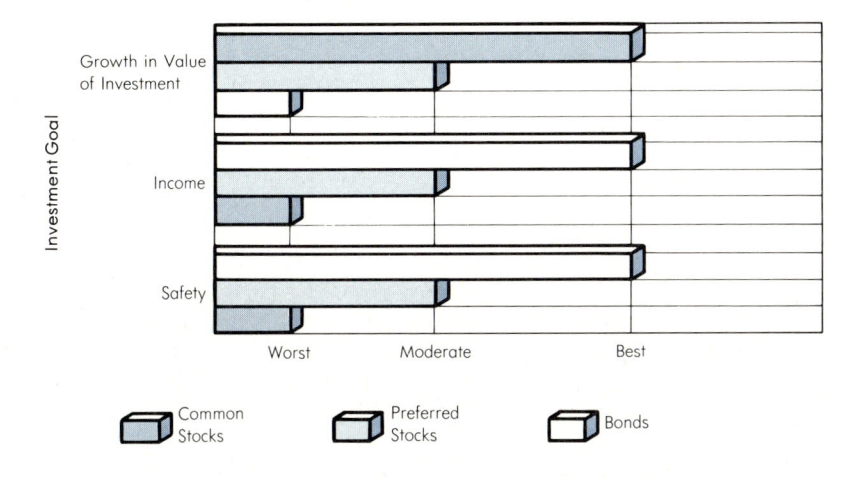

WHY DO INVESTORS PURCHASE COMMON STOCK?

The best way to answer the question of why investors purchase common stock is to consider the formation of a new business. Suppose that you have a great new business idea. You have invented a product—a shoeshine kit that polishes shoes all by itself. You know there is a demand. All you need is the capital to get started.

After carefully analyzing major production and sales costs, you decide that $100,000 is needed to get the business under way. Unfortunately, you do not have that kind of money, nor do you know anyone who would be willing to lend it. The banks have refused to grant a loan. As a young and as yet unproven business person, you are not a good credit risk.

With all these sources of capital closed to you, there is only one other way to raise money. You can incorporate, "go public," and sell shares in the company. You decide that you will attract the largest number of investors by offering the stock at $1 a share. A higher price might discourage the small investor (who would be priced out of the market) as well as the large investor (who might wonder whether your as-yet-unproven company is worth the gamble). So you draw up a *prospectus*—a document that formally announces a stock issue. You offer 100,000 shares, hoping that the promise of a labor-free shoeshine will attract investors.

Before the firm is allowed to issue the stocks, approval must be obtained from state and/or federal regulatory agencies. Once this is accomplished, investors can be offered the opportunity to purchase a fractional share of your corporation—Easy Shine. But why would they invest their funds in your—or

prospectus: *a document that makes the formal announcement of a stock issue.*

any—company? What do they expect from their investment? In most cases, their investment objective is appreciation in value. In other instances, they may desire income in the form of dividends. And in all cases, common stockholders expect to have a voice in the operation of the firm in the form of voting rights.

Appreciation. As noted earlier, investors hope that their stock will increase in value as the company grows and prospers. The appreciation of common stocks is possible only because stockholders have the right to sell their property on the open market any time they wish.

Dividends. Stockholders also hope that company profits will be distributed to shareholders in the form of *dividends*. Dividends are not at all certain in established companies and are questionable in newly organized corporations. Even if your firm realizes a $50,000 profit after its first year of operation, top management may decide to plow all the money back into the company to finance additional growth. These profits are called *retained earnings*. If only $25,000 is reinvested, the remaining $25,000 is distributed to shareholders in the form of dividends. The shareholder with 1,000 shares will then receive $250.

Dividends are expressed in dollar amounts. To compute a stock's *yield*, you divide the annual stock dividend by the stock's market value. A stock selling at $40 a share with a dividend of $4 a share yields a dividend of 10 percent.

Common-stock dividends frequently rise and fall with company profits. Each quarter the board of directors decides whether to declare a dividend and, if so, how large it will be. Companies try to avoid cutting dividends because doing so shakes investor confidence. But if poor earnings force a company into a tight financial bind, it may eliminate all shareholder dividends for as long as necessary.

Dividends may be issued in the form of cash or additional stock. Stock dividends grant a stated amount of free stock for every share of stock already owned. Although many investors prefer stock dividends over cash because of the opportunity for future appreciation of their newly acquired stock, these dividends represent no net gain for shareholders and may even depress the stock's market value. Because the number of outstanding shares increases in the same percentage as an investor's stock, their ownership percentage remains the same. And with more shares outstanding or available, demand will decrease, thus lowering the stock's price.

Some 1,300 companies across the country issue stock dividends through *dividend reinvestment plans (DRPs)*, which offer current stockholders the opportunity to automatically reinvest their cash dividends in additional common stock without paying brokerage commissions on the transaction. Many DRPs offer shares at 95 percent of their current market value, thus providing stockholders with an additional incentive to reinvest and the company with additional capital.

---

dividends: company profits that are distributed to shareholders.

retained earnings: company profits that are plowed back into the corporation rather than being distributed as dividends.

yield: the dividend divided by the stock's market value.

dividend reinvestment plans (DRPs): programs that give current stockholders the opportunity to automatically reinvest their dividends in additional common stock without paying brokerage fees on the transaction.

STOCKS AND BONDS

Voting Rights. In addition to the opportunity to share in the profits of the company, common stockholders have the right to vote at certain corporate meetings. Stockholders elect a board of directors to establish overall policy for the company. The directors then hire the management. These elections take place at the company's annual meeting, which all common stockholders are invited to attend. Stockholders who are dissatisfied with company management or policy can voice their sentiments at this meeting. If they have a concrete proposal they want all stockholders to consider, they can make a motion to the board to submit the issue for a vote. Figure 15-4 gives shareholders notice of AT&T's ninety-eighth annual meeting and lists the purpose of the meeting.

Votes are apportioned according to the number of shares held: 10 shares means 10 votes; 100 shares, 100 votes; and so on. So the small investor with just a few shares will not be able to exert much influence in an election; the main influence will be wielded by someone with controlling interest—a percentage of the stock that is larger than that held by any other individual. Nevertheless, the small investor does have a say in the process. Questions are decided by a simple majority.

Figure 15-4
NOTICE OF AT&T ANNUAL MEETING

Notice of Meeting
The 99th Annual Meeting of Shareholders of American Telephone and Telegraph Company will be held in the Milwaukee Exposition and Convention Center, 505 West Kilbourn Avenue, Milwaukee, Wisconsin, on Wednesday, April 18, 1984 at 9:30 A.M. for the following purposes:

1. To elect directors for the ensuing year;
2. To ratify the appointment of auditors to examine the Company's accounts for the year 1984;
3. To authorize the AT&T 1984 Stock Option Plan; and
4. To act upon such other matters, including shareholders' proposals (beginning on page 19 of the accompanying proxy statement), as may properly come before the meeting.

Holders of common shares of record at the close of business on February 28, 1984 will be entitled to vote at the meeting or any adjournment thereof.

Thomas O. Davis
Corporate Vice President and Secretary

February 28, 1984

Source: American Telephone and Telegraph Company, 1983.

PLACING A VALUE ON COMMON STOCK

Consider for a moment how the value of the common stocks of Easy Shine, our hypothetical company, is determined. Suppose that after three years of operation, the company is booming. One million kits have already been sold and consumer demand shows no signs of easing up. A soon-to-be-completed factory promises to boost production and sales even more. As a result, the price of a share of common stock has zoomed by $10 a share—boosting the value of a share way above its original $1 cost to $11. The $11 price of the stock is certainly an indication of its value. However, other methods of valuation are also used.

Par Value. The arbitrary value assigned to each share by the company's charter is referred to as its *par value*. This value is often a nominal amount—$1 or $2, for example. Although at some earlier time par value may have had some meaning, it is typically ignored by investors today and is really just a convention. Par value is such an inaccurate guide to even a newly issued stock that many companies issue stock at "no par." *Does have meaning*

par value: the arbitrary value often assigned to each share of common stock by the company's charter.

book value per share: the value determined by adding up the original cost of all that the company owns, subtracting all that it owes, and dividing by the number of outstanding common-stock shares.

Book Value. If over a period of time, the value of a firm's assets—equipment, land, plant facilities, and inventory—increases without a corresponding increase in the amount the company owes, then the book value of each share also increases. *Book value per share* is an accounting term for the value arrived at by adding up all that the company owns, subtracting all that it owes, and

net val. of co. on books

Owners of common stock can express their opinions on company performance and on corporate decisions at the annual stockholders' meeting.

dividing the remaining net worth by the number of outstanding common-stock shares.

The book value of the company is the minimum price someone should pay for the company if it were liquidated, just as the book value of a used car is the minimum that should be paid if it were sold. Unlike cars, however, most corporations have the potential for making money, and so the book value is probably lower than a realistic selling price for a going concern. And, because it is based on a single point in time, it does not indicate whether the company's total value has been increasing or declining. In as short a time period as a year, the picture may change dramatically.

Although book value provides an assessment of the cost of assets owned by the company, it is of little value in assessing the worth of a going concern. It leaves investors with no idea of the company's profitability. It does not indicate the kind of dividends the shareholders have been receiving or can reasonably expect to receive in the future, nor does it indicate whether the supply-and-demand forces of the stock market will push the stock's value even higher or cause a sudden drop in price.

Market Value. In the final analysis, a share of stock is worth what people in the market think it is worth. Remember the book value of your car: it may be $5,000, but it really has little value as a source of needed funds if you cannot find a buyer.

STOCKS AND BONDS

"You're down 2 ⅜."

Market Values Fluctuate Constantly on Wall Street, the Home of the Stock Market.

Source: *Grin and Bear It* by George Lichty. Copyright News Group Chicago, Inc. Courtesy of News America Syndicate.

Potential investors are always looking toward the future, and their opinion of the company's potential for growth and future profits will cause the stock to increase or decrease in price. Indeed, anticipation of future profits is often much more important to investors than current earnings per share, for when future prospects are good, investor demand pushes up the market value of the stock.

DETERMINING VALUE IN DOLLARS AND CENTS

Although the book and market values of a stock provide important information, they reveal little about company earnings. This information is available by analyzing two other measures of a stock's worth: earnings per share and the price-earnings ratio.

Earnings per Share (EPS). Corporations vary greatly in both the size and the number of shares of common stock outstanding, so some technique is required to make meaningful comparisons. *Earnings per share (EPS)* is a ratio designed to make such comparisons. EPS is determined by dividing the corporation's total earnings for a specific time period by the number of shares outstanding. Consider, for example, a small corporation with 400,000 shares of outstanding common stock and earnings last year of $80,000. Its EPS would be calculated as follows:

earnings per share (EPS): the company's total annual earnings divided by the number of shares outstanding.

$$\text{Earnings per share} = \frac{\text{Total net company earnings}}{\text{Total common stock outstanding}} = \frac{\$80,000}{400,000} = 20 \text{ cents per share}$$

The earnings-per-share ratio is widely used as an indicator of company profitability. These earnings function to finance future growth and serve as a source of dividends for the corporation's stockholders.

price-earnings (P/E) ratio: the current price of a share of stock divided by its earnings per share for a 12-month period.

Price-Earnings (P/E) Ratio. In its simplest terms, the *price-earnings (P/E) ratio* is the current price of a share of stock divided by its earnings per share for a 12-month period. A company that sold stock for $50 a share but earned $5 a share during the past year has a price-earnings ratio of 10. The market value of the stock is 10 times its current earnings.

What does this mean to investors? Price-earnings ratios commonly range from 10 to 20, with the average probably closer to the lower figure. In rapidly growing companies, however, a P/E ratio of 50 is not uncommon. In general, a high P/E ratio indicates investor optimism about a company. Investors are willing to pay a relatively high price for shares because they see the possibility of continued growth and large earnings in the future.

Analysts believe that by studying a company's price-earnings ratio over a relatively long period of time, one can determine whether a company is a good investment. If, for example, over a five-year period, the P/E ratio ranged from 10 to 40 and the stock's current ratio is 15, the stock would be desirable if the investor were fairly certain of the company's financial health. In the light of its historical pattern, this low ratio suggests that the stock is now a good buy. If, on the other hand, the current P/E ratio is 39 or 40 (which is at the high end of its historical pattern), there is a good chance that the stock will drop. Too high a P/E ratio may also be a sign of speculative fever. A stock whose market price is 80 to 100 times its current earnings may lose investor interest unless it continues to grow rapidly.

A company's price-earnings ratio must also be analyzed in terms of current market conditions. What may be considered a low at one point may be a high at another due to such economic factors as rising unemployment, deepening recession, or high interest rates. If, for example, the interest rates of high-quality bonds are only 5 or 6 percent, investors may be drawn to growth stocks, where they have a possibility of earning much more for their money. Under these conditions, they may be willing to pay 25 or 30 times the company earnings for the stock. When interest rates are high, however, and bonds yield 10 or 11 percent, these same growth stocks and the risks surrounding them may seem less attractive. When this happens, the P/E ratio may fall to 15 or 20.

The price-earnings ratio is so commonly used that it even appears with the stock quotations in daily newspapers. However, despite its acceptance as a measure of company performance, it provides no guarantee of distinguishing with great accuracy between winners and losers. The market often fluctuates in response to such intangibles as investor enthusiasm and the tastes of the moment. One year investor tastes may boost semiconductor, computer, and other high-technology stocks; the next, they support oil and utilities. Such tastes are difficult to predict, but taste will often determine the current market favorites.

TYPES OF COMMON STOCK

Stocks perform in different ways and are intended for different investment purposes. Some investors are attracted to current income, while others are interested in future growth. Some stocks are speculative, while others are solid but conservative. It is important to clarify these stock types in order to find the stock that best meets your investment needs.

Blue-Chip Stocks versus Growth Stocks. In the game of poker three different color chips are used to bet on a game; the blue chip has the highest value of all. Similarly, in the stock market, *blue-chip stocks* are those that are considered to be of the highest quality on the market. They represent such industrial giants as IBM, General Motors, and AT&T. A blue-chip stock can be recognized by its solid earnings history and its future prospects.

Although the earnings of blue-chip companies may not be spectacular, they are usually steady, even during recessionary periods. Solid prospects for future earnings and dividends make blue-chip stocks some of the most desirable stocks on the market. Thus, investors tend to hold on to these stocks even when earnings are slow. This tendency makes it even more likely that blue chips will maintain their market value when times are bad.

Growth stocks, on the other hand, show a record of superior earnings growth per share, which ultimately translates into rapidly rising stock prices. This

blue-chip stocks: stocks issued by large companies with solid earnings.

growth stocks: stocks with records of superior earnings growth per share and rising share values.

growth, which may be as high as 10 percent a year or more, is fueled by continued growth in demand for the company's products. This demand may continue for a number of years since growth companies usually outperform other companies in their field. Eventually they may become the market leaders.

Unlike blue chips, growth stocks offer investors the chance for spectacular future profits but little or no opportunity for current income. Current earnings are usually plowed back into the business to finance future growth by improving technology, increasing production capacity, expanding market coverage, and perhaps seeking out international markets.

Growth stocks are often found in newly emerging fields, such as computer technology and energy conservation. When a firm develops a new product in an established field, it is considered a growth company. Polaroid was such a company when it first developed its instant photography process.

Since growth companies are often relatively new, it is important to analyze carefully the abilities of the company's management before investing. This investigation is critical for an investment in a small firm that has only a few key people making the major decisions.

In general, growth stocks are only appropriate for those investors who seek large capital gains and are willing to wait for the right time to sell. If you can afford to forgo current dividends in order to invest in a dynamic, emerging company, you should consider growth investments.

Income versus Speculative Stocks. *Income stocks,* which include the blue chips, offer investors the highest possible current income and stability. Investors face minimal risk, but they also have little chance to see the market value of their investment appreciate rapidly.

At the other end of the spectrum, *speculative stocks* are ultraperformance growth stocks, or at least they are perceived as such by investors. In the hope that a stock will double or triple in value in a short time, investors take higher-than-average risks. They face the chance of a sharp decline in the market price of the stock and even the possibility of company bankruptcy.

These potential profits and risks are tied to the uncertain prospects of the company. It may be new and unproven, or its success may depend on the discovery of oil or diamonds or on the changing fortunes of a changing industry, such as gambling.

Because of the uncertainty that surrounds speculative stocks, they are not for everyone. One must have the temperament as well as the money to be a successful speculator. Although many of yesteryear's speculative stocks and the money investors poured into them are nothing but faded memories, some issues overcame the risks and are now established leaders on the stock market. Investors willing to risk their money may take comfort in the fact that when first issued, General Electric and IBM were both considered speculative stocks.

---

income stocks: stocks with high current income and stability; this classification includes blue chips.

speculative stocks: stocks that are perceived as ultra-performance growth stocks but also carry considerable risk.

STOCKS AND BONDS 435

Cyclical versus Defensive Stocks. The movement of a stock's price can be seen in relation to the overall movement of the stock market. Two common indicators (discussed in Chapter 16) are the Dow Jones Industrial Average and Standard & Poor's 500. *Cyclical stocks* are issues whose ups and downs most closely follow the general movement of the market. Manufacturing companies in the auto and chemical industries, for example, will follow general market trends. There will always be exceptions, but on the whole these stocks typically lose value when the market declines.

Some stocks "defend" investors from market downtrends. They remain stable when the market fluctuates, or they may even be countercyclical, faring better when the market is on the way down. Generally, these *defensive stocks* are issued by companies that are regulated by outside agencies (government-supervised utilities, for example) or provide essential goods and services, such as food and drugs.

ADDITIONAL FEATURES OF COMMON STOCK

Holders of common stock may receive certain benefits that increase the value of their investments. These benefits include rights, warrants, and stock splits.

Rights. A corporation in need of additional funds may issue additional securities. To entice its existing stockholders to buy these securities, it may offer them at below-market prices for a limited period of time in the form of *rights*. The number of rights stockholders receive is in direct proportion to the number of shares of stock they own.

When AT&T wanted to raise $1.2 billion in new capital in the 1970s, it told its several million shareholders that they would receive one right for every share of stock they owned and that 20 rights plus $100 would entitle them to purchase one additional share of stock. At the time AT&T was trading for about $140 a share, so the below-market-value rights that the stockholders received had a value over and above the value of the stock itself.

AT&T stockholders who wished to take advantage of this offering had the choice of purchasing additional shares on the company's terms (20 rights plus $100) or selling their rights, which were valued at $2.30 each on the open market ($46 — the difference between the market value of a share and its cost under the rights offering — divided by 20, the number of rights needed to purchase one share). Thus, stockholders with fewer than 20 shares could buy the rights that they needed to purchase one more share of AT&T at the below-market price.[7]

Warrants. Like rights, *warrants* are a promise by the company to sell common stock at some future date at a stated price. But unlike rights, warrants are sometimes issued to company stockholders and nonstockholders alike for

---

cyclical stocks: stocks whose movements closely follow what is happening on the overall stock market.

defensive stocks: stable issues of firms regulated by government agencies or companies that provide essential goods and services.

rights: company authorizations that allow current stockholders to buy additional securities at below-market prices for a limited period of time.

warrants: a promise by a company to sell common stock at some future date at a stated price.

terms that may be as long as one to five years and at prices that may exceed the current value of the stock.

Warrants become valuable only when the market price of the stock increases. For example, each share of $5 stock you purchase might be accompanied by a warrant to purchase one more share at $10 within two years. This warrant becomes valuable only if the price of the stock climbs above $10. If it climbs to $20, for example, a share of stock can be purchased for $10 less than it is actually worth.

Because of their potential value, warrants are traded just as shares are and become attractive investments should the price per share rise above the price stated on the warrant. Speculators may purchase them in the hope that stock prices will climb—which is by no means certain. The future value of warrants issued by high-risk companies is especially doubtful. These companies are often so shaky that the only way they can sell their stock is by issuing warrants, which give investors an extra incentive to buy.

Stock Splits. Occasionally a company will split its total outstanding stock issue—simply called a *stock split*—effectively doubling or tripling its number of outstanding shares. In a 2-for-1 split, the holder of 10 shares will receive 10 additional shares. Splitting resembles a stock dividend on a grand scale; it gives shareholders more stock but does not necessarily add to the value of their holdings. Their proportional share of the company is still the same.

A stock split in a well-functioning stock market usually indicates a healthy company whose stock price is very high due to great demand. To stimulate trading, the company effectively reduces the price of its stock (by one-half in the above example) so that small investors can afford to buy. Such snowballing demand ultimately benefits those who hold on to all their stock after the split takes place. Corporations like AT&T have had numerous stock splits over the years.

Stock prices may even rise in anticipation of a split and continue to rise after the announcement of the split is made. For example, when on January 19, 1983, the Dun & Bradstreet Corporation recommended a 2-for-1 split (subject to shareholder approval), the stock rose to a record high of $109 per share. By February 17, 1983, the stock had climbed even higher, to $114 per share, even though the actual split had not yet taken place. (The previous year, Dun & Bradstreet stock had sold for as low as $58.50 per share.)[8]

EVALUATING COMMON STOCKS AS AN INVESTMENT VEHICLE

A careful analysis of your investment goals and the risks involved in the purchase of common stock is the starting point in the development of an investment strategy. It is often difficult to maintain this cautious, deliberate approach when reading about boom markets that take the price of General Motors

---

stock split: a decision to increase the number of shares outstanding in order to reduce the current market price of each share.

STOCKS AND BONDS

common stock from 33 to 65 and those of IBM from 57⅛ to over 130 within a few months. These kinds of gains can make one want to jump into the market without first specifying financial needs, risks involved, and investment objectives.

The right common stock can provide current income or the chance to parlay an investment into a more generous nest egg in future years. This nest egg is nurtured by the federal tax structure. If you hold on to common stock for more than one year and if the stock value rises, the net gain from the sale of the stock (the *capital gain*) is taxed at a lower rate than ordinary income.*(The profits from stock sold within one year of its purchase is taxed at the full income tax rate.) In addition, $100 of dividend income ($200 for a joint return) is exempt from taxes each year. In effect, the government encourages the purchase of common stock through these tax breaks. Without individual investors risking their capital in the nation's businesses, these businesses could not survive.

Clearly, the soundness of the American economy is an issue for individual investors as well as for government. If a person believes in the current strength of the economy and in its future growth, investing in common stocks for income, growth, or a combination of both should be considered.

*may be changing — all gains rated ordinary rate?

INVESTING IN PREFERRED STOCKS

Many investors want to own stock in a company but wish to avoid some of the risks present in common stock. They turn instead to preferred stock. Preferred stock is also an equity security—that is, it represents partial ownership in a corporation—but it differs from common stock in several important ways.

POSITIVE FEATURES OF PREFERRED STOCK

As its name implies, *preferred stock,* which is issued by relatively few companies, receives certain preferred treatment over common stock, particularly in terms of rights to company assets and dividends.

Prior Claim on Corporate Assets. If a company goes out of business, one's risk of losing money is smaller if one owns preferred rather than common stock. The law requires that the claims of preferred stockholders be paid ahead of those of common stockholders. Although all the company's debt must be paid first, the investor's chances of seeing his or her investment capital again are certainly better with preferred than with common stock.

Dividend Payments. Holders of preferred stock also receive their full dividends before any dividend payments to common stockholders. Moreover, these dividends are fixed by the company, typically at a higher rate of return than common-stock dividends. Thus, investors know in advance exactly how

preferred stock: an issue that grants its holder certain preferred treatment over common stock such as a prior claim on assets and first right to dividends.

much they will receive in dividends and are fairly certain that their payments will be on time. In this respect, preferred stocks are similar to bonds.

Dividend payments are expressed as a percentage of the original investment. Thus, a preferred stock paying 9 percent on a $1,000 investment yields $90 a year. Dividends are paid four times a year.

Conversion Feature. In order to attract investors who are interested in receiving fixed dividends for the next few years but who also want the opportunity to participate in increased market prices of stock should the company continue to grow and operate profitably, some corporations offer convertible preferred stock. Such stocks are sold with the agreement that within a specified period of time, the investor can exchange his or her shares for a predetermined amount of common stock. This is called a *conversion feature*. The value of these convertible preferreds depends largely on the quality and value of the common stock. If the common stock increases in value, the value of the convertible preferreds will also rise.

NEGATIVE FEATURES OF PREFERRED STOCK

Although the above-described features make preferred stock a good choice for many investors, other investors will avoid preferreds because of several limitations. These include dividend limitations, possible call features, and the lack of voting rights except in unusual situations.

Dividend Cap. Common stockholders benefit when company earnings rise. They frequently share in the company's good fortune by receiving larger dividend payments. Preferred stockholders do not. Their dividends remain the same even in boom times. This dividend cap affects the market value of the stock. Consequently, those investors seeking the potential for higher earnings tend to shy away from preferreds, while those seeking dependable dividends tend to hold on to their stock. The result is a market with few dips and rises in stock value.

Call Provision. Most preferred stocks contain a *call provision*—that is, the issuing company has the right to buy back the shares at a specified price at any time it chooses. This price is often slightly above the stock's market value. Companies generally call in an issue of preferred stock when falling interest rates enable them to offer another issue at a lower dividend—a move that can substantially reduce the dividends they must pay their stockholders. Unfortunately, shareholders who would prefer to hold on to their high-income shares are penalized by this feature.

Lack of Voting Rights. Unlike holders of common stock, owners of preferred stock usually have no voting rights in the corporation. They cannot elect

---

conversion feature: a preferred stock or bond issue that allows the investor to convert his or her shares into a predetermined amount of common stock.

call provision: a feature of a preferred stock or bond that allows the company to buy it back at a specified price.

members of the company's board of directors or vote on corporate policy questions that are placed before common stockholders. They exchange this right for the stability of dividends and the relative security of their investment. In some corporations, the no-vote rule may be broken when dividends are withheld from shareholders. When this happens, owners of preferred stock get voting rights for the election of board members as long as dividends remain unpaid.

TYPES OF PREFERRED STOCK

Preferred stock is either cumulative or noncumulative, participating or nonparticipating. Each type affects the investor in a different way.

Cumulative versus Noncumulative. Although preferred-stock dividends are much more likely to be paid than common-stock dividends, they may be decreased or even eliminated at the discretion of the board of directors. Whether preferred stockholders will eventually receive the withheld dividends depends on the type of preferred stock purchased: cumulative or noncumulative.

Owners of *cumulative preferred stock* ultimately receive all dividends that are omitted. These payments accumulate and must be paid in full before any common-stock dividends are paid. Owners of *noncumulative preferred stock,* on the other hand, have no such guarantees. They receive dividends only when they are declared by the board of directors. And when part or all of a dividend is omitted, shareholders simply lose their right to that dividend payment forever. Most preferred stock is cumulative.

Participating versus Nonparticipating. In the vast majority of cases, preferred stocks are *nonparticipating*—that is, they do not earn additional dividends even if the corporation has a banner year. However, a few companies offer *participating preferred stock,* which entitles stockholders to dividend increases when times and profits are good. These increases are issued only if earnings surpass a specified level.

EVALUATING PREFERRED STOCKS AS AN INVESTMENT VEHICLE

Investors seeking a more secure, higher-income investment than common stock provides, with some possibility of capital gains if the market value of their stock increases, are attracted to preferred stocks. Yet, however substantial these benefits are to some investors, the disadvantages discussed earlier make preferreds unattractive investment vehicles to many more investors.

The decision to buy preferred stock should, of course, be based on individual financial needs. If you have major expenses or if you do not expect your income to increase as much as your future financial needs, preferred stocks may offer the steady, high income needed without the market fluctuations and

cumulative preferred stock: an issue whose dividends accumulate and must be paid in full before any common-stock dividends are paid.

noncumulative preferred stock: an issue that receives dividends only when declared by the board of directors.

nonparticipating preferred stock: an issue with a set preferred-stock dividend and no provision for increasing the dividend.

participating preferred stock: an issue that allows for an increase in preferred dividends if profits surpass a certain level.

risk of common stock. If finances are not a problem, common stocks offer more opportunity and higher potential profits.

INVESTING IN BONDS

When you purchase a bond, you become a creditor to the corporation or government body issuing the bond. As indicated earlier, you lend your money in exchange for a contractual promise from the debtor to repay the original investment plus interest. These payments are made at regularly scheduled intervals—typically every six months. Unlike common and preferred stocks, which represent ownership in a corporation, bonds are a form of indebtedness, a negotiable IOU, entered into by a company or government body.

CORPORATE BONDS

Corporations seeking to raise additional funds but wishing to avoid diluting the ownership rights of current stockholders by issuing additional shares may choose to borrow money by issuing corporate bonds. The debt that the corporation enters into may be secured by specific corporate assets or merely by the corporation's promise to pay. Corporate bonds are issued by thousands of corporations, both large and small, across the country. They are usually issued in denominations of $1,000, although many are more costly, for terms of 2 to 30 years or even longer. Although there are at least a dozen different types of corporate bonds, we will examine only those of most interest to individual investors.

Mortgage Bonds. Mortgage bonds are secured bonds. Among the safest bonds issued by corporations, *mortgage bonds* are backed by the corporation's fixed property. Just as a homeowner puts his or her house up for collateral when receiving a mortgage, the corporation issuing mortgage bonds puts up its plants, equipment, real estate, and other tangible assets. If the corporation defaults—that is, if it cannot make good on its obligations—bondholders have a primary and indisputable claim on these assets.

The safest mortgage bonds are called *closed-end bonds*. These bonds guarantee that the bondholder will have first claim on the property even if the corporation issues additional bonds pledging the same security. The bondholders are in the same position as the holder of a first mortgage on a house. Even if a second mortgage is issued using the house as security, the claim of the first mortgage holder is primary if the mortgage payments are not met.

Collateral Trust Bonds. Collateral is property pledged by a borrower to secure repayment of a loan. The corporation issuing a *collateral trust bond* puts up security in the form of its own stock and bond holdings. This portfolio is kept

---

mortgage bonds: corporate bonds secured by the corporation's fixed property.

closed-end bonds: mortgage bonds that guarantee the holder first claim on property even if it is used to back other bonds.

collateral trust bonds: secured bonds backed by a corporation's own stock and bond holdings.

in trust by a commercial bank and may be awarded to the creditor in the event of default.

If the value of the securities portfolio goes below a certain level, the trustee will, according to an agreement known as an *indenture,* require the company to add money or securities to ensure that the bond continues to be backed by adequate collateral. Because of these safeguards, collateral trust bonds are a desirable, secure investment.

indenture: *an agreement whereby a company is required to back their collateral trust bonds with adequate collateral.*

Debentures. *Debentures* are unsecured obligations; they are IOUs in their purest form, backed only by the "general assets" of the corporation. No mortgage, lien, or specific property secures the loan. Very often these intangible assets consist of nothing more than the reputation of the issuing corporation. With such intangible backing, only debentures of the highest-rated companies are attractive to investors. When issued by a well-established, financially secure corporation, debentures are no less credit-worthy than secured obligations.

debentures: *unsecured corporate obligations backed by the firm's general assets.*

Subordinated Debentures. *Subordinated debentures* are unsecured obligations backed by the "general assets" of the issuer, but they are riskier than debenture bonds. If claims are made against the company, holders of subordinated debentures must wait in line for their money until all regular debenture holders have been paid. They are subordinate, or junior, in regard to claims; regular debentures take priority in case of default.

subordinated debentures: *unsecured corporate obligations backed by the corporation's general assets but subordinate to regular debentures.*

GOVERNMENT BONDS

Every level of government—federal, state, and local—borrows money from investors to help pay for government services and finance government debt. This borrowing takes place at the federal level in the form of treasury bills, notes, and bonds, which were discussed in Chapter 6. At the state and city levels, it takes the form of municipal bonds.

Municipal Bonds. *Municipal bonds* are debt obligations issued by a state, city, town, village, or U.S. territory or possession. They are also issued by various local government agencies that provide such public services as schools and public housing. The main attraction of municipal bonds—or *munis* as they are called—is the exemption of bond interest from federal income tax. In most cases, they are also free of state and local taxes if the bondholder lives within the jurisdiction of the local government issuing the bond.

municipal bonds: *debt obligations of a state, city, town, village, or U.S. territory or possession.*

Investors seeking this tax-saving feature have poured increasingly large sums of money into munis in recent years. As noted in Figure 15-5, tax-exempt bond sales are on the rise. In 1982, for example, sales were 70 percent higher than in 1981.

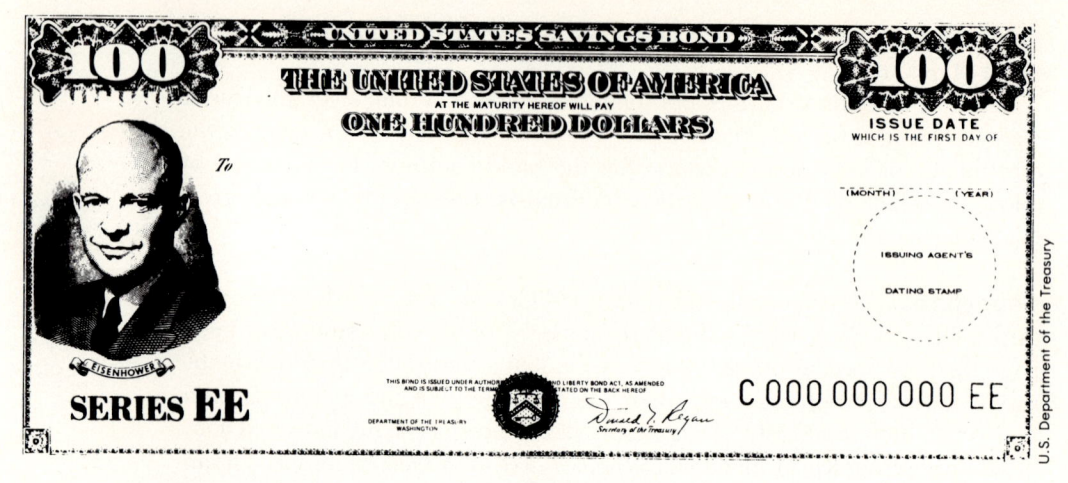

When an individual buys a U.S. government bond, he or she in effect lends the government money to help it pay for goods and services.

The tax-exempt status of a municipal bond means that the real rate of return is higher than that on a taxable bond with the same stated rate of interest. The following equation can be used to find a tax-exempt bond's taxable equivalent yield, or the interest percent a taxable bond would need to equal the earning power of a municipal bond:

$$\text{Taxable equivalent yield} = \frac{100 \times \text{Tax-free-yield percent}}{100 - \text{Tax-bracket percent}}$$

Thus, if a person were in the 30-percent tax bracket and his or her tax-exempt bond yielded 12 percent, the formula would indicate a taxable equivalent yield of 17.14 percent.

$$\frac{100 \times 12}{100 - 30} = \frac{1200}{70} = 17.14 \text{ percent}$$

In general, financial analysts recommend tax-free municipals for those in the 30-percent tax bracket and above. Those with smaller incomes receive higher after-tax yields with competitive taxable bonds.

general obligation bonds: *municipal bonds backed by the full faith and credit as well as the full taxing power of the issuer.*

revenue bonds: *municipal bonds secured by income from a particular source.*

There are two general types of municipal bonds. *General obligation bonds* are backed by the full faith and credit as well as the full taxing power of the state, city, or other municipality that issues them. They are typically used to finance non-revenue-producing projects. By contrast, *revenue bonds*—which account for two-thirds of all tax-exempt bonds—are secured by income from a particular source, such as a toll road or a state college dormitory. The full interest and principal owed bondholders is paid from these sources, not from the general revenue. If there is insufficient revenue and interest cannot be paid temporarily, the bonds are not in default.

Figure 15-5
STATE AND LOCAL BORROWING SINCE 1970

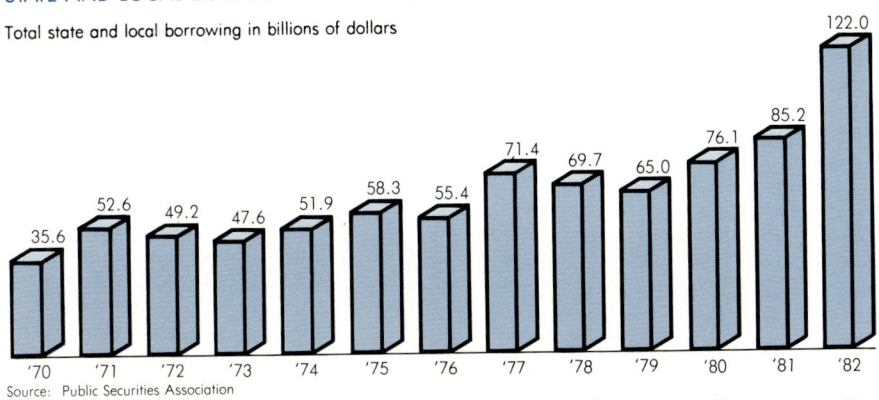

Total state and local borrowing in billions of dollars

'70	'71	'72	'73	'74	'75	'76	'77	'78	'79	'80	'81	'82
35.6	52.6	49.2	47.6	51.9	58.3	55.4	71.4	69.7	65.0	76.1	85.2	122.0

Source: Public Securities Association

Source: Michael Quint, "The Boom in Municipal Bonds," *New York Times*, March 17, 1983, p. D1. Copyright © 1982/83 by The New York Times Company. Reprinted by permission.

Many investors consider well-chosen revenue bonds a better investment than general obligation bonds. Depending on the general taxing power of the municipality, the ability of general obligation bonds to repay their obligations may be weakened when the municipality's general tax revenues are low, as they are during recessions and periods of high unemployment. Revenue bonds that are linked to essential income-producing services such as water and sewage are considerably safer investment vehicles.

BOND CHARACTERISTICS

Investors should be aware of a number of bond characteristics that may affect their suitability as an investment vehicle. These include fixed-interest payments and two other characteristics shared by some preferred stocks: conversion features and call features.

Fixed-Interest Payments. When a corporation or government body issues a bond, it promises to pay back the sum it borrowed plus a fixed rate of interest. This interest is paid at regular intervals until the bond matures. No matter what happens to the bond market after the bond is issued, the interest payments are fixed for the life of the bond.

The method by which bondholders collect interest payments depends on the type of bond they own. *Registered bonds* are assigned directly to the bondholders; their name and address are listed on the face of the bond, and the issuing corporation mails interest payments directly to them. By contrast, holders of *coupon* (or bearer) *bonds* must take several steps in order to collect interest payments. First, they must clip a coupon that is attached to the bond. This coupon is then deposited in the bond issuer's bank or in the holder's own

registered bonds: bonds that are assigned directly to the bondholder, with interest payments issued directly to the bondholder by mail.

coupon bonds: bearer bonds that include coupons that can be deposited like checks when interest is due.

Figure 15-6
CORPORATE BOND AND EXAMPLES OF BOND COUPONS

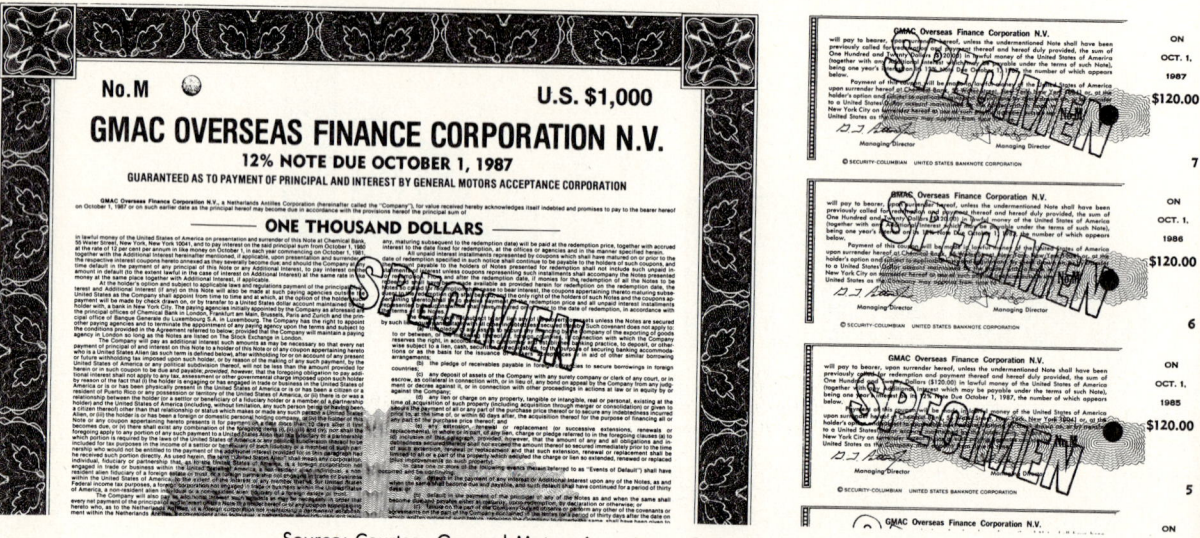

Source: Courtesy General Motors Acceptance Corporation.

bank, just as a check would be. Figure 15-6 shows a coupon bond issued by GMAC Overseas Finance Corp., N.V. and three coupons from the bond dated October 1, 1985; October 1, 1986; and October 1, 1987. The maturity date shown on the face of the bond is October 1, 1987, so these are the last remaining coupons to be used before the bond matures.

Conversion Features. In some instances, bondholders have the privilege of converting their holdings into a specified amount of common-stock shares in the corporation. In other words, they can change the very nature of their holdings from a debt obligation to equity. If the price of the common stock increases greatly, so will the market price for the convertible bonds.

Call Features. Like preferred stocks, bonds may have call features. In such cases the issuer may decide to call back the bond issue if falling interest rates make it possible to issue new bonds with a lower rate of interest. A 20-year bond paying 13 percent interest is considered expensive by the corporation when interest rates are 10 percent. If these bonds contain a call feature, the company is likely to retire the bond issue.

Most types of bonds provide call protection, which guarantees that the bond will not be called for a limited number of years. This protection is generally available for 5 years from utilities and 10 years from industrial corporations. Longer protection is possible only for purchases of treasury bonds and notes, which usually cannot be called, and general obligation municipal bonds.

FACTORS AFFECTING BOND PRICES AND INTEREST RATES

The amount paid for a bond is linked to three major factors: interest rates, the bond's rating, and its length or maturity.

Interest Rates. A decision by the Federal Reserve System to tighten credit, thereby holding down the money supply and discouraging inflation, sends interest rates up. The opposite decision, to expand the amount of money in the economy to encourage business activity, lowers interest rates. Both decisions have an impact on the price paid for a bond, for when interest rates rise, bond prices fall, and vice versa.

The reason for this relationship is simple: supply and demand. If a bond pays 11 percent and interest rates fall to 9 percent, your bond will be worth more than its face value should you try to sell it before it matures. This difference—called a *premium*—is directly tied to the fact that a large number of investors want the bond since it is paying higher-than-market rates. Conversely, when interest rates rise, the value of the bond will fall since few people are willing to purchase a bond when they can receive higher rates elsewhere. When this happens, the bond will sell at a *discount*. Its market value will be less than its face value.

premium: *the value of a bond in excess of its face value.*

discount: *the amount that a bond's face value exceeds its market value.*

Interest rates and bond prices are also affected by the amount of borrowing in the marketplace. More borrowing means greater demand for money and higher bond prices. As Figure 15-7 reveals, the largest borrower by far is the federal government.

Bond Ratings. Analysts' opinions of the credit worthiness of a company or government body influence the price of the bonds that are issued. These opinions are expressed in bond ratings, which give investors an idea of the amount of risk they take when they buy a bond. In essence, these ratings tell investors the likelihood of receiving their interest payments on schedule and their principal at maturity.

Two organizations, Standard & Poor's Corporation and Moody's Investors Service, Inc., provide a bond-rating service. Table 15-2 explains the categories used by the two firms to rate the credit worthiness of various bonds.

Bonds in the four top rating categories are considered the most secure investments. Those in the next two grades (BB/Ba and B) are less secure investments. In the analysts' opinion these bonds may or may not be able to pay interest when due or repay the principal at the bond's maturity. The remaining rating categories contain *junk bonds,* which may pay no interest or be issued by companies that are already in default. The descent is from investment grade to speculative, which includes junk bonds. The risk of losing part or all of your money grows increasingly larger at each rung of the speculative-ratings ladder. Ratings address credit risk, not market risk. Even a triple-A bond will drop in price if market interest rates rise.

junk bonds: *bonds that pay no interest, or that represent high investor risk.*

446 INVESTMENTS

Figure 15-7

THE FEDERAL GOVERNMENT'S SHARE OF ALL U.S. BORROWING

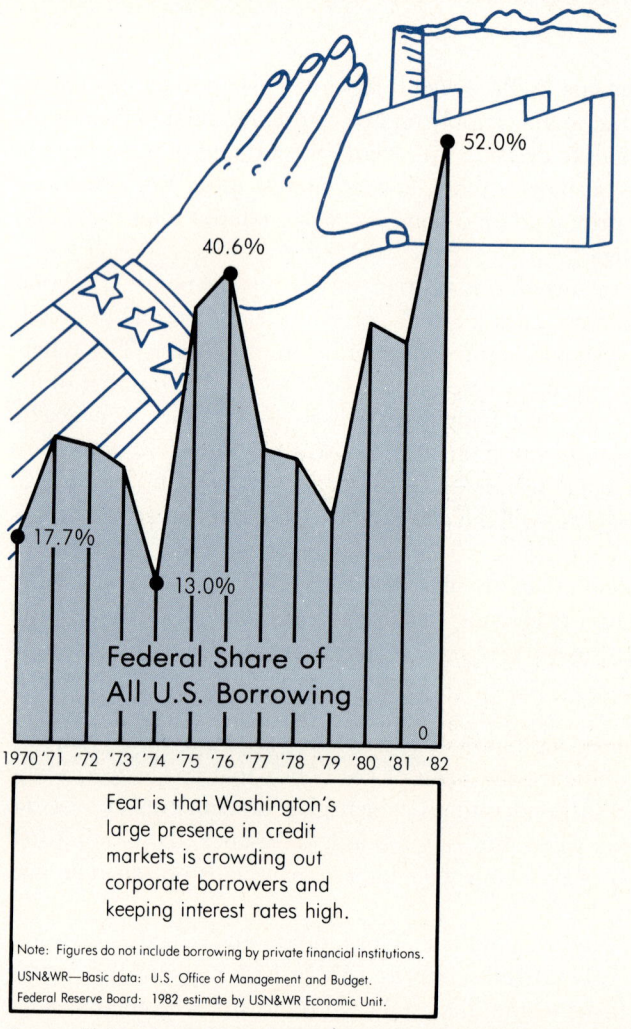

52.0%
40.6%
17.7%
13.0%

Federal Share of All U.S. Borrowing

1970 '71 '72 '73 '74 '75 '76 '77 '78 '79 '80 '81 '82

Fear is that Washington's large presence in credit markets is crowding out corporate borrowers and keeping interest rates high.

Note: Figures do not include borrowing by private financial institutions.
USN&WR—Basic data: U.S. Office of Management and Budget.
Federal Reserve Board: 1982 estimate by USN&WR Economic Unit.

Source: "When National Debt Gets Out of Control." Reprinted from the June 14, 1982 issue of *U.S. News & World Report*; Copyright 1982, U.S. News & World Report, Inc.

Generally, the higher the bond rating, the more expensive the bond. The fact that people are willing to pay a premium for more secure investments pushes the price of the bond up and the interest rate down. Looked at in another way, this means that the more costly, high-quality bonds have a lower yield than the relatively inexpensive, low-quality bonds.

Although the ratings issued by Standard & Poor's and Moody's usually agree, they may be a grade apart. Both organizations generally review bond

Table 15-2
MOODY'S AND STANDARD & POOR'S BOND RATINGS

Moody's	Interpretation	Standard & Poor's	Interpretation
Aaa	Prime Quality	AAA	Bank Investment Quality
Aa	High Grade	AA	
A	Upper Medium Grade	A	
Baa	Medium Grade	BBB	
		BB	
Ba	Lower Medium Grade or Speculative	B	Speculative
B	Speculative	CCC	
		CC	
Caa	From Very Speculative	C	
Ca	to near or in Default		
C		DDD	In Default (Rating Indicates the Relative Salvage Value)
		DD	
		D	

Source: Courtesy of Standard & Poor's Corporation and Moody's Investors Service, Inc.

ratings on an annual basis, downgrading or upgrading bonds that are already on the market according to the condition of the issuer. These ratings are available from banks and brokers. Important changes in the ratings of big issues are announced in the financial section of newspapers.

Maturity. In most cases, the longer it takes for a bond to mature, the higher the interest rate the bond pays. If, for example, there are two bonds from the same company, one of which matures in 10 years and the other in 50, the longer loan will probably provide a higher rate of interest despite the fact that both loans are with the same borrower. The reason is that the longer one's money is tied up, the greater the uncertainty about future developments that might affect the stability of the borrower and the interest-rate climate.

CALCULATING BOND YIELDS

Yield is a measure of return on investment—that is, the money actually earned on a stock or bond. There are two ways to determine yield—by looking at current yield and at yield to maturity.

Current Yield. Suppose that soon after a company issues a 30-year bond with a face value of $1,000 and an interest rate of 8 percent, interest rates rise and the next bond issue carries an interest rate of 8.5 percent. While the older bond pays $80 a year ($1,000 × 8 percent), the newer issue pays $85

The Allure of Junk Bonds

On the surface, investing in junk bonds—the bonds rated in the cellar of the Standard & Poor's and Moody's rating systems—makes no sense, especially in these uncertain economic times. Yet thousands of people jump at the chance to put their money in these high-risk investments and, surprisingly enough, they have several good reasons for doing so.

Most investors buy junk bonds because of their higher yields. These yields outpace the rate of inflation, which is something low-risk, triple-A bonds typically do not do. In the early 1980s, for example, when interest rates were at an all-time high, Metropolitan Edison's BB-rated bonds, maturing in the year 2008, yielded 16.4 percent, while some companies' triple-As yielded only 10.7 percent.

In addition to high yields, junk-bond investors also profit from the fact that these bonds are issued at deep discounts from their face value. If investors hold the bonds until maturity, they will earn a large capital gain (the difference between the face value of the bond and the amount they actually paid for it).

Many investors also find junk bonds attractive because of their conversion features. At the same time they are earning a high rate of interest, investors have the option of converting their shares into common stock if the company prospers. Even though investors have to sacrifice several points in interest for this conversion right, they are attracted to a convertible bond's flexibility.

---

current yield: a bond's annual interest divided by its market price.

($1,000 × 8.5 percent). This rise in interest rates will cause the price of the older bond to fall to perhaps $960, although the interest stays the same. This decline brings the bond into line with the going market rate, for an $80 return on $960 is close to the current interest rate of 8.5 percent. This interest payment expresses the bond's current values, or its current yield. *Current yield* is expressed in following equation:

$$\text{Current yield} = \frac{\text{Annual interest in dollars}}{\text{Market price of bond}}$$

yield to maturity: the capital gain or loss on a bond plus its interest payments.

Yield to Maturity. Suppose you decide to sell the bond for $960 and take a $40 loss. If the buyer holds it until its maturity, the full $1,000 will be received—a gain of $40. What one gains or loses in this process—including the interest rates earned, the price actually paid for the bond, and the amount received when it is redeemed—is called the *yield to maturity*.

EVALUATING BONDS AS AN INVESTMENT VEHICLE

Before deciding to invest in bonds, one should carefully consider how their advantages and disadvantages will affect investment goals. It is interesting to note that while the bond market is considerably larger than the stock market, it is dominated by institutional investors. The typical investor is more likely to be interested in common stocks than in bonds—particularly corporate and municipal bonds. The limited involvement of typical investors is indicated by the fact that the average number of daily trades for a typical bond is about five.

SUMMARY

Stocks and bonds are the instruments used to finance privately owned enterprises. Common stocks are the units of ownership interest in a corporation. The number of shares issued is specified by the corporation's charter, a document that governs the firm's formation. Money can also be raised by selling bonds—agreements to pay back money plus interest in a specified period of time.

People invest for two primary reasons: to see their money grow or appreciate and to receive a steady stream of income. The risks associated with investing include purchasing-power risk, market risk, business risk, and interest-rate risk. The individual investor should assess the risks he or she can afford at a particular point in life. Factors like age, one's life situation, and personality should enter into the decision.

Most corporations begin by issuing common stock. A prospectus outlining the stock issue is made available to potential investors. Common stocks can be classified in a variety of ways. Blue-chip stocks are issued by large firms with long histories of solid earnings, while growth stocks come from firms with superior earnings growth per share and rising share values. Income stocks, which include blue chips, are those with high current income and stability. Speculative stocks, on the other hand, are perceived as ultra-performance growth stocks that also possess considerable risk. Cyclical stocks are those whose movements closely follow what is happening in the overall market for stocks. Defensive stocks are stable issues of firms regulated by government agencies or companies that provide essential goods and services.

Certain additional features of common stocks are important to investors. Rights are company authorizations that allow current stockholders to buy additional securities at below-market prices for a limited period of time. By contrast, warrants are a promise by a company to sell common stock at some future date at a stated price. Companies sometimes use a stock split to increase the number of shares outstanding. All of these factors can affect the value of a common-stock investment.

Preferred stock is another option open to investors. Preferred stock is an issue that grants its holders certain preferred treatment over holders of common stock, such as a prior claim on corporate assets and first right to dividends. Some preferred issues also have a conversion feature, which allows the conversion of the preferred shares into common stock. The negative features of preferred stock are the cap on dividends; a call provision, which allows the company to buy back the stock at a specified price; and the lack of voting rights. Classifications of preferred stocks include cumulative, noncumulative, participating, and nonparticipating.

Bonds are still another investment option. Corporate bonds may be classified as mortgage bonds, collateral trust bonds, debentures, and subordinated debentures. Government bonds are also available, in the form of treasury bills, notes, and bonds. Municipal bonds are the debt obligations of a state, city, town, village, or U.S. territory or possession.

The values of all bonds—both corporate and government—can be affected by interest rates, the bond's rating, and its length or maturity. The current yield of a bond can be calculated by dividing the annual interest by the bond's market price. The so-called yield to maturity is the capital gain or loss on the bond if held to maturity as well as its interest payments.

REVIEW QUESTIONS

1. Briefly define the following terms:

common stock	dividends	book value per share	income stocks
charter	retained earnings	earnings per share (EPS)	speculative stocks
bonds	yield		cyclical stocks
investing	dividend reinvestment plans	price-earnings (P/E) ratio	defensive stocks
appreciation		blue-chip stocks	rights
prospectus	par value	growth stocks	warrants
			stock split

preferred stock
conversion feature
call provision
cumulative preferred stock
noncumulative preferred stock
nonparticipating preferred stock
participating preferred stock
mortgage bonds
closed-end bonds
collateral trust bonds
indenture
debentures
subordinated debentures
municipal bonds
general obligation bonds
revenue bonds
registered bonds
coupon bonds
premium
discount
junk bonds
current yield
yield to maturity

2. Why do people invest in stocks and bonds despite the risks of doing so?
3. What factors should be considered when making a decision to invest?
4. What are the most important features of common stock? List and briefly explain the major categories of common stock.
5. Identify both the positive and negative features of preferred stock. What are the major types of preferred stock?
6. Describe the major types of corporate bonds. How can municipal bonds be categorized?
7. The stock of Horizon International Corporation is currently selling for $40 per share. Five years ago it sold for $35. It has undergone two 2-for-1 stock splits during this period. If you had purchased 25 shares five years ago and wanted to sell your holdings today, how much profit would you earn?
8. Suppose that when you calculated your income taxes last year, you discovered that you were in the 30-percent tax bracket. If you bought a tax-exempt municipal bond this year with a stated 8-percent annual interest rate, what would the taxable equivalent be for you?
9. Twenty-First Century Mining has declared bankruptcy, and its assets are being liquidated and the resulting cash distributed. The claimants include holders of mortgage bonds, preferred shareholders, holders of debentures, holders of subordinated debentures, and common-stock holders. Who receives money first? What order of preference will follow?
10. Explain the major characteristics of bonds and the factors that affect bond prices.

CASES AND EXERCISES

1. Assume that you have just inherited $10,000. Analyze your current situation and describe how you would invest this money. Explain why you selected this particular approach to investing.
2. Pick an industry and look up the price-earnings ratios of the various firms involved in it. What does this tell you about the industry's future prospects?
3. Identify two or three firms that would fall into each of the following stock categories: blue-chip, growth, income, speculative, cyclical, and defensive.
4. Many people argue that corporate dividends are taxed twice: once as part of corporate profits, then again as personal income when they are received as a dividend (except for a $100 exclusion on an individual return and $200 on a joint return). One proposal would exempt from corporate taxation all profits declared as dividends. How would the implementation of such a proposal affect investing?
5. In 1983 the Washington Public Power and Supply System (WPSS) went into default on some bonds issued to pay for nuclear power plants. How is this default likely to affect investors' perceptions of municipal bonds?

ANSWERS TO PERSONAL FINANCE I.Q. TEST
1. Fact. 2. Fiction. 3. Fact. 4. Fiction. 5. Fiction. 6. Fact.

HOW LINDA GRIFFIN REACHED HER PERSONAL FINANCIAL DECISION

To gain an even clearer picture of the Griffins' current financial needs, Professor Baird sits down with Linda to analyze a monthly budget. Because the Griffins' income just covers their expenses, Professor Baird advises Linda not to speculate with her $10,000 insurance proceeds. At this point in time, Linda and her family should not be taking risks with their money. Even blue-chip stocks present a certain risk. If, for instance, the Griffins suddenly needed extra money, they might be forced to sell stock at a low point on the market and thus might lose on their investment.

Essentially, Professor Baird indicates, Linda already has the right idea in managing her money. He recommends that Linda keep her $10,000 in an interest-bearing account with a six-month maturity so that the funds are available to meet medical bills and unexpected expenses. Of course, she should shop around for the best rates.

After Linda returns to work and her husband receives his disability settlement, she will be in a better position to assume a higher risk with her $10,000. At that time she can reinvest for a higher return.

LEARNING OBJECTIVES

1. To differentiate between primary and secondary markets. / *2.* To discuss the role of different securities exchanges and over-the-counter markets. / *3.* To explain the role of the Securities and Exchange Commission in regulating markets. / *4.* To describe how an investor buys and sells securities. / *5.* To examine the functions performed by stockbrokers and how to go about selecting a broker. / *6.* To identify the various sources of investment information. / *7.* To show how stock indexes are used in personal financial decisions. / *8.* To outline the steps involved in developing a successful investment strategy.

TESTING YOUR PERSONAL FINANCE I.Q.

	FACT	FICTION
1. Every time the price of IBM stock increases by $1, the corporation receives $1 for each share traded.	☐	☐
2. The forerunner of the New York Stock Exchange (NYSE) started meeting under a buttonwood tree in 1792.	☐	☐
3. An investor with a margin account at Dean Witter Reynolds needs to pay the brokerage house only $10,000 on a purchase of $20,000 worth of Exxon stock.	☐	☐
4. Over a billion shares of stock change hands every day in the United States.	☐	☐
5. Spokane, Washington, has a stock exchange just like those in such larger cities as New York, Chicago, and Philadelphia.	☐	☐
6. Only one out of every thousand U.S. corporations is listed on the Big Board, but these NYSE-listed firms control over 40 percent of the assets of American business.	☐	☐

The materials in this chapter assist in separating fact from fiction. Your answers can be checked on page 492.

CHAPTER SIXTEEN

BUYING AND SELLING SECURITIES

**SHARING A PERSONAL FINANCIAL DECISION WITH
PROFESSOR RUSSELL OGDEN OF EASTERN MICHIGAN UNIVERSITY**

When Jennifer Powell's grandmother died, she left her favorite granddaughter $10,000. Jennifer is concerned about making good use of this unexpected inheritance. As a student in Professor Russell Ogden's personal finance class, she has already learned about the importance of planning in making any financial decisions. To get additional advice, she approached Professor Ogden during his office hours.

Jennifer explained that she and her boyfriend Nick plan to get married at the end of the school year, when they both graduate. Although it's still some time in the future, eventually they want to buy their own home and raise children. For now, though, they're both anticipating good job offers, and they've already set up a savings account to cover emergencies.

"After talking it over with Nick, I thought investing in a safe and sound stock would be the best way to use the $10,000," Jennifer indicated. "Obviously, I want the money to grow. From what you said in class, the stock market seems to offer the most growth potential. But I'm not looking for a quick return. In addition, I'd like to get my original investment back in about 10 years—when Nick and I will probably need money to buy a house."

Jennifer stressed that she doesn't want to take big risks. "My real question is: How do I go about finding a safe stock to invest in? I don't want to lose money. How can I make the best choice?"

If you were Professor Ogden, what suggestions would you make?

To find out how Professor Ogden helped Jennifer with her personal financial decision, turn to page 492.

"How to get rich in the stock market: Take all your savings and buy some good stock and hold it till it goes up and then sell it. If it don't go up, don't buy it."
Will Rogers

Investing in motion-picture stocks has made Sheldon Starkman a rich man. Here is how he struck it rich:

"I'm a movie fan and I got addicted to the stock market," says Sheldon Starkman, explaining his curious accomplishment. He is a Los Angeles freelance artist who draws magazine ads and movie posters for a living. But for fun, he has been buying up—single-mindedly and staggeringly—shares of two major motion-picture companies, Warner Communications and 20th Century-Fox. Like many another virtuoso performance in Hollywood history, it sounds crazy but it worked.

When Denver oilman Marvin Davis bought Fox . . . , company officials were astonished to discover that Starkman was Fox's largest individual shareholder. From an initial investment of $130 in 1974, he'd managed to pyramid his holdings to 48,080 shares in the company. That was worth $5.1 million after Davis' offer. Subtracting his enormous loans in his margin account, Starkman received $3.2 million from the Fox sale. (His Warner stock would net him an additional $1.3 million if he sold it.)

Starkman, 49, has stuck stoically with his investments, even when the stocks declined. To keep on buying, he borrowed heavily. "I was putting just about every cent I was earning into the stocks," he says. "Along the way I did everything but hock my house." To pay for all those shares in the two movie companies, he dug deeply into his $15,000-to-$30,000 annual income. He took out personal loans. When things were really tight, he even ate some of his meals free at an uncle's restaurant.

Over the years, he was able to borrow more than $2.3 million from the brokerage house that handled his trades. Much of his leverage came from increases in the value of his stocks. John P. Graner, manager of the Beverly Hills office of Bache Halsey Stuart Shields, where Starkman does his trading, analyzes his success this way: "He has a staying power that very few of us ever have. . . ."

In the six weeks after *Star Wars* came out, he bought 4,900 shares of Fox at an average price of $22 each. Starkman spent $107,800 in all. But he wrote checks for just $15,187. Of that, he borrowed $5,000 from an uncle and $4,300 from a bank, withdrew $2,000 from his savings and took $3,887 from his income. The other $92,613 came from the increasing purchasing power in his margin account as the stock rose from $11 to $24.50.

By 1980, Starkman had accumulated 32,535 shares of Fox. Then the stock split four for three. His equity had increased so much that he was able to relax a little. So he borrowed from his broker against his holdings in order to begin spending some money on himself. His major extravagance: a house in gilt-edged Bel Air on which he and Donna are spending $950,000. Admits Sheldon Starkman, "By all the laws of logic and probability, I was supposed to be wiped out. Instead, I'm rich."[1]

Although it is possible to join Sheldon Starkman as a successful investor without skill, experience, advice, or expertise (credit sheer luck and perseverance), it is not likely. In fact, poor results are much more likely within a short period of time. Only by knowing the basics of buying and selling securities—the subject of this chapter—can you feel confident that your investment plans will have at least a reasonable chance of success. And, even then, you should keep in mind that there are no guarantees when it comes to investing in securities. Even the experts lose at least part of the time.

SECURITIES MARKETS

Once you have made the decision to invest in a specific security, how do you acquire it? How do you make it part of your investment portfolio? Stocks and bonds are bought and sold in two marketplaces: primary markets, which deal in the initial distribution of offerings, and secondary markets, which trade these offerings once they have been purchased. The secondary market is much larger in annual dollar volume and is the market in which you are likely to do most of your investing.

PRIMARY MARKETS

Primary markets are markets in which new issues of bonds, preferred stocks, or common stocks are sold by businesses and governmental units to acquire new funds. Figure 16-1 shows an advertisement announcing the issuance of $200 million worth of bonds by Hospital Corporation of America. Although the convertible subordinated debentures being issued by Hospital Corporation represent debt capital, the firm could have issued equity capital in the form of shares of common or preferred stock. In either case, the reason for the issue would be to raise additional needed funds.

How do the primary markets work? Let's take a look at a hypothetical example to find out. Easy Shine, the hypothetical shoeshine-kit manufacturer introduced in the last chapter, wants to raise $10 million of new capital by issuing 1 million additional shares of common stock.

To accomplish this, Easy Shine's president contacts a specialized financial institution called an *investment banker,* which agrees to acquire the total issue from the firm and then resell it to other investors. The investment banker is referred to as the underwriter of a stock or bond offering. In addition to finding buyers for the issue, the underwriter gives advice to the company selling

primary markets: *markets in which new issues of securities are sold to the public.*

investment banker: *a financial institution specializing in selling new issues of stocks and bonds for business firms and government agencies.*

Figure 16-1
ANNOUNCEMENT OF A BOND OFFERING

This announcement is neither an offer to sell nor a solicitation of an offer to buy these securities.
The offer is made only by the Prospectus.

New Issue / March 4, 1983

$200,000,000

HCA Hospital Corporation of America

8½% Convertible Subordinated Debentures Due 2008

Interest on the Debentures is payable semiannually on March 1 and September 1 beginning September 1, 1983. The Debentures are convertible at any time prior to maturity, unless previously redeemed, into Common Stock of the Company at $51.875 per share, subject to adjustment.

Price 100% and accrued interest from March 1, 1983

Copies of the Prospectus may be obtained in any State in which this announcement is circulated only from such of the undersigned as may legally offer these securities in such State.

Salomon Brothers Inc
Prudential-Bache Securities

Atlantic Capital Corporation
The First Boston Corporation
Basle Securities Corporation
Bear, Stearns & Co.
Blyth Eastman Paine Webber Incorporated
J. C. Bradford & Co.
Dillon, Read & Co. Inc.
Donaldson, Lufkin & Jenrette Securities Corporation
Drexel Burnham Lambert Incorporated
Goldman, Sachs & Co.
E. F. Hutton & Company Inc.
Kidder, Peabody & Co. Incorporated
Lazard Frères & Co.
Merrill Lynch White Weld Capital Markets Group Merrill Lynch, Pierce, Fenner & Smith Incorporated
L. F. Rothschild, Unterberg, Towbin
Shearson/American Express Inc.
Smith Barney, Harris Upham & Co. Incorporated
Warburg Paribas Becker A. G. Becker
Wertheim & Co., Inc.
Dean Witter Reynolds Inc.
Nomura Securities International, Inc.
ABD Securities Corporation
Advest, Inc.
Allen & Company Incorporated
Arnhold and S. Bleichroeder, Inc.
Sanford C. Bernstein & Co., Inc.
Alex. Brown & Sons
Daiwa Securities America Inc.
Dominion Securities Ames Inc.
F. Eberstadt & Co., Inc.
A. G. Edwards & Sons, Inc.
EuroPartners Securities Corporation
Robert Fleming Incorporated
Hambros Bank Limited
Janney Montgomery Scott Inc.
Kleinwort, Benson Incorporated
Ladenburg, Thalmann & Co. Inc.
Cyrus J. Lawrence Incorporated
McLeod Young Weir Incorporated
Montgomery Securities
Moseley, Hallgarten, Estabrook & Weeden Inc.
The Nikko Securities Co. International, Inc.
Oppenheimer & Co., Inc.
Robertson, Colman & Stephens
Robinson Humphrey/American Express Inc
Rothschild Inc.
Thomson McKinnon Securities Inc.
Tucker, Anthony & R. L. Day, Inc.
Wood Gundy Incorporated
Yamaichi International (America), Inc.
Burns Fry and Timmins Inc.
Butcher & Singer Inc.
Cazenove Inc.
Cowen & Co.
Fahnestock & Co.
First of Michigan Corporation
Furman Selz Mager Dietz & Birney Incorporated
Gruntal & Co.
Interstate Securities Corporation
Johnson, Lane, Space, Smith & Co., Inc.
Johnston, Lemon & Co. Incorporated
Josephthal & Co. Incorporated
Legg Mason Wood Walker Incorporated
Neuberger & Berman
Richardson Greenshields Securities Inc.
Wheat, First Securities, Inc.
Craigie Incorporated
Shelby Cullom Davis & Co.
Doft & Co., Inc.
First Albany Corporation
First Harlem Securities Corporation
Herzfeld & Stern
Moore & Schley Capital Corporation
Silberberg, Rosenthal & Co.

Source: Courtesy of Hospital Corporation of America.

the security on such subjects as the general legal requirements of such an offering, its pricing, and the timing of the offering.

A firm that is involved in making a stock or bond offering, as Easy Shine is, compensates the underwriter for its efforts and for the risk it takes in locating buyers. It does this by selling its stock or bonds to the underwriter at a discount. In general, the greater the difficulty the underwriter expects to encounter in selling the issue, the larger the discount it receives from the issuing company. Sometimes when the offering is large, the stock or bond sale is a two-step process: the underwriter might choose to resell the stock or bonds to other investment companies that, in turn, sell them to the public. Thus Easy Shine's underwriter might purchase the 1 million share issue from the shoeshine manufacturer for $10 a share and sell it to various underwriters for $10.75. The second group of underwriters would then offer it to investors for $11 a share.

America's Investors: Myths and Realities

The New York Stock Exchange's ninth survey of share-ownership dispels a number of common misconceptions about investments and investors. Here are some common myths:

- *Myth #1. Very few people invest in stocks.* On the contrary, about one out of seven Americans owns shares in publicly traded corporations. This amounts to more than 32 million people and represents one out of every four U.S. households.

- *Myth #2. Only rich people own stocks.* Not so, according to the survey. Half of all stockholding households have incomes of $29,200 or less. Although this income is higher than the national average, younger, middle-income people who are buying securities for the first time are reducing the overall income average. Each year it reflects more and more the general U.S. population.

- *Myth #3. Only rarely would people own stocks and not know it.* On the contrary, the nation's 32 million *direct* shareholders represent a small fraction of the total number of corporate stockholders in the U.S. Approximately 135 million additional Americans own stocks indirectly through the money they save in insurance companies, mutual savings banks, and profit and pension funds. These funds are invested for them in public corporations.

In addition to dispelling myths, the shareownership survey also revealed a number of facts about owners of stock:

- *Fact #1. Shareowners are more educated than the general population.* Nearly 75 percent of the shareholders have attended or graduated from college. The average shareholder had 15 years of formal schooling; fewer than 6 percent had not received a high school diploma.

- *Fact #2. More men than women own stock.* In 1981 male shareholders outnumbered female shareholders by 5 percent; adult males comprised 49 percent of the total and adult females accounted for another 44 percent. (The remaining stocks are held by children.)

- *Fact #3. People are investing more than ever before.* The survey revealed that the average investor owned $5,450 in stocks—26 percent more than the previous year. Although almost one-half of the investor population had a portfolio worth less than $5,000, a significant number—22 percent—owned more than $25,000 worth of stock.

Source: Data from *Shareownership 1981* (New York: New York Stock Exchange, 1982).

SECONDARY MARKETS

Most stock and bond trades occur on the *secondary markets,* where previously issued shares of stocks and bonds are traded. These markets serve only as convenient locations for buyers and sellers to make exchanges. Neither the exchanges nor the companies whose securities are traded receive proceeds from such transactions. Gains and losses affect only current and potential owners of the securities.

The ease of trading on the secondary markets makes the nearly 15,000 corporations listed on the various stock exchanges and traded in the over-the-counter markets especially attractive investments. Sellers are not left holding unwanted shares of stock with no means of reselling them, and buyers have a convenient means of acquiring securities they seek. The next section focuses

secondary markets: markets in which previously issued stocks and bonds are bought and sold.

on the nation's major securities exchanges and how they function to meet the needs of investors who buy and sell securities.

THE SECURITIES EXCHANGES

The securities exchanges are among the few remaining open markets run almost entirely by the forces of supply and demand. Buyers and sellers bidding with one another for the best price determine the market price of securities. Trading requirements imposed by the exchanges are designed to permit orderly trading and to provide protection for brokerage firms, purchasers, and sellers. Specifically:

- They guard against secret trades by requiring that all transactions be publicly posted.
- They maintain a sophisticated record-keeping system that alerts exchange officials to manipulated price swings.
- They require companies listed on the exchanges to meet certain minimum financial standards.
- They set rules that both brokers and investors must follow when buying or selling securities.

In a single year some 20 billion shares, worth more than $500 billion, are traded on registered exchanges throughout the United States. These exchanges include the New York and American stock exchanges, which are considered national exchanges, as well as several regional exchanges.

THE NEW YORK STOCK EXCHANGE

Big Board: the New York Stock Exchange, the largest and most prestigious organized securities exchange in the world.

Known to investors as the *Big Board,* the New York Stock Exchange (NYSE) is the most important and prestigious stock exchange in the world. Although only one out of every 1,000 corporations qualifies for listing on the exchange, these firms account for more than 40 percent of the assets held by all U.S. companies. Each year more than 20 billion shares of common stock are traded on the Big Board. The 1,499 issues of common and 726 issues of preferred stock represent 85 percent of the market value of all stocks sold on U.S. exchanges. In addition, over 3,000 bond issues are traded on the NYSE. In order to be listed on the New York Stock Exchange, a firm must meet a number of rigorous requirements, which are intended to weed out most companies before they even apply.

Only individuals and firms who have an individual working for them who is an exchange member can trade securities on the floor of the exchange. In effect, a seat is a license to do business in the most exclusive stock exchange in the world. Seats are rare and expensive. Since 1953 there have been only

The New York Stock Exchange, right, traces its beginnings to 1792, when stockbrokers began meeting under this buttonwood tree, left, a few blocks from its present location.

1,366 exchange seats, and very few have turned over each year. In 1982 only 34 seats changed ownership, at prices that ranged from $190,000 to $340,000.

THE AMERICAN STOCK EXCHANGE

The second largest stock exchange in the world, the American Stock Exchange (Amex), traces its origins to 1849, when a group of dealers in unlisted securities began meeting unofficially on a Wall Street corner. Originally called the Outdoor Curb Exchange, many still refer to the Amex as *The Curb*. In many ways this exchange is virtually indistinguishable from its older, larger counterpart. However, the less stringent listing requirements of the Amex give it a reputation as a "seasoning exchange" for companies that are not quite ready for listing on the Big Board. In general, the Amex lists the common and preferred stock of medium-sized companies. It also lists corporate bonds, warrants, put-and-call options, and the common and preferred stock of a number of very large corporations that have chosen to list their securities either exclusively on the Amex or concurrently with listings on the regional stock exchanges.

The Curb: the American Stock Exchange (Amex), the second largest organized securities exchange in the United States.

Actively Traded Securities Are Widely Reported.

Source: Drawing by Stan Hunt; © 1970 The New Yorker Magazine, Inc.

REGIONAL EXCHANGES

Although investors spend most of their time closely watching the New York and American stock exchanges, a great deal of investment activity occurs each business day on the regional exchanges. In total, there are seven regional exchanges: the Boston, Cincinnati, Intermountain (located in Salt Lake City), Midwest (in Chicago), Pacific (with trading floors in San Francisco and Los Angeles), Philadelphia, and Spokane. The Pacific and Midwest are the largest regional exchanges.

Originally organized to provide a marketplace for relatively small, regional companies that were unable to meet the more stringent listing requirements of the two national exchanges, the regional exchanges have since become a more "mature" investment marketplace. Today, the regional exchanges deal in many of the same stock issues as the national exchanges. Approximately nine out of ten stocks listed on the regional exchanges are also found on the New York Stock Exchange. Although the regional exchanges continue to list small, local companies, these companies are no longer their primary business.

OVER-THE-COUNTER (OTC) MARKETS

listed securities: stocks and bonds traded on organized securities exchanges.

Thus far, the discussion has been limited to *listed securities*—those traded on the national and regional exchanges. Although these stocks and bonds represent the most prestigious companies, they do not represent the majority of securities traded in the United States. The securities of the vast majority of corporations are bought and sold in a very different kind of marketplace: the over-the-counter market.

Unlike the organized exchanges, the *over-the-counter (OTC) market* is not a place, but a way of doing business. Whereas shares on the organized exchanges are traded by means of an open auction, stocks and bonds listed on over-the-counter markets are privately traded by securities dealers who are often not affiliated with any securities exchange.

over-the-counter (OTC) market: an unorganized securities market in which transactions are between securities dealers.

With no trading floor on which to conduct business, these dealers do most of their buying and selling by teletype and computer terminals. They "make a market" by quoting a *bid*—what they will pay for a security—and an *asked*, or selling, *price*. Individual investors who decide to purchase over-the-counter stock will contact their brokers, who in turn contact the dealers handling the stock in order to search for the best price. When a market is made—that is, when the investor and the dealer agree on a price—the purchaser buys directly from the dealer. In many instances, however, large brokerage firms such as Merrill Lynch, Dean Witter, and Paine Webber make a market for their clients and those of other brokerage firms. Giant financial institutions such as Salomon Brothers and Goldman Sachs also serve as leading OTC bond firms.

bid: the price at which a seller will purchase a share of a stock or bond.

asked price: lowest price at which a stock or bond can be purchased.

Most stocks traded on over-the-counter markets are not listed on any organized exchange. Some of the firms have too few shares, others too few stockholders, and still others insufficient earnings to trade on any of the regional or national exchanges.

Trading NASDAQ Securities. To minimize the risk of trading OTC stock, many investors limit their transactions to the approximately 4,500 securities listed on the National Association of Securities Dealers Automatic Quotation (*NASDAQ*) System. This system deals with the most widely traded OTC issues. As Figure 16-2 indicates, a total of 15.9 billion shares of NASDAQ-listed companies were traded in 1983, more than seven times the share volume of the American Stock Exchange and approximately three-fourths the share volume of the New York Stock Exchange.

NASDAQ: the national system of over-the-counter securities price quotations.

The 441 dealers participating in NASDAQ report their market prices to a central computer, which is linked to all other dealers as well as to the various brokerage houses. This system gives dealers constant access to their competitors' price quotes. As a result, the quotation received from one dealer is approximately the same as that from any dealer. Indeed, NASDAQ rules require market makers to issue quotes that are "reasonably related to the prevailing market in the security."[2]

In addition to speculative issues, the over-the-counter market includes many bank and insurance company stocks, U.S. government bonds, municipal bonds, and the stocks and bonds of some large national corporations. Almost half the companies traded on NASDAQ meet the requirements for listing on either the New York or American stock exchange.

Figure 16-2

ANNUAL SHARE VOLUME OF ORGANIZED STOCK EXCHANGES AND OVER-THE-COUNTER MARKETS

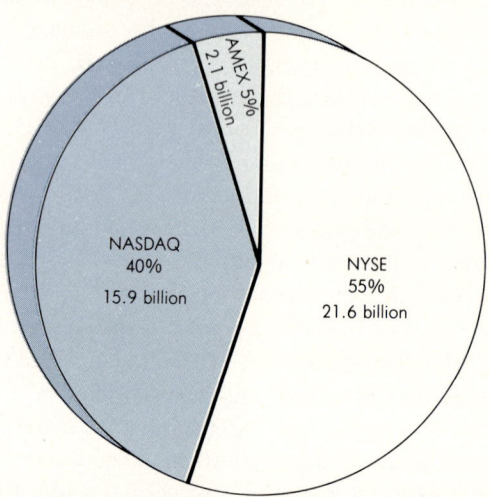

- AMEX 5% — 2.1 billion
- NASDAQ 40% — 15.9 billion
- NYSE 55% — 21.6 billion

Source: Data from *1983 NASDAQ Fact Book* (New York: National Association of Securities Dealers, 1984), p. 12.

REGULATING THE SECURITIES MARKETS

In 1929 the stock market collapsed, partially as a result of the market manipulation that had become an everyday fact of investment life. Since then, several federal laws have been passed to prevent the occurrence of a similar economic catastrophe. The keystone of this federal regulation is the Securities and Exchange Commission.

THE SECURITIES AND EXCHANGE COMMISSION

Securities and Exchange Commission (SEC): the federal agency that enforces federal securities laws and regulates information disclosure on and the operation of the organized securities exchanges and over-the-counter markets.

In 1934 Congress passed the Securities Exchange Act, which created a special commission to regulate the securities markets. The *Securities and Exchange Commission (SEC)* is a presidentially appointed, five-member body charged with overseeing federal securities regulations. All securities listed on the national and regional exchanges must be registered with the SEC, as must large over-the-counter offerings.

The activities of the exchanges and of member brokerage houses are also subject to SEC regulation. The Maloney Act of 1938 extended the SEC's policing powers to the over-the-counter markets. In addition, the Investment Company Act of 1940 brought under SEC authority investment companies that are involved in the investing, reinvesting, and trading of securities. Finally, as a result of the Investment Advisers Act of 1940, persons whose business is to advise investors concerning securities are regulated by the SEC.

In general, the SEC controls six aspects of the securities market:

1. The issuance of new securities.
2. Trading on all the national and regional exchanges and over-the-counter markets.
3. Financial statements issued by publicly owned corporations.
4. The practices of investment companies.
5. Most corporate reorganizations.
6. The complete financial status of public utility holding companies.

OTHER SOURCES OF REGULATION

The SEC receives assistance in its watchdog role from the individual states and from the exchanges and brokerage houses, which maintain strict standards for their members. The approximately 54,000 full-time, registered representatives of the New York Stock Exchange, for example, must pass comprehensive qualifying examinations and adhere to a strict code of ethics.

These regulations help safeguard investors' funds from loss due to manipulation and other illegal activities. They do not, however, guarantee that investors will be protected should a brokerage house fail. This protection is provided by the Securities Investor Protection Corporation.

SECURITIES INVESTOR PROTECTION CORPORATION

The *Securities Investor Protection Corporation (SIPC)* was created in 1970 to protect investors from losses due to the collapse of brokerage houses—just as the FDIC and the FSLIC protect savers from financial losses due to the collapse of banks and thrifts (see Chapter 6). SIPC differs from these banking agencies, however, in one important way: FDIC and FSLIC are federal agencies, while SIPC is a membership organization composed of all the registered brokers and members of national securities exchanges.

Should an SIPC member firm fail, SIPC provides the following protections against loss:

1. Clients of the failed stockbrokerage firm with securities registered in the firm's name will receive these securities. They will also receive any of their securities that are in the process of being registered.

2. All remaining cash and securities held by the firm are distributed on a prorated basis to investor clients of the failed firm. Thus, an investor with an unsettled claim of $10,000 will receive ten times as much as an investor with a $1,000 outstanding claim.

3. All remaining claims that are linked to the loss of securities are insured to a maximum of $500,000. Claims for cash are insured to a maximum of $100,000.

Securities Investor Protection Corporation (SIPC): *a membership organization that insures the accounts of brokerage firm clients to a maximum of $100,000 in cash in case of bankruptcy of the firm.*

The Crash of '29

On Black Tuesday—October 29, 1929—the stock market collapsed, marking the official beginning of the worst economic catastrophe in U.S. history: the Great Depression. The Great Crash took place in an era of high expectations, domestic prosperity, wild stock market speculation, and a booming Dow Jones Industrial Average. Stock values had more than doubled between 1926 and 1929 and, with a 25-percent spurt during the summer of 1929, the Dow reached its peak of 381 on September 3, 1929.

Realizing that the weak national economy could not sustain these levels, a few market analysts echoed warnings by the Federal Reserve Board for investors to be wary of market weaknesses. This warning sent a shock wave through Wall Street and prices began to plummet.

The actual panic began on Thursday, October 24. Plunging stock prices forced brokers to issue margin calls for additional funds from investors. If they could not contribute additional cash to maintain their holdings, they would have to be sold at huge losses. A selling panic followed and a collapse was prevented that day only when the nation's five leading banks made major stock purchases in an attempt to shore up the market.

But these measures were to prove futile. By the following Monday, the market had dropped by 13 percent. Then came Black Tuesday, when the market dropped another 12 percent on an unprecedented volume of 16.4 million shares. By the time the downward spiral ended in July 1932, the Dow had reached an all-time low of 41. Stocks had lost nearly 90 percent of their September 1929 values, and investor losses totaled more than $74 billion—or more than $300 billion in today's prices.

Why did the crash occur? A major reason was the loose margin requirements that allowed investors to buy stocks with only a 10-percent cash payment. Easy credit lured both the rich and the poor, seasoned investors and amateur speculators to the market as a place to make their fortune, using little money of their own. Like a house of cards, when the market turned down, their portfolios built on borrowed funds collapsed. The pre-Crash market also suffered from bank speculations, pyramiding schemes, and "pool" operations that illegally manipulated stock prices.

Could a similar market disaster happen today? Most experts feel that safeguards built into the system would prevent it. Margin requirements are far more stringent today: they are 50 percent of the stock purchase price rather than the 10 percent of 1929. Laws have been enacted prohibiting stock schemes and manipulations, and banks can no longer take part in market speculation. Finally, with institutions rather than individuals comprising a large percentage of the total market, the speculative fever and panic selling are greatly reduced.

The Crash of '29: the *Variety* headline says it all.

The procedures are applied in a sequential manner. After investors receive their registered securities and their prorated share of whatever customer properties remain, SIPC settles investor claims depending on the value of their losses in securities and cash. Here are several examples:

- If you lose $485,000 in securities and $100,000 in cash, SIPC will cover all but $85,000 of your losses.

- If you lose $600,000 in securities and $200,000 in cash, you will receive the maximum SIPC benefit of $500,000.
- If you lose $150,000 in cash and $90,000 in securities, you will receive $190,000.

The formation of SIPC was at least partially a reaction to the 1967–1970 crisis on Wall Street that threatened the collapse of many brokerage firms and the loss of investor securities and cash. Many large brokerage firms provide additional insurance to protect their customers against the possibility of losses that exceed the SIPC ceiling.

MAKING SECURITIES TRANSACTIONS

Millions of times each day, individual investors call their local brokers to determine the latest price of a stock or bond or to place an order to buy or sell. They tell their brokers to buy 200 shares of Apple Computer at the market, to buy 100 shares of Chrysler at 20, to sell 200 shares of Disney if the price drops to 40, to buy 100 shares of Xerox on margin, to sell short 300 shares of American Motors, and so on. Each of these orders has a specific meaning and is executed in a different way.

In order to learn how a typical order is handled, we will follow the path of a market order, which allows the broker to execute a purchase or sale at the prevailing market price.

THE MECHANICS OF MAKING AN ORDER

Suppose you are interested in buying 100 shares of Wang Laboratories, Inc., a high-technology stock listed on the American Stock Exchange. You call your broker, who, after punching up the stock symbol for Wang on her desk-top computer terminal, informs you that the last sale price of the stock was 33; the *bid* price, or the price some buyer has offered for his stock, is 33; and the *asked* price, or the lowest offer to sell, is $33\frac{1}{2}$. If you decide to buy the stock at the best possible market price (as you will see later, this is not the only way to buy), you simply tell your broker to buy 100 shares of Wang at the market.

This simple order sets the following series of events into motion. Since time is of the essence (a delay of even a few minutes can mean a higher—or lower—price), the broker immediately transmits your order to the main office, where the message is then relayed to the firm's booth on the trading floor. There a clerk informs a floor broker, whose job is to buy and sell stocks for his or her firm's customers. The floor broker quickly walks your order to the trading post where Wang is traded. (The Amex has 19 trading posts on its trading floor. Each stock trades at only one post.) The floor broker then asks the *specialist* (who handles a limited number of stocks) for the latest quote on Wang.

The 219 specialists with seats on the American Stock Exchange and the approximately 400 specialists on the New York Stock Exchange perform two important functions. First, they step in when the forces of supply and demand are at odds with one another and help restore the order of the market. When there is a temporary imbalance between buyers and sellers, specialists buy or sell their own holdings to get the market moving. Second, they act as "brokers' brokers." That is, they represent the broker who was instructed to buy at 20 a stock that now is selling for 30. A specialist takes the order from the broker and executes it if the stock price declines to 20, thus freeing the broker to continue with other business.

After the specialist informs your broker of the latest bid and asked prices, your firm's representative on the trading floor turns to the other brokers standing around the post and attempts to make a deal. Even though all the sellers' brokers are asking 33½—50 cents higher than your broker is willing to pay—a seller is located who is willing to accept your bid. He will sell 100 shares of Wang for 33¼ a share—halfway between the bid and asked prices. Both the buying and selling brokers are satisfied, since they have gotten their clients the best possible market price.

Within seconds after the transaction is made, the sale is entered into the Amex computer system and appears on the ticker tape. The sale is officially concluded when you are notified by your broker that you have purchased 100 shares of Wang at 33¼.

Market Orders. The transaction just described involved the placement and execution of a *market order*. This type of order gives the broker complete discretion to execute a purchase or sale at the prevailing market price. If the investor wants to maintain some control over the transaction even after it is on the trading floor, there are several other types of orders from which to choose.

Limit Orders. A *limit order* specifies the exact price at which a stock can be bought or sold. A limit order to buy at 50 cannot be executed at any price higher than 50, just as a limit order to sell at 50 cannot be executed at any lower price.

Because the floor broker cannot wait at the trading post until the stock declines or rises to the price you have specified, he or she normally leaves your order with the specialist handling that stock. Your order takes its place in the specialist's books behind all other limit orders for the stock at the $50-a-share price. When the market price reaches 50, your order becomes a market order and is executed like any other market order received at the trading post for the first time.

Limit orders may be appropriate when a stock's volatility (extreme price fluctuation) or inactivity (lack of trading) makes its market price unpredictable. However, if you feel that a particular stock is a good buy, it is probably not a good idea to try saving a dollar or two per share by using a limit order. If

---

market order: the investor's instruction to purchase or sell stock or bonds at the best price available at the time the order is placed.

limit order: the investor's instruction either to purchase a security at or below a specified price or to sell a security at or above a specified price.

its price should fall to your limit price, the execution of other limit orders received before yours might well drive up the price again, preventing the execution of your order.

Stop Orders. Stop orders are intended to protect your profits or limit your losses. A *stop order* to sell protects the value of your holding from a price decline. If, for example, you buy 100 shares of CBS stock at 50 and are unwilling to lose more than $1,000 if the value of the stock drops, you can place a stop order to sell at 40. Should CBS drop to 40, your order automatically becomes a market order to sell. This does not guarantee that the order will be executed at exactly 40, since the broker must then find a buyer who is willing to pay the best possible market price. In most cases, however, you will receive the approximate price. Alternatively, if the 100 shares of CBS you purchase at 50 rise to 70, you are guaranteed at least $1,000 in profits (less commissions) by placing a stop order at 60.

Stop orders to buy are sometimes placed to limit losses when selling short, as you will see later in the chapter.

stop order: the investor's instruction to sell a security if its market price reaches or drops below a specified level; also called a "stop-loss order."

Timing of Orders. Market orders are normally executed in a matter of minutes on the day they are received. Limit and stop orders are often placed as *period orders*, expiring if they are not executed within a certain time span. Day orders are good until the close of the business day; week orders remain in force until the close of the Friday session of the week in which they are placed; and month orders are good through the last trading day of the month. Good-'til-canceled orders remain in force until they are canceled by the customer.

period order: the investor's instruction to purchase or sell securities within a specified period.

MARGIN PURCHASES AND FINANCIAL LEVERAGE

In the financial as well as the physical sense, *leverage* represents borrowed strength. Just as the leverage provided by a tire jack allows you to lift a car, the leverage provided by your broker when you purchase securities on margin permits you to trade in dollar volumes above and beyond what you could otherwise manage. As Chapter 15 pointed out, this borrowed strength is a double-edged sword, for it makes possible both larger profits and larger losses.

leverage: the use of borrowed funds to magnify financial returns.

Margin Requirements. In essence, *margin*—the percentage of the purchase you must deposit—allows you to use the broker's credit to buy stock. Under current Federal Reserve System rules, you must pay your broker at least 50 percent of the stock's market value or deposit securities worth as much as the stock you are buying. (The Federal Reserve permits only half of the current market value of these stocks to be applied to the margin requirement.) Figure 16-3 shows how margin requirements have varied over the years since World War II.

margin: the percentage of funds investors must deposit in order to purchase specified dollar amounts of securities; the remaining funds are borrowed from the brokerage firm.

Figure 16-3

CHANGES IN MARGIN REQUIREMENTS, 1947–1985

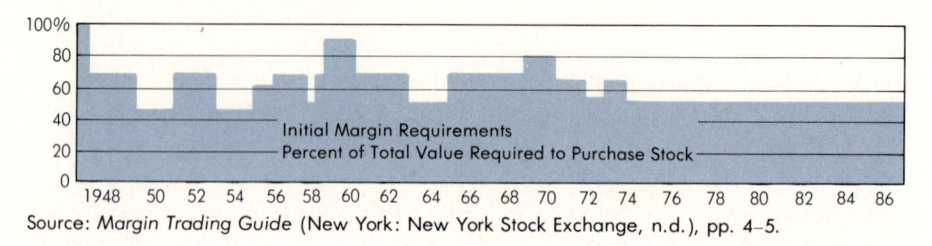

[Bar chart showing Initial Margin Requirements — Percent of Total Value Required to Purchase Stock, from 1948 to 1986, ranging from about 40% to near 100%]

Source: *Margin Trading Guide* (New York: New York Stock Exchange, n.d.), pp. 4–5.

In addition to the Federal Reserve requirement, exchanges and brokerage firms establish margin requirements of their own. Member firms of the New York Stock Exchange require a minimum initial cash deposit of $2,000. In certain situations, this increases the margin requirement to more than 50 percent. If, for example, you purchase $3,000 worth of securities, the $2,000 minimum margin requirement would mean that you are actually depositing 66.7 percent of the stock's value rather than 50 percent. Brokerage houses commonly set their own higher requirements if you buy low-priced stocks on margin or if you buy only a single security. Many over-the-counter issues cannot be bought on margin.

Interest is charged on the amount borrowed during a margin transaction. The exact interest rate is tied to the current cost of money and to the kind of customer you have been over the years. Clients with large, active accounts may pay less interest on borrowed funds than those who have just opened an account.

Once you satisfy the Federal Reserve's margin requirement (this must be done within five business days of the transaction), the Federal Reserve is no longer interested in the ratio between the market value of the stock you purchased and the amount kept on deposit in your account. However, the New York Stock Exchange requires that the margin equity of its members' customers be at least 25 percent of the market value of the securities held in their account. Many firms require more. Merrill Lynch, for example, has a 30-percent maintenance requirement. If the 100 shares of CBS you originally purchased at 50 drop to 35, the total market value of your stock is now $3,500 — $1,500 less than it was before the stock declined. Since you still owe your broker $2,500 — half of the original stock price — your margin equity is only $1,000, or 20 percent of the stock's value, which falls below the NYSE margin maintenance requirement. When this happens, you are undermargined, and a *margin call*, directing you to increase your margin deposit, is made. Failure to respond to this call gives your broker the right to liquidate your securities or demand full payment of your debt. (Technically, your broker can ask you to settle your account at any time.)

margin call: *a request by a brokerage firm that the investor deposit additional funds into his or her margin account; this occurs when the value of the margin account drops below some specified minimum.*

Knowing When to Sell

Every investor knows the feeling: the stock purchased at 40 is now 35 and falling. Deciding whether to hold on to it and hope for a turnaround or whether to sell before things get even worse is enough to make many people swear off the stock market—at least for a while.

Why do people have such difficulty in deciding when—and whether—to sell? Experts point to the psychological defense of *denial* as the culprit: investors think in terms of profits when stock is sold, not losses. Consequently, they have problems in coming to grips with how to handle a losing stock—until it is too late. Embarrassment also complicates the issue. Many investors see the sale of a losing stock as admission of a mistake or of investment ineptness, and thus as a poor reflection on the individual's overall abilities.

Three simple rules should aid the investor in avoiding the emotional problems that surround selling a losing stock. They should also help to keep losses to a minimum:

1. *Decide before you buy any stocks how much you are willing to lose.* Many investment advisers suggest that you limit your losses to 10 percent. For example, if you buy a stock at 40, you should sell it if it drops as low as 36 in order to avoid an even larger loss later on. If you can't bear the thought of a loss soon after purchasing the stock, you should at least seek environmental factors, such as a major stock market "correction" that pulled down the prices of all shares temporarily, to justify its retention. Don't just sit on your remaining funds when you sell; reinvest them in a more promising stock.

2. *Compare your shares' performance to the performance of the overall market to determine whether you are winning or losing.* If your stocks consistently underperform the Dow Jones Industrial Average or the Standard & Poor's Index of 500 Stocks, sell before they lose even more ground.

3. *Set a price-appreciation goal when you first buy a stock.* Will you be satisfied with a 10 or 20 percent gain? Are you hoping for even more? If the stock fails to live up to your expectations within a reasonable time period—if, for example, internal company problems are continuing to depress company profits—sell before others reach the same conclusion.

Investors who make the mistake of sticking with a losing stock fail to realize that it is impossible to pick a winner every time. Even investment professionals consider themselves fortunate if they are right only half the time. They also understand that their current paper losses will eventually turn into even larger real losses when they decide to sell. Most important, they view their losses dispassionately, realizing that in the long run the ability to sell at a small loss separates the successful investor from the one who never makes it.

Sources: The issue of deciding when to sell is discussed in William C. Bryant, "Knowing When to Sell," *U.S. News & World Report*, March 8, 1982, p. 77; *10 Questions to Ask—Before You Buy* (New York: New York Stock Exchange, 1981); and Jane Bryant Quinn, *Everyone's Money Book* (New York: Dell, 1980), pp. 604–606.

The Benefits and Risks of Margin. If the stock you buy on margin increases in value, leverage works in your favor. Your investment dollar has nearly twice the strength it would have if you had purchased the stock for cash. Without leverage you can purchase only 100 shares of $10-per-share stock for $1,000. If the price climbs to $13 a share, your profit will be $300—30 percent of your original $1,000 investment. With leverage, you can use the same $1,000 to purchase 200 shares. Should the stock rise to 13, your profit doubles: you earn $600, or 60 percent of your original investment. The ability to purchase twice as many shares also gives you the potential for twice the dividend income.

Unfortunately, if the stock drops in value the risks are twice as great. Purchasing a declining stock on margin can be extremely costly. You stand to lose twice as much and are responsible for costly interest charges.

Margin, then, is a powerful but potentially dangerous tool. It also enables you to trade stocks in an unconventional way—by selling short.

THE LONG AND SHORT OF SELLING STOCK

Until now, the discussion has been limited to the most common way of buying and selling stock: buy when the price is low and sell later when it is high—a method known as *selling long*. There is another, less conventional, way of selling stocks that enables speculators to profit when a stock drops in price. This system is called *selling short*. It involves the selling of unowned shares, promising a later delivery date, and in the meantime buying the shares at a price that is lower than the selling price.

selling long: the traditional investment technique of purchasing shares of stock or bonds and selling them at a later date—after their prices have risen.

selling short: a speculative technique in which the investor sells shares he or she does not yet own with the intent of actually delivering them at a later date by purchasing them—at a lower price than the price at which they were sold short originally.

How You Can Profit. Suppose that you have been following CBS stock for several months and have concluded that its recent upswing is about to peak. You instruct your broker to sell 100 shares of CBS at the current market price of 50—*even though you do not own a single share*. To deliver the stock to the purchaser, the broker has to borrow it, putting up as collateral a portion of the stock's market value equal to the current margin requirement. (You cannot sell short unless you have a margin account.)

Meanwhile, CBS stock begins to fall in price. At 40, you close out the transaction by purchasing the 100 shares you previously "sold" to replace those your broker borrowed. By selling at 50 and then buying at 40, you realize a profit of $1,000 less commissions, and any dividends earned during the time the stock was borrowed. (These dividends belong to the person who actually owned the borrowed stock.)

How You Can Lose. If, however, the market value of CBS begins to rise instead of fall, you face a very different situation. As the cost of replacing the borrowed stock rises (the higher the market value, the more you owe), your broker will require that you increase the deposit in your account. Since there is no limit to the potential price increase, you may find yourself depositing more and more into your account. If the stock rises to 60, you owe $1,000 plus commissions and other costs. At 70 you owe $2,000; at 75, $2,500; and so on. To protect yourself from catastrophic losses, you can place a stop order to buy if the stock rises by a certain amount. (This amount is determined by how much you can afford to lose.) If in this case you place a stop order to buy at 60, you limit your potential loss to $1,000. Figure 16-4 traces the steps involved in selling short.

Regulation of Short Sales. To ensure that unscrupulous investors do not illegally manipulate the market by selling short, the SEC as well as the securities exchanges have stringent rules for its use. Short sales are permitted only when the price of stock is increasing. In addition, the sale must be identified as

Figure 16-4
HOW PROFITS AND LOSSES CAN RESULT FROM SELLING SHORT

March 15
Investor sells 100 shares of CBS common stock "short" at the current market price of $50.

April 1
CBS shares drop in price to $40. Investor purchases 100 shares at $40 to cover his "short" position.

Profit
Short Sale: $5,000
Purchase Cost: 4,000
Gross Profit $1,000
(before paying brokerage commissions and taxes)

Or:

March 15
Investor sells 100 shares of CBS common stock "short" at the current market price of $50.

April 1
CBS shares have risen steadily in price since March 15 and now are selling at $60 per share. Rather than risking further increases in price and greater losses, the investor purchases 100 shares at $60 to cover his "short" position.

Loss
Short Sale: $5,000
Purchase Cost: 6,000
Loss (not ($1,000)
including brokerage commissions and taxes)

a short account and officers of the company issuing the stock are prohibited from selling short. Before these regulations were established, "pool" operators created intense public interest in a stock by means of "wash sales." Large blocks of the stock were simultaneously bought and sold, creating the illusion of activity. This activity attracted the attention of unsuspecting investors, who purchased the stock—driving up its price even higher. The pool operators then sold short huge volumes of the stock, which drove the price so low that they could buy it back at a tremendous profit.

WHAT YOU CAN EXPECT FROM YOUR BROKER

Next to your doctor and lawyer, your stockbroker may be the most important professional in your life. Essentially, a *stockbroker* (or "account executive") is a financial go-between who buys and sells securities for clients and also provides

stockbroker: the financial intermediary who buys and sells securities for clients and provides information and advice; frequently called an "account executive."

information and advice. If you trust his or her advice—and take it—your stockbroker can assist you in turning even a small investment into a large nest egg.

Because of the crucial role stockbrokers may play in your financial life, it is important to understand exactly what you can expect from the stockbroker-client relationship, including services and fees. We will examine these concerns within the context of the two major types of brokerage houses—full-service and discount.

FULL-SERVICE BROKERS

The giants of the brokerage business—Merrill Lynch, Pierce, Fenner & Smith; Shearson/American Express; Paine Webber Mitchell Hutchins; and Smith Barney, Harris Upham, just to name a few—are all full-service brokers. As the name suggests, full-service brokers offer their customers a wide range of sophisticated investments, including stocks and bonds, money-market accounts (see Chapter 17), options and commodities (see Chapter 18), retirement annuities and individual retirement accounts (see Chapter 20), tax shelters, and asset-management accounts. They also offer expert investment advice. Your broker will guide you through the maze of investment alternatives to find the right investment for you. Many of his or her recommendations are based on the findings of the firm's research department, which analyzes industries and specific corporations and writes investment reports.

commission: *the fee charged by stockbrokerage firms for purchasing and selling securities.*

Fees reflect the full-service approach. You pay for the advice and attention you receive in the form of the broker's *commission,* the amount the brokerage firm charges to buy or sell securities. Commissions vary according to the type of security sold. For example, there is a higher commission attached to stocks than to Treasury bills. In general, the larger the trade, the smaller the percentage rate of the commission. Although fees vary from firm to firm, competition keeps most full-service brokerage fees in the same range. (You can ask your broker for a copy of the firm's commission schedule, which will indicate exactly what the firm charges for various transactions.) These fees, however, are higher than those charged by discount brokers.

DISCOUNT BROKERS

Since their introduction in 1975, when the Securities and Exchange Commission deregulated brokerage commission fees, discount brokerage houses have offered investors a real alternative to full-service brokers. Instead of paying for expensive research and investment advice, investors who know exactly what they want to buy or sell can do business with a discount broker, who simply executes their order for 40, 50, and sometimes 70 percent below what full-service firms charge.

Table 16-1
COMPARISON OF COMMISSIONS CHARGED BY SELECTED DISCOUNT AND FULL-SERVICE BROKERAGE FIRMS

The Discounting Difference

Discount brokers are in the shaded areas. The others listed are full-service firms.

Commission for Buying A.T. & T. Stock at $58 a Share

Broker	100 Shares	1,000 Shares
Charles Schwab & Co.	$45	$225
Quick & Reilly Inc.	40	161
Fidelity Brokerage	40	204
Ovest Securities	40	110
George A. Brown	33	105
Merrill Lynch, Pierce, Fenner & Smith	87	575
Shearson/American Express	97	626
Paine Webber Mitchell Hutchins	90	645

Commission for Buying A.T. & T. Option Contracts at 2¼ ($225 per 100 Shares)

Broker	One Contract	Ten Contracts
Charles Schwab & Co.	$18	$ 56
Quick & Reilly Inc.	30	72
Fidelity Brokerage	30	57
Ovest Securities	24	56
George A. Brown	21	56
Merrill Lynch, Pierce, Fenner & Smith	30	125
Shearson/American Express	25	119
Paine Webber Mitchell Hutchins	29	122

Source: Leslie Wayne, "The Discounters Storm Wall Street," *New York Times,* December 26, 1982, sec. 3, p. 8. Copyright © 1982/83 by the New York Times Company. Reprinted by permission.

In 1982 full-service firms charged an average of $90 for each securities transaction, while discount brokers charged approximately $55.[3] Discount brokerage houses are also less expensive because they do not use commissioned salespeople. Table 16-1 shows how brokerage fees vary among discount and full-service brokers who have executed stock and options trades.

Attracted to these lower fees, investors have flocked to discount brokers. In 1982 the nation's approximately 100 discount brokerage firms accounted for about 10 percent of the approximately $2.7 billion in retail commissions. By 1990 this figure is expected to reach 30 percent. As a result of this competition, full-service brokers have begun to offer an even more sophisticated package of investment services. Many discounters, in turn, have extended their scope from mere order taking to offering money-market and other mutual funds, IRA and Keogh retirement accounts, annuities, and tax shelters as well as other services—still at a discount price because no individualized service is offered. For example, Charles Schwab & Company, with 52 offices, the nation's largest discount broker, offers an asset-management account, individual retirement account, money-market accounts, and 24-hour order taking.

In general, discount brokers should be used by highly knowledgeable investors who are actively managing their own accounts. Investors who are relying on advice from an independent investment adviser may also process their transactions through a discount broker.

ROUND-LOT AND ODD-LOT TRANSACTIONS

Whether you use a full-service or discount broker, the fee you pay depends on whether you make a round-lot or an odd-lot transaction. *Round-lot transactions* are trades in even multiples of 100 shares. (The unit of trading on the major stock exchanges is generally 100 shares.) Trades of any amount of stock less than a round lot are considered *odd-lot transactions*. Brokers generally charge proportionately higher fees for these trades.

round-lot transactions: purchases or sales of securities in units of 100.

odd lot transactions: purchases or sales of securities in quantities of less than 100.

SELECTING A STOCKBROKER

When you choose a stockbroker, you are choosing a brokerage house as well as a personal adviser. The choice of a specific stockbroker is typically far more difficult than choosing the brokerage house.

CHOOSING A BROKERAGE HOUSE

Most people choose a brokerage house because of its general reputation, the specific services it offers, and its fees—an objective selection process that has little to do with people or personalities. In most instances, investors limit their choice to one of the 617 members of the New York Stock Exchange. These firms are the most prestigious in the country and must meet strict SEC and New York Stock Exchange standards. All member firms are required to provide customers with the firm's most recent financial statement; maintain at all times a specified amount of capital in a reserve fund; undergo a yearly audit by an independent accountant; submit to spot financial reviews by the Exchange; file as many as 12 financial reports every year; disclose to the Exchange whether any partners or officers in the firm have certain types of loans outstanding; and carry fidelity insurance on all firm members. In addition, individual brokers are required to complete a four-month training program and pass a rigorous New York Stock Exchange examination as well as state tests.

CHOOSING A BROKER

Unless you ask for a specific broker by name, most brokerage houses will simply give your account to the next broker on their list. A better approach involves preliminary discussions with the manager of the brokerage office. After discussing your investment goals and the services you require, the manager is in a better position to recommend an appropriate broker.

Before agreeing to this choice you can ask the manager about the broker's educational background, experience, and specialty. You can even ask to interview more than one broker. Even in a short meeting you can make a general assessment and decide whether you are comfortable with his or her personality and credentials. Do you prefer a young broker who has been recently trained or an older broker with years of experience? Is he or she too businesslike or too personal? You can also ask each candidate some probing questions about investment philosophies and strategies: What kinds of investment does he or she recommend? What kind of return is considered satisfactory? How successful has he or she been in the past? You can even ask to see his or her customer records (no names, of course).

When making your choice, the advice of friends and co-workers whose financial judgment you respect may be sought. "I don't know of any way [to find a good broker] except to talk to friends to see what their experience has been," says Thomas O'Hara, president of the National Association of Investment Clubs.[4]

After working with a broker for a period of time, you should ask yourself some more questions about his or her performance and your relationship. Do you get the feeling that the broker is overselling in order to increase commissions? Are you pressured to buy or sell without receiving information? Does the broker keep informed about the latest investment information? Is he or she well organized? Does this broker accurately present the pluses and minuses of an investment and analyze its risks? Is he or she patient when explaining a new investment? Finally, and most important, has the relationship proven profitable for you? Has the value of your investment grown?

Regardless of your choice, it is important to remember that you can always change your mind. "If you feel that you're not getting the kind of service you should have," says Henry P. Perrine of E. F. Hutton and Company, "ask the manager to reassign your account."[5] If you are still not happy, you can move your account to another office or change brokerage firms.

OPENING AND USING A BROKERAGE ACCOUNT

Before you can actually buy or sell a security through a broker, you must open an account. You are required to provide such personal information as your name, address, Social Security number, citizenship, and age. You are

cash account: *an investor's account in which all security purchases are fully paid for when they are made.*

margin account: *an investor's account in which payment for security purchases is made partially in cash, with the remainder covered by funds loaned to the investor by the brokerage firm.*

street name: *the practice of allowing the brokerage firm to register in its name securities purchased by the investor and to retain the stock or bond certificates.*

also required to provide some facts about your finances and credit history. (If you open a joint account, both parties on the account must supply this information.)

This information is used by the brokerage firm in deciding whether you are likely to be responsible for orders executed on your behalf and are able to pay for the securities you buy and deliver the securities you sell. You can open a *cash account,* buying and selling securities in full when the transaction is made, or a *margin account,* using the broker's credit to buy and sell. For obvious reasons, brokers have more stringent requirements for margin accounts.

Once your account is open, you can conduct all future business with your broker by phone or mail. After a transaction is made, you have five business days to settle your account—that is, to pay for the securities you have purchased or to deliver the certificates you have sold. Soon after a purchase your broker will tell you exactly how much you owe, and you will receive written confirmation within a few days of your order. Similarly, you can expect to receive the proceeds of a sale within a few days.

When you buy a security, you can choose to keep the certificate yourself or leave it with your broker. If your broker keeps it in the firm's vault, it is registered in the broker's name. These securities are said to carry the broker's *street name.* If you request that the certificate be sent to you, it is registered in your name—that is, your name appears on the front of the certificate. When you sell it, you must endorse it just as you would a check. It is a good idea to deliver all stock certificates to your broker by hand or to send them by registered mail to guarantee their safety.

In most cases, where you keep your certificates is a matter of personal preference and convenience. Generally, active investors prefer that their brokers retain their certificates, while long-term investors take possession. People who purchase stock on margin must leave their certificates with their broker. When deciding how to handle your certificates, it is a good idea to keep in mind the SIPC insurance protection ceiling of $500,000 on all unsatisfied claims involving securities left in the hands of a broker.

SOURCES OF INVESTMENT INFORMATION

Anyone interested in investing in stocks and bonds will have no trouble finding information on the subject. Thousands of books, magazine and newspaper articles, stock price reports, annual reports, and stock market letters are published every day. None of these will help you, however, if you do not know exactly what you are looking for. To avoid confusion, you must approach the subject of investments and investment information in a systematic way. You must know where to look, and what you can expect to find.

BUYING AND SELLING SECURITIES

CORPORATE INFORMATION

You can learn a lot about a company's financial health from its annual report. The annual report is a formal financial statement that summarizes the company's finances for the entire year, including its assets, liabilities, revenues, expenses, and earnings. It tells you in a nutshell where the company stood financially at the close of the business year. If you own stock in a firm, a copy of the annual report will be mailed to you each year. If you are thinking of buying stock, you can locate a copy of the most recent annual report at your brokerage house or local library, or by writing or calling the respective company.

Despite its accessibility, many investors ignore the annual report as a source of financial information. According to financial writer Sylvia Porter, investors who discard an annual report "are junking the single most important account of the financial health of your company and your single best measure of how well (or how poorly) your savings are now invested."[6]

Why, then, is this document ignored? The simple reason is that most people do not know what the report contains or how to read it. Even though understanding an annual report will never be easy, it is not as difficult as it once was. Here are several key sections to look for:

1. *President's letter to the stockholders* (which may also be called the letter from the chairman): One of the first things you see when you open the report, this letter highlights what you will find as you read on. It summarizes how the company has done in the past year and may discuss plans for the year ahead. In general, the tone is optimistic, so pay attention to the letter's phrasing. Sentences that start with "Except for . . ." or tell you that the year "was a period of adjustment" may indicate that all is not well.

2. *Text:* This part summarizes the activities in each of the company's major branches and presents the short- and long-term outlook.

3. *Income statement or earnings report:* Here the company's year is translated into dollars and cents—its income, costs, and net profits and losses for the year are compared with figures from the previous year. In effect, you learn how much the company has earned or lost during the year and how favorably or unfavorably this performance compares with the past. You can determine, for example, whether net sales are increasing faster than inflation. (If they are not, the company is not growing.)

4. *Balance sheet:* Here a comparison is offered showing how the company's current assets (such as cash, receivables, inventory, equipment, and other property) stack up against its current liabilities (loans, notes, and other payables) at the close of the year. The difference between these two figures is referred to as the net working capital. A decline in this figure may be a strong warning. You can also determine the value of what stockholders own

Investors' Most Common Mistakes

It may give the small investor some small comfort to know that even their worst investment mistakes have been made before. In fact, certain mistakes are so common that experienced advisers can predict them before they actually occur. Here are the most common pitfalls:

- *Expecting too much too soon.* Those who expect to invest money on Monday and make their fortunes by the following Friday are almost always disappointed. Moreover, in most cases, investors purchase stocks for the wrong reasons, acting on impulse instead of solid information from professional advisers. With visions of earning a quick fortune, many investors overextend their budgets and take foolish risks. Others seek only those stocks that are completely safe, pay large dividends, and grow in value within a very short period of time. No stock fits this description.
- *Investing without a long-term plan.* According to financial writer Thomas W. Phelps, "Most people try to make a few points quickly . . . but not one in one thousand seriously plans and acts as one must to make a fortune." Investors fail to ask and answer such basic questions as: Am I looking for income or growth? What is my patience level? How long am I willing to wait to get what I want?
- *Deciding that research is time-consuming and unnecessary.* Investing without adequate research often proves both foolish and costly, especially since firm and industry data are readily available from stockbrokers, industry trade associations, and the company itself. Always read the corporate annual report *before* you buy.
- *Taking more risks than you have to.* Too many investors possess the belief that low-quality investments increase their chances of quick profits. In reality, high-quality stocks in a fast-growing industry offer much better long-term investments.
- *Avoiding high-priced stocks.* Many investors believe that they are more likely to double or triple their investment with a $5 stock than with a $50 stock. Although this may prove correct in some instances, the lower-priced stock is typically a much riskier investment.
- *Unwillingness to invest when stock prices are low.* Most people fear the worst when the market is down: they expect things to get even worse. But if stock selections are carefully made, this is an excellent time to buy. Those who wait are forced to pay significantly higher prices for the same stock when the market rebounds.
- *Selling a stock simply to earn short-term profits.* If a firm is on the upswing and the price of its stock is rising, it is shortsighted to sell for a quick profit. In addition to being unable to participate in the company's future growth, the investor is forced to pay regular income taxes on the gain rather than lower capital gains taxes had the stock been held for one year or more. In addition, the brokerage fees for the purchase and sale further dilute the earnings of frequent sellers. And the seller is faced with the need to select another firm that will outperform the previous company.

Source: Phelps quotation from John W. Hazard, "12 Mistakes Investors Make," *U.S. News & World Report,* January 10, 1983, p. 69.

(referred to as stockholders' equity) and the size of the long-term debt. By dividing long-term liabilities by stockholders' equity, the debt-to-equity ratio can be calculated. If the ratio is high, you should be sure that company sales are growing fast enough to support it. If sales are increasing slowly, a high debt-to-equity ratio may be a sign of trouble.

5. *Notes to financial statements:* Although this section is frequently the most important part of the entire annual report, it is worded in such technical terms that many investors skip it. The notes may tell you whether the firm's

record profits resulted from a one-time-only transaction or reflected continued growth. This section typically covers such topics as research and development, lawsuits, foreign-currency transactions, lease commitments, and changes in accounting practices.

6. *Auditor's letter:* This letter tells you whether the accountants who examined the firm's books found them satisfactory. It will mention any potential problems uncovered. Professional investors often turn to this section first.

PUBLISHED ARTICLES AND SUBSCRIPTION MARKET LETTERS

Investors interested in keeping abreast of ongoing economic events that might affect their current or future investments should consider reading several business periodicals, watching special television programs, and subscribing to a market letter.

Business Periodicals and Special Television Programs. When read on a regular basis, such periodicals as *Barron's, Money, Business Week, Changing Times, Fortune, Forbes,* and the *Wall Street Journal* will provide a wealth of valuable information. In addition, specialty or trade journals are available in many fields. If you are thinking of investing in McDonald's or Burger King, for example, you could subscribe to *Restaurants and Institutions,* which cites industry trends and analyzes corporate successes and problems long before the news reaches the mass media. Similarly, if you own stock in an advertising agency, you can keep up with corporate events by reading *Advertising Age.*

If you want to learn more about a company before investing or reevaluating your current investments, you can check several periodical indexes at your library for relevant articles. The *Readers' Guide to Periodical Literature* lists the articles written in such popular business publications as *Fortune, Money,* and *U.S. News & World Report.* The *Business Periodicals Index* lists these sources as well as sources for the trade only, including *Restaurants and Institutions* and *Beverage World.* Three excellent general industry references are *Standard & Poor's Industry Survey, Moody's,* and *Value Line Investment Survey,* which periodically evaluate a wide range of industries. Your broker may be able to supplement this information with other investment sources.

A growing number of television programs specialize in business news and market trends. Two of the most popular of these are the *Nightly Business Report* and Louis Rukeyser's *Wall Street Week.*

Subscription Market Letters. Millions of investors pay for expert advice in the form of subscription market letters, which analyze the market and pinpoint which stocks to buy and sell. One of the most popular market advisory services is the weekly *Value Line Investment Survey,* which ranks 1,700 stocks in terms of their probable market performance and yield in the next twelve months, their investment safety, and their estimated appreciation potential in the next three to five years. Other influential services include *The Outlook,* a weekly investment advisory service published by Standard & Poor's Corporation, which recommends various stock issues and creates sample portfolios for investors with different objectives; the *Moody's Stock Survey* and *Moody's Bond Survey,* which recommend specific securities and analyze general market trends; the weekly *United Business & Investment Report,* which contains a list of 150 closely watched stocks as well as recommendations on many other securities; and the weekly *Trendline's Current Market Perspectives,* which follows the price fluctuations of nearly 1,500 stocks and ranks their performances.

Many of these letters are written for the experienced, professional investors, not for beginners. Because of this, their success is dependent, at least in part, on your willingness to study and learn the investment field.

Market letters are generally expensive; most cost more than $100 a year. Investors are therefore cautioned to shop around in order to seek out market letters with a long history of respectability and success. If possible, the investor should examine back issues at the public library to determine how right—or wrong—the advice has been. If after subscribing, you do not profit from the letter's suggestions, cancel the subscription and investigate other alternatives.

DAILY STOCK AND BOND PRICE REPORTS

The acid test for how well a stock or bond is performing is its market value—how much investors are willing to spend for it on the open market. This information is readily available in the business section of daily newspapers throughout the country. There you will find price information for stocks listed on the New York, American, and many regional exchanges as well as on over-the-counter markets. You will also find New York Stock Exchange bond prices and prices for options.

Stock Listings. Figure 16-5 describes in detail how to read a stock table. The table provides a great deal of valuable information in addition to reporting the latest selling price of the stock. It reveals at a glance the stock's market performance over the past 52 weeks, the regular annual dividend per share, the yield, the price-earnings ratio, the net change in price from the closing price of the day before, and more. The symbol *pf* identifies preferred stock.

Over-the-Counter Listings. The National Association of Securities Dealers uses a different system to report the current trading prices of over-the-counter stocks. As Figure 16-6 reveals, their quotations contain the following information:

1. *Stock and dividend:* the company name in its abbreviated form and the regular annual dividend per share.

Figure 16-5
HOW TO READ A NEWSPAPER STOCK QUOTATION

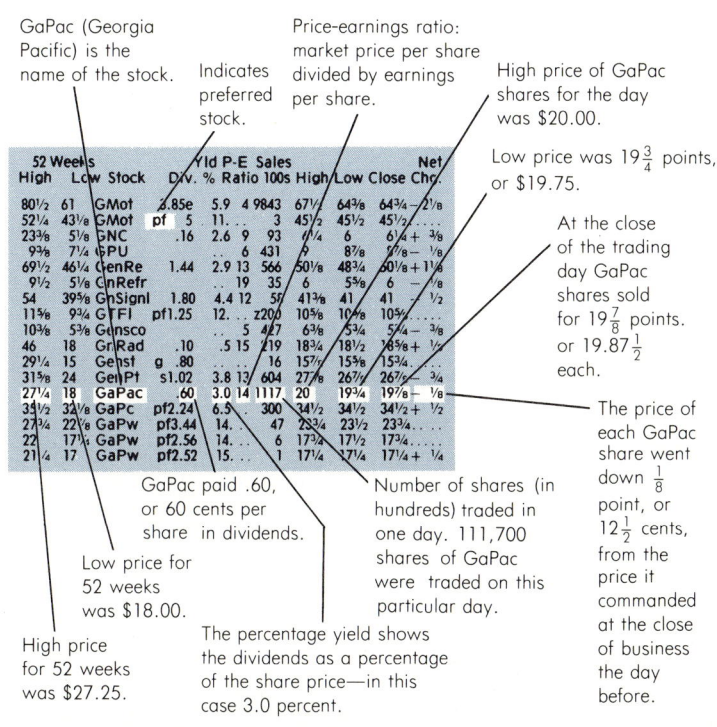

GaPac (Georgia Pacific) is the name of the stock.

Indicates preferred stock.

Price-earnings ratio: market price per share divided by earnings per share.

High price of GaPac shares for the day was $20.00.

Low price was $19\frac{3}{4}$ points, or $19.75.

At the close of the trading day GaPac shares sold for $19\frac{7}{8}$ points. or $19.87\frac{1}{2}$ each.

The price of each GaPac share went down $\frac{1}{8}$ point, or $12\frac{1}{2}$ cents, from the price it commanded at the close of business the day before.

GaPac paid .60, or 60 cents per share in dividends.

Number of shares (in hundreds) traded in one day. 111,700 shares of GaPac were traded on this particular day.

Low price for 52 weeks was $18.00.

High price for 52 weeks was $27.25.

The percentage yield shows the dividends as a percentage of the share price—in this case 3.0 percent.

Source: Adapted from David J. Rachman and Michael H. Mescon, *Business Today* 4th ed. (New York: Random House, 1985), p. 405.

2. *Sales in 100s:* trading on OTC markets is much lighter than on the national and regional exchanges. Superior Electric, for example, traded only 5,800 shares.

3. *Bid:* the approximate amount per share that market makers are willing to pay for the stock. This is the price originally quoted when you are ready to sell.

4. *Asked:* the approximate amount per share you must pay to purchase the stock. As you can see, the asked price is always higher (usually by only a fraction of a point) than the bid price.

5. *Net change:* how much the stock has changed in price from the close of business on the previous day. This figure is expressed in terms of the movement of the stock price up or down and is written as " + " or " − " points or fractions of points per share. Thus, Superior Electric gained $37\frac{1}{2}$ cents.

Approximately 2,000 NASDAQ stocks are traded on a new NASDAQ National Market System. This system gives investors the day's high, low, and

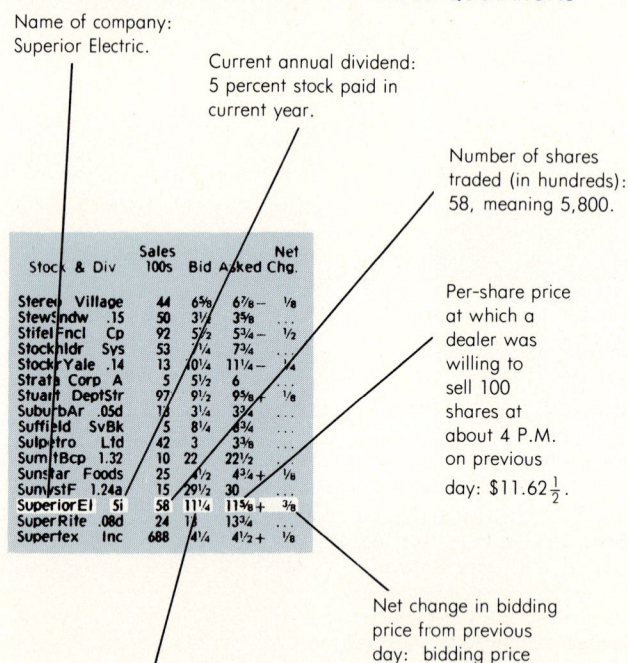

Figure 16-6

HOW TO READ OVER-THE-COUNTER STOCK QUOTATIONS

Name of company: Superior Electric.

Current annual dividend: 5 percent stock paid in current year.

Number of shares traded (in hundreds): 58, meaning 5,800.

Per-share price at which a dealer was willing to sell 100 shares at about 4 P.M. on previous day: $11.62½.

Stock & Div	Sales 100s	Bid	Asked	Net Chg.
Stereo Village	44	6⅝	6⅞	−⅛
StewSndw .15	50	3½	3⅝	...
Stifel Fncl Cp	92	5½	5¾	−½
Stockhldr Sys	53	7¼	7¾	...
StockrYale .14	13	10¼	11¼	−¼
Strata Corp A	5	5½	6	...
Stuart DeptStr	97	9½	9⅝	+⅛
SuburbAr .05d	18	3¼	3¾	...
Suffield SvBk	5	8¼	8¾	...
Sulpetro Ltd	42	3	3⅜	...
SumItBcp 1.32	10	22	22½	...
Sunstar Foods	25	4½	4¾	+⅛
SunystF 1.24a	15	29½	30	...
SuperiorEl 5i	58	11¼	11⅝	+⅜
SuperRite .08d	24	13	13¾	...
Supertex Inc	688	4¼	4½	+⅛

Per-share price at which a dealer was willing to purchase 100 shares at about 4 P.M. on previous day: $11.25.

Net change in bidding price from previous day: bidding price has increased $\frac{3}{8}$, meaning 37½ cents. (Therefore bidding price of previous day was $10.87½.)

Source: Adapted from David J. Rachman and Michael H. Mescon, *Business Today* 4th ed. (New York: Random House, 1985), p. 406.

closing trade prices as well as the traditional bid and asked prices. Securities included on this list must meet financial criteria similar to those used by the New York and American stock exchanges.

Bond Listings. Although the majority of bonds and all municipal bonds are traded on over-the-counter markets, the leading bonds are traded on the New York and American stock exchanges, where the following quotation system is used (see Figure 16-7):

1. *Bond name:* the same corporate abbreviation as in the stock tables.

2. *Description:* the coupon rate (the bond's original rate of interest) and its maturity (when the bond will mature). The latter is usually expressed in terms of the last two digits of the year of maturity. Thus, the shaded Southern Bell Telephone bond in Figure 16-7 has a coupon rate of 8⅛ and matures in the year 2017.

BUYING AND SELLING SECURITIES

Figure 16-7
HOW TO READ BOND QUOTATIONS

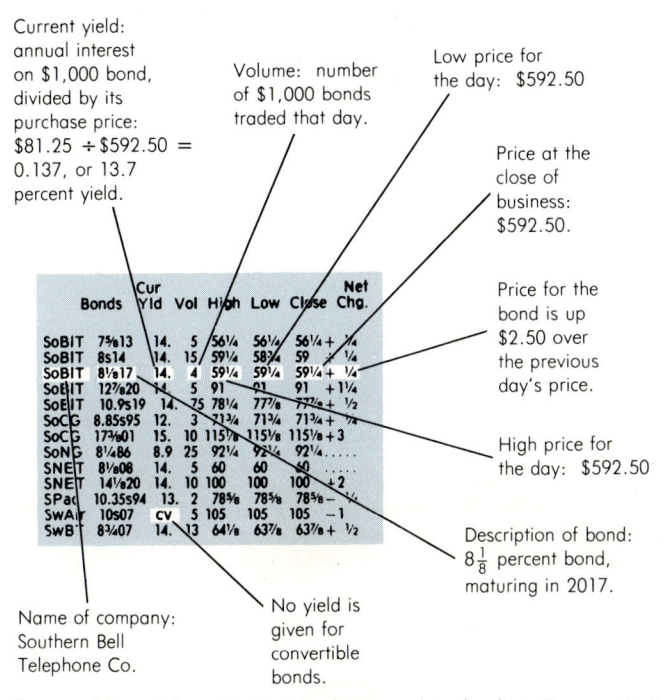

Current yield: annual interest on $1,000 bond, divided by its purchase price: $81.25 ÷ $592.50 = 0.137, or 13.7 percent yield.

Volume: number of $1,000 bonds traded that day.

Low price for the day: $592.50

Price at the close of business: $592.50.

Price for the bond is up $2.50 over the previous day's price.

High price for the day: $592.50

Description of bond: $8\frac{1}{8}$ percent bond, maturing in 2017.

Name of company: Southern Bell Telephone Co.

No yield is given for convertible bonds.

Source: Adapted from David J. Rachman and Michael H. Mescon, *Business Today* 4th ed. (New York: Random House, 1985), p. 405.

3. *Current yield:* the relationship of the coupon or interest rate to how much the bond is actually selling for on the open market. The Southern Bell bond yields 14 — a figure higher than the actual coupon rate of the bond. When the current yield column has the notation *cv* instead of a figure, the bond is convertible to common stock under certain conditions.

4. *Volume:* the number of bonds that changed hands. Thus, 4 Southern Bell bonds were traded on this day.

5. *High, low, close:* the bond's range of prices during the day. "Close" refers to the bond's price at the close of the business day. Since the face value of almost all bonds is $1,000, a zero is added to the end of each of these figures to determine the actual price of the bond. Thus, both the day's lowest price and the closing price of the Southern Bell bond was $592.50. The high price of the day was $592.50 as well. As Chapter 15 explained, these price changes directly affect the bond's yield.

6. *Net change:* how much the bond has risen or fallen in price since the previous day. An increase of ¼ means the bond has actually risen $2.50 in value. Since the numbers are expressed as a percentage of the bond's face value and the face value is almost always $1,000, 1 is equal to $10.

STOCK INDEXES

In addition to printing the prices of individual securities, most newspapers publish one or more of the market averages that have been devised to chart general market movement. Though the formulas used to compile them and their usefulness in predicting future trends are often questioned, the various averages continue to hold the attention of investors.

The Dow Jones Industrial Average

> LATE RALLY SENDS DOW UP 12.86
> SPECULATION ON OPEC PACT SPURS ADVANCE
>
> DOW FALLS BY 21.96 TO 1,219.78
> RATE FEARS AND PROFIT TAKING MAJOR FACTORS

These headlines indicate a truism on Wall Street: daily stock market activity is judged by the up-and-down movement of the Dow Jones Industrial Average (DJIA), which is the most widely published stock market index. The DJIA (also referred to as the Dow) consists of the stocks of 30 major industrial corporations listed on the New York Stock Exchange. This list—shown in Table 16-2—has changed little over the years, although occasionally companies have been dropped and others added for financial reasons. In 1982, for example, the bankrupt Manville Corporation was replaced by American Express. In addition to the industrial index, the Dow Jones average also measures the activity of 20 transportation stocks, 15 utility stocks, and a composite of all the stocks contained in the four averages. These averages receive little attention in comparison with the DJIA.

Part of the popularity of the DJIA is its longevity: the Dow has been around longer than any other stock market barometer. Starting with 12 stocks in 1896, the Dow expanded to 30 stocks in 1928. Its popularity is also influenced by the reputation of its publisher, Dow Jones and Company, which publishes the widely respected *Wall Street Journal,* and to the Dow Jones wire service, to which almost all newspapers and broadcasting firms subscribe.

But the Dow is not without its critics. Some argue that the DJIA contains too few stocks to reflect accurately what is going on in the entire market. The Dow's 30 stocks represent only 23 percent of the New York Stock Exchange market value. Critics contend that these distortions are compounded by the fact that the Dow is weighted by the prices of the 30 listed companies. The price fluctuations of a stock selling at $100 a share have twice the effect on the average as the fluctuations of a stock selling at $50; yet, ironically, it is the low-priced stocks that often create the most activity. Finally, critics point to the disproportionately large number of "smokestack" stocks included in the DJIA. They argue that the Dow reflects the nation's industrial past and ignores the enormous changes that have turned the United States into a service and high-technology economy.

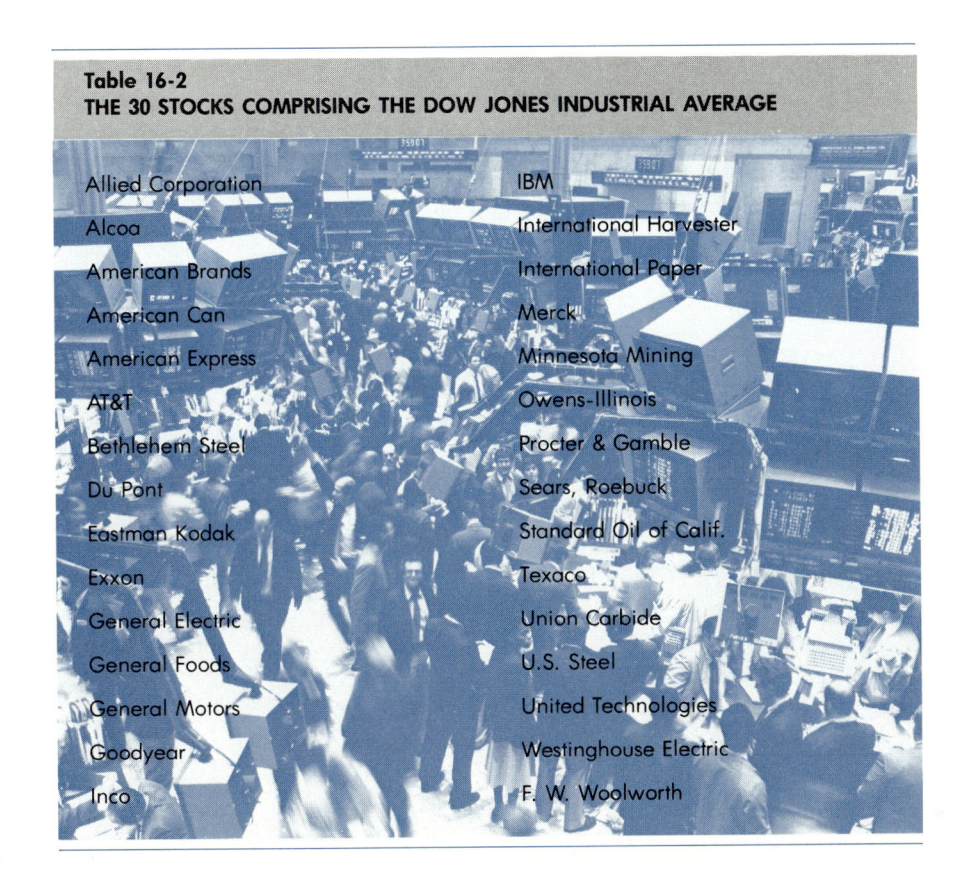

Table 16-2
THE 30 STOCKS COMPRISING THE DOW JONES INDUSTRIAL AVERAGE

Allied Corporation	IBM
Alcoa	International Harvester
American Brands	International Paper
American Can	Merck
American Express	Minnesota Mining
AT&T	Owens-Illinois
Bethlehem Steel	Procter & Gamble
Du Pont	Sears, Roebuck
Eastman Kodak	Standard Oil of Calif.
Exxon	Texaco
General Electric	Union Carbide
General Foods	U.S. Steel
General Motors	United Technologies
Goodyear	Westinghouse Electric
Inco	F. W. Woolworth

Yet despite these criticisms, the Dow continues to capture the headlines and the public's attention. Americans chart the Dow (see Figure 16-8) and look to it for signs that a sick economy is recovering or that a healthy economy is losing its vitality. When, for example, in 1983, the Dow broke through the 1,200 mark for the first time in its history, market analysts began talking of a resurgence of business confidence, marking an economic recovery.

Standard & Poor's Index of 500 Stocks. The Standard & Poor's Index of 500 Stocks is a lesser-known measure of stock market performance. But, despite its low profile, this index is considered by market professionals to be a far better index of stock market activity than the DJIA. There are several reasons why. With a broader base of 500 stocks, including 400 industrial, 40 financial, 40 utility, and 20 transportation issues, the Standard & Poor's Index is more representative of total market activity. With listings from the New York Stock Exchange, the Amex, and over-the-counter markets, it cuts across different markets and different types of stock. More than 90 industry subgroups,

Figure 16-8

CHARTING THE DOW JONES INDUSTRIAL AVERAGE: A 60-YEAR PERSPECTIVE

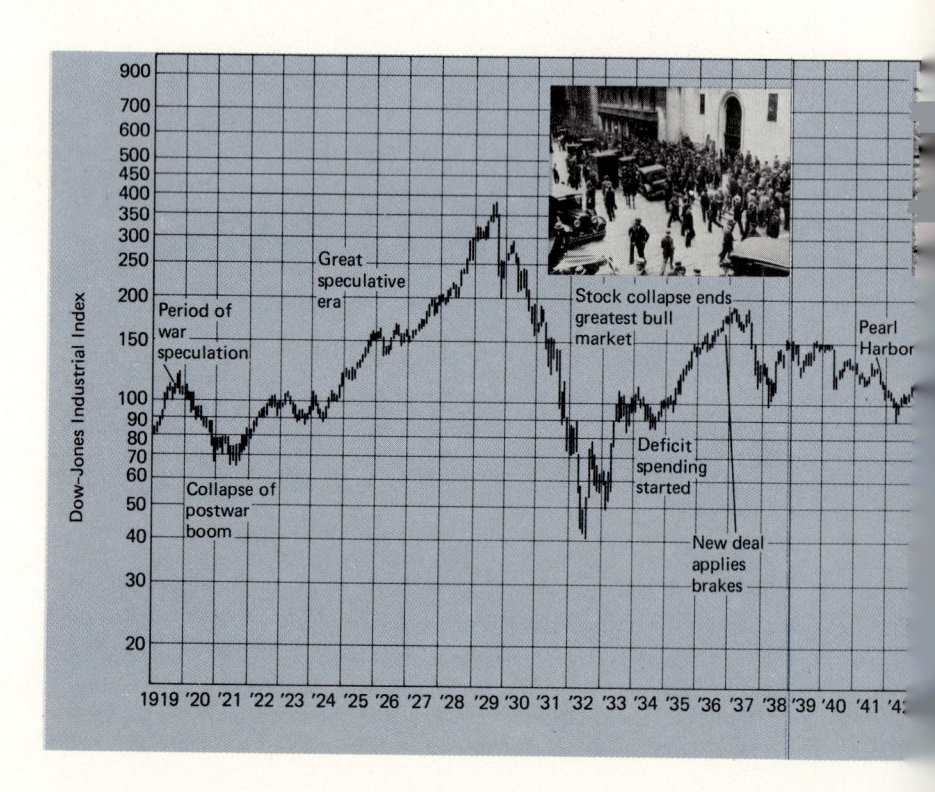

Source: David J. Rachman and Michael Mescon, *Business Today* 3rd ed. (New York: Random House, 1982), pp. 418–419. Reprinted by permission.

ranging alphabetically from aerospace to toys, are followed, giving investors a way of tracking daily industry performance and trends.

Other Indexes. The *New York Stock Exchange Index* measures the activity of the more than 1,500 common stocks listed on the exchange. It includes a composite index of all common stocks as well as indexes for industrial, transportation, utility, and financial issues. Similarly, the *American Stock Exchange Index* is based on the market activity of all the common stock shares on the Amex. In both cases, stocks are weighted according to their total market value, giving the larger companies a greater effect on the average than the smaller ones. Finally, the *National Association of Securities Dealers Automated Quotations (NASDAQ) Index* measures the activity of the most important companies listed on the over-the-counter market.

BUYING AND SELLING SECURITIES 487

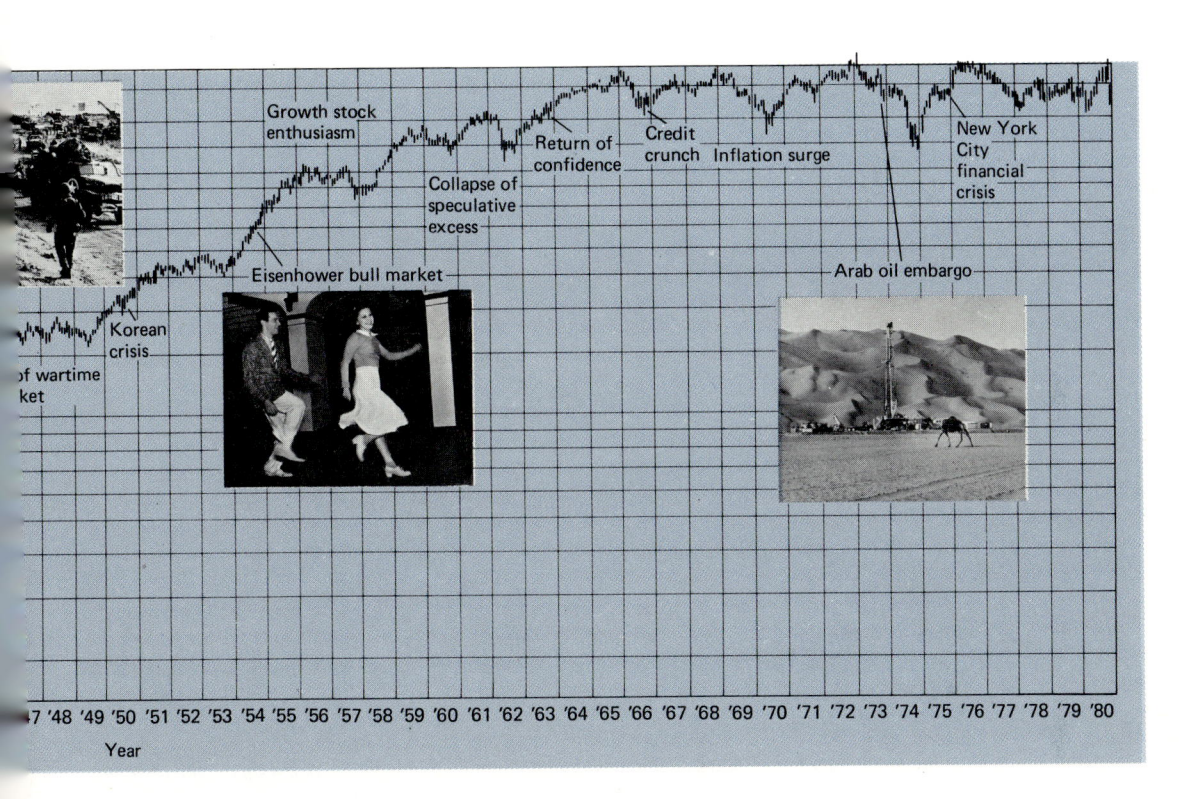

DEVELOPING A SUCCESSFUL INVESTMENT STRATEGY

Although there are as many investment strategies on Wall Street as there are investors, there are few that pay off consistently year after year. The variety of these approaches brings home the point once again that the hardest part of investing in securities is doing it successfully.

THE EFFICIENT-MARKET HYPOTHESIS

"Mkt is efficient only when investors cannot consistently outperform it."

Many investors believe that they can beat the market through a quick series of trades: buy a stock on Monday for 10 and sell it on Friday for 12. Instead of buying and holding securities in the hope of long-term gains, they move in and out of the market with the aim of outdoing the market averages. After paying broker commissions, they usually fall short of their goal.

INVESTMENTS

The main reason for their failure is the efficiency of the market. Security analysts believe that the market operates on the basis of complete information about individual companies, industries, the market, and the general economy. Market prices reflect this efficiency and are therefore completely accurate. Price changes occur only in response to new information. In a self-adjusting process, the market moves up or down to reflect what it has learned.

Analysts believe that the market's efficiency makes predicting a stock's short-term movement impossible. Both the direction and magnitude of change are completely random. A stock can rise one day and for no apparent reason drop the next. This independent, erratic behavior is termed *random walk*. Long-term behavior, on the other hand, depends on complete information and usually varies around a point determined by company earnings and dividends.

THE BETA CONCEPT

How can an investor minimize the risk that his or her stock will fall faster than the market itself? One way is to understand and apply the beta concept to the investor's entire portfolio. According to this concept, some stocks maintain relatively stable prices while others rise and fall more sharply than the market itself. The *beta concept* is a mathematical coefficient that measures relative price pattern of a stock.

beta concept: a mathematical coefficient measuring the volatility of a stock's price relative to the overall market.

When the movement of a stock is in line with overall market trends, it is assigned a beta of 1. If the market rises or falls 10 percent, a stock with a beta of 1 will also experience a 10-percent rise or fall. A stock that moves twice as fast as the overall market is given a beta of 2. A stock that is only half as volatile is assigned a beta of 0.5.

Most experts advise against deciding whether to buy an individual stock just on the basis of its beta. At any given time, the price of a stock may have little relationship to its past performance. But a person may use betas to assess the risk of their entire stock portfolio. If an investor owns 10 or more stocks, the betas of his or her stock will be an accurate risk measure.

The beta of a portfolio can be determined by multiplying the current market price of each stock by the stock's beta, adding these results, and then dividing by the total value of all stock holdings. This will indicate whether one's portfolio is more risky than the market itself. It is important to remember that the more volatile stocks create the highest losses and the highest rates of return. If the investor can accept the risk, these stocks have the greatest chance of turning into a bonanza.

The betas of individual stocks are calculated by the Value Line Index. Table 16-3 shows some of the values assigned to various stock in 1982. Value Line reports, which are published quarterly, are available through stockbrokers or in the business section of the public library.[7]

Table 16-3
BETAS OF SOME LEADING COMPANIES

Company	Beta	Company	Beta
Alcoa	1.05	General Motors	.90
Allied Stores	.85	Gulf Oil	1.15
American Brands	.70	Ingersoll-Rand	.90
AT&T	.65	IBM	.95
Bethlehem Steel	1.25	Johnson & Johnson	.95
Burroughs	.95	McDonald's	1.05
Campbell Soup	.65	J. C. Penney	1.00
Caterpillar Tractor	.95	Philip Morris	.90
Coca-Cola	.85	Polaroid	1.20
Dow Chemical	1.25	Safeway Stores	.80
Du Pont	1.10	Sears, Roebuck	.90
Eastman Kodak	1.00	J. P. Stevens	.75
Exxon	.90	Texaco	.95
Ford Motor	.85	U.S. Steel	1.00
General Electric	.95	Winn-Dixie Stores	.55
General Foods	.75		

Note: A figure of 1.00 means price of stock usually changes about as much as the Value Line index. A stock above 1.00 is more volatile than the index.

Source: William C. Bryant, "One Way to Reduce Risk," Reprinted from *U.S. News & World Report*; April 19, 1982, p. 105 , Copyright 1982, U.S. News & World Report, Inc.

DETERMINING ACCEPTABLE RISK

As discussed in Chapter 15, many different factors determine whether a risk is acceptable to you. An individual's age, life situation, personality, health, income level, assets, and more influence investment decisions. This analysis helps determine how much risk an investor should be willing to take.

DOLLAR-COST AVERAGING

The timing of investment decisions is a subject of continuing concern to most investors. It is impossible to predict the lowest price for a security during a market reverse or the peak price during a market rally, so how does the investor decide when to purchase and when to sell?

Rather than attempting to outguess the market, many investors choose to make a number of fixed-dollar investments in a given security over a period of time. This technique—called *dollar-cost averaging*—means that the investor may sometimes pay relatively higher prices for the stock and sometimes pay quite low prices for it. On balance, however, it should permit the investor to acquire the desired number of shares at a reasonable level. Figure 16-9 shows how this approach would work over a one-year period.

dollar-cost averaging: *a method of timing investment decisions by purchasing a specified dollar amount of securities at fixed time intervals.*

Figure 16-9

DOLLAR-COST AVERAGING

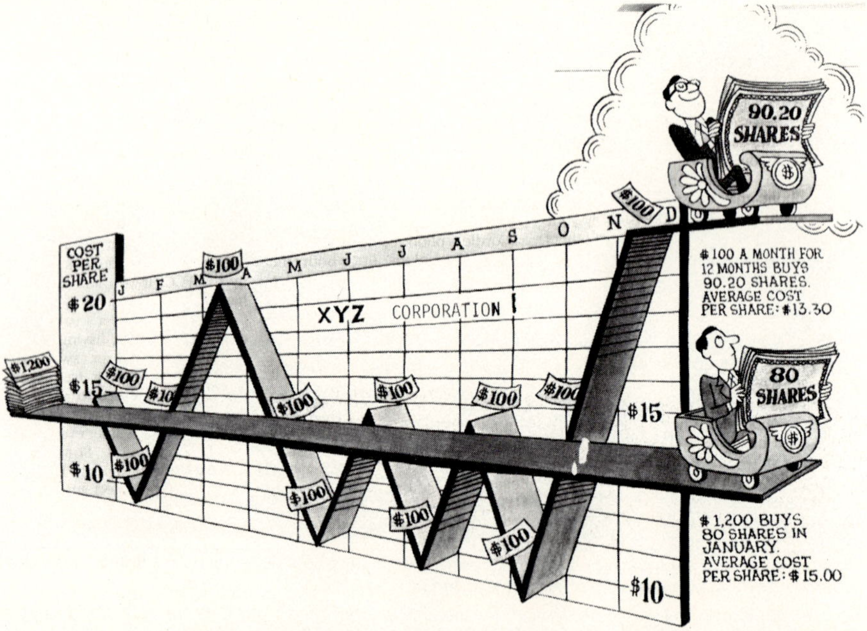

Source: Excerpted with permission from "Investment Formulas That Cut Your Risk," *Changing Times*, July 1983, p. 34. Artwork by Roy Doty.

Dollar-cost averaging is particularly effective for highly volatile investments, where rapid price changes are common. It should be seriously considered by those investors who are able to invest about the same amount of money at regular intervals.

SPREADING RISK THROUGH A PORTFOLIO OF DIFFERENT SECURITIES

One of the risks in the purchase of a stock is that the stock will decline even while the market is booming. To protect against this, it is important to diversify one's holdings.

The investor can also diversify by industry sector and type of stock in order to protect against slowdowns in various parts of the economy. For example, a portfolio of blue-chip and growth stocks in manufacturing, transportation, and financial companies is less risky than putting all your funds in one industry.

Diversification is limited by the number of stocks one can comfortably afford and follow. The goal is to extend investment horizons, not to overextend your budget or investment-management ability.

SUMMARY

Two types of securities markets exist. The primary market is used by businesses and governmental units selling *new* issues of stocks or bonds in order to raise needed capital funds. Such issuing firms and agencies typically utilize the services of a securities marketer called an investment banker in selling the issue and in providing advice concerning offering price and other details. The secondary market is the market in which previously issued stocks and bonds are bought and sold.

Securities exchanges are locations where stocks and bonds are sold. The two largest exchanges in the United States are the New York Stock Exchange (the Big Board) and the American Stock Exchange (Amex, or the Curb). Several regional securities exchanges also exist. Stocks and bonds not listed on one of the organized exchanges are traded over-the-counter through securities dealers who operate largely by telephone and computer terminals.

The Securities and Exchange Commission, created by the Securities Exchange Act of 1934, is the federal agency charged with enforcing federal security laws and regulating disclosure of information by firms to the investing public. In addition, the SEC regulates operation of the organized securities exchanges, over-the-counter markets, and mutual funds industry.

Stockbrokers are employed by brokerage firms to handle securities transactions and provide advice and information for their clients. Discount brokers usually charge a smaller commission on securities transactions than do full-service brokers, but the personal services, research facilities, and advice provided to their clients are limited.

Investors may use cash accounts and pay for all of their securities purchases at the time of purchase, or they may open a margin account, which allows them to pay a fraction—as little as 50 percent—of the total cost of the securities purchased and borrow the remainder from the brokerage firm. Use of margin accounts allows investors to practice the financial concept of leverage, whereby they attempt to magnify their return on their investment through the use of borrowed funds.

Shares are usually traded in round lots of 100 units. Odd-lot purchases, or sales of less than 100 units, typically involve higher commission charges. Stocks can be held personally in the name of the investor, or they can be held by the brokerage firm in its street name. Margin purchases are always held by the brokerage firm.

Numerous sources of investment information are available. These include corporate information in the form of annual reports, published articles and subscription market letters, specialized television programs, daily stock and bond price reports, and reports of stock indexes such as the Dow Jones Industrial Average and the Standard & Poor's Index of 500 Stocks.

In developing a successful investment strategy, the investor should determine acceptable risk and then attempt to spread that risk through a portfolio of different securities.

REVIEW QUESTIONS

1. Briefly define the following terms:

   primary markets
   investment banker
   secondary markets
   Big Board
   The Curb
   listed securities
   over-the-counter (OTC) market
   bid
   asked price
   NASDAQ
   Securities and Exchange Commission (SEC)
   Securities Investor Protection Corporation (SIPC)
   market order
   limit order
   stop order
   period order
   leverage
   margin
   margin call
   selling long
   selling short
   stockbroker
   commission
   round-lot transactions
   odd-lot transactions
   cash account
   margin account
   street name
   beta concept
   dollar-cost averaging

2. Compare and contrast the primary and secondary markets for securities.

3. What is the role of the various securities exchanges and the OTC market?

4. List and briefly comment on the legislative framework within which U.S. securities markets must operate.

5. Describe the process an investor goes through when buying or selling a security.

6. Explain the functions performed by a stockbroker. How should a new investor select a broker?

7. What sources of investment information are available to the investor?

8. Identify and describe the several different stock indexes. How are they used in personal financial decisions?

9. Outline the sequence involved in developing a successful investment strategy.

10. Explain the efficient-market hypothesis. What is the relationship of this hypothesis to the distinction between investors and speculators?

CASES AND EXERCISES

1. Sharon Goldfine asked her broker to buy 80 shares of Stymin Corporation stock selling at 55½. The broker executed the order and billed Goldfine $4,460 plus commission, taxes, and other fees. Did the broker make a mistake in Goldfine's billing? Discuss.

2. The local paper showed the following for Baker Enterprises:

52 Weeks High	Low	Stock	Div.	Yld. %	P/E Ratio	Sales 100s	High	Low	Close	Net Chg.
44½	21 1/8	BKZ	1.00	4.0	10	47	25 5/8	23½	25	+¼

Discuss what this quotation tells a potential buyer of Baker Enterprises stock.

3. The following information about Dauphin Industries—an OTC stock—recently appeared in the newspaper:

Stock & Div.	Sales 100s	Bid	Asked	Net Chg.
Dauphin IN 2.24	60	37 5/8	38	—

Discuss what this quotation tells a potential buyer of Dauphin Industries stock.

4. The Colorado Company's bonds were recently quoted as:

Bonds	Cur. Yld.	Vol.	High (if actual no.)	Low	Close	Chg. Chg.
CoLoCo 7½ 06	10	7	76¼	74	75	+1½

Discuss what this quotation tells a potential buyer of bonds issued by the Colorado Company.

5. Consider the following scenario. The stock market is moving up rapidly. Your broker calls with a suggestion that you invest $5,000 of the funds now in your money-market mutual fund in either one of two popular high-tech issues. Both stocks sell for about $7 per share. Neither currently pays a dividend. The broker also mentions that one stock—Storwell-Addison, Inc.—has a beta of 2.5. The other issue—Frayer Co.—has a beta of .8. Do you agree with the broker's suggestions? If so, which stock would you pick? Why?

ANSWERS TO PERSONAL FINANCE I.Q. TEST

1. Fiction. 2. Fact. 3. Fact. 4. Fiction. 5. Fact. 6. Fact.

HOW JENNIFER POWELL REACHED HER PERSONAL FINANCIAL DECISION

Professor Ogden's first comment to Jennifer is that *no investment in the stock market is absolutely safe.* "If you want absolute safety," he warns, "don't go into the world of buying and selling securities. On the other hand, no place offers the same potential profits. In fact, in good times, buying and selling stock can be an exhilarating experience."

Jennifer has the right idea in setting up a 10-year run for her investment, according to Professor Ogden. Many newcomers to the stock market expect miracles overnight. Usually that doesn't happen. "Don't expect too much too soon," he cautioned.

"The best way to go about investing," Professor Ogden explained, "is to select a reputable broker. Most of us don't have the time to study all the ins and outs of the stock market ourselves—unless, of course, that's our full-time job. Especially when you're new to the stock market, choosing a good brokerage firm is essential. Your broker will have looked into different companies and will help you assess the risks involved; he or she will also have good advice on when to buy and when to sell. But even with a broker, you need to keep yourself informed. That way you'll know what questions to ask."

Professor Ogden made one final point: "Because investing in the stock market always carries some risk, it's important to develop a philosophy that accepts that risk. One way of looking at it is to see your investment as extra money—if worst came to worst and you lost it, you'd still be able to carry on your present lifestyle."

LEARNING OBJECTIVES

1. To explain how investment clubs operate and the benefits provided to club members. / *2.* To compare monthly investment plans and employee stock purchase and option plans. / *3.* To distinguish between bull markets and bear markets. / *4.* To identify the primary benefits mutual fund investments offer to individual investors. / *5.* To differentiate load from no-load mutual funds. / *6.* To outline the advantages provided for an investor through a family of mutual funds. / *7.* To describe the specialized services offered by many mutual funds.

TESTING YOUR PERSONAL FINANCE I.Q.

	FACT	FICTION
1. SEC regulations limit investment club participants to wealthy investors, since the minimum investment allowed is $100 per month.	☐	☐
2. Bull markets typically occur during periods of rising beef prices.	☐	☐
3. No-load mutual funds do not charge management fees.	☐	☐
4. IBM is the most widely held stock by mutual funds.	☐	☐
5. The existence of a family of mutual funds increases investor flexibility.	☐	☐
6. Mutual fund shares can be bought and sold only through licensed stockbrokers.	☐	☐

The materials in this chapter assist in separating fact from fiction. Your answers can be checked on page 521.

CHAPTER SEVENTEEN

INVESTMENT CLUBS AND MUTUAL FUNDS

SHARING A PERSONAL FINANCIAL DECISION WITH MARK BASS, CPA, OF TEXAS TECH UNIVERSITY

He can't quite believe it himself, but Sam Johnson is eager for the start of classes. He has a question he wants to ask his personal finance teacher, Mark Bass, CFP, CPA. Last year Sam listened with interest to Mr. Bass's lectures on investment possibilities. But learning about the investment decision was one thing. Now Sam has the chance to make it work for him.

During the summer between his freshman and sophomore years, Sam earned $6,000. Because his parents are paying for all of his expenses while he is in school, he has decided to invest the money. Already Sam has tried to sort out his personal objectives. Essentially, he wants the money to grow. With this $6,000 he hopes to lay the foundation for an investment portfolio he can manage for years to come.

Because this is the first opportunity Sam has had to invest, he wants to do it right. He knows that Mr. Bass, who is also a financial planner with Pennington/Bass Companies in Lubbock, Texas, will offer sound advice.

If you were Mr. Bass, what investments would you suggest to Sam?

To find out how Mr. Bass helped Sam with his personal financial decision, turn to page 521.

"A bull can make money on Wall Street; a bear can make money on Wall Street; but a hog never can."
Anonymous

From his "collegiately cramped" dorm room in Princeton University's Lockhart Hall, 20-year-old Jim Lavelle runs a mutual fund with, at last count, 14 clients and $130,000 in assets. "Pin Stripe Investments, Inc.," reads the Princeton junior's business card, "J. Francis Lavelle, President."

Such embellishments would have been judged mortally unhip on campus a decade ago, and even now might mark someone of lesser talents as a nerd. But Lavelle wears his credentials like a Savile Row suit. "People get involved in my fund because they think that if I'm doing this at 20, by the time I'm 30 they will have created a small fortune," he explains. "To a great extent, that's true."

Just a year ago Lavelle had started an informal stock advisory service for friends and relatives. He turned it into an SEC-registered corporation last October. His fund's assets nearly doubled recently in the wake of an Associated Press story on the fund. In response to about 100 ensuing inquiries, he mailed information about his fees (from 2½ to 4 percent) and portfolio (heavy right now on People Express, Home Health Care of America, and Sunrise Savings & Loan of Florida).[1]

Jim Lavelle is a 20-year-old Princeton student who runs a booming mutual fund from his dorm room.

For the thousands of investors who want to put at least some of their investment dollars in stocks and bonds but do not want to make each selection themselves, a number of options exist. Some prefer to make decisions about security choices with a group of interested investors rather than relying solely on their own individual judgment. In these instances, they may decide to join an investment club. In other cases, they may prefer to invest in a mutual fund similar in structure to the one developed by Jim Lavelle. These investment alternatives are explored in this chapter.

INVESTMENT CLUBS

Investing can be a lonely, uncertain activity. But approximately 325,000 to 400,000 people across the country have avoided this investor-isolation syndrome by joining *investment clubs*. Each of the estimated 4,500 clubs throughout the United States is made up of an average of 15 people, who join forces to invest in the securities market. Each group member contributes an agreed-upon amount of money each month (usually $25) to a central investment fund. This fund functions as a self-run mutual fund, enabling investors to pool their money and make purchases they could not make on their own. According to Thomas O'Hara, president of the National Association of Investment Clubs (which represents an estimated 25 percent of all U.S. clubs), the average investment club owns 20 to 40 different stock issues with a total value of approximately $60,000. These investments have an average annual yield of 21 percent.[2]

investment clubs: organizations in which members pool their funds to make investments in selected securities.

MAKING PURCHASE DECISIONS

Before a decision is made concerning specific investments by the club, members present research reports on specific companies. A vote is then taken to decide on the most-preferred investments. Once securities are acquired, club members are typically assigned the task of collecting and regularly updating financial information related to each stock. The box on page 502 shows how such information is used in analyzing each stock on a regular basis and in deciding when to sell.

BULL MARKET OR BEAR MARKET?

The willingness of investment club members to invest additional funds in securities or to place them in interest-earning savings instruments such as certificates of deposit, money-market funds, or government or corporate bonds depends considerably on general market conditions. These conditions result from such factors as current levels of economic activity, inflation rates, levels of unemployment, investor attitudes concerning the future, and current governmental actions aimed at either slowing the economy or stimulating additional

Stock Analysis Checklist

Inexperienced investors can use some of the same techniques that professional analysts employ in deciding whether a stock is worth buying. One revealing test compares a company with the rest of its industry on the basis of vital balance-sheet and stock market performance data. The worksheet below is designed to help you make key comparisons that will tell you whether a stock deserves further consideration.

You'll find the numbers you need in the stock market listings of your newspaper (if it's skimpy, use the *Wall Street Journal*) and in the Value Line Investment Survey, available in well-stocked libraries. Value Line makes earnings estimates and compiles some of the industry averages. Calculate the others from Value Line reports on companies in specific industries. You'll also have to work out the percentage change in earnings. To determine if the stock is widely held by financial institutions, divide the number of shares they own (listed in Value Line under "institutional decisions") by the total shares outstanding (found under "capital structure"). Check your newspaper to make sure the stock price Value Line used for such data as price/earnings ratio isn't out of date.

In addition to earnings growth, a company's financial strength shows up in its net profit margin, which is the rate of return on sales; in its return on net worth, another gauge of profit; and in its cash flow per share, which indicates how much money the company is generating to finance further growth. Give the company a plus for each of these values if it is higher than the industry average. The last three measures on the worksheet give you an idea of the relative value of the stock. Give the stock a plus if any of these ratios is *below* average. When you've scored the company on each item, tally the pluses and minuses. Plus three or better is encouraging.

Once you've isolated a promising stock, more work needs to be done. Check with your broker for late news about the company. Though its balance sheet looks rock solid, its stock price may be down for an important reason. In the case of SmithKline Beckman, the company's drug Tagamet, which gave it a virtual monopoly in the antiulcer market, is about to meet competition from Zantac, the product of an English company, Glaxo. Some analysts find SmithKline less attractive than before.

BASICS ABOUT A STOCK

Example: SmithKline Beckman
Industry: Drugs
Ticker symbol: SKB

	SKB	Your stock		SKB	Your stock
Latest price	$63.75		Last year's per-share earnings	$5.51	
52-week range	$57–$77		This year's estimated earnings	$6.40	
Annual dividend	$2.60		Estimated change	+15.6%	

THE FINANCIAL ANALYSIS

The following should be above the industry average:	SKB	Industry average	Above or below average	Score	Your stock	Industry average	Above or below average	Score
Five-year average annual earnings growth	33%	17%	above	+				
Net profit margin	15.3%	11.4%	above	+				
Return on net worth	24.7%	18%	above	+				
Cash flow per share	$6.58	$3.51	above	+				
The following should be below the industry average:								
Price/earnings ratio	11.5	24	below	+				
Ratio of price to book value	311%	474%	below	+				
Institutional stockholdings	61%	46%	above	−				
			Net score:	+5			Net score:	

Source: Jordan E. Goodman, "Stock Analysis Checklist." Reprinted by special permission from *Money*, September 1983, p. 6.

economic activity. When the trend of the stock market is up, it is called a *bull market*. On the other hand, a *bear market* is one in which the prices of stocks are generally falling as a result of an economic downturn, government restrictions on growth, and general pessimism among investors. Although the volume of securities traded tends to increase during a bull market, some stocks are countercyclical. That is, they tend to increase in price during bear markets and may even decline during bull markets. Gold stocks such as Dome Mines and Homestake Mining Company have followed this pattern during some recent stock market reverses.

bull market: a period of general increases in stock market prices; it is characterized by investor optimism, favorable economic conditions, and/or governmental policies designed to stimulate the economy.

bear market: a period of general decreases in stock market prices; it is characterized by investor pessimism, unfavorable economic conditions, and/or governmental policies designed to slow economic growth rates.

DECIDING WHEN TO SELL

As the previous chapter pointed out, two major decisions causing investor anxiety are when to purchase a desired stock and when to sell it. Investors learn of their stock's annual low price and high price only after the year is over, but the desire to avoid selling too soon or too late is understandable. Investment club members typically spend part of each month's meeting reviewing their current portfolio and discussing candidates for sale. Such decisions are made jointly by all club members following discussions of the merits and shortcomings of each stock.

In some instances, stocks acquired years earlier may become sentimental favorites, and club members refuse even to consider selling them. But if the investment club is to accomplish its financial objectives, its portfolio must be reviewed regularly and some stocks pruned from the list. In some instances, sale of a stock is due to failure of the company to produce expected growth and profit performance. In other cases, new firms with stronger expected-market performance than that of currently held stocks are identified. In order to perform an objective review of all stocks in the club's portfolio, many clubs use a checklist of rating factors. Figure 17-1 shows a portfolio checklist and how to evaluate the answers to each question.

Even though an investment club does not permit each member-contributor the absolute discretion he or she would enjoy by investing alone, it may offer benefits in addition to the collective investment judgment and wisdom of club members. Two additional advantages are the potential for greater stock diversification and lower commission costs resulting from pooled investment funds. Detailed information on forming and operating an investment club can be obtained from the National Association of Investment Clubs, 1515 East Eleven Mile Road, Royal Oak, Mich. 48067.

SPECIAL PURCHASE ARRANGEMENTS

Two additional methods of making stock purchases with limited investments are monthly investment plans and employee stock purchase and option plans.

Figure 17-1

A STOCK SELLER'S CHECKLIST

DIRECTIONS: In deciding when to sell, you need to consider a variety of factors. Here are ten questions you can apply to each stock you own. The first six involve broad economic and stock market indicators. The final four questions involve your particular stock. If you can answer yes to seven or more of the ten questions, it's time to seriously consider selling.

	Yes	No		Yes	No
1. Has an economic recovery been in progress for at least a year?	☐	☐	7. Is your stock's price/earnings ratio significantly above its 10-year average?	☐	☐
2. Is a current bull market two years old?	☐	☐	8. Is the ratio of its book value to the price of its shares 5 or higher?	☐	☐
3. Is this the year after a presidential election?	☐	☐			
4. Have more stocks been declining than advancing over the past two months?	☐	☐	9. Has the stock's price recently fallen below its 30-week average?	☐	☐
5. Are professionals heavily using short sales?	☐	☐	10. Is the stock's price increasing more slowly—or falling more rapidly—than the Dow Jones Industrial Average?	☐	☐
6. Are mutual fund managers almost fully invested in stocks?	☐	☐			

Source: Reprinted by special permission from *Money*, January 1984, p. 75.

For millions of investors, these special purchase arrangements permit stock purchases that would not be possible under typical purchase arrangements.

MONTHLY INVESTMENT PLANS

Investors who prefer to make long-term contributions of a fixed amount each month or quarter frequently participate in a *monthly investment plan*. To establish one, a person simply signs an agreement with a broker and agrees to deposit a specified amount between $40 and $1,000 each month or quarter. These funds are used to purchase shares in a specified security listed on the New York Stock Exchange. Because the participant in a monthly investment plan invests a fixed-dollar amount each period, fractional shares are purchased. If, for example, the investor deposits $100 each month for use in purchasing Exxon stock and the current price is $40, the investor will purchase 2.5 shares. Brokerage commissions are charged on each transaction.

The monthly investment plan agreement may be canceled at any time, and there are no penalties for missing payments. Such plans serve as a form of fixed-dollar-cost averaging, since the investor continues to purchase shares throughout the year. For investors seeking long-term acquisition of shares, the monthly investment plan may prove an effective method.

monthly investment plan: an arrangement permitting investors to make specified monthly or quarterly investments in securities listed on the New York Stock Exchange.

employee stock purchase plans: employee benefits provided by some companies that permit employees to obtain a specified number of shares in company stock, often at a discount below current market prices.

EMPLOYEE STOCK PURCHASE AND OPTION PLANS

People who work for a large corporation like American Telephone and Telegraph can purchase company stock through special *employee stock purchase plans*. These plans allow employees to apply a certain percentage of their regular salary to stock purchases. Because the purchases are made through the company, no brokerage fees are involved. Some companies sell their stock to employees at a discount from market value. At AT&T, for eample, employees pay 95 percent of the market value for shares of common stock. According to a recent New York Stock Exchange survey, one-third of the nation's shareholders participate in an employee stock purchase plan and nearly half have obtained stock through such a plan at some time in the past.

Like any other investment, the decision to participate in an employee stock purchase plan should depend on market conditions. If you buy the stock when its value is low, the investment will increase along with the market. But if the purchase is made after the stock's value has peaked, you will experience a reduction in the value of your investment just as you would in a non-company-related investment.

Some companies also offer stock option plans, which allow employees to purchase a stated number of stocks at a given price. Like all stock options, this employee benefit has value should the market price of the stock exceed the option price. If an employee receives an option to buy 100 shares of stock at $40 a share, it pays to exercise the option if the stock climbs above $40. Unless it exceeds the $40 level, the stock option has little or no value.

WHAT ARE INVESTMENT COMPANIES?

Over 20 million people in the United States have chosen an indirect method of investing in stocks and bonds. Rather than purchasing them directly, they own shares in specialized financial firms called investment companies. An *investment company* is a commercial enterprise formed for the purpose of investing in securities for profit. It secures its investment funds from the numerous investors who purchase shares of its stock. In return, investors own a share of a diversified portfolio of securities managed by experts. As the value of the securities owned by the investment company increases, so does the value of each investor's share in the investment company. Investment companies can be categorized as either closed-end or open-end.

investment company: a company that pools investment money from purchasers who buy shares in the fund and uses the money to acquire a diversified portfolio of securities.

CLOSED-END INVESTMENT COMPANIES

About 10 percent of all investment company assets are owned by *closed-end investment companies.* These firms issue a fixed number of shares and use the funds generated by this sale to finance the purchase of a portfolio of securities. Once the closed-end fund is organized, no additional shares are offered for sale to investors by the company. Following the initial sale of shares to investors, the shares can be traded only in secondary markets, such as the organized exchanges or over-the-counter markets. Trading is handled much like the purchase and sale of common stock, and brokerage commissions are paid

closed-end investment companies: investment companies organized by issuing a fixed number of its shares to investors in order to raise funds that are used to purchase a diversified portfolio of securities. No additional shares are issued, and outstanding shares are not redeemed.

on each transaction. The value of shares in such closed-end companies as Madison Fund and Lehman Corporation is determined by the value of the securities owned by the firm.

OPEN-END INVESTMENT COMPANIES (MUTUAL FUNDS)

open-end investment companies: *investment companies that issue and redeem their shares on demand based on the current value of their securities portfolio; also referred to as mutual funds.*

Unlike closed-end funds, *open-end investment companies,* also known as mutual funds, will sell and redeem their shares at any time. They do not have a fixed amount of shares. The price at which they will buy back their own shares or sell additional shares is based on the current value of the securities that the fund owns. Since open-end investment companies, or mutual funds, are the dominant form of investment company, they are discussed in detail in this chapter. Table 17-1 describes their general characteristics.

WHY PURCHASE MUTUAL FUNDS?

Mutual funds are particularly appropriate for the person who has a modest amount of money, time, and expertise and wishes to invest in the securities market. As one writer points out, "Just as there is no perfect person or painting

Table 17-1
CHARACTERISTICS OF MUTUAL FUNDS

Factor	Description
Pricing	Net assets divided by total number of shares outstanding.
Market for Shares	Directly from the fund through a securities broker or mutual fund selling organization.
Share Price	Varies directly with the total of all assets owned by the fund.
Volatility	As volatile as the fund's assets.
Commissions	Varies considerably. May pay a commission when buying the fund of up to 8.5%; no commission on sales ordinarily.
Marketability of Shares	Guaranteed market to buy or sell shares at any time in any amount.
Size of Fund	Varies with amount invested and value of assets.
Shares Outstanding	No limit.
Shareholder Services	Record keeping of purchases and sales, tax notification, dividend notification.

Source: Richard P. Halverson, *Financial Freedom: Your New Guide to Economic Security and Success* (San Francisco: Harbor Publishing Company, 1982), p. 334. Copyright 1982 by Richard P. Halverson.

or poem, so there is no perfect investment. But the one that comes closest for most people is the mutual fund."³

Not only are mutual funds appropriate vehicles during a rising securities market, they also offer numerous options for an investor during market declines. Factors supporting mutual funds as an investment choice for millions of investors include the mutual fund industry's track record of financial returns and its diversified portfolio, liquidity, professional management, and convenience. Some funds have no minimum investment amount; others require minimum investments as low as $100.

Record of Return. A mutual fund investment has the potential to grow in two ways—through dividends and capital gains. Dividends, when earned, are distributed quarterly to all investors. Capital gains are declared when the fund sells one of its investments at a profit. These profits may be taxed as long-term or short-term capital gains, depending on how long the fund has held the stock. In addition, if the value of the fund has increased during your ownership of its shares and you sell them after one year or more, your profits are taxed as capital gains. If the value has declined, it is taxed as a capital loss.

During the late 1970s and early 1980s, investors made substantial profits in mutual funds—profits that outpaced the market itself. While the Standard & Poor's Index of 500 Stocks rose 93.2 percent over a four-year period ending in 1982, stock mutual funds gained an average of 120.5 percent if all dividends were reinvested. At the same time, the Consumer Price Index rose only 59.4 percent.⁴ Over the ten-year period between 1973 and 1983, the best-performing mutual funds—Twentieth Century Select and Fidelity Magellan—grew approximately 700 percent.

Figure 17-2 is an advertisement emphasizing the performance of a major mutual fund. Potential investors who respond to such ads will receive a prospectus describing the fund's complete portfolio.

This is not to say that mutual funds always outperform the market or even that they always earn money. On the contrary, in the late 1960s and early 1970s, the track record of many funds was poor—and some lost a great deal of their investors' money. Part of the reason for this was the lackluster performance of the stock market, in which most funds were heavily invested. In the end, the overall performance of a mutual fund does nothing more than reflect how well or how poorly its primary investments are doing. When the market is down, high-risk funds are often the most susceptible to losses. During the 1973–74 and 1980–82 recessions, many of the more speculative funds took an inevitable fall. As a result, annual net sales of mutual fund shares declined seven times during the 1970s and increased only three times.

Diversification. The wisdom behind mutual fund diversification is as simple and logical as the old proverb that warns against putting all your eggs in

Figure 17-2

MUTUAL FUND ADVERTISEMENT

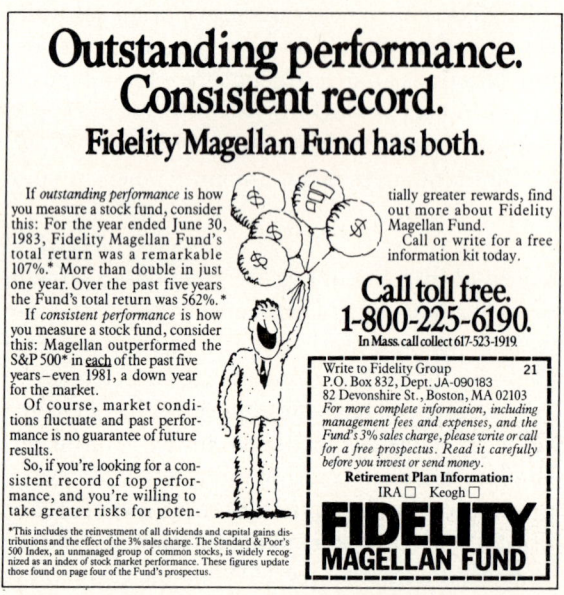

Outstanding performance. Consistent record.
Fidelity Magellan Fund has both.

If *outstanding performance* is how you measure a stock fund, consider this: For the year ended June 30, 1983, Fidelity Magellan Fund's total return was a remarkable 107%.* More than double in just one year. Over the past five years the Fund's total return was 562%.*

If *consistent performance* is how you measure a stock fund, consider this: Magellan outperformed the S&P 500* in each of the past five years—even 1981, a down year for the market.

Of course, market conditions fluctuate and past performance is no guarantee of future results.

So, if you're looking for a consistent record of top performance, and you're willing to take greater risks for potentially greater rewards, find out more about Fidelity Magellan Fund.

Call or write for a free information kit today.

Call toll free.
1-800-225-6190.
In Mass. call collect 617-523-1919.

Write to Fidelity Group   21
P.O. Box 832, Dept. JA-090183
82 Devonshire St., Boston, MA 02103
For more complete information, including management fees and expenses, and the Fund's 3% sales charge, please write or call for a free prospectus. Read it carefully before you invest or send money.

Retirement Plan Information:
IRA ☐   Keogh ☐

FIDELITY MAGELLAN FUND

*This includes the reinvestment of all dividends and capital gains distributions and the effect of the 3% sales charge. The Standard & Poor's 500 Index, an unmanaged group of common stocks, is widely recognized as an index of stock market performance. These figures update those found on page four of the Fund's prospectus.

Source: © 1984, Courtesy of Fidelity Investments.

---

one basket: if you put your entire investment in one or two stocks and they fall flat or backslide, you have a much more serious financial problem than if you invest in a mutual fund whose portfolio contains dozens of well-chosen stocks. Even if several of these stocks lose money, the others may keep your investment profitable. Table 17-2 ranks the 20 companies most widely held by mutual funds. Over 350 different mutual funds have IBM stock in their portfolios with a total overall value of more than $2 billion.

A diversified investment is not the same as a random investment. You control exactly where your money is being invested through your fund choice. If you are interested in investing in computer companies, you can find a fund that specializes in them. If you are interested only in blue chips, you will find many funds that fill the bill. In addition, even if you know what you're doing—if, for example, you have zeroed in on a hot industry—diversification prevents you from investing all your money in the one company in the industry that develops serious, unexpected problems.

Professional Management. More than anything else, when you buy a mutual fund, you buy its management expertise—the collective experience and judgment of fund managers who select the fund's numerous investments and decide when to buy and sell.

Table 17-2
TWENTY COMPANIES MOST WIDELY HELD BY MUTUAL FUNDS

Company	Value of Holdings	Number of Funds
IBM	$2,016 million	351
AT&T	875 million	214
General Electric	616 million	165
Philip Morris	509 million	132
Eastman Kodak	500 million	178
Schlumberger	488 million	213
General Motors	431 million	109
Digital Equipment	394 million	144
Atlantic Richfield	383 million	162
Minnesota Mining	358 million	115
Hewlett-Packard	351 million	104
Exxon	341 million	142
Tandy	338 million	78
MCI Communications	338 million	75
Hospital Corp.	287 million	77
SmithKline Beckman	279 million	86
McDonald's	278 million	94
Motorola	276 million	83
Johnson & Johnson	265 million	121
Ford	257 million	62

Note: Figures are as of December 31, 1982.
Source: "A Bull Market in Mutual Funds, Too." Reprinted from *U.S. News & World Report*, March 21, 1983, p. 73; Copyright 1983, U.S. News & World Report, Inc.

Each fund is headed by a portfolio manager, who makes the final investment decision. Some managers are autonomous, choosing investments at their own discretion, while others are constrained by the investment philosophy and choices of their investment company. At Value Line, for example, fund managers base their investment decisions on the system developed by Arnold Bernhard, the company's founder. This system, known as the Value Line Investment Survey, analyzes 1,700 stocks each week and rates the stocks in terms of their anticipated performance and safety over the next 12 months. After the analysis is complete, fund managers choose from the top 100 performers. Their record of success has been extraordinary. The Value Line Special Situations Fund grew by nearly 225 percent in five years while, during the same period, the Value Line Fund and Income Fund grew by 189 percent and 122 percent respectively.

By contrast, after considering analysts' advice, fund managers at the Oppenheimer Management Corporation are in total control of their funds' investment decisions. Donald W. Spiro, president of the company, describes its philosophy in this way: "Our portfolio managers have complete discretion to operate their funds as they see fit."[5] Here, too, the results are impressive: the Oppenheimer Special Fund grew 292 percent in five years and the Oppenheimer Time Fund grew 171 percent.

Convenience. For people who have limited time to manage their own investments, mutual funds eliminate many of the headaches involved in investing. You don't need to follow the ups and downs of individual companies and industries or pay brokerage fees when buying or selling individual securities. Mutual funds are also easy to use—in most cases you can make all of your transactions by phone.

LOAD VERSUS NO-LOAD MUTUAL FUNDS

More than 540 stock and bond mutual funds are currently operating in the United States. In addition, there are approximately 300 money-market mutual funds. All of these funds provide their investors with professional management, and all charge a management fee. These fees typically amount to 0.5 percent per year and are deducted from earnings. However, the funds differ greatly in whether they charge sales commissions to purchasers of their own shares. If purchasers pay a sales commission for mutual fund shares, they are buying *load funds*. The sales commission, or "load," represents compensation for the stockbroker or financial planner who handles the transaction. If no sales commission is involved, the mutual fund is referred to as a *no-load fund*. In addition, some funds charge no fees for purchases but impose a fee of up to 5 percent if the investors sell their shares in less than five years.

load funds: *mutual funds that charge purchasers a sales commission (or "load") in order to compensate stockbrokers and financial analysts for their marketing efforts.*

no-load fund: *a mutual fund that does not charge a sales commission to purchasers of its shares.*

EVALUATING LOAD FUNDS

Purchasers of such well-known mutual funds as Oppenheimer, Dreyfus, Kemper, and Keystone pay a sales commission ranging from 1 to 9 percent. Unlike an individual broker's commission, the load covers both the purchase and the eventual sale of the mutual fund shares; no additional commission is charged when the shares are sold. Still, loads reduce the yield on the investment, particularly when the investor makes a number of small individual purchases. The commission declines with large volume, just as commissions charged by stockbrokers for stocks and bonds decline when large purchases are made.

Approximately 350 of the nation's mutual funds are load funds. However, analysis of mutual fund performance reveals that load funds as a whole do not perform better than no-loads, despite the claims of many brokers. The major advantage of purchasing a load fund is personal service. Investors who prefer to rely on the advice of stockbrokers or financial analysts are more likely to purchase load funds and pay commissions for this expertise. If they have questions about their investment, their financial advisers are available to discuss the matter and make recommendations. This can be particularly comforting to investors as financial times become increasingly complex. Investors who do not require these services are more likely to purchase no-load funds in order to avoid paying the commission.[6]

EVALUATING NO-LOAD FUNDS

With a no-load mutual fund, rather than dealing with a salesperson, you purchase shares directly from the fund's management, by telephone or through the mail. Althogh the service is less personal in a load fund, the comparable overall market performance has made no-load funds a popular investment vehicle. In 1982 there were over 14 million shareowners in the nation's 500 no-load funds, accounting for nearly half of the total dollar volume of mutual fund share purchases. By contrast, ten years earlier only 160 no-load funds existed, and they represented only 1.2 million shareholders.[7]

A number of major no-load funds such as Fidelity, Scudder, Stevens & Clark, and Stein Roe Farnham have opened customer service offices in major cities. These offices give investors the opportunity to buy and sell shares and resolve problems and complaints on a person-to-person basis. They also serve a marketing function by giving interested newcomers an opportunity to learn about their operations. The sales practices of the no-load Vanguard Group may provide a glimpse of the future for the mutual funds industry. Vanguard's sales representatives now operate in kiosks located inside a number of Kroger supermarkets, marketing their mutual funds directly to food shoppers.

DIFFERENT TYPES OF MUTUAL FUNDS

A major consideration in investing in a mutual fund is securing a match of your individual investment objectives with those of the mutual fund. Funds differ not only in being load or no-load but also in the kinds of portfolio they own and the investment objectives they pursue. David Silver, president of the Investment Company Institute (the trade association of mutual funds), emphasizes the choices facing investors: "There are mutual funds across the entire financial spectrum from the most conservative kind of investment to the most speculative. It's the whole idea of risk-adjusted investments."[8]

Speculators interested in a high rate of return may consider funds specializing in gold and precious metals, natural resources, or options. More conservative investors can choose bond funds or those specializing in blue-chip stocks. Figure 17-3 shows how the assets of mutual funds are divided by various investment objectives.

This section reviews the major types of portfolios and objectives. However, new types of funds are constantly being formed in response to trends in the

Figure 17-3

MUTUAL FUND ASSETS CLASSIFIED BY INVESTMENT OBJECTIVES

September 1982 assets of all mutual funds excluding money market funds by broad category of investment objective. Dollar amounts in billions, percentages are of total.

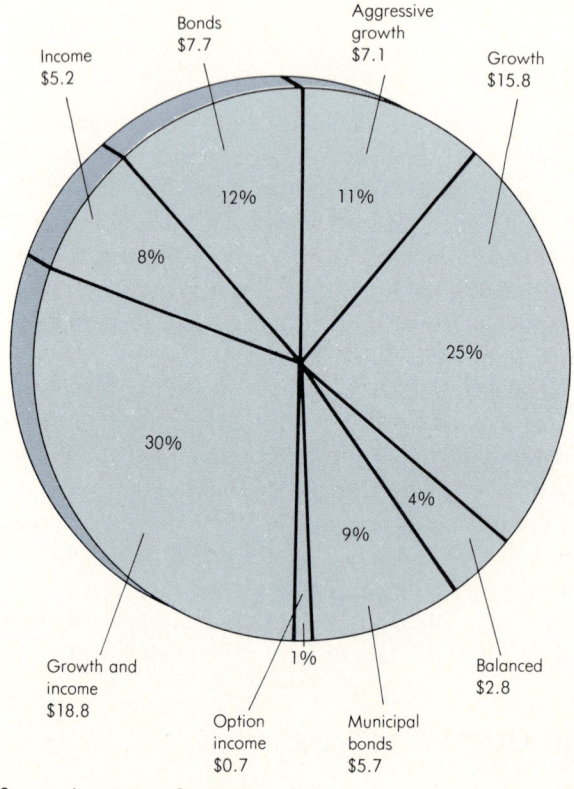

- Income $5.2 — 8%
- Bonds $7.7 — 12%
- Aggressive growth $7.1 — 11%
- Growth $15.8 — 25%
- Balanced $2.8 — 4%
- Municipal bonds $5.7 — 9%
- Option income $0.7 — 1%
- Growth and income $18.8 — 30%

Source: Investment Company Institute.

economy. Consequently, careful investors should study current financial publications and seek advice from experts in order to remain knowledgeable about these trends.

Aggressive Growth Funds. The main objective of aggressive growth funds is maximum capital appreciation through the purchase of such risky investments as the common stock from small, newly emerging companies; options; and warrants. Stocks are also purchased on margin to increase the fund's leverage, and selling short is common. These funds tend to outperform a rising market and fall more sharply than a declining market. Aggressive growth funds may also be called maximum capital gains funds, capital appreciation funds, or maximum appreciation funds.

Growth Funds. Growth funds usually hold portfolios of diversified common stocks that provide the opportunity for substantial gain. Their primary objective is long-term growth rather than rapid appreciation.

Growth and Income Funds. Both high income and long-term capital gains are the objectives of the growth and income funds, which invest mainly in blue-chip stocks paying high dividends. They give investors who need current income the chance to see their money grow over a long period of time.

Balanced Funds. As the name implies, balanced funds are balanced between bonds and preferred stock and the riskier common stock. The proportion is usually 30 to 40 percent in bonds and preferreds, with the rest in common stock. These funds are generally conservative, having as their aim steady, gradual growth over a long period of time, with corresponding steady income.

Income Funds. Income funds invest in securities that offer high current income rather than capital gains. They invest mainly in corporate bonds, government-insured mortgages, and preferred stocks, all of which offer investors a high degree of safety.

Index Funds. The portfolio of an index fund is made up of common stocks that are chosen to represent and perform like the stock market as a whole. Decisions on the portfolio are usually based on Standard & Poor's Index of 500 Stocks, the objective being a rate of return that parallels that of the stock market as a whole and allows the small investor access to the same kind of return an investor with a large, diversified portfolio could expect. [betas ≈ 1.0]

Bond Funds. The portfolios of these funds are made up of income-producing bonds. Some bond funds specialize in tax-exempt municipals, issued by states, cities, and government agencies, which give investors tax-free current income. Investors interested in municipals that mature in two years or less can invest in a short-term municipal bond fund, which is also known as a tax-exempt money-market fund.

Money-Market Funds. In recent years the most popular type of mutual fund has been the money-market fund, which invests in U.S. government securities, bank certificates of deposit, and commercial paper. The primary objective of these funds is immediate income and safety.

Industry Funds. Also known as specialty funds, industry funds buy only the common stocks of companies in a particular industry or economic area, such as electronics or computers, although some also hold preferred stocks and bonds. The funds can be attractive to the investor who is interested in a particular industry but unsure of which companies are likely to be winners. Like other mutuals, industry funds can be conservative or aggressive. These funds are classified on the basis of such investment objectives as maximum capital gains, long-term growth, growth and income, income, bond funds, and money-market funds.

MUTUAL FUND FAMILIES

In order to serve investors with evolving objectives and to attract new investors who may have investment objectives widely different from those of current investors, a number of large mutual funds serve as umbrella organizations for several different mutual funds designed to match specific investor objectives. These numerous smaller funds, which operate as separate organizations within a larger umbrella organization, are referred to as a *mutual fund family*.

mutual fund family: numerous smaller funds operating as separate organizations within a larger umbrella mutual fund organization.

Each fund's portfolio and objectives are described in its prospectus. For example, T. Rowe Price contains 10 funds in its family of funds. Its New Horizons Fund seeks long-term growth by purchasing shares of small, growth companies with the potential of becoming major companies in the future. Its Tax-Free Income Fund invests in municipal bonds in order to produce the highest tax-exempt income consistent with preservation of principal. Its New Era Fund invests primarily in stocks of companies developing natural resources and seeks long-term growth. Figure 17-4 identifies the 11 funds in the Oppenheimer family. Each is shown on a scale ranging from most aggressive to least aggressive, permitting investors to consider specific funds that best match their own investment objectives.

SWITCHING WITHIN A FAMILY

The advantage of investing in a mutual fund such as Fidelity (with its 26-fund family) or Vanguard (with its 22 separate funds) is flexibility. Should your fund fail to achieve your investment objectives or your objectives change, you

Figure 17-4
THE OPPENHEIMER MUTUAL FUND FAMILY

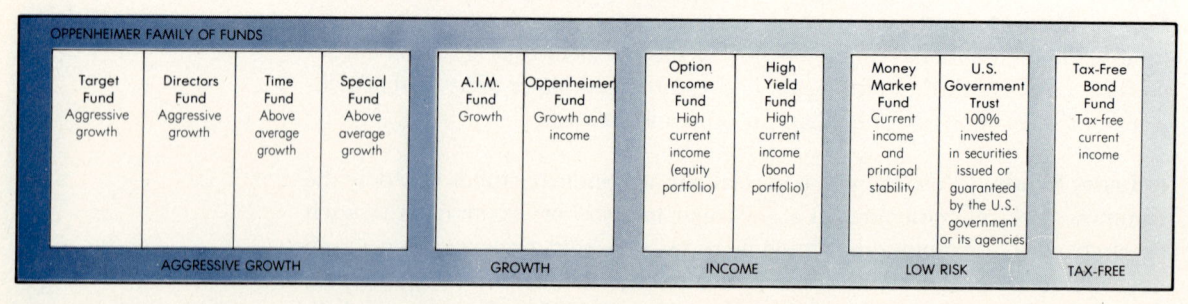

OPPENHEIMER FAMILY OF FUNDS										
Target Fund — Aggressive growth	Directors Fund — Aggressive growth	Time Fund — Above average growth	Special Fund — Above average growth	A.I.M. Fund — Growth	Oppenheimer Fund — Growth and income	Option Income Fund — High current income (equity portfolio)	High Yield Fund — High current income (bond portfolio)	Money Market Fund — Current income and principal stability	U.S. Government Trust — 100% invested in securities issued or guaranteed by the U.S. government or its agencies	Tax-Free Bond Fund — Tax-free current income
AGGRESSIVE GROWTH				GROWTH		INCOME		LOW RISK		TAX-FREE

Source: Courtesy Oppenheimer Management Corporation.

can switch into a different fund made up of a totally different portfolio of investments. In most instances, such a conversion can be accomplished with a telephone call. Such switches may produce a tax liability, however, since the Internal Revenue Service typically interprets a switch as a sale.

Some funds require a transfer form, which includes a guaranteed signature witnessed by an officer of a commercial bank or brokerage house. Even if telephone transfers are permitted, the investor should note the name of the fund representative called together with the date and time of the call. This information is needed if a mistake is discovered in the transaction. (To protect themselves against possible complaints, many mutual funds record the calls they receive from clients.)

SPECIAL FEATURES TO LOOK FOR IN MUTUAL FUNDS

Both the stated objectives and actual performance of mutual funds are major considerations in selecting an appropriate fund. However, the investor should also consider the services offered by the fund. These may include automatic reinvestment, systematic withdrawal, insurance against loss, retirement accounts, and check-writing privileges.

AUTOMATIC REINVESTMENT

Some funds allow shareholders to reinvest their gains automatically. Money earned in the fund (income or growth) is added to the original investment. This is usually a contractual arrangement made with the initial purchase. Automatic reinvestment provides the advantage of increasing one's holdings slowly and painlessly without paying an additional sales commission for each increment. Administrative and management fees still apply, however, and the IRS considers the reinvested funds income, just as if they had been received in cash.

SYSTEMATIC WITHDRAWAL

Funds pay out earnings annually or on a variable schedule and in amounts that reflect performance over the period. If an investor wants to receive a uniform amount at regular intervals, some funds provide what is called a systematic withdrawal plan.

These plans vary. Some pay out a fixed amount; some provide for the sale of a certain number of shares at regular intervals, so dollar amounts of the payment vary; and some provide for reinvestment of any excess earned on the account during the period. Administrative and management fees are charged for this service, and there is a minimum initial investment to participate.

"You missed the gold play, you missed the real-estate boom and the market upturn, and you're probably missing something else this very minute."

The Ability to Switch among a Family of Mutual Funds Increases Investor Flexibility.

Source: Drawing by Wm. Hamilton; © 1983 The New Yorker Magazine, Inc.

Systematic withdrawal plans may be especially attractive to investors seeking an additional source of retirement income. Moreover, unlike an annuity, at least part of the original investment is likely to remain for survivors.

In a rising stock market, the systematic withdrawal plan enables a person's capital to grow at a faster pace than it would at a bank while providing a regular income. In a declining market, the advantages of the plan are less clear; the investor might earn more at a bank or corporate bond fund.

INSURANCE PROTECTION

Some funds offer an insurance policy that guarantees that the investor will suffer no loss in redeeming shares if they are held for a specified period of time, usually between 10 and 15 years. To be eligible, all your earnings over this period must be reinvested. There is also an annual premium. Both insurance and premiums are forfeited if there is a sale before the end of the term. The major disadvantage of this plan is that people are forced to tie up their money for a long period of time—a restriction that makes impossible investing in better opportunities when they come along.

RETIREMENT PLANS

As inflation erodes the value of money, and as the security of Social Security becomes more and more tenuous, the federal government has encouraged individuals to set up their own retirement plans in the form of Keogh and individual retirement accounts, or IRAs (discussed in Chapter 20). Individuals may invest these tax-deferred savings in certain types of mutual funds as well as in savings accounts or other instruments. Many financial experts believe that mutual funds are ideal for an IRA or Keogh retirement plan. They point to the long-term performances of many funds, which have outpaced the stock market; to the advantage of professional management; and to the flexibility of belonging to a family of funds.

CHECK-WRITING AND TELEPHONE PRIVILEGES

Some funds, particularly the money-market funds, enable the investor to write checks against his or her account as if it were a regular bank account. However, these check-writing privileges are usually restricted to checks of at least $500 or even $1,000 or more. Telephone transaction privileges enable investors to manage their accounts by telephone.

EVALUATING THE VARIOUS MUTUAL FUNDS

How do you decide which mutual fund is best for you? Should a fund be chosen on performance alone, or should you also consider such diverse factors as fund objectives, size, management structure, services, investment requirements, and your own personal style and investment objectives? Experts agree that to be successful, the choice must be based on all of these factors.

PERFORMANCE

When evaluating performance, look at the fund's long-term record. Says financial writer Sylvia Porter: "A fund can produce large gains—or losses—over any short-term period, but it never was intended for short-term speculation, and if you try to use it [for this purpose], you are misusing it. Funds are meant for long-term investing objectives."[9]

Taking a long-term view, you should analyze whether the fund has outperformed the Standard & Poor's or Dow Jones averages and how it compares with other funds seeking similar objectives. A number of information sources are also available to help one evaluate just how well the various funds have performed:

- Wiesenberger Financial Service publishes an annual volume on mutual fund performance entitled *Investment Companies* and the monthly *Wiesenberger Investment Companies Service,* which present the most current statistics and news. These publications are usually available at a brokerage house or library, or they can be purchased directly from the company.

- *Johnson's Investment Company Charts* analyze fund performance. They are also available at a brokerage house or library or for sale by the company.

- Moody's Investor Service publishes *Moody's Bank and Finance Manual,* which describes in detail the nation's 100 largest mutual funds.

- The Investment Company Institute (1775 K Street, N.W., Washington, D.C. 20006) publishes an annual industry *Fact Book* (available to the public) as well as a news magazine entitled *Mutual Fund Forum.*

- The No-Load Mutual Fund Association, Inc. (11 Penn Plaza, Suite 2204, New York, N.Y. 10001), publishes a complete directory to hundreds of no-load mutual funds as well as numerous consumer pamphlets. The directory is available from the association for $1.

- Major financial publications, such as *Forbes, Fortune, Barron's,* and the *Wall Street Journal,* provide current price movement information as well as periodic ratings and performance reviews. Consumer-oriented financial publications like *Money* and *Changing Times* do the same and also carry articles on various companies and types of funds.

- Numerous mutual fund newsletters give professional advice on buying, selling, and switching mutual funds. These newsletters, which also rate the funds' performance, range in price from $75 to $175 a year.

- A fund's formal prospectus provides valuable information about its past performance and current investment objectives.

INVESTMENT OBJECTIVES

One question you should ask is whether you would buy the securities in a fund if you were investing independently. Are you comfortable with the number of companies in the portfolio, the industries they represent, their size and track record? Do you want a fund that specializes in common stocks or one that also invests in bonds, preferreds, warrants, or options? The advertisement for the Twentieth Century Investors family of funds shown in Figure 17-5 emphasizes the usefulness of a mutual fund family in matching evolving investor objectives.

Figure 17-5
ADVERTISEMENT EMPHASIZING FLEXIBILITY OF A MUTUAL FUND FAMILY

> **A family of funds that offers flexibility.**
>
> Each investor has a slightly different objective: some want long-term capital growth, some need income, and some like to jump from one strategy to another as their needs and the market conditions change. Whatever your objective happens to be, you should know about Twentieth Century Investors—a no-load mutual fund company that offers a family of four different funds, each with a slightly different investment strategy. Perhaps one will fit your particular objective.
>
> *Want to know more? For more complete information about Twentieth Century's funds (Growth Investors, Select Investors, Ultra Investors, and U.S. Governments) including charges and expenses, send for a free prospectus. Please read the prospectus carefully before investing.*
>
> **TWENTIETH CENTURY INVESTORS — No-Load Mutual Funds**
>
> Please send a free prospectus to:
> Name ___
> Address ___
> City ___
> State ___ Zip ___
>
> FBS830509   P.O. Box 200, Kansas City, Missouri 64141 • (816) 531-5575

Source: Courtesy of Twentieth Century Investors, Inc.

SIZE

How large or small a fund is can determine how successfully it meets its objectives. A large fund has the advantage over a smaller fund of being able to buy a larger selection of securities and, as a result, may provide more stable income to investors. A small fund, on the other hand, may concentrate its resources on a few growth companies whose explosive performance can drastically increase the fund's profits. Large funds have a more difficult time achieving this kind of payoff from a few winning securities.

Some financial analysts recommend that investors choose mutual funds with at least $100 million in assets. If a fund is too small, it may not be able to attract first-rate analysts.[10]

MANAGEMENT STRUCTURE

The type of management style you choose depends, to a great extent, on your own personality. If you are more comfortable with a team approach that minimizes human judgment, a company like Value Line is for you. If you are intrigued by the genius and skill of a single manager, a group like Oppenheimer is ideal.

Good Advice for a Price

One of the many conveniences of investing in mutual funds instead of directly in stocks or bonds is that a fund is vastly easier to follow. You don't have to evaluate a long list of products or services or assess the competition. But you probably will want to monitor the fund's performance to make sure you know when it's time to hold on, buy more—or cut losses and sell. Dozens of newsletter advisory services stand ready to help you track mutual funds for tax-deductible annual fees of up to $125. Among the most helpful:

Fundline (P.O. Box 663, Woodland Hills, Calif. 91365; monthly, $77 a year). Editor David Menashe ranks and charts 38 top-performing funds over the past nine months and recommends those he thinks have the greatest potential.

Growth Fund Guide (Growth Fund Research Building, P.O. Box 6600, Rapid City, S.D. 57709; monthly, $79 a year; sample copy, $2). This 24-page publication emphasizes investing in solidly proven funds and sticking with them as long as they continue to do well. Funds are ranked according to the volatility of the stocks they buy.

Mutual Fund Specialist (P.O. Box 1025, Eau Claire, Wis. 54701; monthly, $48 a year; $15 for three issues). Editor Royal LeMier tracks the performance of more than 60 families of funds over a variety of periods and pinpoints the top equity fund in each family. He also ranks top individual funds, as well as 200 money-market and income funds.

NoLoad Fund X (235 Montgomery St., San Francisco, Calif. 94104; monthly, $77 a year; $27 for three issues). Publisher Burton Berry provides a scorecard for no-load stock, bond, and money-market funds. He also tells you how all 280-plus of the funds he covers fared in past markets. Berry encourages frequent switching among fund families to get the very top performers.

Switch Fund Advisory (8943 Shady Grove Ct., Gaithersburg, Md. 20877; monthly, $125 a year; sample copy, $10). This letter is designed for those who want to switch from one fund to another within a family of funds. Editor James Schabacker profiles various funds, listing their major stock holdings and then recommending a buy or no-buy. He bases his switching advice on 14 criteria, ranging from the percentage of cash that mutual funds hold to the presidential election cycle.

Telephone Switch Newsletter (P.O. Box 2538, Huntington Beach, Calif. 92647; monthly, $97 a year). Editors Dick and Douglas Fabian advocate investing in aggressive funds when they see the market going up and money-market funds when they see a downturn ahead. They recommend only about five funds at any one time and provide a telephone hot line to inform subscribers of any changes in their picks.

United Mutual Fund Selector (United Business Service Co., 210 Newbury St., Boston, Mass. 02116; semi-monthly, $75 a year). Every other issue overflows with performance data on most mutual funds. Intervening issues focus on a high-performing fund or fund family.

Source: Jordan E. Goodman, "Good Advice for a Price," Money, November 1983, p. 78. Reprinted by permission.

Financial writer Sylvia Porter sums up the need to investigate and understand the structure of a fund's management in this way: "You owe it to yourself to find out precisely what sort of management you are buying when you buy mutual fund shares. Since you're buying your shares for the long term, you should make sure your fund has a management structure that can operate successfully over the long term."[11]

Find out whether the fund can accommodate all or at least most of your investment needs. Can you buy, sell, and switch funds by phone? Does the fund have automatic reinvestment and systematic withdrawal plans?

INVESTMENT REQUIREMENTS AND SERVICES PROVIDED

The minimum investment requirements of funds differ a great deal, and it is important to find out what these requirements are before opening an account. The Fidelity Equity-Income Fund, for example, which specializes in growth and income securities, requires at least a $1,000 investment on opening an account and at least $250 for additional deposits. The Stein Roe & Farnham Balance Fund, on the other hand, requires a minimum initial investment of $2,500 and subsequent investments of at least $100.

YOUR PERSONAL STYLE AND FINANCIAL NEEDS

Deciding which mutual fund is right for you has as much to do with your own personality and personal financial needs as it does with the investment itself—or at least it should. David Silver of the Investment Company Institute sums up this view: "The fundamentals in choosing a mutual fund is your own circumstances. Look at your age and your financial resources. What is your personal style? How will you sleep best at night?"[12]

The cardinal rule of investing is: Be honest with yourself about your personal and financial needs. This applies as strongly to mutual funds as to other investments. If you are young and have few financial responsibilities, you can probably afford to take greater risks than if you are about to retire. But some people, no matter how young and independent they are, cannot deal with even small amounts of risk, while some older people thrive on the excitement. The need to know yourself is especially important when investing in mutual funds because of the vast number of choices available.

One of the most important considerations in choosing a fund should be the amount of time and energy you are willing to put into your investment over the years. If you want to put your money into a fund and then forget it until you are ready to take it out, you should choose one that keeps pace with the market during good times and does not suffer too badly during bad times. These middle-of-the-road funds should provide a middle-of-the-road return whether you watch their investment performance or not. On the other hand, if you normally spend some time following the market and the general economy, read the financial pages of the daily newspaper, and are willing to switch your money from one fund to another occasionally when the timing is right, you should seek a fund that has outperformed the market during bad times.

HOW TO READ MUTUAL FUND LISTINGS

Investors can follow the daily market performance of mutual funds by consulting the mutual fund listings found in the business section of most daily

Figure 17-6
HOW TO READ A NEWSPAPER MUTUAL FUND QUOTATION

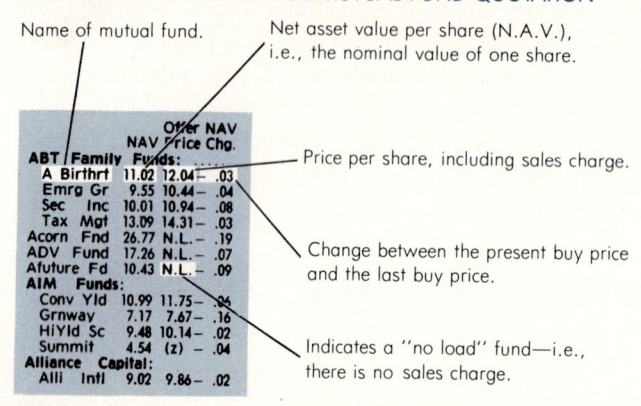

- Name of mutual fund.
- Net asset value per share (N.A.V.), i.e., the nominal value of one share.
- Price per share, including sales charge.
- Change between the present buy price and the last buy price.
- Indicates a "no load" fund—i.e., there is no sales charge.

	NAV	Offer NAV Price	Chg.
ABT Family Funds:			
A Birthrt	11.02	12.04 −	.03
Emrg Gr	9.55	10.44 −	.04
Sec Inc	10.01	10.94 −	.08
Tax Mgt	13.09	14.31 −	.03
Acorn Fnd	26.77	N.L. −	.19
ADV Fund	17.26	N.L. −	.07
Afuture Fd	10.43	N.L. −	.09
AIM Funds:			
Conv Yld	10.99	11.75 −	.05
Grnway	7.17	7.67 −	.16
HiYld Sc	9.48	10.14 −	.02
Summit	4.54	(z) −	.04
Alliance Capital:			
Alli Intl	9.02	9.86 −	.02

Source: Adapted from David J. Rachman and Michael H. Mescon, *Business Today* 4th ed. (New York: Random House, 1985), p. 407.

net asset value (NAV) per share: the current worth, or book value, of a share in a mutual fund; calculated by dividing the current value of all securities owned by the mutual fund by the number of shares.

newspapers. The worth, or book value, of a share in a mutual fund, called the *net asset value (NAV) per share,* is calculated by adding the total value of all the securities the firm owns and dividing by the number of shares. The NAV is the price a mutual fund shareholder would receive by selling the share on a given day. It is shown in the first column of Figure 17-6. The second column shows the *offer price,* the price an investor would have to pay to buy a share of the fund. For no-load funds, this price is the same as its net asset value, and the column is marked *NL.* The buy price for load funds equals the NAV plus the sales commission. Thus the net asset value of the American Birthright Fund is $11.02 and its buy price, including commissions, is $12.04.

The final column in Figure 17-6 shows the change in net asset value from the previous day. The American Birthright Fund, for example, lost three cents a share while the ADV Fund lost seven cents a share.

BUYING AND SELLING MUTUAL FUNDS

If you are interested in a load mutual fund, you can buy shares through a stockbroker or through a fund salesperson. No-load funds can be purchased directly from the fund's management. Coupon ads for both types of funds can be found in the business section of daily newspapers.

BUYING MUTUAL FUNDS

If you wish to make single purchases and regulate their timing yourself, you should buy through what is called a *regular account*: you decide the amount of your purchase (which of course must meet the fund's minimum requirement);

pay the sales commission, if any; and make the payment. When you want to add to your investment, you simply repeat this procedure.

If you want to make regular additions to your investment, most funds give you the option of setting up a savings accumulation plan. These plans are of two types:

1. *The voluntary plan*: Here you make regular purchases within a specified dollar range and pay the full commission on each purchase. You do not have to make these purchases—there is no penalty if you do not—and you can make purchases larger than your regular amount whenever you wish.

2. *The contractual plan*: Under this plan, you are obligated to make a certain minimum purchase; to make regular purchases over a definite period, often ten years; and sometimes to pay the whole commission first in a payment system known as *front-end load*. Criticism of front-end loading has led to some modifications in the penalty incurred if the investor cannot fulfill the whole contract. If, for example, you pay the entire fee up front and then find after two years that you must abandon the plan, you stand to lose, not gain, from the investment. Some companies have voluntarily made adjustments to reduce the penalties; some have been forced to do so by state laws; and some offer insurance to guard against loss.

SELLING SHARES

The exact procedure for redeeming, or selling, shares differs from fund to fund. Some funds allow you to sell by phone; others require a written order; and still others need a signature in the presence of a banker or broker. The fund's formal prospectus clearly describes the procedures to follow when you decide to redeem shares.

SUMMARY

For a number of investors, investment clubs represent an effective approach to investing in securities. Each member contributes an agreed-upon amount of money each month into the club. Club members collect research on investment candidates and vote on purchase decisions. In addition, they monitor securities in the club's portfolio and decide when sales should be made. Benefits include the collective investment judgment of the club members, potential for greater stock diversification, and lower commission costs resulting from pooled investment funds. Another investment alternative is participation in such special purchase alternatives as monthly investment plans and employee stock purchase and option plans.

Over 20 million U.S. investors choose investment companies—companies formed for the purpose of investing in securities for profit. They are an indirect method of investing. Shareholders purchase shares in the company, which, in turn, uses the funds to purchase securities. A closed-end investment company issues only a fixed number of shares, which are traded on an organized securities exchange or over-the-counter market. The open-end investment company, or mutual fund, issues and repurchases its shares as demanded. Mutual funds are the dominant type of investment company. They offer investors the advantages of diversification, professional management, convenience, and flexibility. Moreover, their operations are regulated by the Securities and Exchange Commission.

Mutual funds can be broadly categorized as load and no-load, depending on whether a sales commission is charged to purchasers. Both types, however, charge management fees. Beyond this distinction, a wide diversity of mutual funds is available, ranging from aggressive growth funds to income funds. In addition, mutual fund families allow investors to switch their investments from fund to fund as their personal needs and objectives change.

In evaluating a mutual fund as an investment vehicle, you should consider the importance of its services, including automatic reinvestments, systematic withdrawal, insurance protection, retirement plans, and check-writing and telephone transfer privileges. You should also compare funds in terms of current portfolio of securities, investment objectives, size, management structure, and investment requirements. As in all investment decisions, the fit with your personality and financial needs is a key factor.

Current listings of mutual funds are found in the business section of most daily newspapers. The price of a mutual fund is called the net asset value (NAV) per share. It is calculated by adding the total value of the securities owned by the fund and dividing by the number of shares. If the fund is a load fund, a sales commission is added to the NAV to determine the purchase price.

REVIEW QUESTIONS

1. Briefly define the following terms:
   - investment clubs
   - bull market
   - bear market
   - monthly investment plan
   - employee stock purchase plans
   - investment company
   - closed-end investment company
   - open-end investment companies
   - load funds
   - no-load fund
   - mutual fund family
   - net asset value (NAV) per share

2. What are the primary motivations for joining an investment club? How does an investment club operate?

3. Distinguish between a bull market and a bear market. What types of stocks are more likely to increase in price during a bear market?

4. What types of investors are likely to benefit from monthly investment plan programs? What are the limitations in using such plans?

5. Why do investors purchase shares in mutual funds? What benefits are present that cannot be obtained from direct investment in individual stocks and bonds? How do closed-end and open-end funds differ?

6. Distinguish between load and no-load mutual funds. Why do many investors choose load funds over no-loads?

7. Identify the special services provided for investors by many mutual funds.

8. How should an investor go about deciding which mutual fund is most appropriate for his or her needs?

9. What advantages exist for investors who choose to invest in a mutual fund family?

10. Distinguish between the net asset value (NAV) per share of a mutual fund and the fund's offer price. Under what conditions are the two identical?

CASES AND EXERCISES

1. Consider two stocks of your choice. These may be shares of companies that either you or your parents currently own or companies you admire for their past and present industry growth, profits, and market performance. Refer to the checklist shown on page 498. Complete as much of the list

as possible, depending on available information. Then make recommendations concerning the two stocks.

2. Less than 50 percent of eligible employees participate in employee stock purchase and option plans. Develop an argument that might be used to convince more employees to participate. Why do you think firms make such plans available to their employees?

3. Comment on the following statement: "I see no reason to invest in a mutual fund with a load when no-load funds are readily available."

4. Review the firms listed in Table 17-2. What common characteristics do you see that make these firms mutual funds' favorites? What industries are represented? Give an example from the list of an income-oriented firm. Which are examples of high-growth firms?

5. Given your current personal and financial status, which of the mutual funds shown in the Oppenheimer Family of Funds (see page 510) is most appealing? Why did you select this particular fund?

ANSWERS TO PERSONAL FINANCE I.Q. TEST

1. Fiction. 2. Fiction. 3. Fiction. 4. Fact. 5. Fact. 6. Fiction.

HOW SAM JOHNSON REACHED HIS PERSONAL FINANCIAL DECISION

Mr. Bass first suggested that Sam keep the money liquid. Flexibility is important because Sam is still young and faces many uncertainties before he becomes established in a career. With this in mind, Mr. Bass based his advice on Sam's desire for money growth, as well as his own awareness that Sam needs a safe investment because he does not have additional funds to fall back on. Here is what Mr. Bass suggested:

"Invest $3,000 in a money-market fund, which you can also think of as an emergency fund. If something unexpected comes up, you'll be able to get your hands on some extra money quickly. Then invest the remaining money in growth funds. For instance, you might put $1,000 in a gold fund and $2,000 in a growth stock fund. I think there will be a nice increase in gold in the next year or two. Besides, it's a good idea to have 10 to 15 percent of your money in an asset like metals that acts as an inflation hedge—where prices rise and fall with inflation. But diversification is always important; you don't want to put all your eggs in one basket. As a start, you should have at least two options in growth funds. Both the stock fund and the gold fund will be diversified in their holdings. This, combined with your low-risk money-market account, will give you the balance you need to accomplish your investment objectives."

Sam was thrilled to get such clear advice, and he planned to follow it exactly. Yet he was disappointed that not all his money would be in growth funds. After talking this over more with Mr. Bass, he came up with a way to increase his growth accounts systematically. Each month he'd save $50 from his paycheck as a part-time assistant manager at the bookstore and add it to one of the growth funds. With this kind of head start, Sam expects to be in a strong financial position when he graduates.

LEARNING OBJECTIVES

1. To compare the various investment alternatives to stocks, bonds, and mutual funds. / 2. To outline the alternative methods of investing in real estate and the advantages and disadvantages of such an investment. / 3. To explain how a person can invest in commodities. / 4. To discuss the role of stock options in personal finance. / 5. To identify the advantages and disadvantages of precious and strategic metals as an investment alternative. / 6. To describe the role of collectibles in an investment portfolio.

TESTING YOUR PERSONAL FINANCE I.Q.

	FACT	FICTION
1. Not only are diamonds "a girl's best friend," but they have also proved to be an investor's best friend during the past five years.	☐	☐
2. Frozen pork bellies are attractive investment alternatives for thousands of Americans.	☐	☐
3. Real estate offers important tax advantages not available in other investment alternatives.	☐	☐
4. Gold was a very popular investment alternative during the 1960s, but its popularity has faded since 1974.	☐	☐
5. Collectibles have consistently outperformed strategic metals in price appreciation since 1975.	☐	☐

The materials in this chapter assist in separating fact from fiction. Your answers can be checked on page 554.

CHAPTER EIGHTEEN

OTHER INVESTMENT ALTERNATIVES

SHARING A PERSONAL FINANCIAL DECISION WITH PROFESSOR JAMES W. BAIRD OF COMMUNITY COLLEGE OF THE FINGER LAKES

Five years ago, Ed Murphy, a former student of Professor James Baird, opened his own landscape architecture business in upstate New York. His wife, Marie, works as the firm's bookkeeper. It's been hard work, but this family business has done very well. It also enjoys a solid reputation in the community. Ed and Marie have built up considerable assets, and have managed to pay off all of the loans for the building and equipment. But as business profits have grown, so have the couple's income taxes. The Murphys do not have dependents and their limited deductions do not go far in reducing their annual tax bills. While they have made some investments in common stocks and in interest-bearing savings accounts, they would like to develop a more diversified portfolio of assets. In addition, they are seeking a secondary source of income to offset to some extent the seasonality of their landscaping business. Finally, they are beginning to think about retirement planning. When they retire, they plan to move to the Sunbelt where they can enjoy their favorite sport, golf.

Ed recalls Professor Baird's lectures on investing, and he wonders if there is a way to invest his and Marie's earnings and at the same time lower taxes. To find out, the Murphys went to Professor Baird for advice.

If you were Professor Baird, what would you recommend?

To find out how Professor Baird helped the Murphys with their personal financial decision, turn to page 554.

"If you sell diamonds, you cannot expect to have many customers. But a diamond is a diamond even if there are not customers."
Swami Prabhopada[1]

commodities: staples such as agricultural products that are bought and sold in relatively large quantities.

Don Skinrood once worked as an electrical engineer for the Atomic Energy Commission, but now he is a full-time investor and trader in the commodities market. *Commodities* are staples such as agricultural products that are bought and sold in bulk lots. Grain, soybeans, and pork bellies are examples.

Skinrood works out of his waterfront home on Puget Sound's San Juan Islands. He gets up early to catch the 5 A.M. (Pacific Time) opening of the commodity markets. For the first half-hour each day, Skinrood studies 30 commodities, comparing each transaction to the commodity's normal range. Then he places his orders through a Chicago discount broker. His investment decisions hinge on the coded radio signals he receives over an unused portion of a Seattle FM radio station's licensed frequency. The commodity service, which costs from $180 to $385 a month, requires that Skinrood maintain a certain type of radio receiver and a computer capable of decoding the signals. The output is then printed on a TV screen.

Skinrood's personal finances and even his lifestyle are based on this alternative investment vehicle. As he puts it, "with my little system here in my house, looking east toward Lopez Island is a very nice setting to do your trading in."[2]

AN OVERVIEW OF INVESTMENT ALTERNATIVES

There are almost as many alternatives for investors seeking profits as there are ways to lose a needle in a haystack. As the three previous chapters have pointed out, people frequently invest in stocks and bonds. Others purchase shares of mutual funds. But the investor who is willing to accept more risk in the hope of spectacular returns has dozens of choices—participating in the commodities market, trading in stock options, purchasing property, investing in a real estate syndicate that owns buildings in several states, buying gold coins, purchasing art or collectibles, speculating in diamonds, and more.

The chosen alternative depends on the investor's investment strategy, current and future needs, and personality as well as the opportunities available. In the last 20 years, and particularly in the last 10, all sorts of new opportunities to make money in not so conventional ways have developed. This chapter will analyze a number of more speculative investment possibilities. All offer advantages and disadvantages, and all carry varying levels of risk.

REAL ESTATE

When most people think of investing in real estate, they think only in terms of purchasing a home. Whether it be a single-family house on two acres in suburbia or a condominium in an urban high-rise, they see home ownership as a way to build equity while legally reducing their tax bill.

Their philosophy is both correct and appropriate—as a starting point. But for many millions of investors, owning a place in which to live is just the beginning. These investors see real estate in the same way they see any other promising investments: they buy property in order to receive current income and possible future capital gains.

Real estate became a popular investment vehicle during the 1970s when inflation caused values to soar. The slowdown in growth rates of real estate values in recent years has made a careful, thorough analysis of potential investments more important today than ever before.

And, as with any other investment, you must also consider your lifestyle, abilities, financial situation, and goals before you invest. Expert advice is available to aid in distinguishing among alternative real estate offerings. As an investor, you should seek out several sources of expertise: a knowledgeable real estate broker; an engineer to inspect the property; an experienced real estate appraiser, who will use the engineer's inspection report as a guide; a real estate attorney to ensure that your rights and money are protected; and an accountant to evaluate the seller's profit, expense, and depreciation statements and determine whether they are realistic. In addition, the accountant can assist in analyzing cash inflows and outflows and in estimating the return on the investment.

Real estate provides a number of different investment choices. The investor can purchase raw land, single-family rental units, small and large apartment buildings, or commercial properties like stores and office buildings. In addition, it is possible to invest indirectly by buying into a real estate partnership, syndicate, investment trust, or specialized mutual fund.

PROS AND CONS OF INVESTING IN REAL ESTATE

Potential real estate investors should consider certain special features of this investment tool in addition to their own situation and goals. Some of these features make real estate appealing; others may tarnish its glamorous image.

Liquidity and Cash Flow. Real estate is generally a long-term, relatively *illiquid* investment. That is, in most cases, you cannot easily and quickly convert the investment into cash, as you can with stocks and mutual funds. *Cash flow*—the timing of receipts and payments—is another important consideration. If an investment makes you a millionaire on paper but leaves you unable

cash flow: *the timing of cash receipts and payments.*

to find the cash with which to buy groceries or pay bills, you may need to reconsider the wisdom of your investment strategy.

Risk. There is considerable risk involved in real estate as well. That bargain tract of land may never be in the path of a new highway or a new commercial development; the blighted neighborhood may not turn around; the shopping mall may be in the wrong geographic location or face too much competition. Moreover, it may take 20 years for the expected return to be realized.

As millions of investors learned in the early 1980s, general economic factors—especially upward and downward swings in interest rates—can play havoc with the real estate market. In 1982, for example, when interest rates for fixed-rate mortgages peaked at 18 percent, owners trying to sell their property discovered just how illiquid real estate can be. Unable to find buyers who could qualify for a mortgage, many were forced to hold on to their property for months longer than they wanted and to lower the price to stimulate buyer interest.

There is also the risk that values will not increase as fast or as much as expected. According to Anthony Downs, a housing expert with the Brookings Institution in Washington, D.C., "the fantastic [real estate] investments in the 1970s were unsustainably good." Price increases that sent real estate values skyrocketing 20 percent or more each year drew investors with high expectations to the real estate market. When the market softened under the pressure of high interest rates, these investors were left with far less than they had hoped for. In the years ahead, comments Downs, real estate "will continue to be a good investment, but I'd be surprised if it significantly outperforms other investments."[3]

Investing in the U.S. Postal Service?

Few people realize that most U.S. post offices are really owned by private investors, who then lease the facility to the government. In fact, the U.S. Postal Service has used this arrangement throughout its history. Today, 88 percent of the nation's 28,000 post offices are leased. One California investor is reported to own 350 post offices in 49 states.

Back in 1963, P. J. Wise, a hospital maintenance engineer, and Jimmy Carter, a peanut farmer, both bid for the right to build a new $20,000 post office in Plains, Georgia. Carter won but later changed his mind. He traded the deal to Wise, who built the post office and signed a 20-year, fixed-rate lease for $156 per month. By the time Jimmy Carter got to the White House, in 1976, similar commercial property in Plains rented for four times what Wise collected for his post office.

Inflation has made many post office investments like Wise's unprofitable. But when these leases come up for renewal, substantial increases can be negotiated with the government.

Source: Data on Wise from Jeff Blyskan, "The Broker Always Rings Twice," *Forbes*, September 4, 1981, p. 36.

Expenses. There are many different expenses associated with owning real estate. First of all, during the early years of a mortgage, the great bulk of the payments goes toward the interest on the loan; almost none of it repays the *principal*—the amount originally borrowed. The result benefits your income tax situation, since interest payments are totally deductible. But your *equity*—the portion of the property you actually own—does not grow.

Moreover, property owners are responsible for real estate taxes, which can be considerable if the property is valuable, and for special assessments such as the installation of sewers. Insurance also adds to the cost of ownership. Property insurance must be carried to protect yourself against damage due to fire, storms, electrical problems, and other perils. You must also carry liability insurance to cover damages stemming from personal injuries that might occur on your property.

In addition, maintenance costs can be considerable. You may have to patch a leaking roof, replace a worn-out oil burner, keep up the grounds, add energy-saving windows, and more. Although expensive, an adequate maintenance program is necessary if one hopes to sell the property at a profit.

Tax Advantages. Despite these expenses, there are a number of special tax advantages to owning real estate. Real estate investments are particularly attractive to investors seeking to reduce their income tax bill, since property taxes, interest payments, depreciation allowances, and the cost of maintaining business property all represent tax-deductible items. In addition, investors who acquire depreciable property such as apartment and office buildings, shopping centers, and other commercial buildings are eligible for special tax credits. Depreciation deductions are based on the *accelerated cost recovery system (ACRS)* created by the Economic Recovery Tax Act of 1981. As Table 18-1 indicates, purchasers of apartments and commercial buildings can recover the cost of their property over an 18-year period by deducting a specified percentage of their cost each year.

The investor who purchases a $250,000 building in January will be able to deduct $24,250 in depreciation that year ($250,000 × the 9.7-percent year-1 deduction); $22,000 in year 2; $19,750 in year 3; and lesser amounts in subsequent years until the eighteenth year. In addition, the *property tax deduction* allows the investor to deduct state and local property taxes from federal and state income taxes. The *interest deduction* on funds borrowed to finance the real estate purchase gives the property owner a further tax break.

accelerated cost recovery system (ACRS): a schedule used to determine the amount of tax deduction generated by purchasing business property.

Leverage. Real estate has yet another tempting advantage—*leverage*. When you invest in real estate, you generally do so with borrowed funds; only a fraction of the money invested is actually yours. The return on your investment can therefore be greatly increased as the value of the property appreciates since you receive all the profits even though you invested only part of the money.

leverage: the magnified return on an investment resulting when an investor uses a substantial amount of borrowed funds to finance the purchase of investment property.

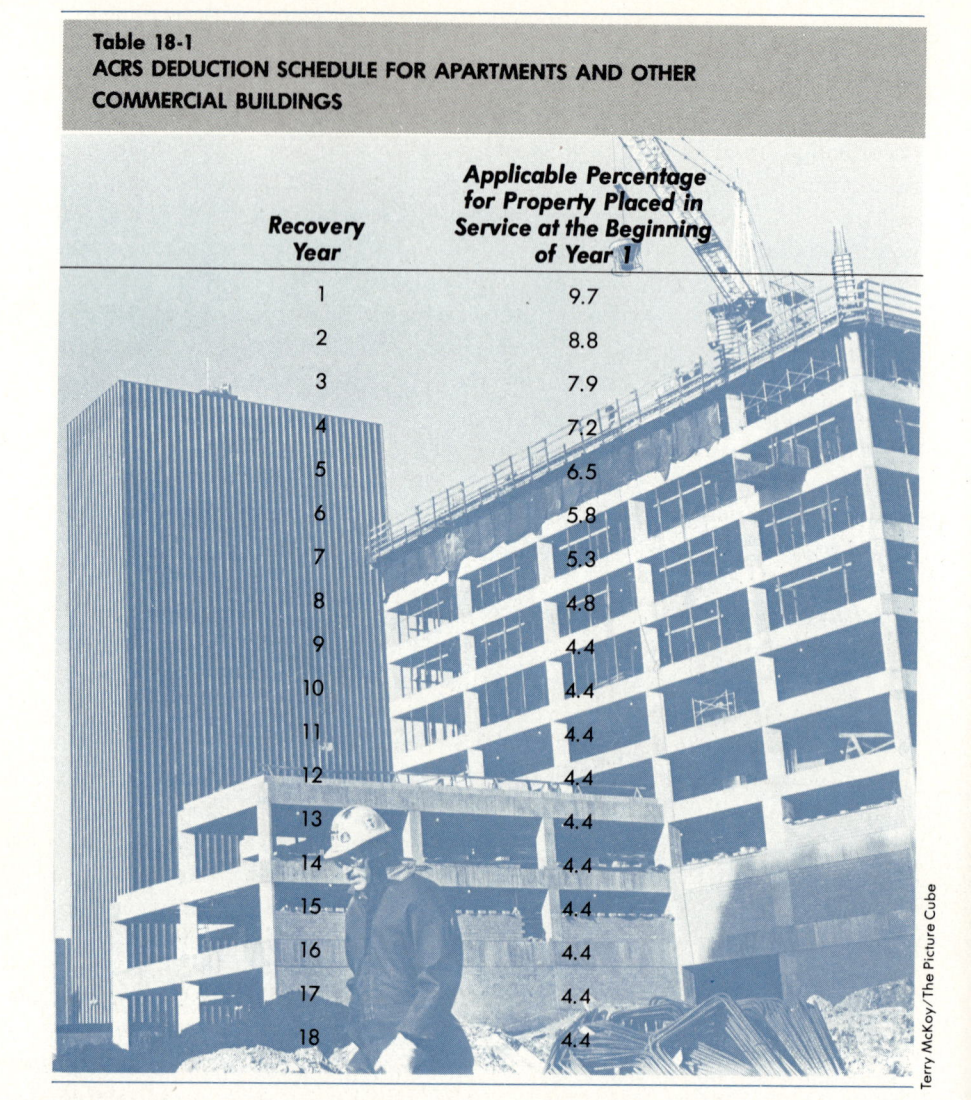

Table 18-1
ACRS DEDUCTION SCHEDULE FOR APARTMENTS AND OTHER COMMERCIAL BUILDINGS

Recovery Year	Applicable Percentage for Property Placed in Service at the Beginning of Year 1
1	9.7
2	8.8
3	7.9
4	7.2
5	6.5
6	5.8
7	5.3
8	4.8
9	4.4
10	4.4
11	4.4
12	4.4
13	4.4
14	4.4
15	4.4
16	4.4
17	4.4
18	4.4

Leverage works for you when you first purchase property. With only $20,000 in your pocket, you might borrow $80,000 from a bank and purchase a $100,000 rental property. It also works for you when you receive the property's rental income. The $4,000 you may receive as net proceeds each year after expenses are paid is only 4 percent of the $100,000 purchase price—a return few would be satisfied with. But that same $4,000 is 20 percent of the actual $20,000 investment.

Finally, leverage works for you when you sell. Imagine that another investor offers to purchase the rental property from you for $118,000 at the end of the first year. Table 18-2 analyzes the impact of leverage on this sale. At first glance, you see that the interest paid on the borrowed funds reduces the size of the profit from the sale. Assuming a 10-percent annual interest rate on the $80,000 mortgage loan, your profits are reduced by $8,000 to a $10,000 gain. Had you supplied all of the $100,000 initial purchase price, your profits would have been $18,000. But now consider the return on your investment. In the first instance, with borrowed funds, the relatively small initial investment generates a 50-percent return. Only an 18-percent return is realized when no borrowed funds are involved. This is the power of leverage.

Leverage also allows investors to participate in more projects than would otherwise be possible. Suppose, for example, you put all your investment money—$100,000—into a condominium, which you might resell at a good profit. In the meantime, however, all your money is tied up, and you may miss other attractive investment opportunities. Moreover, if the investment produces poor or negative returns, you stand to lose heavily. But, say you use only $10,000 of your own funds and borrow the remainder to purchase the condo. Now you have both the real estate investment and the remaining $90,000 for use in making other investments.

Risks of Using Leverage. Of course, too much leverage—too much borrowing—carries the risk of losing everything should you default on the loans. *Pyramiding*—building larger and larger investments on the basis of leverage—can be very exciting, but it can also be extremely dangerous because leverage also works in reverse. A small decline in value is magnified many times when borrowed funds are used to finance an investment. Because of this danger, highly leveraged investments should be avoided unless you are a knowledgeable professional and can afford the risks.

DOES THE PROPERTY GENERATE INCOME?

Some properties, such as building lots and rural acreage, are *non-income-producing properties*—they generate no income and yield an investment return only when sold. Others—*income-producing properties*—offer a return in the form of rent during the time the property is owned while also appreciating in value. These characteristics affect the relative attractiveness of different types of real estate and, consequently, their price.

Non-Income-producing Properties. Raw land and residential lots are usually bought to be resold. That is, they are a speculative investment whose return comes not in the form of regular income over a period of time but in the profit (or loss) that results from reselling.

Because no income is generated from such an investment, it makes sense to purchase raw land only if you expect it to increase in value. If a shopping center, housing development, office building, or recreational facility is planned

non-income-producing properties: building lots and raw land that may appreciate in value but do not produce rental income.

income-producing properties: rental property—residential and commercial—that generates income for its owners while holding the possibility of value appreciation.

Table 18-2
USE OF LEVERAGE IN A REAL ESTATE INVESTMENT

	Leverage	No Leverage
Initial Purchase		
Owner investment	$ 20,000	$100,000
Borrowed funds	80,000	0
Total	100,000	100,000
Sale of Property		
Selling price	$118,000	$118,000
Minus interest	8,000	0
Amount received	110,000	118,000
Profit on Sale	$ 10,000	$ 18,000
Return on Investment	$10,000 / $20,000 = 50%	$18,000 / $100,000 = 18%

Forms courtesy of Julius Blumberg, Inc.

for the land sometime in the future, its value will increase and the investment will pay off. If nothing is planned and the land is located in a remote area, you must ask yourself why someone would pay more for it than you originally did. If you have no answer, do not buy. Moreover, even if you expect the value to appreciate, the land may still be a poor investment. Property purchased for $100,000 and held for 10 years should produce considerably greater returns than an alternative investment due to the risks involved. If you sell it for only a few thousand dollars more than you paid, it is not worth the risk.

Clearly, purchasing non-income-producing property is a risky venture for the nonprofessional or small investor, and it demands a knowledge of local as well as national economic conditions and trends. Impressive returns are possible from such ventures, but you must be prepared for the windfall's not materializing.

Income-producing Properties. Investors seeking a stream of income from their real estate investments may be attracted to a number of income-producing properties:

- *Small rental dwelling units*: For many fledgling investors, small rental units such as a single-family house, duplex, or triplex may represent attractive investment vehicles. Research conducted by Century 21's nationwide network of real estate agencies reveals that approximately 20 percent of home purchases are for use as rental property. According to Martin Rueter, director of Century 21's investment services, "this is seen as an entry level into real estate investment. It's something that new investors feel they can handle and are familiar with."[4]

- *Large apartment complexes*: Owning a large apartment complex requires both a larger investment and a more serious approach to its operation, maintenance, and management. These additional expenses must be considered in evaluating such investments.
- *Commercial shopping centers*: The thousands of shopping centers, large and small, that dot America are generally owned by real estate investors seeking a higher income than they could get from owning an apartment building. However, despite their allure, commercial shopping centers frequently cost more than apartments to own and operate. And owners face the risk of a prolonged, substantial loss if a major tenant moves out and another tenant cannot be found immediately.
- *Commercial and professional office buildings*: Commercial and professional office buildings rent space to businesses and professional people. Like commercial shopping centers, they frequently generate higher income than apartment buildings but may also cost more to purchase and operate. Both commercial shopping centers and office buildings generally issue long-term leases to reduce the risk of losing a major tenant.

THE PITFALLS OF DIRECT INVESTMENT

Direct investment in real estate by an individual is risky and requires a great deal of time, effort, and money. If, for example, you do not have the time or skill to manage a property yourself, you must hire others to do it. In addition, many investors have serious cash-flow problems during their first years of operation. Unless they have established a cash reserve, they may face the possibility of losing the entire investment.

In recent years a number of well-publicized success stories have described how one or two people have started with very little money—perhaps only $2,000 or $3,000—and built up their holdings to six figures and even beyond. But, almost invariably, these investors had put in years of hard work before realizing this profit. To match their successes, you have to be willing to invest an equal amount of time and labor. This could mean constantly checking real estate listings, brokers, and neighborhoods to find good opportunities; repairing, rehabilitating, inspecting, and maintaining the property; analyzing the continuing costs of the property; locating affordable financing for building improvements; dealing with and choosing tenants and solving tenant problems;

and scouring garage sales and auctions for items that can be refinished or repaired and used in the building. Your real estate investment frequently becomes your primary focus in life if you seek major gains in income and value.

All these factors make direct investment in real estate by a nonprofessional an expensive proposition. But other methods of securing a return from this investment vehicle spread the risk and take less time and attention.

SPREADING THE RISK

Because real estate investments frequently involve large sums of money, real estate partnerships are often used. A group of three or four investors may pool their available investment funds to make the down payment on a larger property. In addition, their combined wealth and potential earnings may be needed to persuade a lending institution to grant a mortgage. Such partnerships are structured on the basis of a formal partnership agreement specifying the objectives of the partnership and the duties of each partner. It typically specifies the time period during which the partnership will exist and its purpose.

Unlimited or general partners are liable for any debts or expenses of the business, so it is possible for them to lose much more than they actually invest. For this reason, many investors seek other techniques for investing in real estate that limit their liability and may also spread their investment risk over a greater number of properties. Investment devices for accomplishing these objectives include syndicates, real estate investment trusts, and mutual funds specializing in real estate.

Real Estate Syndicates. A *syndicate* is an investment group formed for a specific objective, such as investing in real estate. Organizers sell shares in the syndicate to other investors. The syndicate is dissolved at the end of a specified period or when its objectives have been attained.

The syndication industry experienced major growth during the past decade. In 1973 syndicators raised $100 million in publicly offered deals; in 1983 the number had soared to $4.7 billion. During 1983 syndicated partnerships acquired such major properties as the Boca Raton Hotel in Florida for $100 million and the Seafirst Center building in Seattle for $123 million.

Although some syndicates are corporations, many are organized as a *limited partnership*. In this case, one or more members of the syndicate serve as the *general partners*: they assume the major management responsibility for managing the organization and also have unlimited liability for the debts of the partnership. Investors join as *limited partners,* with limited liability.

Syndicates can be organized to purchase one or more specific properties (a *single-property pool*) or to invest in certain types of properties, with decisions concerning the specific properties to be acquired left to the syndicate's managers (a *blind pool*). Syndicates may be large or small, public or private. Those with 35 or fewer limited partners can avoid registration with the Securities and

---

syndicate: an investment group formed for a specific purpose such as investing in real estate.

limited partnership: a partnership agreement between general partners (with management responsibility and general liability exposure) and limited partners (who have no management responsibility and limited liability).

blind pool: a form of syndicate in which the syndicate's managers decide on the specific properties to be acquired.

OTHER INVESTMENT ALTERNATIVES 533

Figure 18-1
ADVERTISEMENT FOR REAL ESTATE PARTNERSHIP

IS EQUITEC A MISSING LINK IN YOUR PORTFOLIO?

COMPLETE YOUR PORTFOLIO WITH AN INVESTMENT IN EQUITEC REAL ESTATE INVESTORS FUND XIII

Equitec Real Estate Investors Fund XIII is a real estate limited partnership which intends to invest in or develop income producing properties.

If you would like to explore this investment opportunity call Donald Mitchum at either of the toll free numbers or send in the coupon for a prospectus. Read it carefully before you invest.

1-800-445-9020
800-445-9052 (In California)

Equitec Real Estate Investors Fund XIII
$75,000,000 of limited partnership interests; $500 per unit.
Minimum investment is $3,000 (6 units); $2,000 (4 units) for IRAs or Keogh plans; requirements vary in some states.

This announcement is neither an offer to sell nor a solicitation of an offer to buy these securities. Such an offer is made by the Prospectus only copies of which are obtainable only in those states in which these securities may lawfully be offered and only from Equitec Securities Company, the Dealer Manager or from other securities dealers who may lawfully offer these securities in such states. Neither the Attorney General of the State of New York, nor the Attorney General of the State of New Jersey nor the Bureau of Securities of the State of New Jersey has passed on or endorsed the merits of this offering. Any representation to the contrary is unlawful.

EQUITEC

Equitec Real Estate Investors
Fund XIII
P.O. Box 2470, Dept.
Oakland, CA 94614

Name _____
Address _____
City _____
State _____ Zip _____
Telephone ( ) _____
Or call Donald Mitchum:
1-800-445-9020
800-445-9052 (In California)

Source: Courtesy of Equitec.

Exchange Commission. All, however, issue a prospectus and can—and should—be evaluated carefully. Shares in larger syndicates are offered through real estate brokers, stockbrokers, and newspaper advertising. Figure 18-1 is an advertisement for a real estate syndication by Equitec of Oakland, California.

On the plus side, real estate syndicates offer a potentially high return on investment as well as tax-shelter benefits, professional management, convenience, and access for the small investor. The syndicator handles all the day-to-day management issues and maintenance problems. Yet the limited partner has the same tax advantage as a direct investor.

There are, however, potential disadvantages. The success of the syndicate depends on the experience, business judgment, and ability of those who will make the buying, managing, and selling decisions. In addition, the investment is relatively illiquid: investors cannot easily sell their shares if circumstances change. And they receive little or no monetary returns until the syndicate is liquidated. An investor must expect to wait the entire term of the investment for its reward.

Syndicators also receive substantial fees for forming the syndicate, managing the properties, and arranging for their eventual sale. There is usually a 20-to 25-percent fee when the syndication is formed, as well as management fees (typically 9 percent of operating profits or cash flow). When the property is sold, syndicators retain a percentage share (often about 17 percent) of the final profits.[5] This percentage share serves to reduce the overall returns of the investors. Thus, although this approach to investing in real estate may reduce some of the inherent risks, it also reduces the potential gains for the individual investor.

Real Estate Investment Trusts. Many investors, desiring to invest relatively small sums of money in real estate and seeking a more liquid form of investment than the typical real estate syndicate, consider a *real estate investment trust (REIT)*. The REIT is an unincorporated business that sells shares to small investors and invests these funds in real estate ventures or mortgages. *Equity REITs* own such property as apartment buldings, hotels, retail stores, office buildings, and condominiums. *Mortgage REITs* provide long-term mortgages and short-term construction loans. Mortgage REITs frequently structure mortgage loans so that they receive a fractional ownership of the property they finance in addition to interest on the loaned funds.

real estate investment trust (REIT): an unincorporated business that sells shares to small investors and invests these funds in real estate ventures or mortgages.

REITs are frequently organized by commercial banks, insurance companies, and mortgage banking firms. Since their shares are often traded on the New York or American stock exchanges or on the over-the-counter markets, not only can investors purchase shares in firms directly involved in real estate investments, but they can quickly convert their shares to cash by selling them. Investors have a choice of some 80 larger REITs whose shares are actively traded. Their combined assets total more than $8 billion.

As specialized investment companies regulated under the Real Estate Investment Act of 1960, REITs are designed to provide smaller investors with access to real estate investments and to attract additional capital for this industry. REITs are not taxed. Instead, owners of shares in REITs pay taxes — ordinary income or capital gains — on income when it is distributed to them.

Although they form a substantial part of all real estate investments, REITs are risky. Subject to the lows in the real estate and housing industries, they suffered serious setbacks during the 1970s. Between 1974 and 1976, for example, the REIT industry nearly collapsed, losing half its assets to the recession. The hardest hit were the mortgage trusts; those that invested in actual properties fared somewhat better.

Today, REITs are showing signs of a comeback. The new mortgage trusts operate differently from their predecessors, which proved so vulnerable to economic downturns. They add restrictions to their loans to protect themselves from loss, are well managed, and often partially own the property they finance. One mortgage REIT, for example, makes loans only on new apartment buildings that can be converted into condominiums, buys from the developer at the end of the mortgage period, and then manages the conversion from rental property to condominiums. The equity trusts are turning to new items, such as miniwarehouses, and are offering tax shelter benefits like those to be had from limited partnerships.

Despite these changes, REITs continue to be a risky investment and require careful study. Special attention should be paid to dividend yields. You should seek only those REITs selling at average or better-than-average price-earnings ratios for the REIT industry. In 1984 REITs paying 8 or 9 percent were considered attractive investments.

Real Estate Investment Companies. Specialized mutual funds for real estate are another investment vehicle. These funds sell shares of stock and use this money to acquire real estate. They differ from REITs in that they must pay corporate income taxes on earnings. Unlike REITs, the distribution of earnings to shareholders is not regulated. In short, real estate investment companies are similar to any other firm whose shares are bought and sold on the securities exchanges. They may plow back their earnings into additional real estate acquisitions in order to continue to grow, or they may decide to pay out most of their earnings in the form of dividends. Published statistics are available on their past performance, projected growth, and other corporate information. These data should be analyzed carefully by the potential investor.

IS REAL ESTATE FOR YOU?

Real estate can be an excellent and rewarding long-term investment, but it is risky and not ordinarily liquid. Moreover, despite the belief that real estate values only go up, their pattern is actually more cyclical. Although 1976, 1979, and 1984 proved to be boom years, for example, 1975, 1980, 1981, and 1982 were bad years. Real estate investors who look back and see only rapidly escalating prices may fall into the trap of believing that these gains will continue forever.

Real estate is a long-term investment strategy. Its long-term nature must fit with your financial resources and future needs. Timing and judgment can be important. Rental properties, for instance, have experienced financial problems because expenses have risen faster than rent increases, making it difficult for the owner to maintain a sufficient profit. And some investors have found themselves locked into their rental properties for longer than they had planned due to high mortgage rates that have limited the pool of potential buyers.

INVESTMENTS

COMMODITIES

Manufacturers use a variety of raw materials such as wheat, cotton, soybeans, and other farm products; animal products such as milk, skins, and eggs; and minerals and metals such as coal, silver, and copper in producing their wares. As noted earlier, these raw materials—animal and farm products, minerals and metals—are known as *commodities*.

Because the price and availability of commodities affect both the cost and manufacturing schedules of the businessperson's goods, some means must be available to guarantee their steady supply at known prices. Thus, the trading of commodities is similar to that for stocks and bonds. Members of commodity exchanges meet on a floor to trade contracts calling for the delivery of a specific amount of a commodity at a specific time. The New York Mercantile Exchange and the Chicago Board of Trade are two of the largest commodity exchanges.

In some cases, commodities trading is for immediate delivery of the particular product at a specified price. This is known as *spot trading,* or cash trading. Figure 18-2 shows a report of spot prices for a partial list of traded commodities.

In most cases, however, the trading involves future delivery—typically several months or even a year or more in the future. When the trading involves

spot trading: *commodity trading involving contracts for immediate delivery of a specified amount of a commodity for a specified price.*

Figure 18-2
HOW TO READ COMMODITIES LISTINGS

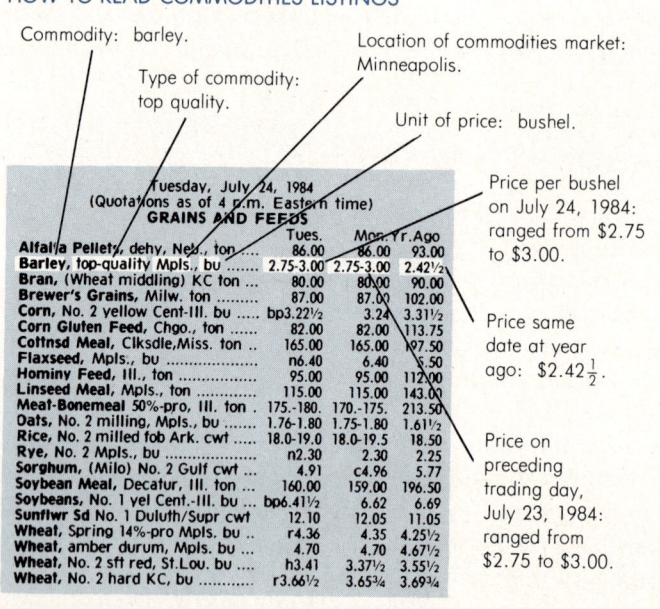

Commodity: barley.

Type of commodity: top quality.

Location of commodities market: Minneapolis.

Unit of price: bushel.

Price per bushel on July 24, 1984: ranged from $2.75 to $3.00.

Price same date at year ago: 2.42\frac{1}{2}$.

Price on preceding trading day, July 23, 1984: ranged from $2.75 to $3.00.

Source: Adapted from David J. Rachman and Michael H. Mescon, *Business Today* 4th ed. (New York: Random House, 1985), p. 408.

contracts for delivery of a specified amount of a commodity at a certain future date at a stated price, it is called *futures trading*. Although the original purpose of commodity trading was to allow producers and consumers of commodities to protect themselves against major price changes, a number of speculators participate in the commodities market in order to earn a profit. When they buy a futures contract for such commodities as Maine potatoes, Kansas wheat, or frozen orange juice, they do not actually buy the potatoes, wheat, or orange juice. Rather, they speculate on price changes and expect to sell their contract at a profit long before the actual delivery date.

futures trading: commodity trading involving contracts for delivery of a specified amount of a commodity at a certain date for a specified price.

THE RISKS OF FUTURES TRADING

Trading in futures contracts is a fast, tricky business. In most cases, the speculator's goal is to buy low and sell the contracts at a higher price before the delivery date. You can also sell short, selling the commodity futures contract at the current market price and buying it later at a lower price to cover the obligation to deliver. This strategy works if the price of the commodity declines. If it increases, you are forced to pay more for the contract than the price at which you sold the original contract.

Futures traders must keep an almost hour-by-hour watch on both futures and spot-price movements and trends. In order to minimize the risk and maximize the investment, they must give a broker precise and detailed purchase and sell instructions. They must be aware of such environmental factors as changes in the weather, in political power, and in consumption patterns; and they must be extremely knowledgeable about the past price trends and behavior of the particular commodity. Even then, the risk is high, as Figure 18-3 points out.

Commodity futures transactions are often highly leveraged. Investors need only put up between 5 and 20 percent of the contract's total value in order to make the purchase. And, unlike margin transactions on stocks, the amount borrowed is interest-free, since no money is paid to the seller until the commodity is actually delivered. Obviously, if you put up very little of your own money to buy futures contracts worth many thousands of dollars, you can make a great deal if the investment is successful. The catch, however, is that if you do not sell in time, or if prices suddenly drop, you stand to lose that much more. In commodities, you can be rich at 11 A.M. and poor by 3 P.M.

COMMODITIES EXCHANGES

The 12 commodities exchanges in the United States are arenas of frenzied activity. The largest of these exchanges is the Chicago Board of Trade, which is the central trading ground for futures contracts in such agricultural commodities as soybeans, wheat, and corn. The second largest exchange is the Chicago

Figure 18-3
ADVERTISEMENT DISCUSSING MANAGING RISK IN COMMODITIES MARKETS

Risk Is Not A Four-Letter Word

Today more than ever, risk is a fact of life. Avoiding risk is impossible. Recognizing the opportunities it presents is the mark of a smart investor.

Managing risks and taking advantage of them is what futures and options trading on the Chicago Mercantile Exchange is all about.

The CME is the world's most diverse marketplace, offering actively traded contracts on the Standard & Poor's 500 Stock Index futures, S&P 500 options, and futures contracts in three short-term interest-rate products, seven foreign currencies, cattle, hogs, pork bellies, gold and lumber.

These contracts, along with the background on how to use them effectively, can help investors and businessmen alike treat risk as other than a four-letter word. With CME contracts, it's possible to diversify a commodity portfolio... manage interest-rate volatility...or even hedge the value of an equities portfolio.

To learn more about futures and options trading at the CME, contact your broker. He or she can give you a copy of "Trading in Tomorrows: Your Guide to Futures" and "Options on Futures: A New Way to Participate in Futures," and show you videotapes featuring Louis Rukeyser, the host of public television's "Wall Street Week."

Together, they can help today's investor recognize the opportunity side of risk. ■

Markets For Today's Investor

CHICAGO MERCANTILE EXCHANGE®
International Monetary Market®
Index and Option Market

444 W. Jackson Blvd. ■ Chicago, IL 60606 ■ 800/843-6372
Offices in New York and London

Source: Courtesy of the Chicago Mercantile Exchange.

Mercantile Exchange, which trades contracts in live cattle and hogs and frozen pork bellies (bacon). These exchanges—along with the Commodity Futures Trading Commission (CFTC), the federal agency that regulates commodities trading—establish rules to ensure fair market activity.

These rules are extremely important because of the high cost of commodities contracts. You cannot just buy a contract for one bushel of wheat or five pounds of sugar. Rather, the minimum wheat contract is 5,000 bushels; the minimum sugar contract, 12,000 pounds; the minimum cotton contract, 50,000 pounds; and so on. These huge volumes make futures contracts extremely sensitive to even minor market swings caused by such factors as changes in the weather, political upheaval, inflation, recession, the rate of export, and so on. A cocoa contract, for example, issued in 30,000 pound units would increase by $300 if the price per pound rose by just one penny. Only expert traders can carefully weigh these factors to determine a commodity's selling price.

So the caution for small investors is a strong one: 80 to 90 percent of traders in commodities are professionals, and even they lose 75 percent of the time, according to a *Barron's* report.[6] This kind of investing should be done with money you can well afford to lose, and only if you are the kind of person who can tolerate high risk and uncertainty.

FINDING OUT MORE

Commodities futures contracts can be bought and sold through a brokerage house, which charges a commission on each trade. Information on commodities, including daily price quotes, is available every day in the *Wall Street Journal* and in most newspapers. In addition, the Commodity Futures Trading Commission publishes periodic reports on commodities as well as other information on these markets. Major brokerage firms and the exchanges themselves are also good sources of information.

OPTIONS

Options are contracts that allow an investor to buy or sell a specified amount of securities at a certain price—called the *striking,* or *exercise, price*—within a certain period of time. Traders of options are buying and selling *opportunities* to buy and sell shares; they are not trading the actual shares themselves. Like the commodity futures traders, they are betting that prices will change to their advantage long before the term of the contract (the option) expires.

To understand how stock options work, it may be helpful to think of yourself in the midst of a real estate transaction. You are interested in purchasing a piece of property worth $100,000 but want more time to investigate the deal. So instead of purchasing the property outright, you take an option on it. For $1,000 you purchase the right to buy the property for $100,000 at any time during the next 30 days. If during that time you learn that a major shopping center developer is seriously considering this location and is willing to pay you double your purchase price, you would undoubtedly exercise your purchase option. Even if the seller learns of the proposed shopping center, he or she is forced to go through with the sale at $100,000 as long as you complete the transaction within 30 days. If, on the other hand, you learn that a toxic dump site has just been discovered next to your property and decide not to buy, you lose only the $1,000 value of the option rather than the full $100,000 value of the property.[7] In many cases, the option price can be applied to the purchase price if you exercise the option.

These principles can be applied to the securities market. Stock options are traded in two different forms: options to buy and options to sell. A *call* option gives the owner the right to buy 100 shares of a security at a given price within a given time period. A *put* option gives the owner the right to sell 100 shares of a security at a given price within a given time period. Most options are written

options: contracts that allow the holder to buy or sell a specified amount of a security at a certain price within a specified time period.

call: an option to purchase 100 shares of a security at a certain price within a specified time period.

put: an option to sell 100 shares of a security at a certain price within a specified time period.

for three, six, or nine months. It is the task of the options trader to make a profitable trade or to limit a loss during this time period as the stock moves up and down in value.

CALL OPTIONS

Imagine that you are interested in buying a stock (called the underlying security) that is now trading at 47, but need more time to make your final decision. You decide instead to purchase a call option, which gives you the right to purchase 100 shares of the stock at a guaranteed price of 45 within six months. Since this option has a value of its own, you pay $4.50 for each option. (The option price depends on two major factors: how the current price of the underlying security compares with the striking price and the length of time remaining on the option. Because these factors are constantly changing, the price of the option fluctuates.) In order for you to profit from your option, the stock price must rise above $49.50 a share (the $45.00 striking price plus the $4.50 premium) within six months. As Table 18-3 shows, there are other possible outcomes as well. They range from loss of your total $450 premium to making an enormous profit. The amount you lose is limited to the relatively small amount of your premium. Most investors who anticipate a loss sell their call option before the expiration date and lose only a portion of their investment.

In fact, win or lose, in most cases, investors do not play their options out to the bitter end. When the stock is rising, they sell their option for a much greater percentage profit than they would earn if they bought and sold the stock itself. If, for example, you are convinced that a stock will rise from its current price of $29 and are willing to pay $2 a share for the option to buy 100 shares at $30 each, you might sell the option after one month if the stock climbs to 33. The investor who purchases your option may either exercise it when it expires, buying the stock for the bargain price of $30 a share, or resell it to another investor if the stock continues to climb. Because of the stock's increased value, you might be able to resell the option for $4.50—a 125-percent gain over the original $2 you paid for it. Had you bought the stock instead, your gain would have been significantly less. Buying at 29 and selling at 33 represents only a $4, or 14-percent, gain per share.

PUT OPTIONS

The opposite conditions apply for a put option. In order to gain, the value of the underlying security must fall. If you are convinced, for example, that a stock now priced at 40 is on the way down, you might pay $2.50 a share for the right to sell 100 shares of the stock at 40 within the next three months. (In a put option, you *sell short* since you do not actually own the stock.) If the stock falls to 35, the selling price of your option would climb to perhaps $5 a share—

Table 18-3
WHAT CAN HAPPEN WHEN YOU TRADE IN OPTIONS

	Possible Outcomes			
	1	2	3	4
Price on expiration date	$60.00	$49.50	$47.00	$40.00
Value of 100 shares	6,000.00	4,950.00	4,700.00	4,000.00
Cost of exercising option to buy at $45	4,500.00	4,500.00	4,500.00	4,500.00
Gross profit on exercising option (if negative, you will not exercise the option to buy)	1,500.00	450.00	200.00	0.00 (Won't exercise)
Less premium already paid	450.00	450.00	450.00	450.00
Net profit (or loss)	1,050.00	0.00	(250.00)	(450.00)
Return on original investment	133% Profit	0% Profit	(−56%) Loss	(−100%) Loss

Source: Richard P. Halverson, *Financial Freedom: Your New Guide to Economic Security and Success* (San Francisco: Harbor Publishing, 1982), p. 344. Copyright 1982 by Richard P. Halverson. Reprinted by permission.

double what you paid for it. You would probably then sell the option to someone looking for an even greater price decline before the contract expires.

Put options in gold-mining issues became extremely valuable in 1983, when the bottom of the gold market dropped out, at least temporarily, causing the price of gold to plunge $42.50 in a single day. Homestake Mining, the largest gold producer in the United States, dropped from 59⅞ to 48⅛. At the same time, the April 50 put—which gave option owners the right to sell their stock at 50 until the options contract expired in April—increased in value from 1 1/16 to 4¾.[8]

HOW TO TRADE IN STOCK OPTIONS

Trading in options can be done through dealers or brokers or through the relatively new options exchanges. The Chicago Board Options Exchange (CBOE), where more than 100 million contracts are traded each year, is the

Figure 18-4
HOW TO READ OPTIONS LISTINGS

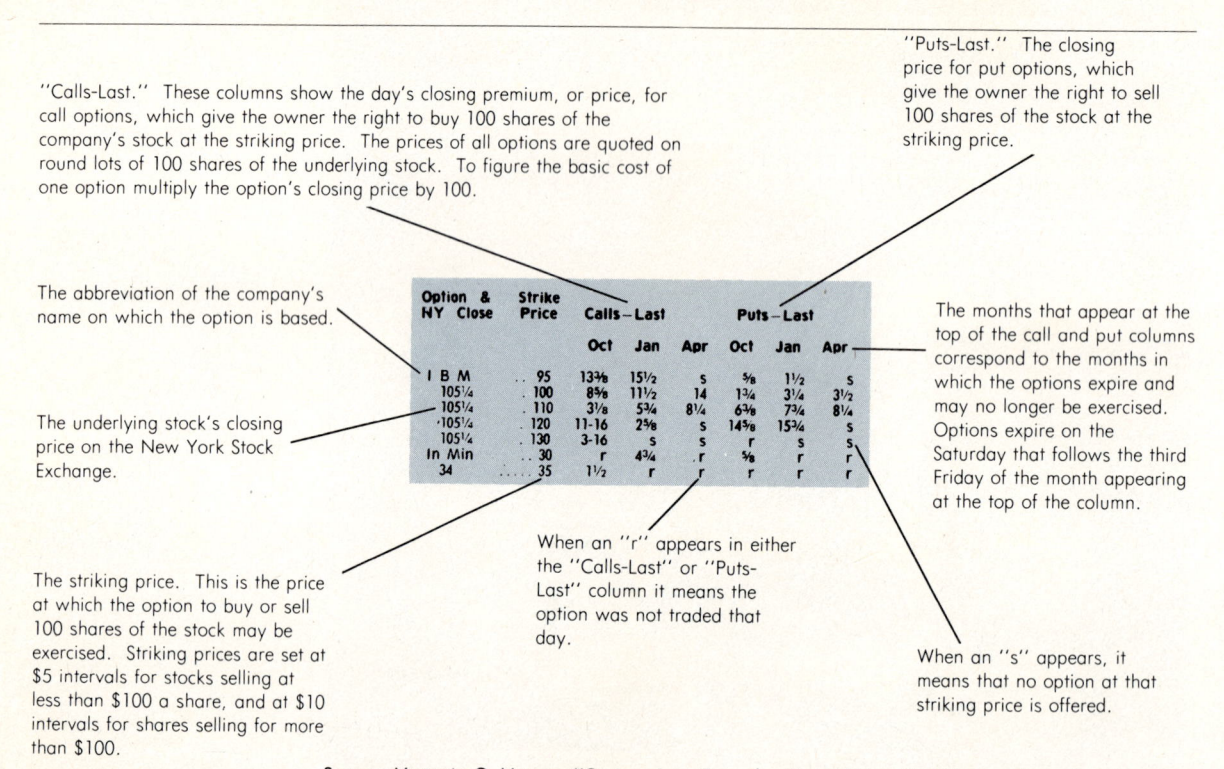

"Calls-Last." These columns show the day's closing premium, or price, for call options, which give the owner the right to buy 100 shares of the company's stock at the striking price. The prices of all options are quoted on round lots of 100 shares of the underlying stock. To figure the basic cost of one option multiply the option's closing price by 100.

"Puts-Last." The closing price for put options, which give the owner the right to sell 100 shares of the stock at the striking price.

The abbreviation of the company's name on which the option is based.

Option & NY Close	Strike Price	Calls—Last			Puts—Last		
		Oct	Jan	Apr	Oct	Jan	Apr
I B M	.. 95	13⅜	15½	s	⅝	1½	s
105¼	. 100	8⅝	11½	14	1¾	3¼	3½
105¼	. 110	3⅛	5¾	8¼	6⅜	7¾	8¼
105¼	. 120	11-16	2⅝	s	14⅝	15¾	s
105¼	. 130	3-16	s	s	r	s	s
In Min	.. 30	r	4¾	r	⅝	r	r
34	 35	1½	r	r	r	r	r

The months that appear at the top of the call and put columns correspond to the months in which the options expire and may no longer be exercised. Options expire on the Saturday that follows the third Friday of the month appearing at the top of the column.

The underlying stock's closing price on the New York Stock Exchange.

The striking price. This is the price at which the option to buy or sell 100 shares of the stock may be exercised. Striking prices are set at \$5 intervals for stocks selling at less than \$100 a share, and at \$10 intervals for shares selling for more than \$100.

When an "r" appears in either the "Calls-Last" or "Puts-Last" column it means the option was not traded that day.

When an "s" appears, it means that no option at that striking price is offered.

Source: Vartanig G. Vartan, "Options Lure Even the Timid," *New York Times*, December 12, 1982, p. 54. Copyright © 1982/83 by the New York Times Company. Reprinted by permission.

largest, but a number of others are available. In addition, options are traded on the American, Pacific, and Philadelphia stock exchanges. Price quotations for options appear daily in the *Wall Street Journal* as well as in the business sections of other major newspapers. Figure 18-4 explains how to read an options listing.

There are also option-income mutual funds that purchase high-yield stock and sell calls on these same stocks. While their objective is high current income for shareholders, they also charge relatively high commissions. As a result, they may offer investors lower total returns over the long run than would other, more conservative investment choices.

A Word of Warning. Despite the possibility of enormous profit, virtually all discussions of put and call options include strong warnings about the extremely high risk. "The options experience," says Edwin Burton of Smith Barney, Harris Upham & Company, "has chastened a lot of speculators."[9]

OTHER INVESTMENT ALTERNATIVES   543

The main reason experts caution investors away from options trading is the extreme volatility of the market. Although minor fluctuations have only a small effect on your percentage of profits on a stock, they may wipe out half or more of a gain on an option before you realize what is happening. Because of the speed of these changes, options investors have to follow closely the price of their investment on a daily basis. They must also be willing to sell an option—even if it means losing money—before it expires. If they do not sell, continuing to cling to the hope that the price of the stock will turn around may leave them holding an option with absolutely no value.

Most market professionals agree that greed is responsible for most investor failures with options. "If you see a small gain," says financial writer Gordon Williams, "grab it before it gets away rather than gamble on a bigger killing down the road."[10]

PRECIOUS AND STRATEGIC METALS

The Midas touch has fascinated people for thousands of years; almost all of us are dazzled by the sight of gold and silver. But gold and silver, plus other precious and strategic metals, are not just the stuff of legend; they are also investment vehicles.

GOLD

Precious metals are those with intrinsic value. Gold is the best-known precious metal. Since the end of 1974, when Americans were permitted to buy, sell, and own gold for the first time since 1933, ordinary investors have been able to participate in gold trading. This most durable of precious metals became *the* hedge against inflation, and sales of bullion, coins, gold certificates, gold futures, and mining stock boomed. The price of an ounce of gold, once set at $35 by the U.S. government, soared to a record $850 an ounce in 1980. It then began to fluctuate slowly downward but still remained in the $400 range during the mid-1980s.

precious metals: metals such as gold and silver with intrinsic value.

Why Buy Gold?

Investors in gold, known as "gold bugs," flock to this precious metal for several reasons. First, they believe that it protects them against the erosion of their assets as a result of inflation. Paul A. Sarnoff, director of the metal department at Paine, Webber, Jackson & Curtis, has observed: "Of all the hedges against inflation down through the ages, nothing compares with gold because it remains the most widely accepted store of value, and it is portable and easily transferable."[11]

Second, they see gold as a hedge against falling interest rates. When interest

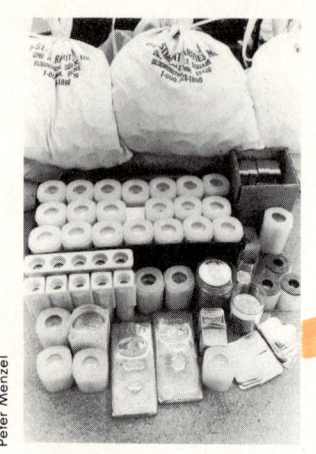

Gold is more than a precious metal; it is an investment vehicle, even in the unusual forms shown here. People may buy gold to protect themselves against inflation, falling interest rates, and, in many foreign countries, political instability. However, the recent volatile fluctuations in the price of gold have tended to offset these advantages for the average investor.

rates decline, so does the return on bank certificates of deposit, Treasury bills, money-market funds, and other investments. During such periods, gold bugs move their money from these paper investments to gold.

Third, investors, especially those in many foreign countries, purchase gold as a protection against political instability. A change in government, a currency devaluation, or a shift in the balance of power could make gold an extremely attractive commodity.

As recent history has shown us, gold's sheen quickly dulls when any of these factors change. When the inflation rate drops, so does investor interest in gold. Moreover, even when inflation is high, the high interest rates offered by money-market funds, bank CDs, and other investments compete with gold for investors' limited dollars. These paper investments have the advantage of being more liquid and more stable than gold. Political and economic instability may act against the price of gold as well. When gold plummeted $105.20 an ounce during the last week of February 1983, a one-day drop of $42.50 an ounce, the market decline was directly related to bullion sales by Middle East oil-producing countries, which saw declining oil prices as a signal that another round of inflation was unlikely, at least for a while.

Because gold is so volatile (price swings of several hundred dollars or more in a period of months are not uncommon), most investors make little or no use of gold as a component of their investment portfolios. Although over the ten-year period ending in 1982, gold outperformed inflation (consumer prices rose at an annual rate of 8.6 percent while gold rose at a rate of 18.6 percent), it did poorly in the following year. During that period consumer prices increased 6.6 percent, while gold decreased in value by 34 percent.[12]

How to Buy Gold. Gold is available in several different forms. *Bullion coins*—such as the South African Krugerrand, U.S. gold medallions, the Mexican 50-peso piece, and the Canadian Maple Leaf—are among the most popular gold investments because they are so easily traded. Sold for their gold value rather than their value as a collector's item, these coins require no assay expenses to determine their purity and no expensive written appraisal. Their worth is evident based on their face value and the current market price.

The Krugerrand, which contains exactly one troy ounce of gold, is especially easy for investors to trade, although prices vary a great deal depending on one's trading partner. Krugerrands can be bought and sold through private dealers or through the American Gold Exchange, which is part of the American Gold Stock Exchange. A commission ranging from 2 to 4 percent of the price of the coin is typically charged for each transaction. Figure 18-5 discusses the merits of including gold as part of a diversified investment portfolio and methods of acquiring gold coins.

The United States sells gold coins in the form of gold medallions, which are minted in one-ounce and half-ounce weights. These coins, which bear the

Figure 18-5
GOLD COINS AS AN INVESTMENT ALTERNATIVE

Source: Courtesy of International Gold Corporation, Ltd.

likenesses of such noted Americans as jazz musician Louis Armstrong, architect Frank Lloyd Wright, and opera singer Marian Anderson, are available through precious metals dealers and their nationwide network of coin dealers, banks, and brokerage houses.

Rare coins with value beyond their gold content are another investment vehicle. The value of these coins is dependent on the rarity of the coin (its age and type), its condition, and the current market. Uncirculated, undamaged coins are the most valuable to collectors.

You can also purchase gold in the form of *gold bullion*—gold ingots ranging in size from a fraction of a troy ounce to several hundred ounces. They are available from dealers and selected brokerage houses and banks. These bars, however, are often more difficult to sell than gold coins. They may require an

Economists Pick Tomorrow's Winners

Which investments will be the stars of tomorrow? *Blue Chip Economic Indicators*, published in Sedona, Arizona, asked 34 economists... to indicate how they thought the assets listed here will perform, using a scale of 1 (very poorly) to 10 (excellently). The figures are averages of their ratings, not anticipated percentage returns.

Source: "Economists Pick Tomorrow's Winners," *Changing Times*, January 1984, p. 38. Reprinted with permission from *Changing Times* Magazine, © Kiplinger Washington Editors, Inc., 1984.

	1 Year	5 Years
Stocks	7.4	7.4
Bonds	6.8	6.1
Treasury bills	6.1	5.7
Housing	5.7	6.2
Foreign exchange	5.5	5.2
Farmland	4.9	5.9
Silver	4.5	5.2
Gold	4.1	4.8
U.S. coins	4.0	4.8
Oil	3.7	4.9
Old Masters	3.7	5.1
Diamonds	3.6	4.2
U.S. stamps	3.6	4.9
Chinese ceramics	3.4	4.4

assay to prove their purity, and large bars are not easily divided if you want to sell only part of your holdings.

In addition, gold is available in less tangible forms. When you buy a *gold certificate*, you purchase a specific amount of gold, which is stored in some specified place. You do not physically take possession of the gold but must pay storage and insurance fees. The advantage of the gold certificate is that it allows you to purchase and sell the gold in quantities smaller than those that are usual for the bullion itself. Merrill Lynch, for example, has marketed gold certificates for as little as $100.

Gold stocks invest in gold-mining issues and offer the advantage of possible dividends as well as capital gains. *Gold mutual funds*, which invest in a range of gold-related stocks, offer this advantage as well. They also lessen the risk of total loss by offering a diversified portfolio. The major gold and precious-metal funds include the United Services Gold Shares, Strategic Investments, Fidelity Select Portfolio–Precious Metals, International Investors, and Research Capital. Speculators may also choose to invest in *gold futures* or in options in gold-mining stocks.

SILVER

Like gold, silver is subject to major variations in value, and its price can be battered by such diverse factors as inflation, interest rates, and political upheaval. "When gold catches a cold," said one dealer, "silver catches pneumonia."[13]

Starting from $1.79 an ounce in 1969, the price of silver has fluctuated dramatically over the years. By 1978 the price had risen to $5.40 an ounce; in 1979 it increased sharply to over $40 an ounce; and in 1980 it reached an astounding $48 an ounce. But following the same pattern as gold, silver prices then took a precipitous drop before they stabilized during the early 1980s at between $5 and $12 an ounce.

Silver is available in 5-pound bags of U.S. silver coins, 100-ounce silver bars, and silver certificates (which sell for as little as $1,000 from precious-metals dealers and selected banks and brokerage houses). In addition, silver can be purchased on the Commodity Exchange and the Chicago Board of Trade or acquired via flatware, tea sets, jewelry, and so on. Because price fluctuations can be severe, the small investor needs professional help to be successful in investing in silver.

STRATEGIC METALS

During the past five years, a number of investors have turned to more exotic investments in search of profits. For some, strategic metals have served as the focus of interest and speculation. *Strategic metals* are the approximately 36 non-fuel minerals considered essential to the U.S. economy. Of these 36, about 20 are imported. For example, the United States imports 97 percent of its tantalum and manganese, 93 percent of its cobalt, and 91 percent of its chromium.

Strategic metals are crucial to manufacturers of jet engines, semiconductors, many defense-related products, infrared lenses, missile nose cones, and high-quality steel. Chromium, for example, is widely used in oil refining, power plants, gas turbines, and stainless steel. As Figure 18-6 indicates, it comes mostly from the Soviet Union and South Africa. Because of their importance to the security of the United States, most of these metals are stockpiled by the federal government in predetermined amounts.

Strategic metals rank among the riskiest of investments. No organized market exists, and prices are reported on a sporadic basis. Some metals come in varying grades of purity, and grades may be difficult to determine. In addition, sales commissions and storage charges add to their cost.[14] Such metals are accessible to the small investor through a few brokers, who typically add sales commissions, insurance costs, and assay fees to the cost of the metal. Although brokers may split large units into smaller, more affordable units, these odd lots may prove more expensive to purchase and more difficult to sell.

Given the fact that most people do not even know the names of these materials much less how they are used, the opportunities for fraud are great. Investors should remember that cash transactions are not regulated by the SEC or the Commodity Futures Trading Commission.

strategic metals: *metals considered essential to the U.S. economy; they frequently involve importation from other producing countries.*

DIAMONDS AND GEMS

During the 1970s, one of the most highly sought investments by precious-stone speculators was the one-carat D-flawless diamond. At its peak in early

Figure 18-6

MAJOR U.S. STRATEGIC METAL IMPORTS

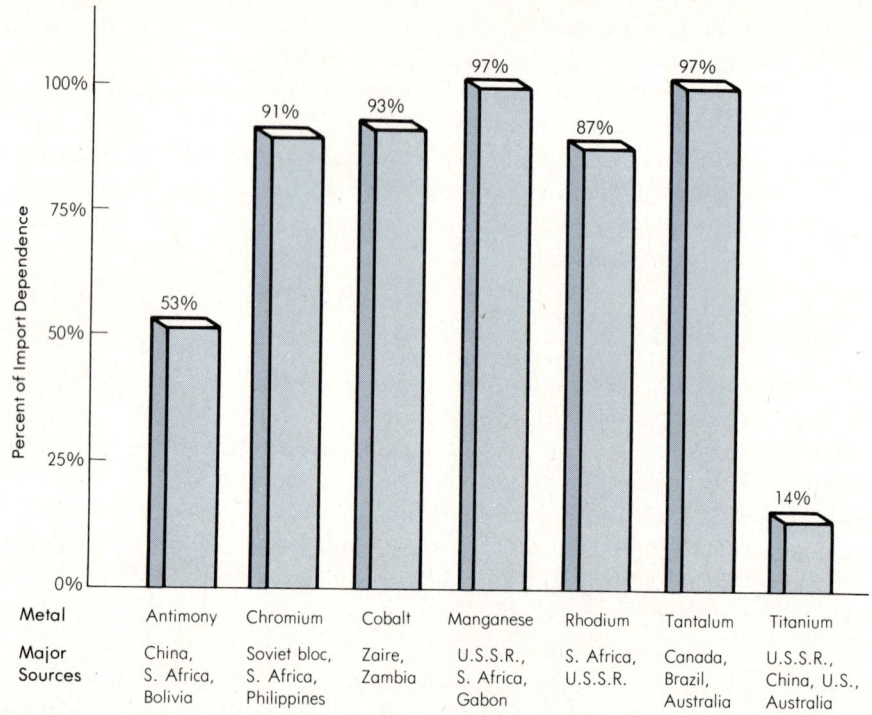

Metal	Antimony	Chromium	Cobalt	Manganese	Rhodium	Tantalum	Titanium
Percent of Import Dependence	53%	91%	93%	97%	87%	97%	14%
Major Sources	China, S. Africa, Bolivia	Soviet bloc, S. Africa, Philippines	Zaire, Zambia	U.S.S.R., S. Africa, Gabon	S. Africa, U.S.S.R.	Canada, Brazil, Australia	U.S.S.R., China, U.S., Australia

Source: Richard Buck, "Strategic Metals," *Seattle Times,* December 1, 1981, p. F1. Reprinted by permission from the *Seattle Times.*

1980, this diamond commanded a price of $63,000. But within a two-year period, its price had plunged to $15,000 or less. Less-perfect diamonds as well as colored gems such as rubies and emeralds experienced similar highs and lows during this period.

The price of diamonds declined for many of the same reasons that the price of gold dropped. An easing of inflation and increasing interest rates encouraged investors to abandon diamonds, gold, and other tangible assets that paid no interest or dividends in favor of such high-yielding paper investments as money-market funds. In addition, the wild speculation that turned diamond jewelry into a money-making investment finally ran out of steam, partially as a result of the unscrupulous business practices of firms trying to take advantage of a vulnerable public. These speculators undermined the nearly total market control of De Beers Consolidated Mines, the South African cartel that has controlled the production and sale of diamonds for decades. "The company has already lost control of the D-flawless market," comments David E. Koskoff, author of *The Diamond World,* "and the investor can no longer confidently assume an ever-upward trend."[15] Rather than having the assurance that the value of diamonds will never fall because of De Beers' iron control, many investors have learned the hard way that these values are even more fragile than the stones themselves.

Part of the reason experts warn investors away from diamonds is their questionable resale market. Resale prices vary greatly due to honest differences of opinion among appraisers: a high-quality stone in one expert's opinion may be a flawed stone in the opinion of another. In addition, investors must sell stones they purchase at retail prices at or below wholesale, which means they take an immediate 50-percent loss. "We usually can't pay more than a maximum of 90 percent of the current wholesale price," said Jack Brod, president of Empire Diamonds Corporation, one of the most respected diamond wholesalers in New York. "In most cases we have to pay less. . . . We have to leave a margin for error in our evaluation."[16]

One dealer paints the following worst-case scenario to describe what could happen if speculators rushed to sell:

> Investment diamonds are bought for $30,000 a carat, not because any woman wants to wear them on her finger, but because the investor believes they will be worth $50,000 a carat. He may borrow heavily to leverage his investment. When the price begins to decline, everyone will try to sell their diamonds at once. In the end, of course, there will be no buyers for diamonds at $30,000 a carat or even $15,000. At this point, there will be a stampede to sell investment diamonds, and the newspapers will begin writing stories about the great diamond crash. Investment diamonds constitute, of course, only a small fraction of the diamonds held by the public, but when women begin reading about a diamond crash, they will take their diamonds to retail jewelers to be appraised and find out that they are worth less than they paid for them. At that point, people will realize that diamonds are not forever, and jewelers will be flooded with customers trying to sell, not buy, diamonds. That will be the end of the diamond business.[17]

Although no one knows for certain whether diamonds will ever reclaim the value they had in the 1970s, most experts encourage investors to avoid them. David E. Koskoff sums up this view in his book *The Diamond World*: "Diamonds are traded in an arcane world in which the investor, the nonexpert dabbler, is . . . fair game. . . . The investor must buy in a seller's market. He must pay a substantial initiation fee. . . . Almost nobody in the world diamond community—whatever they may say publicly—really thinks much of diamonds as an investment for the nonexpert."[18]

While diamonds are the most commonly-purchased precious stone, a number of alternatives exist for the person seeking gems as an investment vehicle. These include precious and semiprecious stones ranging from rubies, sapphires, emeralds, and opals to jade. With each of them, the potential for appreciation—and the risks—are similar to that for diamonds.

ART, ANTIQUES, AND OTHER COLLECTIBLES

collectibles: any tangible items people seek out for collecting and investment purposes because they are perceived to be in short supply.

The 1970s was a decade of rapid appreciation in the prices of fine art, antiques, and other items called *collectibles*. Collectibles are anything that people decide to seek out because it is perceived to be in short supply. Dabblers and serious investors alike began buying everything from comic books to Coke bottles. They grabbed Oriental rugs, Tiffany lamps, antique furniture, first-edition books, vintage autos, rare coins, stamps, and even rarer wines in the hope that their value would climb. In fact, their value went through the roof. The list below features some very different examples.

- The rare eighteenth-century Goddard-Townsend kneehole desk, valued at $18,500 in 1958, commands between $350,000 and $450,000 today.
- The first *Daredevil* comic by popular artist Frank Miller sold for 40 cents in May 1979. Today it can be bought for $30.
- A 24-cent U.S. stamp known as the Inverted Jenny, minted in 1918 with a printer's error, sold for $160,000 in 1981.
- A 1934 publication of Aristophanes' erotic comedy *Lysistrata* illustrated by Pablo Picasso originally sold for $10 a copy. Today the price is $1,000.
- The elaborately illustrated *Gospels of Henry the Lion*, a twelfth-century manuscript, set an all-time auction record in 1983 when the West German government purchased it at Sotheby's for more than $10.7 million.

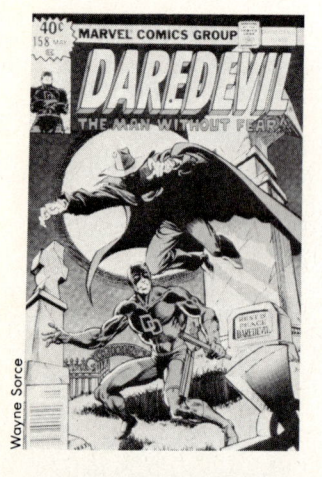

These price increases not only outstripped inflation, they also surpassed almost all stocks and bonds. Those watching from the sidelines, who believed that the market could maintain this feverish level, invested money in collectibles in the hope of a quick and substantial profit. But they were in for a rude awakening. Except in the case of extremely rare and valuable individual items (the Goddard-Townsend kneehole desk; the paintings of such masters as Rembrandt, Renoir, Monet, and Cézanne; the Inverted Jenny stamp), collectibles have not maintained the gains that they made between 1978 and 1981. As a result of slowing inflation and rising interest rates, many collectible prices quickly fell to their 1978 levels and below. Investors no longer feared the erosion of the dollar's buying power, so there was no reason to put their money only into investments they could touch and see. With the price drop, a quick profit was no longer likely. When investors sold their collectibles back to a dealer, they typically received a wholesale price amounting to only about half of the item's retail value. Thus, in order to make even a small profit, the item had to double in value.

Price declines affected nearly every collectible. According to Salomon Brothers, a major New York investment banking firm, prices for Oriental rugs

How to Sell Your Collectibles and Come Out Ahead

If you purchase collectibles as an investment, your aim is to sell them—rather than hold on to them—when the price goes up. The best way to do this is to follow three basic steps:

1. *Know the market value:* Make sure you have a good sense of how much the item is worth *before* you take it to a dealer or auction house. If you have any doubts have the item appraised.

   Finding a competent, qualified appraiser may be harder than you think. Appraisers are specialists, so you must find someone who knows a lot about what you have to sell and who has years of experience sizing up the value of collectibles. Ask your lawyer, banker, antique dealer, or anyone else you might know who deals in collectibles for a recommendation. You can also contact the American Society of Appraisers (Dulles International Airport, PO Box 17265, Washington, D.C. 20091) or the Appraisers Association of America (60 East 42nd Street, New York, N.Y. 10165) for a list of their members. Although these groups certify appraisers in specific areas such as antiques, fine arts, coins, gems, and jewelry, careful screening is still required.

   "Also, ask to see a client list," says Dexter MacBride of the American Society of Appraisers. "Many appraisers have worked for museums, and you want to see some credits that make you comfortable." Big-ticket items should be analyzed by at least two appraisers to be sure that the price finally settled on is correct.

   Some appraisers charge by the hour while others charge a flat fee. Never agree to pay a percentage of the appraised value since the appraiser may inflate the item's value just to fatten the fee. In the end, warns MacBride, "it is *caveat emptor* in dealing with appraisers. There is no state or federal licensing at all."

2. *Investigate auction possibilities:* Auction houses charge a percentage of the item's purchase price either to the seller or to both the buyer and seller. For example, some houses charge the seller 20 to 25 percent, while others charge the buyer and seller 10 percent each.

   Auction houses fall into three categories. The top ones, like New York's Sotheby Parke Bernet and Christie's, are the best places to sell highly specialized antiques or those dating from the eighteenth century or earlier. Regional auction houses like Butterfield and Butterfield in San Francisco and Sloan's and Wexler's in Washington, D.C. are qualified to meet almost all the auction needs of collectors selling items that range in value from a few hundred dollars to $50,000 or more. Finally, country auctions (which sell more items at auction than any other type of auction house) specialize in small items with a value of a few hundred dollars or less—especially those that date from the nineteenth or twentieth century.

3. *Evaluate dealers:* Collectibles can be sold directly through a dealer, who will either give you money on the spot or take the item on consignment. You can expect to receive from 50 to 75 percent of the item's retail value if you choose cash and 70 to 90 percent if you consign the article to the dealer. The higher percentage with consignment is due to the fact that the dealer does not pay you until he or she actually sells the item. Of course, if you choose consignment, there is no guarantee when, if ever, the sale will occur.

Source: MacBride quotations from "Liquidating Your Investment in Collectibles," *Business Week*, June 11, 1979, p. 136.

---

dropped 10 percent between 1981 and 1982. In that same period, coin prices dropped 28 percent and even the value of Old Masters dropped 22 percent.[19] In addition, Persian rugs that once sold for $16,000 to $22,000 sold for as little as $1,500 in 1982. And in 1983, a bronze and marble nineteenth-century French mantle clock valued at $400 and $600 sold at auction for only $176.[20]

"Are you sure they're a hedge against inflation?"

Various Collectibles Have Been Used as Investment Alternatives.
Source: Drawing by Stevenson; © 1981 The New Yorker Magazine, Inc.

These swings in market value are a warning to investors who intend to dabble in collectibles to stay away. Consistent profits are possible only if you are a serious collector and only if you buy top quality and hold it for a number of years.

SUMMARY

A variety of investment alternatives exist in modern personal finance. The major alternatives to stocks, bonds, and mutual funds are real estate, commodity futures, options, precious and strategic metals, diamonds, and collectibles.

Real estate offers investors the opportunity for significant profits as well as tax advantages. But there are also considerable risks involved, and illiquidity is a major disadvantage. Real estate investors may choose between non-income-producing property, such as raw land, or income-producing property, such as rental dwelling units, apartment buildings, shopping centers, and commercial buildings. Investments can be made directly or through limited partnerships, real estate syndicates, real estate investment trusts (REITs), or specialized real estate investment companies.

A different investment alternative is to enter the commodities market and engage in futures trading, with contracts that call for the delivery of a specified amount of a commodity at a certain date at a certain price. Stock options—contracts that allow the holder to buy (call) or sell (put) a specified amount of stock at a certain price within a certain period of time—are another possibility. Precious and strategic metals are another popular investment alternative. Diamonds and other gems are also purchased as investment vehicles, although resale may be difficult. Finally, collectibles may be used as an investment alternative.

REVIEW QUESTIONS

1. Briefly define the following terms:
   - commodities
   - cash flow
   - accelerated cost recovery system (ACRS)
   - leverage
   - non-income-producing property
   - income-producing property
   - syndicate
   - limited partnership
   - blind pool
   - real estate investment trust (REIT)
   - spot trading
   - futures trading
   - options
   - call
   - put
   - precious metals
   - strategic metals
   - collectibles

2. Explain the major tax advantages of investing in real estate.

3. How does the concept of leverage apply to real estate investments? Does it also apply to commodities trading? To precious and strategic metals? To collectibles?

4. Compare and contrast real estate syndicates and real estate investment trusts (REITs).

5. Describe the various methods available for investing in real estate.

6. How does a person invest in commodities futures?

7. How are stock options used in modern personal finance? Distinguish between puts and calls, and give an example of when each might be an appropriate strategy.

8. Distinguish between precious and strategic metals. What is the underlying rationale for investing in such products? What inherent problems face the investor in precious and strategic metals?

9. Identify the major alternative methods of making gold purchases.

10. What are the benefits and problems involved in the use of collectibles as an investment vehicle?

CASES AND EXERCISES

1. Since income-producing property has important investment advantages over non-income-producing property, why would investors choose the latter? Which type of investors would be more likely to be attracted to non-income-producing real estate?

2. Develop an argument for including gold in an investment portfolio. How could the problems involved in such an investment be reduced?

3. Assume that you bought a $200,000 commercial building three years ago for $50,000 down. The previous owner carried the balance on long-term contract. A buyer has now offered you $240,000 if you will carry the same contract that the first owner carried. The balance of the purchase price will be paid in cash. Is $240,000 a good price for a property you paid $200,000 for three years ago?

4. Analyze a prospectus of a publicly offered real estate limited partnership. Would you invest in this program? Why or why not?

5. In 1984 Sotheby's of London auctioned a number of art works from the estate of Sir Kenneth Clark. The most important work, a painting by the nineteenth-century artist J. M. W. Turner, set an all-time auction record with a winning bid of $10 million. The new record far eclipsed the previous record of $6 million for another Turner painting, *Juliet and Her Nurse*. What, if anything, does this suggest about collectibles as an investment alternative?

ANSWERS TO PERSONAL FINANCE I.Q. TEST

1. Fiction. 2. Fact. 3. Fact. 4. Fiction. 5. Fiction.

HOW ED AND MARIE MURPHY REACHED THEIR PERSONAL FINANCIAL DECISION

Professor Baird suggested that the Murphys consider an investment in income-producing real estate. The real task was finding an investment vehicle that would accomplish the diverse objectives of the Murphys and not exceed their available investment funds.

"Why not consider a condominium in the Carolinas or Florida as a rental unit?" he asked. "As long as you do not occupy the condo for more than 14 days a year or—if greater—no more than 10 percent of the number of days it is rented that year, you are eligible for a number of tax breaks. You may, for instance, deduct the mortgage interest payments, insurance, maintenance, and management fees as expenses. These expenses can then be used to offset your condo rental income and the earnings from your landscaping business."

Professor Baird pointed to another tax advantage of such an investment: Ed and Marie can depreciate the cost of the real estate investment over an 18-year period. Moreover, by the time the condo is fully paid for, the Murphys will be ready to give serious consideration to retirement. At that time they would have the option of making the condo their retirement residence or selling it and purchasing another property. By creating a second small business in the form of rental property, they can use its tax-deductible expenses to offset their tax liabilities and build equity in the condominium at the same time. Since real estate values in the Sunbelt states have tended to increase more rapidly than in the Northeast, they will probably realize greater investment growth than they would with a comparable investment closer to home.

PART SEVEN

FINANCIAL PLANNING FOR TOMORROW

LEARNING OBJECTIVES
1. To explain the role of the Social Security system in modern personal finance. / 2. To identify the several programs administered by the Social Security Administration. / 3. To describe the evolution of the Social Security Act. / 4. To explain the status of the Social Security system today. / 5. To discuss the various controversies over Social Security and the proposals that have been advanced to modify the system.

TESTING YOUR PERSONAL FINANCE I.Q.

	FACT	FICTION
1. Approximately 1 in every 10 people in the labor force is covered by Social Security.	☐	☐
2. Medicare was part of the original Social Security Act of 1935.	☐	☐
3. Divorced wives of 10 or more years of marriage can claim Social Security benefits based on their ex-husband's coverage.	☐	☐
4. New federal employees are now required to belong to Social Security.	☐	☐
5. Fifty million people in the United States are Social Security recipients.	☐	☐
6. College students are eligible for substantial Social Security benefits.	☐	☐

The materials in this chapter assist in separating fact from fiction. Your answers can be checked on page 573.

CHAPTER NINETEEN

SOCIAL SECURITY

**SHARING A PERSONAL FINANCIAL DECISION WITH
PROFESSOR GEORGE L. GRANGER OF EAST TENNESSEE STATE UNIVERSITY**

Senior Estelle Cooper had begun planning for her future career. She has just accepted an attractive job offer in a management training program, and she is now busy figuring out how to put her prospective salary to good use. One thing troubling her is the amount that will be taken out of her paycheck each week. She understood the need for taxes. But what about Social Security? Even though her employer would be paying more than half, her share totaled more than $1,000 per year. Estelle figured she could do better investing on her own. Why did she need Social Security?

The next day she approached George Granger, her personal finance instructor, during his office hours. "I know Social Security is required," she began, "but I don't fully understand the need for it. From what I've learned about retirement planning, it seems as if I might do better on my own."

Estelle explained that, for her, it was important to understand where her money was going. "Is the Social Security system really an economical way of providing basic financial security?" she asked. "I guess I'm not convinced that there needs to be a government program at all," she concluded.

If you were Professor Granger, how would you respond to Estelle's concerns?

To find out how Professor Granger helped Estelle answer her personal financial question, turn to page 573.

"Today a hope of many years' standing is in large part fulfilled. We can never insure 100 percent of the population against 100 percent of the hazards and vicissitudes of life, but we have tried to frame a law which will give some measure of protection to the average citizen and to his family . . . against poverty-ridden old age."
President Franklin Delano Roosevelt
(on signing the Social Security Act)[1]

Social Security: the United States' social insurance plan covering retirement, disability, and other protections.

Ida Fuller, a law clerk from Ludlow, Vermont, got the first Social Security check—number 00-000-001—in 1940. At that time employers and employees each paid a 1 percent tax on the first $3,000 earned each year. Participation in the *Social Security* system—the U.S. social insurance plan—was probably the best investment Ida Fuller ever made. She paid a grand total of $22 into the system and collected over $20,000, as she lived to age 100.[2]

Compare Fuller's wise investment to the current situation. In 1984 employers were required to pay 7 percent of the first $37,800 in earnings; employees paid 6.7 percent on the same base amount; and 0.3 percent came from general tax revenue. Technically, the 0.3 percent paid from general funds is a one-time-only tax credit to workers, since employers and employees make equal contributions to Social Security. The total maximum contribution was $5,292 in 1984. However, an Associated Press–NBC poll indicated that most Americans thought their contributions to the Social Security system were wasted. Some 74 percent of the people polled did not believe that they would ever receive a retirement benefit from Social Security.[3] Clearly, the Social Security system has experienced drastic changes since check 00-000-001 was issued. Indeed, it has become the focus of one of the most critical debates in the field of personal finance.

THE IMPORTANCE OF THE SOCIAL SECURITY SYSTEM

Thirty-five million Americans now receive monthly Social Security checks. The bulk of these recipients are people 62 or more years of age who receive retirement benefits—the program for which Social Security is most widely known. Other recipients include disabled workers and surviving spouses, children, and elderly parents of deceased workers. In 1983 the Social Security system accounted for 30 percent of all federal expenditures. Back in 1960, the comparative figure was 12 percent.[4]

By contributing to programs established by the federal Social Security Act, about nine out of ten workers in the United States are currently earning protection against economic insecurity.[5] Each covered worker and his or her employer make compulsory contributions to these programs by means of a payroll tax. The bulk of this tax goes to pay current beneficiaries. The remainder pays for administrative costs or goes into trust funds. Since current wage earners must depend on future workers to pay their benefits, many experts fear that the Social Security system is on the brink of bankruptcy.

THE COMPLEXITY OF THE SOCIAL SECURITY SYSTEM

The Social Security system is both enormous and complex. The Social Security Administration has over 1,300 offices located across the United States, and the Social Security Act requires a 457-page handbook to explain it.[6] The system undergoes almost continual legislative, administrative, and judicial change requiring that people already in the system be treated by one set of schedules and formulas while people entering the system be treated by another set. Thus, the eligibility of prospective beneficiaries must be determined on a case-by-case basis.

The Social Security Act covers several programs:

1. Retirement (old-age) insurance
2. Survivors (life) insurance
3. Disability insurance
4. Hospital and medical insurance for the aged and disabled (Medicare)
5. Black-lung benefits
6. Supplemental security income
7. Unemployment insurance
8. Public assistance and welfare services
   a. Aid to families with dependent children
   b. Medical assistance (Medicaid)
   c. Maternal and child-health services
   d. Services for physically handicapped children
   e. Child welfare services
   f. Food stamps
   g. Energy assistance

The first six programs are operated by the federal government, while the remainder are operated by the states with federal assistance. The federal agency responsible for the federal programs is the Social Security Administration (SSA) within the Department of Health and Human Services.

Because so many people receive such significant amounts of money under Social Security for so many reasons, it is an important part of personal financial planning. Yet the role of Social Security in protecting against adversity has changed since its inception in 1935 and will probably change further in the future. In order to take proper account of Social Security in personal money matters, something must be known of its historical development.

SSA: *Social Security Administration, the federal agency that administers the U.S. Social Security programs.*

THE EVOLUTION OF THE SOCIAL SECURITY ACT

In 1934 Robert J. Myers took on a two-month assignment with the Committee on Economic Security set up by President Franklin Roosevelt. The 22-year-old actuary developed the formula used as the basis of the Social Security

560   FINANCIAL PLANNING FOR TOMORROW

These brochures, published by the Social Security Administration, suggest the wide range of government-assistance programs that is available to the retired, the disabled, the unemployed, and other needy groups in America.

system. He later served as the system's chief actuary, from 1947 to 1970. A decade later, the Reagan administration hired him back as deputy commissioner of Social Security.[7]

Social Security Act of 1935: the original legislation setting up the nation's Social Security system.

The *Social Security Act of 1935* set up this nation's Social Security system, which originally was meant to supplement other retirement funds. But over the years Social Security has become a primary source of retirement income for most Americans. The initial legislation was formulated during the Great Depression, when about three-quarters of a million senior adults were on federal relief rolls. The traditional view that individuals could rely on their savings and families for retirement had been destroyed by the nation's economic collapse. The problem was compounded by the fact that an increased life expectancy had greatly increased the number of senior adults. Some states passed mandatory pension bills, many of which were inadequate, while other states took no action. Then, in an address to Congress on June 8, 1934, President Roosevelt pointed out the need for such social security measures. The Social Security Act of August 4, 1935, was the direct result of his appeal.[8]

PROVISIONS OF THE EARLY SOCIAL SECURITY LAW

The original Social Security Act stipulated that eligibility for retirement income be based on participation in the program, not on a demonstration of a need for benefits. In 1939, before the program was truly operational, the act was amended to include life insurance by extending benefits to survivors of deceased workers. Minimum benefits for low-wage earners were established, and benefits were also extended to certain dependents of retired workers.[9]

To be classified as fully insured, a worker had to contribute for 40 quarters

In 1935, President Franklin D. Roosevelt signed the Social Security Act into law.

on wages of at least $50. These contributors were entitled to a so-called primary benefit. The legislation assumed that husbands were a household's primary wage earner, but it provided 50 percent of the primary benefits to wives, and 75 percent to widows.

Although actuarial experts had determined that to provide moderate retirement annuities, at least a 5-percent combined payroll tax was needed, the original figure for the combined employee-employer tax was only 2 percent.[10] The prevailing opinion in the year 1934–35 was that Depression-burdened taxpayers could not handle the higher rate, nor was it deemed desirable to siphon off consumer buying power needed to revitalize the economy. The act did provide, however, that the rate would go up gradually until it stood at 6 percent after 1948. Future wage earners were to make up the difference. The initial funding of the program was further handicapped by the inclusion of people who were already old at the time of its enactment and who obviously had not paid a full share into the program. This, too, was to be handled by future taxpayers.

AMENDMENTS TO THE SOCIAL SECURITY LEGISLATION: 1950–1977

In 1950 coverage was extended to farm and household workers, the self-employed, employees of nonprofit organizations, and on a voluntary basis to state and local government workers. The early objections of inadequate record-keeping capabilities, states' rights, and separation of church and state subsided.[11]

Also in 1950, survivors' insurance was extended to husbands and children of female workers contributing to the program, many of whom had come into the work force and earned credits during World War II. In 1956 the program for disability insurance was enacted. In 1965 dependent children's benefits were extended beyond age 18 if the child was a full-time student. Also in 1965, *Medicare,* a program of hospital and medical insurance (discussed in

Medicare: hospital and medical insurance for the aged and disabled begun in 1965.

"Retirement plan? I wouldn't worry about that. You'd be out of your mind to work here that long."

Social Security Provides a Retirement Income—Even If You Do Switch Jobs Often!
Source: From the *Wall Street Journal*—Permission, Cartoon Features Syndicate.

Chapter 13), was begun, to protect people age 65 and over. Disabled widows and widowers were added to the list of eligibles in 1967. In 1973 Medicare was extended to those under 65 who had been entitled to disability checks for two or more consecutive years and to people with permanent kidney failure in need of dialysis or transplants.

In 1972 Social Security benefits were linked to the cost-of-living index. The highest cost-of-living adjustment was made in 1980, when Social Security checks were increased 14.3 percent. In 1977, figures used to compute benefits were also indexed to reflect the growth of average earnings. The 1977 legislation set the benefit for a worker with an average salary at 41.4 percent of his or her earnings just before retirement. This percentage of the ending salary is known as the *replacement ratio*.[12] The 1977 amendments also built future tax increases into the system. The 1985 tax rate is 7.05 percent of base earnings. The earnings base was raised to $39,300 as of 1985 and will be subject to formula increases thereafter. For instance, in 1986 the base will be $41,400, and the tax rate will be 7.15 percent. Further increases with the 1983 amendments have had a major impact on personal finances.

replacement ratio: method of determining Social Security benefits by calculating monthly benefits as a percentage of a recipient's earnings just before retirement.

THE 1983 AMENDMENTS

The 1983 amendments to the Social Security Act were based largely on suggestions of a National Commission on Social Security Reform. Contributions were increased to save the Social Security system from collapse. These new revenues are being funneled into the financially insolvent Federal Old-Age and Survivors Insurance Trust Fund—the largest of the three Social Security funds, which provides monthly benefits to retirees. Before revenues were increased, the Social Security Administration was paying out $16,667 per minute more in benefits than it was collecting.[13]

There are several parts to the Social Security bail-out plan, including delayed cost-of-living increases and the first-time inclusion of new federal workers in the system. But the plan's success is tied to substantial increases in Social Security contributions and the initiation of taxes on Social Security benefits. By 1990 contributions for wage earners will climb to 7.65 percent, and the wage base will grow to $57,000. Although increases were already scheduled before the 1983 law was passed, the new law has accelerated many of them. These new contributions will increase the funds the Social Security system has on hand between 1983 and 1990 by $40 billion.

In an attempt to raise another $30 billion, the Social Security bail-out plan also began taxing half of a recipient's benefits if he or she earned over a certain amount in that year from other income sources. Starting in 1984, individuals with an adjusted gross income of at least $25,000 and couples with an adjusted gross income of $32,000 felt the new tax bite. The income used to calculate these amounts does not include the Social Security benefits themselves, nor does it include income from such tax-exempt investments as municipal bonds. Architects of the plan justify this abrupt departure from one of the basic principles of the Social Security system by pointing out that Social Security taxes are contributed by both workers and their employers, so no new taxes are placed on the worker's share. Rather, the tax is levied on the employer's contribution alone.

SOCIAL SECURITY TODAY

Most employment is included under the current Social Security system. Indeed, only 10 percent of all jobs are not covered. The exceptions are federal employees hired before January 1, 1984; some local and state employees who are covered by other systems; certain agricultural and domestic workers (mostly transients); and employees of some nonprofit organizations. The bulk of the American population makes considerable contributions to the Social Security system.

CONTRIBUTIONS

The *FICA* (Federal Insurance Contributions Act) heading on an employee's pay stub lists the amount that a person contributes to the Social Security system. In 1985 an employee's FICA contribution could reach $2,770.65 if he or she earned the maximum amount ($39,300) subject to Social Security. For

FICA: *Federal Insurance Contributions Act.*

self-employed people, the maximum was $5,541.30 since they in effect must pay both the employer and employee contributions.

Employers, who pay an amount equal to the employee's contribution, are responsible for sending all money withheld to the government. They are also required to maintain certain records and to provide employees with reports of their annual FICA contributions. The self-employed report their Social Security earnings on their tax returns. Anyone self-employed and earning $400 or more is required to file IRS Schedule SE (Computation of Social Security Self-Employment Tax). Individuals can check their contributions by filing a request with the Social Security Administration. These forms can be obtained from any SSA office. Experts recommend that individuals check their records every three years.

Social Security contributions are pooled into three federal trust funds: the Federal Old-Age and Survivors Insurance Trust Fund, the Federal Disability Insurance Trust Fund, and the Federal Hospital Insurance Trust Fund. Medicare premiums and matching government funds go into the Supplementary Medical Insurance Trust Fund.

BENEFICIARIES

Retired workers over 62 years of age are Social Security's best-known beneficiaries. But there are numerous other categories of beneficiaries: disabled workers under age 60; dependent spouses; spouses of retired or disabled workers; surviving spouses regardless of age who are caring for a child 16 or under; disabled surviving spouses age 50 to 59; surviving spouses who are 60 or over; divorced wives of retired or disabled workers whose marriage lasted 10 years or more; children age 19 or under whose parent is disabled or retired; and disabled dependent adults.

In order to be eligible for Social Security benefits a worker must have credit for at least a minimum amount of work. These credits are called quarters of coverage. The 1939 amendments provided that a quarter was earned whenever a worker was paid $50 or more in covered wages in a calendar quarter. Before 1978 most Social Security reports were filed quarterly by employers. To simplify record keeping, the 1977 amendments permitted annual reporting and so required that the definition of a quarter be changed. In 1984 a worker earned one quarter of coverage for each $390 of covered annual earnings up to a total of not more than four quarters. The amount of covered earnings needed for a quarter of coverage will increase automatically each year to keep pace with increases in average wage levels.[14]

For retirement benefits, a worker must have enough quarters of coverage to be "fully insured." The minimum of quarters needed is 40, or 10 years of covered work—about one fourth of an average work career. However, when the 1951 amendment extended coverage to people who had less than a full working lifetime ahead of them, the requirement was converted to a smaller number of quarters for life or disability insurance.[15] For example, a 25-year-old who became disabled would need 2½ years of coverage to qualify for disability benefits. The *Social Security Handbook* defines as *disabled* anyone who is unable "to engage in any substantial gainful activity by reason of any medically determinable physical or mental impairment which can be expected to result in death or which has lasted or can be expected to last for a continuous period of not less than 12 months."[16]

disabled: *a person whom the Social Security Administration determines is unable to engage in substantial gainful activity.*

COMPUTING THE BENEFIT

The amount of Social Security benefits is related to a worker's average monthly earnings in covered work. For people who were first eligible for benefits prior to January 1, 1979, their actual past earnings were used to determine benefits. The 1977 amendments provided for a new method, which indexes past wages. This approach better reflects living conditions just before a worker's eligibility. The law intends that the monthly benefit should be a reasonable proportion—the 41.4-percent replacement ratio—of monthly wages being earned in the years just before retirement. Now past earnings are adjusted so that they will be stated in current dollars.

A worker's average indexed monthly earnings (*AIME*) is ordinarily computed from 1950 (or after age 21, if that date is later) to the year in which he or she reaches age 60, or a later retirement age, becomes disabled, or dies. The five years of lowest earnings or no earnings at all are dropped. No year can exceed the maximum earnings covered by Social Security for that year. A formula is then applied to the AIME to yield the primary insurance amount (*PIA*). This formula changes annually, and there are maximum amounts. For example, in 1984 a 65-year-old retiree could expect to collect $703.60 per month.

AIME: *The average indexed monthly earnings of workers used in computing a Social Security benefit.*

PIA: *the primary insurance amount used in calculating Social Security benefits.*

Covered workers at age 65 receive 100 percent of the primary insurance amount. Those who work beyond age 65 can get more than 100 percent of their primary insurance benefit. Their dependents aged 65 and their children are eligible for 50 percent of the PIA. Certain maximum family benefit restrictions apply. Survivors of deceased workers can receive 75 to 100 percent of the PIA, depending on the circumstances. A $255 lump-sum death payment is also paid to a surviving spouse, and a child can also get this payment under Social Security rules.[17]

Social Security payments are an important segment of the U.S. economy. In 1984 they amounted to some $180 billion a year. At the beginning of the 1980s, it was estimated that a 65-year-old recipient would collect some $120,870 over his or her remaining lifespan. The worker's net contribution prior to retirement —a mere $8,324![18] The Social Security Administration forecasts that a 65-year-old retiree may collect as much as $21,418 annually by the year 2000.[19]

BENEFIT RESTRICTIONS

retirement test: *the Social Security Administration's determination of a person's eligibility for retirement benefits.*

Several restrictions apply to the payment of Social Security benefits. The primary one is the *retirement test,* a determination of a person's eligibility for retirement benefits. People who are substantially employed will have their Social Security benefits reduced. In 1984 retirees 65 or over could earn up to $6,960 before their Social Security benefits were reduced. Those younger than 65 have a lower limit, and those over 70 have no limit. The self-employeds' retirement is assessed on the amount of work they actually perform. Income from investments and the like do not count. Survivors face similar earnings limits. But this applies only to a particular individual's earnings, so children are not affected.[20]

Students can receive 75 percent of a deceased worker's PIA and 50 percent of a retired or disabled worker's PIA. Students attending high school full-time can receive checks until age 19. As of April 1985, college students aged 18 to 22 can no longer receive benefits. Students are also subject to earnings restrictions similar to those for retired workers.[21]

FILING A CLAIM

Whether or not they intend to retire, people should contact one of the 1,300 Social Security offices three months prior to their 65th birthday. Medicare is available to all 65-year-olds, working or not. Others who should contact Social Security include disabled workers, survivors, 60-year-olds who intend to retire, or families who have a member with permanent kidney failure. Failure to contact the Social Security Administration promptly can result in the loss of some benefits that otherwise would have been paid.

The SSA office will want your Social Security number or that of the person on whose record the claim is based. Social Security personnel may also want some proof of age, such as a birth certificate or marriage certificate, and other information. Your local SSA office will tell you the exact information required for any particular claim, or you can call the Social Security Administration on one of its toll-free telephone lines.

SUPPLEMENTAL SECURITY INCOME

supplemental security income: *a program designed to guarantee disabled, blind, or retired persons a minimum monthly income.*

Supplemental security income is designed to guarantee disabled, blind, or retired persons a minimum monthly income. The Social Security Administration operates the program, but the funds come from general tax revenues. Needy persons who meet income and asset eligibility standards can receive up to $314 per month, or $472 for a couple. A few states—Washington, for example—supplement these amounts.

THE SOCIAL SECURITY CONTROVERSY

Social Security has always been a controversial subject. Although most people believe that government should help people meet financial adversity, there is considerable debate over how big a role it should play. Just when does an individual's responsibility end and society's responsibility begin?

Robert Ball, former commissioner of Social Security, argues that compulsion is the only sure way to prevent large-scale economic insecurity. He insists that most people simply do not save sufficiently for old age and that without a system of social insurance large numbers of people would become dependent on public charity. He points out that all industrial countries today—free-enterprise, socialist, and communist—have compulsory social insurance programs.[22]

Nobel-Prize-winning economist Milton Friedman, by contrast, favors abolishing the Social Security system altogether and replacing it with a negative income tax that guarantees everyone a minimum amount on which to live. Friedman thinks that Social Security discourages employment, so he

Our Social Security system is now at the heart of a major controversy. Advocates of the system insist that it provides insurance for people who may not have saved enough for their old age and that all segments of our society benefit from it. Opponents, though, claim that Social Security discourages employment and is an unfair burden on employed taxpayers.

favors a program that would honor current commitments but phase out the system in the future.[23]

IS SOCIAL SECURITY INSURANCE OR WELFARE?

The longstanding controversy has been over whether Social Security is insurance or welfare. Americans have traditionally viewed it as insurance, but recently they have been reminded of its welfare aspects. An earlier study by Lewis Meriam concluded that because the system depended on congressional appropriations due to the low initial contributions, it was never actually sound. Meriam states: "If this system were private voluntary insurance or a private retirement system, bankruptcy would be inevitable."[24]

Similarly, Friedman notes that while the system allows workers to earn protection credit, it depends on current taxes to pay benefits. He terms this arrangement a "compact between generations."[25] Many critics question whether this compact will break down in the next century. The current workers-retiree ratio is 100 to 31, but in 30 years the Social Security Administration estimates it could be as high as 100 to 73.

Robert Ball counters that Social Security is really an extensive insurance network. He points out that it covers all ranges of the income spectrum, not just the needy, as a welfare program does. Ball adds that contributions determine eligibility and provide the financing for the system.[26]

Today, the most pressing debate concerns what to do about the financial crisis affecting the system. Numerous viewpoints have been expressed. Some are directed at alleviating short-term funding difficulties; others are concerned with a long-term overhaul of the system.

WHAT NEXT FOR SOCIAL SECURITY?

Ultimately, the soundness of Social Security is a political, not an actuarial, matter. There are always those who would expand the system and those who would cut it back or eliminate it altogether. The 1983 amendments, which were designed to ensure the system's solvency into the next century, highlighted the political decisions involved in this crucial area of personal finance. The cause of many of the problems faced by Social Security in the 1980s can be found in the system's recent past.

During the late 1970s a funding crisis occurred. Social Security suffered from the economic paradox called *stagflation*—the situation that arises when recession and high unemployment cause low payroll taxes to be collected while inflation increases benefits. Consideration was given to supplementing the program from general tax revenues, but the crisis was averted or delayed by scheduling increases over succeeding years in the contribution rates and wage base.

stagflation: *an economic condition characterized by both high unemployment and inflation.*

Politics and public opinion have also interacted with the economic factors. According to a 1977 study by the American Enterprise Institute for Public Policy Research, a relatively small number of people (35 million) receive a substantial monthly benefit, which in most cases is a very important source of income for them. These people clamor for bolstering the system. In contrast are the taxpayers, who number over 100 million but who each have a relatively small tax burden. The taxpayers tend to be apathetic about Social Security for several reasons. First, they see only half the true tax deducted from their earnings. Because the deductions are made regularly, for most taxpayers there is no attention-getting April 15. Moreover, the deductions are made under the heading FICA, which evidently many employees do not really understand. Indeed, according to this study, few taxpayers realized that nearly half of them paid more money into Social Security than they did in income taxes. But, in any case, the taxpayers know that someday they too will be beneficiaries.[27]

Since this study, however, public opinion and political moods have shifted. The 1981 tax cut provided an interesting contrast. Withholding taxes fell while FICA amounts escalated. *Fortune* magazine estimated that combined Social Security contributions could be as high as 36.3 percent in 2030 if present trends continue.[28]

Various proposals have been advanced for saving the Social Security system. A sampling of these proposals is discussed below.

PROVIDING UNIVERSAL COVERAGE

Robert Ball, among others, favors universal coverage of all workers.[29] The 10 percent of the labor force not covered by Social Security consists primarily of federal civilian employees hired before 1984 and some local and state employees. According to Ball, state and local governments have not been compelled to join because the federal government would have to force these other governments to pay the employer's tax, a questionable practice. As a result, voluntary coverage has been permitted. Some fire and police employees resist coverage because they have early retirement programs that permit them to draw a pension after 20 years and then start working in other jobs that provide Social Security. Federal civilian employees were exempt because they already had a pension plan, but new federal employees were included under Social Security as a result of the 1983 amendments.

FURTHER ALTERING THE INDEXING SYSTEM

Social Security benefits are now indexed to the Consumer Price Index. The wage base is also indexed via the so-called replacement ratio. The purpose is to let recipients maintain their standard of living, but this system has been criticized for being too generous.

Many critics contend that Social Security beneficiaries receive excessive adjustments because the indexing system has been tied to the Consumer Price Index (CPI). The CPI has traditionally been weighted toward housing and other costs that may not be relevant to a retiree's circumstances. Some people advocate setting up a separate "retiree's index of living cost."

As of 1983, the Bureau of Labor Statistics (BLS) revised the index so that sharp shifts in mortgage costs and housing prices were no longer reflected in the CPI. In their place, the BLS used estimated rental values of housing. This figure is based on taxes, repairs and maintenance, and insurance. If this new approach had been applied during the early 1980s, reported inflation figures would have dropped slightly.[30] The change became effective for Social Security benefits in 1985.

CHANGING THE RETIREMENT AGE

The retirement age of 65 was set in the 1930s, and several proposals have argued that a later retirement age would be appropriate now and in the future. Robert J. Myers, the man who originally helped set up the Social Security system, believes that age 68 in the year 2000 would be the equivalent of 65 in 1935. It is estimated that such a change would mean a 20-percent cut in total benefits paid.[31] Current law says that starting in the year 2000, the age at which full benefits are payable will be increased gradually until it reaches 67.

CRACKING DOWN ON FRAUD

Fraud is another favorite target of Social Security reformers. The SSA's Office of Security and Program Integrity has recently beefed up its investigative efforts. Usually the government simply stops payments for those wrongly receiving money and tries to get reimbursement. Because intentional cheating is

---

"But I Am Alive and Well"

An Ohio resident's wife was notified that since her husband had died the previous fall, she was now entitled to survivor's benefits. Meanwhile the Treasury Department plucked $1,392 in overpayments from the deceased's direct-deposit account at a bank. These actions bothered 68-year-old James Badgero. Contrary to the Social Security Administration's claim, he was still alive and well and living in Worthington, Ohio.

Although a mistake was made in this case, it should be noted that the government can take money out of direct-deposit accounts if benefits were paid in error after a person's death. However, beneficiaries must be notified and given the right to appeal. In 1983 some 331,000 bank accounts were subject to such recoupment procedures.

Source: "'Dead' Man Tells Horror Story of Social Security Foul-Ups, Bureaucracy," *Journal-American* (Bellevue, Wash.), November 30, 1983, p. A8.

difficult to prove, only 5 percent of the cases end up as criminal prosecutions. Methods used by investigators include checking tax and other government records, conducting audits, following up on citizen complaints about recipients, and having claims personnel spot suspicious cases.[32]

DEVELOPING AN ALTERNATIVE SYSTEM

Several people have proposed replacing Social Security with some alternative system. One interesting proposal comes from David Fischer, a social historian at Brandeis University, who suggests that the government invest $1,300 for every newborn. An 8-percent return would provide an $18,000 annual pension for every 65-year-old retiree.[33]

Although such drastic revisions are unlikely, it seems clear that the Social Security system will be modified further in the years ahead, probably several times. From its inception, the system has been subject to continual adaptation and modification. But whatever the changes, Social Security will continue to play an important role in people's financial planning.

SUMMARY

Social Security—the U.S. social insurance plan—covers 90 percent of all Americans. Of the 35 million Americans now receiving Social Security benefits, the bulk are retirees. In addition to retirement, Social Security is concerned with survivors insurance, disability insurance, Medicare, black-lung benefits, supplemental security income, employment insurance, and public assistance and welfare services. Most of these programs are operated by the Social Security Administration (SSA).

The Social Security Act of 1935 was a legislative response to changes in traditional retirement patterns and the dire economic conditions of the Great Depression. Amendments since 1935 have served to expand the system's coverage and role in our economic society.

Contributions are made by both employees and employers, with the self-employed paying their Social Security through their federal income tax returns. These contributions go into various trust funds to pay benefits.

Benefits are paid on the basis of participation to retirees, disabled workers, various dependents (spouses, children, and parents), and divorced wives. Eligibility is based on quarters of coverage. The actual benefit received is based on the average wages earned, which are indexed to current levels. The benefits themselves are then indexed annually to the Consumer Price Index. In some cases, retirees, the disabled, or the blind can also claim supplemental security income, a program designed to provide all Americans with a minimum monthly income. Social Security claims can be filed through any of the 1,300 SSA offices.

Social Security benefits are subject to several restrictions. A primary one is the retirement test, which limits the earnings of 60- to 70-year-olds. The retirement test for self-employed workers is based on the amount of work they have actually performed. In either case, there is no limit for workers over 70. Survivors face similar earnings limits. Student benefits are restricted to full-time high school students under age 19. Earnings limits are also applicable.

Social Security has always been controversial. Two traditional debates concern the size of Social Security's role in the U.S. economy and whether social security is insurance or welfare. The current debate is over how best to maintain the system's solvency. Critics have noted that the system was incomplete from the beginning. The 1983 amendments addressed some of the financial problems. Other proposals include universal coverage of all workers, altering the indexing system, raising the retirement age to 68, cracking down on fraud, and developing alternative systems. But whatever changes are made in the future, Social Security will continue to play a pivotal role in personal financial planning.

REVIEW QUESTIONS

1. Briefly define the following terms:

   Social Security
   SSA
   Medicare
   Social Security Act of 1935
   replacement ratio
   FICA
   disabled
   AIME
   PIA
   retirement test
   supplemental security income
   stagflation

2. What is the role of the Social Security system in modern personal finance?

3. Why is the Social Security system so complex?

4. Describe the evolution of the Social Security Act.

5. How are Social Security taxes collected?

6. Who benefits from Social Security? What restrictions are applicable?

7. How are Social Security benefits computed?

8. Is Social Security insurance or welfare? Why or why not?

9. Discuss the various proposals for modifying the current social security system.

10. In your opinion, what is the single biggest issue facing the Social Security system today? Explain.

CASES AND EXERCISES

1. Prepare a report on the national retirement system used in another nation. Point out similarities and differences between the foreign plan and our social security system. Are there any features of the other nation's plan that should be adopted in the United States?

Questions 2–5 Are Based on the Following Discussion

THE FREEDOM PLAN

A. Haeworth Robertson, who spent four years as Chief Actuary of the Social Security Administration, has written a book entitled *The Coming Revolution in Social Security.* In it, Robertson proposes a "Freedom Plan." He argues that major changes must occur if Social Security is to avoid future problems. Robertson's Freedom Plan would operate in the following manner.

The current system would be retained in its entirety for all persons 45 or over as of July 4, 1984. The existing program would thus apply to some 46 million people between 45 and 65, another 28 million over 65, and dependents. All others—approximately 168 million people younger than 45 on that date—would participate in the proposed Freedom Plan. The plan itself would consist of three elements:

1. A compulsory senior citizen benefit program.
2. A voluntary retirement savings bond program—"Freedom Bonds."
3. A supplement to private pension plans that would adjust for the cost of living.

Senior citizen benefits would provide an economic safety net for the elderly. Each citizen would receive a tax-free, uniform benefit at age 70 that approximates the subsistence level (about $350 per month in 1983). Robertson estimates that while two-thirds of all Social Security recipients now receive higher amounts, the lower third would actually get an increase under the system. Age 70 was selected to reflect the longer lifespans of today, and this figure could be adjusted periodically to reflect changing life expectancies. Retirement before age 70 would have to be funded entirely from personal resources. The senior citizen benefit would be paid from some form of general revenue directly linked to the benefit. Thus, citizens could comprehend the costs associated with changes in the benefit level.

The second part of Robertson's plan is the Freedom Bond Program. The author notes that inflation can wreck even the best-laid retirement plans. To alleviate this problem, Robertson proposes that the government offer Freedom Bonds to anyone participating in the new system. Citizens between ages 45 and 70 could buy the bonds if they were under 45 as of July 4, 1984. Ten percent of a person's taxable earnings or 10 percent of the average U.S. earnings—whichever was higher—could be used for these bonds. People in nonpaid employment would also be eligible. The bonds would pay no interest, but their value would be adjusted to compensate for any increases in the cost of living. The Freedom Bonds would be paid out of general revenues, and would not be subject to taxation. The bonds would be redeemable—in full or in part—at age 60, or in the event of death, disability, or a severe emergency. Robertson estimates that anyone who made a 10 percent contribution between 45 and 70 would acquire enough bonds to pay 20 to 30 percent of their average annual earnings at age 70.

The third part of the Freedom Plan recognizes that private pension plans cannot protect against inflation. So Robertson proposes that general tax revenues be used to adjust all approved private pension benefits after age 70. A cost-of-living index designed to reflect the expenditures of elderly persons would be used to determine these supplemental payments. Robertson concludes that his Freedom Plan will provide the economic safety net society demands as well as protect against inflation.[34]

2. What is your assessment of the Freedom Plan?

3. Can you identify any loopholes or inequities in the system that Robertson proposes?

4. Can you suggest any modifications that might improve the Freedom Plan?

5. How would congressional adoption of the Freedom Plan change personal financial planning?

ANSWERS TO PERSONAL FINANCE I.Q. TEST

1. Fact. 2. Fiction. 3. Fact. 4. Fact. 5. Fiction. 6. Fiction.

HOW ESTELLE COOPER REACHED HER PERSONAL FINANCIAL DECISION

"A lot of people have questions about Social Security," Professor Granger told Estelle. "The first thing to remember is that the Social Security Administration covers more than just retirement income for the aged and their spouses. It also provides benefits to widows or widowers and orphans, as well as disability income and Medicare. When people argue that they could do better on their own, they're usually considering only the retirement aspect. They forget the other kinds of protection involved. And they do not allow for the fact that no physical exam is required for this social insurance. That may not seem a problem now, when you're young and healthy, but it can be when you're older."

Thinking over Professor Granger's comments, Estelle admitted, "I didn't realize Social Security protected me in so many different ways. From what you say, it does seem that some method is needed to make working people share with people who can't work anymore. Maybe the present system could be improved, but I guess it shouldn't be eliminated. It's true that the issue of security for the aged isn't just going to go away. I see now how my Social Security payments are serving a need and giving me a kind of insurance I couldn't buy elsewhere."

LEARNING OBJECTIVES

1. To outline the decisions involved in retirement planning. / **2.** To discuss the sources of retirement income. / **3.** To explain the various types of annuities and how they are used. / **4.** To describe the different aspects of estate planning: wills, probate, trusts, and various tax considerations.

TESTING YOUR PERSONAL FINANCE I.Q.

	FACT	FICTION
1. Kalahari bushmen probably initiated retirement planning as we know it today.	☐	☐
2. Intestate is a disease that affects older Americans.	☐	☐
3. About half of all Americans are not covered by an employee retirement program.	☐	☐
4. Speeding will probably cut a year off your expected life.	☐	☐
5. The Economic Recovery Tax Act of 1981 increased estate taxes—once again proving that "you can't take it with you."	☐	☐
6. IRAs are restricted to people who do not have employer retirement plans.	☐	☐
7. Seventy percent of all Americans do not have a will.	☐	☐

The materials in this chapter assist in separating fact from fiction. Your answers can be checked on page 604.

CHAPTER TWENTY
RETIREMENT, WILLS, AND ESTATE PLANNING

SHARING A PERSONAL FINANCIAL DECISION WITH
PROFESSOR GEORGE L. GRANGER OF EAST TENNESSEE STATE UNIVERSITY

Cindy Donovan has come to realize how carefully her grandmother must plan to live within her limited income. Although Cindy's grandmother gets some help from her children, her main source of income is her Social Security check. But Cindy's parents are now approaching retirement age. They are both teachers so they will receive income from their pension fund in addition to Social Security. The Donovans also have a modest asset management account and the two individual retirement accounts (IRAs) they have set up. Even so, Cindy knows that they, like her grandmother, will need to plan carefully in the years ahead. She'd like to help them work out a retirement budget and, in the process, gain insight into her own financial planning.

A few years ago, in college, Cindy took Professor George Granger's personal finance course. One thing that stood out for her was how much inflation could add to future costs. Even with a low rate of inflation—say, 5 to 6 percent—prices would double every 12 to 13 years. Cindy realizes that once you retire, you cannot count on salary increases as a hedge against inflation. As a nurse, Cindy also realizes that as you get older, your health care needs tend to increase.

Cindy decides to call Professor Granger and ask him how best to advise her parents. She also wonders how much she should save each year for her own retirement. Recognizing her parents' and grandmother's situations has made her very conscious of the importance of insuring her own future.

If you were Professor Granger, what would you tell Cindy?

To find out how Professor Granger helped Cindy with her personal financial decision, turn to page 604.

"Retirement at sixty-five is ridiculous. When I was sixty-five I still had pimples."
George Burns[1]

For 35 years Chester Oldakowski of Erie, Pennsylvania, rose at 5 A.M. and headed for the American Meter plant. Oldakowski worked in a corner of the third floor, nicknamed the "Penthouse." It was cold in winter; hot in summer. Classified as an assembler, Oldakowski put tubing in a machine that produced parts for gas meters. His seniority eventually permitted him five weeks of annual vacation. His decision to retire was a happy one. Oldakowski's American Meter pension and Social Security benefits allow for few luxuries, but he no longer has to punch the time clock at the factory.[2]

Chester Oldakowski is probably typical of a lot of people. Retirement is a time to enjoy leisure pursuits. In fact, a retired employee benefits director at General Motors, Victor Zink, has commented: "Those retirement parties, they used to be sad affairs. They're darn happy ones now."[3] Personal financial planning can go a long way toward making an individual's retirement years a rich and rewarding stage of life.

RETIREMENT PLANNING

Retirement planning is largely a product of advanced societies. A Kalahari bushman has no need for retirement planning. When he is deemed too elderly to work any longer, he lies beneath a thorn tree and wills his own death. The American Express Company offered one of the earliest retirement plans in the United States. The wording of the 1875 plan was amusing. It provided a pension for 20-year employees who were "worn-out or disabled."[4]

American Express's early plan has few similarities to retirement programs of the late 1980s. Retirement planning has become an important aspect of personal financial planning, and it is likely to increase in national importance as our population grows older. Today, people over 75 make up the fastest-growing segment of the population. By 2010, when people who were born in the late 1940s and early 1950s begin to retire, one out of two Americans will be 40 or over. For many people, the result of these demographic changes will be postponed retirement and the need to save and invest on one's own to provide an adequate retirement income.[5]

Retirement is not a priority in the financial planning of most young adults, but one should develop a concern as soon as possible. Too many people put off retirement planning until the years just before their retirement.

How Long Will You Live?

Start With the Number 72

Personal Facts:

If you are male, **subtract 3.**
If female, **add 4.**
If you live in an urban area with a population over 2 million, **subtract 2.**
If you live in a town under 10,000 or on a farm, **add 2.**
If any grandparent lived to 85, **add 2.**
If all four grandparents lived to 80, **add 6.**
If either parent died of a stroke or heart attack before the age of 50, **subtract 4.**
If any parent, brother or sister under 50 has (or had) cancer or a heart condition, or has had diabetes since childhood, **subtract 3.**
Do you earn over $50,000 a year? **Subtract 2.**
If you finished college, **add 1.** If you have a graduate or professional degree, **add 2 more.**
If you are 65 or over and still working, **add 3.**
If you live with a spouse or friend, **add 5.** If not, **subtract 1** for every ten years alone since age 25.

Running Total _____

Life-Style Status:

If you work behind a desk, **subtract 3.**
If your work requires regular, heavy physical labor, **add 3.**
If you exercise strenuously (tennis, running, swimming, etc.) five times a week for at least a half-hour, **add 4.** Two or three times a week, **add 2.**
Do you sleep more than ten hours each night? **Subtract 4.**
Are you intense, aggressive, easily angered? **Subtract 3.**
Are you easygoing and relaxed? **Add 3.**
Are you happy? **Add 1.** Unhappy? **Subtract 2.**
Have you had a speeding ticket in the past year? **Subtract 1.**
Do you smoke more than two packs a day? **Subtract 8.** One to two packs? **Subtract 6.** One-half to one? **Subtract 3.**
Do you drink the equivalent of $1\frac{1}{2}$ oz. of liquor a day? **Subtract 1.**
Are you overweight by 50 lbs or more? **Subtract 8.** By 30 to 50 lbs? **Subtract 4.** By 10 to 30 pounds? **Subtract 2.**
If you are a man over 40 and have annual checkups, **add 2.**
If you are a woman and see a gynecologist once a year, **add 2.**

Running Total _____

Age Adjustment:

If you are between 30 and 40, **add 2.**
If you are between 40 and 50, **add 3.**
If you are between 50 and 70, **add 4.**
If you are over 70, **add 5.**

ADD UP YOUR SCORE TO GET YOUR LIFE EXPECTANCY.

Source: Robert F. Allen, with Shirley Linde, *Lifegain* (Englewood Cliffs, N.J.: Appleton Books, 1981). Reprinted with permission by HRI, Human Resources Institute, Morristown, N.J. 07960.

Longer lifespans mean that retirement takes up a longer segment of the human life cycle. The average lifespan of a female born in 1983 is 78.3 years; that of the average male born in 1983 is 70.9 years.[6] There are now some 25 million

theoretical limits of biological longevity: the maximum age that could be obtained if all diseases were cured.

Americans aged 65 or over—approximately 11.6 percent of the U.S. population. There are 2.4 million Americans over 85, and about 32,000 over 100.

Some writers have discussed the *theoretical limits of biological longevity,* the maximum age that could be obtained if all diseases were cured. The current estimate of this limit is 115 years, but some believe the limit can be pushed to 140 years or more.[7] In any case, a 65-year-old American considering retirement next year can look forward to a long retirement. A male who reaches age 64 in the mid-1980s can expect to live another 19.4 years; a woman can expect another 22.8 years.[8]

Inflation and longer lifespans require careful financial planning if the retiree is to have adequate purchasing power during these important years of life. For example, a 6-percent inflation rate can cut a retirement check in half in about 12 years.

TWO CRITICAL RETIREMENT DECISIONS

Retirement planning starts with a thorough self-analysis that answers the basic question: What kind of life do I want to lead when I retire? To answer this question, you must decide where to live after retirement and when to retire.

Choosing a Retirement Location. The choice of a retirement location depends on many factors—some financial, others involving lifestyle. Since retirement income usually does not equal preretirement earnings, cutting overhead

When a person chooses where to live after retirement, he or she should consider a location that will offer opportunities for socializing, community involvement, or part-time work.

Table 20-1
THE 12 BEST METROPOLITAN AREAS FOR RETIREES

Rank	Metropolitan Area
1	Asheville, NC
2	Knoxville, TN
3	Johnstown, PA
4	Charleston, WV
5	Utica-Rome, NY
6	Lexington-Fayette, KY
7	Wheeling, WV
8	Louisville, KY
9	Erie, PA
10	Nashville-Davidson, TN
11	Greensboro-Winston-Salem-High Point, NC
12	Evansville, IN

Source: Adapted from *Places Rated Almanac* by Richard Boyer and David Savageau. Copyright 1981 by Rand McNally & Company.

Courtesy of the Asheville, N.C., Chamber of Commerce

is an important concern. To make ends meet, many people try to minimize their fuel and clothing costs by moving to Florida and other Sunbelt states. In fact, in Florida 17.3 percent of the population is 65 or over—the highest such percentage in the nation.[9]

In addition to climate and terrain, the *Places Rated Almanac* considers such factors as availability of housing, health care, transportation, and educational and recreational facilities; crime; and economic factors. Table 20-1 shows the 12 best metropolitan areas for retirees. Interestingly, none are in Sunbelt states. According to the *Places Rated Almanac,* this is because of extreme summer temperatures, better housing buys in non-boom areas, high energy costs in the Sunbelt, and rising crime rates in prime retirement areas.[10] A U.S. Department of Labor survey of 25 metropolitan areas concluded that the highest cost of living for retired couples was in Anchorage, Boston, Honolulu, New York, and Seattle. By contrast, the bottom five were Atlanta, Dallas, San Diego, Denver, and Houston.[11]

"She drives me crazy. Since she retired she wanders around the house with nothing to do."

Experts Advise Retirees to Remain Active.
Source: From the *Wall Street Journal*—Permission, Cartoon Features Syndicate.

Lifestyle is another important factor in choosing a place to live during retirement. Most retirement experts recommend that, if at all possible, a person should remain busy and involved in some form of part-time work or community activity. Retirement counselor Jack Wright, whose insight into retirement adjustment comes from his own personal experience, advises: "To achieve peace of mind, stay in circulation. Get out of your own limited environment and see what is going on elsewhere. Keep alert to new things, and try them. Talk to people and listen to people. Be a friend and you will have friends to join you in the things you like to do."[12]

Often, a retiree must decide whether to stay close to family and friends or move to an area with better climate and lower taxes. This decision should be made well in advance of retirement so as to avoid the pitfalls of a hasty decision.

Deciding When to Retire. Timing one's retirement is another issue to be considered. Federal laws now prohibit the use of age as a factor in forcing retirement earlier than age 70. Many people continue working past the traditional retirement age of 65, particularly during periods of economic uncertainty.

Whether one chooses to postpone retirement or combine it with some form of continuing employment depends on the person's health, job skills, employment opportunities in the area, and similar factors. Whatever the decision, it should make one's later years more emotionally and financially rewarding.

CALCULATING RETIREMENT NEEDS

Where and when an individual retires is also a function of the amount of his or her retirement income. Here are some stark realities to consider in retirement planning:

- Most pensions are fixed—that is, the amount received in the eighteenth year of retirement is the same as that received in the first. Unfortunately, as the years pass, the purchasing power of this fixed amount grows smaller.
- Even though Social Security payments are tied to the rate of inflation through cost-of-living increases, maximum benefits bring a person only to the poverty level.
- Retirement at age 65 is probably more of a dream than a reality for most workers. Three out of four workers who responded to a survey sponsored by the American Council of Life Insurance stated that they could not save enough money for retirement. Forty-four percent were convinced that they would not be able to afford to retire when they reached 65.[13]

The best way to deal with these restraints on successful retirement is to begin planning well in advance of one's retirement date. Approach it in a systematic way, analyzing your projected income and expenses. Table 20-2 presents a useful worksheet for such an analysis.

In filling out the worksheet in Table 20-2, an important consideration is how your expenses will change with retirement. Will you need the same income as before retirement? Actuaries (professional people who do statistical work related to pensions and the like) estimate that a retired person will need only a portion of his or her preretirement earnings. As Table 20-3 indicates, this amount ranges from 44 to 69 percent, depending on the preretirement income level. For example, a retiree would need only $23,656 to match a preretirement income of $40,000.

SOURCES OF RETIREMENT INCOME

In planning for retirement, you need to consider a variety of potential sources of retirement income. As Chapter 19 described, Social Security is a government safety net that most retirees could not do without. But even with this protection, retirees may require additional income to retain their standard of living. Private pension plans, individual retirement accounts (IRAs), and Keogh plans can be important elements in providing for your retirement years. In addition, retirees may gain income from part-time employment, savings and investments, or the sale of a home. Annuities, another option, will be discussed in the next section.

HOW MUCH WILL SOCIAL SECURITY REPLACE?

Many middle-income retirees find that Social Security replaces a good portion of the money they took home during their last year of work. Social Security accounts for 33.2 percent of the income of families headed by someone 65 or older.[14] While Social Security provides a significant portion of what retirees

Table 20-2
WORKSHEET FOR PROJECTING RETIREMENT CASH FLOW

	Yourself	Spouse	Combined
Social Security	$	$	$
Pension plan			
Profit sharing			
IRA/Keogh			
Private annuity			
Savings bank interest			
Bond interest			
Stock dividends			
Rental income			
Other			
Total estimated annual income			$

Less:
EXPENSES
- Food $ _____
- Transportation _____
- Clothing _____
- Home maintenance & improvement _____
- Utilities _____
- Mortgage interest _____
- Real estate taxes _____
- Contributions _____
- Entertainment _____
- Interest expense _____
- Medical (unreimbursed) _____
- Insurance premiums _____
- Personal _____
- Other _____
- Total expenses $ _____

Debt Amortization
- Bank debt $ _____
- Mortgage principal _____
- Installment debt _____
- Other _____
- Total debt amortization $ _____

Taxes
- Federal income $ _____
- State and city income _____
- Total taxes _____

Total disbursement $ _____

NET CASH FLOW
(Income minus disbursements) $ _____

Source: Copyrighted by the Research Institute of America and reprinted with permission.

Table 20-3
WHAT YOU'LL NEED WHEN YOU RETIRE

The table below shows how much income you should plan for after retirement to maintain your standard of living. The column labeled Retirement Standard is the sum, after subtracting taxes, of work-related expenses, savings and investments, that someone in your income bracket typically spends each year. As the figures make clear, you can attain the same standard of living in retirement from a much smaller income—assuming, however, that it keeps pace with inflation.

Pre-Retirement Income	Pre-Retirement Taxes	Work-Related Expenses	Savings & Investment	Retirement Standard	Post-Retirement Taxes	Post-Retirement Income
$ 20,000	$ 3,861	$ 968	$ 1,291	$13,880	$ 0	$13,880
40,000	11,151	1,731	3,462	23,656	479	24,135
60,000	18,891	2,467	6,577	32,065	2,342	34,407
80,000	27,771	3,134	10,446	38,649	5,854	44,503
100,000	37,073	3,776	15,102	44,049	11,297	55,346

Source: Gus Hedberg, "Planning for Your Post-Job Job," Money, December 1983, p. 162. Reprinted by permission.

need, the percentages may be changing as a result of recent tax legislation. As of 1984, half of the Social Security benefits of single retirees with incomes over $25,000 are taxable. The figure for married persons is $32,000.

Some time before one retires it is important to calculate exactly how large your monthly Social Security check will be. As noted in Chapter 19, this depends on a number of factors, including retirement age and the number of work credits accumulated. If you have doubts about what your Social Security income will be, check with your local Social Security office for the exact amount.

PRIVATE PENSION PLANS

Approximately 45 million Americans are protected through their employers by private pension plans, which are intended to replace a part of the worker's preretirement income.[15] A typical private pension plan may replace 16 percent of a preretirement salary if a person worked for the firm for 20 years, 31 percent after 25 years, and 50 percent after 30 years.

Consider someone 40 years old, with 5 years of tenure at a company, earning $35,000 a year and receiving an 8-percent annual raise. At the age of 55, after 20 years of service, this individual would have a preretirement salary of $102,800 and a pension of $16,900 a year. If the employee waited 5 more years and retired at age 60, his or her annual income would be $151,000 with a retirement pension of $47,000. After 30 years, at age 65, the person would be earning $222,000, and Social Security and pension benefits would equal $110,300 a year. (Social Security and pension benefits are integrated with one another to produce a retirement income equal to a given percentage of your preretirement working salary.) Although this pension may sound huge, inflation will whittle down its buying power just as significantly as it escalated the base pension figure. Overall, private and government pension plans provide 13.3 percent of the income of families headed by someone 65 or older.[16]

Where the Money Comes From. Many pension plans are fully funded by employers. Other plans require employee contributions that are matched, at least in part, by the employer. If your plan falls into the latter category, you should begin making contributions as soon as possible. Some plans exclude part-time workers and workers with less than a specified period of seniority.

Most companies, however, require that employees put in five or ten years of service before they become "vested." To be vested means that your pension benefits are guaranteed at retirement and that if you leave the job, the company must pay the vested pension rights in a lump sum. This money can then be rolled over into an individual, tax-sheltered pension plan to continue deferring taxes. Employees who leave the firm before vesting will receive their own contributions back (but not those of the company) plus interest. Or a partially vested employee may take a reduced amount on a monthly basis at age 65.

Employee Retirement Income Security Act (ERISA): legislation passed in 1974 that provides several important retirement guarantees for workers with private pension plans.

Pension Benefit Guaranty Corporation (PBGC): a provision of ERISA that guarantees pension payment if the employer goes bankrupt.

How ERISA Protects You. The *Employee Retirement Income Security Act—ERISA*—was passed by Congress in 1974 to reform the nation's private pension system. ERISA gives workers some basic protections:

1. *Vesting*: most pensions are now guaranteed after five to ten years of employment.

2. *Guarantees against bankruptcy*: the *Pension Benefit Guaranty Corporation*, or *PBGC*, guarantees pension payment if the employer goes bankrupt, although it may limit the guarantee.

3. *Limitation of penalties because of a break in service*: ERISA limits the loss of pension credits if the employee takes time off from the job. (Before 1974, all pension credits could be lost.)

4. *A plain-language, written explanation of employee pension rights.*

5. *A statement upon retirement of how much the employee will receive.*

6. *An annual statement of how the pension money is invested.*

7. *The right to go to court if the employee believes he or she was fired or discriminated against in order to deprive him or her of a pension.*

Key Questions to Ask. First of all, employees should find out whether they are covered by a private pension plan. Approximately 50 percent of all workers are not so covered. Other important questions to ask are:

- What are the company's vesting requirements?
- What benefits have been credited to your pension account as of now? (These benefits depend on your meeting vesting requirements.)
- What is the minimum age for a full pension? What is the age for early retirement?
- Are pension rights protected during leaves of absence, layoffs, and disability?
- What death benefits are paid to a spouse?
- Where are the pension funds invested, and how are individual benefits determined?[17]

A major problem is that half of the employees who *are* covered will never be vested. As they jump from company to company, they continually lose their pension rights. A study done by Heidrick and Struggles, the country's largest executive search firm, showed that among employees in the 50 to 54 age group who had reached the vice-presidential level or above, most had already worked for three different employers, making a job change about once every ten years. Job longevity was even lower for managers in the 40 to 44 age group, who had jumped once every seven years—often, three years short of being vested. The problem of lost pension rights is especially acute among women employees who interrupt their careers to have children.[18] "Private pensions are a lot like horse races," comments Professor Merton Bernstein of the Washington University Law School. "The winnings of a few are based on the losses of the many."[19]

The Underfunding Controversy.[20] A pension fund whose obligations significantly exceed its assets is termed an *underfunded pension plan*. Overall, firms put about 8 percent of payroll costs into their retirement programs. Underfunding often occurs when the employer is unable to properly fund its *past-service liability* (the years of employee service prior to the beginning of the plan), and it is particularly crucial when companies have a cash-flow problem during recessionary periods. Many retirement programs for government employees are also underfunded.

The government's Pension Benefit Guaranty Corporation agrees to support corporate pension funds if the firms fail. But it often lacks sufficient funds to back its pledge. One possible solution to this national dilemma is simply to prohibit the underfunding of pension funds. Arguments in favor of banning the practice of underfunding include the following: (1) Employees would be assured that their retirement funds were secure; (2) another element of fairness would be introduced into the private pension system; (3) there would no longer be a need for a federal guarantee; and (4) employers would be forced to be more responsible in planning and promoting their retirement programs. A variety of arguments can also be made against such legislation. These include the following: (1) Many established companies would be unable to start

underfunded pension plan: a situation in which a pension fund's obligations significantly exceed its assets.

past-service liability: the number of years of employee service prior to the beginning of a pension plan.

pension funds because they could not fund past-service liabilities; (2) the immediate funding of all liabilities would cut retirement benefits; and (3) firms would not be allowed to exercise adequate financial flexibility in economically depressed times.

INDIVIDUAL RETIREMENT ACCOUNTS[21]

Many people now elect to supplement their employer's retirement program with an individual retirement account (IRA). These accounts were once used primarily by employees working in firms without pension plans, but the Economic Recovery Tax Act of 1981 liberalized their availability. Beginning in

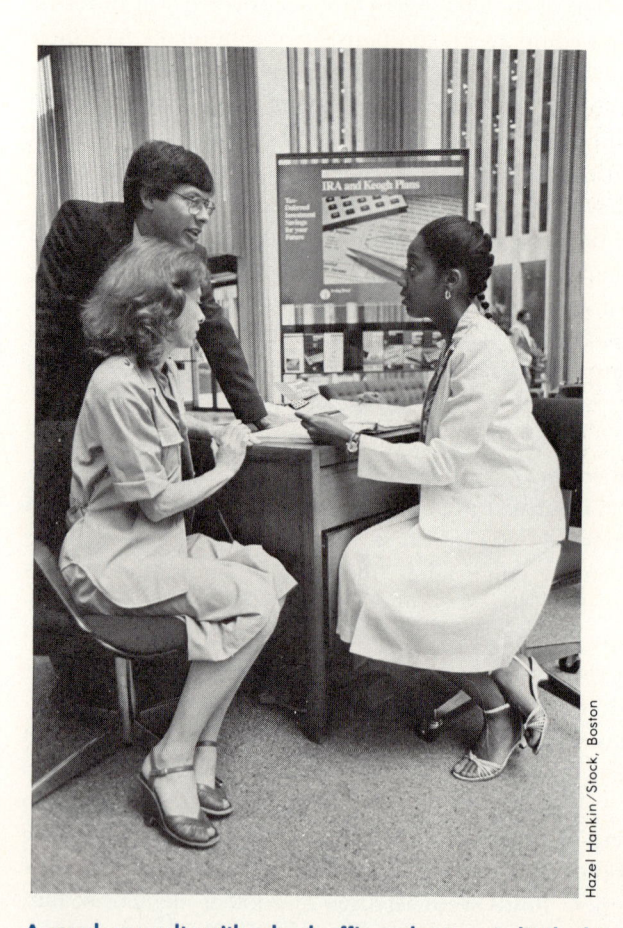

A couple consults with a bank officer about an Individual Retirement Account (IRA). As of 1982, any employee can open an IRA and can deposit up to $2,000 annually or 100 percent of his or her income, whichever is less, into such an account. Funds placed in an IRA are not taxed until they are withdrawn.

1982, all employees could set up an IRA regardless of whether they participated in a company's retirement program.

The *IRA* — or *individual retirement account* — is a tax-deferred account designed to provide supplemental retirement funds. Individuals (under 70½) with earned income from wages or professional fees can put up to $2,000 a year or 100 percent of their earned wages, whichever is less, into an IRA. A worker with a nonworking spouse can contribute up to $2,250; when both husband and wife work, a $4,000 annual contribution is allowed. Unearned income from such sources as interest, dividends, and gifts cannot be used to calculate one's IRA contribution. Contributions to an IRA are deductible from current income. Thus, an IRA is a tax shelter that defers taxes on the contributions (and the earnings of these contributions) until the funds are withdrawn. If you are in the 40-percent tax bracket, your $2,000 annual contribution actually costs only $1,200.

According to one survey, over $40 billion is invested annually in IRA accounts; some 25 million households participate in an IRA; and 53 percent of IRA investments come from earnings and the remainder from savings. The study also characterized the typical IRA investor as 48 years of age with a household income of $30,000. Fifty-seven percent of the IRA investors are male.[22]

individual retirement account (IRA): a tax-deferred account designed to provide supplemental retirement funds.

How Your Money Grows. Because the money put aside in an IRA and the compounded interest it earns over the years are not taxed until they are withdrawn, the potential payoffs can be substantial. If a working couple puts $4,000 a year away for 30 years at 12 percent interest, they will have over $1,300,000 upon retirement (see Figure 20-1).

Figure 20-1
THE EFFECT OF COMPOUND INTEREST ON AN IRA

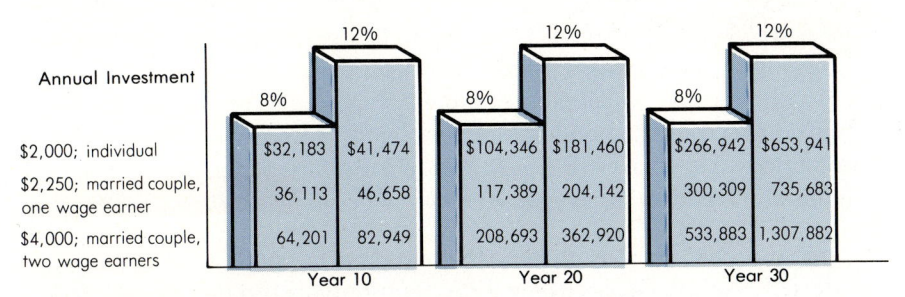

Annual Investment	Year 10 8%	Year 10 12%	Year 20 8%	Year 20 12%	Year 30 8%	Year 30 12%
$2,000; individual	$32,183	$41,474	$104,346	$181,460	$266,942	$653,941
$2,250; married couple, one wage earner	36,113	46,658	117,389	204,142	300,309	735,683
$4,000; married couple, two wage earners	64,201	82,949	208,693	362,920	533,883	1,307,882

These projections assume a constant 12% and 8% annual interest rate, compounded daily to yield 12.94% and 8.45%, respectively, each year over the term of the investment.

Source: Adapted from Thomas L. Friedman, "Where to Open a Retirement Account," *New York Times,* December 6, 1981, p. F15.

Banks and other institutions offering IRAs are quick to point out in their advertisements the mathematics of compound interest. Financial writer Jane Bryant Quinn agrees that an IRA could make young couples millionaires in the future, but she also notes that "a dozen apples that year will cost you $120."[23]

Withdrawals. Withdrawals from an IRA cannot begin before the year in which a person turns 59½, unless he or she dies or becomes disabled, but they must start by the year the person turns 70½. As the retiree takes the money out of the IRA, it is taxed as ordinary income even if it otherwise would qualify for the lower capital gains rate. Of course, most people's tax rates when they retire are lower than when they made the actual contribution. A 10-percent penalty is charged on money withdrawn before age 59½.

IRA Investment Opportunities. IRAs must be deposited with a trustee who meets government standards. A wide range of opportunities exist, each with its own set of advantages, disadvantages, and costs. Among the primary IRA investment opportunities, outlined in Table 20-4, are:

1. *Commercial and savings banks*: Various kinds of accounts are available, including long- and short-term accounts, ones with fixed or adjustable rates, and more. New York's Citibank, for example, gives IRA depositors the choice of an 18- or 30-month fixed-rate account, a daily passbook account, or a $10,000 six-month certificate of deposit. The bank also gives depositors the option of having Citibank act as the custodian for a portfolio of stocks and bonds. The main advantage of opening an account in a commercial or savings bank is that all funds not invested in stocks and bonds are federally insured.
2. *Insurance companies*: Many offer IRA investment opportunities, such as annuities (discussed later in this chapter) and mutual funds.
3. *Mutual funds*: Firms like Oppenheimer Management Corporation and Dreyfus Service Corporation offer money-market, stock, and bond accounts.
4. *Brokerage houses*: Firms like Merrill Lynch give depositors the option of investing in money-market funds, stocks, bonds, real estate, and oil and gas partnerships. As market conditions change, the funds can be moved from one account to another without penalty. However, brokerage-house accounts are similar to IRA accounts in insurance companies and mutual funds and bank accounts invested in securities in that they are not insured.

For many people, there is another IRA investment option. The company in which they work will collect their IRA contributions through payroll deductions and then invest them in a plan that meets government standards. This is a convenient way to accumulate tax savings and additional retirement funds. Be sure, however, to examine the investment results of the company's plan

RETIREMENT, WILLS, AND ESTATE PLANNING

Table 20-4
IRA INVESTMENT OPPORTUNITIES

	Investment Choices	Fees	Early Withdrawal Penalties
Banks, Thrifts & Credit Unions	Certificates of Deposit & Savings Accounts	Usually none to open Up to $25.00 Annual Maintenance	Minimum six months interest on CD's, none on Savings
Insurance Companies	Fixed Premium Annuities .... Variable Premium Annuities	Percentage of Investment to Open .... No Sales Charge Up to $30.00 Annual Maintenance	Usually None .... Percentage of Investment
Mutual Funds	Money Market Stocks, Bonds, Stocks and Options	$5.00 to Open .... $10.00 a Year Some Sales Charges	NONE
Stockbrokers	Stocks, Bonds, Real Estate, Oil and Gas, Equipment Leasing	Up to $30.00 to Open $25.00 to $50.00 Annual Maintenance	NONE

Source: Bruce Kitts, "A Variety of Investments with Variety of Risk, Return," *Journal-American* (Bellevue, Wash.), December 28, 1981, p. C1.

carefully before deciding to invest in it. Company plans are only one option, and you may be able to do better on your own.

THE KEOGH PLAN

The *Keogh plan* enables self-employed people to set up pension plans. The legislation, passed in 1962, is named after its sponsor, the former New York Representative Eugene J. Keogh. It can be used by anyone with a source of outside income. This income must come from work-related services, not investments. You can belong to a corporate pension plan and still be eligible for a Keogh if you work for yourself part-time. Keogh participants are also allowed to have IRA accounts.

How the Plan Works. Those people qualified for a Keogh can set aside 20 percent of their income, up to a maximum contribution of $30,000 as of January 1, 1984. The contribution is deducted from taxable current income. A

Keogh plan: a retirement program set up by self-employed people.

person in the 50-percent tax bracket can end up with up to a $15,000 tax savings. Like an IRA, a Keogh contribution and the amount it earns are untaxed until they are withdrawn some time between the ages of 59½ and 70½. (Withdrawals earlier than 59½ are subject to a 10-percent penalty.) Gradual withdrawals are taxed at ordinary rates. A lump-sum distribution may qualify for a special ten-year averaging formula that will cut the effective tax rate. Keogh funds can be invested in a number of areas: certificates of deposit, stocks, bonds, mutual funds, and so on. Most of the institutions involved with IRA accounts also offer investment vehicles for Keogh plans.

Defined Benefit Plan. A *defined benefit plan* is an actuarially determined type of Keogh plan based on the size of the retirement benefit one seeks rather than on a percentage of earnings. The defined benefit contribution can be any percentage of earned income to a ceiling of $90,000. As of 1986, the ceilings for both regular and defined benefit Keogh plans are adjusted by the cost-of-living increase given recipients.[24]

defined benefit plan: a type of Keogh plan based on the size of the retirement benefit one seeks, rather than a percentage of earnings.

401(K) Plans. Named after a tax law section, *401(k) plans* permit tax-deferred salary reductions. These plans can substitute for an IRA or may be set up in addition to an IRA. You are taxed when you withdraw the money, but the tax is divided over a 10-year period. This is a significant advantage over IRAs which do not receive such favorable tax treatment. Financial hardship or leaving the employer are the only allowable reasons for withdrawing 401(k) funds prior to age 59½.[25]

401(k) plans: named after a tax law section, they permit tax-deferred salary reductions up to 10 percent of earnings.

PART-TIME EMPLOYMENT

Many retired people continue to work on a part-time basis. For some, part-time work provides the activity and stimulation they need to remain happy; after working all their adult lives, not working may become a burden rather than a relief. In addition, many retired people, faced with today's economic realities, have a hard time making ends meet on their retirement income alone. They must work to pay their bills. Unfortunately, the decision to take part-time work may affect the amount of Social Security income they receive.

As Chapter 19 indicated, retirees are subject to a "retirement test," which sets an income ceiling. In 1984 people aged 65 to 70 could earn $6,960 without having their benefits reduced. Those under 65 had to stay within a $5,160 income ceiling. Those over age 70 continued to receive Social Security benefits no matter how much money they earned. In any year that earnings exceed the income ceiling, the Social Security Administration will deduct $1 from the benefit amount for every $2 earned. This formula enables people to continue working while receiving some Social Security payments. It should be noted that unearned income—for instance, interest on savings—is not counted in the retirement test.

RETIREMENT, WILLS, AND ESTATE PLANNING

SAVINGS AND INVESTMENTS

Savings and other assets are the source of 17.5 percent of the income of families headed by someone 65 or older.[26] Savings and investments provide a significant portion of retirement income, so they deserve appropriate attention in personal financial planning.

Everyone should establish savings and investment goals early in their working life. One's goals should account for the ravages of inflation and should be reviewed periodically. The object should be to establish a fund sufficiently large for you not to outlive the withdrawals made during retirement. Many senior adults fear that they will "outlive their money," and this fear has a negative impact on what should be some of the most rewarding years of their lives.

The retiree should calculate exactly how long his or her savings will last given specified withdrawal and earnings rates. If, for instance, a 65-year-old retired man has all of his money in a 5.25-percent passbook account and withdraws 10 percent of it annually, he can expect to run out of money during his retirement years. By moving the money to some other higher-earning instrument, he will have adequate funds for his remaining years.

SELLING A PRIMARY RESIDENCE

A major source of income for many retired people is the tax-exempt money they get from the sale of their home. Americans can exclude as much as $125,000 of capital gains from taxes when they sell their principal residence. In order to take advantage of this exemption, one must be at least 55 years old and have lived in the house at least three out of the five years before the sale. A 65-year-old is also eligible if he or she lived in the house for five of the last eight years. If a person dies before taking advantage of the exclusion, the estate receives no benefit. This is a one-time exclusion, but it is cumulative in that the capital gains from several primary residences can be included.[27] Nevertheless, retirees should give considerable thought to selling their homes. They need to be sure that they can obtain alternative housing at an affordable price.

ANNUITIES

An *annuity* is a financial instrument that is issued by an insurance company and guarantees a lifetime income. The primary use of annuities is to provide income to people during their retirement years, usually in the form of a monthly check.[28]

annuity: a financial instrument issued by an insurance company that guarantees a lifetime income.

PAYMENT OPTIONS

There are three basic payment options for annuities:

1. A *straight life annuity* pays benefits until death. No payments are due the person's estate. The advantage of this type of annuity over the other options

straight life annuity: an annuity that pays benefits until death.

is that the recipient will get larger payments. Some people will receive considerably more than they paid in, although those who die early will collect less than their initial payment.

2. An *annuity with period certain* guarantees an annuity income for a specified period of time, such as 5, 10, or 20 years. People living beyond this time period will still be paid. If the person dies early, the benefits will be paid to the estate for the remainder of the guarantee period.

3. A *refund annuity* pays regular annuity installments during the person's lifetime and refunds any balance in the annuity fund to a beneficiary if the person dies.

annuity with period certain: an annuity that guarantees income for a specified period of time.

refund annuity: an annuity that pays regular installments during the person's lifetime and refunds any balance to a beneficiary upon death.

TYPES OF ANNUITIES

Whatever the payment option, annuities come in two basic forms: immediate payment life annuities and deferred annuities.

Immediate-Payment Life Annuities. As the name suggests, an *immediate-payment life annuity* begins paying benefits right away. These annuities are generally purchased by people at retirement age who want to be sure that they receive a specified amount of money for the rest of their lives. The primary advantage of this type of annuity is the stability that it provides.

immediate-payment life annuity: an annuity that begins payment immediately; it is usually purchased by a retiree.

Deferred Annuities. In a *deferred annuity,* the purchaser does not receive the first annuity payment until some predetermined time in the future—say, 20 years from now, when the person retires. Deferred annuities may be purchased in two ways: by paying regular annual premiums or by paying a single large premium. With the *annual-premium deferred annuity,* you are able to accumulate annuity funds over the years. The annual premiums are invested until your annuity installments begin. The *single-premium deferred annuity,* on the other hand, is designed for people who have a large sum of money on hand and want to earmark it for use some time in the future.

deferred annuity: an annuity that does not begin payment until some time in the future.

One of the major advantages of both types of deferred annuities is that the interest earned on the money is not taxed until it is withdrawn. There are other advantages as well. Since the purchaser already paid the taxes on the funds deposited into the annuity, the money can be withdrawn at any time and no more taxes are due. In addition, annuities deposited with an established insurance company are extremely secure, and the funds are nearly as liquid as they would be if they were deposited in a money-market fund or savings account.

FIXED-RATE AND VARIABLE-RATE DEFERRED ANNUITIES

In recent years the growing competition for investor funds has forced insurance companies to guarantee fixed-rate yields that are close to those offered by

A Landmark Decision:
Norris vs. Arizona Governing Committee

When Nathalie Norris, an Arizona state employee, discovered that her contribution to a state-sponsored annuity program with Lincoln National Life Insurance Company provided $34 less a month than it did for a male counterpart, she filed a class-action suit. Norris argued that the Civil Rights Act of 1964 prohibited discrimination based on sex, race, religion, or ethnic origin. The insurer argued that the difference stemmed from actuarial calculations based on the fact that a man's life expectancy was seven years below that of a woman. In 1983 the U.S. Supreme Court upheld Norris's position but did not make the ruling retroactive. Some 16 million people with employer-sponsored annuities were affected.

Source: Adapted from "Turning the Sexual Tables," *Time*, July 18, 1983, p. 34.

---

money-market funds. In 1984, for example, most insurance companies offered fixed rates of 10.5 percent guaranteed for two years. After the initial guaranteed interest period, many fixed-rate annuity plans also guarantee a minimum interest rate for an intermediate period of, say, two to ten years. After that period is over, most fixed-rate annuities protect one's investment by offering a minimum interest-rate guarantee that lasts for the life of the annuity. This guarantee is usually 5 percent or less. In addition, if interest rates fall below a certain point, the person can withdraw the money without a withdrawal charge.

Although deferred annuities tied to fixed-dollar investments offer a guaranteed income that will meet an individual's retirement needs during economically stable times, inflation can deteriorate the purchasing power of a fixed-dollar annuity investment. The holder may be left with a steadily declining standard of living. To deal with this problem, insurance companies have developed the variable-rate annuity, which guarantees that it will pay benefits during the person's lifetime but does not guarantee how much each payment will be. The amount received fluctuates according to the market value of the investments, which are mainly in common stocks but may also be in money-market funds and bond funds. Variable-rate annuities provide a choice of funds, and the investor can switch from fund to fund whenever he or she wishes. Nevertheless, the fluctuation in monthly income is unacceptable to some retirees.

CHOOSING AN ANNUITY

Annuities vary as much in price and quality as any consumer purchase. So, in addition to deciding on the type of annuity and payment option most suited to one's needs, here are three factors to consider in buying an annuity:

1. *Sales commission*: Most annuities charge a *load* fee when the person first opens the account. This charge varies from company to company. No-load

(no-commission) annuities are available, but they may charge a hefty withdrawal fee.

2. *Withdrawal penalties*: If the investor takes all or part of the money out of the annuity, a withdrawal penalty may be charged. In many cases, withdrawal fees decline over the earlier years of the annuity and disappear completely after some point. But some companies continue to penalize withdrawals throughout the life of the contract. There are also companies with no withdrawal penalties.

3. *Rates and annual charges.* The rates offered and the annual charges vary significantly. Comparison shopping is required to get the best buy.

ESTATE PLANNING

A person's *estate* is essentially his or her net worth at death. Estate planning involves the creation and conservation of wealth as well as decisions on how the property will be divided upon death. It attempts to maximize the inheritance through tax reduction and other steps that are the legal right of all Americans.

The starting point in estate planning is to calculate what one has. Chapter 3 explained how to determine your net worth. It is important that these personal financial statements be updated periodically.

estate: a person's net worth at death.

THE IMPORTANCE OF A WILL

Henry Bernier of Minneapolis knows the value of a will. A handyman at the Continental Hotel, Bernier took care of its 92-year-old owner when he was ill. When the owner passed away, his will left Bernier the hotel and other property worth $1.3 million.[29]

A *will* is a legal document that specifies how a person wants his or her property distributed after death. Creating a will is a simple, inexpensive process — the vast majority of wills range in price from $35 to $350 — yet seven out of ten American adults die without one.[30] The existence of a valid will is essential to effective estate planning.

will: a legal document that specifies how a person wants his or her property distributed upon death.

The best way to describe the importance of a will is to look at what happens if a person dies without one — a situation that the law calls *intestate*. The case of Howard Hughes is a classic example. With an estate estimated as high as $2 billion, the reclusive Howard Hughes died in 1976 while being rushed to Houston from Acapulco for emergency medical treatment. He was declared "intestate" — he had left no will. There were no readily recognized wives (Hughes was twice divorced), children, brothers, or sisters. So the estate had to go to distant relatives. But here the case became complex. There were about 800 claimants.

intestate: a situation when someone dies without a will.

In 1978 some 24 of the relatives made an agreement to divide the estate

Although it is simple and inexpensive to prepare a will, most Americans die without one. As a result, their heirs may be left with fewer assets than careful estate planning would have provided for.

among themselves if the court rejected the claims of the others. One of the debates was whether a woman who died in the 1940s was the daughter of Hughes's uncle Rupert, or whether Rupert's child actually died as an infant; alternatively, the woman may have been the illegitimate daughter of the wife Rupert divorced for adultery in 1904. Other rejected claims included those by two women who asserted they had married Hughes and a man who said Hughes adopted him in 1953. The last claim to be resolved was that of the actress Terry Moore, who claimed Hughes married her aboard a ship in 1949. Despite the fact that she had since married three times (all those marriages ending in divorce) and Hughes had also been married after 1949, Moore claimed that she and Hughes were never divorced. Her suit was before the Nevada Supreme Court when the 24 heirs agreed to a sizable settlement. While the heirs were now in line for estate distributions, the federal government stood to get a 77-percent tax settlement. There seems little doubt that the big winner was an uncle named Sam.[31]

The case of Howard Hughes illustrates the confusion that arises when someone dies intestate, particularly a person of considerable wealth. An attorney's proverb puts it this way: "Where there's a will there are relatives, and where there's no will there are even more relatives."[32]

Minor-age children present another problem. Without a specific direction provided in a will, the court will pick a guardian for the children. This choice may or may not have been the intention of the deceased. Dying intestate also means that the settlement of the estate will probably be delayed and costly.

Some people avoid preparing a will because they fear that their privacy will be invaded. But probably the primary reason is an unwillingness to recognize one's own mortality. A more reasoned approach is to treat one's will as just another aspect of personal financial planning.

THE PROBATE SYSTEM

probate: *a legal process by which a court carries out the dictates of one's will.*

As a legal document, a will must meet the standards and rules of the court system. Upon death, wills pass through a legal process called *probate,* which is designed to ensure that a person's final wishes are carried out.[33] Probate is the process of submitting the will to the proper court, where it is examined and declared valid. The deceased's assets are listed and their value determined. Real property is appraised; the value of stocks and bonds assessed; and so on. In many cases, the will's executor appoints a lawyer to handle the probate process. It can be a lengthy and expensive process indeed.

For their legal and administrative work, lawyers, appraisers, and others generally receive 6 to 10 percent of the estate's total value, but fees are sometimes higher. In one case, legal fees alone consumed $8,300 of a Chicago man's $12,000 estate, and the lawyer handling the $38,000 estate of a Cincinnati schoolteacher received $8,625.[34]

Because of these problems, many people try to avoid the probate process. They arrange their estate so that property is not left by will. They resort to joint ownership of property, insurance policies, bonds and various other assets paid directly to their beneficiaries, trusts whose proceeds are distributed immediately, and other legal devices that circumvent the legal system.[35]

Uniform Probate Code: *a standard code concerning probate that has been adopted by many states.*

The Uniform Probate Code.   Many states have adopted all or parts of the *Uniform Probate Code.* The code's main goals are to give family members, rather than the courts, the main responsibility for settling the estate, to reduce estate settlement costs, and to ensure that surviving spouses will inherit all or most of an estate when there is no will.

TYPES OF WILLS

Wills take several forms. They may be either individual or joint, handwritten (in some states) or formally drawn by a lawyer, and added to or changed slightly in a codicil.

individual will: *a will involving the estate of just one individual.*

An *individual will* involves the estate of one individual. Financial experts recommend that every adult have a will of his or her own. Conrad Teitell, who has written extensively on wills and estates, cites the example of a married

Silent Cal's Will—Brief as Usual

President Calvin Coolidge was a man of few words. His will reflects his lifelong passion for expressing himself in the fewest possible words. In its entirety Coolidge's will was only 18 words: "I leave my entire estate to my wife, Grace, and request that she be appointed executrix without bond."

Source: "What You Should Know about Wills," *Consumer Reports*, July 1981, p. 434.

---

woman who saw no need to have her own will since all the family's property was in her husband's name. The woman did not realize that if her husband died before her and left all his property to her, the family estate would be dispersed according to the state's intestacy laws when she died. Thus, no matter how many plans the husband and wife made for their children, grandchildren, other relatives and friends, the state would take over the property distribution when the wife died.[36]

A different alternative is chosen by many husbands and wives. They draw up a *joint will*, which leaves the bulk or all of the estate to one spouse if the other should die first or to beneficiaries if they should die together.

Not everyone uses a lawyer to prepare a will. A *holographic will* is a handwritten will drawn without the advice of an attorney. Such wills are recognized in some states if certain conditions are met. All but a few of those states require that your handwritten will be witnessed, and nearly half the states do not recognize handwritten wills at all.

In order to avoid any legal pitfalls, it is a good idea to have a *formally drawn will*—one prepared by an attorney. This is especially important if the person has a very large or complicated estate, if a dependent will need lifetime care, or if a child or relative is to be disinherited. Lawyers understand the complexity of legal regulations regarding wills and use precise legal phrases to state one's last wishes.

Minor changes can be made in a will by a written amendment known as a *codicil*. The codicil must be treated in the same formal way as the will itself. Its signature and dating must be witnessed, and the witnesses must sign the document.

Whatever their form, most wills contain certain standard ingredients to cover legal requirements, debt payments (including taxes and funeral expenses), property dispersement, trusts (if any), and the naming of an executor and guardians (if necessary). Here are some important points to remember:

1. *Identification:* The person's name, address, and intention to write a last will and testament and to revoke any existing wills or codicils are stated in the will's first paragraph. The person writing the will is referred to as the *testator*.

---

joint will: a will used by couples whereby the estate of each spouse goes to the other, or to beneficiaries if they die together.

holographic will: a handwritten will drawn without the advice of an attorney.

formally drawn will: a will prepared by an attorney.

codicil: a written amendment to a will.

testator: a person making a will.

2. *Debt payment*: Instructions are then given to pay any outstanding debts, taxes, funeral expenses, and estate administration costs. These expenses must be paid before any property is distributed.

3. *Property distribution*: A will can make a specific legacy to a relative or friend; that is, it can direct that a particular item of personal property—a gold watch, for example—be given to that person. One can also give a general legacy—$10,000 to a favorite uncle, for example. A general legacy does not indicate a particular fund from which the money must come. The principal heir or heirs receive what is called the residual estate, which is made up of all the money and property that remain after these legacies have been paid.

4. *Trusts*: Any trust set up for your spouse and children is listed, as is the name of the trustee who will administer the assets. (Trusts are discussed later in this chapter.)

5. *Executor*: The name of the chosen executor is included. The *executor* of a will is a person or institution with the responsibility for carrying out the will's provisions. The executor must guide the will through the probate process; itemize the person's property, pay taxes and debts, including funeral expenses; and distribute the property according to the will. The executor submits a final estate statement to the probate court and to the beneficiaries. The selection of an executor is an important estate-planning decision. The executor should be a trusted person or institution experienced in financial matters. In some cases, banks and individuals may be co-executors.

6. *Guardian*: Couples with children should appoint a guardian in case both parents die at once.

7. *Burial arrangements*: Many testators include a paragraph on the kind and cost of the funeral.

8. *Witnesses*: A will should close with the testator's signature and the date. An attestation clause follows. This states that witnesses (their names and addresses are included) observed the signing and dating of the will. All witnesses must affix their signature one time. State laws vary as to the number of witnesses required.[37]

Attorneys and estate planners also recommend that a letter of instruction be prepared. This letter discusses funeral instructions, the location of one's will, the rationale for various aspects of the will, and other information that might aid one's survivors. The letter should then be given to the estate's executor.

Wills and letters of instructions should be reviewed periodically to be sure that they continue to reflect the person's desires. Original copies of wills should be kept in a safe location, identified in the separate letter of instruction. Safe-deposit boxes are not recommended for storage of a will because in many states they are sealed upon one's death and cannot be opened without a court

---

executor: a person or institution charged with the responsibility for carrying out the provisions of a will.

RETIREMENT, WILLS, AND ESTATE PLANNING

authorization. However, individuals may want to keep an extra copy of their will in a safe-deposit box for easy reference.

A SPECIAL CASE: SIMULTANEOUS DEATHS

Sometimes when an auto or air tragedy is the cause of death, it is impossible to tell which spouse died first—and therefore how their wills should be executed. The issue of the order of death has tied up some estates in court for years.

For example, suppose a husband and wife with no children die in a common accident and it is impossible to determine who died first. Had the wife died first, all her assets might pass to her husband and when he died, the family estate would pass to his brother. If, instead, the husband died before his wife, the wife's sister might receive the bulk of the estate.

To avoid this problem, most states use the *Uniform Simultaneous Death Act*, which provides that if spouses die in a common accident and there is no way to prove that one died before the other, their separate property is distributed in accordance with what would have happened had the other spouse survived.

TRUSTS

A *trust* is a legal format by which a trustee holds and disperses funds on behalf of a person's beneficiaries. A trust may go into effect after death or during a person's lifetime. Trusts have three primary purposes: to handle the money of a minor, inexperienced, or otherwise limited person; to limit the way in which the beneficiary can use the money; and to provide tax advantages. There are, however, several different types of trusts.

Testamentary Trusts. A *testamentary trust* is written into someone's will and becomes operational at death. The money left to a beneficiary is given to a trustee, who handles and distributes it according to provisions of the will. Testamentary trusts are often designed to provide for the care of minor children.[38]

Living Trusts. A *living trust* empowers a trustee to handle and distribute assets according to instructions while a person is still living. People put their money in living trust for a variety of reasons, including the fear of becoming disabled or incompetent and unable to handle their money on their own, the desire to avoid probate, and the desire to shift their income to someone in a lower tax bracket and therefore save on taxes.

A living trust may be either revocable or irrevocable. A revocable living trust can be changed at any time during the person's life and as often as he or she wishes without the consent of beneficiaries. An irrevocable living trust ties one to the gift even if one's desires change.

Uniform Simultaneous Death Act: standard legislation that provides that if both of the spouses die in a common accident and there is no way to prove that one died before the other, their separate property is distributed in accordance with what would have happened had the other spouse survived.

trust: a legal format by which a trustee holds and dispenses funds on behalf of a person's beneficiaries.

testamentary trust: a trust included as part of a will that becomes operational upon death.

living trust: a trust set up and operational while a person is still living.

Clifford trusts: a short-term trust frequently used for a child's education.

Clifford Trusts. A special kind of living trust is a *Clifford trust,* which is often used to provide for children's college tuition or the support of elderly, retired parents. While the Clifford trust is in effect (a minimum of 10 years) the income from the principal is taxable to the trust beneficiary. If the beneficiary is a young child or an elderly parent with no income, the tax savings can be tremendous. At the end of the trust period, the trust is dissolved and the property reverts to the person who set it up.

insurance trust: a trust set up to administer the proceeds of a life insurance policy.

Insurance Trusts. It is also possible to set up an *insurance trust* to administer the proceeds of one's life insurance according to one's written wishes. Set up during a person's lifetime, insurance trusts are usually revocable at any time.

Uniform Gifts to Minors Act: a law that authorizes trust accounts for minors.

Uniform Gifts to Minors. A form of the *Uniform Gifts to Minors Act* exists in every state. It gives one the right to give money, stocks, bonds, and sometimes life insurance and annuity contracts to a custodian, who manages the trust account for the child. Since the property is held in the child's name, the child must pay the taxes on any income the asset earns. Since a child is almost certainly in a much lower tax bracket, this gift has significant tax advantages for many parents.

Gifts made under the Uniform Gifts to Minors Act are irrevocable. When the child reaches the age of majority—18 or 21—he or she is legally entitled to receive the entire principal plus any unused income. Before that time, all the income from the account must be used for the child's benefit but not for child support. It can, for example, be used to pay for college tuition but not for food and clothing.

TAX CONSIDERATIONS

Conrad Teitell, a national authority on wills and estates, cites a character in a play by Paddy Chayefsky who epitomized the American obsession with avoiding estate taxes. The character turns to the audience and says something like this: "Did you ever hear about the man who got married in order to take advantage of the joint return, who then got divorced in order to preserve his Liechtenstein tax status, and who finally, on the advice of his accountant, kills himself?"[39]

Teitell's point is clear: Inevitably, avoiding taxes is an important part of estate planning, but it should not guide one's plans. First determine what you want to accomplish with the estate, and then look at the tax considerations.

Economic Recovery Tax Act of 1981: tax legislation that resulted in tax cuts, and significantly affected estate planning by reducing the amount of estate tax that is due upon death.

The Effect of the Economic Recovery Tax Act. The *Economic Recovery Tax Act of 1981* (discussed in Chapter 5) has had a profound effect on estate taxes. The net result is that only the very wealthy need be concerned about federal estate taxes. Prior to 1982, all estates over $175,625 were taxed at rates ranging from a low of 32 percent up to 70 percent for those over $5 million. The Economic Recovery Tax Act increased the tax-free exemption to $400,000 in

1985; $500,000 in 1986; and $600,000 in 1987. Furthermore, a new scale of tax rates went into effect. The new rates range from a minimum of 37 percent up to 50 percent for estates over $2.5 million.[40]

The new law also enables a person to pass an estate on to his or her spouse completely tax-free through the *free marital transfer*. That is, upon a person's death, the spouse can inherit the estate completely tax-free. Free marital transfers can also be made in the form of gifts during one's lifetime. Under this new law, husbands and wives are treated as a single economic unit. Estates are no longer taxed twice—at the death of each spouse. Rather, taxes are collected only when both husband and wife die.

free marital transfer: a provision that allows one to pass an estate on to one's spouse free of estate taxes.

It is estimated that by 1987, this tax legislation will have eliminated taxes on 95 percent of all estates.[41] Good estate planning thus also requires a review of one's life insurance. Policies purchased in order to provide one's heirs with the cash to pay estate taxes may no longer be needed. However, insurance designed to pay off debts is still a good idea.

State Taxes. All states except Nevada levy estate or inheritance taxes. State estate taxes vary substantially and are not deductible from federal estate taxes. Retirees who are considering a geographical move may want to consider the estate taxes levied by their new home states (see Table 20-5).

Gift Taxes and Exclusions. Gift giving—before you die—is another way to minimize taxes. This is especially true since the 1981 changes in the federal tax rates made larger tax-free gifts possible, although many states do levy gift taxes. Annual gifts of $10,000 are now free of federal taxes, and if both spouses make a gift together, $20,000 can be excluded.

In addition to the gift-tax exclusions, people can give their spouses as much money or property as they choose tax-free and take deductions for paying anyone's medical expenses or tuition. The estate-tax exclusion allows you to give away up to the specified amount in lifetime gifts or bequests. If a person gives away $60,000 during his or her lifetime—aside from the $10,000 tax-free gifts permitted annually—a $540,000 estate could be left tax-free at death.[42]

SPECIFYING ONE'S FINAL ARRANGEMENTS

The natural conclusion to estate planning is the individual's own funeral arrangements. Because this involves the inevitability of one's own death, it is the most difficult part of estate planning.

There are basically two concerns. The first involves the service, burial place, and method of handling the remains. Many people have strong feelings about such matters, and these should be spelled out in their letter of instruction. The second factor is cost. Funerals now cost an average $2,000 nationwide. There is a general trend toward less expensive funerals, particularly on the West Coast. For example, in Washington State cremation accounts for 40 percent of all funerals.[43] The funeral industry is also stressing pre-need

Table 20-5
A STATE-BY-STATE COMPARISON OF DEATH TAXES

An *estate tax* is levied on the value of the entire estate normally at one tax rate in a manner similar to the federal estate tax. An *inheritance tax* is levied on the share of each heir at rates that vary with the heir's relationship to the deceased person. A *pickup tax* for estates with a federal tax liability allows the state to collect a tax equal to the full amount of the credit permitted on the federal estate tax return. In some states the names used for estate and inheritance types of tax do not clearly describe them; the pickup tax is also called the credit estate tax.

	Estate Tax	Inheritance Tax	Pickup Tax
Alabama			●
Alaska			●
Arizona			●
Arkansas			●
California			●
Colorado			●
Connecticut		●	●
Delaware		●	●
District of Columbia		●	●
Florida			●
Georgia			●
Hawaii		●	●
Idaho			●
Illinois			●
Indiana		●	●
Iowa		●	●
Kansas		●	●
Kentucky		●	●
Louisiana		●	
Maine*		●	
Maryland		●	●
Massachusetts	●		●
Michigan		●	
Minnesota	●		●
Mississippi	●		●
Missouri			●
Montana		●	●
Nebraska		●	●
Nevada†			
New Hampshire		●	●
New Jersey		●	●
New Mexico			●
New York	●		●
North Carolina		●	●
North Dakota			●
Ohio	●		●
Oklahoma	●		●
Oregon††	●		
Pennsylvania		●	●
Rhode Island	●		●
South Carolina	●		●
South Dakota		●	●
Tennessee		●	●
Texas			●
Utah			●
Vermont			●
Virginia			●
Washington			●
West Virginia		●	●
Wisconsin		●	●
Wyoming			●

*Maine's inheritance tax will be phased out by July 1, 1986, when a pickup tax will begin.
†Nevada has no death taxes as mandated by the state constitution.
††Oregon's estate tax will be phased out by January 1, 1987, leaving only a pickup tax.

Source: From "You're Named in the Will," *Changing Times*, November 1983, p. 60. Reprinted with permission from *Changing Times Magazine*, © Kiplinger Washington Editors, Inc., 1983.

arrangements. Such arrangements should be noted in a letter of instruction. These concerns may result in agonizing decisions, but they are a final, critical aspect of estate planning.

SUMMARY

Increased lifespans have made retirement planning more important than ever in personal finance. Retirement planning involves several decisions: choosing a retirement home, determining when to retire, and calculating retirement needs. The main sources of retirement income include Social Security, private pension plans, individual retirement accounts (IRAs), Keogh plans, part-time employment, savings and investments, and the sale of one's primary residence.

Annuities are financial instruments that are issued by insurance companies and guarantee a lifetime income. They are an important element of retirement planning. Annuities offer three payment options: straight life, which pays benefits until death; annuity with period certain, which guarantees an income for a specified period of time; and a refund annuity, which pays regularly during the person's lifetime and refunds any balance to the estate at death. There are also two major types of annuities: immediate-payment life annuities (lump-sum investments at retirement that pay a lifetime income) and deferred annuities (which pay out at some future time either in a single payment or in a series of annual premiums). Annuities can carry fixed or variable rates.

A person's estate is essentially his or her net worth at death. Everyone should have a will that specifies how the estate should be distributed upon death. A person without a will is referred to as being intestate. Wills are processed through a court system known as probate to assure that a person's last wishes are carried out correctly. Many states have adopted the Uniform Probate Code. There are several categories of wills: individual wills, joint wills (used by couples), holographic (handwritten) wills, and formally drawn wills (prepared by an attorney).

Many people use trusts in their estate planning. Trusts are a legal format by which a trustee holds and dispenses funds on behalf of a person's beneficiaries. A typical use is to handle money for a minor. Testamentary trusts are part of one's will and become operational at death. Living trusts are set up during a person's lifetime. They can be revocable or irrevocable. Clifford trusts are short-term trusts set up for a child's education. Insurance trusts are sometimes used to handle the proceeds of an insurance policy. The Uniform Gifts to Minors Act provides for trust accounts for children.

The Economic Recovery Tax Act of 1981 has had a profound effect on estate taxes. It expanded the tax-free exclusions and changed the rate structure so that most Americans no longer have to pay estate taxes. The gift-tax exemption was also expanded.

REVIEW QUESTIONS

1. Briefly define the following terms:

theoretical limits of biological longevity
Employee Retirement Income Security Act (ERISA)
Pension Benefit Guarantee Corporation (PBGC)
underfunded pension plan
past-service liability
individual retirement account (IRA)
Keogh plan
defined benefit plan
401(k) plans
annuity
straight life annuity
annuity with period certain
refund annuity
immediate-payment life annuity
deferred annuity
estate
will
intestate
probate
Uniform Probate Code
individual will
joint will
holographic will
formally drawn will
codicil
testator
executor

Uniform Simultaneous Death Act
trusts
testamentary trust
living trust
Clifford trusts
insurance trust
Uniform Gifts to Minors Act
Economic Recovery Tax Act of 1981
free marital transfer

2. What types of decisions are involved in retirement planning?
3. What protections were provided by the Employee Retirement Income Security Act of 1974?
4. Discuss the various sources of funds for retirement.
5. Outline the different types of annuities and different payment options.
6. What is the purpose of the probate system?
7. Explain the various types of wills.
8. What should be included in a will?
9. Discuss the various trusts and how they are used in estate planning.
10. How did the Economic Recovery Tax Act of 1981 affect estate planning?

CASES AND EXERCISES

1. Complete the "How Long Will You Live?" questionnaire on page 577. How can this information be used to improve your life expectancy? How can it be used in your personal financial planning?
2. Interview a recent retiree. Find out what this person finds rewarding about retirement and what he or she finds troubling.
3. Where do you plan to retire? Why? Discuss what factors might alter your decision in the future?
4. How much income do you think you will need when you retire? Where do you expect to obtain this income? Discuss.
5. Prepare a report on the IRA plans (individual retirement accounts) that are available in your area. Which one would you select? Why?

ANSWERS TO PERSONAL FINANCE I.Q. TEST

1. Fiction. 2. Fiction. 3. Fact. 4. Fact. 5. Fiction. 6. Fiction. 7. Fact.

HOW CINDY DONOVAN REACHED HER PERSONAL FINANCIAL DECISION

Professor Granger suggested some ideas on how Cindy can help her parents with their retirement budget. "A good working plan," he suggests, "is to figure on using only 50 percent of your parents' total income for actual living expenses, including housing, food, automobile maintenance, and routine medical expenses. Then you might designate 25 percent for travel or other recreational interests and put aside the remaining 25 percent as money to be added to the asset management account each year. This provides a kind of cushion. If, for instance, poor health becomes a problem, you can reduce or eliminate the travel budget. If more money is needed for health care, you can decrease the percentage put into the asset management account and eventually use a portion of the asset management account to supplement Medicare. With luck, the asset management account will have doubled before that's necessary."

"It's really important," Professor Granger stresses, "that your parents start out using only 50 percent of their income for living expenses. They'll need the cushion I mentioned not only for health care but also to combat inflation. What you have to work out, then, is how much income they'll need so that only 50 percent is required for their lifestyle."

Professor Granger gives Cindy a hypothetical example to clarify how to do this. "Let's say," he conjectures, "that your parents need $1,500 a month to live on. The income they need is $3,000 a month. If their pension and Social Security checks come to $2,400 a month, they should be planning on $600 a month from investments."

Professor Granger explains that to earn $600 a month at an average interest rate today, you should have accumulated $80,000 to $100,000 in retirement savings. "If that figure sounds high," he adds, "think of it this way: over a work life of 40 years, if you save only $386 per year at an interest rate of 8 percent, you'll have $100,000 by the time you retire."

NOTES

CHAPTER ONE

1. J. Paul Getty, quoted in Barbara Rowes, *The Book of Quotes* (New York: Ballantine Books, 1979), p. 10.
2. The royal couple's finances are outlined in Bonnie Angelo, "An Inside Look at Royal Riches," *Money,* July 1981, pp. 28-34. See also "Walter Scott's Personality Parade," *Parade,* January 29, 1984, p. 2.
3. Similar discussions of the functions of money appear in Louis E. Boone and David L. Kurtz, *Contemporary Business,* 4th ed. (Hinsdale, Ill.: Dryden Press, 1985); and David J. Rachman and Michael H. Mescon, *Business Today,* 3rd ed. (New York: Random House, 1982).
4. "Rate of Inflation Is Lowest in 11 Years," *Seattle Times,* January 24, 1984, p. A1.
5. "Briefs," *Wealthbuilding,* February 1984, p. 27.
6. "Health—Not Wealth—Is the Best Measure of Success, Poll Says," *Seattle Times,* September 23, 1983, p. E5.
7. Ibid.

CHAPTER TWO

1. Jacques Plante, quoted in *On the Upbeat,* vol. A, no. 8A (Fairfield, N.J.: Economic Press).
2. Randall Poe, "Moneyball," *Across the Board,* September 1981, pp. 12-20 (Ruth quote from pp. 13-14). Inflation update based on "Rate of Inflation Is Lowest in 11 Years," *Seattle Times,* January 24, 1984, p. A1.
3. U.S. Department of Commerce, Bureau of Economic Analysis.
4. See Malcolm N. Carter, "Opportunities for Young Americans," *Money,* June 1981, pp. 32-33.
5. Studs Terkel, *Working* (New York: Pantheon Books, 1974), p. 312.
6. See Ralph E. Winter, "Survey Indicates Bosses Savor Jobs, Fear Inflation's Effect on Income," *Wall Street Journal,* May 12, 1981, sec. 2, p. 25.
7. Terkel, *Working,* p. 589.
8. W. Vance Grant and Leo J. Eiden, *Digest of Education Statistics* (National Center for Education Statistics, May 1982, p. 189.
9. See Jan Fildenhar, "It's a Shocker: College Education for Two Children Tops $150,000!," *Seattle Times,* August 31, 1981, p. B5; and Judson Gooding, "Slashing Your Way through College Costs," *Money,* September 1981, p. 104.
10. See *The Student Guide: Five Federal Financial Aid Programs: 1983* (Washington, D.C.: U.S. Department of Education, 1983); *Financial Aid Form: School Year 1983-1984* (Washington, D.C.: College Entrance Examination Board, 1982); *The College Aid Checkbook* (Washington, D.C.: Army ROTC). See also Joseph Michalak, "Loan Program Will Soon Go to 14 Percent," *New York Times,* August 11, 1981, pp. C1, 3; Gooding, "College Costs," pp. 104-106, 108; A. O. Salzberger, Jr., "Students Hurry to Get Loans Before U.S. Limits Eligibility," *New Times,* August 23, 1981, pp. 1, 64, and "New Federal Aid to Help Pay for College," *U.S. News & World Report,* February 2, 1981, p. 67; George M. Stoddart, "Easy College Credit," *Money,* February 1981, pp. 87-89, and "Meeting College Costs—Part 3," *Forbes,* February 16, 1981, pp. 111-113. The references also list some of the sources of financial aid information cited in this section.

CHAPTER THREE

1. Ayn Rand, quoted in Barbara Rowes, *The Book of Quotes* (New York: Ballantine Books, 1979), p. 15.
2. This estimate is based on the Consumer Price Index reported in U.S. Bureau of Labor Statistics, "Current Labor Statistics," *Monthly Labor Review,* December 1981, p. 87; and "Rate of Inflation Lowest in 11 Years," *Seattle Times,* January 2, 1984, p. A1.
3. These uses are suggested in Carol Pucci, "Your Net Worth," *Seattle Times,* March 12, 1981, p. F1; and W. Thomas Porter, "Up-to-Date Fiscal Profile Is Vital in Inflationary Time," *Seattle Business Journal,* April 20, 1981, pp. 2-3.
4. George Watson Smith, "Tax Tips," *Journal-American* (Bellevue, Wash.), December 21, 1981, p. D1.
5. Porter, "Fiscal Profile," p. 2.
6. An excellent discussion appears in "Personal Financial Planning: Taking the First Step—Data Gathering," *National Tax Shelter Digest,* October 1981, pp. 17-19.
7. "Put a Finger on Your Financial Pulse," *Changing Times,* January 1979, p. 38.
8. See, for example, Pucci, "Your Net Worth," p. F1.
9. Theodore J. Miller, ed., *Make Your Money Grow* (New York: Dell, 1981), p. 447.
10. See Stephen W. Lewis, "Seven Serious Mistakes with Your Money," *Money,* November 1981, pp. 101-104.
11. Ibid.

CHAPTER FOUR

1. Benjamin Franklin, quoted in "Getting Spending Under Control," *Wealthbuilding,* September 1983, p. 11.
2. Barbara Hanna, "She Can Live within a Budget Because It's All on Paper," *Journal-American,* January 11, 1982, P. C1.
3. The Alcalas' story is excerpted from "Young Couple with Two Incomes: How to Manage All That Money," *Changing Times,* March 1981, p. 29.
4. See George E. L. Barbee, "Personal Financial Planning: The Role of Advisors," *National Tax Shelter Digest,* December 1981, pp. 18-21.
5. Tamar Lewin, "Lively Debate on Bankruptcy," *New York Times,* August 9, 1983, p. D2.
6. Jan Gildenhar, "Carefree? Jim, 34, Should Increase Savings," *Seattle Times,* September 28, 1981, p. B1.

CHAPTER FIVE

1. Arthur Godfrey, quoted in Marilyn Passell Goldsmith, "Observations & Opinions," *Tax Shelter Digest,* April 1982, p. 7.
2. "When the Rich Fill Out Returns," *U.S. News & World Report,* November 15, 1982, p. 93.
3. Adam Smith, *An Inquiry into the Nature and Causes of the Wealth of Nations* (Oxford, England: Oxford University Press, Bicentennial Ed., 1976), p. 825.
4. "Do We Really Need an Income Tax?" *U.S. News & World Report,* April 18, 1983, p. 41.
5. Tax Foundation (Washington, D.C.), "News Release," July 30, 1983.
6. "Do We Really Need an Income Tax?" p. 41.
7. "Standing Up to the IRS," *U.S. News & World Report,* March 26, 1984, p. 40.
8. "Cheating by the Millions," *Time,* March 28, 1983, p. 27.
9. "Cheating by Millions," p. 27.
10. Jerry Edgerton, "Ten Terrific Tax-Saving Ideas," *Money,* June 1983, p. 56.
11. Reported in Marilyn Passell Goldsmith, "Observations & Opinions," *National Tax Shelter Digest,* April 1982, p. 7.

CHAPTER SIX

1. Nick the Greek, quoted in Barbara Rowes, *The Book of Quotes* (New York: Ballantine Books, 1979), p. 20.
2. Frederick Kempe, "Poles Survive Collapse of Currency by Using Own System of Barter," *Wall Street Journal,* October 23, 1981, pp. 1, 25.
3. Frederick Amling and William G. Droms, *The Dow Jones-Irwin Guide to Personal Financial Planning* (Homewood, Ill.: Dow Jones-Irwin, 1982), p. 65.
4. Ibid.
5. John Helvar, "In Spite of Low Yields Savings Accounts Still Satisfy Many People," *Wall Street Journal,* April 15, 1981, p. 1.
6. H. Erich Heinemann, "Assets of Money Funds Off a Record $8.3 Billion," *New York Times,* December 24, 1982, p. D1; and "The Money Funds Are Gearing Up," *New York Times,* December 27, 1982, p. D1.
7. Amling and Droms, *Dow Jones-Irwin Guide,* p. 78.
8. "Is Your Money Safe in a Savings and Loan?" *U.S. News & World Report,* August 17, 1981, p. 72.
9. Robert A. Bennett, "Savings Institutions Are Healthier But Now Face Further Challenges," *New York Times,* December 30, 1982, p. D4.
10. "Streamlined S&Ls Are Back in the Black," *U.S. News & World Report,* December 19, 1983, p. 77.
11. *Facts about Credit Unions* (Washington, D.C.: Credit Union National Association, n.d.).
12. "Where America Will Bank," *Newsweek,* October 19, 1981, p. 80.
13. "Merrill Lynch Plays Bank—Again," *Business Week,* June 28, 1982, p. 92.
14. James D. Robinson, III, "The Growing Competition in the Financial Service Industry," *Vital Speeches of the Day,* December 15, 1981, p. 150.
15. "Automatic Teller Foils Two Would-Be Robbers," *New York Times,* January 2, 1983, p. 30.
16. "Electronic Banking," *Business Week,* January 18, 1982, p. 71.
17. Margaret Daly, "What Are Your Rights When You Bank by Machine?" *Better Homes and Gardens,* February 1981, p. 18.
18. Ibid., p. 19.
19. "Banking's Crumbling Image," *Time,* August 2, 1982, p. 50.

20. "What Big Losses Mean to Safety of S&Ls," *U.S. News & World Report,* December 7, 1981, p. 76.
21. "Exploring the Money-Fund Option," *Newsweek,* March 15, 1982, p. 52.
22. Ibid.
23. John W. Hazard, "Keeping an Eye on Your Money," *U.S. News & World Report,* September 6, 1982, p. 75.
24. "Fewer Freebies," *Time,* April 12, 1982, p. 60.
25. Orania Papazoglou, "Consumer Bank Errors," *Working Woman,* April 1982, p. 24.

CHAPTER SEVEN

1. Dr. Joyce Brothers, quoted in Barbara Rowes, *The Book of Quotes* (New York: Ballantine Books, 1979), p. 19.
2. Frederick Case, "His Spuds Were Duds So U.S. Grant Got Battle Fatigue," *Seattle Times,* October 20, 1981, p. 81.
3. "Credit Card Not Assured Even If You've Very Rich," *CPA Client Bulletin,* June 1983, p. 4.
4. Robert D. Hershey, Jr., "Credit Card Impact Minimized by Fed," *New York Times,* August 12, 1983, p. D4.
5. "Big Fight for Credit-Card Market," *U.S. News & World Report,* August 29, 1983, p. 61.
6. U.S. Bureau of the Census, *Statistical Abstract of the United States* (Washington, D.C.: U.S. Government Printing Office, 1983), p. 513.
7. John W. Slocum, Jr., and H. Lee Mathews, "Social Class and Income as Indicators of Consumer Behavior," *Journal of Marketing,* April 1970, pp. 69–74. See also Gillian Garcia, "Credit Cards: An Interdisciplinary Survey," *Journal of Consumer Research,* March 1980, pp. 327–337.
8. Sylvia Porter, *Sylvia Porter's New Money Book for the 80s* (New York: Avon Books, 1979), p. 822.

CHAPTER EIGHT

1. President John F. Kennedy, quoted in Barbara Rowes, *The Book of Quotes* (New York: Ballantine Books, 1979).
2. "Jury Awards $408,000 to Couple 'Bumped' from Overbooked Flight," *Journal-American* (Bellevue, Wash.), October 7, 1981, p. A8.
3. "Typical U.S. Family Is Earning Less," *Consumers' Research,* November 1982, p. 25.
4. Sylvia Lazos Terry, "Unemployment and Its Effect on Family Income in 1980," *Monthly Labor Review,* April 1982, p. 35.
5. "America's Mood Today," *Changing Times,* April 1982, pp. 28–29.
6. Ibid., p. 27.
7. *U.S.A. Today,* April 2, 1984, p. A1.
8. Charles M. Schaninger and Chris T. Allen, "Wife's Occupational Status as a Consumer Behavior Construct," *Journal of Consumer Research,* September 1981, pp. 189–196.
9. Reprinted from "Two-Income Families: A Bittersweet Lifestyle," *U.S. News & World Report,* November 2, 1981, p. 85. Copyright, 1981, U.S. News & World Report, Inc.
10. Ibid., pp. 85–86.
11. Fran R. Schumer, "Downward Mobility," *New York,* August 16, 1962, p. 22.
12. John B. Lansing and Leslie Kish, "Family Life Cycle as an Independent Variable," *American Sociological Review,* October 1957, pp. 512–519.
13. "'Tis the Season to Be Wary of Crooks," *U.S. News & World Report,* December 6, 1982, p. 78.
14. "Behind Moves to Ease Regulations on Business," *U.S. News & World Report,* August 2, 1982, p. 63.
15. David W. Cravens and Gerald G. Hills, "Consumerism: A Perspective for Business," *Business Horizons,* August 1970, p. 21.
16. "Head of Consumer Affairs Assesses First Year on Job," *New York Times,* January 30, 1983, p. 22.
17. "When Business Tries to Regulate Itself," *U.S. News & World Report,* May 17, 1982, p. 65.
18. Ibid.

CHAPTER NINE

1. *Time,* December 28, 1981.
2. "118 Room Post Mansion Nation's Costliest Home," *Journal-American* (Bellevue, Wash.), February 13, 1984, p. A8; "A Place by the Sea," *Forbes,* April 30, 1984, pp. 8, 10; "At $13.5 Million, Florida Real Estate Built by Post Is a Tough Sale," *Wall Street Journal,* June 27, 1984, sec. 2, p. 9.
3. "Housing's Storm," *Business Week,* September 7, 1981, p. 63.
4. See, for example, Earl G. Gottschalk, Jr., "The Affordable Home Turns Out to Be Tiny and Not Really Cheap," *Wall Street Journal,* December 17, 1983, pp. 1, 20; and "Dollhouses in Texas," *Time,* November 30, 1981, p. 63.
5. Nancy Way, "Renters Receive the Red Carpet," *Journal-American* (Bellevue, Wash.), August 22, 1981, p. C1.
6. This section is based on Jane Bryant Quinn, *Everyone's Money Book* (New York: Dell, 1980), pp. 298–299.

7. Robert Guenther, "Changes in Financing Improve Manufactured Home Outlook," *Wall Street Journal,* October 21, 1981, sec. 2, p. 25.
8. Michael Sumichrast and Ronald G. Shafer, *The Complete Book of Home Buying* (Princeton, N.J.: Dow Jones Books, 1980), p. 153.
9. "For Consumers, a Year of Modest Price Hikes," *U.S. News & World Report,* January 9, 1984, p. 49.
10. Deeds are discussed in many real estate sources. See, for example, Daniel J. De Benedictis, *The Complete Real Estate Adviser,* new rev. ed. (New York: Pocket Books, 1977), pp. 166–168; and Sylvia Porter, *Sylvia Porter's New Money Book for the 1980's* (New York: Avon Books, 1979), p. 172.
11. Land leases are discussed in Theodore J. Miller, ed., *Make Your Money Grow* (New York: Dell, 1981), pp. 110–111.
12. Sumichrast and Shafer, *Home Buying,* pp. 197–199.
13. See ibid., p. 202.
14. For an excellent discussion of this type of mortgage, see Nancy R. Hess, *The Home Buyer's Guide* (Englewood Cliffs, N.J.: Prentice-Hall, 1976), pp. 21–25. See also ibid., pp. 201–207.
15. Sumichrast and Shafer, *Home Buying,* p. 199.
16. These new mortgage formats are outlined in numerous sources. See, for example, William Baldwin, "Where Will the Money Come From?" *Forbes,* September 14, 1981, pp. 150–154; Edward R. Wolfe, "Adjusting to Adjustables," *Money,* December 1981, pp. 119–120; Merle Dowd, "Fixed- versus Adjustable-Mortgage Loans," *Seattle Times,* November 12, 1981, p. E1; Miller, *Make Your Money Grow,* pp. 101–111; Porter, *Money Book,* pp. 190–193; Sumichrast and Shafer, *Home Buying,* pp. 208–214; "Beating the Cost of Mortgages," *Time,* May 18, 1981, pp. 66; "If You Have to Accept One of Those New Mortgages . . . ," *Medical Economics,* November 2, 1981, pp. 221, 224, 228, 230, 233, 236; C. Christian Hall, "How Floating Rates on Mortgages Affect More Home Purchases," *Wall Street Journal,* May 6, 1981, pp. 1, 20; and Robert Guenther, "Adjustable Rate Mortgages Gaining Favor among Buyers," *Wall Street Journal,* November 16, 1983, p. 29.
17. These provisions are discussed in a variety of sources: see Porter, *Money Book,* p. 188; Hess, *Home Buyer's Guide,* pp. 26–29; and Sumichrast and Shafer, *Home Buying,* pp. 207–208.
18. See Robert Guenther, "High Interest Rates May Pop 'Balloons' in Home Financing," *Wall Street Journal,* September 23, 1981, sec. 2, p. 33.
19. Building a home is discussed in Hess, *Home Buyer's Guide,* pp. 176–185; and Porter, *Money Book,* pp. 172–183.
20. "Canadians Find Success with Accelerated Payment Schedule," *Journal-American* (Bellevue, Wash.), October 23, 1983, pp. G1, G2.

CHAPTER TEN

1. Earl Wilson, quoted in Barbara Rowes, *The Book of Quotes* (New York: Ballantine Books, 1979), p. 17.
2. Personal interview with Janet Guthrie, May 16, 1983.
3. U.S. Bureau of the Census, *Statistical Abstract of the United States* (Washington, D.C.: U.S. Government Printing Office, 1983), p. 605.
4. "Retiring Autos at 14," *New York Times,* April 3, 1983, sec. 3, p. 1; "Autorama U.S.A.," an advertising supplement sponsored by the Motor Vehicle Manufacturers Association, *Time,* May 10, 1982, p. S9.
5. "The Great American Transportation Mess," *U.S. News & World Report,* August 31, 1981, p. 20.
6. *Bus Facts: Intercity Bus Industry in 1981 and Decade of 70s* (Washington, D.C.: American Bus Association, 1982), p. 2.
7. U.S. Bureau of the Census, *Statistical Abstract,* p. 622.
8. *Transit Fact Book* (Washington, D.C.: American Public Transit Association, 1981).
9. Telephone interview with James McCarthy, spokesperson for the Air Transportation Association of America, February 16, 1984.
10. "Now That the Brakes Are Off the Bus Industry," *U.S. News & World Report,* April 18, 1983, pp. 87–88.
11. "Prices Are Headed Up, But So Is Quality," *Changing Times,* January 1984, p. 58.
12. Marsha Taylor, "Price Gap between New and Used Cars Is Closing," *Seattle Times,* January 28, 1984, p. B1.
13. Gail Bronson, "Owning vs. Leasing," *Money,* August 1982, p. 50.
14. Clint Willis, "Lease for Less," *Money,* May 1983, p. 40.
15. Lani Luciano, "Getting a Good Deal," *Money,* August 1982, p. 56. Reprinted by permission.
16. Angela Fox Dunn, "When Is the Best Time to Buy, Shop for a New Car?" *Seattle Times,* December 31, 1981, p. C1.
17. Janet Guthrie, "Nuts and Bolts: Financing," *Working Woman,* April 1982, p. 84.
18. "The Real Cost of Driving Your Car and How to Control It," *Changing Times,* September 1980, pp. 21–22.
19. *What It Costs to Run a Car* (Wellesley, Mass.: ALA Auto and Travel Club, 1983), p. 8.
20. Ibid.
21. "How to Get the Most MPG's," *Consumer Reports,* April 1980, p. 229.
22. U.S. Bureau of the Census, *Statistical Abstract,* p. 620.
23. Ibid.
24. Ibid., p. 617.
25. Ibid., p. 618.

26. "Behind the Surge in Auto Recalls," *U.S. News & World Report,* August 25, 1981, p. 54.

CHAPTER ELEVEN

1. "People," *Journal-American* (Bellevue, Wash.), August 3, 1981, p. A10.
2. "The Price Women Would Pay for Unisex Pensions," *U.S. News & World Report,* May 9, 1983, p. 169.
3. See Daniel Seligman, "Insurance and the Price of Sex," *Fortune,* February 21, 1983, pp. 84–85.
4. *Insurance Facts* (New York: Insurance Information Institute, 1983), pp. 22, 58; and "Traffic Deaths Hit 20-Year Low," *U.S. News & World Report,* February 20, 1984, p. 13.
5. *Insurance Facts,* p. 70.
6. Andrew Tobias, *The Invisible Bankers: Everything the Insurance Industry Never Wanted You to Know* (New York: Simon and Schuster, 1982), p. 39.

CHAPTER TWELVE

1. Philip Slater, quoted in Barbara Rowes, *The Book of Quotes* (New York: Ballantine Books, 1979), p. 12.
2. The four paragraphs above were reprinted from "A Premium on Fear," *Newsweek,* December 17, 1979, p. 86. Copyright 1979, by Newsweek, Inc. All rights reserved. Reprinted by permission.
3. Andrew Tobias, *The Invisible Bankers: Everything the Insurance Industry Never Wanted You to Know* (New York: Simon and Schuster, 1982), p. 74.
4. *Life Insurance Fact Book* (Washington, D.C.: American Council on Life Insurance, 1982), p. 14.
5. Jane Bryant Quinn, *Everyone's Money Book* (New York: Dell, 1980), p. 363.
6. "The Reckoning," *Money,* April 1982, p. 134. Reprinted by permission.
7. "Managing Your Money: Borrowing on Life Insurance," *U.S. News & World Report,* January 29, 1980, p. 28.
8. Brendan Jones, "Your Money: Insurance Loans: Pros and Cons," *New York Times,* February 23, 1980, p. 28.
9. Jane Moss Snow, "Whole Life or Term? It Depends on Needs," *USA Today,* May 4, 1984, p. 7B.
10. "Credit Life Insurance: Oversold and Overpriced," *Changing Times,* March 1980, p. 63.
11. Ibid., p. 64.
12. Quinn, *Everyone's Money Book,* p. 394.
13. *Life Insurance Fact Book,* p. 14.
14. Telephone conversation with Bob Waldron of the American Council of Life Insurance, May 2, 1983.
15. Edward E. Scharff, "How Sweet Is Universal Life?" *Money,* May 1983, p. 113.

CHAPTER THIRTEEN

1. Quoted in Barbara Rowes, *The Book of Quotes* (New York: Ballantine Books, 1979), p. 228.
2. "The Vet's Healing Touch," *Newsweek,* November 9, 1981, pp. 82–84.
3. "Americans Now Living Longer, But Paying Higher Price for It," *Journal-American* (Bellevue, Wash.), January 18, 1984, p. A12; "How Investors Can Profit from the Health Care Boom," *Changing Times,* June 1983; and "Soaring Hospital Costs," *U.S. News & World Report,* August 22, 1983, pp. 39–42.
4. "Soaring Hospital Costs," p. 40.
5. Types of health insurance are described in *Policies for Protection* (Washington, D.C.: American Council on Life Insurance, 1978), pp. 10–13; *What You Should Know about Health Insurance* (Washington, D.C.: Health Insurance Institute); and *Source Book of Health Insurance Data* (Washington, D.C.: Health Insurance Association, 1981).
6. "Hospital Costs State by State," *U.S. News & World Report,* October 24, 1983, p. 13.
7. Indemnity and service plans are discussed in Carolyn Jabs, "Health Insurance Policies Are Not All Alike," *Ms.,* June 1978, pp. 85–87.
8. Robert Pride, "Softing a Disabling Blow," *Money,* November 1983, p. 185.
9. "Dental Insurance: A Fringe Benefit That's Spreading," *U.S. News & World Report,* September 3, 1979, p. 76.
10. Carrie Tuhy, "Toning Up Your Health Policy," *Money,* August 1981, p. 72.
11. "Health Maintenance Organizations: Going against Tradition," *Wealthbuilding,* May 1984, p. 10.
12. "HMO Will Pay Bonus for Cut in Hospital Stay," *American Medical News,* October 16, 1981, p. 23.
13. "Could an HMO Give You Better, Cheaper Health Care?" *Changing Times,* June 1980, p. 29.
14. Ibid., p. 30.
15. Medicare is discussed in "What Medicare Will and Won't Do for You," *Changing Times,* January 1979, pp. 39–42; *What You Should Know about Health Insurance When You Retire* (Washington, D.C.: Health Insurance Institute, March 1979), pp. 4–6; Social Security Administration, "A Brief Explanation of Medicare," SSA Publ. No. 05-10043 (May 1980); "How Medicare Helps during a Hospital Stay," SSA Publ. No. 05-10039; and "Home Care under Medicare," SSA Publ. No. 80-10042.

16. "Elderly and Disabled Given Most of Medicaid," *New York Times,* October 18, 1981, p. 46.
17. "Has Success Spoiled the Medicare Program?" *U.S. News & World Report,* October 10, 1983, pp. 87–88.
18. U.S. Bureau of the Census, *Statistical Abstract of the United States* (Washington, D.C.: U.S. Government Printing Office, 1983), p. 412.
19. Sylvia Porter, *Sylvia Porter's New Money Book for the 80s* (New York: Avon Books, 1979), pp. 462–463. New York Workers Compensation discussion from *On-the-Job Injury* (Workers Compensation Board, March 1980).
20. New York Workers Compensation Board, *On-the-Job Injury,* March 1980.
21. Ellen Sweet, "Before You Pick Sides—What You Need to Know about National Health Plans," *Ms.,* August 1979, p. 79.
22. "Battle Begins over National Health Insurance," *U.S. News & World Report,* June 25, 1979, pp. 62–63; and James J. Kilpatrick, "National Health Needs a Private Prescription," *Nation's Business,* July 1979, pp. 13–14.
23. Tuhy, "Toning Up Health Policy," p. 71.
24. "Does Your Medical Insurance Really Cover Enough?" *Changing Times,* October 1980, p. 38.
25. This section based on Jane Bryant Quinn, *Everyone's Money Book* (New York: Dell, 1980), pp. 466–474.
26. Information for this section from "Does Your Medical Insurance Really Cover Enough?" p. 39.
27. Robert Guenther, "Employers Try In-House Fitness Centers to Lift Morale, Cut Cost of Health Claims," *Wall Street Journal,* November 10, 1981, sec. 2, p. 1.

CHAPTER FOURTEEN

1. Henny Youngman, quoted in Barbara Rowes, *The Book of Quotes* (New York: Ballantine Books, 1979), p. 196.
2. "Grid Fan Sues Bears for Misrepresenting Team as Professionals," *Seattle Times,* October 15, 1981, p. B6; and "Bear Facts: Fumbles Not Misrepresentation," *Seattle Times,* November 10, 1981, p. G1.
3. *A Family Guide to Auto and Home Insurance* (New York: Insurance Information Institute, 1978), p. 18.
4. Data in this section and some of the later sections were provided by Tena Perry of the Justin Agency, Inc., Redmond, Wash. See also "Homeowners Insurance: Part I," *Consumer Reports,* August 1980, pp. 484–485.
5. U.S. Bureau of the Census, *Statistical Abstract of the United States* (Washington, D.C.: U.S. Government Printing Office, 1983), p. 615.
6. See Jane Bryant Quinn, *Everyone's Money Book* (New York: Dell, 1980), pp. 211–212; and *Family Guide,* pp. 3–5.
7. See Mary Williams, "No-Fault Auto Policies Are Widely Attacked as Costly, Ineffective," *Wall Street Journal,* November 16, 1983, pp. 1, 21.
8. Quinn, *Money Book,* pp. 2–3, 12. The factors impacting premiums are also from this source, pp. 16–21.
9. *Sharing the Risk: How the Nation's Businesses, Homes and Autos Are Insured* (New York: Insurance Information Institute, 1981), p. 15.
10. Ibid., pp. 16–17.
11. Ibid.
12. See Quinn, *Money Book,* p. 226.
13. This section and the previous one are based on Insurance Information Institute, *Sharing the Risk,* pp. 6–8.
14. See ibid., p. 96.
15. "Uncle Sam Bribes Town to Buckle-up for Safety," *Journal-American* (Bellevue, Wash.), November 15, 1983, p. A7.

CHAPTER FIFTEEN

1. Bennett Cerf, *At Random: The Reminiscences of Bennett Cerf* (New York: Random House, 1977).
2. Richard P. Halverson, *Financial Freedom: Your New Guide to Economic Stability and Success* (San Francisco: Harbor Publishing, 1982).
3. Ibid., p. 296.
4. Ibid., p. 297.
5. William G. Shephard, Jr., "Variety, New Risks Complicate Decisions," *New York Times,* December 12, 1982, sec. 12, p. 11.
6. Jane Bryant Quinn, *Everyone's Money Book* (New York: Dell, 1980), pp. 562–564.
7. Sylvia Porter, *Sylvia Porter's New Money Book for the 80s* (New York: Avon Books, 1979), pp. 1026–1027.
8. Vartanig G. Vartan, "Advantages of Stock Splits," *New York Times,* February 17, 1983, p. D8.

CHAPTER SIXTEEN

1. Robert Runde, "Money Makers of the '80s," *Money,* September 1981, p. 51. Reprinted by permission.
2. *1982 NASDAQ Fact Book* (New York: National Association of Securities Dealers, 1982), p. 57.
3. Robert L. Gould, "Discount Brokers Branch Out to Wide Variety of Services," *New York Post,* January 24, 1983, p. 34.

4. Terry Brown, "Which Broker Is Right for You?" *Orlando Sentinel,* November 9, 1981, p. 8D.
5. Donald H. Dunn, "The Delicate Task of Choosing the Right Broker," *Business Week,* June 15, 1981, p. 113.
6. Sylvia Porter, *Sylvia Porter's New Money Book for the 80s* (New York: Avon Books, 1979), p. 1019.
7. William C. Bryant, "One Way to Reduce Risk," *U.S. News & World Report,* April 18, 1982, p. 105.

CHAPTER SEVENTEEN

1. "Cum Laude." Reprinted by permission of *Forbes* magazine, January 30, 1984. © Forbes Inc., 1984.
2. "Investment Clubs Stage Comeback," *USA Today,* March 7, 1983.
3. Jerry Edgerton, "Streaking Ahead with the Mutual Funds," *Money,* April 1983, p. 56.
4. Ibid.
5. Tyler Mathisen, "Moving Around in the Best of Families," *Money,* April 1983, p. 70.
6. Allen Sloan, "How to Find the One for You," *Money,* November 1983, p. 75.
7. *Fact Sheet* (New York: No-Load Mutual Fund Association, 1983).
8. Quoted in Leonard Sloane, "Back in Vogue with Mutual Funds," *New York Times,* December 12, 1982, sec. 12, p. 34.
9. Sylvia Porter, *Sylvia Porter's New Money Book for the 80s* (New York: Avon Books, 1979), p. 1067.
10. Nancy Dunnan, "Mutual Funds: The Easy Way to Ride the Bull Market," *Consumers Digest,* November/December 1983, p. 21.
11. Porter, *Money Book,* p. 1067.
12. Quoted in Sloane, "Back in Vogue," p. 34.

CHAPTER EIGHTEEN

1. Quoted in Barbara Rowes, *The Book of Quotes* (New York: Ballantine Books, 1979), p. 24.
2. Hall Glatzer, "Local Commodity Dealer Stays in Tune with Markets via Radio Band," *Seattle Business Journal,* October 19, 1981, pp. 6-7.
3. Daniel F. Cuff, "The High Return under Your Own Roof," *New York Times,* December 12, 1982, sec. 12, p. 82.
4. Ibid., p. 83.
5. Charley Blaine, "Teaming Up on Real Estate," *USA Today,* February 3, 1984, p. 3B.
6. "Exciting Futures," *Barron's,* December 1, 1969, p. 3.
7. Based on Gordon Williams, *Financial Survival in the Age of New Money* (New York: Simon and Schuster, 1982), p. 222.
8. Vartanig G. Vartan, "Option Trades: Allure, Risks," *New York Times,* March 3, 1983, p. D6.
9. Vartanig G. Vartan, "Options Lure Even the Timid," *New York Times,* December 12, 1982, sec. 12, p. 52.
10. Williams, *Financial Survival,* p. 226.
11. Quoted in H. J. Maidenberg, "Inflation Fears and the Advance of Gold," *New York Times,* February 20, 1983, p. F16.
12. H. J. Maidenberg, "Gold Loses Its Bad Name," *New York Times,* December 12, 1982, sec. 12, p. 72.
13. "Behind the Long Slide in Gold Prices," *U.S. News & World Report,* March 22, 1982, p. 69.
14. Richard Buck, "Strategic Metals," *Seattle Times,* December 1, 1981, p. F1.
15. "Investment Gems: Will They Ever Sparkle Again?" *Changing Times,* April 1982, p. 38.
16. Quoted in Edward Jay Epstein, "Have You Ever Tried to Sell a Diamond?" *The Atlantic Monthly,* January 1982, p. 30.
17. Ibid., p. 32.
18. Quoted in "Investment Gems," p. 39.
19. Shona McKay, "The Downward Mobility of Collectibles," *Macleans,* October 18, 1982, p. 64.
20. John W. Hazard, "Time to Start a Collection," *U.S. News & World Report,* April 26, 1982, p. 87; and "Collectibles: Still Some Bargains," *Money,* April 1983, p. 40.

CHAPTER NINETEEN

1. President Franklin Delano Roosevelt, quoted in "The Crisis in Social Security," *Newsweek,* June 1, 1981, p. 25.
2. Nancy Shulins, "Retirement Riddle: The Bill for Social Security Promises Is Due," *Journal-American* (Bellevue, Wash.), October 6, 1981, pp. C1, C2.
3. "Can You Afford to Retire?" *Newsweek,* June 1, 1981, p. 24; and "Crisis in Social Security," p. 26.
4. "Biting the Bullet on Social Security," *U.S. News & World Report,* November 8, 1982, p. 43.
5. Social Security Administration, *Your Social Security* (Washington, D.C.: U.S. Government Printing Office, April 1983), p. 5.
6. U.S. Department of Health and Human Services, *Social Security Handbook,* 7th ed. (Washington, D.C.: U.S. Government Printing Office, June 1982).
7. John H. Fialka, "Man Who Helped Get Social Security Started Now Strives to Save It," *Wall Street Journal,* September 22, 1981, pp. 1, 21.
8. See Paul H. Douglas, *Social Security in the United States: An Analysis and Appraisal of the Federal Social Security Act,* 2nd ed. (New York: McGraw-Hill, 1939), pp. 3-4, 6-9, 26. See also Mary Ross, *Why Social Security?* rev. ed., Publ. No. 15 (Washington, D.C.: Social Security Board, 1940).
9. Lewis Meriam, *Relief and Social Security* (Washington, D.C.: Brookings Institution, 1946).
10. Douglas, *Social Security,* p. 56.
11. Robert M. Ball, *Social Security Today and Tomorrow* (New York: Columbia University Press, 1978), pp. 218-221.
12. "Benefits May Fall by Fourth in Long Run," *Seattle Times,* May 15, 1981, p. A1.
13. Calculated from "Biting the Bullet," p. 43.
14. See Social Security Administration, *Social Security Credits—How You Earn Them,* SSA Publ. No. 10072 (Washington, D.C.: U.S. Government Printing Office, January 1980).
15. Ball, *Social Security Today,* pp. 112-113.
16. DHHS, *Social Security Handbook,* p. 81.
17. SSA, *Your Social Security,* p. 11.
18. Nancy Shulins, "Early Retirement's Promise Fades as Social Security Falters," *Seattle Times,* October 8, 1981, pp. A4-A5.
19. Ball, *Social Security Today,* p. 235.
20. See Social Security Administration, *How Work Affects Your Social Security Check* (Washington, D.C.: U.S. Government Printing Office, May 1983); and Social Security Administration, *Social Security Survivors Benefits,* SSA Publ. No. 05-10084 (Washington, D.C.: U.S. Government Printing Office, July 1980).
21. Social Security Administration, *Social Security Checks for Students* (Washington, D.C.: U.S. Government Printing Office, January 1983).
22. Ball, *Social Security Today,* pp. 5-6.
23. Milton Friedman and Rose Friedman, *Free to Choose* (New York: Avon Books, 1980), pp. 110-111, 114.
24. Meriam, *Relief,* p. 83.
25. Wilbur J. Cohen and Milton Friedman, *Social Security: Universal or Selective?* (Washington, D.C.: American Enterprise Institute for Public Policy Research, 1972), pp. 24-25, 38.
26. Ball, *Social Security Today,* pp. 2, 7.
27. William C. Mitchell, *The Popularity of Social Security: A Paradox in Public Choice* (Washington, D.C.: American Enterprise Institute for Public Policy Research, 1977).
28. A. F. Ehrbar, "How to Save Social Security," *Fortune,* August 25, 1980, pp. 34-39.
29. See Ball, *Social Security Today,* pp. 187-207.
30. "Cost of Living Increases Will Shrink with Altered Consumer Price Index," *Seattle Times,* October 27, 1981, p. A1; and "Price Index Revision Could Reduce Pay Raises," *Journal-American* (Bellevue, Wash.), October 28, 1981, p. A8.
31. See "Delay Social Security till Age 68?" *U.S. News & World Report,* February 19, 1979, pp. 49-50.
32. "Now, Crackdown on Scams in Social Security," *U.S. News & World Report,* November 3, 1980, p. 66.
33. "Crisis in Social Security," p. 27.
34. A. Haeworth Robertson, "The Freedom Plan for Old Age," *Across the Board,* July/August 1981, pp. 48-54; "The Social Security Fix," *Across the Board,* April 1983, pp. 35-36.

CHAPTER TWENTY

1. George Burns, quoted in Barbara Rowes, *The Book of Quotes* (New York: Ballantine Books, 1979), p. 17.
2. Nancy Shulins, "Call It Quits," *Journal-American* (Bellevue, Wash.), October 5, 1981, p. D1.
3. Ibid.
4. James Gallin, *The Star Spangled Retirement Dream* (New York: Charles Scribner & Sons, 1981), pp. 1, 38-39.
5. Robert Runde, "Planning Now for Your Longer Life," *Money,* March 1981, p. 52.
6. "Good News: We'll Be Living Longer," *U.S. News & World Report,* May 14, 1984, p. 13.
7. Steven Findley, "New Wrinkles in the Aging Debate," *USA Today,* September 22, 1983, p. 3D.
8. "Early Retirement—Could You Pull It Off?" *Changing Times,* February 1984, p. 31.
9. William Graeburn, "U.S. Is Reversing Itself on the Promise of Retirement," *Seattle Times/Seattle Post Intelligencer,* October 9, 1983, p. A2.
10. Richard Boyer and David Savageau, *Places Rated Almanac* (Chicago: Rand McNally, 1981).
11. "Retirees' Costs—25-Area Survey," *U.S. News & World Report,* August 24, 1981, p. 7.
12. Frederick Case, "Retirement's First Lesson: Learn How to Come Down," *Seattle Times,* June 21, 1981, p. E1.
13. John W. Hazard, "Planning Now for Retirement," *U.S. News & World Report,* July 20, 1981, pp. 70, 76; and "Your Company Pension: Will It Go Far Enough?" *U.S. News & World Report,* March 9, 1981, p. 76.

14. "Facing the Pension Dilemma," *Time,* October 19, 1981, p. 76.
15. Tom Redburn, "Retirement," *Seattle Times,* October 20, 1983, p. E1.
16. "Pension Dilemma," p. 76.
17. Based, in part, on Jane Bryant Quinn, *Everyone's Money Book* (New York: Dell, 1980), pp. 768–774.
18. "Putting Together a Portable Pension," *Business Week,* May 11, 1981, p. 42.
19. Quoted in Runde, "Planning Now," p. 60.
20. This section is based on "Facing the Pension Dilemma," *Time,* October 19, 1981, pp. 76–77; and James Gallin, *The Star Spangled Retirement Dream* (New York: Charles Scribner & Sons, 1981), pp. 55–57, 98–100.
21. The individual retirement accounts discussion is based on these sources: Jill Bettner, "To Decide Where to Put Your IRA Dollars, Look at Risk, Management and All the Fees," *Wall Street Journal,* December 14, 1981, p. 46; Richard Eisenbert, "Where to Start Your IRA," *Money,* December 1981, pp. 70, 72, 74; Merle David, "Looking at IRA's," *Seattle Times,* October 29, 1981, p. F1; Jane Bryant Quinn, "All You Need to Know about the New IRA's," *Newsweek,* December 21, 1981, pp. 66–67; Gary Heberlein, "Investing IRA Funds," *Seattle Times,* December 24, 1981, pp. D1–D2; Nancy Way, "IRA's: A Nest Egg and Tax Shelter for All Wage-Earners," *Journal-American* (Bellevue, Wash.), December 28, 1981, p. C1; William A. Doyle, "Reagan Tax Bill," *Journal-American* (Bellevue, Wash.), September 29, 1981, p. B4; "What the New IRA Rules Do for You," *Business Week,* September 14, 1981, pp. 122–123, 126; John M. Berry, "IRA: Saving for Your Retirement," *Seattle Times,* November 26, 1981, pp. C1–C2 (*Washington Post* story), and Thomas L. Friedman, "Where to Open a Retirement Account," *New York Times,* December 6, 1981, p. F15.
22. "Original IRA Estimate Off the Mark," *Wealthbuilding,* November 1983, p. 5.
23. Jane Bryant Quinn, "All You Need to Know about the New IRA's," *Newsweek,* December 21, 1981, p. 67.
24. Ed O'Toole, "Financing the Leisure Years," *Forbes* (Special advertising supplement).
25. "10 Terrific Tax-Savings Ideas," *Money,* June 1983, p. 60.
26. "Facing the Pension Dilemma," p. 76.
27. See Michael Sumichrast and Ronald G. Shafer, *The Complete Book of Home Buying* (Princeton, N.J.: Dow Jones Books, 1980), pp. 256–257; and "Personal Business," *Business Week,* March 26, 1979, p. 101.
28. The section on annuities is based on Laurie Cohen, "Annuities Spark New Consideration as Tax Shelters," *Seattle Times,* June 15, 1981, p. B1; Paul Gross, "The Advantages of a Single Premium Deferred Annuity," *House and Garden,* May 1981, pp. 46–48; *1980 Life Insurance Fact Book* (Washington, D.C.: American Council of Life Insurance, 1980), pp. 37–38; and "Turning a Hunk of Cash into Lifetime Income," *Changing Times,* March 1980, pp. 57–59. See also Theodore J. Miller, ed., *Make Your Money Grow* (New York: Dell Books, 1979).
29. "Winners and Losers of the Year," *Money,* January 1982, p. 91.
30. William L. Eppley, "Where There's a Will There's a Way," *Aging,* January/February, 1981, p. 28.
31. "People," *Time,* June 6, 1983, p. 67; "Hearing to Begin on Hughes Estate," *New York Times,* July 12, 1981, p. 38; "Judge Dismisses Claims of 4 to Hughes Estate," *New York Times,* July 14, 1981; and "Winners and Losers of the Year," *Money,* January 1982, p. 91.
32. Richard Wolkomir, "The High Cost of Neglecting Your Will," *McCalls,* April 1980, p. 90.
33. Probate is discussed in sources like Melvin Jay Schwartz, *Don't Die Broke,* rev. ed. (New York: E. P. Dutton, 1978), pp. 103–124.
34. "Beating the High Cost of Probating a Will," *Changing Times,* May 1981, p. 46.
35. See "Don't Lose It in Probate," *50 Plus,* February 1981, pp. 30–31.
36. "Planning Your Family's Financial Future," *U.S. News & World Report,* December 8, 1980, p. 45.
37. This listing is based on Sylvia Porter, *Sylvia Porter's New Money Book for the 80s* (New York: Avon Books, 1979), pp. 967–968.
38. See *Planning with Your Beneficiaries* (Washington, D.C.: American Council of Life Insurance, 1980), p. 4.
39. "Planning Family's Financial Future," p. 45.
40. William Doyle, "New Tax Law Easier on Gifts," *Journal-American* (Bellevue, Wash.), September 30, 1981, p. C7.
41. Nancy L. Ross, "Insurers Fear Effect of Shift in Estate Tax," *Washington Post,* August 13, 1981, p. D15.
42. Doyle, "New Tax Law," p. C7; and Karen W. Arenson, "Estates and Gifts: Planning Simplified," *New York Times,* September 4, 1981, p. D1.
43. Peter Neuroth, "Funeral Homes Close Ranks to Help Deal with High Cost of Dying," *Seattle Business Journal,* January 11, 1982, pp. 8–9.

INDEX

Definitions appear on pages indicated by boldface numbers.

ability-to-pay philosophy of taxation, **88**
accelerated cost recovery system (ACRS), 527–528, **527**
accidental death clause, **358**
actuarial method, 189–190, **189**
add-on method, **189**
adjustable-rate mortgages, **261**
adjusted gross income, **108**
advertising, deceptive, 224–225
Agriculture Department, 223, **229**
Ahern, Michael J., III, 271, 301
Aid to Families with Dependent Children, 381
AIME (average indexed monthly earnings), **565**
air travel, 277–279
ALA Auto and Travel Club, 295
Alcala, Tom and Kim, 67
Alfred A. Knopf, Inc., 416
Allen, Frank, 77
Allen, Robert F., 577
Allstate Insurance Company, 319
American Automobile Association, 297–298
American Bankers Association, 137
American Cancer Society, 330
American Council of Life Insurance, 351, 581
American Dental Association, 376
American Enterprise Institute for Public Policy Research, 569
American Express Company, 576
American Express Gold Card, 144, 174
American Family Life Assurance Company, 330
American Gas Association Laboratories Seal of Approval, **236**
American Gold Exchange, 544
American States Insurance Company, 395
American Stock Exchange (Amex), 459, 465–466, 482
American Stock Exchange Index, 486
American Telephone and Telegraph (AT&T), 424–425, 429, 435, 504–505
Amtrak, 276–277, **276**, 279
annual percentage rate (APR), **188**, 197
annuities, 591–594, **591**
  choice of, 593–594
  fixed-rate and variable-rate deferred, 592–593
  payment options for, 591–592
  types of, 592
annuities with period certain, **592**

Applewhite, Marrily, 66
appliances, life expectancy for, 223
appreciation, **248**, **419**
Arizona Bank, 158
asked price, **461**
assets, 53–54, **53**
  fixed, 54
  liquid, 54
  quick, 54
assigned risk pool, 406–407, **406**
Associated Press, 558
assumable-mortgage clauses, **262**
Astin, Alexander, 21
ATMs (automated teller machines), 151–152, **151**
AUTOCAP, 232–233
automatic overdraft accounts, **183**
automobile insurance, 195, 318, 400–407
  assigned risk pool for, 406–407
  auto usage and, 406
  for bodily injury and property damage liability, 401
  for collisions, 402–403
  for comprehensive physical damage, 403
  compulsory liability insurance laws and, 404
  driving record and, 406–407
  financial responsibility laws and, 403–404
  for medical payment, 402
  no-fault, 404
  personal characteristics and, 406
  place of residence and, 406
  premiums for, 404–407
  type of car and, 407
  for underinsured motorists, 402
automobiles, 271–301
  "blue book" for, 286
  choice of, 279–287
  dealers and, 272–273, 284, 288–291
  domestic vs. imported, 283
  drunken drivers and, 405
  financing for, 291–292
  fixed expenses for, 293–295
  insurance for, *see* automobile insurance
  leasing of, 286–287
  Lemon Laws for, 284
  need for, 274–275
  options on, 282
  preference questionnaire for, 281
  price of, 282–291
  purchase negotiations for, 290
  purchase of, 279–292

  real cost of, 292–297
  sale of, 273–274
  servicing of, 273, 297–299
  summary for, 299–300
  theft of, 403
  trade-ins, 291
  used, 273, 283–286
  variable expenses for, 293, 295–297
  warranties for, 297–299
auto recalls, 299
Auto Repair for Dummies (Sclar), 273
Auxiliary Loans to Assist Students, 23

Badgero, James, 570
Baird, James W., 415, 451, 523, 554
bait and switch, **225**
balance sheet, **47**, 53–56
  assets on, 53–54
  liabilities on, 53–55
  net worth on, 53, 56
Ball, Robert, 567–569
balloon payments, **264**
bankruptcy, 80–81, **80**
banks, 130–131
  commercial, 137–138, 140, 149–150
  electronic funds transfer (EFT) by, 151–154
  errors by, 153–154
  loans from, 179
  money-market accounts from, 133
  mortgages from, 263
  mutual savings, 140
  resolving problems with, 165–167
  safe-deposit boxes in, 150
  safety of, 154–157
  services offered by, 146–151
  trustee services of, 150
  wire transfers by, 151
Barash, Samuel T., 92
Barnes, Joseph W., 51
Barnhart, Dennis R., 423
Barron's, 544
barter, **126**, 128
Bass, Mark, 495, 521
bear markets, 497–499, **499**
Beneficial Finance, 116, 173, 179
beneficiary, 353–354, **353**, 356
benefits-received philosophy of taxation, 88
Bensman, Joseph, 214
Benson, Ann, 339
Berg, Adriane G., 324
Bernhard, Arnold, 505

610

INDEX

Bernier, Henry, 594
Bernstein, Merton, 593
Best's Insurance Guide, 325
beta concept, 488-489, **488**
Better Business Bureau, 221, **232**
   arbitration program of, 234
Bickelhaupt, David L., 311
bid, **461**
Big Board, **458**
blank endorsement, **162**
blind pools, **532**
Block, Robert L., 55
Blue Chip Economic Indicators, 550
blue-chip stocks, 433-434, **433**
Blue Cross/Blue Shield, 372, 377-378, **378**
Blyskan, Jeff, 526
bodily injury and property damage liability insurance, **401**
Bohn, Robert, 125, 169, 329, 365-366
bonds, 417-418, **417**, 440-448
   characteristics of, 443-447
   collateral trust, 440-441
   corporate, 440-441
   daily listings of, 480, 482-483
   debentures, 25, 441
   government, 441-443, 446
   interest rates on, 417-418, 443-448
   as investment vehicles, 448
   junk, 445, 448
   mortgage, 440
   municipal, 441-443
   ratings for, 445-448
   yields on, 447-448
book value per share, 429-430, **429**
borrowing, 171-204
   from consumer finance companies, 179
   cost of, 185-190
   from family and friends, 180-181
   from government, 180
   from life insurance companies, 180
   limits of, 190-192
   from loan sharks, 181
   from pawnbrokers, 181
   promissory notes for, 185-186
   from retailers, 180
   right reasons for, 191-193
   from sales finance companies, 179
   summary of, 201-202
   wrong reasons for, 194-196
   see also credit; finance charges; interest rates; loans
bracket creep, 113-114, **113**, 214
Brainerd, Thomas S., 144
Brod, Jack, 549
brokers, **409**
Bronstein, Harvey, 391, 411-412
Brothers, Joyce, 172
Bryant, William C., 489
Buck, Richard, 548
budgeting, 15, 65-67, **66**, 71-77
   components of, 71-72

consumer spending patterns and, 72
fixed expenses in, 71, 76
income in, 73-76
preliminary matters for, 69-70
sample, 73-74
summary of, 81-82
variable expenses in, 71, 76-77
variance in, 73
bullion coins, 544
bull markets, 497-499, **499**
Bureau of Labor Statistics, 27, 72, 570
burglary insurance, **318**
Burns, George, 576
Burr, William, 243, 269
Burton, Edwin, 542
business, self-regulation by, 232-233
bus travel, 278-279

call provisions, **438**
calls, 539-540, **539**
capacity, **174**
capital gains, 108-109, **108**, 439
capital losses, 108-109, **108**
Capone, Al, 102
car-buying services, 288-290, **289**
career choice, 14, 19-41
   decision in, 39
   hiring interview in, 39
   job availability and, 27-28
   job location and, 31
   job satisfaction and, 21
   money and, 21
   occupational clusters and, 31
   occupational potential and, 28-31
   personal goals and, 20-22, 25
   personal inventory for, 25-27
   self-employment as, 31-33
   social contribution and, 21
   summary of, 39
   vocational counseling for, 27
   working at home as, 33
   see also job search
Car/Puter International Corporation, 289
Carter, Jimmy, 383, 530
cash accounts, 476
cash allowances (spending money), 50
cash flow (in budgeting), 71-72, **71**
cash flow (for real estate), 525-526, **525**
cashier's checks, 165-166, **165**
cash management accounts (CMAs), 143-144
cash-out period, **264**
cash value, 341-342, **341**
Census Bureau, 274
Cerf, Bennett, 416
certificates of deposit (CDs), 131-133, **131**, 143
certified checks, 165-166, **165**
certified public accountants (CPAs), 117
Changing Times, 347-348, 361
character, 174-175, **174**

charge accounts, 178
   regular (30-day), 184
   revolving (open-end), 182-183
Charles, Prince of Wales, 4
Charles Schwab & Company, 474
charter, **417**
checking accounts, 7-8, 146-147, 159-164
   automatic overdraft for, 183
   check clearing and, 160
   deposits for, 160
   individual vs. joint, 159
   monthly statement for, 163-164
   NOW accounts vs., 148
   opening of, 159-160
   overdrafts in, 160-161
   record keeping for, 160
   stopping checks and, 161
   types of, 147
   writing and endorsing checks for, 161-163
   see also NOW accounts
checks, special types of, 163-166
Chemical Bank, 158
   PRONTO system of, 152-153
Chicago Bears, 392
Chicago Board of Trade, 536, 537, 553
Chicago Board Options Exchange, 541-542
Chicago Mercantile Exchange, 537-538
Chicago World's Fair, 51
Christmas club accounts, 131
chronological résumés, 36-37, **36**
Chrysler Corporation, 297, 421
Citibank, 187
Civil Rights Act of 1964, 593
Clark, Barney B., 385
Clifford trusts, 600
closed-end bonds, **440**
closed-end installment purchase plans, **183**
closed-end investment companies, 501-502, **501**
closed-end leases, **287**
closing costs, **259**
clothing expenditures, 50
codicils, **597**
coinsurance, **375**
collateral, **175**
collateral trust bonds, 440-441, **440**
collectibles, 550-552, **550**
College Work Study, **24**
collision insurance, 402-403
Commerce Department, 47
commercial banks, **137**, 149-150
   interest rates at, 138, 140
commissions, 472-473, **472**
commodities, **524**, 536-539
   futures trading of, 536-537
   information on, 539
   risks of, 537
   spot trading of, 536
commodities exchanges, 537-539
Commodity Exchange, 547

INDEX

Commodity Futures Trading Commission (CFTC), 538
common stock, **416**, 426–437
  appreciation of, 428
  blue-chip vs. growth, 433–434
  book value of, 429–430
  cyclical vs. defensive, 435
  dividends on, 428
  earnings per share of, 432
  income vs. speculative, 434
  as investment vehicle, 436–437
  market value of, 430–431
  par value of, 429
  price-earnings (P/E) ratio for, 432–433
  prospectus and, 427
  reasons for investment in, 427–429
  retained earnings and, 428
  rights on, 435
  splits of, 436
  value of, 429–433
  voting rights and, 429
  warrants for, 435–436
  yield on, 428
community property states, **56**
comparison shopping, **217**
comprehensive personal liability insurance, 394–395, **394**
comprehensive physical damage insurance, **403**
compulsory liability insurance laws, **404**
condominiums, 252–253, **252**
Congressional Budget Office, 384
conspicuous consumption, 194–195, **194**
consumer action panels, 232–233, **232**
Consumer Credit Counseling Service, 196
Consumer Credit Protection Act of 1968, *see* Truth in Lending Act of 1968
consumer finance companies, **179**
consumerism, **226**
Consumer Leasing Act of 1976, **287**
consumer loans, 149–150
Consumer Price Index (CPI), 9–11, **9**, 113, 503, 569–570
Consumer Product Safety Commission (CPSC), **228**
Consumer Reports, 217, 234–235, 280, 297, 325
consumer rights, **226**
consumers, 207–241
  appliance and auto repairs and, 222–223
  bait and switch and, 225
  business self-regulation and, 232–233
  children's influence on, 219, 221
  comparison shopping by, 217
  complaints by, 221, 237–239
  credit used by, 209–210
  deceptive advertising and, 224–225
  deceptive sales practices and, 225
  decision-making process for, 216–219
  door-to-door selling schemes and, 224
  downward mobility and, 214
  family life cycle and, 214–216
  fraud and abuse of, 219–226
  have-nots among, 212–213
  haves among, 212
  help for, 234–237
  inflation and, 208–210
  land sales and, 224
  mail and telephone fraud and, 222
  marital roles and, 219–220
  media and, 237
  occupational and professional licensing boards and, 233–234
  price abuses and, 225–226
  product labels and, 229
  product warranties and, 230–231
  purchases postponed by, 209–210
  regulation and, 226–234
  small-claims court and, 239
  spending patterns of, 72
  step-by-step approach for, 217–219
  summary for, 239–240
  third-party action for, 239
  two-income families as, 210–214
  unemployment and, 209
Consumers' Research, 235
Consumers' Resource Handbook, 237–238, **237**
Consumers Union, 234–236, **234**
contingent beneficiary, **354**
continuing education, 25
conversion feature, 438
conversion privilege, **379**
Coolidge, Calvin, 597
cooperative apartments, 253–254, **253**
cooperative education programs, 24
Council of Better Business Bureaus, 222, 232
counteroffers, **256**
coupon (bearer) bonds, 443–444, **443**
Court of Claims, U.S., 102
Crash of 1929, 464
creative financing, 263–264, **263**
credit, 171–204, **173**
  agreements for, 184–185
  automatic overdraft accounts and, 183
  capacity for, 174
  character and, 174–175
  charge accounts and, 178
  closed-end installment purchase plans as, 183
  collateral for, 175
  consumer use of, 209–210
  counseling on, 196–197
  denial of, 176–178
  establishment of, 176, 178
  installment, 182–184
  lines of, 183
  obtainment of, 174–178
  sources of, 178–181
  summary of, 201–202
  total consumer installment, 173
  types of, 181–184
credit abuse, 78–81
  bankruptcy and, 80–81
  repossession and, 78–79
  wage garnishment and, 78
credit bureaus, 175–177, **175**
credit-card fraud, 198
credit cards, 150
credit counselors, 196–197, **196**
credit files, 175–177
credit life insurance, 347–349, **347**
credit unions, 141–142, **141**, 149
  auto loans from, 291–292
  insurance from, 156
  loans from, 179, 291–292
cumulative preferred stock, 439
CUNA Mutual, 348
Curb, The, **459**
current yield, **448**
cyclical stocks, **435**

Dade County, Fla., 231
Davis, Harry L., 220
Davis, Katherine Bement, 51
Davis, Marvin, 454
DeBari, Tom, 174
De Beers Consolidated Mines, 548–549
debentures, 25, **441**
debit cards, 144
declarations page, **408**
declining-balance method, **189**
decreasing term insurance, 337–338, **337**
deductible provision, 374–375, **374**, 398–399, **398**
deeds, 257
default, **78**
defensive stocks, **435**
deferred annuities, **592**
deficiency judgment, **79**
defined benefit plans, **590**
delinquency clauses, **262**
Delta Airlines, 208
demand deposits, **7**
Denenberg, Herbert S., 330
Depository Institutions Deregulation Committee, 137
deposit term insurance, **340**
Depression, Great, 131, 464, 560
Dewey, John, 218
diamonds and gems, 547–549
Diana, Princess of Wales, 4
Dictionary of Occupational Titles, **25**, 33
disability income insurance, **371**
disability waivers, **376**
disabled, **565**
discount method, **189**
discounts, **445**
discretionary income, **9**
disposable income, **9**
dividend reinvestment plans (DRPs), **428**
dividends, **428**
Dohan, Michael, 19, 40–41

INDEX

Dole, Robert F., 383
dollar-cost averaging, 489–490, **489**
Donoghue, William E., 156
door-to-door selling schemes, 224
Dow Jones Industrial Average, 435, 484–485
down payment, **254**
Downs, Anthony, 526
downward mobility, 214
Dunn, Angela Fox, 290

earnest money provision, **256**
earnings per share (EPS), **432**
Economic Recovery Tax Act (ERTA) of 1981, 112–114, **112**, 527, 586, 600–601, **600**
Edgerton, Jerry, 104
education:
  continuing, 24
  cost of, 22–23
  financing of, 22–25
  income potential and, 22–25
effective rate of interest, **129**
effective tax rate, 110–112, **111**
Einstein, Albert, 104
Eisenberg, Richard, 112–113
electronic funds transfer (EFT), 151–154, **151**
  safeguards for, 153–154
emergency funds, 69–70, **70**
Employee Retirement Income Security Act (ERISA) of 1974, **584**
employee stock purchase plans, 500–501, **500**
endorsements, 399–400, **399**
endowment insurance, 346–347, **346**
entrepreneurship, 32–33, **32**
Environmental Protection Agency (EPA), 296–297
Equal Credit Opportunity Act of 1975, 200–201, **200**
equity, **248**
escrow, **255**
estate planning, 594–604
  funeral arrangements in, 601–603
  summary of, 603
  taxes and, 600–602
  trusts and, 599–600
  see also wills
estates, **594**
Europe, value-added taxes in, 93–94
excise taxes, **94**
exclusions, **408**
exclusive agents, **409**
executors, **598**
expenditures, 14, 48–52
  on income statements, 48–52
  monitoring of, 15

Failure Analysis Associates, 394
Fair Credit Billing Act of 1974, 199–200, **199**

Fair Credit Reporting Act of 1970, 198–199, **198**
Fair Debt Collection Practices Act of 1978, **201**
family life cycle, 214–216, **214**
Federal Bankruptcy Reform Act of 1978, 80–81, **80**
Federal Deposit Insurance Corporation (FDIC), 154–156, **155**
Federal Housing Authority (FHA), 253–255, 259–260
Federal Insurance Administration (FIA), 400
Federal Insurance Contributions Act (FICA), 91, 563–564, **563**
federal regulatory agencies, 227–231
Federal Reserve Board, 183
Federal Reserve System, 467–468
Federal Savings and Loan Insurance Corporation (FSLIC), 154–156, **155**
Federal Supply Service, 223
Federal Trade Commission (FTC), 225, **228**, 231, 253, 345
fee simple, **257**
Ferrara, Connie, 19, 40–41
FICA (Federal Insurance Contributions Act), 91, 563–564, **563**
FIFO (first-in, first-out), 129
finance charges, 187–190, **187**, 197
  actuarial method for, 189–190
  add-on method for, 189
  declining balance method for, 189
  discount method for, 189
  rule of 78s method for, 190
financial institutions, 137–146
  choice of, 157–159
  convenience of, 157
  fees of, 158
  insurance for, 158–159
  services of, 157–158
financial planning, 15–16, 65–83, **66**
  credit abuse vs., 78–81
  emergency fund in, 69–70
  goals in, 67
  insurance in, 70
  by professionals, 67–69
  review of, 69
  summary of, 81–82
  see also budgeting
financial responsibility laws, 403–404, **403**
financial statements and records, 45–63, **47**
  frequency of, 47
  how long to keep, 58
  importance of, 47
  personal computers for, 59–61
  record keeping and, 56–58
  software for, 61
  summary of, 61
Financial Strategies, 73
financial supermarkets, 142–146, **142**
Fireman's Fund Insurance Company, 306–308

Fischer, David, 571
fixed assets, **54**
fixed expenses, **71**, 76, **293**
float, **153**
floater policies, **400**
Food and Drug Administration (FDA), **228**
food expenditures, 48–50
Forbes, 128
Ford Credit, 292
foreclosure, **259**
formally drawn wills, **597**
Form 1040, **108**
Form 1040A, 106–108, **106**
Form 1040EZ, 105–106, **105**
Fortune, 569
401(k) plans, **590**
Franklin, Benjamin, 66
Frazee, Harry, 20
free marital transfer, **601**
Friedman, Milton, 567–568
Friedman, Thomas L., 587
Fulco, Michael, 333–335
Fuller, Ida, 558
full warranty, **231**
functional résumés, **36**, 38
futures trading, 536–537, **537**

Gallup polls, 77
Gardner, Robert A., 112
garnishment, **78**
gender, insurance and, 315–316
General Accounting Office (GAO), 81, 102
General Electric, 24, 375
General Electric Credit Corporation, 179
General Motors, 256
General Motors Acceptance Corporation, 179, 292, 444
general obligation bonds, 442–443, **442**
Getty, J. Paul, 4
goals, personal, 5–7
  career choice and, 20–22, 25
  in financial planning, 67
  for savings, 127–128
  setting of, 6–7
Godfrey, Arthur, 86
gold, 543–546
  forms of, 544–546
Good Housekeeping Seal of Approval, **236**
Goodman, Jordan E., 498, 520
graduated-payment mortgages, **261**
Grafton, Marvin, 128
Graner, John P., 454
Granger, George L., 557, 573, 575, 604
Grant, Ulysses S., 172
Gray, Mary, 316
Greyhound, 278
gross income, **105**
gross national product, 8–9, **8**
Group Health Cooperative of Puget Sound, 380

613

INDEX

group health insurance, **379**
group life insurance, 348–350, **349**
growth stocks, 433–434, **433**
guaranteed insurability clause, **359**
Guaranteed Student Loan Program (GSLP), 22–23, **22**, 180
Guthrie, Janet, 272–274, 292
Gybbons, William, 337

H & R Block, 115–116
Haitch, Richard, 95
Halverson, Richard P., 418, 502, 541
Hand, Learned, 103–104
Harris, Marlys, 74
Hauser, Robert, 214
Hayes, Linda Snyder, 52
Hazard, John W., 478
health care:
    costs of, 50, 370–371
    hospice programs for, 375
health care industry, 370–371
health insurance, 369–389
    coinsurance and, 375
    conversion privilege for, 379
    coverage provided by, 372, 375
    deductible provision in, 374–375, 387
    dental insurance as, 376–377
    disability definition for, 387
    for disability income (salary continuation insurance), 371, 375–376
    group, 379
    HMOs and, 379–380
    hospital expenses and, 372–373
    individual, 378
    initial and secondary claims for, 376
    length of payment for, 376
    for medical expenses, 371, 374–375
    Medigap as, 382
    national, 383–384
    personal health care protection plan and, 384–387
    physician expenses and, 373
    policy evaluation for, 385–387
    premiums for, 387
    protection plans for, 377–383
    stop-loss feature in, 386
    summary for, 387–388
    surgical expenses and, 372–373
    waiting period for, 376
    workers' compensation as, 382–383
Health Insurance Association of America, 373
Health Maintenance Organization of Pennsylvania, 380
health maintenance organizations (HMOs), 379–380, **379**
Heberlein, Greg, 52
Hedberg, Gus, 591
Heidrick and Struggles, 585
Hertz Corporation, 295
Hiland, Teresa and Mike, 212–213

holographic wills, **597**
Home Accountant, 61
homeowners insurance, 395–400, **395**
    all-risk policies as, 397–398
    deductible in, 398–399
    endorsements for, 399–400
    floater policies for, 400
    standard formats for, 398–399
Home Owners Warranty (HOW) Program, 233
Hometax, 61
hospice programs, 375
Hospital Corporation of America, 455–456
hospital costs, 372–373
Household Finance, 173, 179
housing, 243–269
    asking prices and counteroffers for, 256
    closing costs and, 259
    condominiums as, 252–253
    construction of, 264–265
    cooperative apartments as, 253–254
    down payment on, 254, 258
    expenditures on, 48
    final sale price for, 256
    financing of, 257–264
    land leases for, 257
    leases on, 250
    location of, 244–245
    maintenance and operating expenses for, 255
    manufactured homes as, 251
    money in escrow and, 255
    monthly payment limitations and, 246–247
    new home buyer profiled, 247
    owner sale of, 256
    personal requirements for, 244–254
    purchase contract for, 257
    purchase of, 254–257
    real estate agents and, 255
    rental of, 247–251
    renting vs. buying, 247–248
    sale of, 265–266
    second homes as, 266–267
    summary of, 267–268
    tandem units as, 246
    taxes and, 245, 248, 253, 255
    time shares as, 267
    titles and deeds for, 257
    type of, 245–246
    where to look for, 255–256
    see also mortgages
Hughes, Howard, 603–604
Hummel, Dean L., 31
Hutton Life, 351
Hyatt Regency Hotel, Kansas City, Mo., 394

immediate-payment life annuities, **592**
impulse purchases, 195
income:
    adjusted gross, **108**

    in budgeting, 73–76
    gross, 105
    taxable, 105
    of two-income families, 210–214
income potential, 22–25
    occupational patterns for, 25
income-producing properties, **529**, 530–531, **534**, 535–536
income statement, **47**, 48–53
    expenditures on, 48–52
    income on, 48
    savings and investment on, 52–53
income stocks, 434
income taxes, 90–91, **90**
    federal, 90
    state and local, 90–91, 93
indemnity plans, **372**
indentures, **441**
independent agents, **409**
indexing, 113–114, **113**
Individual Retirement Accounts (IRAs), 150, 586–587, **587**
    interest and, 587–588
    investment opportunities for, 588–589
    withdrawals from, 588
individual wills, 596–597, **596**
industrial life insurance, 348
inflation, 9–11, **9**
    consumers and, 208–210
    savings and, 209–210
initial claims, **376**
installment credit, 182–184, **182**
insurable interest, 313–314, **314**
insurable risk, 311–315, **311**
insurance, 70, 305–366, **306**, 391–412
    amount of, 324–325
    basic elements of, 319–323
    burglary, robbery, and theft, 318–319
    cancer, 330–331
    choice of, 325
    for credit unions, 156
    duration of, 325
    for financial institutions, 158–159
    fire, 317–318
    gender and, 315–316
    interest rates and, 351
    law of large numbers for, 311–314
    liability and, 392–395, 399
    major policy provisions for, 407–408
    mortality tables for, 311–313
    for mutual funds, 516–517
    private mortgage, 258
    property, 317–319
    purchase decision for, 409
    purchase process for, 323–325
    rates for, 322–323
    risk and, 308–315
    specific policy conditions for, 408–409
    summaries for, 326, 409–410
    types of, 311, 317–319
    what to insure, 323

INDEX

see also automobile insurance; health insurance; homeowners insurance; life insurance
insurance agents, **320**, 324–325, 409
insurance companies, 320–323, **320**
   mortgages from, 263
   mutual, 321
   stock, 321–322
Insurance Information Institute, 395
insurance policies, 320–321, **320**, 407–409
insurance premiums, 319 320, **319**
insurance trusts, **600**
insuring agreement, **408**
interest, 129–130
   day-of-deposit-to-day-of-withdrawal method for, 130
   effective rate of, 129
   FIFO method for, 129
   IRAs and, 587–588
   LIFO method for, 129
   low balance method for, 130
   real rate of, 134
interest rates, 185–190
   annual, 188, 197
   on auto loans, 291–292
   on bonds, 417–418, 443–448
   calculation of, 187–190
   at commercial banks vs. S&Ls, 138, 140
   at credit unions, 142
   insurance and, 351
   for mortgages, 260–262
   on NOW accounts, 147–149
   on super-NOW accounts, 149
   usury laws and, 187
   see also finance charges
Internal Revenue Service (IRS), 86, 96–103, **96**, 511
   audits by, 97–102
   as information source, 115, 117–118
interviews:
   employment, 36
   hiring, 39
intestate, **594**
investing, **420**
Investment Advisers Act of 1940, 462
investment bankers, 455–456, **455**
investment clubs, 495–499, **497**
   bull vs. bear markets and, 497–499
   purchase decisions in, 497
   sale timing and, 499–500
   summary of, 519
investment companies, 501–502, **501**
   closed-end, 501–502
   open-end, 502
   see also mutual funds
Investment Company Act of 1940, 462
investments, 14, 52–53, 415–554
   acceptable risk for, 489–490
   age and, 425–426
   beta concept for, 488–489
   business risk for, 424

   capital growth from, 419
   common mistakes in, 478
   corporate information for, 477–479
   dollar-cost averaging for, 489–490
   efficient-market hypothesis for, 487–488
   future financial gain from, 419
   goals of, 426
   income from, 419–421
   intentions and, 418–419
   interest-rate risk for, 424
   life situation and, 426
   market risk for, 423, 424
   periodicals and TV programs on, 479
   personality and, 426
   purchasing-power risk for, 423
   pyramiding of, 529
   reasons for, 419–421
   in retirement planning, 591
   risk-return ratio for, 422
   risks of, 421–426
   risk spread in, 490
   sale timing for, 469
   speculators vs. investors and, 421
   strategy for, 487–490
   subscription market letters for, 479–480
   summaries for, 449, 491, 552–553
irrevocable beneficiary, 354

J. C. Penney, 142, 145
job satisfaction, 21
job search, 33–39
   interview in, 36
   résumé in, 34–38
   where to look in, 34
job service centers, **34**
Johnson, Edward F., 158
joint wills, **597**
junk bonds, **445**, 448
Justice Department, 416

Kadzis, Peter, 101, 144
Kane, Maryanne, 267
Katz, Michael, 321
Keck, Peggy, 3, 17
Kennedy, Edward M., 370, 383–384
Kennedy, John F., 208, 226–227
Keogh, Eugene J., 589
Keogh plans, 150, 589–590, **589**
Kero-Sun, Inc., 236
Kitts, Bruce, 589
Klopfer, Donald, 416
Knepper, Mike, 284
Koskoff, David E., 548–549
Kroger Company, 146
Krugerrands, 544–545

Labor Department, 9–11, 25
land leases, **257**, 286–287
land sales, 224
Lavelle, Jim, 496

law of large numbers, 311–314, **311**
leasehold, **257**
leases, **250**, 286–287
Lehman Corporation, 506
level term insurance, **337**
leverage, **467**, 527–530, **527**
Levering, Robert, 321
Lewis, Jerry Lee, 103
Lewis, Stephen, 56–58
liabilities (on balance sheets), 53–55, **53**
liability (in insurance), 392–393, **392**
   negligence and, 392–394
   personal, 393–395
   strict, 393
   vicarious, 393
liability insurance, 393–395, **393**, 399
   for bodily injury and property damage, 401
licensing boards, occupational and professional, 233–234
licensing taxes, **94**
Lichty, George, 431
life insurance, 150, 317, 329–366, **331**
   accidental death clause for, 358
   amount of, 332–335
   beneficiary clause with, 353–354, 356
   borrowing from, 342–343
   cash value of, 341–342
   changes in policies for, 360
   choice of, 353
   contract for, 353–360
   cost indexes for, 362–364
   cost of, 340–341, 344–345, 347, 360–364
   credit, 347–349
   disability waiver in, 376–377
   dividend clause for, 357–358
   endowment, 346–347
   guaranteed insurability clause for, 359
   group, 348–350
   for homemakers, 339
   human life value approach to, 332
   industrial, 348
   mail order, 361
   multiple earnings approach to, 332–333
   need for, 332
   nonforfeiture option for, 359
   policy loans and, 359–360
   policy reinstatement clause for, 359
   premium payment clause for, 356–357
   sample policy for, 363
   Savings Bank, 361
   settlement options for, 354–357
   shopping for, 360–361
   straight, 341–342
   suicide clause for, 358
   summary for, 364
   term, 337–340, 345
   term vs. whole, 344–346
   types of, 336–353
   universal, 351–355
   variable, 351–352

life insurance *(continued)*
  variables in, 336
  waiver-of-premium clause for, 358–359
  whole, 340–346
  worksheet for, 334
Life Insurance Buyer's Guide, 362–364
life insurance companies, 180
life insurance expenditures, 50
Life Insurance Marketing and Research Association, 343
lifestyle, 5–6, **5**
lifestyle score, **55**
LIFO (last-in, first-out), 130
limited partnerships, **532**
limited-payment whole life insurance, 343–344, **343**
limited warranty, **231**
limit order, 466–467, **466**
Linde, Shirley, 577
lines of credit, **183**
liquid assets, **54**
listed securities, **463**
Listerine, 225
listings, **255**
living trusts, **599**
load funds, 506–507, **506**
loan organization fees, **259**
loan payments, 52
loans:
  consumer, 149–150
  see also borrowing
loan sharks, **181**
Long, Russell, 383
Loomis, Gilbert, 404
Louis XI, King of France, 224
Lubin, Joann S., 375

MacBride, Dexter, 551
McNulty, Barry, 298
MADD (Mothers Against Drunk Drivers), 405
Madison Fund, 506
Magnuson-Moss Warranty Act of 1975, **231**
mail fraud, 222
Major Appliance Consumer Action Panel (MACAP), 233
major medical expense insurance, 374–375, **374**
Malloy, Ethel C., 65, 83
Maloney Act of 1938, 462
manufactured homes, **251**
Mar-a-Lago, 244
margin, 467–470, **467**
margin accounts, **476**
marginal tax rate, 110–114, **111**
margin calls, **468**
market orders, **466**
MARTA (Metropolitan Atlanta Rapid Transit Authority), 276
mass transit, 275–276, **275**
MasterCard, 150, 182–183

media, consumers and, 237
Medicaid, **381**
medical expense insurance, **371**
medical payment insurance, **402**
Medicare, **381**, 561–562, **561**
  diagnostic-related groups (DRGs) for, 382
Medwed, Butch, 306–308
Melton, William C., 157
mergers, **416**
Meriam, Lewis, 568
Merrill Lynch, 142–144, 546
Metcalf, Ellen, 209
Metropolitan Life, 343, 346–347, 363–364
Michigan University Institute for Social Research, 219
Miller, James C., III, 225, 233
Miller, Merl, 59–60
Miller, Theodore J., 599
Millers Casualty Insurance Company, 407
money, **7**, 126–127
  career choice and, 21
  convenience of, 127
  in the economy, 8–9
  functions of, 8
  impact of, 7–11
  relative value of, 9–11
Money, 73, 280, 325
money management, 125–169
  balances maintained in, 126–127
  choosing institution for, 157–159
  summary of, 167–168
  see also checking accounts; investments; savings
money-market accounts, 133
money-market mutual funds, 133–134, 142, 156–157
Moneythink: Financial Planning Finally Made Easy (Berg), 324
monthly investment plans, **500**
Moody's Investors Service, Inc., 445–447
Moon, Sun Myung, 103
Moore, Terry, 595
mortgage bonds, **440**
mortgages, 138–139, 182, **184**, 254–255, **254**, 257–264
  closing costs and, 259
  conventional, 259
  down payment and, 258
  from FHA, 253–255, 259–260
  fixed-rate vs. floating-rate, 261
  foreclosure of, 259
  graduated-payment, 261
  interest rates on, 260–262
  money sources for, 263–264
  1980s rates for, 260–262
  private insurance for, 258
  provisions of, 262–263
  second, 262–263
  shared-appreciation, 262
  sources of, 259–260

  types of, 261–262
  from VA, 253–255, 259–260
mortgage companies, 263
mortgage deeds, 184
mortgage notes, 184
mortgage table, 248–249, **248**
Moskowitz, Milton, 321
Mueller Group, 248
multiple listing services, **255**
municipal bonds, 441–443, **441**
Murray, Donna, 21
mutual funds, 502–521
  advice on, 516
  automatic reinvestment by, 511
  characteristics of, 502
  check-writing and telephone privileges with, 513
  convenience of, 506
  diversification in, 503–505
  families of, 510–512, 515
  front-end load in, 519
  insurance protection for, 512–513
  as investment, 502–506, 514, 519
  listings for, 517–518
  load, 506–507
  management structure of, 515–516
  net asset value per share of, 518
  no-load, 506–507
  performance evaluation of, 513–514
  personal style and needs and, 517
  professional management of, 504–506
  purchase of, 518–519
  rate of return on, 503
  retirement plans and, 513
  sale of shares in, 519
  services provided by, 517
  size of, 515
  summary of, 519–520
  systematic withdrawals from, 511–512
  types of, 507–510
mutual fund families, 510–512, **510**, 515
mutual insurance companies, **321**
mutual savings banks, **140**
Myers, Robert J., 559, 570

NADA Official Used Car Guide, **286**, 291, 295
Nader, Ralph, 226
NASDAQ (National Association of Securities Dealers Automatic Quotation) System, **461**, 480–482, 486
National Advertising Review Board, 232
National Association of Insurance Commissioners (NAIC), 362
National Association of Investment Clubs, 499
National Association of Securities Dealers, 484
National Automobile Theft Bureau, 403
National Broadcasting Company (NBC), 558

INDEX

National Commission on Social Security Reform, 562–563
National Credit Union Administration, 156
National Direct Student Loans, **24**, 180
National Foundation for Consumer Credit, 196
National Highway Traffic Safety Administration (NHTSA), **229**, 299
National Labor Relations Board, 379
National Railroad Passenger Corporation, 276–277
National Safety Council, 406
Nationwide Auto Brokers, Inc., 289
negligence, 392–393, **392**
net asset value (NAV) per share, **522**
net worth, **53**, 56
   quick, 55
New York City Department of Consumer Affairs, 231
New York State, usury ceiling in, 187
New York Stock Exchange (NYSE), 420, 457–460, 463–469, 474, 482, 485, 500–501
New York Stock Exchange Index, 486
Nick the Greek, 126
Nixon, Richard, 229, 254
no-fault insurance, **404**
no-load funds, 506–507, **506**
noncumulative preferred stock, **439**
nonforfeiture clause, **359**
non-income-producing properties, 529–530, **529**
nonparticipating preferred stock, **439**
Norris, Nathalie, 593
NOW accounts, 147–149, **147**
   checking accounts vs., 148
   share-draft accounts as, 149
   super-, 149

Occidental Fire and Casualty Company, 394
occupational cluster, **31**
Occupational Outlook Handbook, 33
odd-lot transactions, **474**
Office of Consumer Affairs, U.S., 229–230, **229**, 237
Ogden, Russell, 305, 327, 453, 492–493
O'Hara, Thomas, 475, 497
Oldakowski, Chester, 576
Old Republic Life Insurance of Chicago, 321
open-end investment companies, **502**
   see also mutual funds
open-end leases, **287**
Oppenheimer Management Corporation, 505–506
options, 539–543, **539**
   call, 539–540
   put, 539–541
   trading in, 541–543
overdrafts, 160–161, **160**
over-the-counter (OTC) market, **461**

Pacific Express, 278
participating preferred stock, **439**
par value, **429**
passbook savings accounts, 130–131
past-service liability, **585**
Patrick, Tom, 21
pawnbrokers, **181**
Pell Grants, **22**
Pension Benefit Guaranty Corporation (PBGC), 584–585, **584**
pension plans, 150, 583–586
Pepper-McFadden Act, **146**
period orders, **467**
Perrine, Henry P., 475
personal computers, **5**, 59–61
   banking with, 152
   choices in, 60
   cost of, 60
personal finance:
   environmental factors and, 11–13
   importance of, 4–5
   model for, 11–13
   personal decision factors and, 11–13
personal income, **9**
personal property, **91**
Pfeister Barter, 128
Phelps, Thomas W., 480
PIA (primary insurance amount), **565**
Places Rated Almanac, 579
Plante, Jacques, 20
points, **259**
Poland, money in, 126
policy conditions, **408**
policy loans, 342–343, **342**, 359–360
Porter, Sylvia, 477, 513, 516
Postal Service, U.S., 222, 530
Post Foundation, 244
Post, Marjorie Merriweather, 244
Prabhopada, Swami, 524
precious metals, 543–548, **543**
preferred stock, 437–440, **437**
   as investment vehicle, 439–440
   negative features of, 438–439
   positive features of, 437–438
   types of, 439
premiums, **445**
prepayment clauses, **262**
price-earnings (P/E) ratio, 432–433, **432**
primary beneficiary, **354**
primary markets, 455–456, **455**
priorities, personal, 15
private mortgage insurance, **258**
private pension plans, 591–594
   questions for, 592–593
   underfunding of, 593–594
probate, **596**
Proctor and Gamble, 224–225
progressive taxes, 88–89, **88**
promissory notes, 185–186, **185**
property insurance, 317–319, **317**
property taxes, 91–92

prospectus, **427**
Publication 17: Your Federal Income Tax (IRS), 117–118
purchase contracts, **257**
pure risk, **308**
puts, 539–541, **539**
pyramiding, 533–534

quick assets, **54**
quick net worth, **55**
Quinn, Jane Bryant, 331, 348, 588
Quint, Michael, 445
quit-claim deeds, **257**

Rand, Ayn, 46
Random House, Inc., 416
rare coins, 545
RCA (Radio Corporation of America), 375, 418
Reagan, Nancy, 86–87
Reagan, Ronald, 86–87, 111–112, 316
real estate, 525–535
   accelerated cost recovery system and, 527–528
   direct investment in, 531–532
   expenses of, 527
   illiquidity of, 525–526
   income-producing, 530–531
   investment companies for, 353
   investment partnerships for, 532–534
   leverage and, 527–530
   non-income-producing, 529–530
   risk of, 526, 532
   taxes and, 527
real estate agents, **255**
real estate investment trusts (REITs), 534–535, **534**
real property, **91**
reasonable care, **393**
recession, 208–210
recreation expenditures, 50
refund annuities, **592**
registered bonds, **443**
regressive taxes, **89**
regular (30-day) charge accounts, **184**
renegotiable-rate mortgages, **261**
repairs, for autos and appliances, 222–223
replacement cost, **54**
replacement ratio, **569**, 576
repossession, 78–79, **78**
Reserve Officers Training Corp (ROTC), 24
restrictive endorsement, **162**
résumé, 34–38, **34**
   chronological, 36–37
   functional, 36, 38
retailers, borrowing from, 180
retail installment contracts, **185**
retained earnings, **428**
retirement, 127

INDEX

retirement planning, 575–594, 603–604
  annuities in, 591–594
  income sources and, 581–594
  IRAs and, 586–589
  Keogh plans and, 589–590
  lifespan and, 577–578
  location choice in, 578–580
  needs calculated in, 580–583
  part-time employment and, 590
  private pension plans and, 583–586
  sale of primary residence and, 591
  savings and investments in, 591
  Social Security income and, 581–583
  summary of, 603
  timing of retirement and, 580
retirement test, **566**
revenue bonds, 442–443, **442**
revolving (open-end) charge accounts, 182–183, **182**
Rhodes, Elizabeth, 76
Rigaux, Benny P., 220
rights, **435**
Rinde, Robert, 354
risk, 308–315, **308**
  insurable, 311–315
robbery insurance, 318–319, **318**
Rockefeller, Nelson, 46, 53
Rogers, Will, 102, 454
Rohmann, Laura, 128
Roosevelt, Franklin Delano, 558, 560–561
ROTC (Reserve Officers Training Corp), 24
round-lot transactions, **474**
Rubin, Jim, 21
rule of 78s, **190**
Runzheimer and Company, 293
Ruth, Babe, 20

safe-deposit boxes, 58
sales finance companies, **179**
sales taxes, 91–93, **91**
Salomon Brothers, 558
Sarnoff, Paul A., 543
savings, 52–53, 127–128
  alternatives evaluated, 136–137
  bank money-market accounts for, 133
  CDs and, 131–133
  Christmas club accounts for, 131
  goals of, 127–128
  importance of, 127–128
  inflation and, 209–210
  instruments for, 130–139, 149
  interest on, 129–130, 591
  money-market mutual funds for, 133–134, 142
  passbook accounts for, 130–131
  in retirement planning, 591
  treasury bills, bonds, and notes for, 135
  in U.S., compared to other countries, 52
  U.S. savings bonds for, 135–136

savings and loan associations (S&Ls), 137–140, **137**
  interest rates at, 138, 140
Savings Bank Life Insurance, 361
savings bonds, U.S., 135–136
Sayer, Steve and Nancy, 212
Schreiner, Tim, 221
Sclar, Deanna, 273
Sears, 142–143
secondary claims, **376**
secondary markets, 457–458, **457**
second mortgages, 262–263, **262**
securities, 453–476
  bid vs. asked prices for, 461
  brokerage accounts for, 475–476
  leverage with, 467
  limit orders for, 466–467
  listed, 460
  margin and, 467–470
  market orders for, 466
  NASDAQ and, 461
  orders for, 465–467
  period orders for, 467
  stop orders for, 467
  summary for, 491
  see also bonds; common stock; preferred stock; stocks
Securities and Exchange Commission (SEC), 462–463, **462**, 472
Securities Exchange Act of 1934, 462
securities exchanges, 458–461
  Amex as, 459, 465–466, 482
  OTC markets as, 460–461
  regional, 460
  see also New York Stock Exchange
Securities Investor Protection Corporation (SIPC), 463–465, **463**
securities markets, 455–458
  bull vs. bear, 497–499
  Great Crash and, 464
  making transactions in, 465–471
  primary, 455–456
  regulation of, 462–465
  secondary, 457–458
self-employment, 31–33
selling long, 470–471, **470**
selling short, 470–471, **470**
Senate Health and Scientific Research Subcommittee, 383
service plans, **372**
shared-appreciation mortgages, **262**
share-draft accounts, **149**
Shepherd, William G., Jr., 421
silver, 546–547
Silver, David, 507, 517
Simplified Employee Pension (SEP) plans, 150
Skinrood, Don, 524
Slater, Philip, 330
small-claims court, **239**
Smith, Adam, 88

Smith, Greg V., 95
Social Security, 381–382, **381**, 557–574, **558**
  AIME and, 565
  alternatives to, 571
  beneficiaries of, 564–565
  benefit restrictions for, 566
  complexity of, 559
  computing benefit from, 565
  controversy over, 567–568
  direct deposit of, 152
  disability coverage of, 375–376, 381, 382, 565
  FICA contributions to, 91, 563–564
  filing claims with, 566
  fraud and, 570–571
  importance of, 558–559
  indexing system for, 569–570
  as insurance, 568
  Medicaid and, 381–382
  Medicare and, 381, 561–562
  PIA and, 565
  replacement ratio for, 562, 569
  retirement age change suggested for, 570
  retirement planning and, 581–583
  retirement test for, 566
  stagflation and, 568
  summary for, 571–572
  supplemental security income and, 566
  universal coverage proposed for, 569
  as welfare, 568
Social Security Act of 1935, 558–563, **560**
  amendments to (1950–1977), 561–562
  evolution of, 559–560
  1983 amendments to, 562–563
  original provisions of, 560–561
Social Security Administration (SSA), 559
Social Security disability income, **381**
Social Security Handbook, 565
software, for personal finance, 61
South Dakota, usury ceiling in, 187
special endorsement, **163**
speculative risk, **308**
speculative stocks, **434**
Spiro, Donald W., 505–506
spot trading, **536**
stagflation, **568**
Standard & Poor's Corporation, 445–447
Standard & Poor's Index of 500 Stocks, 435, 485–486, 503
Standard & Poor's Register of Corporation Directors and Executives, 238
Starkman, Sheldon, 454–455
stockbrokers, 471–475, **471**
  commissions of, 472–473
  discount, 472–474
  full service, 472–474
  selection of, 474
  specific, 475
  street name of, 476
stock insurance companies, 321–322, **321**

INDEX

stocks, 416-418
  analysis of, 498
  daily price reports and, 480-482
  employee purchase plans for, 500-501
  as equity, 417
  indexes for, 484-486
  long vs. short sales of, 470-471
  monthly investment plans for, 500
  ownership myths and facts for, 457
  round-lot vs. odd-lot transactions with, 474
  sale timing for, 499-500
  special purchase arrangements, 499-501
  see also common stock; options; preferred stock; securities
stock splits, **436**
stop orders, **467**
straight life annuities, 591-592, **591**
straight life insurance, 341-342, **341**
strategic metals, 547-548, **547**
street name, **476**
strict liability, **393**
sublease clause, **250**
subordinated debentures, **441**
suicide clause, **358**
super-NOW accounts, **149**
Supplemental Education Opportunity Grants (SEOG), **24**
supplemental security income, **566**
Supreme Court, U.S., 593
survival score, **55**
syndicates, 532-533, **532**

take-home pay, **9**
taxable income, **105**
tax accountants, 117
tax audits, 97-102, **97**
  appeals of, 102
  recommendations for dealing with, 101
tax avoidance, 103-104, **103**
tax credits, 109-110, **109**
taxes, 85-121, **86**
  advice on, 114-117
  bracket creep and, 113-114, 214
  capital gains and losses and, 108-109
  collection of, 96-104
  crime and, 95
  effective rate of, 91
  estate planning and, 600-602
  excise, 94
  housing and, 245, 248, 253, 255
  on income, 90-91, 92, 93
  indexing and, 113-114
  licensing, 94
  marginal vs. effective rates of, 110-111
  marriage penalty and, 113
  municipal bonds and, 443-445
  philosophies for, 88
  progressive, 88-89
  on property, 91-92, 527

  regressive, 89
  on sales, 91-93
  for Social Security, 91
  summary of, 119
  tips for saving on, 118-119
  for two-income families, 213-214
  types of, 86-95
  underground economy and, 103
  value-added, 93-94
tax evasion, 102-103, **102**
Tax Manager, 61
tax planning, 14-15
tax preparation agencies, 115-117, **115**
tax returns, 96-102
  deductions on, 108, 111
  filing conditions for, 104-105
  Form 1040 for, 108
  Form 1040A for, 106-108
  Form 1040EZ for, 105
  preparation of, 104-111
  zero-bracket amount on, 108
telephone fraud, 222
Telling, Edward, 143
Terkel, Studs, 21
term insurance, 337-340, **337**, 345
  conversion and renewable features of, 338-340
testamentary trusts, **599**
testators, **597**
theft insurance, **319**
theoretical limits of biological longevity, **578**
Thomas Registry, 238
thrifts, **130**, 149-150
  loans from, 179
titles, **257**
Tobias, Andrew, 315
Toffler, Alvin, 27, 33
Touche Ross, 47
Trailways, 278
transfer payments, **9**
transportation, 271-301
  air travel as, 277-279
  Amtrak as, 276-277, 279
  bus travel as, 278-279
  mass transit as, 275-276
  summary of, 299-300
  see also automobiles
transportation expenditures, 50
traveler's checks, 165-166, **165**
Travelers Insurance Company, 306
treasury bills, **135**
treasury bonds, **135**
Treasury Department, 136
treasury notes, **135**
trusts, 599-600, **599**
Truth in Lending Act of 1968, 78, 181, 184-185, 187-188, 197-198, **197**
Twain, Mark, 96
two-income families, 210-214
  added expenses of, 213-214

  have-nots among, 212-213
  haves among, 212

umbrella policies, **395**
underfunded pension plans, 585-586, **585**
underground economy, **103**
underinsured motorist insurance, **402**
Underwriters Laboratories (UL), **235**
unemployment, consumers and, 209
Uniform Gift to Minors Act, **600**
Uniform Probate Code, **596**
Uniform Residential Landlord and Tenant Act, 250-251, **250**
Uniform Simultaneous Death Act, **599**
United Airlines, 278
universal life insurance, 351-355, **351**
U.S. News & World Report, 212
usury laws, **187**

value-added tax (VAT), 93-94, **93**
Value Line Index, 492
Value Line Investment Survey, 498, 505
values, personal, 15
VanCaspel, Venita, 345
variable expenses, **71**, 76-77, **293**
variable life insurance, 351-352, **351**
variable-rate mortgages, **261**
variance, **73**
Vartan, Vartanig G., 542
Veterans Administration (VA), 253-255, 259-260
veterinary medicine, 370
vicarious liability, **393**
Visa cards, 150, 174, 182-183
vocational counselors, **27**

waiting periods, **376**
waiver-of-premium clause, 358-359, **358**
Wall Street Journal, 77, 484, 539, 542
Warner-Lambert, 225
warranties, 230-231, **230**
  for autos, 297-299
warrants, 435-436, **435**
warranty deeds, **257**
Watt, Sarah, 37-38
Wayne, Leslie, 473
Wealth of Nations (Smith), 88
Westinghouse, 375
Westwood, Clyde P., 85, 121, 171, 204
whole life insurance, 340-346, **340**
  arguments against, 344-345
  arguments for, 345-346
Wiesenberger Investment Companies Service, 514
Williams, Gordon, 543
wills, 594-599, **594**
  codicils to, 597
  executors of, 598
  probate system and, 596
  simultaneous deaths and, 599

wills *(continued)*
    testators of, 597
    types of, 596–599
Wilsker, Ira, 207, 241
Wilson, Earl, 272
Wise, P. J., 530
women, 200

Woodcock, John, 284
workers' compensation insurance, 382–383, **382**
Working (Terkel), 21
Worosz, Gregory, 45, 62–63, 369, 389
Wright, Jack, 580

yield, **428**
yield to maturity, **448**
Youngman, Henny, 392

zero-bracket amount, **108**
Zink, Victor, 576